Urgent Applications
in the Court of Protection

Second Edition

Urgent Applications in the Court of Protection

Second Edition

Her Honour Nazreen Pearce

District Judge Sue Jackson
Nominated Judge of the Court of Protection

JORDANS

Published by
Jordan Publishing Limited
21 St Thomas Street
Bristol BS1 6JS

British Library Cataloguing-in-Publication Data

A catalogue record for this book is available from the British Library.

ISBN 978 1 84661 809 3

Typeset by Letterpart Ltd, Caterham on the Hill, Surrey, CR3 5XL

Printed in Great Britain by CPI Antony Rowe, Chippenham and Eastbourne

FOREWORD TO THE FIRST EDITION

It is now over two years since the implementation of the Mental Capacity Act 2005. Despite some well-publicised criticisms, it has achieved the fundamental objectives of improving perceptions of incapacity and how they should be approached. It has settled the principles which underpin decision making for those who lack capacity by incorporating common law jurisprudence and best practice into statute. It has unified the previously disparate areas of finance and personal welfare (including medical treatment), and brought them under the jurisdiction of a new Court of Protection with its own specialist judges. The legislation is supported by a statutory Code of Practice, and the court procedure has a framework of rules and practice directions.

This work introduces the practitioner to the new legislation and the approach of the courts. It explores current case law. It provides a practical guide to procedure and drafting, invaluable to practitioners at any level of experience. Its emphasis on the urgent application is of particular importance. The Court of Protection has not been regarded as the first port of call for an emergency remedy. Traditionally, it provided intensive care rather than first aid. However, the new legislation has brought different challenges. Orders resolving emotionally charged disputes about health or personal welfare may need to be sought urgently. Previously, financial orders were highly restrictive and protective of the person who lacked capacity. The move towards empowerment which enables autonomy and flexibility through the use of unrestricted orders, has highlighted associated risks of misuse by the unknowing and abuse by the unscrupulous. The use of emergency powers to protect the welfare and assets of those who lack capacity is therefore of increased significance in the new arena.

This handbook provides an essential easy reference. Its success is attributable to the expertise and experience of its contributors. Nazreen Pearce is a retired circuit judge and well-known writer of legal text books. Susan Jackson is a respected nominated judge of the Court of Protection who worked with me at the Court's Central Registry in Archway for two years overseeing the implementation of the Act.

Denzil Lush
Senior Judge of the Court of Protection

PREFACE

The authors have been pleased to note that the first edition of this title was so well received; hence this updated second edition. New, is the tracking of the unfolding of the Mental Capacity Act 2005, as this new jurisdiction has become embedded in our legal system, and analysis of case law which has underpinned its interpretation.

Good practice is essential in all court proceedings. The Civil Procedure Rules 1998 led the way for reform of procedure and practice across all jurisdictions. The Court of Protection Rules 2007, based on the Civil Procedure Rules, provide simple clearly defined procedures from the start to the finish of the various applications which the court may be called upon to deal with. Each Part of the Rules is supplemented by a Practice Direction, which amplifies the provisions of the rules.

Although the rules are simple to follow and the forms are prescribed for applications made in the Court of Protection, for those who are inexperienced or unfamiliar with the law which applies to this jurisdiction it can still be a maze.

The aim of this book is both to provide professionals who practice in this field and those who are called upon to advise, assist and support 'P', including family and friends, with a step-by-step guide through the law, procedure and remedies in relation to those issues that are likely to arise frequently and which may require immediate action.

We have worked together, bringing our experience from other jurisdictions alongside the publishing team at Jordans, with a view to providing a user-friendly, concise and comprehensive handbook which is accessible to all and to which they may turn to find answers. Precedents and draft orders are provided to give helpful guidance.

The authors wish to express their thanks to the nominated judges and the staff at the Court of Protection.

We also extend our appreciation and thanks to Greg Woodgate for his efforts in paving the way for us to publish this book; to Tracy Robinson for working through the Christmas and New Year break, for her patience, endurance and efficiency in dealing with the amendments we made to the original draft and the proofs often at short notice; to Helen Pettet, marketing executive, for her efforts in marketing this edition, preparing the cover and marketing leaflets; and to Kate Hather, publishing manager, who kept us on track to ensure that we met the deadlines.

We have attempted, where possible, to illustrate the applications and orders by reference to short stories. The characters and factual circumstances relied on are purely fictional. Any apparent similarities to any real person is coincidental.

The law is stated as at 1 February 2014.

Nazreen Pearce
Sue Jackson
1 February 2014

CONTENTS

Part IV
Deprivation of Liberty

Chapter 10
Deprivation of Liberty

Part V
Children

Chapter 11

TABLE OF CASES

References are to paragraph numbers.

TABLE OF STATUTES

References are to paragraph numbers.

TABLE OF STATUTORY INSTRUMENTS

References are to paragraph numbers.

TABLE OF PRACTICE DIRECTIONS AND CODES OF PRACTICE

References are to paragraph numbers.

LIST OF ABBREVIATIONS

ANH	Artificial nutrition and hydration
Code of Practice	Mental Capacity Act (2005) Code of Practice, Issued by the Lord Chancellor on 23 April 2007 in accordance with ss 42 and 43 of the 2005 Act
COP Rules 2007	Court of Protection Rules 2007, SI 2007/1744
CPR	Cardio-pulmonary resuscitation
CPR 1998	Civil Procedure Rules 1998, SI 1998/3132
DoL	Deprivation of liberty
DOLS	Deprivation of Liberty Safeguards
EPA	Enduring powers of attorney
ECHR	European Convention for the Protection of Human Rights and Fundamental Freedoms (1950)
ECtHR	European Court of Human Rights
FLA 1996	Family Law Act 1996
FPR 2010	Family Procedure Rules 2010, SI 2010/2955
IMCA	Independent mental capacity advocate
LPA	Lasting power of attorney
MCA 2005 ('the Act')	Mental Capacity Act 2005
MCS	minimally conscious state
OPG	Office of Public Guardian
PCT	Primary Care Trust
PVS	Persistent vegetative state
RCJ	Royal Courts of Justice

CHAPTER 1

INTRODUCTION

On 1 October 2007 the Mental Capacity Act 2005 introduced a new approach to decision making for those who lack capacity. The Act not only established a new court jurisdiction supported by its own legal framework but also an entirely different way of looking at how capacity is assessed and understood.

Historically, the High Court had exercised its *parens patriae* jurisdiction over the lives, welfare, and property and affairs of those who were deemed to be mentally incapable of making decisions for themselves. The Lunacy Act 1890 gave certain powers to the Office of the Master of Lunacy which included administrative functions in the management of the property and affairs of those who lacked capacity. In 1947 the Office of the Master in Lunacy was renamed the Court of Protection. Its role included administrative and management functions in relation to the property and affairs of those who lacked capacity. It did not include issues relating to health or personal welfare which remained within the High Court's inherent jurisdiction.

The Mental Health Act 1959 established a statutory framework which had the effect of extinguishing the High Court's jurisdiction in relation to all matters concerning an incapacitated adult with a mental disorder. They were catered for under the new legislation. The State assumed responsibility for those who lacked capacity by reason of mental disorder as defined by the Act and to manage their affairs. However, this did not include those who lacked capacity for reasons other than mental disorder, eg due to learning disabilities or dementia. This was confirmed by the House of Lords decision in *Re W*.[1] This significant group was left entirely outside statutory powers or protection.

Over the years, as the elderly population has increased, social conditions have improved and medical advances enabled those with a learning disability to survive childhood. Thus, the number of adults, who lacked capacity to make decisions concerning their personal welfare, health and property and affairs also increased. Health and welfare services have become involved to address the resulting issues. When the Mental Health Act 1983 came into force, the Court of Protection's jurisdiction over the property and affairs of those who were incapable of managing their affairs was retained in Part IV of the Act but not expanded to include health and welfare issues. In 1993, following the introduction of the then government's initiative to refocus adult care under the

---

[1]   [1971] Ch 123.

NHS and Community Care Act 1991, there was wholesale closure of long stay hospitals (known as lunatic asylums) which had detained and treated large numbers of people who lacked capacity under an informal regime. Most were discharged to smaller residential facilities within their communities. Local authorities' social services departments became responsible for assessing and providing for the needs of those who had been discharged into the community and those who were in future to be looked after and treated in the community. The health issues of this group of individuals remained, where appropriate, with the National Health Services. The 1983 Act was sometimes deployed to achieve the detention of and provide medical treatment to those who were not mentally ill but lacked capacity. Most continued to be provided for informally, on the basis that despite incapacity they were compliant with the arrangements made for them. There were no procedures in place for the person informally detained to challenge the decision or a review procedure. There was no formal legal system or any guidelines for those who shouldered these new responsibilities which addressed the multifarious issues which were pertinent to this group, particularly in serious personal welfare and health care matters. The lacuna in the law relating to this category of individuals was filled by the Family Division of the High Court exercising its inherent jurisdiction to make declaratory orders. However, matters were in the main only referred to the High Court in the most serious or extreme cases and related to medical treatment; see *Re F (Sterilisation: Mental Patient)*;[2] *Re T (Consent to Medical Treatment)*.[3]

This jurisdiction became increasingly significant and widely used as more difficult and sensitive decisions came within the domain of health and social care providers, particularly following the decision in *Airedale NHS Trust v Bland*.[4] This jurisdiction was extended to issues concerning personal welfare and injunctive relief: see *Re S (Hospital Patient: Court's Jurisdiction)*;[5] *Re V (Declaration Against Parents)*.[6] The Court over years developed the principles, practice, procedure and guidelines which now underpin the Mental Capacity Act 2005. The overriding principles which form the foundation of the new law have their origins in decisions of the High Court.

In order to resolve the tension between domestic law and the newly adopted European Convention for the Protection of Human Rights and Fundamental Freedoms (ECHR) the High Court continued to fill the gap in the law relating to deprivation of liberty of those who lacked capacity both before and after the Mental Capacity Act came into force. The new provisions of the Mental Health Act 2007 which came into force in April 2009 finally provided the necessary safeguards for the informally detained.

---

2   [1989] 2 FLR 376.
3   [1993] 1 FLR 1.
4   [1993] 1 FLR 1026.
5   [1995] 1 FLR 1075.
6   [1995] 2 FLR 1003.

The Mental Capacity Act 2005 reinvented the Court of Protection. It extended its jurisdiction to enable it to deal exclusively with those who lack capacity but are not mentally ill, and with all issues relating to them. It has wide powers to deal with the personal welfare medical treatment and property and affairs of those who lack capacity to make decisions for themselves. The jurisdiction is not dissimilar to the High Court's inherent jurisdiction. The Court has its own unique procedure which is governed by its own Rules, Practice Directions, Forms and Code of Practice. Initially the Court maintained its historic links with the Public Guardian (OPG), the body responsible for supervision of deputies and the registration authority for enduring and lasting powers of attorney. In April 2009 the administration of the Court was absorbed into HM Court Service and its separation from the Office of the Public Guardian was completed.

Currently the Court receives on average about 2000 applications a month. The overwhelming majority are for appointment over or dealings with property and affairs. It is also apparent from the recent attention that the Court has received in the media that abuse of those who lack capacity is not unusual and is an increasing problem both in relation to personal welfare and property and financial issues. Abuse concerning the property and affairs of those who lack capacity is estimated to range from between 10%–15% of all cases and the OPG has recently strengthened its approach to supervision

All the indications suggest that, as with the Children Act 1989 and the family justice system, the law relating to those who lack capacity will be a fast developing specialist branch of the law, with the Court of Protection taking a prominent position in the hierarchy of specialist courts. When problems or conflicts arise it will be to the lawyers that those involved will turn for advice and, where necessary, to take action. In some instances the decision will need to be made as a matter of urgency. Those who do not regularly practice in this jurisdiction and do not have an in-depth knowledge of the new law and practice and procedure may find the process unfamiliar.

This book does not seek to be an academic study of the new law. Its aim is to provide a step-by-step guide to practitioners and professionals involved with those lacking capacity, in order to deal with most issues that are likely to arise and, in particular, those which may require an urgent application. It also provides an overview of the new legislation for those who have no or little specialist knowledge.

The book is divided into eight parts. The first deals with the general principles which must be considered and applied in every case by the decision maker whenever a decision has to be made, no matter how trivial or serious the issue may be. The second, third and fourth parts deal with matters relating to property and affairs and personal welfare, including health and deprivation of liberty respectively, with examples of the relief or remedy or declaration which can be applied for. Part V deals with matters relating to children. Part VI deals with all issues relating to publication and its restriction including, restrictions on the attendance of the media at hearings and disclosure. Mandatory and prohibitive orders which can be made by the Court and which are also likely to form part of the substantive orders applied for and, the appeal process are all dealt with in Part VII. Finally the Mental Capacity Act 2005 and the recent Practice Guidance: *Transparency in the Court of Protection – Publication of Judgments* issued on 16 January 2014 are included in Part VIII of the book. It should also be noted that 'the person lacking capacity' is referred to as 'P' in the statute and subsidiary legislation and throughout this publication.

PART I

GENERAL

CHAPTER 2

GENERAL PRINCIPLES

LAW AND PRACTICE

2.1 INTRODUCTION

The Mental Capacity Act 2005 (the Act) came into force in two stages on 1 April 2007 and on 1 October 2007. Further significant changes were introduced in April 2009. It provides an entirely new and comprehensive statutory framework for decision making for adults who lack capacity to make decisions for themselves, and for those who have capacity but want to make advance decisions for a time when they may lack capacity to make those decisions in the future. It covers issues and decisions relating to personal welfare, health care, property and financial affairs.

The Act builds upon best practice and guidelines laid down in case law and common law principles relating to those who lack capacity and those who have the responsibility to make decisions on their behalf.

The Act was amended by the Mental Health Act 2007 to introduce procedural safeguards where a person lacking capacity may be deprived of his/her liberty in his/her best interest and to make such actions compliant with Art 5 of the European Convention for the Protection of Human Rights and Fundamental Freedoms (ECHR). These provisions came into force on 1 April 2009.

The Act, in ss 42 and 43, provides for one or more Codes of Practice to be issued by the Lord Chancellor for the guidance of those who have responsibility in relation to a person who lacks capacity and the issues identified in the section. These include:

(a) those involved in assessing capacity in relation to any matter;

(b) persons acting in connection with the care or treatment of a person lacking capacity;

(c) donees of lasting powers of attorney;

(d) deputies appointed by the Court ie the Court of Protection;

(e) persons carrying out research in reliance on any provision made by or under the MCA 2005 concerning persons who lack capacity;

(f) independent mental capacity advocates;

(g)   with respect to the issues relating to advance decisions and apparent advance decisions to refuse treatment;

(h)   persons involved in using deprivation of liberty procedures and those who are appointed as representatives of the person deprived of his/her liberty;

(i)   any other matter concerned with the Act as the Lord Chancellor thinks fit.

Section 42(4) of the Act imposes a legal duty on certain categories of persons to have regard to any relevant code if acting, in relation to a person who lacks capacity, in one or more of the following ways:

(a)   as the donee of a lasting power of attorney;

(b)   as a deputy appointed by the Court;

(c)   as a person carrying out research in reliance on any provision made by or under the Act;[1]

(d)   as an independent mental capacity advocate;

(e)   in exercising procedures relating to deprivation of liberty;

(f)   as a representative of a person deprived of his/her liberty;

(g)   in a professional capacity;

(h)   for remuneration.

Section 42(5) provides that a provision of a Code of Practice or a failure to comply with the code may be taken in to account by a court or tribunal conducting any criminal or civil proceedings where it is relevant to a question under consideration in the proceedings.

2.2   TO WHOM DOES THE ACT APPLY?

The Act applies to:

(a)   all adults who lack capacity; and

(b)   young persons, aged between 16 and 18 years, who lack capacity.

Decisions relating to persons between the ages of 16 and 18 years of age can be dealt with under the provisions of the Children Act 1989 in the county court (family court from April 2014) as the definition of a 'child' in s 105 of the 1989 Act includes a child under the age of 18 years, and under the High Court's inherent jurisdiction relating to children. However, the Court's jurisdiction under the Children Act 1989 in relation to children over 16 years of age is restricted by s 9(5)–(7) and more specifically in relation to specific issue and prohibited steps orders, unless it can be established that the circumstances are exceptional. When a young person lacks capacity and the issues relate to property and finance, or are of a testamentary nature which may involve the management of the person's affairs on a continuing basis into adulthood, the Court of Protection is the more appropriate venue to deal with such matters. Section 18(3) of the Act also provides that the Court of Protection may exercise

---

[1]   See MCA 2005, ss 30–34.

jurisdiction in relation to a person's property and affairs even though that person has not reached the age of 16 years, if the Court considers it likely that the person will still lack capacity to make decisions in respect of that matter when he/she reaches adulthood. Additionally, s 21 of the Act makes provision for the transfer of proceedings relating to a person under the age of 18 years from the Court of Protection to a court having jurisdiction under the Children Act 1989 and vice versa.

2.3   KEY PRINCIPLES THAT UNDERPIN THE ACT

The Act, in s 1, sets out the fundamental principles to which regard must be had in every decision made under the Act. These are:

(a)   a person must be assumed to have capacity unless it is established that he lacks capacity;

(b)   a person is not to be treated as unable to make a decision unless all practicable steps to help him to do so have been taken without success;

(c)   a person is not to be treated as unable to make a decision merely because he makes an unwise decision;

(d)   an act done, or decision made, under this Act for or on behalf of a person who lacks capacity must be done, or made, in his best interests;

(e)   before the act is done, or the decision is made, regard must be had to whether the purpose for which it is needed can be as effectively achieved in a way that is less restrictive of the person's rights and freedom of action.

The Act thus reinforces the common law presumption that an adult person has full capacity to make decisions for himself/herself unless it is shown that he/she does not have capacity to do so. In order to assist a person in making a decision the Act provides that all practical assistance must be offered to that person. The Code of Practice[2] also draws attention to this principle by emphasising that a person should not be assumed to be unable to make a decision simply because he/she needs help or support to make and communicate the decision. Paragraphs 3.15–3.22 of the Code also alert and guide those who have to deal with a person who appears to have difficulty in making or taking a decision, to take appropriate steps to assist that person to make his/her decision. The key principle (d) (above) reaffirms previous case law (see *Re T (An Adult) (Consent to Medical Treatment)*;[3] *Sidaway v Board of Governors of the Bethlem Royal Hospital and the Maudsley Hospital*[4]) that a person is not to be regarded as lacking capacity by reason of the fact that he/she has come to a decision which is different from that which most people would make. This is further emphasised in s 2(3) which provides that a lack of capacity cannot be established merely by reference to a person's age or appearance or a condition of his, or an aspect of his behaviour, which might lead others to make

---

2   Mental Capacity Act (2005) Code of Practice, issued by the Lord Chancellor on 23 April 2007 in accordance with ss 42 and 43 of the 2005 Act.
3   [1992] 2 FLR 458.
4   [1985] AC 871.

unjustified assumptions about his capacity. The Code of Practice however, draws attention to decision making which is out of character and which therefore may be evidence of P lacking capacity. Section 1(5) enshrines the common law 'best interests' practice established in *Re F (Mental Patient: Sterilisation)*.[5] Finally the principle set out in s 1(6) seeks to achieve a balance between assisting and enabling a person to make some decisions and ensuring that when the decision is taken on behalf of the person lacking capacity there are safeguards which protect that person's rights and the person from abuse.

2.4   THRESHOLD TEST OF CAPACITY

The jurisdiction of the Court of Protection is engaged only if a person lacks capacity. The Court has no power to make decisions on behalf of vulnerable adults unless they also lack capacity to make decisions for themselves. The test for whether a person (P) has capacity to make a specific decision at the material time is set out at s 2(1) of the Act and provides that:

> 'a person lacks capacity in relation to a matter if at the material time he is unable to make a decision in relation to the matter because of an impairment of, or a disturbance in, the functioning of the mind or brain.'

Section 3 (see below **2.4.2**) then goes on to consider the circumstances in which P is regarded as being unable to make a decision. So this provides for a two stage test, a diagnostic test of the nature of the impairment or disturbance and a functional test of how decision making is affected. In the Court of Appeal decision of *PC & NC v City of York Council* the Court concluded that this should not be regarded as a series of two free-standing tests. Instead it was more appropriate to consider first the decision to be made and why P cannot make it, in the context of diagnosis. Any other interpretation would ignore the nexus between the two and in particular the words 'because of' in s 2(1). Per McFarlane LJ:

> 'There is, however, a danger in structuring the decision by looking to s 2(1) primarily as requiring a finding of mental impairment and nothing more and in considering s 2(1) first before then going on to look at s 3(1) as requiring a finding of inability to make a decision. The danger is that the strength of the causative nexus between mental impairment and inability to decide is watered down. That sequence – "mental impairment" and then "inability to make a decision" – is the reverse of that in s 2(1) – "unable to make a decision ... because of an impairment of, or a disturbance in the functioning of, the mind or brain". The danger in using s 2(1) simply to collect the mental health element is that the key words "because of" in s 2(1) may lose their prominence.'

2.4.1   Diagnostic stage

Despite some debate about how the requirements of the test should be applied there is no doubt that a diagnosis of impairment of the mind or brain is

---

[5]   [1990] 2 AC 1, [1989] 2 FLR 376, HL.

essential in assessing capacity. Further there is no doubt that s 2(1) recognises that the issue of capacity is issue/decision (including acts and persons) specific and time specific.

The main categories of people lacking capacity who come before the Court of Protection are elderly people suffering from dementing illnesses, victims of strokes or accidents causing brain injury and those with learning disabilities. The Code of Practice, para 4.12 helpfully sets out some of the conditions which could result in such impairment or disturbance. It includes conditions associated with some forms of mental illness, dementia, significant learning difficulties, long term effects of brain damage, physical or mental conditions which cause confusion, drowsiness or loss of consciousness, delirium, concussion following a head injury and the symptoms of alcohol and drug abuse. In order to determine this issue it may be necessary to obtain expert medical, psychiatric and/or psychological assessment of the incapacitated person (see below under 2.4.8) unless the person is known to have been diagnosed with a well established medical condition which is not in dispute.

If an impairment of the mind or brain is diagnosed, the legislation goes on to ask whether or not the impairment affects P's ability to make that particular decision at 'the material time'. It is thus acknowledged that a person's capacity may fluctuate. This is further affirmed in s 2(2), which provides that it does not matter whether the impairment or disturbance is permanent or temporary. Therefore, if the impairment is temporary and there is no urgency in making the particular decision, then applying the key principle set out in s 1(3), that all *practicable* steps to help the person must be taken and found to have failed before any decision is taken on his behalf, it may be appropriate to wait until the person is able to make a decision for himself/herself. The Code of Practice supports this interpretation as it defines 'practicable' as 'practical and appropriate' and according to 'personal circumstances', ie the kind of decision that has to be made and the time available to make that decision.

Where the circumstances require an urgent decision to be taken the Act permits the decision to be taken on behalf of the person lacking capacity but emphasises that the act done or decision made must be in P's best interests.

2.4.2 The functional stage

The other requirement of the test of capacity must demonstrate that the impairment or disturbance renders the person unable to make the decision in question for himself/herself.

Case law[6] had established that a person may be considered as lacking capacity to make a decision when:

---

[6] *Masterman-Lister v Brutton & Co* [2002] EWCA Civ 1889.

(a) P is unable to comprehend and retain the information which is material to the decision, especially as to the likely consequences of having or not having the treatment in question;

(b) P is unable to use the information and weigh it in the balance as part of the process of arriving at the decision.[7]

The Act, in s 3(1), confirms this test by providing that a person is unable to make a decision for himself if he is unable:

(a) to understand the information relevant to the decision;

(b) to retain that information;

(c) to use or weigh that information as part of the process of making the decision; or

(d) to communicate his decision (whether by talking, using sign language or any other means).

It is important to note that the legislation establishes jurisdiction on the basis of capacity only. Attempts have been made to imply into the legislation an additional threshold gleaned from a reading of the ECHR and subsequent case law. In *G v E and A Local Authority*[8] Baker J rejected the proposition raised by way of analogy with s 31 of the Children Act 1989, that ECHR, Art 5 established a threshold condition or conditions which had to be satisfied over and above the test of capacity.

2.4.3   (a) The person's ability to understand the information provided

Section 3(2) provides that a person is not be regarded as unable to understand the information relevant to a decision if he is able to understand an explanation of it given to him in a way that is appropriate to his circumstances. The information relevant to a decision includes information about reasonably foreseeable consequences of deciding one way or another or failing to make the decision.[9] In order to enable the person to understand the consequences of his decision the person must be given information about the nature of the decision to be made, the reason why the decision needs to be taken and the likely effects of making it and of refusing to make it. The extent to which P may need to forsee the consequence of his/her decision has been held to be time limited. In *A Local Authority v Mrs A*[10] the Court considered the forceable administration of contraception to a married woman whose children were removed at birth under care orders. By reason of serious learning difficulties she had no understanding of the duties and responsibilities of parenthood. This was held to be beyond the scope of the information needed. The information needed to reach a decision about contraception was limited to pregnancy and the subsequent birth.

---

[7]   *Re C (Refusal of Medical Treatment* [1994] 1 FLR 31.
[8]   [2010] EWHC 621 (Fam).
[9]   MCA 2005, s 3(4).
[10] [2010] EWHC 1549 (COP), [2010] COPLR Con Vol 138.

2.4.4   (b) The ability to retain information[11]

The fact that a person is able to retain the information relevant to a decision for a short period only does not prevent him/her from being regarded as able to make the decision.[12]

2.4.5   (c) The ability to use or weigh the information as a test of capacity

This has been considered in a number of decisions (for example *Re MB (Medical Treatment)*,[13] where the patient had a phobia of needles and was held to be incompetent at the point of proceeding with surgery due to the phobia, and *Bolton Hospitals NHS Trust v O*[14]).

P is not expected to have a comprehensive understanding of all the ins and outs of the information available. In *CC v KK and STCC*[15] Baker J in a case concerning welfare issues said:

'I bear in mind and adopt the important observations of Macur J in *LBL v RYJ and VJ* [2010] EWHC 2665 (COP), [2010] COPLR Con Vol 795, [2011] 1 FLR 1279, at para [24], that:

"it is not always necessary for a person to comprehend all peripheral details ..."'

That would of course confer a test with which most of the population would be unable to comply!

The easier or more straightforward it is for P to use or weigh the information is also relevant. For instance despite a diagnosis of an impairment of the mind or brain, P may have capacity to make decisions regarding routine financial transactions such as the payment of bills but not the selling of a portfolio of stocks and shares. The example in *PC & NC v York City Council*[16] was of information required to decide to take a holiday abroad being easier to use and weigh than that required to decide to emigrate.

2.4.6   (d) The ability to communicate

If there is any indication that the person is unable to communicate this inability may be overcome with the appropriate support and assistance. In such cases, there is an obligation to provide the required support and, where appropriate, by a person who has the necessary skills. In other instances the failure to

---

[11]   MCA 2005, s 3(1)(b).
[12]   MCA 2005, s 3(3).
[13]   [1997] 2 FLR 426.
[14]   [2002] EWHC 2871 (Fam), [2003] 1 FLR 824.
[15]   [2012] EWHC 2136 (COP).
[16]   [2013] EWCA Civ 478.

communicate may be due to a physical condition, eg unconsciousness or other such condition. The issue in such cases will be an assessment by a qualified and experienced professional on the person's condition and the likelihood of him/her regaining consciousness or the ability to communicate the information within the time limit which is relevant to the circumstances.

2.4.7   Threshold of incapacity in cases of urgency (interim orders)

In cases where a decision needs to be made and an act done as a matter of urgency in the best interest of a person who appears to lack capacity, but before it is possible to assess the person's capacity comprehensively, the Court is empowered, following an application, to exercise its powers on an interim basis by applying a lower threshold if the conditions set out in s 48 of the Act are met.

Section 48 provides:

> 'The court may, pending the determination of an application to it in relation to a person (P), make an order or give directions in respect of any matter if:
> (a)   there is reason to believe that P lacks capacity in relation to the matter;
> (b)   the matter is one to which its powers under this Act extend; and
> (c)   it is in P's best interest to make the order or give directions.'

Thus the Court may determine the issue without a finding of lack of capacity but it must still apply the key principles set out in s 1 of the Act when deciding what order/s to make on the issue under consideration.

The application of s 48 was considered in *Re F*[17] by HHJ Marshall a nominated circuit judge of the Court of Protection who said:

> '... it is obvious that situations can arise where the obtaining of a formal declaration or decision ... will take time, but common sense suggests that some action may be needed in the interim. Common sense also suggests that if lack of capacity in relation to any particular matter or decision is in issue (notwithstanding the presumption of capacity) then the Court should have any necessary powers to enable the proper consideration and determination of that issue, even (and in fact inevitably) if this means making orders or directions which affect the person whose capacity is in issue, before that issue has been determined.
>
> It is the intention of s 48 to provide for those situations and to authorise the taking of urgent decisions which appear to be necessary in P's best interests "without delay" before there has been an actual determination that P does lack capacity.
>
> The "reason to believe" test is therefore met if there is evidence to suggest that there is a real possibility that P may lack capacity ...'

The test to be applied in such cases was considered by the judge and it was held that:

---

[17]   (Unreported) 28 May 2009.

'the proper test for the engagement of Section 48 in the first instance is whether there is evidence giving good cause for concern that P may lack capacity in some relevant regard. Once that has been raised as a serious possibility the Court then moves on to the second stage to decide what action, if any, it is in P's best interest to take before a final determination of his capacity can be made.'

2.4.8 Assessment of capacity

There is no specific requirement in the Act for a professional, whether medical or otherwise, to carry out the assessment. In the majority of cases the assessment will be undertaken by the person who is responsible for providing the care or treatment and directly concerned with the person lacking capacity, and therefore has to make the decision. A special visitor may however, be called upon to provide an assessment. Pursuant to s 61 of the Act and for the purposes of the new jurisdiction, the Lord Chancellor has appointed two panels of Court of Protection visitors, namely a panel of special visitors and a panel of general visitors. A special visitor must be a registered medical practitioner or, appear to the Lord Chancellor to have other suitable qualifications or training and, to have knowledge of and experience in cases of impairment of or disturbance in the functioning of mind or brain.[18] They are usually psychiatrists who specialise in this area of work. By reason of their experience and qualification, special visitors are qualified to provide reports on the issue of whether or not P has capacity and to assist in ascertaining the wishes and feelings of P when there are communication difficulties.

In order to protect those who provide care and treatment and who have to make decisions on a regular basis in providing the care and treatment, s 5 provides that if a person does an act in connection with the care or treatment of another person (P) he/she will not incur any liability in relation to the act provided, before doing the act, the person takes reasonable steps to establish whether P lacks capacity in relation to the matter in question, and, when doing the act, the person reasonably believes that P lacks capacity in relation to the matter and that it will be in P's best interest for the act to be done. The nature of the care and treatment to which such acts relate are not defined in the section. The definition of 'treatment' provided in s 64(1), namely as including a 'diagnostic or other procedure' is not specific. Paragraph 6 of the Code of Practice sets out guidelines which must be followed and para 6.5 includes a list of some actions that might be covered by s 5. These involve action related to the personal care of the person concerned and health care and treatment. The latter includes:

- carrying out diagnostic examinations and tests (to identify an illness condition or other problem);
- providing professional medical, dental and similar treatment;
- giving medication;
- taking someone to hospital for assessment or treatment;
- providing nursing care (whether in hospital or in the community);

---

[18] MCA 2005, s 61(2).

- carrying out any other necessary medical procedures (for example, taking blood sample) or therapies (for example, physiotherapy or chiropody);
- providing care in an emergency.

The protection is available only if the person providing the care and treatment reasonably believed that the patient lacked capacity to give consent and the actions taken are considered to be in the best interests of the patient after having applied the key principles (see further under the Code of Practice, paras 6.8–6.39).

The steps that are accepted as 'reasonable' will depend upon the circumstances and the urgency of the decision. Again guidance is provided in the Code of Practice (in paras 4.44–4.54) on how to assess the situation and the factors that may affect the nature of the assessment and when a professional assessment may be necessary, before any decision is made or act done.

Where the decision relates to complex and or disputed issues (see the Code of Practice, paras 3.37–4.42 and 4.53–4.54) the assessment should be undertaken by a professional who has the necessary expertise in the particular field, eg a psychiatrist, psychologist etc. In some instances an assessment by more than one expert may be needed. Where the intervention of the Court of Protection is sought, a formal assessment by an appropriately qualified professional will be required.

When assessing capacity or lack of it, the person required to carry out the assessment must be given information relating to the background history and circumstances and the details of the specific decision that needs to be made by P. It is also necessary to ensure that the principles set out in the Act and the requirement of assisting P to make the decision is considered and undertaken. The assessment should also consider how the person can be encouraged to participate, or to improve his ability to participate as fully as possible in any act done for him and any decision affecting him.[19] In deciding the issue of capacity, the factors which will need to be considered are the proposed treatment, the risk involved and the benefit to P. It will also be necessary to establish whether the condition is permanent or temporary. If temporary, the assessment should give an indication when it is likely that the person will regain capacity.

If there is any doubt about capacity, or lack of capacity, a declaration may be sought from the Court of Protection under s 15 of the Act which gives the Court power to make declarations as to:

(a) whether a person has or lacks capacity to make a decision specified in the declaration;

(b) whether a person has or lacks capacity to make decisions on such matters as are described in the declaration;

(c) the lawfulness or otherwise of any act done, or yet to be done, in relation to that person.

---

[19]   MCA 2005, 4(4).

The Court may also be asked to make the decision(s) on P's behalf in relation to any specific matter(s), or to appoint a deputy to make the decisions on P's behalf, in relation to the specific matters under s 16(1) and (2) of the MCA 2005.

2.5 BEST INTERESTS – S 4

Where lack of capacity has been established, case law has recognised and established that any act undertaken or decision made must be in the best interests of P (see *Wyatt v Portsmouth NHS Trust*;[20] *Re Y (Mental Incapacity: Bone Marrow Transplant*[21]) and in so doing that the wishes of P, his religious beliefs and of those close to him are considered. However, the approach to a best interests decision on behalf of P was then very different. There was a leaning towards the substituted judgment approach. Best interests were represented as what P him/herself would decide rather than an objective assessment. In Re *D(J)*[22] the leading case on statutory wills pre 2007, Sir Robert Megarry V-C formulated a framework of principles upon which the Court should act. These imagined that P was having a lucid interval and relied upon what was known of P and the decisions he/she may take during such a lucid interval. However, following the implementation of the Act, it was held that the substituted judgment approach could no longer be supported. In *Re P*[23] Lewison J considered the past guidance of *Re D(J)* and set out the way in which the Act now requires the Court to assess P's 'best interests'. This is different from inquiring what P would have wanted if he or she had capacity.

> 'The Act does not require the counter-factual assumption that P is not mentally disordered. The facts must be taken as they are. It is not therefore necessary to go through the mental gymnastics of imagining that P has a brief lucid interval ... The goal of the inquiry is not what P "might be expected" to have done; but what is in P's best interests. This is more akin to the "balance sheet" approach than to the "substituted judgment" approach.'

That case also involved the making a of a statutory will. In deciding its terms Levinson J rejected the approach of *Re D(J)* because it is not automatic that P's wishes in this context will always be followed – it was:

> 'Part of the overall picture and an important one ... but what will live on after P's death is his memory; and for many people it is in their best interests that they be remembered with affection by their family and as having done "the right thing" by their will.'

P's own wishes will however be a magnetic component in assessing best interests but not paramount. In *Re S and S*[24] HHJ Marshall in considering an appeal from a district judge about a dispute over the appointment of an

---

[20]   [2006] 1 FLR 554.
[21]   [1996] 2 FLR 787.
[22]   [1982] 2 All ER 37, ChD.
[23]   [2009] EWHC 163 (Ch).
[24]   Lawtel Case No AC0119248.

attorney said that if P's views were reasonable rational and responsible then there was a presumption that they would be followed. Levinson J went on in *Re P* to consider this and said:

> 'The only imperative is that the decision must be made in P's best interests ... and ... although P's wishes must be given weight, if as I think, Parliament has endorsed the "balance" sheet approach they are only one part of the balance. I agree those wishes are to be given great weight but I would prefer not to speak in terms of presumption.'

The views of third parties, eg parents and those with responsibility for caring for P should also be taken into account, although not always followed, if it is not considered to be in the interests of P (*Re A (Male Sterilisation)*[25] – where the wish of a mother of a young man with Down's syndrome, who was on the borderline between significant and severe impairment of intelligence, was that he should be sterilised on the ground that it was in his best interest, but her application was refused on the basis that the best interests of P encompassed medical, emotional and all other welfare issues. Neither the birth of a child nor disapproval of his conduct was likely to impinge on him to a significant degree other than in exceptional circumstances).

The Supreme Court decision in *Aintree University Hospitals NHS Foundation Trust v James*[26] suggests that although the MCA 2005 does not directly provide for the 'substituted judgment' to be applied there are elements in the provisions in s 4(6) which make P's own wishes central to best interests decision making on his behalf. The Court seems to have rejected the objective test or the test of what a reasonable patient' would wish. The position is however not entirely clear as Baroness Hale placed greater emphasis on 'best interests' test rather than 'substituted judgment' but stated that in applying the best interests 'the preference of the person concerned are an important component in deciding where his best interests lie'.

Section 1(5) of the Act establishes that an act done or a decision made under this Act for or on behalf of a person who lacks capacity must be done or made in his best interests. Section 4 furthers this principle by setting out the best interests criteria to be applied when making any decision relating to a person who lacks capacity. The person making the determination is required to consider all the relevant circumstances (of which that person is aware and which it would be reasonable for him to regard as relevant) and in particular:

(a)   he must consider whether it is likely that the person will at some time have capacity in relation to the matter in question and if it appears likely that he will, when that is likely to be.

(b)   he must consider so far as is reasonably ascertainable:

(i)   the person's past and present wishes and feelings (and, in particular, any written relevant statement made by him when he had capacity) (see *MM; Local Authority X v MM (By the Official Solicitor) and KM*[27]);

(ii) the beliefs and values that would be likely to influence his decision if he had capacity, and the other factors that he would be likely to consider if he were able to do so.

(c)   he must take into account, if it is practicable and appropriate to consult them, the views of:

(i)   anyone named by the person as someone to be consulted on the matter in question or on matters of that kind;

(ii) anyone engaged in caring for the person or interested in his welfare;

(iii) any donee of a lasting power of attorney granted by the person;

(vi) any deputy appointed for the person by the Court as to what would be in the person's best interests.

(d)   where the determination relates to life-sustaining treatment the person carrying out the assessment must not, in considering whether the treatment is in the best interests of P, be motivated by a desire to bring about his death. Life-sustaining treatment means treatment which in the view of a person providing health care for the person concerned is necessary to sustain life. Reference should be made to the Code of Practice, paras 5.29–5.36 which gives guidance on how the best interests of P should be considered. (See also under chapter 9.)

These considerations are reinforced in the Code of Practice, para 5 and more particularly paras 5.47–5.48 in relation to the weight to be given to the interests of third parties. It also provides guidance in dealing with problematic cases. For instance, where there may be conflict of interests and concerns, where decisions are challenged. Where problems may be experienced when consulting and dealing with family members, carers and their views, guidance is provided in paras 5.62–5.69.

Section 4(4) of the Act also requires the decision-maker, so far as is reasonably practicable, to permit and encourage the person to participate, or to improve his ability to participate, as fully as possible in any act done for him and any decision affecting him.

In *Re P (Adult Patient) (Medical Treatment)*[28] the Court of Protection considered the issue of whether the best interests of P required immediate admission to a residential unit for assessment or delayed assessment at a chronic fatigue unit. P's mother's preferred option was an admission to a chronic fatigue unit. The judge approved the assessment at the chronic fatigue unit. The mother subsequently withdrew her consent. The PCT made an interim application for the immediate admission of P as an in-patient to a local unit of the PCT relying on the urgency of the need for an assessment and the

---

[27]   [2009] 1 FLR 443.
[28]   [2009] 1 FCR 567.

risk of interference from the mother. It was considered by the experts, that overall admission to the chronic fatigue unit was the preferred option since it would involve a degree of consent rather than coercion. The Court agreed that on balance it was in P's best interests to be admitted to the chronic fatigue unit, provided that the mother was willing to co-operate and would not interfere with the proposed treatment or resist any restrictions which might be imposed on her. The Court also provided that, if admission to the chronic fatigue unit was unable to proceed due to the mother's lack of co-operation, P should be admitted to the local unit immediately without recourse to a further application to the Court.

In assessing P's best interests, decision makers including the Court must have regard to P's rights under the ECHR. These will include the right to life (Art 2); prohibition of torture and inhuman or degrading treatment (Art 3); the right to liberty and security (Art 5); the right to a fair trial (Art 6); the rights to respect of private and family life (Art 8); the right to marry (Art 12). In appropriate cases the rights protected under the UNCRPD and the principles protected under the Recommendation No R (99)4 of the Committee of Ministers of the Council of Europe concerning the legal protection of incapable adults (23 February 1999) may also be relevant and a factor to be considered in undertaking the balancing exercise.

2.6   INDEPENDENT MENTAL CAPACITY ADVOCATES – SS 35–39

An independent mental capacity advocate (IMCA) is the creation of the Act. The purpose of this provision is to provide an additional safeguard for P's interests in two specific situations namely:

- where serious medical treatment is proposed for P; and/or
- where a change in P's residence is proposed by a NHS body or the local authority.

However, the appointment of an IMCA is only available where P has no family or friend whom it would be appropriate for the NHS body or the local authority to consult in determining what is in P's best interests (for an example of a case where an IMCA was appointed see *Re M (Best Interests: Deprivation of Liberty)*[29] and for a further discussion see **9.15.1** and **9.1.3**).

2.7   PERMISSION TO APPLY

In order to invoke the jurisdiction of the Court there is a general requirement to apply for permission as a preliminary to intervening. Section 50 of the Act sets out the categories of persons who do not require the permission of the Court before issuing an application for relief or order under the Act. They are:

(a)   a person who lacks capacity;

---

[29]   [2013] EWHC 3456 (COP).

(b)   a person who has parental responsibility for a person who lacks capacity who is under the age of 18 years;

(c)   the donor of a lasting power of attorney to which the application relates;

(d)   a deputy appointed by the Court for a person to whom the application relates;

(e)   a person named in an existing order of the Court if the application relates to that order.

The Act, in Sch 3, para 20(1) and (2), also provides that an interested person may apply to the Court for a declaration as to whether a protective measure taken under the law of a country outside England and Wales is to be recognised in England and Wales without first seeking permission to apply.

Pursuant to s 50(2) and the COP Rules 2007, r 51, the Official Solicitor and the Public Guardian also do not require permission.

Permission is also not required:

* (subject to certain exceptions set out in r 52) where the application concerns P's property and affairs;

* for a lasting power of attorney which is, or purports to be, created under the Act;

* for an instrument which is, or purports to be, an enduring power of attorney;

* for an application made in the course of proceedings and where an acknowledgement is filed which seeks an order different from that sought in the substantive application (see Part 10 of the Rules).

All other applications require permission.[30] The Act and the Rules read together therefore require that issues relating to health and welfare will require permission even where orders relating to urgent medical treatment or withholding of such treatment are sought, unless the exemptions referred to in s 50 apply.

Where part of the application relates to a matter which requires permission and part of it does not, the applicant has a choice to either make two separate applications or one application. Provision is made for permission to be sought for that part of it which requires permission in the main application.[31] The advantage of seeking both permission and the order which does not require permission in one application is that only one fee will be payable.

---

[30]   MCA 2005, 50(2).
[31]   COP Rules 2007, r 53(2) and PD 8A, paras 2 and 3.

2.7.1   Factors which the Court must take account of when considering an application for permission

The factors which the Court must take into consideration include:

(a)   the applicant's connection with the person to whom the application relates;

(b)   the reasons for the application;

(c)   the benefit to the person to whom the application relates of a proposed order or directions; and

(d)   whether the benefit can be achieved in any other way.

These factors ensure that any application which is made is motivated by the need to promote the interest of the person who lacks capacity and to protect that person from frivolous applications. The requirement that the Court should consider whether there are other means of achieving the end result also ensures that an application is made to the Court as a last resort after all other ways of achieving the desired outcome have been tried without success. In determining such application the Court thus weighs up the advantages and disadvantages to P and the motives of the applicant in making the application. The provisions in s 50(3) require the Court to prevent not only the frivolous and abusive applications but those which have no realistic prospect of success or bear any sense of proportional response to the problem that is envisaged by the applicant (per Macur J in *NK v VW and Others*[32] where permission was refused). The Court in such an application must of course consider the Convention rights of both the applicant and P. In this context, the Art 8 rights of both P and the applicant family member is very relevant but that must be determined with the priority given to P's rights as is clear from the terms of s 50(3) (see also *Re S (Adult Patient) (Inherent Jurisdiction: Family Life)*).[33])

2.7.2   Procedure for application for permission

The application must be made on Form COP2 and filed with all the supporting information and documents; ie a draft of the application in Form COP1, which the applicant seeks permission to have issued and an assessment of capacity in Form COP3 (in its new form), where this is required.[34] If the applicant is unable to file an assessment of capacity he must file a witness statement explaining the reasons for the absence of the assessment; the efforts that have been made to obtain an assessment; and the reason why it is believed that the person lacks capacity to make a decision in relation to the subject of the proposed application. The application form must state the capacity in which the applicant is making the application if it is made in a representative capacity and state the issues which he/she requires the Court to determine and the order/s sought. It must identify the person whom lacks capacity and any person

---

[32]   [2012] COPLR 105 (COP).
[33]   [2002] EWHC 2278 (Fam), [2003] 1 FLR 292.
[34]   COP Rules 2007, r 54 and PD 8A.

who the applicant reasonably believes may have an interest in the matter under consideration and any person who ought to be notified under r 70.

Within 14 days of the application for permission being filed the Court will consider the application and either grant the application in whole or in part, or subject to conditions without a hearing, and may also give directions in connection with the issue of the application form or refuse the application or fix a date for a hearing of the application or simply order the filing of further information.[35] The Court may also give directions for the appointment of a special visitor to assess P's capacity and ascertain, in so far as it is practicable, his/her wishes and feelings. If the Court grants permission without a hearing it will give directions for the filing of all the relevant documents required under r 64 unless these have already been provided.

If the Court fixes a date for the permission hearing it will serve notice of the hearing to the applicant and any other interested party.

Any person who is notified of the application for permission and who wishes to be heard at the permission hearing must file an acknowledgement of notification within 21 days of the date on which the notification was given. The acknowledgement which must be signed by the person or his/her legal representative; must state whether the person consents to the application or opposes it, setting out the grounds for the opposition; state what if any order is considered to be more appropriate; and provide an address for service. If the person notified of the permission hearing does not file an acknowledgement he will not be able to take part in the proceedings unless the Court permits him to do so.

The order granting or refusing permission will be served by the Court on the applicant and any other person notified of the application who filed an acknowledgement of notification.[36]

Any person who is aggrieved by the decision of the Court has the right to appeal. The appeal must be dealt with in accordance with Part 20.

2.8 ALLOCATION – R 86

Before the Act came into force the jurisdiction over the affairs of a person who lacked capacity was divided between the Court of Protection and the Family Division of the High Court. The Court of Protection dealt with matters relating to the person's property and affairs. The Family Division dealt with issues relating to medical treatment and personal welfare.

The two courts approached issues in different ways. Cases heard in the Family Division involved a full hearing with oral evidence including evidence from

---

[35] COP Rules 2007, r 55.
[36] COP Rules 2007, r 59.

experts taken. The person who lacked capacity was a party to the proceedings and represented by the Official Solicitor. In the old Court of Protection most cases were dealt with without an oral hearing and even when such hearings did occur they were relatively short.

Since 1 October 2007 all issues relating to an incapacitated person's property and financial affairs and personal welfare and medical treatment are now dealt with in the Court of Protection.

The Central Registry for the Court of Protection was based at the Thomas More Building at Royal Courts of Justice in the Strand, and where all applications were processed. The Court has now moved to First Avenue House on High Holborn. Regional Courts are located in Birmingham, Bristol, Cardiff, Manchester, Newcastle and Preston. In practice, regional judges will travel to courts convenient for the parties. The President of the Family Division is also the President of the Court of Protection. Denzil Lush, the former Master of the Court of Protection, is the Senior Judge. A number of High Court judges, circuit and district judges have also been nominated to hear Court of Protection cases. There is thus a three-tier judiciary who are nominated to sit in the Court of Protection. The Court of Protection's Practice Direction provide that all cases involving serious medical treatment must be heard by a nominated judge of the Family Division of the High Court. In practice, financial and management decisions are usually dealt with by district judges with the right of appeal to a nominated circuit judge. Personal and welfare decisions are generally dealt with by the Senior Judge of the Court or a nominated circuit judge. The COP Rules 2007 apply across all tiers but the pattern followed continues to be the same as before the Act came into force. The more serious cases are assigned to the High Court as follows:

(a) An application involving the lawfulness of withholding or withdrawing artificial nutrition and hydration from a person in a permanent vegetative state, or minimally conscious state or a case involving an ethical dilemma in an untested area must be heard by the President of the Court of Protection or by a judge nominated by the President (including permission, the giving of any directions and any other hearing).[37]

(b) An application in relation to serious medical treatment or where a declaration of compatibility pursuant to s 4 of the Human Rights Act 1998 is sought (including permission, the giving of any directions, and any hearing) must be conducted by the President of the Family Division, the Chancellor or a puisne judge of the High Court.[38]

(c) A judge to whom a serious medical treatment case or a case where a declaration of incompatibility is sought under the Human Rights Act is allocated may determine that the matter is one which can be dealt with by a judge of the court other than a designated High Court judge.[39]

---

[37] PD 12A, para 2.
[38] PD 12A, para 3.
[39] PD 12A, para 5.

Tension may however arise where there are mixed property and finance issues and difficult welfare issues to be determined. The allocation of such cases will depend on the facts of the individual case but in most cases the Court will apply commonsense and consider issues such as proportionality; the need to avoid delay and to deal with the case expeditiously; saving the parties incurring unnecessary costs and expense; the complexity of the issues; and judicial availability and the Court's resources.

2.9 FEES AND COSTS

2.9.1 Court fees

With effect from 7 October 2013 a universal fee remission scheme was adopted in all courts nationwide to include COP. The forms 160A and 160B can be downloaded from the website (for web-link see under Part VIII). It is important to note that Form 160B which enables applicants for urgent orders, to give an undertaking either to pay the fee or apply for remission so the payment of fees does not operate as a bar to bringing proceedings in an emergency. Further applicants have a period of 3 months from the making of a final order to make a backdated claim for fees to be remitted in the event that the financial information required is not immediately forthcoming.

2.9.2 Charging

Fixed fees maybe chargeable by professionals although most opt for assessment of their costs. Expenses can be claimed by lay persons managing P's property and affairs and or health and welfare subject to scrutiny by the Public Guardian.

2.9.3 Costs

The provisions relating to the payment of costs are set out in s 55 of the Act and COP Rules 2007, rr 155–168. Subject to the COP Rules, the costs of and incidental to all proceedings in the Court are in the Court's discretion. The Court has full power to determine by whom and to what extent the costs are to be paid. It may also disallow or order the legal or other representatives concerned to meet the whole of the wasted costs or such part of them as may be determined in accordance with the rules.[40]

'Wasted costs' means any costs incurred by a party:
(a)   as a result of any improper, unreasonable or negligent act or omission on the part of any legal or other representative or any employee of such a representative; or

---

[40]   MCA 2005, 55(1)-(4).

(b) which, in the light of any such act or omission occurring after they were occurred, the Court considers it is unreasonable to expect that party to pay.[41]

The Act, in s 56, provides for the COP Rules 2007 to make provision as to the way in fees and costs are to be paid; or charging fees and costs upon the estate of the person to whom the proceedings relate; and for the payment of fees and costs within a specified time of the death of that person to whom the proceedings relate, or the conclusion of the proceedings.

The general rule is that, where the proceedings concern the incapacitated person's property and affairs, the costs of the proceedings, or of that part of the proceedings that concerns his or her property and affairs, shall be paid by him or her or charged to his estate.[42] Where the proceedings concern the incapacitated person's personal welfare there will be no order as to costs of the proceedings or of that part of the proceedings that concern his or her personal welfare.[43] Where the proceedings concern both property and affairs and personal welfare the Court, insofar as practicable, will apportion the costs as between the respective issues.[44]

The Court may however depart from this general rule if the circumstances so justify. In deciding whether to depart from the general rule the Court will have regard to all the circumstances, including:

(a) the conduct of the parties;

(b) whether a party has succeeded on part of his case, even if he has not been wholly successful; and

(c) the role of any public body involved in the proceedings.

'Conduct' of the parties includes conduct before as well as during, the proceedings and whether it was reasonable for a party to raise, pursue or contest a particular issue. It includes the manner in which a party has conducted the litigation and whether a party who has succeeded in his application or response to an application, in whole or in part, exaggerated any matter contained his application or response. Conduct therefore includes both the general conduct of the parties and conduct during litigation.[45]

COP Rules 2007, r 160 also extends Parts 44, 47 and 48 of the Civil Procedure Rules 1998 with certain modifications to proceedings in the Court of Protection, where appropriate.

If the Official Solicitor is involved in the proceedings his costs in relation to the proceedings, or in carrying out any direction given by the Court and not provided for by remuneration under r 167, must be paid by such person or out

---

[41] MCA 2005, s 55(6).
[42] COP Rules 2007, r 156.
[43] COP Rules 2007, r 157.
[44] COP Rules 2007, r 158.
[45] COP Rules 2007, r 159.

of such funds as the Court may direct.[46] Costs may also be ordered against or in favour of a third party but before doing so that person must be added as a party to the proceedings for the purposes of costs only and be given a reasonable opportunity to attend a hearing at which the Court intends to consider the matter.[47]

---

[46] COP Rules 2007, r 163.
[47] COP Rules 2007, r 166.

PRECEDENT

PRECEDENT FOR AN ORDER MADE WITHOUT A HEARING REFUSING PERMISSION WITH REASONS FOR THE REFUSAL

IN THE COURT OF PROTECTION

IN THE MATTER OF THE MENTAL CAPACITY ACT 2005

AND IN THE MATTER OF ALFONO MARIO

BETWEEN

	AB	Applicant
	And	
	XY	Respondent

ORDER

Made by District Judge Wise

At First Avenue House 42-49 High Holborn London WC1A 9JA (*insert address if sitting at a regional court*)

On ....

WHEREAS

1.   Jacqueline Peacock, the 'applicant' has sought permission to apply to the Court to be appointed joint deputy to make personal welfare decisions for Alfonso Mario.

2.   The applicant has sought to be appointed joint deputy to make property and affairs decisions for Alfonso Mario.

3.   Section 5 of the Mental Capacity Act 2005 confers general authority to act without the need for any formal authorisation by the Court if a person does an act in connection with the care or treatment of a person who lacks capacity and acts in that person's best interests.

4.   Section 16(4) of the Act provides that, when deciding whether it is in a person's best interests to appoint a deputy, the Court must have regard to the principles that (a) a decision of the Court is to be preferred to the

appointment of a deputy and (b) the powers conferred on a deputy should be as limited in scope and duration as is reasonably practicable in the circumstances.

5. In the permission Form COP2, witness statement dated .... day of .... 2010 and documents filed, the applicant has not identified with sufficient particularity the reasons why it is necessary at this stage to appoint a deputy to make personal welfare decisions and what specific personal welfare powers are sought.

IT IS ORDERED THAT

1. The application for permission to apply to the Court to be appointed deputy to make personal welfare decisions for Alfonso Mario is refused.

2. For the avoidance of doubt, if an issue arises upon which a personal welfare decision or direction of the Court is sought this decision does not preclude the applicant from re-applying at the material time, nor does it prejudice the applicant's application to be appointed a deputy to make decisions regarding Alfonso Mario's property and financial affairs which application is continuing.

3. This order was made of the Court's own initiative without a hearing and without notice, pursuant to rule 89 of the Court of Protection Rules 2007. Any party or any other person affected by this order may apply to the Court for reconsideration of the order made provided any such application is made within 21 days of the order being served.

PART II

PROPERTY AND AFFAIRS

Of the 2000 or so applications received each month by the Court of Protection, by far the overwhelming majority concern the management of P's property and affairs. Typical applications are, for the appointment of deputies; the making of a statutory will; issues regarding property and the restriction or enhancement of the powers of an attorney. Some of those applications can arise from an emergency or are otherwise urgent. For instance the making of a will for P who is terminally ill or the restraint of a deputy or attorney in the light of alleged financial abuse. In all cases an order of the Court will be required.

CHAPTER 3

APPOINTMENT OF A DEPUTY BY THE COURT, OBJECTION TO THE APPOINTMENT OF A DEPUTY OR SUSPENSION AND DISCHARGE OF A DEPUTY

LAW AND PRACTICE

3.1 POWERS OF THE COURT

Where a person (P) lacks capacity in relation to decisions concerning his or her personal welfare or property and affairs, the Court of Protection is given wide powers under s 16(2) of the Act. It may either make an order on an interim basis pending investigations or a single full order, by making the decision(s) on P's behalf, or appointing a person known as a (formerly a receiver) to make decisions on P's behalf, where there are ongoing decisions to be made for P, who is likely to lack capacity for the forseable future, to make such decisions for himself. The Court's power, however, is subject to the principles set out in s 1 and the best interests provisions set out in s 4 (for a detailed discussion of best interests see chapter 2). When deciding whether it is in P's best interests to appoint a deputy the Court must have regard to P's best interests, to the principle that a decision by the Court is to be preferred to the appointment of a deputy to make a decision, and that powers conferred on a deputy should be as limited in scope and duration as is reasonably practicable in the circumstances.[1] In cases where there is no enduring or lasting power of attorney (E/LPA) in place and a financial decision or a statutory will needs to be made immediately as a matter of urgency, the Court will take the decision on behalf of P. Situations concerning welfare decisions are considered under Part III.

Circumstances in which an appointment of a deputy is appropriate will vary according to whether the decision to be made relates to property and affairs of P or his/her welfare. Much will depend on the circumstances of P whether future and ongoing decisions are likely to be necessary. In matters concerning property, a deputy is likely to be necessary where P has sufficient income, capital assets and property which needs to be dealt with and managed.[2]

---

[1]   MCA 2005, s 16(4).
[2]   See Code of Practice, paras 8.27 and 8.35.

When deciding to appoint a deputy the Court may appoint one or more deputies to make all decisions or specify the decisions that may be undertaken by the deputy/deputies which may relate only to personal welfare or property and affairs or both. It may make restricted or unrestricted orders or one-off single orders.

3.2 THE COURT'S APPROACH WHEN APPOINTING A DEPUTY

On appointing a deputy the Court has wide powers to identify the duties and responsibilities of the deputy and to impose restrictions on the deputy's powers. The Court may:

- Confer powers or impose duties on a deputy as it thinks necessary or expedient for giving effect to, or otherwise in connection with, an order or appointment made by it.[3]
- Make the order, give the directions or make the appointment on such terms as it considers are in P's best interests, even though an application is before the Court for an order, directions or an appointment on those terms.[4]
- Vary or discharge an order made by a subsequent order[5] but subject to the provisions of para 6 of Sch 2 to the Act.[6]
- Revoke the appointment of a deputy or vary the powers conferred on him/her, where there are concerns for the conduct of the deputy.[7]
- Restrict the deputies powers[8] (see **7.7**).

The Court has similar powers in relation to the appointment of deputies for personal welfare (including health) which are dealt with in this book in Part III.

3.3 COURT'S POWERS IN RELATION TO PROPERTY AND AFFAIRS

The Court's powers in relation to property and affairs include:

(a)   the control and management of P's property;

(b)   the sale, exchange, charging, gift or other disposition of P's property;

(c)   the acquisition of property in P's name or on P's behalf;

(d)   the carrying on, on P's behalf, of any profession, trade or business;

(e)   the taking of a decision which will have the effect of dissolving a partnership of which P is a member;

---

[3]   MCA 2005, s 16(5).
[4]   MCA 2005, s 16(6).
[5]   MCA 2005, s 16(7).
[6]   MCA 2005, s 18(5).
[7]   MCA 2005, s 16(8).
[8]   MCA 2005, s 20.

(f)   the carrying out of any contract entered into by P;

(g)   the discharge of P's debts and of any of P's obligations, whether legally enforceable or not;

(h)   the settlement of any of P's property, whether for P's benefit or for the benefit of others and such other consequential vesting or other orders as the case may require, including in the exercise of such a power, any order which could have been made in such a case under Part 4 of the Trustee Act 1925.[9] If a settlement has been made, the Court may by order vary or revoke it if the settlement makes provision for its variation or revocation; or the Court is satisfied that a material fact was not disclosed when the settlement was made or if it is satisfied that there has been a substantial change of circumstances;[10]

(i)   the execution for P of a will;

(j)   the exercise of any power (including a power to consent) vested in P whether beneficially or as trustee or otherwise;

(k)   the conduct of legal proceedings in P's name or on P's behalf.

A deputy may be given all these powers save in relation to the settlement of any of P's property ((h) above) the execution of a will on P's behalf ((i) above) or the exercise of any power (including the power of consent) vested in P whether beneficially or as trustee or otherwise.[11] The Court may also confer on a deputy powers to take possession or control of all or any specified part of P's property and to exercise all or any specified powers in respect of it, including such powers of investment as the Court may determine.[12]

These powers may be exercised even though P has not reached 16 years of age, if the Court considers it likely that P will still lack capacity to make decisions in respect of that matter when he or she reaches 18 subject to the usual restrictions which apply to deputies.

3.4   WHO CAN BE A DEPUTY?

A deputy appointed by the Court in relation to P's welfare must be an individual who has reached the age of 18. In relation to matters of property and affairs a deputy may be an individual who has reached the age of 18 or a trust corporation.[13] The consent of the individual to be appointed must be obtained.[14]

When the issue of the appointment of a deputy is being determined whether on an interim basis or otherwise, the Court will usually be faced with deciding between an application by a family member and that made by a local authority

---

[9]   MCA 2005, Sch 2, para 5.
[10] MCA 2005, Sch 2, para 6.
[11] MCA 2005, s 20(3).
[12] MCA 2005, s 19(8).
[13] MCA 2005, s 19(1).
[14] MCA 2005, s 19(3).

or a professional body. The Court will necessarily take into account all the circumstances of the case but of significance will be the size of the assets to be managed, the skills required, avoidance of conflict and delay in the decision making process. How the Court approaches this issue and the criteria which are considered relevant is illustrated by the case of *Re HA*.[15] In that case although the application before the Court was for directions under s 27A MCA 2005, it also included an application by P's daughter to be appointed property and affairs and welfare deputy of P. The Official Solicitor was acting as P's litigation friend. It was agreed that P lacked capacity to make decisions as to where she should live, her medical care and as to her property and affairs and relating to litigation. The issue of where P should live required considerable and thorough investigation of the options identified by the Court. The Court took the view that the local authority was best placed to undertake the investigations and enquiries pursuant to its statutory duties. Additionally, in order to make its final decisions the Court required to be informed of P's full financial position which had hitherto been under the control of P's daughter. The Court thus had to decide whether an interim deputy should be appointed in respect of property and affairs and if so whether that deputy should be P's daughter and or the local authority. The family was agreed that it should be the daughter. The Court however ruled in favour of the local authority for the following reasons:

(a)   Speed and avoidance of delay and resulting problems. The Court took the view that the appointment of the daughter would cause delays, for example in arranging visits and visits to P's property.

(b)   Since the deputyship included a direction for an investigation to be carried out this would best be undertaken by the local authority. The issue of expenditure at this stage was not relevant. What was relevant was that a full and informed investigation was made. It was also relevant that the daughter had incurred expenditure which she should be able to reclaim and that this should be dealt with by the Court in the context of the application for the appointment of a deputy on a long term basis. The local authority's expenditure was one for future determination having regard to, amongst other things, the decision concerning P's medium and long term care.

(c)   Potential of conflict arising between siblings and the need to avoid any such risk.

(d)   The Court also took into account the stance taken historically by the daughter who had been obstructive in respect of relevant steps that needed to be taken about her mother's financial affairs and to gain access to the property. This had caused delay. The Court took the view that:[16]

> 'if the financial purse strings are controlled by members of the family it is likely that this will cause further delay and it seems to me that the balance between the competing factors, including the point now raised by Mrs C, favours the order that I have made.'

---

[15]   [2012] EWHC 1068 (COP).
[16]   Ibid, at para 25.

The Court considered that it was only once the full investigation was complete and all the parties had an opportunity to respond and put forward their options would it be possible for the Court to make an informed decision. The Court thus stayed the application for a welfare deputy and adjourned the application for a property and affairs deputy to be determined with the s 21A application.

Guidance was also provided in *Re P (Vulnerable Adult: Deputies)*[17] on the appointment of a deputy. Hedley J stated that applications by family members should be viewed sympathetically by the courts provided that the family members are not embroiled in conflict and appear to be able to carry out the functions and duties of a deputy appropriately. Hedley J went on to state that:[18]

> 'it must be appreciated that section 16(4) has to be read in the context of the fact that, ordinarily, the court will appoint deputies where it feels confident that it can. It is perhaps important to take one step back even than that, and for the court to remind itself that in a society structured as is ours, it is not the State, whether through the agency of an authority or the court, which is primarily responsible for individuals who are subjects or citizens of the State. It is for those who naturally have their care and wellbeing at heart, that is to say, members of the family, where they are willing and able to do so, to take first place in the care and upbringing, not only of children, but of those whose needs, because of disability extend far into adulthood. It seems to me at least that the Act ought to be read subject to that overriding policy aim.

> Therefore the court ought to start from the position that, where a family member offer themselves as deputies, then in the absence of family dispute or other evidence that raises queries as to their willingness or capacity to carry out these functions, the court ought to approach such an application with considerable openness and sympathy ...'

This principle was applied by Senior Judge Lush in *Re AS; SH v LC*.[19] In that case the Court had to decide between appointing SH a solicitor on the panel of approved deputy or LC, a niece. In determining the issue and exercising the Court's discretion the judge applied the best interests test and stated that the pre-2005 authorities on the appointment of a receiver are probably still relevant to the appointment of deputies. They showed that there was an order of preference. Generally speaking the order of preference is: (a) P's spouse or partner; (b) any other relative who takes a personal interest in P's affairs; (c) a close friend; (d) a professional adviser, such as the family's solicitor or accountant; (e) a local authority's social services department; and finally (f) a panel deputy, as deputy of last resort (para 23). The judge also applied Hedley J's observations in *Re P* (above) and referred to the statistics which showed that in the majority of cases the Court appoints a person who has a relationship with P as his/her deputy. He noted:[20]

---

[17] [2010] EWHC 1592 (Fam), [2010] COPLR Con Vol 922.
[18] At paras 8 and 9.
[19] [2013] COPLR 29.
[20] At para 24.

'The court prefers to appoint a family member or close friend, if it is possible. This is because a relative or friend will already be familiar with P's affairs, and wishes and methods of communication. Someone who already has a close personal knowledge of P is also likely to be better able to meet the obligation of a deputy to consult with P, and to permit and encourage him to participate, or to improve his ability to participate, as fully as possible in any act done for him and any decision affecting him. And, because professionals charge for their services, the appointment of a relative or friend is generally preferred for reasons of economy.'

But he acknowledged that there are cases in which the Court would not countenance appointing a family member as deputy. These would include for example cases where (a) there has been financial abuse or some other kind of abuse; (b) there is a conflict of interests; (c) the proposed deputy has an unsatisfactory track record in managing his own financial affairs; (d) there is on gong family friction (para 26) (for other relevant factors see also *Re Rodman* (below at **3.7**)).

(Judge Lush also referred to an unreported case of *Re Bridge*,[21] where he had applied the concept of deputyship of last resort.)

Recently, in *Re M; N v O and P*,[22] Judge Lush, whilst acknowledging that the order of preference referred to by him in *Re AS; SH v LC* (see above) was still relevant and that under that order a spouse is the first choice when appointing a deputy, nevertheless, stated that the Court would not automatically appoint him or her. P's past and present wishes were relevant factors of 'magnetic importance' as were the wishes of others who were close to P who were unanimous in their view that the appointment of N, whom P had shown a preference for and who had known P for 40 years, would be in P's best interests. In determining the issue the judge applied the balance sheet approach to the competing claims and their respective strengths and weaknesses when applying the factors, which he considered were relevant, namely: the willingness to act; ability to act; qualification; place of residence; security; conduct before as well as during the proceedings; nature of the relationship with P; P wishes and feeling; the views of others; the effect of hostility; conflict of interests, remuneration and the terms of P's will.

The Court may appoint two or more deputies to act jointly, jointly and severally or jointly in respect of some matters and jointly and severally in respect of others.[23] Provision may also be made for one or more other person to succeed the existing deputy/deputies in such circumstances or on the happening of such events, as may be specified in the order or for such period as may be so specified.[24]

---

[21]   (No 11579443) 15 August 2011.
[22]   [2013] COPLR 91.
[23]   MCA 2005, s 19(4).
[24]   MCA 2005, s 19(5).

3.5 COSTS

A deputy is entitled to be reimbursed out of P's property for his reasonable expenses for discharging his function and the Court when making the appointment may also direct that the deputy's remuneration for discharging his function be paid out of P's property.[25] Where a Court appoints a solicitor to act as a deputy for P, the fixed rates of remuneration will apply.[26]

The Court may require a deputy to give to the Public Guardian such security as the Court thinks fit for the due discharge of his functions before any action is taken by the deputy[27] and to submit to the Public Guardian such reports at such times or at such intervals as the Court may direct.[28] The Court will almost invariably require a deputy who is being replaced or suspended to submit such a report.

3.6 RESTRICTIONS ON DEPUTIES

In addition to the restrictions referred to above the following further restrictions apply to a deputy appointed by the Court:

- He/she may not make a decision on behalf of P in relation to a matter if he knows or has reasonable grounds for believing that P has capacity in relation to the matter.[29]
- He/she may not refuse life sustaining treatment on P's behalf.[30]
- His/her authority is subject to the principles embodied in s 1 and the best interests as defined in s 4 of the Act.
- He/she may not do any act which is inconsistent with a decision made under a lasting power of attorney conferred by P.
- He/she may not do any act that is intended to restrain P unless the four conditions set out in s 20(8)-(11) are met namely:
  (i) in doing the act, the deputy is acting within the scope of an authority expressly conferred on him/her by the Court;
  (ii) the deputy must reasonably believe that P lacks capacity in relation to the matter in question;
  (iii) the deputy reasonably believes that it is necessary to do the act in order to prevent harm to P;
  (iv) the act must be a proportionate response to the likelihood of P's suffering harm and the seriousness of that harm.

'Restrain' is defined in s 6(4) of the Act and may take many forms. It may be verbal eg shouting or physical, forcibly holding P down or restraining P by means of a restraint device such as a belt, or by locking the person in a confined

---

[25] MCA 2005, s 19(7).
[26] See PD 19B – Fixed Costs in the Court of Protection.
[27] COP Rules 2007, r 200.
[28] MCA 2005, s 19(9).
[29] MCA 2005, s 20(1).
[30] MCA 2005, s 20(5).

area. A deputy will be treated as restraining P if he/she uses, or threatens to use, force to secure the doing of an act which P resists or restricts P's liberty of movement, whether or not P resists, or if he authorises another person to do any of those things.[31] A deputy will be regarded as doing more than restraining P if he/she deprives P of his or her liberty within the meaning of Art 5(1) of the European Convention for the Protection of Human Rights and Fundamental Freedoms (ECHR) (whether or not the deputy is a public authority)[32] (see chapter 10 and 10.3).

3.7   OBJECTION/SUSPENSION/DISCHARGE OF THE APPOINTMENT

In some cases families, friends or public authorities may not agree upon who should be appointed as P's deputy. The usual procedural path for objection is for the objector to indicate his/her intention to object when returning the acknowledgment of service. The Court will then adopt the same procedure set out below for intervention post appointment. Where the objector has not been notified but becomes aware of the application having been made but not granted, an application is necessary. Where the order has already been made, no objection can be raised and any application must be for the discharge of the deputy. Furthermore, it is unfortunately the case that despite the rigours of the application some deputies are unable to carry out their duties. Some are simply dishonest. In those circumstances the Court has the power to remove their authority or alternatively to restrict their influence. The Court applies the same criteria in approaching both applications. There are few reported cases that indicate the test that the Court will apply when considering whether to remove a deputy. The test applied in the recent decision of Newey J in *Re Rodman; Long v Rodman & Others*[33] is thus relevant to an application for the removal of a deputy notwithstanding the fact that the judgment only deals with the Court's powers under s 16(7) and makes no reference to s 16(8) (see below). In that case Mrs R and her late husband who were both USA citizens had settled in London and had substantial assets in England. At the time of Mr R's death Mrs. R was suffering from advanced Alzheimer's Disease and lacked mental capacity. In 2009 Mr L, a solicitor, experienced in COP and administration of estates was appointed property and affairs deputy for Mrs R and in 2010 he was appointed an administrator of Mr R's estate. In 2010 the Court made an order for Mrs R to be transferred to New York with an undertaking by her daughters that they would apply to be appointed as welfare guardians for her and to appoint a 'financial guardian (or conservator)'. Without any further order Mrs R was in fact moved to Nevada to live in Las Vegas. In January 2011 S was appointed as general guardian of Mrs R's estate. He applied to the Court to be appointed deputy in place of L and, in proceedings commenced in the Chancery Division he sought an order for L to be replaced as Mr R's personal

---

[31]   MCA 2005, s 20(12).
[32]   MCA 2005, s 20(13).
[33]   [2012] COPLR 433.

representative. The application for removal of L as Mrs R's deputy was transferred from the Court to the Chancery Division.

In considering the application Newey J considered the Court's power under s 16(7) and stated that the exercise of the Court's power under s 16(7) necessarily concerned s 1(5) of the Act, ie that the decision taken must be in the best interest of P. In determining that issue the Court must consider all the relevant circumstances as required by s 4(2) of the Act and in that regard applying s 4(7) the Court must in particular take into account the views of 'anyone engaged in caring for the person or interested in [Mrs Rodman's] welfare' which included her daughters.

Newey J then went on to consider other relevant factual matters, which were that:

(a) L was better qualified than S to act as Mrs R's deputy. He had considerable experience and expertise in matters relating to the British dimensions of the case and court process and in particular matters relating to the administration of estates and the Court of Protection.

(b) S's 'hostile approach' to date did not inspire confidence that he would be an appropriate deputy.

(c) Replacement of L would inevitably result in costs as the new deputy and, probably, lawyers acting on his behalf would need to familiarise themselves with Mrs R's affairs.

(d) It would prove inconvenient and expensive to have different people handling Mrs R's affairs and Mr R's estate.

(e) There was good reason to fear that if S was appointed as deputy he would nonetheless seek to involve himself in matters relating to Mr R's estate as his appointment as deputy would give him a platform to do so. This would be 'a recipe for conflict and cost.

(f) If L was replaced both as deputy and administrator it would inevitably result in increased costs of handover.

(g) It would engender other difficulties for a replacement to take over satisfactorily 'midstream'.

By virtue of s 16(8) the Court may suspend or discharge the appointment of a deputy or vary the powers conferred on him/her if it is satisfied that the deputy:

(a) has behaved, or is behaving, in a way that contravenes the authority conferred on him by the Court or is not in P's best interests; or

(b) proposes to behave in a way that would contravene that authority or would not be in P's interests.

(See how the Court in *Re J*[34] applied the provisions of s 22(3)(b) to the revocation of a LPA which are similar to those under s 16(8).)

---

[34] [2011] COPLR Con Vol 716.

Hence, if the deputy or applicant for an appointment is found to contravene any of the directions or orders specified in the order appointing him/her or if he/she is failing to comply with the order, or it is found or reasonably believed that the deputy is misappropriating P's property or mismanaging P's affairs it would be a ground for seeking his/her replacement. In such cases the circumstances may be such that an urgent application needs to be made to the Court and dealt with expeditiously. The Court will also bear in mind that the appointment of a friend or relative in the case of a modest estate should be preferred to a charging professional. Where a local authority is involved, the officer with responsibility for Court of Protection affairs can be appointed. In the case of a large estate a trust corporation solicitor or accountant will be considered better placed than an individual. As a last resort or in particularly acrimonious cases the Court has available the option of appointing a solicitor from a panel of deputies, as an independent deputy.

3.8   HOW TO MAKE THE APPLICATION FOR OBJECTION/SUSPENSION/DISCHARGE

3.8.1   Is permission required

Permission to make the application will be required unless it is made by:

(a)   P;

(b)   if P has not reached the age of 18 years, by anyone with parental responsibility for him/her;

(c)   by the donor or a donee of a lasting power of attorney to which the application relates;

(d)   by a deputy appointed by the Court;

(e)   by a person named in an existing order of the Court if the application relates to the order;[35]

(f)   by the Official Solicitor;[36]

(g)   by the Public Guardian;[37]

(h)   where the application concerns P's property and affairs, unless the application is of a kind specified in COP Rules 2007, r 52 or a lasting power of attorney which is or purports to be created under the Act or an instrument which is or purports to be an enduring power of attorney.

Therefore in practice it is unlikely that permission will be required.

3.8.2   How to apply

If permission is required the application for permission should be made in Form COP2 and filed with the substantive application in Form COP1. In addition the

---

[35]   MCA 2005, s 50.
[36]   COP Rules 2007, r 51(1)(a).
[37]   COP Rules 2007, r 51(1)(b).

following accompanying forms should be filed namely Form COP1A (ie all the supporting information). Form COP3 to confirm that P continues to lack capacity should also be filed.

The Court fee of £400 will have to be paid when the application is issued.

3.8.3   Urgent application

If the matter is urgent the applicant must file an application in Form COP9 with a draft of the orders sought and if possible a disc of the order.

3.8.4   The Court

Where permission is required the Court is required to deal with the application within 14 days. It may grant or refuse the application or list the application for a hearing and give directions including specifying who should be given notice of the hearing.[38] If a hearing is listed a person who is notified of the hearing should file an acknowledgement of service in Form COP5.

If permission is given the substantive application will be issued by the Court. The applicant will receive from the Court Form COP5 (the acknowledgement of service), Form COP14 (the notice of proceedings to P) with the guidance notes in Form COP14A, notice in Form COP15 and guidance notes of the issue of the application and the certificate of service Form COP20. The Court in an emergency may make an interim order suspending the deputy pending the final hearing. This may be done at a hearing, on notice or without notice or on the papers depending on the urgency. It is important to specify in the forms what order is required and when. If an order is made without notice, the Court may give directions for a reply from the deputy and fix an interim directions hearing. It may be necessary to apply at the same time in the same application form for a freezing order or an injunction to protect P's assets in the interim (see chapter 14 below).

3.8.5   Service

It is the duty of the applicant to:
- Serve all the necessary documents and Forms on the respondents within 21 days.
- Serve P with Forms COP14 and 14A and COP5.
- Notify any other relevant person of the application in Forms COP15 and COP5.
- File the certificate of service within 7 days of service in Form COP20.

---

[38]   See COP Rules 2007, rr 55, 56 and 89.

3.8.6   The respondent/s to the application

Every respondent and any person who wishes to take part in the proceedings must file the acknowledgment of service within 21 days. The Court will then either give directions without a hearing or list the matter for a directions hearing.

3.9 PROCEDURAL GUIDE FOR OBJECTION/SUSPENSION/DISCHARGE OF A DEPUTY

Permission to apply	An objection can be raised in COP5 by a notified person returning the form All other applications require permission everyone except by the person lacking capacity	MCA 2005 s 50 COP Rules 2007, Part 8
	If the person lacking capacity is under 18 anyone with parental responsibility	
	Donee of a LPA to which the application relates	
	Deputy appointed by the Court	
	A person named in an existing order	
	Official Solicitor/Public Guardian	
Objector must file Applicant for suspension or discharge must file	Objection in COP5 Form **COP2** if permission is required	COP Rules 2007, Part 9 PD 9A and COP Rules 2007, rr 62–64
	Forms **COP1, COP1A, COP1B, COP3**	
	Form **COP4** where a deputy has been assigned	
	Copy of a LPA if relevant	
	If the application is urgent Form **COP9** and draft of order and disc	
Court Office	(1) Issues application and gives to the applicant:	
	• Form **COP5**	
	• Forms **COP14** and **COP14A**	
	• Forms **COP15** and **COP15A**	
	• Form **COP20**	
	(2) Judge considers the application and decides whether to give directions or list for directions/disposal hearing	COP Rules 2007, r 89
	(3) May decide to make order without a hearing in which case order Court will serve order on all the parties and direct the deputy to file a reply and consider an application for a freezing order if made	
What the applicant must do	(1) Serve on the respondent/s within 21 days Forms **COP1, COP1A, COP5, COP15** and **COP15A**	
	(2) Notify P on Forms **COP14, COP14A** and **COP5** of the application	COP Rules 2007, r 69

	(3) Notify any relevant party on Forms **COP15** and **COP15A**	
	(4) File certificate of service and notification in Form **COP20**	
	(5) If an urgent application is required file Form **COP9**	COP Rules 2007, Part10 PD 10A and 10B
What the respondent must do	File an acknowledgement of service in Form **COP5** within 21 days or such shorter period as may be directed	PD 9C(3)
What the person notified must do	File an acknowledgement of notification in Form **COP5**	PD 9C(4)
Hearing	The Court will consider the application	
	Give directions	COP Rules 2007, r 85
	Allocate the case	
	Set the time table and trial window or if urgent list for a disposal hearing	
	Make any other appropriate orders	
Orders that the Court may make at the interim hearing	(1) Declare whether a person lacks capacity to make a particular decision specified in the declaration	MCA 2005, s 15
And at the final hearing	(2) Declare whether the person lacks capacity on the matters set out in the declaration	
	(3) Declare the lawfulness or otherwise of any act done or yet to be done	
	(4) Any other consequential or protective orders	

PRECEDENTS

STATEMENT IN SUPPORT OF APPLICATION
TO DISCHARGE A DEPUTY

IN THE COURT OF PROTECTION   CASE NO ....

IN THE MATTER OF THE MENTAL CAPACITY ACT 2005

AND IN THE MATTER OF P [*insert forename and surname*]

BETWEEN

HELLINIC COUNTY   Applicant
COUNCIL

And

GREEDY SCROUGE   1st Respondent

And

PATIENCE FRAIL   2nd Respondent

(by her litigation friend the
Official Solicitor)

**STATEMENT OF RUBY JOLLY IN SUPPORT OF AN APPLICATION FOR
THE REMOVAL OF A DEPUTY**

I, RUBY JOLLY of Bright House in the County of Hellinic will state as follows:

1. I am a care manager employed by the Hellenic County Council. My Qualifications are as follows: [*set these out*]

2. I have been the allocated care manager for the second respondent since she was placed at Bright House by her son Greedy Scrouge in January 2004. On 6 June 2004 he was appointed receiver to manage the property and affairs of his mother by the Court. He became a deputy by operation of law on 1 October 2007.

3. I make this statement in support of the applicant's application for the removal of the first respondent as a Deputy for the second respondent.

4. Since her placement at Bright House I have observed the first respondent's behaviour towards his mother on every occasion that he has visited her. I have heard him speak to her in a very harsh and aggressive way and seen her being quite intimidated by him. On many occasions I

have had to intervene and those occasions he has been aggressive and abusive towards me and other members of staff at Bright Home.

5. More recently he has insisted on seeing his mother in her room and on some of those occasions she has been heard to cry out in distress.

6. I have recently observed him getting the first respondent to sign what appeared to me to be legal documents. When he has left the second respondent has appeared very withdrawn. Last week when I was assisting her to get ready for bed she disclosed to me that she was concerned and confused about some documents that her son had got her to sign.

7. I reported the incident to my employers. I understand that they reported the matter to the Public Guardian who confirmed that his office had been sent a report alleging that Greedy Scrouge the second respondent's son has mortgaged his mother's property and that he has also withdrawn a large sum of money from her building society account at Prudence Provident Society.

8. An investigation has been lodged by the Public Guardian. The investigation has revealed some inappropriate dealings with the second respondent's assets and more particularly that the first respondent has not filed any returns since his appointment.

9. It is therefore in the best interests of the second respondent that an independent person be appointed to manage her financial and personal affairs pending a full investigation in order to protect the second respondent and to prevent her assets being dissipated dishonestly by the first respondent.

DRAFT ORDER WHERE A DEPUTY HAS DIED, WISHES TO RETIRE OR IS UNABLE TO ACT

THIS DOCUMENT IS NOT VALID UNLESS IT BEARS THE IMPRESSED SEAL OF THE COURT OF PROTECTION ON ALL PAGES

IN THE COURT OF PROTECTION   NO ... << CASE NUMBER>>
MENTAL CAPACITY ACT 2005

In the matter of

<<P_FULL_NAME_IN_BLOCK CAPS>>

ORDER APPOINTING A NEW DEPUTY
FOR PROPERTY AND AFFAIRS

made by <<JUDGES_NAME>>/<<AUTHORISED_OFFICERS_NAME>>, an authorised officer of the Court

at First Avenue House, 42-49 High Holborn, London WC1A 9JA

on <<ORDER_DATE>>

WHEREAS

(1)   By an order dated the <<ORDER_DATE>> <<OLD_DEPUTY_FULL-_NAME>> was appointed as deputy for property and affairs for <<P_FULL_NAME>>.

(2)   And it appearing that the said <<OLD_DEPUTY_FULL_NAME>> (died on the <<DATE OF DEATH>>) (is unable to continue as deputy) (desires to retire from the deputyship), and an application has been made for an order under the Mental Capacity Act 2005 ("the Act").

(3)   The Court is satisfied that <<P_FULL_NAME>> continues to lack capacity to make various decisions for himself/herself in relation to a matter or matters concerning his/her property and affairs, and that the purpose for which the order is needed cannot be as effectively achieved in a way that is less restrictive of his/her rights and freedom of action.

IT IS ORDERED that:

DISCHARGE OF DEPUTY

[If the former deputy is still alive]

(a)   The said <<OLD_DEPUTY_FULL_NAME>> is discharged from the deputyship and his/her powers are terminated.

(b)   The said <<OLD_DEPUTY_FULL_NAME>> is to provide the (deputy hereinafter appointed) (new deputy as and when appointed) with a final account to the date of this order by the «DATE».

(c)   The said <<OLD_DEPUTY_FULL_NAME>> shall disclose to the (deputy hereinafter appointed) (new deputy as and when appointed) copies of all documents, correspondence or records that he/she holds, or has access to, that relate to <<P_FULL_NAME>>'s property and affairs.

(d)   The said <<OLD_DEPUTY_FULL_NAME>> is to transfer all property belonging to <<P_FULL_NAME>> which remains under his/her control to the (deputy hereinafter appointed) (new deputy as and when appointed).

[Or, if the former deputy is deceased]

(a)   The personal representatives of the late <<OLD_DEPUTY_FULL-_NAME>> are to provide the (deputy hereinafter appointed) (new deputy as and when appointed) with a final account to the date of this order by the <<DATE>>.

(b)   The personal representatives of the late <<OLD_DEPUTY_FULL-_NAME>> shall disclose to the (deputy hereinafter appointed) (new deputy as and when appointed) copies of all documents, correspondence or records held by the late <<OLD_DEPUTY_FULL_NAME>> that relate to <<P_FULL_NAME>>'s property and affairs.

(c)   The personal representatives of the late <<OLD_DEPUTY_FULL-_NAME>> are to transfer all property belonging to <<P_FULL-_NAME>> which remains under the control of the late <<OLD_DEPUTY_FULL_NAME>> to the (deputy hereinafter appointed) (new deputy as and when appointed).

APPOINTMENT OF NEW DEPUTY

(a)   «NEW_DEPUTY_FULL_NAME» of «ADRS1», «ADRS2», «ADRS3», «ADRS4», «ADRS5», «POSTCODE» is appointed as deputy ("the deputy") to make decisions on behalf of «P_FULL_NAME» that he/she is unable to make for herself in relation to his/her property and affairs, subject to any conditions or restrictions set out in this order.

(b)   The appointment will last until further order.

(c)   The deputy must apply the principles set out in section 1 of the Act and have regard to the guidance in the Code of Practice to the Act.

AUTHORITY OF DEPUTY

(a)   The Court confers general authority on the deputy to take possession or control of the property and affairs of «P_FULL_NAME» and to exercise the same powers of management and investment, including [selling and] letting property, as he/she has as beneficial owner, subject to the terms and conditions set out in this order.

(b)   The deputy cannot purchase any freehold or leasehold property on «P_FULL_NAME»'s behalf without obtaining further authority from the Court.

(c)   [The deputy must not sell, lease or charge any freehold or leasehold property in which «P_FULL_NAME» has a beneficial interest without obtaining further authority from the Court.]

(d)   If the deputy considers it in «P_FULL_NAME»'s best interests to do so the deputy may appoint an investment manager, who is regulated and authorised to undertake investment business, to manage his/her assets on a discretionary basis under the standard terms and conditions applicable to such service from time-to-time, and to permit the investments to be held in the name of the investment manager nominee company.

(e)   The deputy may make provision for the needs of anyone who is related to or connected with «P_FULL_NAME» if he/she provided for, or might be expected to provide for, that person's needs by doing whatever he/she did, or might reasonably be expected to do, to meet those needs.

(f)   The deputy may, without obtaining any further authority from the Court, dispose of «P_FULL_NAME»'s money or property by way of gift to any charity to which he/she made, or might have been expected to make, such gifts, and, on customary occasions, to persons who are related to or connected with him/her, provided that the value of each such gift is not unreasonable having regard to all the circumstances and, in particular, the size of his/ her estate.

(g)   *[Optional paragraph]* On «P_FULL_NAME»'s behalf the deputy may take such steps as may be necessary to obtain (either alone or with a co-administrator) a grant of representation to the estate of «FULL_NAME_OF_DECEASED» and to use the share to which «P_FULL_NAME» is entitled for his/her benefit.

(h)   For the purpose of giving effect to any decision the deputy may execute or sign any necessary deeds or documents.

(i)   *[Include this paragraph in legacy cases only]* The deputy has permission to inspect all Court records and to make copies of any material which he/she considers necessary to assist in the proper management of «P_FULL_NAME»'s property and affairs, subject to the payment of any relevant fee.

REPORTS

(a)   The deputy is required to keep statements, vouchers, receipts and other financial records.

(b)   The deputy must submit a report to the Public Guardian as and when required.

COSTS AND EXPENSES

(a)   The deputy is entitled to be reimbursed for reasonable expenses incurred provided they are in proportion to the size of «P_FULL_NAME»'s estate and the functions performed by the deputy.(1)

(b)   The deputy is authorised to pay «SOLICITORS» fixed costs for this application, or, where the amount exceeds the fixed costs allowed, the deputy is authorised to agree the costs for making this application and to pay them from funds belonging to «P_FULL_NAME». In default of agreement, or if the deputy or the solicitors would prefer the costs to be assessed, this order is to be treated as authority to the Senior Courts Costs Office to carry out a detailed assessment on the standard basis.(2)

(c)   The deputy is entitled to receive fixed costs in relation to this application, and to receive fixed costs for the general management of «P_FULL_NAME»'s affairs. If the deputy would prefer the costs to be assessed, this order is to be treated as authority to the Senior Courts Costs Office to carry out a detailed assessment on the standard basis.(3)

(d)   The deputy is authorised to agree any outstanding costs of general management and to pay them from funds belonging to «P_FULL-_NAME». In default of agreement, or if the deputy or the solicitors would prefer the costs to be assessed, this order is to be treated as authority to the Senior Courts Costs Office to carry out a detailed assessment on the standard basis.

SECURITY

(a)   The deputy is required forthwith to obtain and maintain security in the sum of £«SECURITY_AMOUNT» in accordance with the standard requirements as to the giving of security.

(b)   The deputy must ensure that the level of security ordered by the Court is in place before discharging any of the functions conferred by this order.

RIGHT TO APPLY FOR RECONSIDERATION OF ORDER

Any person who is affected by this order may apply to the Court for reconsideration of the order within 21 days of the order being served by filing an application notice (form COP9) in accordance with Part 10 of the Court of Protection Rules 2007.

Notes
1.   This clause relates to Lay Deputies only
2.   This clause relates to Lay Deputies where a professional has submitted the application
3.   This clause relates to Professional Deputies only

DRAFT ORDER FOR DISCHARGE OF DEPUTY AND APPOINTMENT OF NEW JOINT DEPUTIES

THIS DOCUMENT IS NOT VALID UNLESS IT BEARS THE IMPRESSED SEAL OF THE COURT OF PROTECTION ON ALL PAGES

IN THE COURT OF PROTECTION   NO ... << CASE NUMBER>>

MENTAL CAPACITY ACT 2005

In the matter of

<<P_FULL_NAME_IN_BLOCK CAPS>>

ORDER APPOINTING NEW JOINT
DEPUTIES FOR PROPERTY AND
AFFAIRS

made by <<JUDGES_NAME>>/<<AUTHORISED_OFFICERS_NAME>>, an authorised officer of the Court

at First Avenue House, 42-49 High Holborn, London WC1A 9JA

on <<ORDER_DATE>>

WHEREAS

(1)   By an order dated the «ORDER_DATE» «OLD_DEPUTY_FULL-_NAME» was appointed as deputy for property and affairs for «P_FULL_NAME».

(2)   And it appearing that the said «OLD_DEPUTY_FULL_NAME» (died on the «DATE_OF_DEATH») (is unable to continue as deputy) (desires to retire from the deputyship), and an application has been made for an order under the Mental Capacity Act 2005 ("the Act").

(3)   The Court is satisfied that «P_FULL_NAME» continues to lack capacity to make various decisions for himself/herself in relation to a matter or matters concerning his/her property and affairs, and that the purpose for which the order is needed cannot be as effectively achieved in a way that is less restrictive of his/her rights and freedom of action.

IT IS ORDERED that:

DISCHARGE OF DEPUTY

[If the former deputy is still alive]

(a)   The said «OLD_DEPUTY_FULL_NAME» is discharged from the deputyship and his/her powers are terminated.

(b)   The said «OLD_DEPUTY_FULL_NAME» is to provide the (deputy hereinafter appointed) (new deputy as and when appointed) with a final account to the date of this order by the «DATE».

(c)   The said «OLD_DEPUTY_FULL_NAME» shall disclose to the (deputy hereinafter appointed) (new deputy as and when appointed) copies of all documents, correspondence or records that he/she holds, or has access to, that relate to «P_FULL_NAME»'s property and affairs.

(d)   The said «OLD_DEPUTY_FULL_NAME» is to transfer all property belonging to «P_FULL_NAME» which remains under his/her control to the (deputy hereinafter appointed) (new deputy as and when appointed).

[Or, if the former deputy is deceased]

(a)   The personal representatives of the late «OLD_DEPUTY_FULL_NAME» are to provide the (deputy hereinafter appointed) (new deputy as and when appointed) with a final account to the date of this order by the «DATE».

(b)   The personal representatives of the late «OLD_DEPUTY_FULL_NAME» shall disclose to the (deputy hereinafter appointed) (new deputy as and when appointed) copies of all documents, correspondence or records held by the late «OLD_DEPUTY_FULL_NAME» that relate to «P_FULL-_NAME»'s property and affairs.

(c)   The personal representatives of the late «OLD_DEPUTY_FULL_NAME» are to transfer all property belonging to «P_FULL_NAME» which remains under the control of the late «OLD_DEPUTY_FULL_NAME» to the (deputy hereinafter appointed) (new deputy as and when appointed).

APPOINTMENT OF NEW JOINT DEPUTIES

(a)   «FIRST_NEW_DEPUTY_FULL_NAME» of «ADRS1», «ADRS2», «ADRS3», «ADRS4», «ADRS5», «POSTCODE» and «SECOND-_NEW_DEPUTY_FULL_NAME» of «ADRS1_2», «ADRS2_2», «ADRS3_2», «ADRS4_2», «ADRS5_2», «POSTCODE2» are appointed as joint deputies ("the deputies") to make decisions on behalf of «P_FULL_NAME» that he/she is unable to make for himself/herself in relation to his property and affairs, subject to any conditions or restrictions set out in this order.

(b)   The appointment will last until further order.

(c)   The deputies must apply the principles set out in section 1 of the Act and have regard to the guidance in the Code of Practice to the Act.

AUTHORITY OF JOINT DEPUTIES

(a)   The Court confers general authority on the deputies to take possession or control of the property and affairs of «P_FULL_NAME» and to exercise the same powers of management and investment, including [selling and] letting property, as he/she has as beneficial owner, subject to the terms and conditions set out in this order.

(b)   The deputies cannot purchase any freehold or leasehold property on «P_FULL_NAME»'s behalf without obtaining further authority from the Court.

(c)   [The deputies must not sell, lease or charge any freehold or leasehold property in which «P_FULL_NAME» has a beneficial interest without obtaining further authority from the Court.]

(d)   If the deputies considers it in «P_FULL_NAME»'s best interests to do so they may appoint an investment manager, who is regulated and authorised to undertake investment business, to manage his/her assets on a discretionary basis under the standard terms and conditions applicable to such service from time-to-time, and to permit the investments to be held in the name of the investment manager nominee company.

(e)   The deputies may make provision for the needs of anyone who is related to or connected with «P_FULL_NAME» if he/she provided for, or might be expected to provide for, that person's needs by doing whatever he/she did, or might reasonably be expected to do, to meet those needs.

(f)   The deputies may, without obtaining any further authority from the Court, dispose of «P_FULL_NAME»'s money or property by way of gift to any charity to which he/she made, or might have been expected to make, such gifts, and, on customary occasions, to persons who are related to or connected with him/her, provided that the value of each such gift is not unreasonable having regard to all the circumstances and, in particular, the size of his/her estate.

(g)   *[Optional paragraph]* On «P_FULL_NAME»'s behalf the deputies may take such steps as may be necessary to obtain a grant of representation to the estate of «FULL_NAME_OF_DECEASED» and to use the share to which «P_FULL_NAME» is entitled for his/her benefit.

(h)   For the purpose of giving effect to any decision the deputies may execute or sign any necessary deeds or documents.

(i)   *[Include this paragraph in legacy cases only]* The deputies have permission to inspect all Court records and to make copies of any material which they consider necessary to assist in the proper management of «P_FULL_NAME»'s property and affairs, subject to the payment of any relevant fee.

REPORTS

(a)   The deputies are required to keep statements, vouchers, receipts and other financial records.

(b)   The deputies must submit a report to the Public Guardian as and when required.

COSTS AND EXPENSES

(a)   The deputies are entitled to be reimbursed for reasonable expenses incurred provided they are in proportion to the size of «P_FULL-_NAME»'s estate and the functions performed by them.(1)

(b)   The deputies are authorised to pay «SOLICITORS» fixed costs for this application, or, where the amount exceeds the fixed costs allowed, the deputies are authorised to agree the costs for making this application and to pay them from funds belonging to «P_FULL_NAME». In default of agreement, or if the deputies or the solicitors would prefer the costs to be assessed, this order is to be treated as authority to the Senior Courts Costs Office to carry out a detailed assessment on the standard basis.(2)

(c)   Any professional deputy is entitled to receive fixed costs in relation to this application, and to receive fixed costs for the general management of «P_FULL_NAME»'s affairs. If the professional deputy would prefer the costs to be assessed, this order is to be treated as authority to the Senior Courts Costs Office to carry out a detailed assessment on the standard basis.(3)

(d)   The deputies are authorised to agree any outstanding costs of general management and to pay them from funds belonging to «P_FULL-_NAME». In default of agreement, or if the deputies or the solicitors would prefer the costs to be assessed, this order is to be treated as authority to the Senior Courts Costs Office to carry out a detailed assessment on the standard basis.

SECURITY

(a)   The deputies are required forthwith to obtain and maintain security in the sum of £«SECURITY_AMOUNT» in accordance with the standard requirements as to the giving of security.

(b)   The deputies must ensure that the level of security ordered by the Court is in place before discharging any of the functions conferred by this order.

RIGHT TO APPLY FOR RECONSIDERATION OF ORDER

Any person who is affected by this order may apply to the Court for reconsideration of the order within 21 days of the order being served by filing an application notice (form COP9) in accordance with Part 10 of the Court of Protection Rules 2007.

Notes
(1)   This clause relates to Lay Deputies only
(2)   This clause relates to Lay Deputies where a professional has submitted the application
(3)   This clause relates to Professional Deputies only

DRAFT ORDER FOR DISCHARGE OF DEPUTY AND APPOINTMENT OF LOCAL AUTHORITY AS NEW DEPUTY

IN THE COURT OF PROTECTION
MENTAL CAPACITY ACT 2005

In the matter of

<<P_FULL_NAME_IN_BLOCK CAPS>>

ORDER APPOINTING A NEW DEPUTY
FOR PROPERTY AND AFFAIRS

made by <<JUDGES_NAME>>/<<AUTHORISED_OFFICERS_NAME>>, an authorised officer of the Court

at First Avenue House, 42-49 High Holborn, London WC1A 9JA

on <<ORDER_DATE>>

WHEREAS

(1)   By an order dated the «ORDER_DATE» «OLD_DEPUTY_FULL-_NAME» was appointed as deputy for property and affairs for «P_FULL_NAME».

(2)   And it appearing that the said «OLD_DEPUTY_FULL_NAME» (died on the «DATE_OF_DEATH») (is unable to continue as deputy) (desires to retire from the deputyship), and an application has been made for an order under the Mental Capacity Act 2005 ("the Act").

(3)   The Court is satisfied that «P_FULL_NAME» continues to lack capacity to make various decisions for himself/herself in relation to a matter or matters concerning his property and affairs, and that the purpose for which the order is needed cannot be as effectively achieved in a way that is less restrictive of his/her rights and freedom of action.

IT IS ORDERED that:

Discharge of deputy

[If the former deputy is still alive]

(a)   The said «OLD_DEPUTY_FULL_NAME» is discharged from the deputyship and his/her powers are terminated.

(b)   The said «OLD_DEPUTY_FULL_NAME» is to provide the (deputy hereinafter appointed) (new deputy as and when appointed) with a final account to the date of this order by the «DATE».

(c)   The said «OLD_DEPUTY_FULL_NAME» shall disclose to the (deputy hereinafter appointed) (new deputy as and when appointed) copies of all documents, correspondence or records that he/she holds, or has access to, that relate to «P_FULL_NAME»'s property and affairs.

(d)   The said «OLD_DEPUTY_FULL_NAME» is to transfer all property belonging to «P_FULL_NAME» which remains under his/her control to the (deputy hereinafter appointed) (new deputy as and when appointed).

[Or, if the former deputy is deceased]

(a)   The personal representatives of the late «OLD_DEPUTY_FULL_NAME» are to provide the (deputy hereinafter appointed) (new deputy as and when appointed) with a final account to the date of this order by the «DATE».

(b)   The personal representatives of the late «OLD_DEPUTY_FULL_NAME» shall disclose to the (deputy hereinafter appointed) (new deputy as and when appointed) copies of all documents, correspondence or records held by the late «OLD_DEPUTY_FULL_NAME» that relate to «P_FULL-_NAME»'s property and affairs.

(c)   The personal representatives of the late «OLD_DEPUTY_FULL_NAME» are to transfer all property belonging to «P_FULL_NAME» which remains under the control of the late «OLD_DEPUTY_FULL_NAME» to the (deputy hereinafter appointed) (new deputy as and when appointed).

APPOINTMENT OF NEW DEPUTY

(a)   The authorised officer for property and affairs deputyships of «COUNCIL», «ADRS1», «ADRS2», «ADRS3», «ADRS4», «ADRS5», «POSTCODE» is appointed as deputy ("the deputy") to make decisions on behalf of «P_FULL_NAME» that he/she is unable to make for himself/herself in relation to his/her property and affairs, subject to any conditions or restrictions set out in this order.

(b)   The appointment will last until further order.

(c)   The deputy must apply the principles set out in section 1 of the Mental Capacity Act 2005 ("the Act") and have regard to the guidance in the Code of Practice to the Act.

AUTHORITY OF DEPUTY

(a)   The Court confers general authority on the deputy to take possession or control of the property and affairs of «P_FULL_NAME» and to exercise the same powers of management and investment, including [selling and] letting property, as he/she has as beneficial owner, subject to the terms and conditions set out in this order.

(b)   The deputy cannot purchase any freehold or leasehold property on «P_FULL_NAME»'s behalf without obtaining further authority from the Court.

(c)   [The deputy must not sell, lease or charge any freehold or leasehold property in which «P_FULL_NAME» has a beneficial interest without obtaining further authority from the Court.]

(d)   If the deputy considers it in «P_FULL_NAME»'s best interests to do so the deputy may appoint an investment manager, who is regulated and authorised to undertake investment business, to manage his/her assets on a discretionary basis under the standard terms and conditions applicable to such service from time-to-time, and to permit the investments to be held in the name of the investment manager nominee company.

(e)   The deputy may make provision for the needs of anyone who is related to or connected with «P_FULL_NAME» if he/she provided for, or might be expected to provide for, that person's needs by doing whatever he/she did, or might reasonably be expected to do, to meet those needs.

(f)   The deputy may (without obtaining any further authority from the Court) dispose of «P_FULL_NAME»'s money or property by way of gift to any charity to which he/she made, or might have been expected to make, such gifts, and, on customary occasions, to persons who are related to or connected with him, provided that the value of each such gift is not unreasonable having regard to all the circumstances and, in particular, the size of his estate.

(g)   *[Optional paragraph]* On «P_FULL_NAME»'s behalf the deputy may take such steps as may be necessary to obtain (either alone or with a co-administrator) a grant of representation to the estate of «FULL_NAME_OF_DECEASED» and to use the share to which «P_FULL_NAME» is entitled for his/her benefit.

(h)   For the purpose of giving effect to any decision the deputy may execute or sign any necessary deeds or documents.

(i)   *[Include this paragraph in legacy cases only]* The deputy has permission to inspect all Court records and to make copies of any material which he considers necessary to assist in the proper management of «P_FULL-_NAME»'s property and affairs, subject to the payment of any relevant fee.

REPORTS

(a)   The deputy is required to keep statements, vouchers, receipts and other financial records.

(b)   The deputy must submit a report to the Public Guardian as and when required.

REMUNERATION

(a)   The deputy is entitled to receive fixed costs in relation to this application and to receive fixed costs for the general management of «P_FULL_NAME»'s affairs.

(b)   The deputy is authorised to agree any outstanding costs of general management and to pay them from funds belonging to «P_FULL-_NAME». In default of agreement, or if the deputy or the solicitors would prefer the costs to be assessed, this order is to be treated as authority to the Senior Courts Costs Office to carry out a detailed assessment on the standard basis.

RIGHT TO APPLY FOR RECONSIDERATION OF ORDER

Any person who is affected by this order may apply to the Court for reconsideration of the order within 21 days of the order being served by filing an application notice (form COP9) in accordance with Part 10 of the Court of Protection Rules 2007.

DRAFT ORDER FOR APPOINTMENT OF A NEW JOINT AND SEVERAL DEPUTIES

THIS DOCUMENT IS NOT VALID UNLESS IT BEARS THE IMPRESSED SEAL OF THE COURT OF PROTECTION ON ALL PAGES

IN THE COURT OF PROTECTION   NO ... << CASE NUMBER>>

MENTAL CAPACITY ACT 2005

In the matter of

<<P_FULL_NAME_IN_BLOCK CAPS>>

ORDER APPOINTING NEW JOINT
AND SEVERAL DEPUTIES FOR
PROPERTY AND AFFAIRS

made by <<JUDGES_NAME>>/<<AUTHORISED_OFFICERS_NAME>>, an authorised officer of the Court

at First Avenue House, 42-49 High Holborn, London WC1A 9JA

on <<ORDER_DATE>>

WHEREAS

By an order dated the «ORDER_DATE» «OLD_DEPUTY_FULL_NAME» was appointed as deputy for property and affairs for «P_FULL_NAME».

And it appearing that the said «OLD_DEPUTY_FULL_NAME» (died on the «DATE_OF_DEATH») (is unable to continue as deputy) (desires to retire from the deputyship), and an application has been made for an order under the Mental Capacity Act 2005 ("the Act").

The Court is satisfied that «P_FULL_NAME» continues to lack capacity to make various decisions for himself/herself in relation to a matter or matters concerning his/her property and affairs, and that the purpose for which the order is needed cannot be as effectively achieved in a way that is less restrictive of his/her rights and freedom of action.

IT IS ORDERED that:

DISCHARGE OF DEPUTY

[If the former deputy is still alive]

(a)   The said «OLD_DEPUTY_FULL_NAME» is discharged from the deputyship and his/her powers are terminated.

(b)   The said «OLD_DEPUTY_FULL_NAME» is to provide the (deputy hereinafter appointed) (new deputy as and when appointed) with a final account to the date of this order by the «DATE».

(c)   The said «OLD_DEPUTY_FULL_NAME» shall disclose to the (deputy hereinafter appointed) (new deputy as and when appointed) copies of all documents, correspondence or records that he/she holds, or has access to, that relate to «P_FULL_NAME»'s property and affairs.

(d)   The said «OLD_DEPUTY_FULL_NAME» is to transfer all property belonging to «P_FULL_NAME» which remains under his/her control to the (deputy hereinafter appointed) (new deputy as and when appointed).

[Or, if the former deputy is deceased]

(a)   The personal representatives of the late «OLD_DEPUTY_FULL_NAME» are to provide the (deputy hereinafter appointed) (new deputy as and when appointed) with a final account to the date of this order by the «DATE».

(b)   The personal representatives of the late «OLD_DEPUTY_FULL_NAME» shall disclose to the (deputy hereinafter appointed) (new deputy as and when appointed) copies of all documents, correspondence or records held by the late «OLD_DEPUTY_FULL_NAME» that relate to «P_FULL-_NAME»'s property and affairs.

(c)   The personal representatives of the late «OLD_DEPUTY_FULL_NAME» are to transfer all property belonging to «P_FULL_NAME» which remains under the control of the late «OLD_DEPUTY_FULL_NAME» to the (deputy hereinafter appointed) (new deputy as and when appointed).

APPOINTMENT OF NEW JOINT AND SEVERAL DEPUTIES

(a)   «FIRST_NEW_DEPUTY_FULL_NAME» of «ADRS1», «ADRS2», «ADRS3», «ADRS4», «ADRS5», «POSTCODE» and «SECOND-_NEW_DEPUTY_FULL_NAME» of «ADRS1_2», «ADRS2_2», «ADRS3_2», «ADRS4_2», «ADRS5_2», «POSTCODE2» are appointed jointly and severally as deputies ("the deputies") to make decisions on behalf of «P_FULL_NAME» that he/she is unable to make for himself/herself in relation to his/her property and affairs, subject to any conditions or restrictions set out in this order.

(b)   The appointment will last until further order.

(c)   The deputies must jointly and severally apply the principles set out in section 1 of the Act and have regard to the guidance in the Code of Practice to the Act.

AUTHORITY OF JOINT AND SEVERAL DEPUTIES

(a)   The Court confers general authority on the deputies to take possession or control of the property and affairs of «P_FULL_NAME» and to exercise the same powers of management and investment, including [selling and] letting property, as he/she has as beneficial owner, subject to the terms and conditions set out in this order.

(b) The deputies cannot purchase any freehold or leasehold property on «P_FULL_NAME»'s behalf without obtaining further authority from the Court.

(c) [The deputies must not sell, lease or charge any freehold or leasehold property in which «P_FULL_NAME» has a beneficial interest without obtaining further authority from the Court.]

(d) If the deputies considers it in «P_FULL_NAME»'s best interests to do so they may appoint an investment manager, who is regulated and authorised to undertake investment business, to manage his/her assets on a discretionary basis under the standard terms and conditions applicable to such service from time-to-time, and to permit the investments to be held in the name of the investment manager nominee company.

(e) The deputies may make provision for the needs of anyone who is related to or connected with «P_FULL_NAME» if he/she provided for, or might be expected to provide for, that person's needs by doing whatever he/she did, or might reasonably be expected to do, to meet those needs.

(f) The deputies may, without obtaining any further authority from the Court, dispose of «P_FULL_NAME»'s money or property by way of gift to any charity to which he/she made, or might have been expected to make, such gifts, and, on customary occasions, to persons who are related to or connected with him/her, provided that the value of each such gift is not unreasonable having regard to all the circumstances and, in particular, the size of his/her estate.

(g) *[Optional paragraph]* On «P_FULL_NAME»'s behalf the deputies may take such steps as may be necessary to obtain a grant of representation to the estate of «FULL_NAME_OF_DECEASED» and to use the share to which «P_FULL_NAME» is entitled for his/her benefit.

(h) For the purpose of giving effect to any decision the deputies may execute or sign any necessary deeds or documents.

(i) *[Include this paragraph in legacy cases only]* The deputies have permission to inspect all Court records and to make copies of any material which they consider necessary to assist in the proper management of «P_FULL_NAME»'s property and affairs, subject to the payment of any relevant fee.

REPORTS

(a) The deputies are jointly required to keep statements, vouchers, receipts and other financial records.

(b)   The deputies must jointly submit a report to the Public Guardian as and when required.

COSTS AND EXPENSES

(a)   The deputies are entitled to be reimbursed for reasonable expenses incurred provided they are in proportion to the size of «P_FULL-_NAME»'s estate and the functions performed by them.(1)

(b)   The deputies are authorised to pay «SOLICITORS» fixed costs for this application, or, where the amount exceeds the fixed costs allowed, the deputies are authorised to agree the costs for making this application and to pay them from funds belonging to «P_FULL_NAME». In default of agreement, or if the deputies or the solicitors would prefer the costs to be assessed, this order is to be treated as authority to the Senior Courts Costs Office to carry out a detailed assessment on the standard basis.(2)

(c)   Any professional deputy is entitled to receive fixed costs in relation to this application, and to receive fixed costs for the general management of «P_FULL_NAME»'s affairs. If the professional deputy would prefer the costs to be assessed, this order is to be treated as authority to the Senior Courts Costs Office to carry out a detailed assessment on the standard basis.(3)

(d)   The deputies are authorised to agree any outstanding costs of general management and to pay them from funds belonging to «P_FULL-_NAME». In default of agreement, or if the deputies or the solicitors would prefer the costs to be assessed, this order is to be treated as authority to the Senior Courts Costs Office to carry out a detailed assessment on the standard basis.

SECURITY

(a)   The deputies are jointly required forthwith to obtain and maintain security in the sum of £«SECURITY_AMOUNT» in accordance with the standard requirements as to the giving of security.

(b)   The deputies must ensure that the level of security ordered by the Court is in place before discharging any of the functions conferred by this order.

RIGHT TO APPLY FOR RECONSIDERATION OF ORDER

Any person who is affected by this order may apply to the Court for reconsideration of the order within 21 days of the order being served by filing an application notice (form COP9) in accordance with Part 10 of the Court of Protection Rules 2007.

Notes
(1)   This clause relates to Lay Deputies only
(2)   This clause relates to Lay Deputies where a professional has submitted the application
(3)   This clause relates to Professional Deputies only

DRAFT ORDER APPOINTING RECEIVER AS DEPUTY PURSUANT TO SCH 5 PARA1(2) OF MCA 2005

THIS DOCUMENT IS NOT VALID UNLESS IT BEARS THE IMPRESSED SEAL OF THE COURT OF PROTECTION ON ALL PAGES

IN THE COURT OF PROTECTION   NO ... << CASE NUMBER>>

MENTAL CAPACITY ACT 2005

In the matter of

<<P_FULL_NAME_IN_BLOCK CAPS>>

ORDER APPOINTING A DEPUTY FOR
PROPERTY AND AFFAIRS

made by <<JUDGES_NAME>>/<<AUTHORISED_OFFICERS_NAME>>, an authorised officer of the Court

at First Avenue House, 42-49 High Holborn, London WC1A 9JA

on <<ORDER_DATE>>

WHEREAS

(1)   By an order dated the «ORDER_DATE» «RECEIVER_FULL_NAME» was appointed as receiver for «P_FULL_NAME».

(2)   By virtue of paragraph 1(2) (a) of schedule 5 of the Mental Capacity Act 2005 ("the Act"), on the 1st October 2007 «RECEIVER_FULL-_NAME» became a deputy for property and affairs.

(3)   An application has been made for an order under the Act.

(4)   The Court is satisfied that the purpose for which the order is needed cannot be as effectively achieved in a way that is less restrictive of his/her rights and freedom of action.

IT IS ORDERED that:

APPOINTMENT OF DEPUTY

(a)   «DEPUTY_FULL_NAME» of «ADRS1», «ADRS2», «ADRS3», «ADRS4», «ADRS5», «POSTCODE» is appointed as deputy ("the deputy") to make decisions on behalf of «P_FULL_NAME» that he/she is unable to make for himself in relation to his/her property and affairs, subject to any conditions or restrictions set out in this order.

(b)   The appointment will last until further order.

(c)   The deputy must apply the principles set out in section 1 of the Act and have regard to the guidance in the Code of Practice to the Act.

AUTHORITY OF DEPUTY

(a)   The Court confers general authority on the deputy to take possession or control of the property and affairs of «P_FULL_NAME» and to exercise the same powers of management and investment, including [selling and] letting property, as he/she has as beneficial owner, subject to the terms and conditions set out in this order.

(b)   The deputy cannot purchase any freehold or leasehold property on «P_FULL_NAME»'s behalf without obtaining further authority from the Court.

(c)   [The deputy must not sell, lease or charge any freehold or leasehold property in which «P_FULL_NAME» has a beneficial interest without obtaining further authority from the Court.]

(d)   If the deputy considers it in «P_FULL_NAME»'s best interests to do so the deputy may appoint an investment manager, who is regulated and authorised to undertake investment business, to manage his/her assets on a discretionary basis under the standard terms and conditions applicable to such service from time-to-time, and to permit the investments to be held in the name of the investment manager nominee company.

(e)   The deputy may make provision for the needs of anyone who is related to or connected with «P_FULL_NAME» if he/she provided for, or might be expected to provide for, that person's needs by doing whatever he/she did, or might reasonably be expected to do, to meet those needs.

(f)   The deputy may (without obtaining any further authority from the Court) dispose of «P_FULL_NAME»'s money or property by way of gift to any charity to which he/she made, or might have been expected to make, such gifts, and, on customary occasions, to persons who are related to or connected with him/her, provided that the value of each such gift is not unreasonable having regard to all the circumstances and, in particular, the size of his/her estate.

(g)   *[Optional paragraph]* On «P_FULL_NAME»'s behalf the deputy may take such steps as may be necessary to obtain (either alone or with a co-administrator) a grant of representation to the estate of «FULL_NAME_OF_DECEASED» and to use the share to which «P_FULL_NAME» is entitled for his/her benefit.

(h)   For the purpose of giving effect to any decision the deputy may execute or sign any necessary deeds or documents.

REPORTS

(a)   The deputy is required to keep statements, vouchers, receipts and other financial records.

(b)   The deputy must submit a report to the Public Guardian as and when required.

COSTS AND EXPENSES

(a)   The deputy is entitled to be reimbursed for reasonable expenses incurred provided they are in proportion to the size of «P_FULL_NAME»'s estate and the functions performed by the deputy.(1)

(b)   The deputy is authorised to pay «SOLICITORS» fixed costs for this application, or, where the amount exceeds the fixed costs allowed, the deputy is authorised to agree the costs for making this application and to pay them from funds belonging to «P_FULL_NAME». In default of agreement, or if the deputy or the solicitors would prefer the costs to be assessed, this order is to be treated as authority to the Senior Courts Costs Office to carry out a detailed assessment on the standard basis.(2)

(c)   The deputy is entitled to receive fixed costs in relation to this application, and to receive fixed costs for the general management of «P_FULL_NAME»'s affairs. If the deputy would prefer the costs to be assessed, this order is to be treated as authority to the Senior Courts Costs Office to carry out a detailed assessment on the standard basis.(3)

SECURITY

(a)   The deputy is required forthwith to obtain and maintain security in the sum of £«SECURITY_AMOUNT» in accordance with the standard requirements as to the giving of security.

(b)   The deputy must ensure that the level of security ordered by the Court is in place before discharging any of the functions conferred by this order.

RIGHT TO APPLY FOR RECONSIDERATION OF ORDER

Any person who is affected by this order may apply to the Court for reconsideration of the order within 21 days of the order being served by filing an application notice (form COP9) in accordance with Part 10 of the Court of Protection Rules 2007.

Notes
(1)   This clause relates to Lay Deputies only
(2)   This clause relates to Lay Deputies where a professional has submitted the application
(3)   This clause relates to Professional Deputies only

DRAFT ORDER APPOINTING JOINT RECEIVERS AS JOINT DEPUTIES PURSUANT TO SCH 1(2)(a) OF MCA 2005

THIS DOCUMENT IS NOT VALID UNLESS IT BEARS THE IMPRESSED SEAL OF THE COURT OF PROTECTION ON ALL PAGES

IN THE COURT OF PROTECTION   NO ... << CASE NUMBER>>

MENTAL CAPACITY ACT 2005

In the matter of

<<P_FULL_NAME_IN_BLOCK CAPS>>

ORDER APPOINTING JOINT DEPUTIES
FOR PROPERTY AND AFFAIRS

made by <<JUDGES_NAME>>/<<AUTHORISED_OFFICERS_NAME>>, an authorised officer of the Court

at First Avenue House, 42-49 High Holborn, London WC1A 9JA

on <<ORDER_DATE>>

WHEREAS

(1)   By an order dated the «ORDER_DATE» «FIRST_RECEIVERS_FULL-_NAME» and «SECOND_RECEIVERS_FULL_NAME» were appointed as joint receivers for «P_FULL_NAME».

(2)   By virtue of paragraph 1(2) (a) of schedule 5 of the Mental Capacity Act 2005 ("the Act"), on the 1st October 2007 «FIRST_RECEIVERS-_FULL_NAME» and «SECOND_RECEIVERS_FULL_NAME» became joint deputies for property and affairs.

(3)   An application has been made for an order under the Act

(4)   The Court is satisfied that the purpose for which the order is needed cannot be as effectively achieved in a way that is less restrictive of his/her rights and freedom of action.

IT IS ORDERED that:

APPOINTMENT OF JOINT DEPUTIES

(a)   «FIRST_DEP_FULL_NAME» of «ADRS1», «ADRS2», «ADRS3», «ADRS4», «ADRS5», «POSTCODE» and «SECOND_DEP_FULL-_NAME» of «ADRS1_2», «ADRS2_2», «ADRS3_2», «ADRS4_2», «ADRS5_2», «POSTCODE2» are appointed as joint deputies ("the deputies") to make decisions on behalf of «P_FULL_NAME» that he/she is unable to make for himself in relation to his property and affairs, subject to any conditions or restrictions set out in this order.

(b)   The appointment will last until further order.

(c)   The deputies must apply the principles set out in section 1 of the Act and have regard to the guidance in the Code of Practice to the Act.

AUTHORITY OF JOINT DEPUTIES

(a)   The Court confers general authority on the deputies to take possession or control of the property and affairs of «P_FULL_NAME» and to exercise the same powers of management and investment, including [selling and] letting property, as he/she has as beneficial owner, subject to the terms and conditions set out in this order.

(b)   The deputies cannot purchase any freehold or leasehold property on «P_FULL_NAME»'s behalf without obtaining further authority from the Court.

(c)   [The deputies must not sell, lease or charge any freehold or leasehold property in which «P_FULL_NAME» has a beneficial interest without obtaining further authority from the Court.]

(d)   If the deputies consider it in «P_FULL_NAME»'s best interests to do so they may appoint an investment manager, who is regulated and authorised to undertake investment business, to manage his/her assets on a discretionary basis under the standard terms and conditions applicable to such service from time-to-time, and to permit the investments to be held in the name of the investment manager nominee company.

(e)   The deputies may make provision for the needs of anyone who is related to or connected with «P_FULL_NAME» if he/she provided for, or might be expected to provide for, that person's needs by doing whatever he/she did, or might reasonably be expected to do, to meet those needs.

(f)   The deputies may (without obtaining any further authority from the Court) dispose of «P_FULL_NAME»'s money or property by way of gift to any charity to which he/she made, or might have been expected to make, such gifts, and, on customary occasions, to persons who are related to or connected with him/her, provided that the value of each such gift is not unreasonable having regard to all the circumstances and, in particular, the size of his/her estate.

(g)   *[Optional paragraph]* On «P_FULL_NAME»'s behalf the deputies may take such steps as may be necessary to obtain a grant of representation to the estate of «FULL_NAME_OF_DECEASED» and to use the share to which «P_FULL_NAME» is entitled for his/her benefit.

(h)   For the purpose of giving effect to any decision the deputies may execute or sign any necessary deeds or documents.

REPORTS

(a)   The deputies are required to keep statements, vouchers, receipts and other financial records.

(b)   The deputies must submit a report to the Public Guardian as and when required.

COSTS AND EXPENSES

(a)   The deputies are entitled to be reimbursed for reasonable expenses incurred provided they are in proportion to the size of «P_FULL-_NAME»'s estate and the functions performed by them.(1)

(b)   The deputies are authorised to pay «SOLICITORS» fixed costs for this application, or, where the amount exceeds the fixed costs allowed, the joint deputies are authorised to agree the costs for making this application and to pay them from funds belonging to «P_FULL_NAME». In default of agreement, or if the joint deputies or the solicitors would prefer the costs to be assessed, this order is to be treated as authority to the Senior Courts Costs Office to carry out a detailed assessment on the standard basis.(2)

(c)   Any professional deputy is entitled to receive fixed costs in relation to this application, and to receive fixed costs for the general management of «P_FULL_NAME»'s affairs. If the professional deputy would prefer the costs to be assessed, this order is to be treated as authority to the Senior Courts Costs Office to carry out a detailed assessment on the standard basis.(3)

SECURITY

(a)   The deputies are required forthwith to obtain and maintain security in the sum of £«SECURITY_AMOUNT» in accordance with the standard requirements as to the giving of security.

(b)   The deputies must ensure that the level of security ordered by the Court is in place before discharging any of the functions conferred by this order.

RIGHT TO APPLY FOR RECONSIDERATION OF ORDER

Any person who is affected by this order may apply to the Court for reconsideration of the order within 21 days of the order being served by filing an application notice (form COP9) in accordance with Part 10 of the Court of Protection Rules 2007.

Notes
    (1)   This clause relates to Lay Deputies only
    (2)   This clause relates to Lay Deputies where a professional has submitted the application
    (3)   This clause relates to Professional Deputies only

DRAFT ORDER APPOINTING JOINT RECEIVERS AS JOINT AND SEVERAL DEPUTIES PURSUANT TO SCH 5(2) OF MCA 2005

THIS DOCUMENT IS NOT VALID UNLESS IT BEARS THE IMPRESSED SEAL OF THE COURT OF PROTECTION ON ALL PAGES

IN THE COURT OF PROTECTION   NO ... << CASE NUMBER>>
MENTAL CAPACITY ACT 2005

In the matter of

<<P_FULL_NAME_IN_BLOCK CAPS>>

ORDER APPOINTING JOINT AND SEVERAL
DEPUTIES FOR PROPERTY AND AFFAIRS

made by <<JUDGES_NAME>>/<<AUTHORISED_OFFICERS_NAME>>, an authorised officer of the Court

at First Avenue House, 42-49 High Holborn, London WC1A 9JA

on <<ORDER_DATE>>

WHEREAS

(1)   By an order dated the «ORDER_DATE» «FIRST_RECEIVERS_FULL-_NAME» and «SECOND_RECEIVERS_FULL_NAME» were appointed as joint receivers for «P_FULL_NAME».

(2)   By virtue of paragraph 1(2) (a) of schedule 5 of the Mental Capacity Act 2005 ("the Act"), on the 1st October 2007 «FIRST_RECEIVERS-_FULL_NAME» and «SECOND_RECEIVERS_FULL_NAME» became joint deputies for property and affairs.

(3)   An application has been made for an order under the Act.

(4)   The Court is satisfied that the purpose for which the order is needed cannot be as effectively achieved in a way that is less restrictive of his/her rights and freedom of action.

IT IS ORDERED that:

APPOINTMENT OF JOINT AND SEVERAL DEPUTIES

(a)   «FIRST_DEP_FULL_NAME» of «ADRS1», «ADRS2», «ADRS3», «ADRS4», «ADRS5», «POSTCODE» and «SECOND_DEP_FULL-_NAME» of «ADRS1_2», «ADRS2_2», «ADRS3_2», «ADRS4_2», «ADRS5_2», «POSTCODE2» are appointed jointly and severally as deputies ("the deputies") to make decisions on behalf of «P_FULL-_NAME» that he/she is unable to make for himself/herself in relation to his property and affairs, subject to any conditions or restrictions set out in this order.

(b)   The appointment will last until further order.

(c)   The deputies must jointly and severally apply the principles set out in section 1 of the Act and have regard to the guidance in the Code of Practice to the Act.

AUTHORITY OF JOINT AND SEVERAL DEPUTIES

(a)   The Court confers general authority on the deputies to take possession or control of the property and affairs of «P_FULL_NAME» and to exercise the same powers of management and investment, including [selling and] letting property, as he/she has as beneficial owner, subject to the terms and conditions set out in this order.

(b)   The deputies cannot purchase any freehold or leasehold property on «P_FULL_NAME»'s behalf without obtaining further authority from the Court.

(c)   [The deputies must not sell, lease or charge any freehold or leasehold property in which «P_FULL_NAME» has a beneficial interest without obtaining further authority from the Court.]

(d)   If the deputies consider it in «P_FULL_NAME»'s best interests to do so they may appoint an investment manager, who is regulated and authorised to undertake investment business, to manage his/her assets on a discretionary basis under the standard terms and conditions applicable to such service from time-to-time, and to permit the investments to be held in the name of the investment manager nominee company.

(e)   The deputies may make provision for the needs of anyone who is related to or connected with «P_FULL_NAME» if he/she provided for, or might be expected to provide for, that person's needs by doing whatever he/she did, or might reasonably be expected to do, to meet those needs.

(f)   The deputies may (without obtaining any further authority from the Court) dispose of «P_FULL_NAME»'s money or property by way of gift to any charity to which he/she made, or might have been expected to make, such gifts, and, on customary occasions, to persons who are related to or connected with him/her, provided that the value of each such gift is not unreasonable having regard to all the circumstances and, in particular, the size of his/her estate.

(g)   *[Optional paragraph]* On «P_FULL_NAME»'s behalf the deputies may take such steps as may be necessary to obtain a grant of representation to the estate of «FULL_NAME_OF_DECEASED» and to use the share to which «P_FULL_NAME» is entitled for his/her benefit.

(h)   For the purpose of giving effect to any decision the deputies may execute or sign any necessary deeds or documents.

REPORTS

(a)   The deputies are jointly required to keep statements, vouchers, receipts and other financial records.

(b)   The deputies must jointly submit an annual report to the Public Guardian as and when required to do so.

COSTS AND EXPENSES

(a)   The deputies are entitled to be reimbursed for reasonable expenses incurred provided they are in proportion to the size of «P_FULL-_NAME»'s estate and the functions performed by them.(1)

(b)   The deputies are authorised to pay «SOLICITORS» fixed costs for this application, or, where the amount exceeds the fixed costs allowed, the deputies are authorised to agree the costs for making this application and to pay them from funds belonging to «P_FULL_NAME». In default of agreement, or if the deputies or the solicitors would prefer the costs to be assessed, this order is to be treated as authority to the Senior Courts Costs Office to carry out a detailed assessment on the standard basis.(2)

(c)   Any professional deputy is entitled to receive fixed costs in relation to this application, and to receive fixed costs for the general management of «P_FULL_NAME»'s affairs. If the professional deputy would prefer the costs to be assessed, this order is to be treated as authority to the Senior Courts Costs Office to carry out a detailed assessment on the standard basis.(3)

SECURITY

The deputies are jointly required forthwith to obtain and maintain security in the sum of £«SECURITY_AMOUNT» in accordance with the standard requirements as to the giving of security.

The deputies must ensure that the level of security ordered by the Court is in place before discharging any of the functions conferred by this order.

RIGHT TO APPLY FOR RECONSIDERATION OF ORDER

Any person who is affected by this order may apply to the Court for reconsideration of the order within 21 days of the order being served by filing an application notice (form COP9) in accordance with Part 10 of the Court of Protection Rules 2007.

Notes
(1)   This clause relates to Lay Deputies only
(2)   This clause relates to Lay Deputies where a professional has submitted the application

(3)   This clause is where one of the deputies is a professional

CHAPTER 4

ENDURING POWERS OF ATTORNEY

LAW AND PRACTICE

4.1 BACKGROUND

The enduring powers of attorney (EPA) are creatures of statute ie the Enduring Powers of Attorney Act 1985 which came into force on 1 March 1986. EPAs differ from ordinary powers of attorney because they endure beyond the onset of incapacity (subject to the requirement of registration). They also enable the attorney to make gifts and make provision for someone whom the donor might have provided for or been responsible for. They are limited in scope in that it relates only to the donor's property and affairs. The attorney does not have any powers in relation to the donor's personal welfare such as residence, care, contact and health. By reason of the fact that they are based on the donor's autonomy to choose the person he wished to manage his affairs, they were open to abuse because of the limited degree of supervision and intervention available to protect the donor when he was unable to make decisions on his own behalf through lack of capacity.

The Mental Capacity Act 2005, s 66 abolished the Enduring Powers of Attorney Act 1985. No EPAs can be made after 1 October 2007.[1] However, all existing EPAs will continue to remain effective, subject to the provision of Sch 4 to the Mental Capacity Act 2005, which in effect incorporates the provisions of the 1985 into the new Act and thus the safeguards introduced by the 1985 Act are preserved. EPAs have been replaced by lasting powers of attorney (LPA), see chapter 4.

4.2 CHARACTERISTIC OF EPAS

To be valid the EPA:

- Must be made in the prescribed form.
- Must be executed in the prescribed manner by the donor and the attorney or attorneys if more than one.
- Must incorporate at the time of execution by the donor the prescribed explanatory information.

---

[1]   MCA, s 66(2).

- Must not appoint an individual as an attorney who has not reached the age of 18 unless it is a trust corporation, and the individual appointed must not be bankrupt.
- Must not give the attorney the right to appoint substitute or successor.

The instrument which creates the EPA will be presumed to have been appropriately executed unless the contrary is proved. An immaterial difference in the form and mode of expression than that which is prescribed will not render the instrument ineffective.[2]

In addition, to the above requirements, the statutory provisions impose a duty on the attorney to register the EPA with the Court of Protection in the prescribed form with the prescribed supporting statement, when he/she believes that the donor is or is becoming incapable of managing his property and affairs. Before making the application the attorney is required to notify the donor personally and at least three relatives in a prescribed order of classes of relatives[3] and any other attorney appointed of his/her intention to do so.

4.3   CONTENTS OF THE NOTICE

The notice to the donor must:
- be in the prescribed form;
- state that the attorney proposes to make an application for registration of the instrument creating the EPA in question; and
- inform the donor that, while the instrument remains registered, any revocation of the power by him/her will be ineffective unless and until the revocation is confirmed by the Court.[4]

The notice to the relatives and to other attorneys (if more than one) must:
- be in the prescribed form;
- state that the attorney intends to register the EPA;
- inform the person concerned that he has a right to object to the registration within 5 weeks of the date of the notice; and
- specify the grounds set out in para 13(9) on which an objection to registration may be made.[5]

4.4   GROUNDS OF OBJECTIONS

Schedule 4, para 13(9) sets out five specific grounds on which objection may be made to the registration of the EPA namely:

---

[2]   MCA, Sch 4, para 2(4).
[3]   MCA, Sch 4, paras 5–7.
[4]   MCA, Sch 4, para 10.
[5]   MCA, Sch 4, para 9.

(a) that the power purported to have been created by the instrument was not valid as an EPA;

(b) that the power created by the instrument no longer subsists;

(c) that the application is premature because the donor has not yet becoming mentally incapable;

(d) that fraud or undue pressure was used to induce the donor to create the power; and

(e) that having regard to all the circumstances and in particular the attorney's relationship to or connection with the donor, the attorney is unsuitable to be the donor's attorney.

4.5 REVOCATION

An EPA is revoked if:

- The donor or the attorney becomes bankrupt.

- The Court exercises it powers to make decisions in respect of P concerning his/her personal welfare and or property and affairs and its powers to appoint deputies under ss 16–20 of the MCA 2005 and directs that the EPA is revoked.

In addition, if the Court is satisfied that any of the grounds set out in para 13(9) above is established it must direct the Public Guardian not to register the instrument. If the Court is satisfied that fraud or undue pressure was used to induce the donor to create the power or that having regard to the all the circumstances and in particular the attorney's relationship or connection with the donor, the attorney is unsuitable to be the donor's attorney, the Court must revoke the power created by the instrument.[6]

If the Court directs the Public Guardian not to register the instrument on any of the grounds set out in para 13(9) the instrument must be delivered up and be cancelled unless the objection has been established on the ground that the application is premature or the Court otherwise directs[7] (see below for the Court's power).

4.6 LEGAL EFFECT OF REGISTRATION

Once registered:

- Any revocation of the power by the donor will be invalid unless and until the Court confirms the revocation.

- Any disclaimer of the power by the attorney is not valid until the attorney gives notice of the disclaimer to the Public Guardian.

---

6   MCA, Sch 4, para 13(11).
7   MCA, Sch 4, para 13(12).

- The donor cannot extend or restrict the scope of the authority conferred by the instrument.

- No instruction or consent given by the donor after registration confers any right or imposes or confers any obligation or right on or creates any liability of the attorney or other persons having notice of the instruction or consent.

Registration of an instrument is evidence of the contents of the instrument and of its registration.[8]

4.7 COURT'S POWERS

Where an instrument has been registered the Court has the following functions with respect to the power.

The Court may:

(a) determine any question as to the meaning or effect of the instrument;

(b) give directions with respect to the management or disposal by the attorney of the property and affairs of the donor; the rendering of accounts by the attorney and the production of the records kept by him for the purpose and the remuneration or expenses of the attorney, whether or not in default or in accordance with any provision made by the instrument, including directions for the repayment of excessive or the payment of additional remuneration;

(c) require the attorney to supply information or produce documents or things in his possession as attorney;

(d) give any consent or authorisation to act which the attorney would have to obtain from the mentally capable donor;

(e) authorise the attorney to act so as to benefit himself or other persons than the donor otherwise than in accordance with para 16(2) and (3) (but subject to any conditions or restrictions contained in the instrument);

(f) relieve the attorney wholly or partly from any liability which he has or may have incurred on account of a breach of his duties as attorney.

4.7.1 The Court's power to confirm revocation on application by the donor

On an application made for the purpose by or on behalf of the donor, the Court must confirm the revocation of the power if it is satisfied that the donor:

(a) has done whatever is necessary in law to effect an express revocation of the power; and

---

8 MCA, Sch 4, para 15.

(b) was mentally capable of revoking a power of attorney when he did so (whether or not he is so when the Court considers the application).[9]

4.7.2 The Court's power to direct cancellation of a registered instrument

The Court must direct the Public Guardian to cancel the registration of an instrument in the following circumstances:

(a) on confirming the revocation of the power (see above under **4.7.1**);

(b) on directing that the power is to be revoked when it exercises its powers under ss 16–20 of the Act in relation to the appointment of a deputy (see above under **4.7.1(b)**);

(c) on being satisfied that the donor is and is likely to remain mentally capable;

(d) on being satisfied that the power has expired or has been revoked by the mental incapacity of the attorney;

(e) on being satisfied that the power was not a valid and subsisting enduring power when registration was effected;

(f) on being satisfied that fraud or undue pressure was used to induce the donor to create the power;

(g) on being satisfied that, having regard to all the circumstances and in particular the attorney's relationship to or connection with the donor, the donor is unsuitable to be the donor's attorney.[10]

4.8 CANCELLATION OF REGISTRATION BY PUBLIC GUARDIAN

The Public Guardian must cancel the registration of an instrument creating an enduring power of attorney in the following circumstances:

(a) on receipt of a disclaimer signed by the attorney;

(b) if satisfied that the power has been revoked by the death or bankruptcy of the donor or attorney or, if the attorney is a body corporate, by its winding up or dissolution;

(c) on receipt of notification from the Court that it has revoked the power;

(d) on confirmation from the Court that the donor has revoked the power.

4.9 PRACTICE AND PROCEDURE

Practice Direction 9H (PD 9H) applies where any person entitled to be given notice of the application to register an instrument wishes to apply to the Court for direction that the instrument should or should not be registered.

---

9 MCA, Sch 4, para 16(3).
10 MCA, Sch 4, para 16(4).

4.9.1 How to apply

The application must be made on Form COP8. The application form must state:

(a) what direction the applicant is seeking;

(b) if the applicant objects to the registration, the grounds on which he does so; or

(c) if the applicant is seeking registration, his reasons for doing so.[11]

The application form must be supported by evidence. This may be contained in either the application form, provided it is verified by a statement of truth, or in a witness statement which must also be verified by a statement of truth.

4.9.2 Service

As soon as practicable after issue, but in any event within 21 days of the application form being issued, the applicant must serve a copy of the application form together with the acknowledgment of service in Form COP5:

(a) unless the applicant is the donor or an attorney, on the donor of the power and every attorney under the power;

(b) if he/she is the donor, on every attorney under the power; or

(c) if he/she is an attorney, on the donor and any other attorney under the power;

(d) where the applicant knows or has reasonably grounds to believe that, the donor of the power lacks capacity to make a decision in relation to the matter that is the subject of the application, he must notify the donor of the application in accordance with COP Rules 2007, r 40 and PD 7A. The applicant in this case must, unless the Court otherwise directs, explain to P who the applicant is; what the application is about; what will happen if the Court makes an order or direction that has been applied for and that P may seek advice and assistance in relation to any matter of which he is notified. This information must be provided to P in a way that is appropriate to P's circumstances (for example using simple language, visual aids or any other appropriate means). The information must be provided to P personally. Every effort should be made to inform P in a way that he/she will understand. The notification should be given on COP14 with COP14A which gives guidance on how to complete Form COP14. P must also be provided with the acknowledgment of notification Form COP5.

4.9.3 Certificate of notification

Once the relevant persons have been notified, the applicant must file the certificate of notification in Form COP20. Where it is apparent that P is unable

---

[11] PD 9H, para 7.

to act on the notification notice the Court should be informed that P is unlikely to return the acknowledgment form or do anything with it. The applicant is obliged to file the COP20 within 7 days of effecting service. If the applicant has difficulty in serving the documents he/she should apply on Form COP9 to the Court for direction for substituted service or service to be dispensed with.

4.9.4 The Court

The Court when required to act in an emergency may:

- make orders on the papers without a hearing;
- make orders at a hearing without notice;
- abridge time for service.

Where an order is made without notice to the attorney the Court will make directions fixing a directions appointment or hearing and give directions for a reply by the attorney.

In cases where there is concern for the misuse of P's assets, application may also be made at the same time for freezing orders or injunctions to protect the position.[12]

An urgent hearing may take place by telephone (PD 9B, para 11) and in an exceptional case an oral application may be made without issue of an application notice (PD 9B, para 9). If the order sought is unusually long a disc should be provided for the Court's use.[13]

---

[12] See COP Rules 2007, r 82 and chapter 11 Enforcement.
[13] PD 9B, para 7.

4.10 PROCEDURAL GUIDE FOR REGISTRATION OF ENDURING POWER OF ATTORNEY AND OBJECTING TO REGISTRATION AND CANCELLATION OF THE POWER

Attorney	Files application to register in Form **EP2G**	MCA 2005, Sch 3, Part 3 Regulations 2007, reg 23 and Sch 7
Attorney notifies donor and relevant relatives	Notice of registration in Form **EP1G**	Regulations 2007, reg 23 and Sch 4, Part 3
Public Guardian	Sends notice of receipt to P and any other attorney and to the attorney if notice of registration is made by P	Regulations 2007, reg 11
Registration	If there are no grounds for Refusing the registration and no objections received within 35 days Public Guardian registers the EPA	MCA 2005, Sch 4
Donor and other relevant persons' objections to the Court by application	Must be made within 5 weeks on prescribed grounds (see **9.4**) on Form **COP8** or **COP1** if the applicant is not entitled to be notified of registration	MCA 2005, Sch 4 COP Rules 2007 PD 9H (6)-(10)
Application to the Court		
Applicant		
Donor (P) Attorney/s Relevant relatives	Form **COP8** and Form **COP24** with a witness statement and supporting evidence and draft order sought	COP Rules 2007 PD 9H PD 9A
Any other person	Form **COP1**	
Service within 21 days on P and other relevant persons	Donor/attorney of Forms **COP14** and **COP14A** and **COP5**	COP Rules 2007 PD 9H(9)
Applicant files	Certificate of notification on Form **COP20** Within 7 days of service	PD 9H
Acknowledgement by persons served	On Form **COP5**	COP Rules 2007, r 72 PD 9H
Orders that Court may make	see **4.7**	

PRECEDENTS

DRAFT DIRECTIONS ORDER ON APPLICATION OBJECTING TO REGISTRATION OF EPA

THIS DOCUMENT IS NOT VALID UNLESS IT BEARS THE SEAL OF THE COURT OF PROTECTION ON ALL PAGES

IN THE COURT OF PROTECTION   NO ... << CASE NUMBER>>
MENTAL CAPACITY ACT 2005

In the matter of

<<P_FULL_NAME_IN_BLOCK
CAPS>>

DIRECTIONS

made by <<JUDGES_NAME>>

at First Avenue House, 42-49 High Holborn, London WC1A 9JA

on <<ORDER_DATE>>

WHEREAS

(1)   On the «DATE_OF_EPA» «P_FULL_NAME» ("the donor") executed an instrument in which he/she appointed «NAME(S)_OF_ATTORNEY(S)» to be his/her sole attorney/joint/joint and several attorneys ("the attorney/attorneys") under an Enduring Power of Attorney ("the EPA").

(2)   On the «DATE_OF_APPLICATION_TO_REGISTER_EPA» an application was made to the Public Guardian by «NAME(S)_OF_ATTORNEY-(S)_WHO_APPLIED_TO_OPG» to register the EPA.

(3)   On the «DATE_COP8_SIGNED» «NAMES_OF_APPLICANTS_FROM-_COP8» ("the objector/objectors") applied to the Court to object to the registration of the EPA.

(4)   The objector has/objectors have filed evidence with his/her/their application.

(5)   Capacity to make/revoke the EPA is/is not in issue.

IT IS ORDERED that:

(1) If they have not yet done so, by 4.00 p.m. on the «14_DAYS» the objector/objectors shall file with the Court and serve on the attorney/attorneys

  (a) all witness evidence in form COP24 (attaching all documentary evidence relied on); and

  (b) if applicable, all medical evidence relied on in respect of the donor's capacity to make and revoke the EPA.

(2) By 4.00 p.m. on the «42_DAYS» the attorney/attorneys shall file with the Court and serve on the objector/objectors

  (a) all witness evidence in form COP24 (attaching all documentary evidence relied on); and

  (b) if applicable, all medical evidence relied on in respect of the donor's capacity to make and revoke the EPA.

(3) The application will be referred to a judge on the first available date after the «63_DAYS» who will decide without a hearing

  (a) whether to uphold or dismiss the objection(s); or

  (b) whether to list the matter for hearing with further directions.

(4) Any person who is affected by this order may apply to the Court for reconsideration of the order within 21 days of the order being served by filing an application notice (form COP9) in accordance with Part 10 of the Court of Protection Rules 2007.

To:

1. «OBJECTOR(S)_OR_OBJECTOR(S)_SOLICITORS_IF_ACTING»

2. «ATTORNEY(S)_OR_ATTORNEY(S)_SOLICITORS_IF_ACTING»

DRAFT ORDER DISMISSING APPLICATION OBJECTING TO REGISTRATION OF EPA

THIS DOCUMENT IS NOT VALID UNLESS IT BEARS THE SEAL OF THE COURT OF PROTECTION ON ALL PAGES

IN THE COURT OF PROTECTION   NO ... << CASE NUMBER>>

MENTAL CAPACITY ACT 2005

In the matter of

<<P_FULL_NAME_IN_BLOCK
CAPS>>

ORDER

made by <<JUDGES_NAME>>

at First Avenue House, 42-49 High Holborn, London WC1A 9JA

on <<ORDER_DATE>>

WHEREAS

(1)   [Staff to insert recitals from the objection directions order as made by the judge]

(2)   The Court has considered the evidence filed.

(3)   The burden of proof is on the objector/objectors.

(4)   Further to the written evidence filed the Court considers that [for judge to insert].

IT IS ORDERED that:

1.   The application dated «DATE_COP8_SIGNED» to object to the registration is dismissed for the reason that none of the grounds of objection to the registration of the EPA has been established to the satisfaction of the Court.

2.   The Public Guardian is directed to proceed with the registration of the EPA.

3.   Any person who is affected by this order may apply to the Court for

reconsideration of the order within 21 days of the order being served by filing an application notice (form COP9) in accordance with Part 10 of the Court of Protection Rules 2007.

To:

1.   «OBJECTOR(S)_OR_OBJECTOR(S)_SOLICITORS_IF_ACTING»

2.   «ATTORNEY(S)_OR_ATTORNEY(S)_SOLICITORS_IF_ACTING»

3.   The Public Guardian, P.O. Box No. 16185, Birmingham, B2 2WH

DRAFT ORDER SEVERING PROVISIONS IN EPA

THIS DOCUMENT IS NOT VALID UNLESS IT BEARS THE SEAL OF THE
COURT OF PROTECTION ON ALL PAGES

IN THE COURT OF PROTECTION   NO ... << CASE NUMBER>>

MENTAL CAPACITY ACT 2005

In the matter of

<<P_FULL_NAME_IN_BLOCK CAPS>>

ORDER

made by <<JUDGES_NAME>>

at First Avenue House, 42-49 High Holborn, London WC1A 9JA

on <<ORDER_DATE>>

WHEREAS

(1)   On the «DATE_OF_EPA» «P_FULL_NAME» executed an Enduring
        Power of Attorney ("the EPA") in which he/she appointed
        «NAME(S)_OF_ATTORNEY(S)» jointly and severally to be his
        attorneys ("the attorneys").

(2)   The EPA contains the provision that "«QUOTE_TEXT_OF_PROVI-
        SION»".

(3)   Pursuant to paragraph 4(5) of Schedule 4 to the Mental Capacity
        Act 2005 the attorneys have referred to the Court for its determination
        the question as to the validity of the EPA.

IT IS ORDERED that:

1.   The Court determines that the provision would be ineffective as part of
        the EPA.

2.   The Court hereby severs the provision.

3.   The Court hereby gives notice to the Public Guardian that it has severed
        the provision and that when the attorneys apply to register the EPA the
        Public Guardian must register the instrument with a note to that effect
        attached to it.

4.   Any person who is affected by this order may apply to the Court for reconsideration of the order within 21 days of the order being served by filing an application notice (form COP9) in accordance with Part 10 of the Court of Protection Rules 2007.

To:

1.   «APPLICANT(S)_OR_APPLICANT(S)_SOLICITORS_IF_ACTING»

2.   The Public Guardian, P.O. Box No. 16185, Birmingham, B2 2WH

CHAPTER 5

LASTING POWERS OF ATTORNEY

LAW AND PRACTICE

5.1 BACKGROUND

A lasting power of attorney (LPA) is a power of attorney which allows the donor (P) to confer on the donee/s authority to make decisions about all or any matters relating to the personal welfare or specified matters concerning P's welfare and P's property and affairs or specified matters relating to P's property and affairs. Its importance is that it includes authority to make such decisions in circumstances where P no longer has capacity.[1] It follows from its nature that it is made by the donor when he/she has capacity and presumes the principles contained in ss 1 and 2 of the Act (see chapter 2), ie that whilst the donor has capacity to make a decision he/she makes that decision himself/herself. In order to prevent abuse, the power of an attorney will be restricted by the terms of the power so that it is exercised only in relation to the specified matters and in certain circumstances identified in the instrument creating the power. The Act also imposes restrictions on this power which are discussed below. The common law restrictions such as the duty of care to P and the duty owed by a person in a fiduciary position to another not to misappropriate P's property or to obtain a gain will also apply. The Court of Protection is now given wide powers which are aimed at preventing abuse of the attorney's powers. The LPA replaces the enduring power of attorney (EPA). No new EPAs can now be created since the MCA 2005 came into force. Those created prior to the Act remain valid so long as they are lawfully created (see chapter 4).

5.2 CHARACTERISTICS OF LPAS

Section 9(2) provides that a lasting power of attorney is not created unless:

(a) section 10 is complied with;

(b) an instrument conferring authority of the kind mentioned in subsection 1 is made and registered in accordance with Sch 1; and

(c) at the time when P executes the instrument, P has reached 18 and has capacity to execute it.

---

[1] MCA 2005, s 9.

The lasting power of attorney must be in the prescribed form and must be registered before it can take effect. Section 9(4) also provides that the authority conferred by a lasting power of attorney is subject to the provisions of the Act and, in particular, the principles set out in ss 1 and 4 of the Act (see **2.3** and **2.5**) and any conditions or restrictions specified in the instrument.

A lasting power of attorney does not authorise the donee/s to do an act that is intended to restrain P unless three conditions are met, namely:

(a)   that P lacks capacity or the donee reasonably believes that P lacks capacity in relation to the matter in question;

(b)   that the donee reasonably believes that it is necessary to do the act in order to prevent harm to P;

(c)   that the act is a proportionate response to the likelihood of P's suffering harm and the seriousness of that harm.

A donee will be treated as using restraint on P if he/she uses, or threatens to use, force to secure the doing of an act which P resists or restricts P's liberty of movements, whether or not P resists or if he/she authorises another person to do any of those things.[2] The donee/s will be treated as doing more than merely restraining P if he deprives P of his liberty within the meaning of Art 5(1) of the European Convention for the Protection of Human Rights and Fundamental Freedoms (ECHR)[3] (see chapter 10 generally for deprivation of liberty).

In relation to any authority given in the instrument relating to decisions about P's personal welfare, s 11(7) and (8) impose the following restrictions, namely, the authority:

(a)   does not extend to making such decisions in circumstances other than those where P lacks capacity, or the donee reasonably believes that P lacks capacity;

(b)   is subject to ss 24–26 (advance decisions to refuse treatment; see under **9.13**).

The power in relation to welfare decisions will extend to giving or refusing consent to the carrying out or continuation of a treatment by a person providing health care for P but it does not authorise the giving or refusing of consent to the carrying out or continuation of life-sustaining treatment, unless the instrument contains express provision to that effect and in such a case it will be subject to any conditions or restriction set out in the instrument.

Where a lasting power confers authority to make decisions about P's property and affairs, s 12 provides that this does not authorise the attorney/s to dispose of P's property by making gifts except to the extent permitted by subs (2). Subject to any conditions or restrictions contained in the instrument, the attorney may make gifts on customary occasions (including to himself) to those who are related to or connected with P or to any charity to whom P made or

---

[2]   MCA 2005, s 11(1)–(5).
[3]   MCA 2005, s 11(6).

might have been expected to make gifts.[4] Customary occasion means the occasion or anniversary of a birth, or marriage or the formation of a civil partnership or any other occasion on which presents are customarily given within families or among friends or associates.

5.3 REGISTRATION OF AN LPA

A lasting power of attorney is ineffective until it is registered. An application to register is made to the Public Guardian in a prescribed form – Form LPA002. It must be accompanied with the original instrument and the appropriate fee.

5.3.1 Persons to whom notice of application to register must be given

The applicant must give notice in Form LPA001 to any person named in the instrument.

If the applicant is the attorney, the Public Guardian is required to give notice of the application to the donor. Where the application for registration is made by the donor the Public Guardian is required to give notice to the attorney/s and if an application is made by one of two attorneys to the other attorney.

5.3.2 Public Guardian's duty to register

The Public Guardian must register the LPA unless one or more of the circumstances set out in Sch 1, paras 13–14 to the Act apply. If the Public Guardian has no grounds for refusing to register or he has not received any objections to the registration within 3 weeks of the notice being given and not less than 4 weeks after notice was given by the Public Guardian, he must register the instrument as a lasting power of attorney.

5.3.3 Grounds on which registration may be refused

The grounds on which the Public Guardian may refuse to register the LPA are those which are inferred from the provisions set out in Sch 1, paras 11–14 to the Act. These include the following:

(a) If it appears that the lasting power of attorney is not valid.

(b) If it appears to the Public Guardian that an instrument accompanying the application is apparently defective or contains ineffective provisions in which case the Public Guardian must not register the power unless the Court of Protection directs him to do so. Where the instrument contains a provision which is ineffective or would prevent the instrument from operating as a valid lasting power of attorney the Public Guardian must apply to the Court for it to determine the matter under s 23(1) of the Act.

(c) If it appears to the Public Guardian that the Court has already appointed a deputy for P and the powers conferred on the deputy by the Court would

---

[4]   MCA 2005, s 12(2).

conflict with the powers of the attorney. In this case the instrument cannot be registered unless the Court directs the Public Guardian to do so.

(d)   If notice is given by an attorney or a named person of an objection to the registration on one or more of the specified grounds in s 13(3) or (6)(a)–(d) which has had the effect of revoking the instrument and the Public Guardian is satisfied that the ground for making the objection is established, unless the Court on the application of the person applying for the registration is satisfied that the ground is established and directs the Public Guardian to register the instrument.

(e)   If the Court of Protection receives a notice of objection from an attorney or a named person on a prescribed ground and notifies the Public Guardian of the application.

(f)   If the donor on receiving the application for registration gives notice to the Public Guardian of an objection to the registration the Public Guardian must not register the instrument unless the Court on the application of the attorney/s is satisfied that P lacks capacity to object to the registration and directs the Public Guardian to register the instrument.

In relation to grounds (1) and (2) many applications are having to be made by the Public Guardian to sever provision in LPAs on the grounds on invalidity. These applications are avoidable if care is taken in drafting the contents of the LPA form. Common invalid restrictions and conditions which have resulted in a referral to the Court for directions include:

- Provision authorising gifts or continuation of regular payments such as helping a donor's child financially which fall outside the statutory powers to make gifts such as 'my handicapped son should be adequately provided for' was held to contravene s 12 of the MCA 2005 and the provision was severed (*Re O'Brien*).[5])

- Appointment of attorneys to act jointly for some decisions and jointly and severally for others are often found to be troublesome. The case of *Re Llewelyn*[6] illustrates this point. In that case the donor appointed attorneys including her husband to act jointly in some matters and jointly and severally in other matters, but identified a list of specified matters which were to be acted on jointly with the proviso that provided her husband was able to act as one on her attorneys all decisions could be made jointly or severally. On the application of the Public Guardian the proviso was severed as being incompatible with an appointment to act jointly in some matters and jointly and severally in others.

- Provisions made for the maintenance of family members. Such a provision can only be valid if the donor has a legal obligation to maintain the family member, such as a child who is under 18 years of age or a spouse or civil partner. In a case where a property and affairs LPA included a direction to the attorney 'I wish my attorney to provide for the financial needs of my husband in the manner that I might have been expected to do if I had

---

5   [2012] MHLO 65 (LPA).
6   [2012] MHLO 61 (LPA).

capacity to do so', the Public Guardian sought the Court's direction on whether the provision contravened s 12 of the Act. The reason for the application was that a wife had no common law duty to maintain her husband and that the husband's duty to maintain his wife would be abolished when s 198 of the Equality Act 2010 came into force. It was held that such clauses should be treated as valid on the basis of the specific maintenance obligations imposed by a number of statutes and the absence of distinction between spouses in the Matrimonial Causes Act 1973 and the Inheritance (Provisions for Family and Dependants) Act 1975 (*Re Strange*).[7] But provisions made to provide for grandchildren or to contribute towards the cost of care for a father have been held to be invalid.

- Where the requirements for making the LPA are not strictly followed. Hence where a LPA appointed two attorneys to act jointly and severally but one attorney's signature was not witnessed and inadvertently the LPA was registered, on the application of one of the attorney for the LPA to be declared valid, the Court directed that the instrument should be returned to the Office of the Public Guardian so that the attorney's appointment could be marked as invalid in accordance with s 10(7) of the Act (*Re Smith*).[8]

- Where one certificate provider is a member of the family of one of the attorneys. The Court has upheld the decision to refuse registration of the LPA. The judge stated that 'anyone who describes himself in this context as the attorney's partner is courting trouble and automatically disqualifies himself from being a person who can give an LPA certificate. This applies regardless of whether he describes himself as the attorney's partner intentionally or inadvertently, whether they live at the same address or at separate locations, whether the relationship is intimate or platonic, and whether the statement is true or false' (*Re Philips*[9]).

- Provisions for the replacement of an attorney which fall outside the events set out in s 13 of the Act such as providing for a replacement if an attorney is not available due to travel difficulties. Provisions for replacements of attorneys who have been appointed to act jointly or jointly for some decisions and jointly and severally for others have also led to provisions being held invalid where for example a donor has provided for replacement of joint attorneys A and B to be replaced by C and D on the first attorney that needs replacing. so that on the first replacement there will be three attorneys. This was held to be invalid because in the event of a replacement C and D would alone replace the original attorneys where decisions have to be made jointly (see *Re Druce*[10] and MCA 2005 s 10(8)(b)).

---

[7] [2012] MHLO 64 (LPA).
[8] [2012] MHLO 63.
[9] [2012] MHLO 60 (LPA).
[10] [2011] COP Order of Judge Lush made 31/5/2011.

- Provisions which contravene s 10(8)(a) of the Act which prohibits a LPA to give a donee or, if more than one, any of them power to appoint a substitute or successor.

Information on avoidance of invalid provisions is available on the OPG's website and the guidance *Avoiding Invalid Provisions in your LPA* (January 2013) prepared by Jill Martin, Legal Adviser to the Public Guardian is a useful tool for those drafting LPAs. If in doubt it is advisable to seek guidance from the OPG and to resolve any issues which may arise in relation to invalid provision by agreement as this avoids delay and the expense of litigation.

5.4   GROUNDS OF OBJECTION

The grounds on which a person named in the instrument or an attorney can object are set out in s 13(3) and (6) and s 22(3). The grounds under s 13 are:

(a)   P has revoked the power;

(b)   it is alleged that P lacked capacity when he executed the instrument;

(c)   P's bankruptcy revokes the power so far as it relates to P's property and affairs;

(d)   the death or bankruptcy of the attorney or if the attorney is a trust corporation its winding up or dissolution;

(e)   the attorney has disclaimed;

(f)   P has died;

(g)   the marriage or civil partnership between P and the attorney has been dissolved;

(h)   the attorney lacks capacity.

The grounds prescribed under s 22(3) are:

(a)   fraud or undue pressure has been used to induce P to create the LPA;

(b)   the attorney has behaved, or is behaving in a way that contravenes his authority or is not in P's best interests; or

(c)   the attorney proposes to behave in a way that would contravene his authority or would not be in P's best interests.

5.5   REVOCATION AND CANCELLATION

Inevitably, as has been described in chapter 3 regarding deputies and chapter 4 regarding attorneys appointed with enduring powers, some will fail to carry out their responsibilities properly. This may be as a result of their own incapacity or dishonesty. In those circumstances an application may need to be made to the Court for the revocation of the instrument creating the power and cancellation of its registration.

The Court's powers to determine issues relating to the validity or operation of a lasting power of attorney are set out in ss 22 and 23 of the Act. The Court has the following specific powers:

- Where P has executed or purported to execute an instrument with a view to creating a lasting power of attorney or an instrument has been registered as a lasting power of attorney conferred by P, the Court is empowered to determine whether one or more of the requirements for the creation of a lasting power of attorney have been met and whether the power has been revoked or has otherwise come to an end (s 22(2)).

- The Court also has power to direct that an instrument purporting to create a lasting power of attorney is not registered, or if P lacks capacity to do so, revoke the instrument or the lasting power of attorney if the Court is satisfied:
  - (a) that fraud or undue duress was used to induce P to execute an instrument for the purpose of creating a lasting power of attorney or to create a lasting power of attorney; or
  - (b) that the attorney/s of a lasting power of attorney has behaved, or is behaving in or proposes to behave in a way that would contravene his/her authority or would not be in P's best interests (s 22(3)).

5.6 COURT'S POWERS

5.6.1 As to validity under s 22

When exercising its powers the Court will consider what is in the best interests of P. This will necessarily involve consideration of the test set out in s 4 of the Act (see **2.5** above) and the provisions of s 1(6) which requires that 'before the act is done, or the decision is made, regard must be had to whether the purpose for which it is needed can be effectively achieved in a way that is less restrictive of the person's rights and freedom of action'. Additionally, the Court must also consider, so far as it is possible to do so to give effect to any decision under the Act, that it is compatible with the European Convention for the Protection of Human Rights and Fundamental Freedoms 1950 (ECHR). These issues were considered by HHJ Marshall QC in *Re J*[11] and by Senior Judge Lush in *Re Harcourt: The Public Guardian v A.*[12] In *Re J* when in deciding whether to revoke a LPA under s 23(3)(b), Judge Marshall held that the Court can 'consider any past behaviour or *apparent* prospective behaviour by the attorney, but depending on the circumstances and the gravity of any offending behaviour found, it can take whatever steps it regards as appropriate in P's best interests (subject to P lacking capacity) to deal with the situation, whether by revoking the power or by taking some other course' (see also Newey J's decision in *Re Rodman* under **3.7** on the issue of other factors which may be relevant).

---

[11] [2011] COPLR Con Vol 716.
[12] [2013] COPLR 69.

In *Re Harcourt: The Public Guardian v A*, P had signed a LPA appointing her daughter to manage her property and affairs. As a result of arrears in the payment of care home charges, failure to pay P pocket money and unaccountable financial transaction, the Public Guardian was required to undertake an investigation pursuant to s 58(1) of the Act under which the Public Guardian's functions include dealing with representation (including complaints) about the way in which a donee is exercising his powers. Additionally, the provisions under the Lasting Powers of Attorney, Enduring Powers of Attorney and Public Guardian Regulations 2007,[13] reg 46, were also engaged in that it empowers the Public Guardian to require a donee to provide information and produce documents where there are circumstances suggesting that the donee of a LPA may have behaved, or may be behaving in a way that contravenes his authority, or is not in the best interests of the donor of the power, or has failed to comply with the requirements of an order made or directions given by the Court (reg 46(1) and (2)). The daughter obstructed the investigation and failed to comply with an order of the Court which led to the Public Guardian applying for an order that the LPA be suspended and for P's bank accounts to be frozen. In determining the issues before him Senior Judge Lush stated that the 'factor of magnetic importance in determining what is in Mrs Harcourt's best interests is that her property and financial affairs should be managed competently and for her benefit' and that by refusing to cooperate with the Court and the OPG the daughter as her mother's attorney was not behaving in her mother's best interests ie the s 4 test and s 1(6) were also engaged. On the facts the Court found that the daughter had behaved in a way that was not in P's best interests (paras 60–65) and that it was appropriate on the facts to revoke the LPA. In addition Senior Judge Lush also considered the impact of the Art 8 rights of the donor and donee to respect for private and family life and the Art 6 rights of the daughter, as the attorney, and of Mrs Harcourt that the issues raised in the case are determined as soon as possible. In doing so he applied Thorpe LJ's conclusion in *K v LBX & Others*.[14] He was satisfied that the daughter had been given ample opportunity to produce the documents and information required of her and that her lack of candour had 'generated deeper concerns that, she has something to conceal and that she may have financially abused her mother'. He found that the revocation of the LPA in order to facilitate the appointment of a deputy was 'a necessary and proportionate response for the protection of Mrs Harcourt's right to have her financial affairs managed competently, honestly and for her benefit, and for the possible prevention of crime' (paras 70–71).

Re Buckley,[15] is another example of a case which fell within the ambit of s 22 and where the Court found that such a revocation was necessary and proportionate and that it was in P's best interest to do so. In that case the LPA was revoked following an investigation by the Public Guardian which revealed that a very substantial sum of P's monies had been used by her niece, who was

---

[13]   SI 2007/1253.
[14]   [2012] EWCA Civ 79, [2012] COPLR 411.
[15]   [2013] COPLR 39.

the attorney under the LPA, that she had invested in a reptile breeding project and transferred £45,000 of P's capital for her own personal benefit.

The decision is also relevant with regard to the responsibilities of an attorney acting under a LPA. Senior Judge Lush identified that there were 'two misconceptions when it comes to investments. The first is that attorneys acting under an LPA can do whatever they like with the donors' funds. And the second is that attorneys can do whatever the donors could – or would – have done personally, if they had the capacity to manage their property and financial affairs'. He stated that neither of these options were open to an attorney acting for an incapacitated donor because of their fiduciary obligations and partly because an attorney is required to act in the donor's bests interests. He went on to give guidance on the responsibilities of an attorney under a LPA when investing a donor's funds (see paras 25–46), which attorneys and those advising them and those advising a donor and drafting a LPA should take into account.

5.6.2   As to operation under s 23

Where there is more than one attorney the Court may revoke the instrument or the lasting power of attorney so far as it relates to any of them.

- The Court may determine any question as to the meaning or effect of a lasting power of attorney or an instrument purporting to create one (s 23(1)).
- The Court may give directions with respect to decisions which the attorney of a lasting power of attorney has authority to make and which P lacks capacity to make (s 23(2)(a)).
- The Court may give any consent or authorisation to act which the attorney would have to obtain from P if P had capacity to give (23(2)(b)).
- The Court may authorise the making of gifts which are not within s 12(2) (s 23(4) and see above at chapter 3).
- The Court may if P lacks capacity:
  (a) give directions to the attorney with respect to the rendering by him of reports or accounts and the production of records kept by him for that purpose;
  (b) require the attorney to provide information or produce documents or things in his possession as an attorney;
  (c) give directions with respect to the remuneration or expenses of the attorney;
  (d) relieve the attorney wholly or partly from any liability which he has or may have incurred on account of a breach of his duties as an attorney (s 23(3)).

5.7   PRACTICE AND PROCEDURE

The Court when required to act in an emergency may:
- make orders on the papers without a hearing;

- make orders at a hearing without notice;
- abridge time for service (see COP Rules 2007, Part 5 – case management powers).

Where an order is made without notice to the attorney the Court will make directions fixing a directions appointment or hearing and give directions for a reply by the attorney.

In cases where there is concern for the misuse of P's assets, application may also be made at the same time for freezing orders or injunctions to protect the position (see chapter 11).

5.8   HOW TO APPLY

A person wishing to object to the registration under one or more of the above grounds must do so by making an application to the Court of Protection in Form COP7 and support the application with a witness statement and other supporting evidence of the objections made. The person making the objections must also inform the Public Guardian of the application to the Court in Form LPA007.

Where the application objecting to the registration is made by a person other than P or an attorney or person named in the instrument, the application must be made in Form COP1.

In the case of an application being made after the lasting power of attorney has been registered any application for the cancellation of the registration or any other directions or order of the Court should be made in Form COP1.

5.9 PROCEDURAL GUIDE FOR REGISTRATION OF LASTING POWER OF ATTORNEY AND OBJECTING TO REGISTRATION AND CANCELLATION OF THE POWER

Attorney	Files application to register in Form **LPA002**	Regulations 2007, reg 11 and Sch 3
Attorney serves person named P in the LPA	Notice of registration in Form **LPA001**	Regulations 2007, reg 10 and Sch 2
Public Guardian	Sends notice of receipt to P and any other attorney and to the attorney if notice of registration is made by P	Regulations 2007, reg 11
Registration	If there are no grounds for Refusing the registration and no objections received within 4 weeks Public Guardian registers the LAP in Form **LPA004**	Regulations 2007, reg 12 and 17 (as amended)
Objections to the Public Guardian	On factual grounds within 3 weeks on Form **LPA001**	Regulations 2007, reg 14(2) and 15(3) (as amended)
Objections to the Court	On prescribed grounds (**see 9.1.3, s 22**) within 5 weeks on Form **COP7**	
Application to the Court		
Applicant Donor (P) Attorney/s Person named in the LPA	Form **COP7** and Form **COP24** with a witness statement and supporting evidence and draft order sought	COP Rules 2007, rr 51(2)(b) and 64 PD 9A
Orders that Court may make	see **5.5**	

PRECEDENTS

WITNESS STATEMENT IN SUPPORT OF AN APPLICATION FOR THE REVOCATION OF AN ENDURING/LASTING POWER OF ATTORNEY AND CANCELLATION OF REGISTRATION

IN THE COURT OF PROTECTION

IN THE MATTER OF THE MENTAL CAPACITY ACT 2005

AND IN THE MATTER OF FREDA FRUMP (D.O.B. 01.12.1917)

BETWEEN

RUM COUNTY COUNCIL   Applicant
SOCIAL AND
COMMUNITY SERVICES
DEPARTMENT

And

FREDA FRUMP   1st Respondent

(By her litigation friend the
Public Guardian)

And

BETSY FRUMP   2nd Respondent

WITNESS STATEMENT OF MELANIS LOVE

I, Melanis Love of Rum County Council Social and Community Services Department, of 22 Acropolis Street, Rum will state as follows:

1. I am a care manager employed by Rum County Council Social and Community Services Department in the Adults' Services Team. I am the allocated care manager for Freda Frump, currently of The Good Samaritan Residential Home in Rum.

2. I qualified as a Social Worker in 1990 with an MSc and Certificate of Qualification in Social Work (CQSW).

3. I have been employed by the Rum County Council since 2003. I had initially worked as a field social worker for different local authorities and in day care and residential units for the elderly. For a period of about 10

years before commencing my employment with Rum County Council I was employed as a social worker for the elderly by Hellinic Borough Council.

4.   I make this statement in support of an application for authorisation for Freda Frump to be placed in residential care at the Good Samaritan Residential Home on a permanent basis subject to the standard residential placement reviewing system and for Betsy Frump to be discharged as Freda Frump's attorney and to appoint a panel deputy to manage the property and affairs of both Freda and Betsy Frump. I make this statement based on my personal knowledge and from information contained on Freda Frump's file. I have also been responsible for Freda's care since her admission to the residential care home and in that capacity have had to discuss the plans for Freda with the medical experts and the Mental Health Team.

5.   Freda and Betsy are sisters. Freda is 92 years of age and Betsy is 95. Neither of them married and have no other siblings or relatives.

6.   Until June 2013 the sisters lived together in their family home. I am aware that they have both executed mutual wills and hold an enduring/lasting power of attorney for each other.

7.   In about 2007 Freda was diagnosed with dementia. Her health deteriorated and it became difficult for Betsy to care for her. On 15 June 2013 Freda fell down the stairs at their home. Fortunately she had minor injuries but she lost all confidence and it became necessary to place her in the residential home. The EPA/LPA had been registered by the Public Guardian and Betsy took over the responsibility for Freda's finances.

8.   Since then it has become apparent that Betsy is becoming disorientated and it appears that she too may be losing capacity.

9.   The local authority's plan for Freda is that she should remain living in and be cared for at the residential home. This plan has been discussed with Betsy but she has refused to co operate and has failed to discharge the fees for the residential care home. She has also refused to pay for the necessary expenses relating to Freda's personal care.

10.   Betsy had been visiting her sister at the care home but more recently she has not done so. Attempts made to engage with her at her home have proved unsuccessful and concerns have been expressed by those who have visited her that she is extremely disorientated. There is now produced and shown to me marked 'ML1' the reports of the assessments carried out on Betsy.

11.   Before making the decision to make this application, I made one last attempt to discuss Freda's care with Betsy but she appeared not to comprehend even the simplest of matters relating to her sister. I too am concerned about Betsy welfare and capacity.

12.   There is now produced and shown to me marked 'ML2' a report of

Dr Wise a consultant psychiatrist for Older Adults and her colleague Dr. Brilliant who have both diagnosed Freda with unspecified dementia.

12.   In those circumstances the local authority applies to the Court of Protection for an order revoking the EPA/LPA and directing the Public Guardian to cancel registration and appointing a panel deputy to manage the property and affairs of both sisters.

13.   The facts stated in this witness statement are true.

Signed

Name ....

Dated ....

ORDER FOR THE REVOCATION OF AN EPA/LPA CANCELLATION OF REGISTRATION AND APPOINTMENT OF A DEPUTY

IN THE COURT OF PROTECTION

IN THE MATTER OF THE MENTAL CAPACITY ACT 2005

AND IN THE MATTER OF .... [*insert P's forename and surname*]

BETWEEN

RUM COUNTY COUNCIL SOCIAL AND COMMUNITY SERVICES DEPARTMENT	Applicant

And

FREDA FRUMP (By her litigation friend the Public Guardian)	1st Respondent

And

BETSY FRUMP	2nd Respondent

DRAFT ORDER

Made by District Judge Felicity Sharp

At ....

On 23 September 2013

UPON hearing Counsel for the applicant and Solicitor for the Public Guardian and for BF respondents

AND UPON considering the trial bundle

WHERAS THE COURT IS SATISFIED [*or See the deputy order and delete para 1-3*]

1. FF lacks capacity to make decisions about her residence and property and affairs.

2. It is lawful in FF's best interests for her to continue to reside at the Good Samaritans Residential Home until further order.

3.   It is lawful, being in FF's best interests for the applicant to arrange contact between FF and her sister BF.

IT IS ORDERED THAT:

[directions]

1.   The applicant local authority do have permission to make the application for an order revoking the EPA/LPA and directing the Public Guardian to cancel registration

2.   FF is joined as first respondent and BF is joined as a second respondent and subject to his consent the O/S is appointed to act for FF OR

3.   [in the case where the attorney has died] It is noted that the attorney .... [*insert name*] appointed by P [*insert name*] by instrument dated [*insert date*] and registered on .... [*insert date of registration*] has died and the instrument is accordingly cancelled.

AND IT IS FURTHER DIRECTED THAT

1   This application and the evidence filed be served on the first and second respondent by the .... day of .... [*service having been abridged*].

2.   The parties do by .... file and serve all the evidence upon which they intend to rely at the hearing.

3.   The hearing be listed on the .... with a T/E of 2 hours.

4.   Pursuant to the Court of Protection Rules 2007 rule 4 the parties shall co operate to agree a trial bundle to be provided to the Court and all parties by the applicant by 12 noon on .... 2014. The parties agreeing the contents by .... skeleton arguments to be filed at Court by ....

5.   BF as attorney for FF shall disclose to the Court all accounts, shares holdings, bonds state benefits and pensions and other investments of FF by ....

6.   BF shall cause the sum of £ .... to be paid from the account of FF with the Prudent bank to be paid into Court Funds Office by ....

8.   BF is forbidden to withdraw, transfer dispose of or in any other way deal with the funds held in the name of FF in the Prudent Bank and any other assets belonging to FF until further order.

[Final Order]

1.   The EPA/LPA dated .... appointing BF as attorney for FF shall be revoked and the Public Guardian is directed to forthwith cancel registration.

2.   A member of the panel maintained by the Office of the Public guardian be appointed deputy in accordance with the procedure set out in the Schedule to this order, to make decisions on behalf of FF that she is unable to make for herself in relation to her property and affairs subject to any conditions or restrictions set out in this order.

3.   (See Precedent in chapter 3 under Deputies).

4.   No order as to costs save detailed assessment of FF's publicly funded costs/ or make an order that costs be paid out P's assets.

DRAFT DIRECTIONS ORDER ON APPLICATION OBJECTING TO REGISTRATION OF LPA

THIS DOCUMENT IS NOT VALID UNLESS IT BEARS THE SEAL OF THE COURT OF PROTECTION ON ALL PAGES

IN THE COURT OF PROTECTION   NO ... << CASE NUMBER>>
MENTAL CAPACITY ACT 2005

In the matter of

<<P_FULL_NAME_IN_BLOCK CAPS>>

DIRECTIONS

made by <<JUDGES_NAME>>

at First Avenue House, 42-49 High Holborn, London WC1A 9JA

on <<ORDER_DATE>>

WHEREAS

(1)   On the «DATE_OF_LPA» «P_FULL_NAME» ("the donor") executed an instrument in which he/she appointed «NAME(S)_OF_ATTORNEY(S)» to be his/her sole attorney/joint/joint and several attorneys ("the attorney/attorneys") under a Lasting Power of Attorney for [property and affairs] [and] [personal welfare] ("the LPA/LPAs").

(2)   On the «DATE_OF_APPLICATION_TO_REGISTER_LPA» an application was made to the Public Guardian by «NAME(S)_OF_ATTORNEY-(S)_WHO_APPLIED_TO_OPG» to register the LPA/LPAs.

(3)   On the «DATE_COP7_SIGNED» «NAMES_OF_APPLICANTS_FROM-_COP7» ("the objector/objectors") applied to the Court to object to the registration of the LPA/LPAs.

(4)   The objector has/objectors have filed evidence with his/her/their application.

(5)   Capacity to make/revoke the LPA/LPAs is/is not in issue.

IT IS ORDERED that:

(1)   If they have not yet done so, by 4.00 p.m. on the «14_DAYS» the objector/objectors shall file with the Court and serve on the attorney/attorneys

    (a)   all witness evidence in form COP24 (attaching all documentary evidence relied on); and

    (b)   if applicable, all medical evidence relied on in respect of the donor's capacity to make and revoke the LPA/LPAs.

(2)   By 4.00 p.m. on the «42_DAYS» the attorney/attorneys shall file with the Court and serve on the objector/objectors

    (a)   all witness evidence in form COP24 (attaching all documentary evidence relied on); and

    (b)   if applicable, all medical evidence relied on in respect of the donor's capacity to make and revoke the LPA/LPAs.

(3)   The application will be referred to a judge on the first available date after the «63_DAYS» who will decide without a hearing

    (a)   whether to uphold or dismiss the objection(s); or

    (b)   whether to list the matter for hearing with further directions.

(4)   Any person who is affected by this order may apply to the Court for reconsideration of the order within 21 days of the order being served by filing an application notice (form COP9) in accordance with Part 10 of the Court of Protection Rules 2007.

To:

1.   «OBJECTOR(S)_OR_OBJECTOR(S)_SOLICITORS_IF_ACTING»

2.   «ATTORNEY(S)_OR_ATTORNEY(S)_SOLICITORS_IF_ACTING»

DRAFT ORDER DISMISSING APPLICATION OBJECTING TO REGISTRATION OF LPA

THIS DOCUMENT IS NOT VALID UNLESS IT BEARS THE SEAL OF THE COURT OF PROTECTION ON ALL PAGES

IN THE COURT OF PROTECTION   NO ... << CASE NUMBER>>

MENTAL CAPACITY ACT 2005

In the matter of

<<P_FULL_NAME_IN_BLOCK CAPS>>

ORDER

made by <<JUDGES_NAME>>

at First Avenue House, 42-49 High Holborn, London WC1A 9JA

on <<ORDER_DATE>>

WHEREAS

(1)   [Staff to insert recitals from the objection directions order as made by the judge]

(2)   The Court has considered the evidence filed.

(3)   The burden of proof is on the objector/objectors.

(4)   Further to the written evidence filed the Court considers that [for judge to insert].

IT IS ORDERED that:

1.   The application dated «DATE_COP7_SIGNED» to object to the registration is dismissed for the reason that none of the grounds of objection to the registration of the LPA/LPAs has been established to the satisfaction of the Court.

2.   The Public Guardian is directed to proceed with the registration of the Lasting Power of Attorney for [property and affairs] [and] [personal welfare].

3.   Any person who is affected by this order may apply to the Court for

reconsideration of the order within 21 days of the order being served by filing an application notice (form COP9) in accordance with Part 10 of the Court of Protection Rules 2007.

To:

1. «OBJECTOR(S)_OR_OBJECTOR(S)_SOLICITORS_IF_ACTING»

2. «ATTORNEY(S)_OR_ATTORNEY(S)_SOLICITORS_IF_ACTING»

3. The Public Guardian, P.O. Box No. 16185, Birmingham, B2 2WH

DRAFT ORDER ON APPLICATION SEEKING WITHDRAWAL OF APPLICATION OBJECTING TO REGISTRATION OF LPA

THIS DOCUMENT IS NOT VALID UNLESS IT BEARS THE SEAL OF THE COURT OF PROTECTION ON ALL PAGES

IN THE COURT OF PROTECTION   NO ... << CASE NUMBER>>
MENTAL CAPACITY ACT 2005

In the matter of

<<P_FULL_NAME_IN_BLOCK CAPS>>

ORDER

made by <<JUDGES_NAME>>

at First Avenue House, 42-49 High Holborn, London WC1A 9JA

on <<ORDER_DATE>>

WHEREAS

(1)   The Court having considered the letter/application notice dated the «DATE» received from the objector/objectors stating that he/she/they withdraw his/her/their application objecting to the registration of the Lasting Power of Attorney for [property and affairs] [and] [personal welfare] ("the LPA/LPAs").

IT IS ORDERED that:

1.   The proceedings are concluded.

2.   The Public Guardian is directed to proceed with the registration of the LPA/LPAs.

3.   Any person who is affected by this order may apply to the Court for reconsideration of the order within 21 days of the order being served by filing an application notice (form COP9) in accordance with Part 10 of the Court of Protection Rules 2007.

To:

1.   «OBJECTOR(S)_OR_OBJECTOR(S)_SOLICITORS_IF_ACTING»

2.   «ATTORNEY(S)_OR_ATTORNEY(S)_SOLICITORS_IF_ACTING»

3.   The Public Guardian, P.O. Box No. 16185, Birmingham, B2 2WH

DRAFT ORDER SEVERING PROVISIONS SET OUT IN LPA

THIS DOCUMENT IS NOT VALID UNLESS IT BEARS THE SEAL OF THE COURT OF PROTECTION ON ALL PAGES

IN THE COURT OF PROTECTION   NO ... << CASE NUMBER>>
MENTAL CAPACITY ACT 2005

In the matter of

<<P_FULL_NAME_IN_BLOCK CAPS>>

ORDER

made by <<JUDGES_NAME>>

at First Avenue House, 42-49 High Holborn, London WC1A 9JA

on <<ORDER_DATE>>

WHEREAS

(1)   On the «DATE_OF_LPA» «P_FULL_NAME» executed Lasting Power of Attorney for [property and affairs] [and] [personal welfare] ("the LPA/LPAs") in which he/she appointed «NAME(S)_OF_ATTORNEY(S)» jointly and severally to be his/her attorneys ("the attorneys").

(2)   The LPA contains/LPAs contain the provision that "«QUOTE-_TEXT_OF_PROVISION»".

(3)   Pursuant to paragraph 4(5) of Schedule 4 to the Mental Capacity Act 2005 the attorneys have referred to the Court for its determination the question as to the validity of the LPA/LPAs.

IT IS ORDERED that:

1.   The Court determines that the provision would be ineffective as part of the LPA/LPAs.

2.   The Court hereby severs the provision.

3.   The Court hereby gives notice to the Public Guardian that it has severed the provision and that when the attorneys apply to register the LPA/LPAs the Public Guardian must register the instrument/instruments with a note to that effect attached to it.

4.   Any person who is affected by this order may apply to the Court for reconsideration of the order within 21 days of the order being served by filing an application notice (form COP9) in accordance with Part 10 of the Court of Protection Rules 2007.

To:

1.   «APPLICANT(S)_OR_APPLICANT(S)_SOLICITORS_IF_ACTING»

2.   The Public Guardian, P.O. Box No. 16185, Birmingham, B2 2WH

CHAPTER 6

STATUTORY WILLS

LAW AND PRACTICE

6.1 INTRODUCTION

Anyone who is 18 years of age or over and who has testamentary capacity can make a valid will. The presumption is that the testator has testamentary capacity unless proved otherwise but he/she must have the mental capacity to do so, both at the time of giving instructions or making the will. If he/she has capacity both at the time of giving instruction and executing the will, then his/her wishes however bizarre or eccentric should be respected.

Before the Act came into force on 1 October 2007 the Court of Protection's powers were limited to all issues relating to an incapacitated person's property and financial affairs. Various Mental Health Acts gave the Court of Protection authority to do everything necessary or expedient for the maintenance or other benefit of an incapacitated person and in relation to his property and affairs and 'for making provision for other persons or purposes for whom or which he might be expected to provide if he were not mentally disordered'.[1] Section 103 of the MHA 1959 empowered the Court to direct the making of settlements. With effect from January 1970, following amendments made to the MHA 1959 by the Administration of Justice Act 1969, the Court was given power to order the execution of a statutory will for a person whom it had reason to believe lacked testamentary capacity. The approach to be taken by the Court in deciding contested applications was aided by guidance of case law, in particular *Re D(J)*,[2] which preferred a substituted judgment approach ie what P would have wanted.

Whilst the power of the Court to authorise the making of wills for those who lack capacity has been retained by Mental Capacity Act 2005 the underlying philosophy of the legislation has operated to change the Court's approach. The Act has introduced the six key principles which must be applied when making any decision relating to an incapacitated person his welfare, property or affairs with the emphasis being on what is in the 'best interest' of the person (see chapter 2). Section 4 sets out a check list of factors which must be considered in deciding what is in the person's best interest.

---

[1] MHA 1959, s 102(1).
[2] [1982] Ch 237, [1982] 2 WLR 373, [1982] 2 All ER 37, ChD.

6.2   POSITION UNDER THE ACT

The Court of Protection is empowered to make a will on behalf of P by virtue of ss 16(2)(a) and 18(1)(i). Section 16(2)(a) provides that the Court may by making an order, make the decision or decisions on P's behalf in relation to the matters and s 18 extends the Court's powers to make such orders which includes the execution for P of a will. The approach the Court must take under the Act was fully considered in *Re P*.[3] Lewison J (as he then was) considered the past guidance of *Re D(J)*[4] and set out the way in which the Act now requires the Court to interpret the 'best interest' test which the Act requires must be applied in all decisions made on behalf of P. He said that 'the overarching principle is that any decision made on behalf of P must be in P's best interests. This is not necessarily the same as inquiring what P would have decided if he or she had had capacity' (para 37):[5]

> 'The Act does not require the counter-factual assumption that P is not mentally disordered. The facts must be taken as they are. It is not therefore necessary to go through the mental gymnastics of imagining that P has a brief lucid interval and then relapse into his former state ... The goal of the inquiry is not what P "might be expected" to have done; but what is in P's best interests. This is more akin to the "balance sheet" approach than to the "substituted judgment" approach.'

The Code of Practice makes this clear. All the relevant circumstances must be taken into consideration in deciding what was in the person's best interest. The Act provides a structured decision making process and:[6]

> 'expressly directs the decision maker to take a number of steps before reaching a decision. These include encouraging P to participate in the decision. He must also "consider" P's past and present wishes and his beliefs and values and must "take into account" the views of third parties as to what would be in P's best interests.
>
> Having gone through these steps, the decision maker must then form a value judgment of his own giving effect to the paramount statutory instruction that any decision must be made in P's best interests.'

6.2.1   Best interest and P's wishes

The Act requires that any decision made or act done for or on behalf of a person who lacks capacity (P) must be one which is in his best interest (s 1(5)) and in determining what is in P's best interests the decision maker is required to consider, so far as is ascertainable, P's past and present wishes and feelings and, in particular, any relevant written statement made by him when he had capacity; the beliefs and values that would be likely to influence his decision if he had capacity and the other factors that he would be likely to consider if he were able to do so. In addition the views of those who are engaged in caring for

---

3   [2009] EWHC 163 (Ch), [2009] COPLR Con Vol 906.
4   [1982] 2 All ER 37.
5   Paragraph 38(i) and (ii).
6   Paragraphs 38(vi) and 39.

P, or interested in his welfare, and any donee of a lasting power of attorney or a deputy appointed by the Court or anyone named by P, must also be taken into account.[7] However, P's wishes and feelings are not the only consideration. It is one of the matters that the Court is required to take account of. Thus, it does not necessarily follow that the person's wishes will in all instances be followed notwithstanding the principle of adult autonomy and that a person has the freedom to dispose of his property as he wishes. In *Re P* (above) Lewison J (as he then was) acknowledged that that was:[8]

> 'part of the overall picture, and an important one … but what will live on after P's death is his memory; and for many people it is in their best interests that they be remembered with affection by their family and as having done "the right thing" by their will. In my judgment the decision maker is entitled to take into account, in assessing what is in P's best interests, how he will be remembered after his death.'

However, when dealing with the issue of P's wishes at para 40 of his judgment Lewison J said that Ps wishes should not be 'lightly overridden'. On the contrary, the Act expressly requires them to be considered; and for particular consideration to be given to wishes expressed by P when he had capacity. He referred with approval to the decision of HHJ Hazel Marshall QC in *Re S and S (Protected Persons)*[9] (an appeal from a district judge of the COP) and her conclusion on the issue of P's wishes when she had said that 'the views and wishes of P in regard to decisions made on his behalf are to carry great weight' and whilst accepting that the Act does not say that P's wishes are to be paramount, she expressed that, by giving prominence to the best interests of P the Act in her judgment recognised that having his views and wishes taken into account and respected is a very significant aspect of P's best interests. Due regard should therefore be paid when doing the weighing exercise of determining what is in P's best interests. She went on to state (at para 57):

> 'And … in my judgment where P can and does express a wish or view which is not irrational (in the sense of being a wish which a person of full capacity might reasonably have), is not impractical as far as its physical implementation is concerned, and is not irresponsible having regard to the extent of P's resources … then that situation carries great weight, and effectively gives rise to a presumption in favour of implementing those wishes, unless there is some potential sufficiently detrimental effect for P of doing so which outweighs this.'

Lewison J agreed with the broad thrust of this but thought that HHJ Marshall QC may have slightly overstated the importance to be given to P's wishes. He gave the following reasons for this:[10]

> 'First, s 1(6) is not a statutory direction that one "must achieve" any desired objective by the least restrictive route. Section 1(6) only requires that before a decision is made "*regard* must be had" to that question. It is an important

---

[7] MCA 2005, s 4(6) and (7).
[8] Paragraph 44.
[9] [2008] COPLR Con Vol 1074.
[10] Paragraph 41.

question, to be sure, but it is not determinative. The only imperative is that the decision must be made in P's best interests, Second, although P's wishes must be given weight, if, as I think Parliament has endorsed the "balance sheet" approach they are only one part of the balance. I agree those wishes are to be given great weight, but I would prefer not to speak in terms of presumption. Third, any attempt to test a decision by reference to what P would hypothetically have done or wanted runs the risk of amounting to a "substituted judgment" rather than a decision of what would be in Ps best interests ... The decision maker must consider the beliefs and values that would be likely to influence P's decision if he had capacity and also the other factors that P would be likely to consider if he were able to do so ...'

Lewison J also relied on the explanation given in para 5.38 of the Code of Practice and pointed out the need for a third party when making a decision on behalf of P to take legal or other advice if appropriate, and to the fact that the decision maker is entitled to take into account, in assessing what is in P's best interests, how he will be remembered after his death.

The decision in *Re P* demonstrates that the Court is likely to balance P's known wishes with other objective considerations in determining what is in his best interests. This will include for instance the Court considering any possible claims for proprietary estoppel and claims under the Inheritance (Provision for Family and Dependants) Act 1975 for financial provision (see *NT v FS & Ors*[11]) and reducing inheritance tax where appropriate. The approach taken in *Re P* was endorsed by Munby J (as he then was) in *In the matter of M*[12] who observed that, P's best interests did not end on death and that the statutory framework of best interests included consideration of how P would be remembered after his death. However, he accepted that this additional factor referred to by Lewison J (as he then was) in *Re P* may not have universal application and could cause some difficulties. Indeed the notion has not proved popular. In *Re G(TJ)*[13] (a case about gifts), Morgan J analysed the case law and concluded that what P would have wanted (ie the substituted judgment approach) was a significant factor for the Court to take into account:

'... in my judgment, P's balance sheet of factors and P's likely decision can be taken into account by the court. This involves an element of substituted judgment being taken into account, together with anything else which is relevant. However, it is absolutely clear that the ultimate test for the court is the test of best interests and not the test of substituted judgment. Nevertheless the substituted judgment can be relevant and is not excluded from consideration.'

These authorities were considered recently in *Re JC; D v JC, JG, A, B, C*[14] by Senior Judge Lush in unusual circumstances. JC's relationship with his four children had been either poor or non-existent. He had denied paternity of A but later his paternity was established. B and C were children of his marriage, which had been short, and D had been conceived by JC raping his ex-wife after

---

[11]   [2013] EWHC 684 (COP), [2013] COPLR 313.
[12]   [2009] EWHC 2525 (Fam).
[13]   [2010] EWHC 3005 (COP).
[14]   [2012] COPLR 540.

the divorce and had been adopted. He had had no relationship with D at all and they had never met. Although JC had indicated that he wished to revoke an earlier will he had made on the ground that he had been tricked into signing it in January 2011, a statutory will was executed dividing his estate between persons who would have been entitled on JC's intestacy and appointing professional executors. Under the terms of the will D, having been adopted, was excluded. D applied for a further statutory will to be executed on the basis that, the 2011 will had not made any provision for her, and A applied for a variation to permit him to decide the devolution of his share of the estate if he pre-deceased JC. In reaching his decision Judge Lush pulled the threads together from previous case law and summarised the principles which the Court is required to take into account when determining on a statutory will as follows:

(a) the check list of factors for best interests decision-making, set out in s 4 of the Act;

(b) the possible application of the 'balance sheet approach' and the identification of 'factors of magnetic importance';

(c) the developed jurisprudence on application of this kind including the recognition that 'for many people it is their best interests that they be remembered with affection by their family as having done the "the right thing" by their will'.

He then went on to observe that:

• Of 11 subsections in s 4, only 4 were of relevance to a statutory will application and that these were subsections (2), (4), (6) and (7) and that these incorporate into the best interests criterion a strong element of substituted judgment, and on that basis on the facts JC would have wished to die intestate had he had capacity to make a will.

• He had doubts about the effectiveness of the 'balance sheet approach' in statutory will applications, although he had applied that test in an application for a gift to save inheritance tax in *JDS; KGS v JDS*,[15] but that there will usually be at least one factor of magnetic importance – as there was in this case – (the absence of any relationship with D) that will assist the judge in reaching a decision.

• Similarly, in relation to the concept of being remembered with affection for having done the right thing was of little assistance because JC had an appalling track record of doing the 'wrong thing' in his relationships with others and that 'his malevolence was such that he would probably relish the prospect of thwarting his children's designs on his estate and would rejoice at being remembered by them with disaffection'.

Applying these factors to the facts before him he concluded that the case presented a combination of substituted judgment and best interests. Applying the former, JC would have preferred to die intestate but, having regard to the nature and extent of the his estate and the family dynamics it was in his best interests to make a will in order to appoint independent professional executors

---

[15] [2012] COPLR 383.

who are familiar with the background and can provide continuity in the administration of his estate before and after his death.

D's application for a statutory will to include her was dismissed but A's application for a variation of the will to include provision permitting him to decide the devolution of his estate if he predeceased JC was allowed and extended to include B and C as well.

In the context of statutory wills it is now important to have regard to the effect of the decision of the Supreme Court in *Aintree University Hospitals NHS Foundation Trust v James*[16] when the Court considers how to assess P's best interests. The entirely objective approach, of what a reasonable person would do, or the concept that it is the best interests of P to be remembered with affection for having done the right thing, should no longer be regarded as the prevailing consideration. The Supreme Court rejected this approach and clarified that best interests should be determined from P's point of view. The Court accepted that it will not always be possible to ascertain P's wishes and that even if it was possible to determine what his wishes and feelings were in the past, they might well have changed. Nevertheless, in 'so far as it is possible to ascertain P's wishes and feelings, his beliefs and values or the thing which were important to him, it is those that should be taken into account because they are a component in making the choice which is right for him as an individual human being'. Whilst the Supreme Court did not go as far as adopting an approach to the concept of best interests which is entirely synonymous with the concept of substituted judgment, it is clear that in future, P's wishes will weigh heavily in the balance sheet.

6.3   CAPACITY

The Act affirms in s 1(1) the common law presumption that a person must be assumed to have capacity unless it is established that he lacks capacity. In order for P to have testamentary capacity, it is not necessary that he/she is able to follow all the provisions relating to the making of the will. It will suffice if at the time of executing the will he/she has an understanding and appreciation that he/she is executing a will. The observations made by Cockburn CJ in his judgment in *Banks v Goodfellow*[17] are often relied on as providing a test of testamentary capacity:

> 'It is essential that a testator shall understand the nature of the act and its effects, shall understand the extent of the property of which he is disposing, shall be able to comprehend and appreciate the claims to which he ought to give effect; and with a view to the latter object, that no disorder of the mind shall poison his affections, pervert his sense of right, or prevent the exercise of his natural faculties – that no insane delusion shall influence his will in disposing of his property and bring about a disposal of it which, if the mind had been sound, would not have been made.'

---

[16]   [2013] UKSC 67.
[17]   (1870) LR 5 QB 549, 39 LJQB 237.

But this test must be applied alongside the principles set out in the Act. Section 1 sets out six fundamental principles which must be applied in every case (see further **2.3**). The Act also sets out the statutory definition or test of incapacity which must be applied and the criteria for assessing what is in the 'best interest' of the person concerned (see **2.4** and **2.5**). The Code of Practice, para 4.32 makes reference to the common law test in relation to capacity to make a will and in para 4.33 confirms that the Act's new definition of capacity is in line with the existing common law tests, and the Act does not replace them. It nevertheless envisages a situation where the new definition will be relevant and more appropriate to apply, as it states:

> 'When cases come before the court on the above issues, judges can adopt the new definition if they think it is appropriate. The Act will apply to all other cases relating to financial, healthcare or welfare decisions.'

It is only if, having applied these principles and criteria, the medical advice establishes that P lacks testamentary capacity that an application will be entertained by the Court of Protection for an order that a statutory will be executed for P.

Cases which are the most troublesome to assess for testamentary capacity are those where P's capacity fluctuates. The case of *A, B, and C v X and Z*[18] best illustrates this point. In that case the Court heard expert evidence from two psychiatrists and neurologist who had reached different conclusions as to X's functioning and capacity. When dealing with the issue of testamentary capacity and applying the test in *Banks v Goodfellow* (above) to the facts Hedley J expressed the difficulty he had in determining the issue when he stated:[19]

> 'I am bound to say that I have found this issue quite difficult. On the one hand, if one looks at X's statement, he demonstrates an understanding of his obligations and makes perfectly sensible and proper proposals as to what should be in his will. On the other hand, I am impressed by the medical evidence, which points out a dramatic decline in executing functioning in the contest of further deterioration, and that seems to me to raise serious concerns as X's own affairs are relatively complicated. I have also borne in mind the differing impressions of the doctors in relation to this question of testamentary capacity and the factors that I set out earlier in this judgment which may have the effect of retarding on the one hand or accelerating on the other the deteriorating progress of this disease.

> In the event I have concluded that I cannot make a general declaration that X lacks testamentary capacity. There will be times when he does lack testamentary capacity. There will be many times when he does not do so. The times when he does lack such capacity are likely to become more frequent. It follows that, in my judgment, any will now made by X, if unaccompanied by contemporary medical evidence asserting capacity, may be seriously open to challenge. I draw attention, if I may, to a helpful passage in ... *Heywood & Massey: Court of Protection Practice*

---

[18] [2012] EWHC 2400 (COP), [2012] MHLO 112.
[19] At paras 36 and 37.

... provided by counsel for the applicants, at para 4046, which deals with borderline capacity. It seems to me that the advice contained in that is very much applicable to this case.'

In all cases where the issue of testamentary capacity raises doubts it is important to follow the *golden rule* and apply the principles set out in the Act alongside the common law test, and where appropriate apply to the Court for a declaration.

Section 42(4) of the Act imposes a legal duty on any person to have regard to any relevant code, if he is acting in relation to a person who lacks capacity and is doing so in one or more of the following ways:

(a)   as the donee of a lasting power of attorney;

(b)   as a deputy appointed by the Court;

(c)   as a person carrying out research in reliance on any provision made by or under the Act;[20]

(d)   as an independent mental capacity advocate;

(e)   in a professional capacity;

(f)   for remuneration.

6.4   FACTORS TO BE CONSIDERED BEFORE MAKING AN APPLICATION

On the basis of the decision in *Re P* details of the incapacitated person's life, interests, relationships, moral obligations, and values which were important to him/her when he/she had capacity will be relevant factors. Before an application to the Court is issued it is important to establish whether P has executed a valid will when he was competent. If such a will exists an application to the Court for a statutory will to be executed on behalf of P is unlikely to succeed, unless it is established that P's circumstances have changed so drastically that the earlier will is no longer in P's best interests and needs to be reviewed and reconsidered. Changes relating to P's personal and marital status, family structure and financial assets may constitute significant reasons to justify a review particularly where it is established that it does not reflect the testator's current wishes. An application may be justified, where P's marriage has been dissolved or where he/she has remarried, or where grandchildren have been born since the earlier will was executed. It may also be justified where a significant beneficiary has died or a previous amicable relationship with a relative or friend has broken down and the wishes of P have therefore changed. It may also be justified where there is doubt regarding the validity of the will purported to have been executed by P or doubts about P's testamentary capacity when he/she made the earlier will. In *Re C (A Patient)*[21] it was shown that P never had testamentary capacity and was therefore unable to make a valid will. Another example is where it can be shown that P executed a will under undue influence

---

[20]   See MCA 2005, ss 30–34.
[21]   [1991] All ER 866.

or duress where in similar circumstances a testator with capacity would not have done so and that it is in his best interests to make a new will, or there is evidence to suggest that the earlier will may have been made under 'a trick', pressure or raises doubts or suspicion about the circumstances in which it was executed, as occurred in *Re JC; D v JC, JG, A, B, C* (above). The application is likely to be received sympathetically in cases where P has not made a valid will particularly if the operation of the intestacy rules would result in the benefit of the estate passing to less deserving persons than those with whom P has a good and caring relationship or worst if it is shown that there are no persons who would inherit in the case of an intestacy and the estate would pass to the Crown as *bona vacantia*.

In a nutshell therefore, the Court is unlikely to accede to an application for a statutory will to be executed on behalf of P unless a significantly good reason is shown for doing so.

When considering whether to make an application for a statutory will to be executed the Court will of course have regard to:

- the key principles which underpin the Act and the requirement that any act done or decision made on behalf of P must be done or made in his best interest; and

- the factors set out in s 4 of the Act – the best interest test (see **2.4** and **2.5**).

6.5 PROCEDURE

The procedure to be followed when making an application for a statutory will is set out in the Court of Protection Rules 2007, Part 9 and Practice Direction 9F.

6.5.1 Who may apply for a statutory will

Section 50 of the Act and the COP Rules 2007, rr 51(1) and 52(2) set out the list of persons who are eligible to apply for a statutory will without first seeking the permission of the Court. They are:

(a) the patient;

(b) a deputy appointed by the Court for the patient;

(c) the Official Solicitor;

(d) the Public Guardian;

(e) a person who has made an application for the appointment of a deputy;

(f) a person who under any known will of the patient or under his intestacy may become entitled to any property of the patient or any interest in it;

(g) a person who is an attorney under an enduring power of attorney which has been registered at the Office of the Public Guardian;

(h) a person who is a donee under a lasting power of attorney which has been registered at the Office of the Public Guardian;

(i)   any person for whom the patient might be expected to provide if had capacity to do so.

Persons not included in the above list must apply for permission to issue an application for an order for a statutory will to be made.

6.5.2   Respondents to an application for a statutory will – PD 9F(9)

The following persons must be joined as respondents to any application for a statutory will:

(a)   any beneficiary under an existing will or codicil who is likely to be materially or adversely affected by the application;

(b)   any beneficiary under a proposal or codicil who is likely to be materially or adversely affected by the application;

(c)   any prospective beneficiary under the patient's intestacy where the patient has not made a will.

6.5.3   Person who must be notified of the application

Rule 70 of the COP Rules 2007 requires the applicant within 21 days of the issue of the application to notify the persons specified in the relevant practice direction that the application has been issued and whether it relates to the exercise of the Court's jurisdiction in relation to the patient's property and affairs or his personal welfare or to both and the orders sought. The notice must be accompanied with a form for acknowledging notification. The applicant is also required to file a certificate of notification within 7 days of service of the notice.[22]

Practice Direction 9B requires notice in Form COP15 to be given to the person listed in PD 9B but acknowledges that the persons who should be notified will vary according to the nature of the application. In relation to an application for a statutory will the applicant must notify at least three people who may have an interest in being notified. These will include members of P's family who are likely to have an interest. The PD specifies the relatives who may have such an interest and should be notified according to the presumed closeness in terms of relationship to P. They should be notified in descending order (as appropriate to the patient's circumstances). They are:

(a)   spouse or civil partner;

(b)   person who is not a spouse or civil partner but who has been living with P as if they were;

(c)   parent or guardian;

(d)   child;

(e)   brother or sister;

(f)   grandparent or grandchild;

---

[22]   COP Rules 2007, r 70.

(g)   aunt or uncle;

(h)   child of a brother or sister;

(i)   step-parent;

(j)   half brother or half-sister; and

(k)   any disadvantaged beneficiary under a previous will or intestacy.

It may well be the case that some of the above relatives would in any event be made respondents to the application and it would be advisable to notify those (if their whereabouts are known) who are not made respondents to the application in any event.

Any deputy appointed by the Court, an attorney appointed under an enduring power of attorney or a donee of the lasting power of attorney (where that person has power to make decisions on behalf of P in regard to his property and affairs) should also be notified.[23]

6.5.4   The application form

The application must be made in Form COP1 with supporting evidence and evidence of the P's incapacity in Form COP3 completed by a medical practitioner who has examined P and who can certify that he has applied the legal test for testamentary capacity. A fee of £400 is payable on issue.

In the case of urgency it would be desirable to make a telephone call to the Judicial Support Unit at the Court (Tel: 020 7664 7178) and inform the Court of the urgency. Consideration should be given to provide for the will to be executed by someone who is available to act on the making of an order eg the Official Solicitor.

6.5.5   Information to be provided with the application form – PD 9F(6)

The Practice Direction sets out the evidence information and documents which must be filed with the application form. These are:

(a)   a copy of the draft will or codicil with a copy;

(b)   copy of any existing will or codicil;

(c)   any consents to act by the proposed executors;

(d)   details of P's family preferably in the form of a family tree, including details of the full name and date of birth of each person included in the family tree;

(e)   a schedule showing details of P's current assets, with up to date valuation;

(f)   a schedule showing the estimated net yearly income and expenditure of P;

---

[23]   PD 9B, para 10(c).

(g) a statement showing P's needs both current and future estimates, and his general circumstances;

(h) if P is living in NHS accommodation, information on whether he may be discharged to local authority accommodation or to other fee paying accommodation or to his own home;

(i) if the applicant considers it relevant, full details of the resources of any proposed beneficiary, and details of any likely changes if the application is successful;

(j) details of any capital gains tax, inheritance tax, or income tax which may be chargeable in respect of the subject matter of the application;

(k) an explanation of the effect, if any, that the proposed changes will have on P's circumstances, preferably in the form of a 'before and after' schedule of assets and income;

(l) if appropriate, a statement of whether any land would be affected by the proposed will or settlement and if so, details of its location and title number, if applicable;

(m) where the application is for a settlement of property or for variation of an existing settlement or trust, a draft of the proposed deed, plus one copy;

(n) a copy of any registered enduring power of attorney or lasting power of attorney;

(o) confirmation that P is a resident of England and Wales; and

(p) an up to date report of P's present medical condition, life expectancy, likelihood of requiring increased expenditure in the foreseeable, and testamentary capacity.

A copy of any existing will

This will inform the Court what the wishes of P were then and how it has changed over the years. It may also identify those persons who have had a meaningful relationship with P and those with whom he has broken all ties. Where there are significant changes or a number of testamentary documents which set out the wishes of P it would be good practice to prepare a schedule to enable a comparison to be made at a glance.

Any consents to act as proposed executors

It is important to provide as much detail as possible relating to those who are prepared to act as executors so that the Court can scrutinise the persons ability and suitability to act as an executor particularly where P's estate is likely to be substantial or complex and difficult to administer or where there is a likelihood of disputes arising or future claims being made against the estate eg under the Inheritance (Provision for Family and Dependants) Act 1975. Consideration should also be given to appointing an existing deputy to act as an executor with others.

Details of family members

It is important to provide the Court with as much information as is possible about the relatives in order for the Court to carry out an informed assessment of the relationship between them and P. Of particular relevance will be information relating to any conflicts and rejection.

Valuation of assets

A professional and comprehensive valuation will only become necessary where the assets are substantial or complex or there is any hint that the valuations will be disputed.

A schedule of the patient's current and future needs

This document will need to be carefully prepared. It is suggested that this document should reflect the information which is often set out in the schedule of special damages in personal injury cases, particularly where P may require special care over a long period or where P is young. A schedule of assets and income and expenditure, such as the schedule prepared in applications for financial relief in matrimonial cases, may also be considered as a way of showing the issues at a glance and to assist the Court.

Details of any capital gains tax etc

The most significant of the taxes listed is of course the inheritance tax liability. An estimate of the liability and evidence of the impact of the liability on the estate will assist those who represent P to present his case and seek professional advice where appropriate on how best to manage and reduce the liability. It will also enable the Court to make an informed decision on what is in the best interest of P.

An explanation of the effect if any, that the proposed changes will have on the patient's circumstances, preferably in the form of 'before and after' schedule of assets and income

Re G (Patients)[24] is an example of the significance of this information.

6.6 EVIDENCE REQUIRED

The Court will require evidence that P lacks capacity to make a valid will for himself/herself. In most cases the Court will require recent evidence as to lack of testamentary capacity.

---

[24] [2007] EWHC 1861 (Ch).

Where a will for P already exists, a copy of that will should be exhibited to the statement filed in support of the application. The statement in support must set out the need for the execution of a further will or codicil.

In the case of a new will, where the draft of the will names the executors, the consent of the executors named in the draft will should be filed with the supporting evidence.

6.7   PROVISION THAT MAY BE MADE IN A WILL

Further provisions which may be included in an order for the making of a statutory will are set out in Sch 2 to the Act. Paragraph 2 of Sch 2 provides that the will may make any provisions (whether by disposing of property or exercising a power or otherwise) which could be made by a will executed by P if he or she had capacity to make it.

6.7.1   Requirements relating to execution

If a Court makes an order under s 16 of the Act or gives directions requiring or authorising a person ('an authorised person') to execute a will on behalf of P the will must:

- state that it is signed by P acting by the authorised person;
- be signed by the authorised person with the name of P and his own name, in the presence of two or more witnesses present at the same time;
- be attested and subscribed by those witnesses in the presence of the authorised person, and
- be sealed with the official seal of the Court.

6.7.2   Effect of execution

Where the will is executed on behalf of P in accordance with the above requirements it has the same effect for all purposes as if P had had capacity to make a valid will and the will had been executed by him in the manner required by the Wills Act 1837 except:

(a)   in so far as it disposes of immovable property outside England and Wales; or

(b)   in so far as it relates to any other property or matter if, when the will is executed, P is domiciled outside England and Wales and under the law of P's domicile any questions of his testamentary capacity would fall to be determined in accordance with the law of the place outside England and Wales.[25]

---

[25]   MCA 2005, Sch 2, para 4(3)–(5).

6.7.3   Procedure on execution of a statutory will

Once a will has been executed on behalf of P, the applicant must send the original and two copies of the will to the Court of Protection for sealing. On receipt of the documents the Court must seal the original and the copy and return both documents to the applicant.[26]

---

[26]   MCA 2005, Sch 2, paras 11 and 12.

6.8 PROCEDURAL GUIDE

Applicant who may apply without permission	(1)	P	
	(2)	A deputy appointed by the Court	
	(3)	The Official Solicitor	COP Rules 2007, r 51(1)
	(4)	The Public Guardian	
	(5)	A person who has made an application for the appointment of a deputy	COP Rules 2007, r 51(4)
	(6)	A person who, under any known will of P or under his intestacy may be entitled to any property of P or any interest in it	COP Rules 2007, r 51(4)(b)
	(7)	An attorney appointed under an EPA/LPA which has been registered in accordance the Act and the regulations referred to in Sch 4 to the Act	COP Rules 2007, r 51(4)(c)
	(8)	Any beneficiary under an existing will or Codicil who is likely to be affected	COP Rules 2007, r 51(4)(d)
	(9)	A person for whom P might be expected to provide if he had capacity to do so	COP Rules 2007, r 51(4)(e)
Respondents	(1)	Any beneficiary under an existing will or Codicil who is likely to be affected	PD9F, para 9
	(2)	Any person who is likely to be a beneficiary under P's intestacy	
	(3)	Any beneficiary under a proposed will or codicil who is likely to be affected by the application	
Applicant must file		Form **COP2** (if permission to apply is required)	COP Rules 2007, r 54 PD8A, para 1
		Forms **COP1** and **COP1A**	
		Written statement in support and providing relevant information	COP Rules 2007, r 64 PD9A, paras 2–9 PD9F para 6–9
		Form **COP3** (assessment of capacity)	COP Rules 2007, r 64(c) PD9A, para 12
		Form **COP4** (deputy's declaration)	
		Copy of EPA or LPA (if applicable)	
Court fee		£400	

Court	Within 14 days must deal with application for permission to apply	COP Rules 2007, r 55
	Judge will either grant or refuse application or fix a hearing and notify any person of the hearing	
	If permission is granted or not required Court will issue application and give the applicant:	
	Form **COP5**	
	Form **COP 14** and **COP14A**	
	Form **COP15** and **COP15A**	
	Form **COP20**	

Service		
The applicant must within 21 days serve Respondents	Form **COP1** and **COP1A** and any other supporting documents Forms **COP5, COP15** and **COP15A**	COP Rules 2007, r 66
Notify and serve P	Forms **COP14, COP14A** and **COP5**	COP Rules 2007, r 69
Notify and serve any other relevant person	Forms **COP5, COP15** and **COP15A**	COP Rules 2007, r 70
Within 7 days of service Applicant must file	Form **COP20**	COP Rules 2007, rr 68(4) and 70(3)

Respondent must if he wishes to respond to the application within 21 days of service file	Form **COP5**	COP Rules 2007, r 72 PD9C, para 3

Persons notified must if they wish to take part within 21 days of notification file	Form **COP5**	COP Rules 2007, r 72 PD9C, para 4
Persons not notified of application who wish to be joined as parties must file	Form **COP9**	COP Rules 2007, r 75 PD10A, para 1

Court must as soon as practicable deal with the application	Court may deal with the application without notice, give directions, fix a direction hearing and give directions and fix final hearing	COP Rules 2007, rr 84 and 85

Orders	On a direction hearing the Court may give any of the orders set out in r 85	COP Rules 2007, r 85
	At a final hearing the Court may authorise the making of Statutory will and direct the terms of the will and its execution and safe custody	

What the applicant must do	File the original executed will with two copies for sealing	PD9F, para 11

	Execution of the will must comply with the requirement of MCA 2005 Sch 2, para 3(2)	PD9F, para 12
Sealing of the will	Court must seal the original will and copy and return both documents to the applicant	

PRECEDENTS

PRECEDENT OF STATEMENT IN SUPPORT OF AN APPLICATION FOR AN ORDER FOR A STATUTORY WILL

IN THE COURT OF PROTECTION   No ....

IN THE MATTER OF THE MENTAL CAPACITY ACT 2005

AND IN THE MATTER OF AB [*insert forename and surname*]

BETWEEN

LUSH COUNTY COUNCIL'S SOCIAL AND COMMUNITY SERVICES DEPARTMENT	Applicant

And

STEPHEN BROWN	1st Respondent

And

JESEBEL BROWN	2nd Respondent

And

AB	3rd Respondent
(by his litigation friend the Official Solicitor)	

I, Alice Goodfellow of Lush County Council will say as follows:

1.   The Lush County Council's Social and Community Services Department was appointed deputy for AB who lacks capacity. A copy of the order is now shown to me marked AG1.

2.   AB is 21-years-old. His parents were violent and neglectful. When he was 6 AB suffered brain damage when he was assaulted repeatedly about the head by his father. He has global developmental delay; functions mentally at about a chronological age of 8 and has limited mobility. An assessment of capacity is now shown to me marked AG2.

3.   Lush County Council took care proceedings in relation to AB and he was made the subject of a care order under s 31 Children Act 1989 when he was 7. He was placed in long term foster care with professional paid carers.

4.   The care plan is for him to remain placed with them. He has a life expectancy of 35 years old and is unlikely to survive his carers.

5.   AB's parents were convicted of criminal offences in relation to their treatment of him. They both received a custodial sentence but have now been released from prison.

6.   AB received an award from CICA of £500,000 2 years ago and the Director of Social Services of Lush CC applied and was appointed deputy for his property and affairs.

7.   Unless a will is executed AB's parents will inherit under the rules of intestacy.

8.   AB loves horses. Despite his mobility problems AB has learned to ride with supervision and attends a stables specialising in horse riding for disabled people. His home with his carer is the only one he remembers. He has no grandparents alive but has an older sister with children of her own who visits regularly and takes him out.

9.   The deputy now seeks an order of the Court:

(a)   For authority to execute a will on AB's behalf urgently.

(b)   To dispense with service on both parents.

Signed ....

Note:

Papers required

- COP 1

- COP3 (from social worker from the learning disability team of Lush CC)

- Draft will (dividing assets into 2 halves, 50% to sister and after her, her children. 50% to be divided between Carers and stables)

- Family tree

PRECEDENT OF STATEMENT IN SUPPORT OF AN APPLICATION FOR AN ORDER FOR A STATUTORY WILL

IN THE COURT OF PROTECTION   No ....

IN THE MATTER OF THE MENTAL CAPACITY ACT 2005

AND IN THE MATTER OF XY [*insert forename and surname*]

BETWEEN

JULIUS ALPHONSO   Applicant

And

JACOBI GODDFELLOW   1st Respondent

And

XY   2nd Respondent

(by his litigation friend the
Official Solicitor)

I, Julius Alphono of 1 Crooked Lane in the County of Barset make oath and say as follows:

1.   I have known XY, who is now 92 years of age, for about 50 years when he and his wife moved to live next door to me at 3 Crooked Lane. We became good friends. He was a solicitor and extremely active.

2.   When his wife died he granted me an Enduring Power of Attorney.

3.   On .... 12 January 2000 he suffered a stroke and suffered brain damage and became partially paralysed. He lost all confidence. He was unable to take care of himself and would not co operate with the daily carers who initially came to take care of his daily needs.

4.   He had to be placed in residential care. His condition has gradually deteriorated. He now has to be helped with feeding toileting washing and dressing. Form COP3 completed by the geriatrician responsible for the care home confirms that XY lacks capacity.

5.   When XY lost capacity I applied to register the enduring power of attorney. A copy of the EPA is now shown to me marked 'JA1'.

6.   XY's home was sold to pay for his care and during the course of clearing the property I was unable to find a will.

7.   Enquiries of Sue & Co produced a copy of XY's will made 25 years previously. It disclosed that XY had left his entire estate to his brother who died three months ago. There is now produced and shown to me marked 'JA2' a certified copy of the death certificate and XY's family tree. There is also now shown to me marked 'JA3' a Schedule setting out XY's assets.

8.   XY did not have any other siblings.

9.   Inquiries have revealed that XY's uncle on his father's side is known to have family. A great nephew survives and lives in Australia. He has never met XY and during the 50 years that I have known XY he never mentioned the existence of any relatives in Australia.

10.   I contacted the great nephew when XY was placed in a residential home but he showed no interest. I have notified him that having regard to XY's deteriorating health it is my intention to apply for a statutory will to be executed. He has made it clear that he would object to any such application.

11.   XY had a companionship with his former housekeeper for 10 years prior to his stroke. Although they did not live together they would go on holiday several times a year birdwatching and spend Xmas and other seasonal holidays together. She visits him 3 times per week in his care home.

12.   In his retirement XY did a lot for the solicitor's benevolent association. His bank accounts also reveal regular standing orders for donations to three charities namely, the NSPCC, The Homeless Centre in Barset and the Barset Hospice.

13.   A draft will is now produced and shown to me marked 'JA3'. It is proposed that that the three charities should receive legacies and the residue of XY's estate be divided between his housekeeper and the RSPB.

14.   As his attorney I apply to the Court for authority to execute a will on behalf of XY. This has now become urgent because XY has suffered a bout of pneumonia and there are concerns that he may not recover.

15.   In view of the urgency and the objections raised by the great nephew I respectfully ask that the Court considers the application as soon as possible at a telephone hearing or by video link.

Signed ....

Signed ....

Papers to be filed

•   COP1

- COP3 (completed by geriatrician responsible for the care home)

- Draft will (legacies to three charities and neighbour. Residue divided between housekeeper and RSPB)

- Family tree

- COP20

- COP5 (from the nephew in Canada objecting to his exclusion)

Court convenes urgent hearing with evidence from the nephew by telephone.

PRECEDENT FOR AN ORDER TO EXECUTE A STATUTORY WILL

IN THE COURT OF PROTECTION   No ......

IN THE MATTER OF THE MENTAL CAPACITY ACT 2005

AND IN THE MATTER OF XY [*insert initials of P's forenames and surname*]

BETWEEN

JULIUS ALPHONSO   Applicant

And

JACOBI GOODFELLOW   1st Respondent

And

XY   2nd Respondent

(by his litigation friend the
Official Solicitor)

DRAFT ORDER TO EXECUTE A STATUTORY WILL

Made by District Judge Wise

At ....

On 23 December 2013

UPON READING the draft of a will proposed to be executed for Cassandra Fragile

(initialled by District Judge Wise for the purpose of identification)

IT IS ORDERED THAT:

1.   The applicant .... [*insert name*] is authorised to execute a will on behalf of XY [*insert P's initials*] in the terms of the draft approved by the Court.

2.   The will when executed is to be held in safe custody in the name of XY [*insert P's initials*] by Messrs Sharp and Swift (the solicitors for the applicant) and is to remain so held subject (during the lifetime of XY [*insert P's initials*]) to the directions of the Court.

3.   A detailed assessment of the costs of and incidental to this application of

the applicant and the Official Solicitor be carried out on the standard basis and the applicant is to pay the certified amounts thereof from the estate of XY [*insert P's initials*].

To: Messrs Sharp and Swift

The Official Solicitor

PRECEDENT FOR EXECUTION OF
A STATUTORY CODICIL

IN THE COURT OF PROTECTION   No ....

IN THE MATTER OF THE MENTAL CAPACITY ACT 2005

AND IN THE MATTER OF XY [*insert initials of P's forenames and surname*]

BETWEEN

JULIUS ALPHONSO   Applicant

And

JACOBI GOODFELLOW   1st Respondent

And

XY   2nd Respondent

(by his litigation friend the
Official Solicitor)

DRAFT ORDER TO EXECUTE A STATUTORY CODICIL

Made by District Judge Wise

At ....

On ....

UPON READING the draft of a statutory codicil proposed to be executed for Cassandra Fragile (initialled by District Judge Wise for the purpose of identification)

IT IS ORDERED THAT:

1.   The applicant .... [*insert name*] is authorised in the name of and on behalf of XY [*insert P's initials*] to execute a statutory codicil in the terms of the draft approved by the Court.

2.   The executed statutory codicil is to be held in safe custody in the name of XY [*insert P's initials*] by Messrs Sharp and Swift (the solicitors for the applicant) and is to remain so held subject (during the lifetime of XY [*insert P's initials*]) to the directions of the Court.

3.   A detailed assessment of the costs of and incidental to this application of the applicant and the Official Solicitor be carried out on the standard basis and the applicant is to pay the certified amounts thereof from the estate of XY [*insert P's initials*].

To: Messrs Sharp and Swift

The Official Solicitor

EXAMPLE OF A FORM OF STATUTORY WILL

THIS IS THE LAST WILL of me AB [*insert name of P*] of .... [*set out the address*] acting by CD the person authorised in that behalf by an Order dated the .... day of .... 2010 made under the Mental Health Act 2005.

I revoke all my former wills and codicils and declare this to by my last will.

1.   I appoint EF and GH to be executors and trustees of this my will.

2.   I give and bequeath .... [*set out the details*]

In witness of which this will is signed by me AB acting by CD under the order mentioned above on the .... [*insert date*]

SIGNED

By the said AB [*insert P's forenames and surname*] by CD [*insert forenames and surname of authorised person*]

And by the said CD with his (or her) own name pursuant to the said order in our presence and attested by us in the presence of CD [*authorised person's name*]

AB [*P's forenames and surname*]

[*authorised person's forenames and surname*]

[*Name and Address of witnesses*]

Sealed with the official seal of the Court of Protection the .... day of .... 2014.

PART III

PERSONAL WELFARE (INCLUDING HEALTH)

CHAPTER 7

WELFARE DECISIONS – MARRIAGE, SEXUAL RELATIONS, RESIDENCE AND CONTACT

LAW AND PRACTICE

7.1 INTRODUCTION

The need for urgent and serious medical treatment are only two of the issues which carers of vulnerable adults encounter and on which a declaration from the Court is often sought. No less important to P are decisions, which need to be undertaken on a day-to-day basis such as where P should live and under what conditions, with whom P should have contact, routine medical attention such as dentistry and of course personal care. P may not have sufficient understanding of the issues or the situation to give such consent. Relatives may not agree between themselves on P's best interests. There are often disputes with professionals. These decisions can become urgent and, in the absence of agreement, may require recourse to a decision or order of the Court.

Additionally, issues relating to all welfare decisions concerning P are problematic since they necessarily involve P's family members and friends and are often connected with P's right to liberty and security under Art 5 of the European Convention for the Protection of Human Rights and Fundamental Freedoms (ECHR) and P's right to respect of private and family life under Art 8 of the Convention (and in what circumstances can it be said to be appropriate and proportionate for the state to intervene). Where there are competing interests and P lacks capacity, his/her right has to be balanced against Y's rights but P's best interests must determine the issue. The Court may be asked to determine that the right should be exercised in the same way as a child's rights take priority over a parent's right.

The definition of a person who lacks capacity, as set out in s 2(1) of the Act, makes it clear that capacity is issue and time specific and must relate to an impairment of, or disturbance in, the functioning of the mind or brain, affecting decision making (see chapter 2 General Principles.) The assessment of P's capacity may differ according to the decision to be made. Although P may lack capacity on major issues it may nevertheless be possible to assist him/her to make a decision for himself or herself in relation to some routine issues, like visiting the GP with a cold or taking paracetamol for a headache. Other decisions such as whether or not it is possible for P to be admitted to or discharged from hospital are more intricate and can arise in crisis. The Act and the Code of Practice specifically provide that efforts should be made to assist P in making the decision. The Act and the Code impose a duty on those who have the care of the vulnerable person, or to make decisions on his or her behalf, to take all reasonable steps to assess the individual in order to establish whether that person lacks capacity to make a decision in relation to the specific issue in question. The Act also sets out when and by whom a formal assessment should be carried out.

Section 3(1) of the Act sets out the test that should be applied in assessing whether or not a person is able to make a decision. A person is unable to make a decision if he or she is unable:

(a)   to understand the information relevant to the decision;

(b)   to retain that information;

(c)   to use or weigh that information as part of the process of making the decision; or

(d)   to communicate his or her decision.

Those who have responsibility for the day-to-day personal care or health needs of a vulnerable person (P), whether that person is a family member or a professional carer or health care professional, will need to make decisions on behalf of the person in their care sometimes without P's consent or agreement. In respect of some of the decisions, s 5 of the Act makes provision to protect the carer if the act done is in connection with the personal care, health care or treatment of the person lacking capacity, provided the conditions in s 5 are satisfied (see chapter 4). Other decisions will require the approval of the Court.

Before an application is made to the Court, P's needs and how it is proposed that those needs should be met or supported must be identified. Where appropriate, consultation with family members should be undertaken and the proposals shared with them and their views given due consideration, with a view to reaching agreement where possible. Where disputes remain, mediation/alternative dispute resolution process should be considered. Referral to the Court of Protection should be made as a last resort.

The Code of Practice, in Chapter 15, specifically imposes an obligation to settle disputes in a conciliatory way when there is a disagreement relating to a person's capacity, their best interests, or any decision or action taken on the person's behalf. Where the dispute arises between the professionals and family members it is good practice to set out the different options available and why the proposed option is considered to be in the person's best interests, and a case conference or meeting should be arranged where not only the options proposed but the views of the family or others who are interested in the care and welfare of the person lacking capacity are aired and discussed and given full consideration. Where appropriate, an advocate to support and represent the person who lacks capacity should be appointed so that the advocate can represent the views and interests of the person lacking capacity to the family carers or professionals and assist where mediation is considered as a way of trying to resolve the disagreement. Unless the issues require an urgent decision to be taken, time for reflection should be allowed. Mediation as a form of settling disagreements is advised (see the Code of Practice, paras 15.1–15.9).

It is obvious that this process is time consuming and therefore it is essential that consideration is given to long-term planning at an early stage. There may however, be cases where, despite attempts made to deal with the issues amicably, P's condition and needs require an immediate decision and an application to the Court as a matter of urgency, if only in the first instance to address and safeguard P's needs.

In relation to marriage issues the most likely recourse to the Courts for an emergency remedy in this context is for an order preventing an unsuitable marriage. However, if it is P who wants to marry he/she will need to be empowered to present his/her views. It is therefore necessary to be aware of the underlying principles associated with the celebration of a marriage by a person whose capacity is in issue.

With regard to P's social relationships, typically an application to the Court for an order urgently intervening in personal relationships, including sexual relationships, will be with the aim of preventing or restricting them. Such applications are usually made where there are concerns about an inappropriate relationship or that P may be exploited – such a situation occurred in *A Local Authority v SY*[1] where the man who was an illegal overstayer deliberately targeted SY because of her learning difficulties and vulnerability, and got her to enter into an Islamic marriage in order to claim asylum. When granting a declaration that SY lacked capacity to enter into a marriage Keehan J sent a clear message that the Courts will 'not tolerate such gross exploitation'. However, P's right to have relationships is an important concept which will be considered by the Court in exercising its discretion.

Although the Court's jurisdiction applies to adults, it is generally accepted that issues relating to those who are between the ages of 16 and 18 may be referred to the Court. In such cases the local authority, which will generally be the body that will be responsible for dealing with issues of care, residence and social and family contact, will need to consider different factors when preparing the care plans from those which apply to adults. However, whatever the issue may be on which a decision or authorisation is required, the overriding principle set out in s 1 of the Act and the best interests of P must dictate the decision taken on P's behalf.

This chapter seeks to deal with such welfare issues relating to those who are in the 16 to 18 year bracket and those who are adults; the steps which should be taken before seeking the Court's intervention; the procedure to be followed when the decision is taken to issue proceedings; and the Court's powers in

---

[1]   [2013] EWHC 3485 (COP).

relation to both categories of incapacitated persons, particularly where interim measures are necessary whilst further investigations are undertaken.

7.2 CAPACITY TO MARRY AND CAPACITY TO HAVE SEXUAL RELATIONS

The presumption that a person possesses capacity and the principle that the issue of capacity is subject/decision specific and time specific is never more relevant than in cases involving the capacity to marry and to make the decision to have sexual relations with a particular person. By reason of this presumption it is not for P to establish that he/she has the capacity to marry or have sexual relations, but for those who assert the contrary to prove that P does not have capacity to marry or to have the intimate relationship that he/she wishes but which is causing concern to those who are responsible for his/her care and protection. In such cases the Court will have to consider how far the person's capacity extends or to which specific areas. It does not follow that because a person is assessed as having capacity in relation to one specific area of a transaction that he/she has capacity in relation to all areas involving the same transaction. For example, a person may have capacity to make a decision in relation to a simple medical procedure but not a more complicated one. P may be able to make a decision to befriend X but lack capacity to decide on a long-term relationship with X. The more serious the decision, the greater the degree of capacity required.

Section 3(1) of the Act applies the same test as that which has been developed at common law in such cases as *Re C (Adult: Refusal of Treatment)*[2] and *Re MB (Medical Treatment)*.[3] This has been affirmed by Munby J (as he then was) in *MM; Local Authority X v MM (by the Official Solicitor) and KM*:[4]

> '... The section 3(1) principle therefore applies to all aspects of "personal welfare".'

This is also confirmed in the Code of Practice, para 4.32 which includes capacity to enter into marriage:

> 'The Act's new definition of capacity is in line with the existing common law tests and the Act does not replace them. When cases come before the Court on the above issues, judges can adopt the new definition, if it thinks it is appropriate. The Act will apply to all other cases relating to financial, healthcare or welfare decisions.'

There is no clear test identified in any of the first instance decisions under the Act on this issue as they are so controversial. Indeed, in *A Local Authority v H*,[5] Hedley J referred to it as a 'legal fog' into which the concept of capacity to

---

[2]   [1994] 1 FLR 31.
[3]   [1997] 2 FLR 426.
[4]   [2007] EWHC 2003 (Fam), [2009] 1 FLR 443.
[5]   [2012] EWHC 49 (COP).

consent to sexual relations has drifted and hoped that 'in the not too distant future this issue may be addressed by the appellate courts' (para 27). The recent Court of Appeal decision in *PC and NC v City of York Council*[6] seeks to provide a clear statement of law but it is at variance with the Supreme Court's decision in *R v C*[7], although it could be argued that *R v C* related to criminal proceedings and the scope of s 30(1) of the Sexual Offences Act 2003. It could also be argued that *PC and NC v City of York* was very much fact-specific and does not provide a test in relation to capacity to marry or to have sexual relations. The Court of Appeal's decision has also caused some consternation as, contrary to what has been the accepted practice supported by the statement in the Code of Practice, it reversed the order of the two stage procedure for assessing capacity. In *IM v LM & Ors*[8] the Court of Appeal considered the test to be applied to consent to sexual relations. It stated that P's ability to use or weigh up the relevant information was much less than in other spheres and that the relevant information does not include remote factors such as the consequences of pregnancy. It also indicated that Baroness Hale's observations in *R v Cooper* as to the person-specific nature of the decision were not inconsistent with the civil approach as the civil and criminal courts were considering different issues. However, this does not provide a clear answer to the difficult cases where there are concerns for those who are easy prey for sexual exploitation and the consequential serious risk to P. In cases where the statutory bodies, who have responsibilities to protect P, consider that the above test leaves P at risk, the possibility of whether the relief sought may be available under the civil law or the court's inherent jurisdiction should not be ruled out.

Until the matter is clarified by the Supreme Court in a case under the Act, it is suggested that the best course, nevertheless is, first to follow s 3 of the Act and in so doing consider the observations made and guidance given in decided cases, and then to consider whether they assist in determining the matter at hand. It is therefore proposed to set out some of the key points that have been made in cases under common law and under the Act.

The test of a vulnerable adult's capacity to consent to marriage and sexual relations was considered in *Re E (An Alleged Patient); Sheffield City Council v E &S*[9] and *X City Council v MB, NB and MAB*.[10]

In *Re E (An Alleged Patient); Sheffield City Council v E & S* the local authority sought to prevent a 21-year-old woman, who was said to function at the level of a 13-year-old and for whom they had responsibility, from marrying a man who was a Schedule 1 offender. The local authority asserted that the woman lacked capacity to make decisions about where she should live, whether she should have contact with the offender or whether she should marry him. The local authority asserted that it was not in the best interests of the woman to

---

6   [2013] EWCA Civ 478.
7   [2009] UKHL 42.
8   [2014] EWCA Civ 37.
9   [2004] EWHC 2808 (Fam), [2005] 1 FLR 965.
10   [2006] EWHC 168 (Fam), [2006] 2 FLR 968.

associate with or marry the offender. A preliminary issue arose as to the appropriate questions to be put to experts in order to establish her capacity to marry. It was held that the test is whether the person has the capacity to understand the *nature* of the *contract of marriage*. The test is not the capacity to understand the *implications* of a *particular marriage*. The contract of marriage is necessarily something shared in common in all marriages. It is not something that differs as between the particular individual that P wishes to marry and is distinct from the question whether P is wise to marry the particular individual. The Court does not have jurisdiction to consider whether a marriage is in an individual's best interests; whether or not that person lacks capacity, nor does it have any role to vet P's choice of suitors. It does not have the power to give consent on behalf of an adult who lacks capacity to give his or her consent. When exercising its inherent jurisdiction the Court does not give a valid consent but declares that something is lawful. The issue is simple in that an adult who lacks capacity cannot marry, so that P's 'best interests' is not relevant. It was also held that the analogy with capacity to consent to medical treatment or capacity to litigate was not appropriate because both those issues were varied, necessarily complex and involved expert advice, whereas marriage was essentially simple and the same for everyone.

Munby J (as he then was) summarised the test as follows:

(a) The question is not whether E has capacity to marry X rather than Y. The question is not (being specific) whether E has capacity to marry S. The relevant question is whether E has the capacity to marry anyone. If she does, it is not necessary to show that she also has capacity to take care of her own person and property.

(b) The question of whether E has capacity to marry is quite distinct from the question of whether E is wise to marry; either wise to marry at all, or wise to marry X rather than Y, or wise to marry S.

(c) In relation to her marriage the only question for the Court is whether E has capacity to marry. The Court has no jurisdiction to consider whether it is in E's 'best interests' to marry or to marry S. The Court is concerned with E's capacity to marry. It is not concerned with the wisdom of her marriage in general or her marriage to S in particular.

(d) In relation to the question of whether E has capacity to marry the law remains the same today as it was set out by Singleton LJ in *The Estate of Park, deceased Park v Park*:[11]

> 'Was the deceased ... capable of understanding the nature of the contract into which he was entering, or was his mental condition such that he was incapable of understanding it? To ascertain the nature of the contract of marriage a man must be mentally capable of appreciating that it involves the responsibilities normally attaching to marriage. Without that degree of mentality it cannot be said that he understands the nature of the contract.'

---

[11]   [1954] P 112 at 127.

(e)   More specifically, it is not enough that someone appreciates that he or she is taking part in a marriage ceremony or understands its words.

(f)   He or she must understand the nature of the marriage contract.

(g)   This means that he or she must be mentally capable of understanding the duties and responsibilities that normally attach to marriage.

(h)   That said, the contract of marriage is in essence a simple one, which does not require a high degree of intelligence to comprehend. The contract of marriage can readily be understood by anyone of normal intelligence.
There are thus, in essence, two aspects to the inquiry whether someone has capacity to marry: (1) does he or she understand the nature of the marriage contract? (2) Does he or she understand the duties and responsibilities that normally attach to marriage?

(i)   The duties and responsibilities that normally attach to marriage can be summarised as follows: marriage, whether civil or religious, is a contract, formally entered into. It confers on the parties the status of husband and wife. The essence of the contract being an agreement between a man and a woman to live together, and to love one another as husband and wife, to the exclusion of all others. It creates a relationship of mutual and reciprocal obligations, typically involving the sharing of a common home and a common domestic life and the right to enjoy each other's society, comfort and assistance.

(See also the cases cited in the judgment.)

In so far as P's right to have a sexual relationship is concerned the issue will relate to:

*   whether P has the understanding of the nature of sexual relationship and the sexual act;
*   whether P understands the risks including the risk of pregnancy and sexually transmitted diseases;
*   whether P is capable of consenting to and refusing sexual intercourse, but it does not necessarily involve the capacity to understand that having a relationship with a particular individual could be harmful.

In relation to capacity to marry it has been stated that it is enough if P has the ability to understand the nature of the marriage contract and the duties and responsibilities that are attached to a marriage. Any assessment of capacity to marry must also take into account the question of capacity to consent to sexual relations (see and *X City Council v MB, NB and MAB*[12] para 64). In assessing capacity to consent to sexual relations the threshold of understanding has been said to be low. It is enough that the person concerned has sufficient 'rudimentary knowledge' of what the act comprises and of its character to enable the person to decide whether to give or withhold consent (see *X City Council v MB, NB and MAB*[13] at paras 74, 84 and 89). This entails P

---

[12]   [2006] EWHC 168 (Fam), [2006] 2 FLR 968.
[13]   [2006] EWHC 168 (Fam), [2006] 2 FLR 968.

understanding the nature of sexual intercourse, the risks of pregnancy and sexually transmitted infections. A refined analysis is less important (see *D County Council v LS*[14] and *YLA v PM and MZ*[15]). The ability to use and weigh information is clearly part of the test but where a sexual partner impedes or undermines or has the effect of impeding or undermining the mental functioning of P it could render P to lack capacity. (For an example see *A Local Authority v SY*[16] where it was declared that P lacked capacity to enter a contract of marriage but had capacity to sexual relations.)

In *MM; Local Authority X v MM (by the Official Solicitor) and KM*,[17] applying the test in *Re E* (above) to capacity to consent to sexual relations, Munby J (as he then was) stated that 'when considering capacity to marry, the question is whether X has capacity to marry, not whether she has capacity to marry Y rather than Z. The question of capacity to marry has never been considered by reference to a person's ability to understand or evaluate the characteristics of some particular spouse or intended spouse ... The same goes and for much the same reasons, in relation to capacity to consent to sexual relations. The question is issue specific, both in the general sense and, as I have already pointed out in the sense that capacity has to be assessed in relation to the particular kind of sexual activity in question, But capacity to consent to sexual relations is, in my judgment, directed to the nature of the activity rather than to the identity of the sexual partner' (para 86) ie it is issue specific and not person or partner specific (the same test applied by Parker J in *YLA v PM and* MZ (above)). However, this approach was doubted in *R v C*.[18] Although the decision in *R v C* relates to criminal proceedings and the scope of s 30(1) of Sexual Offences Act 2003 the ruling is nevertheless relevant because the Supreme Court considered the decisions referred to above and the issue of capacity and held that lack of capacity to choose can be person or situation specific and that an irrational fear that prevents the exercise of choice could amount to a lack of capacity preventing the free exercise of choice and an inability to communicate that choice. The Court doubted that Munby J's (as he then was) observation in MM; *Local Authority X v MM (by the Official Solicitor) and KM* was the correct test. Baroness Hale of Richmond observed that 'it is difficult to think of an activity which is more person and situation specific than sexual relations. One does not consent to sex in general. One consents to this act of sex with this person at this time and in this place. Autonomy entails the freedom and capacity to make a choice of whether or not to do so' (para 27). It is also necessary to consider the impact of Art 12 of the ECHR, which provides that men and women of marriageable age have the right to marry and found a family according to the national law governing the exercise of this right. It is recognised that the lives of those with limited or borderline capacity can still be enriched by marriage and therefore one must be careful not to set the test of capacity too high lest it operates as an unfair,

---

[14]   [2010] EWHC 1544 (Fam).
[15]   [2013] EWHC 3622 (Fam).
[16]   [2013] EWHC 3485 (COP).
[17]   [2007] EWHC 2003 (Fam), [2009] 1 FLR 443.
[18]   [2009] UKHL 42.

unnecessary and discriminatory bar against the mentally disabled. The rights of P to family life under Art 8 is also a relevant factor.

The primary objective in such cases is to make the decision which serves P's best interests. In *Re MM (An Adult)*[19] the High Court applied the test in *X City Council v MB, NB, MAB (By his Litigation Friend the Official Solicitor)*[20] to the issue of whether P had the capacity to consent to sexual relations and whether the care plans of the local authority which imposed restrictions on contact were justified. MM was a 39-year-old woman who suffered from paranoid schizophrenia. She was described as having limited insight into the nature of her illness. She also suffered from moderate learning difficulties and poor cognitive functioning, significantly impaired or non-existent verbal recall and was functionally illiterate. She had been taken into care by the local authority when she was 13. She had a male partner KM of 15 years who was diagnosed with psychopathic personality disorder and alcohol misuse. He had been violent towards MM and used her money to buy alcohol. He had also encouraged her to leave her accommodation and to follow him to various addresses and to disengage from the psychiatric services. In 2006 MM took up residence in supported accommodation at a unit. Certain restrictions were placed on her relating to her movements and inviting KM. Encouraged by KM she failed to comply with those restrictions to the detriment of her health. Without notice orders were obtained declaring that she lacked capacity to decide where she should live and with whom she should associate and that it was not in her best interests to be removed from the unit or to have unsupervised contact with KM. This was later varied to allow her contact with KM not less than twice a week for no less than two hours. Subsequently further orders were made empowering the local authority to terminate contact at its discretion if KM was under the influence of alcohol or if he was abusive or aggressive towards MM and when she went missing ordering KM to assist the local authority to locate her. MM was found but her condition had deteriorated and her placement at the unit was at risk of breaking down. Within 3 months she had to be sectioned pursuant to s 2 of the Mental Health Act 1983. Contact was reduced to once a week for two hours and injunction orders were obtained prohibiting KM from removing her from the family placement and approaching the accommodation and from contacting her. The local authority secured a permanent placement for MM and sought a declaration that MM lacked capacity to conduct litigation and to make decisions as to where and with whom she should live, to determine with whom she could have contact or associate and to manage her financial arrangements and to enter into a contract of marriage. It was eventually conceded that she had capacity to consent to sexual relations with KM. The Court however found that the local authority was seeking to control her relations with KM by imposing a care plan which prevented her from continuing her relationship with KM and hence risked her Art 8 rights. The Court directed the local authority to reconsider its care plans.

---

[19] [2007] EWHC 2689 (Fam), [2009] 1 FLR 487.
[20] [2006] EWHC 168 (Fam), [2006] 2 FLR 968.

In *D County Council v LS*[21] P's capacity fluctuated depending on the circumstances and in consequence it affected her understanding that she could refuse to have sexual relations or alternatively her will could be overborne by others. The Court held that the ability to understand and weigh information was a relevant factor as was the fact that the particular sexual partner impedes or undermines or has the effect of impeding or undermining the mental functioning of P and the decisions she makes so as to render them incapacitous.

In *D Borough Council v AB*[22] the Court ruled that in assessing capacity the relevant factors were an understanding of the mechanics of sexual intercourse, the health risks involved and the risk of pregnancy.

In *A Local Authority v H*[23] the issue was whether a 29 year old woman who suffered from learning difficulties and atypical autism and a low IQ had capacity to consent to sexual relations. She had been sexually exploited by a number of men. She was supervised 1:1 at all times and was made subject of a standard authorisation restricting her freedom of movement for her protection. The Court was asked to determine inter alia whether she lacked capacity to consent to sexual relation. Hedley J in applying the provisions of s 3 referred to the principles in previous decisions and stated that the relevant factors in determining whether a person has capacity are: (i) understanding the relevant information; (ii) a basic understanding of the mechanics of the physical act and an understanding that vaginal intercourse may lead to pregnancy; (iii) a fairly rudimentary grasp of issues of sexual health – ie an understanding that sexual relations may lead to significant ill health and that those risks can be reduced by precautions like a condom; and (iv) an understanding that P has a choice and can refuse to have sexual relations (para 23). Morality although it is an important component in sexual relations can have no specific role in a test of capacity (para 24). Hedley J also held that whilst sexual relations has an emotional component, especially when sexual relations are abused, it cannot be incorporated into a legal test of capacity beyond the requirement of assessing whether the person whose capacity is in question understands that they do have a choice and that they can refuse (para 26). In line with Baroness Hale's observation in *R v C* (above) Hedley J accepted that human sexual relations are particularly person, as well a situation specific (para 26), but considered that the essential protective jurisdiction of the Court of Protection has to be effective to work on a wider canvas and he therefore found himself taking a course which was closer to that taken by MunbyJ (as he then was).

In *PC and NC v City of York* (above) PC married NC whilst he was serving a 13 year sentence of imprisonment for serious sexual offences. PC believed that NC had done no wrong and that the complainants were at fault. Both intended to live together when NC was released. The local authority was concerned about the risk NC posed to PC. There was no dispute about this risk. In those circumstances the local authority issued proceedings for the Court to determine

---

[21]   [2010] EWHC 1544 (Fam).
[22]   [2011] EWHC 101 (COP).
[23]   [2012] EWHC 49 (COP).

whether PC as a married woman had the capacity to decide whether or not she was going to live with NC her husband. Hedley J referred to the above five reported cases and observed that all cases save *R v C* involved first instance decisions and that Baroness Hale's observations in *R v C* were obiter and therefore none of the decisions were binding on a High Court judge sitting in the Court of Protection. It was also accepted that none of the judgments in the cases were reconcilable and this was thus clearly an unsatisfactory situation. Hedley J therefore decided to deal with the issues before him by first analysing the principles set out in ss 1–3 of the Act and applying the s 3(1) test to the facts of the case and then to compare and contrast his conclusions with those reached in the five cases. He eventually found that he was not satisfied that PC was able to understand the potential risk that NC presented to her and therefore she was 'unable to weigh the information underpinning the potential risk so as to determine whether or not such a risk either exists or should be run and should therefore be part of her decision to resume cohabitation'. The couple appealed the decision. The Court of Appeal was required to consider whether in relation to sexual relations the decision is person–specific or act-specific. Although the Court made reference to the differences between the view taken in the civil jurisdiction and criminal jurisdiction and the decision in *R v C* the Court did not go on to adjudicate on the issue save to state:[24]

> 'whilst sexual relations forms part of the wider decision by a spouse whether or not take up full cohabitation with her husband, the two decisions are not precisely the same. The fact that one may be act-specific does not mean that the other, wider, decision cannot be person-specific but in relation to consent to marry appeared to indicate that this was act specific rather than person specific.'

In relation to the wider issue the Court approved the approach adopted by Hedley J as being correct ie to apply the statutory provision without any embellishment or gloss. There was no need to group categories of 'matter' or 'decision' into domains 'save to do so has been established by common law or by the express terms of the MCA 2005'. On this basis the Court applied the s 3(1) test and concluded that on the particular facts of the case, the ability of PC as the wife of NC, to understand the information relevant to the decision to resume cohabitation with her husband included reference to the information that was specifically relevant to NC in the light of his conviction and its potential impact. Since PC clearly had capacity to marry any suggestion that she was unable to decide on the other factors which formed part of the marriage contract would require clear and cogent evidence. On the facts there was insufficient evidence to this effect and therefore the appeal was allowed (see para 60).

Although at first sight the Court of Appeal's decision seems to have clarified the 'legal fog' the issue which it was asked to determine was very much related to the specific facts of the case, and does not provide any guidance on the test which should be applied where capacity to consent to sexual relations is in issue nor, on the difference between the approach adopted under criminal law. It is

---

[24] Paragraph 27.

therefore submitted that the approach adopted by Hedley J when determining the case (see para 19 of his judgment) and approved by the Court of Appeal, however unsatisfactory it might be, remains the only way of dealing with similar issues in future cases until the matter is finally resolved by the Supreme Court. It is nevertheless submitted that the observations made by Baroness Hale in *R v C*, although obiter, should not be considered to be simply persuasive but significant, as the judgments made in the Court of Protection were considered in *R v C* by the Supreme Court.

It is clear that the ability to weigh up the relevant information is one of the elements which needs to be assessed when determining whether P lacks capacity or not but this does not involve a complex abstract or hypothetical information. It simply requires the ability to balance the risks and pleasures both physical and emotional involved. Where the relationship concerns P who is known to be homosexual this will involve the ability to weigh up the emotional consequences of having sexual relations. It is not necessary to establish that P has an understanding or awareness that sexual activity between a man and a woman may result in pregnancy. However where P is attracted to both men and women it will be necessary to establish an understanding and awareness of this fact as part of the assessment of capacity to consent to sexual relations (*A Local Authority v TZ*[25]). In order to assess the evidence and to determine P's understanding of what is involved, the Court should where it is appropriate to do so, hear oral evidence from P (see *A Local Authority v TZ* (above) where although the psychiatrist's assessment had concluded that TZ lacked capacity the Court, on hearing TZ's oral evidence, rejected the expert's assessment).

Where the local authority or those who are responsible for the care of an incapacitated person (P) become aware of the possibility or likelihood of P's parents or relatives intending to arrange a marriage for P it is essential for the local authority to act promptly and apply immediately for a decision on P's capacity to marry and, in the alternative, for a decision on whether the proposed marriage is in the best interests of P (see *YLA v PM and MZ*[26] and the need to inform the Registrar General and/or a Register Officer of concerns relating to incapacity and where appropriate of any proposed application for a declaration of lack of capacity). In such cases an urgent application should also be made for an injunction restraining the family from arranging the marriage until the determination by the Court of the substantive application. Where the indications are that the proposed marriage is likely to be forced, application should be made for a forced marriage protection order. Where a forced marriage protection order is sought it may be possible to persuade the Court to direct any order made prohibiting any person to perform a marriage to include the Register General. Immediate action is necessary as there is no guarantee that in future the Court will grant an annulment of the marriage. Much will depend

---

[25] [2013] EWHC 2322 (COP) paras 31–33.
[26] [2013] EWHC 3622 (Fam).

on the facts of the individual case – contrast the situation in *XCC v AA &
Others*[27] with *Sandwell Metropolitan BC v RG & Others.*[28]

7.3   RESIDENCE

Disagreements regarding residence are common. Family members may not
agree with each other about where P should live. P him/herself may express the
desire to remain at home rather than live in residential care. Local authorities or
health authorities may not agree with P or the family what is in P's best
interests. In those circumstances an application must be made to the Court.
Such applications are often urgent and made in a crisis.

Where the applicant is a local authority or health authority, they must engage
with family members in reaching a decision about where P should live.
Confrontation is to be avoided and a full and comprehensive assessment carried
out, not only of P and his/her capacity, but also an assessment of any person
who puts himself/herself forward as a carer. In so doing, consideration must be
given to all the circumstances including:

- P's vulnerability;
- the effect on P when he/she is residing with the particular carer and
whether it has a damaging effect on P;
- whether if P continues to reside with the carer the support offered would
be accepted;
- whether the support offered would safeguard and promote P's welfare;
- whether the staff have the skills and expertise to manage P's specific needs
problems and disabilities;
- risks involved;
- P's wishes and feelings;
- the level of care available at home and during contact;
- information regarding the psychological and emotional benefit or
satisfaction which the home or contact will provide;
- information relating to any physical, emotional harm which P would
suffer if he/she remained with the carer;
- information on the advantages and disadvantages for P in terms of lifestyle
and opportunities in the long term and medium term which would be
provided;
- any other relevant factors which are specific to P;[29]
- best interests;
- striking a proper balance.

---

[27]   [2012] EWHC 2183 (COP).
[28]   [2013] EWHC 2373 (COP).
[29]   For example, see in *Re MM (An Adult)* [2007] EWHC 2689 (Fam).

It is suggested that a proper balance sheet setting out all the advantages and disadvantages should be prepared to assist the Court. The issue of best interests must also be exercised to ensure that it is compatible with the ECHR with specific reference to P's Art 8 rights, which are central to the issue of protecting a person's family life but subject to Art 8(2) which provides that any restriction in accordance with the law and which is necessary in a democratic society for the protection of health or for the protection of rights and freedoms of others is permissible.

The concept of 'private life' has been described in broad terms, and is not susceptible to an exhaustive definition. It covers physical and psychological integrity of a person. It can sometimes embrace aspects of an individual's physical and social identity. 'Private life' is said to have two elements: (i) the notion of 'inner circle' in which the individual may live his own personal life as he chooses; (ii) the right to establish and develop relationships with other human beings.[30]

Elements such as gender identification, sexual orientation and sexual life fall within the personal sphere protected by Art 8.[31] Article 8 also protects the right to personal development, the right to establish and develop relationships with others and generally the outside world. The right to self determination and the right to personal autonomy is an important principle which underlies the guarantees provided within the Article.

Any intervention must be a proportionate response to the risk presented.[32] Applying this test to adults the assumption has been that a person who lacks capacity would be better living with his/her family than in an institution and if he/she has been cared for by a family member they should continue to do so. This assumption arose as a result of the interpretation given to the observations made in *Re S (Adult Patient) (Inherent Jurisdiction: Family Life)*[33] by Munby J (as he then was) where whilst acknowledging that there was no presumption that mentally incapacitated adults are better off with their families he had stated 'often they will be; and sometimes they will not be. But respect for our human condition, regard for the realities of our society and the common sense to which Lord Oliver of Aylmerton referred in *Re K (A Minor) (Ward: Termination of Access)* surely indicate that the starting point should be the normal assumption that mentally incapacitated adults will be better off if they live with a family rather than in an institution – however benign and enlightened the institution may be, and however well integrated into the community – and that mentally incapacitated adults who have been looked after within their family will be better off if they continue to be looked after within the family rather than by the State' (para 48). McFarlane J in *LLBC v*

---

[30] *Neimietz* v *Germany* (1993) 16 EHRR 97 at para 29; see also *Re S (Adult Patient) (Inherent Jurisdiction: Family Life)* [2002] EWHC 2278 (Fam), [2003] 1 FLR 292; *Re Roddy* [2004] 2 FLR 949.
[31] See *Pretty v UK* (2003) 35 EHRR 1 at para 61.
[32] See *Re L (Care: Threshold Criteria)* [2007] 1 FLR 2050.
[33] [2003] 1 FLR 292.

TG, JG and KR[34] emphasised this assumption when he said that: 'Placement in the family should be at the top of the priority list before alternative non-family placements are considered'. This assumption was applied by Hedley J in *FP v GM and A Health Board*[35] when determining whether GM should be placed at home with his family or into a long term care home and in considering GM's Art 8 rights (para 25). In addition when applying the best interests test Hedley J not only took account of GM's need for physical, personal and health care but also added into the equation GM's emotional needs when he stated:[36]

> 'Those matters give rise to extremely difficult questions of balance. If one asks what has to be taken into account in considering the best interests of any human being, but let us be specific about GM for these purposes, the answer is a very wide ranging one: his health, his care needs, his need for physical care and his needs for consistency. There is, of course, more to human life than that, there is fundamentally the emotional dimension, the importance of relationships, the importance of a sense of belonging in the place in which you are living, and the sense of belonging to a specific group in respect of which you are a particularly important person.'

And:

> 'such a placement contains a formidable emotional component which GM for over 20 years has clearly regarded as being of profound importance to him. These are the single most important relationships in his life. This is the place where he belongs, and where he matters in a sense that he could never matter in an institutional care setting. So in this case, as in many others, the court has this difficult balance to strike, difficult because you cannot compare like with like. This is very much a comparison of apples and pears and trying in the context of it to strike the best interests with as broad a view of those interests as it is possible to do.'

Referring to the relevance of the emotional factor, and considering the advantages and disadvantages of the two placements under consideration, in relation to the care home Hedley J stated that that the emotional component, although not ignored, in a care home cannot begin to be met in the same way that it can if you achieve a placement within a family setting (para 22).

However, in applying the assumption of placement at home and within the family as being the starting point the courts were adopting by analogy the principles that apply in children cases. This was disapproved of by the Court of Appeal in *K v LBX & Others*.[37] The Court held that the proper approach in cases under the MCA 2005 was for the trial judge to ascertain the best interests of the incapacitated person by applying the best interests tests set out in s 4 of the Act and then to ask whether the conclusion reached amounts to a violation of Art 8 rights and if so whether it is a necessary and proportionate interference within Art 8(2). Black LJ in her judgment also doubted whether Munby J (as he

[34]   [2009] 1 FLR 414.
[35]   [2011] EWHC 2778 (COP).
[36]   At para 21.
[37]   [2012] COPLR 411.

then was) in *Re S* (above) established a presumption of a starting point and held
that nothing in subsequent cases elevates what he said in *Re S* to a 'formal and
rigid starting point'. In assessing what is in the best interests of P factual
disputes have to be determined and the recommendations of professionals
evaluated within the powers and duties conferred within the Act. In exercising
their powers and duties neither the courts nor the local authorities as public
bodies should interfere with the exercise of P's Art 8 rights except as provided
for in Art 8(2). It does not require a prescribed starting point to achieve
compliance with that. To do so would deflect 'the decision maker's attention
from one aspect of Art 8 (private life) by focusing on another (family life)' and
in so doing there is a danger of inherent conflicts arising (see para 53). A
balanced consideration of all the circumstances and attention to what is
required by Art 8 is all that is required.

Davies LJ in his judgment also confirmed that the general approach in relation
to incapacitated adults is laid down in the Act and that there was no need to
add a further starting point. To do so would give rise to an unnecessary
complicating factor. In each case the exercise should be fact specific; the
evaluation of all the relevant circumstances and the exercise of the discretion is
to be made by reference to the particular case.

In relation to Art 8 considerations Davies LJ said:[38]

> 'There will undoubtedly be many cases in this context where Art 8 considerations
> will be a very important factor. Where (as here) Art 8 is engaged and where (as
> here) there will be a potential interference with the right to family life which is to
> be respected then the interference has to be justified: that is fundamental. But there
> is no need to move from that to the creation of a legal starting point for the whole
> 2005 exercise. On the contrary the concerns that Mr Armstrong identifies are well
> capable of being altered for by a proper consideration of any Art 8 point arising in
> the s 4 appraisal. The points that need to be identified can, when identified, then
> be weighed appropriately. Where (as here) the family life is long standing, is
> existing and is of high quality, due weight needs to be given to that in assessing
> whether the proposed interference with the family life is justified and
> proportionate and in reaching the overall conclusion on best interests. Where (not
> this case) the family life has been short-lived or has been of very poor quality, less
> weight will be due to that in assessing whether the proposed interference with the
> family life is justified and proportionate and in reaching the overall conclusion on
> best interests.'

This then establishes that in determining residence issues starting points or
other generalised approaches are inappropriate. Each case must be determined
on its own facts applying the principles set out in the Act and with due regard
to P's Art 8 rights. The strength of family ties and the emotional element of such
ties are relevant factors for consideration when applying the principles set out
in s 1 and in applying the best interests tests in s 4. In such a case it is likely to
be considered in P's best interests to allow him to spend his last days within the

---

[38]   At para 63.

family rather than in an institution (see *FP v GM* above) if necessary, with conditions imposed on the carers to enable the authorities to monitor the placement and care that P is receiving.

The burden rests on the local authority to establish on evidence that P lacks capacity to make the specific decision in question and that the care offered to P would be better provided and be in P's best interests in accordance with the proposed care plan, and where appropriate, that there is a need to protect the vulnerable adult. The Court will also be concerned to ensure that by removing P from one type of abuse it does not expose P to the risk of ill treatment at the hands of an institution. In order to intervene to protect a vulnerable adult from future harm there must be a real possibility of such risk, not merely a fanciful risk of such harm. It is therefore essential that the local authority should carry out a full and comprehensive assessment of P and of family members who have cared for P, or are putting themselves forward as possible carers, and to make a genuine and reasonable attempt to carry out a full assessment of capacity of the family to meet P's needs in the community before they invoke the Court's powers to compel a family to place a relative in a residential care home: 'The Court will adopt a pragmatic, common sense and robust approach to the identification, evaluation and management of perceived risk'.[39] In all cases where P's capacity or lack of it is in issue it will be for the Court to assess the evidence and make the ultimate decision. In appropriate cases, eg where P is expressing a strong wish to return home or to a family member it may be necessary notwithstanding expert evidence, where that evidence is challenged and, in order to protect P's Art 6 rights, to hear from P directly before deciding whether or not P lacks capacity to make the decision. In *CC v KK & STCC*[40] P insisted that she wanted to return home. There was a consensus amongst the professionals that she lacked capacity to make decisions concerning where she should live. The Court on hearing her oral evidence found that she was able to give a reasonable explanation for her wish to return home, was aware of and had weighed up the risks of physical harm to her if she returned home and thus did not accept that she lacked capacity to weigh up the information and make a choice. Baker J highlighted the risk of professionals, those involved in treating P and including the Court, being drawn to an outcome that is more protective of P, and in so doing failing to undertake an assessment of capacity that is detached and objective. He emphasised the importance of giving the appropriate weight to P's autonomy; of providing P with the 'relevant information' and identifying ways in which P can be supported as required by the Code of Practice and assisting P to make his/her decision. Where the choice is between living in a nursing home the choice which P should be asked to weigh up 'is not between the nursing home and a return to the bungalow with no or limited support but rather between staying in the nursing home and a return home with all practicable support' (para 68). He also went on to confirm that when considering P's capacity to weigh up the options it is not necessary for P to 'demonstrate a capacity to understand and weigh up every detail of the respective options, but merely the salient factors'.

---

[39] See *NS v MI* [2006] EWHC 1646 (Fam), [2007] 1 FLR 444.
[40] [2012] EWHC 2136 (COP).

Disputes over where P should live often arise when a family member who has been in regular contact with P relocates. In such cases the family member's wish is that P should also be relocated to live within an accessible distance. In general any application for P to be relocated will be declined unless there are exceptional circumstances for the Court to find that it would be in P's interests to be moved (see *HT v CK*[41] and *NK v VW*[42] where permission to bring an application was refused).

In all cases where there is a dispute between what is proposed for P by a public body and the proposals of P's family the issue should be dealt with on notice. In *LLBC v TG, JG and KR* (above) the local authority had obtained an order without notice to the family members, on the basis of inaccurate information and were criticised for failure to communicate adequately with family members, who had been confrontational and at times intractable, and without undertaking an assessment of the family members who had put themselves forward as possible carers. It also highlighted the duty of social workers to check the details of all information given to the Court particularly when draconian orders were sought on an application made without notice to all interested parties. Mcfarlane J endorsed Charles J's observations in *B Borough Council v S (By the Official Solicitor)*[43] that the general approach at a without notice hearing involving vulnerable adults had to be the same as that under s 44 of the Children Act 1989. The local authority's task in both cases was to evaluate, as best it could, the degree of urgency, the risk of intervening by way of making an order and the risks of not intervening at that stage.

In *Re SK*[44] the local authority had applied for a declaration as to P's capacity and injunctive relief against her family. One of the issues for consideration by the Court was the application by the elderly mother of P, who was in her 30s, for her to be returned home into her care in advance of the final hearing. The history was complicated by reason of the fact that the family was of Afghani origins and there were complex family dynamics involved. The local authority had also been involved between 1999 and 2001. The report prepared by the local authority indicated huge conflicts and conflicting and false information, which were of a recurring nature, given by the family. There were allegations that P had been imprisoned within the home, and that she had been kidnapped. There was also police involvement and a place of safety order obtained.

The psychological report concluded that P 'was a vulnerable individual and could be subjected to coercion and is in danger of suffering emotional, physical, sexual and psychological harm if she marries'. The psychiatric report concluded that P was suffering from mental illness within the Mental Health Act 1983 and that she lacked capacity. The assessment of the mother highlighted several concerns. Having reviewed all the evidence, Sumner J concluded that a trial period with her mother was not in P's best interests and referred to the

---

[41]   [2012] EWHC 4160 (COP).
[42]   [2012] COPLR 105.
[43]   [2006] EWHC 2584 (Fam), [2007] 1 FLR 1600.
[44]   [2007] EWHC 3289 (Fam).

conflictual background, the numerous reasons given in the various professional reports, the fact that the mother had had little contact with P and her inadequate housing and inability to cope with the demands of P.

Disputes also arise between family members as to where a loved one should live. Relatives may compete to provide P with a home or disagree about a placement in residential care. The Court in such cases should be asked to make orders in P's best interests settling the issue of residence.

7.4   INDEPENDENT MENTAL CAPACITY ADVOCATE (IMCA) – SS 38 AND 39

In any case where an NHS body or local authority proposes to make arrangements for the provision of accommodation for P in a hospital or care home (in the case of the NHS) or the provision of residential accommodation (in the case of a local authority) or a change in P's accommodation and it is satisfied that there is no family member or friend of P whom it would be appropriate for the NHS body or the local authority, as the case may be, to consult in determining what would be in P's best interests, it must instruct an IMCA to represent P. There are exceptions to this requirement. In the case of an NHS body the provision does not apply if it is satisfied that:

(a) the accommodation is likely to be provided for a continuous period which is less than 28 days, if the accommodation is to be provided in a hospital, or 8 weeks if it is in a care home;[45] or

(b) the arrangements need to be made as a matter of urgency.

In the case of a local authority the provision to instruct an IMCA does not apply if it is satisfied that:

(a) the accommodation is likely to be provided for a continuous period of less than 8 weeks; or

(b) the arrangements need to be made as a matter of urgency.

In either case, if subsequently the NHS body or the local authority (as the case may be) have reason to believe that the accommodation is likely to be provided for a continuous period which is longer than that specified above it must instruct an IMCA to represent P.[46]

In deciding what arrangements to make for P, the NHS body and the local authority (as the case may be) should take into account any information given or submission made, by the IMCA.

(For a further discussion of the role of IMCAs, see **9.14**.)

---

[45] MCA 2005, s 38(3) and (9).
[46] MCA 2005, s 38(3) and (4).

7.5   CONTACT

The principles set out in ss 1–3 (see chapter 2) apply to these decisions as they do to every decision made under the Act. Where lack of capacity has been established any action taken or decision made concerning P must be in the best interests of P. This was recognised and established under common law and has been given embodied in s 4 of the Act. In applying the best interests test the Court must consider so far as is reasonably ascertainable and to take account of if it is practicable and appropriate to do so the factors set out in s 4(6) and (7) of the Act.

Where contact is in issue it is best resolved by agreement and where possible by mediation rather than litigation, which should be considered as the last option. When contact issues are referred to the Court it is because all other means of resolving the conflict or differences of opinions have been tried and failed and thus an emergency arises or the circumstances of the case are complex and urgent action by the Court is needed to protect P. The Court may restrict contact, order that contact be supervised or in extreme circumstances prohibit direct and indirect contact. However, where a public body is providing services and care for P, what the Court does not have power to do is to order the public body to provide a service which it is unable or unwilling to do. The Court has no greater powers than P would have had if he had capacity. Judicial review remains the proper vehicle through which to challenge unreasonable or irrational decisions made by 'care' providers' and other public authorities: see *Aintree University Hospitals NHS Foundation Trust v James*[47] and *ACCG & Anr v MN & Anr*[48] where P's family members sought a declaration in relation to where P should live and for the relevant public body to provide funding to facilitate contact between P and his family at his parents' home. Eleanor King J applying the decision in *Aintree* stated that where public body provides services for a person lacking capacity 'there is a danger of blurring of the distinction between the Court of Protection's statutory duties in a private law context (namely to consider the best interest of an incapacitated adult) with public law challenges in relation to the willingness, unwillingness, reasonableness or rationality of the services a public authority is willing or able to provide (para 34). For the Court to use the best interests decision as a means of putting pressure on a public body to allocate their resources in a particular way would be to go 'against the principle now enshrined in *Aintree*' (paras 52 and 57–86).

Where appropriate the Court may also endorse a penal notice to a contact order and grant injunctive relief to encourage compliance of its order and to ensure that the order can be enforced if its terms are breached. The following cases serve as illustrations of the circumstances which dictate the terms of orders made by the Court. Where a person makes a decision to retain contact only with some of his/her family and not with others and then becomes disabled and lacking capacity, the Court is unlikely to order that contact with the excluded members of the family should be resumed, if it is clear from the

---

[47]   [2013] UKSC 67.
[48]   [2013] EWHC 3859 (COP).

evidence that P's decision was his/her own uninfluenced or overborne by others. P's autonomous wishes should be respected in assessing P's best interests and refusal to make any orders for the resumption of contact would not amount to a breach of Art 8 rights (*PS v LP and RGB v Cwm Taf Health Board & Ors*[49] (below)).

7.5.1 Prohibition on direct contact

Cases of a total prohibition on direct contact are rare because not only the public bodies but also the Court will go to great lengths to facilitate contact and preserve the rights of both P and the third party's rights to family life. In *A Council v X (By her Litigation Friend the Official Solicitor), Y and Z*[50] the Court had previously ordered that contact between X and her daughter Y should be limited and supervised in the hope that given time contact would improve. On a visit for contact the daughter was abusive to the staff of the care home where her mother was residing and the police had to be called. In denying all contact between X and her daughter the Court took into account the following facts:

- that X was immobile and no longer able to recognise her daughter due to dementia which had advanced;

- that moving her elsewhere to another location would be confusing and distressing for X;

- that there was no other place where contact could safely take place;

- an expert instructed to consider the issue of contact had concluded that because of the daughter's behaviour it was not in the best interest of X to continue to have contact; and

- the judge was not satisfied that a replacement of the contact supervisor would have the desired effect of a change in the daughter's behaviour.

In *PS v LP*[51] LP had left her husband and her children due to domestic violence and abuse and went to live with PP. Thereafter she had no contact with her family. Three months after the separation she suffered a cerebral aneurism and had to be placed in a care home and needed 24 hour care. The prognosis was poor. LP's ability in the future to communicate or for an improvement in her condition was slim. Before she suffered the aneurism LP had expressed the wish that she did not want any contact with her family. She had made a will and a letter of wishes a month after she had left her family in which she was critical of her husband and her children. When the family discovered LP's whereabouts they were prevented from contact with her by the local authority in accordance with LP's known wishes. One of LP's children challenged the document relied on by the local authority to deny contact. HH Judge Cardinal after hearing the evidence was in no doubt that LP's wish not to see her family was genuine and expressed voluntarily and there was no evidence to suggest that when the letter

---

[49] [2013] EWHC B23 (COP).
[50] [2011] EWHC B10 (COP).
[51] (Unreported) February 2013, HH Judge Cardinal.

was written by or on behalf of LP and the will was made by her, she lacked capacity to do so. It was held that it was not in LP's best interests to resume contact with her family unless there was a change in her situation and she regained the ability to express a wish as to contact with her family.

In *RGB v Cwm Taf Health Board &Ors*[52] following her separation from her husband in November 2010 Mrs B had clearly expressed that she did not want to see him or for him to be involved in her care. Six months later she issued divorce proceedings against him. Just over a year after the separation she made an advance statement stating that she did not want her husband to be contacted if she became ill and that she did not want to live with him. She was admitted to hospital in June 2012. The husband was not permitted to visit her. He sought a declaration that the health board had acted unlawfully in denying him access to her. Expert evidence established that Mrs B had capacity when she made the advance statement. In determining Mrs B's best interests Moor J held that Mrs B's wishes and feelings as clearly articulated in her advance statement were absolutely central to the matter and stated that 'there would have to be some extremely compelling reason to go against such clearly expressed wishes'. The initial application by Mr B for contact was made without notice and an order was granted against Mrs B's daughter that she should make her mother available for contact. Moor J was rightly critical of both the application and the order that was made and pointed out the dangers of granting without notice application. A without notice application for contact should not be made and if made the Court should err on the side of caution and deal with the matter by abridging time for service.

The Court may prohibit contact where the relationship between P and a third party is considered to have a destructive impact on P *(LB Hammersmith v MW*[53]).

7.5.2   Restrictions on contact

The factors which the Court took into account in restricting contact (and this will be relevant in other cases as well) in *Re MM (An Adult)*[54] included:

- P's vulnerability.
- The volatile and abusive relationship causing harm to P.
- When in the relationship P had been non-compliant with medication and support services were compromised, leading to significant harm to P.
- KM encouraged P to leave the unit and become homeless resulting in neglect to her person.
- P's partner was unable to accept responsibility for his action. He had limited insight into P's needs. He failed to co-operate and did not have the ability to prioritise her needs.

---

[52]   [2013] EWHC B23 (COP), [2013] MHLO 128.
[53]   Judgment of HH Judge Horowitz QC, 29 July 2012.
[54]   [2007] EWHC 2689 (Fam).

- There was a denial of violence towards P.
- P's partner disclosed P's details to her brother who had sexually abused her.
- P's partner undermined her placements.
- P's partner was hostile towards professionals and had failed to comply with the terms of contact.
- Longevity of the relationship.
- Article 8 rights.
- Whether the care plans provided and met the needs of P.
- Whether the restrictions were a proportionate interference with family life and private life.
- Whether the risk was manageable and acceptable.

In determining that the limited and restricted contact offered by the local authority was disproportionate and unjustified the Court relied on the following factors:

- Longevity of the relationship.
- Supervised contact was wholly inappropriate and disproportionate.
- The risks had to be evaluated in a pragmatic and common sense and robust way.
- Balance between the right to respect for P's physical and mental health and safety and her ongoing relationship. The Court found that the risks were not such as to make it necessary for P's contact to be supervised.
- The local authority's plan did not make any provision to facilitate sexual relations between the couple.
- The Court found that 'particularly serious reasons must exist particularly where the relationship has lasted a long time for denying the right to sexual relations and putting obstacles in the way'.

In *LB Haringey v FG & Others (No 2)*[55] H was accommodated by the local authority placed with foster carers until she reached the age of majority. Thereafter the plan was to move her to a residential home. The mother challenged this decision and wanted H to be returned home. The issues before the Court related to residence, contact and finance. It was accepted that H lacked capacity. In relation to contact, the local authority recognised that contact had been significantly restricted to one hour, once a week, after the end of the college day on Mondays, and that that would have to be expanded both in time, possibly in frequency, and manoeuvrability in the sense that it should include activity contact of one sort or another. There was a lack of clarity on the conditions under which contact should take place. It was almost certain that H would want a carer with her, but less clear whether there was also a

---

[55]   [2011] EWHC 3933 (COP).

need for a supervisor to be present as well, to provide some authority over the contact regime. Having considered the oral evidence of the mother Hedley J concluded:

> 'Insofar as contact is concerned, I wish to stress the importance to H's future welfare of contact with family members. Whatever may be the disadvantages, and whatever may be the drawbacks, it is a fact that they will represent for her the one unchanging point in the relationships that she has during the course of her life, and accordingly I not only welcome but positively encourage the development of contact into something much less restricted than there is at the moment. I can well understand that H will wish the presence of a carer if that indeed is her wish. I would very much hope that formal supervision will only be necessary insofar as it is needed to reassure H until she is settled in to a regime of contact.'

7.5.3   Endorsement of penal notice and an injunction

A contact order is not endorsed with a penal notice as a matter or course on orders made in the Court of Protection. It is usually considered as an additional safeguard where there has been a breakdown in the relationship between the local authority and the interested party and or where a contact agreement has not been adhered to; or where court orders have been repeatedly flouted. In *E & K v SB & JB*[56] the Court had approved a consent contact order which provided that the mother was to have pre-arranged supervised contact in a public place. Contact with JB (the step-father) was restricted to provide that it should only take place in accordance with the wishes of E and K and the approval of the local authority. The detailed arrangements for contact were set out in a 'Memorandum of Understanding: Contact'. Both the mother and step father breached the terms of the order which led to the local authority restoring the matter before the Court. Before the application could be heard JB was convicted and sentenced for dangerous driving which had been committed during one of the supervised contact session. It entailed JB colliding with the supervisor who was carried some distance on the bonnet of the car. At the hearing neither parent was present. The contact order was varied on an interim basis to provide that the mother should have contact at the discretion of the local authority but subject to the wishes and feelings of the children. JB was prohibited from talking to E and K on the telephone and from contacting or attempting to contact either of them on the telephone without the express written permission of the local authority and in any event any such contact was to be in accordance with the articulated wishes and feelings of E and K. The Court also made an order prohibiting JB from coming within 100 metres of E and K without the permission of the local authority and prohibiting him from coming within 100 metres of the residential home where E and K were living, or E's and K's work places. The Court found it necessary to attach the penal notice and to grant an injunction due to the repeated breaches of the terms of the contact arrangements, the serious nature of those breaches. Additionally, in relation to the mother the Court found that she was not a passive observer of JB's actions. She was actively involved in aiding JB, and her behaviour, some of

---

[56]   [2012] EWHC 4161 (COP).

which had been pre-meditated, was considered to be harmful to E and K and having regard to the overall history of her involvement in the breaches an undertaking would not have provided sufficient safeguard nor have the effect of ensuring compliance.

7.6   COURT'S POWERS TO MAKE WELFARE ORDERS

Section 16 of the Act sets out the Court's powers to make decisions, in relation to a person (P), who lacks capacity on matters concerning P's welfare. These powers extend to:

- deciding where P should live;
- deciding what contact if any, P should have with any specified person;
- making an order prohibiting a named person from having contact with P;
- giving or refusing consent to the carrying out or continuation of a treatment by a person providing health care for P;
- giving a direction that a person responsible for P's health care allow a different person to take over that responsibility.[57]

Section 16(3) makes the Court's powers subject to the general principles of s 1 and s 4 (best interests). For a discussion of how this is achieved see chapter 2.

The Court's powers, to make interim orders and to give directions under s 48 of the Act, also applies to applications which concern the personal welfare of P. It should be noted that the threshold concerning capacity on an interim application in respect of any matter is whether:

- there is reason to believe that P lacks capacity in relation to the matter;
- the matter is one to which its powers under this Act extend; and
- it is in P's best interests to make the order, or to give directions, without delay.

Pursuant to s 49 the Court may also require reports from several sources to be prepared. It may make consequential directions for the disclosure of medical and other records and specify the scope of such reports.

Section 47 also provides that the Court has, in connection with its jurisdiction, the same powers, rights, privileges and authority as the High Court. It can thus grant injunctions, commit for contempt for non-compliance of its orders and make any other enforcement orders it considers appropriate.

7.7   WELFARE DEPUTIES

Although this is not likely to be effected in an emergency, the Court has a similar power under s 16 MCA 2005 to appoint another person as deputy for

---

[57]   MCA 2005, s 17.

the personal welfare of P as it does for P's property and affairs. Typical powers open to the Court and/or deputies for personal welfare are listed yet not exhaustively in s 17 subject to restrictions imposed on deputies by s 20. So a deputy may not prevent contact with a named person nor exercise restraint, authorise deprivation of liberty nor refuse of consent to life sustaining treatment. These powers are retained by the Court. Generally there is an overriding principle regarding the appointment of deputies in s 16(4) that a decision of the Court is to be preferred to the appointment of a deputy.

On that basis it is difficult to see exactly what was envisaged for the role of a deputy for personal welfare. The Code of Practice envisages that:

> 'Deputies for personal welfare decisions will only be required in the most difficult cases where
> • Important and necessary actions cannot be carried out without the court's authority or
> • There is no other way of settling the matter in the best interests of the person who lacks capacity to make particular welfare decisions.'

The Code of Practice gives examples of the appointment of a deputy for personal welfare in a scenario where there is a history of family dispute and one person needs to be relied upon to make a decision or where a series of health decisions need to be made in respect of someone who has complex health needs.

In *G v E*[58] Baker J considered an application by an adult foster carer to be appointed deputy for the property and affairs and personal welfare of a severely learning disabled young man in her care. He drew the distinction between the common appointment of deputies for property and affairs, where it is desirable to have one person taking what may turn out to be daily decisions about money on behalf of P, which have to be formal and signed for and, decisions about care which are made in an informal and collaborative way between those delivering it in P's best interests. He endorsed the need to preserve that informality and collaborative approach which does not accord with the appointment of a single individual to make welfare decisions. He was further mindful that although there is no formal authorisation for decision making in the absence of an appointment, this is the reality of life and decision makers are in any event protected by s 5 (see above). The case illustrates that appointment of a deputy for personal welfare will be made rarely.

A deputy for personal welfare may be removed from their appointment in the same way as a deputy for property and affairs. See chapter 3 and s 16(8). These applications can be urgent, for example where the deputy may be losing capacity themselves, which is unfortunately becoming common amongst older people appointed deputy for family members.

---

[58]   [2010] EWHC 2512 (COP).

7.8   PRACTICE AND PROCEDURE

Unless the provisions of s 50 of the Act apply, the applicant for any welfare order will need to apply for permission to apply in Form COP2. The Court may refuse permission to the applicant to make the application if the facts clearly disclose that the relief sought under the order is obviously not in the best interests of P. *NK v VW* provides a good example. In *Re VW; NK v VW*[59] NK sought to have his mother removed from her current care home where she was detained under a DOLS authorisation and to place her in one that was more local and accessible to him so that he could have more contact with her than was permitted under the DOLS authorisation. He also proposed that he should be appointed her welfare and financial deputy. His application for permission to apply was refused because medical evidence clearly indicated that to move VW would be detrimental to her welfare.

The substantive application in Form COP1 should be filed at the same time together with all the supporting documents required for personal welfare applications required in Form COP1B Annex B. In addition the Court will require evidence of capacity which should be in Form COP3. Where a deputy has been appointed, Form COP4 (the declaration form), and, if appropriate, a copy of any lasting power of attorney should also be filed.

The Court fee of £400 will have to be paid when the application is issued.

Where permission is required the Court is required to deal with the application within 14 days. It may grant or refuse the application or list the application for a hearing and give directions including specifying who should be given notice of the hearing (see COP Rules 2007, rr 55, 56 and 89). If a hearing is listed, a person who is notified of the hearing should file an acknowledgement of service in Form COP5.

If permission is given, the substantive application will be issued by the Court. The applicant will receive from the Court Form COP5 (the acknowledgement of service) Form COP14 (the notice of proceedings to P) with the guidance notes in Form COP14A, notice in Form COP15 and guidance notes of the issue of the application and the certificate of service Form COP20.

It is the duty of the applicant to:

- serve all the necessary documents and forms on the respondents within 21 days;
- serve P with Forms COP14 and 14A and COP5;
- notify any other relevant person of the application in Forms COP 15 and COP 5;
- file the certificate of service within 7 days of service in Form COP20.

---

[59]   (Unreported) 27 October 2010, Case No 11744555 (Mental Health Law online).

Every respondent and any person who wishes to take part in the proceedings must file the acknowledgement of service within 21 days. The Court will then either give directions without a hearing or list the matter for a directions hearing.

If the matter is urgent the applicant must file an urgent application in Form COP9 with a draft of the orders sought and if possible a disc of the order.

In an emergency the Court may do the following:
- make an order on the papers;
- abridge time for service;
- hold a hearing without notice.

Where orders are made without notice to the respondents, the Court will list a further hearing or directions appointment and give directions for the respondent(s) to reply.

7.9   PROCEDURAL GUIDE FOR WELFARE ORDER

Permission to apply	Required by everyone except by:	MCA 2005 s 50
	The person lacking capacity	COP Rules 2007, Part 8
	If the person lacking capacity is under 18 anyone with parental responsibility	
	Donee of a LPA to which the application relates	
	Deputy appointed by the Court	
	A person named in an existing order	
	Official Solicitor/Public Guardian	
Applicant must file	Form **COP2** if permission is required	COP Rules 2007, Part 9
	Forms **COP1** and **COP1B**	PD 9A and
	Form **COP3**	COP Rules 2007, rr 62–64
	Form **COP4** where a deputy has been assigned	
	Copy of a LPA if relevant	
Court Office	(1) Issues application and gives to the applicant	
	• Form **COP5**	
	• Forms **COP14** and **COP14A**	
	• Forms **COP15** and **COP15A**	
	• Form **COP20**	
	(2) Judge considers the application and decides whether to give directions or list for directions/disposal hearing	COP Rules 2007, r 89
	(3) May decide to make order without a hearing in which case Court will serve order on all the parties	
What the applicant must do	(1) Serve on the respondent/s within 21 days Forms **COP1**, **COP1A**, **COP5**, **COP15** and **COP15A**	
	(2) Notify P on Forms **COP14**, **COP14A** and **COP5** of the application	COP Rules 2007, r 69
	(3) Notify any relevant party on Forms **COP15** and **COP15A**	COP Rules 2007, r 70
	(4) File certificate of service and notification in Form **COP20**	

	(5) If an urgent application is required file Form **COP9**	COP Rules 2007, Part10 PD 10A and 10B
What the respondent must do	File an acknowledgement of service in Form **COP5**	PD 9C(3)
What the person notified must do	File an acknowledgement of notification in Form **COP5**	PD 9C(4)
Hearing	The Court will consider the application	
	Give directions	COP Rules 2007, r 85
	Allocate the case	
	Set the timetable and trial window or	
	If urgent list for a disposal hearing	
	Make any other appropriate orders	
Orders that the Court may make at the interim hearing	(1) Declare whether a person lacks capacity to make a particular decision specified in the declaration	MCA 2005, s 15
And at the final hearing	(2) Declare whether the person lacks capacity on the matters set out in the declaration	
	(3) Declare the lawfulness or otherwise of any act done or yet to be done	
	(4) Authorise deprivation of liberty in certain circumstances	
	(5) Specify where P should live	
	(6) Define the extent of contact between P and others	
	(7) Grant injunctions	
	(8) Appoint a deputy where appropriate	
	(9) Make any other consequential or protective orders	

PRECEDENTS

PRECEDENT FOR A SIMPLE RESIDENCE AND CONTACT ORDER

IN THE COURT OF PROTECTION   CASE NO ....

IN THE MATTER OF THE MENTAL CAPACITY ACT 2005

AND IN THE MATTER OF JOHN SMITH

BETWEEN

HELLINIC COUNTY   Applicant
COUNCIL

And

JOHN SMITH   1st Respondent

(by his litigation friend the
Official Solicitor)

And

JCF   2nd Respondent

DRAFT ORDER

Made by District Judge Wise

At ....

On the day of 2014

UPON HEARING Solicitors for the applicant and the first respondent and the second respondent in person

IT IS HEREBY DECLARED AND ORDERED THAT:

1. JS lacks capacity to make decisions on residence and contact and care provisions.

2. It is in JS's best interests to remain living at the Paradise Residential Home and the application by JCF to remove JS to live with her at .... is dismissed.

3. It is in JS's best interests to have contact with FCF subject to the

conditions set out in the Schedule attached to this order which may only be varied in writing by the Registered Manager of Paradise Residential Home after consultation with a representative of the applicant's Social Services Department.

4.   JCF shall not remove JS from Paradise Residential Home.

5.   No order as to costs save that the costs of the first respondent be subject to detailed assessment.

PRECEDENT FOR AN INTERIM ORDER REFUSING DIRECT CONTACT AND GIVING DIRECTIONS

IN THE COURT OF PROTECTION   CASE NO ....

IN THE MATTER OF THE MENTAL CAPACITY ACT 2005

AND IN THE MATTER OF MARIO SICILIANO

BETWEEN

RAYMOND SCILLIANO   Applicant

and

GLENCARE PCT   1st Respondent

and

NOEL FRY   2nd Respondent

and

MARIO SCILIANO   3rd Respondent

(by his litigation friend the
Official Solicitor)

ORDER

Made by ....

At ....

On ....

UPON hearing the applicant in person and Counsel for the Glencare PCT and the Deputy second respondent and solicitor instructed by the Official Solicitor

AND UPON reading the bundle prepared for this hearing, the letter from the Hellinic County Council (HCC) dated ....

IT IS DECLARED THAT:

1.   MS lacks capacity to decide whether and to what extent he should have contact with his son RS.

2.   The parties to the proceedings shall henceforth be known as 'RS' 'NF' 'MS'.

IT IS ORDERED THAT:

1.   Pursuant to ss 48,16(2)(a) and 17(1)(b) & (c) of the Mental Capacity Act 2005, there shall be no direct contact between MS and his son RS save as provided for in paragraph 4 of this order until further order or the determination of the applicant's application dated the ....

2.   The Official Solicitor shall have permitted to disclose to the HCC the bundle prepared for this hearing such disclosure to be made no later than 4pm on ....

3.   The Director of HCC Social Services or some other suitable person must file and serve by .... a report pursuant to s 49 of the Mental Capacity Act 2005 to address the arrangements that can be made to facilitate supervised contact between MS and his son RS outside the Paradise Nursing Home including the provision for travel arrangements and supervision.

4.   HCC shall have permission if they consider it appropriate to be in MS's best interests to arrange one session of supervised contact with a maximum duration of 30 minutes by the .... away from the Paradise Nursing Home and to provide a short report on such contact by ....

5.   The parties must provide updating position statements by ....

6.   The application shall be listed for further directions/final hearing on .... (T/E 1 Hour).

7.   The costs of the Deputy and the Official Solicitor and his solicitors shall be the subject of detailed assessment and shall be paid to the Deputy form the net proceeds of sale of 16 Great Hellinic Road and this order is to be treated as authority to the Supreme Court Costs Office to carry out a detailed assessment on the standard basis. Save as provided herein, costs be in the application.

PRECEDENT FOR A GENERAL FORM OF INTERIM ORDER ON PERSONAL WELFARE APPLICATION

IN THE COURT OF PROTECTION   CASE NO ....

IN THE MATTER OF THE MENTAL CAPACITY ACT 2005

AND IN THE MATTER OF JOHN SMITH [*insert P's forenames and surname*]

BETWEEN

HELLINIC COUNTY COUNCIL   Applicant

And

JOHN SMITH   1st Respondent

(by his litigation friend the Official Solicitor)

And

JCF   2nd Respondent

DRAFT ORDER

Made by ....

At ....

On ....

UPON hearing [*by telephone*] Counsel/Solicitor for the applicant [*or the applicant in person*] and Counsel/Solicitor for the PCT and the Deputy second respondent and Counsel/Solicitor instructed by the Official Solicitor

AND UPON reading the bundle prepared for this hearing, the letter from the Hellinic County Council (HCC) dated .... and considering the submissions made

AND UPON the terms of this order including the declarations having been translated for the first and second respondents [*or as the case may be*] and they having confirmed to the Court that they understand them

AND UPON .... [*insert name*] second respondent undertaking to co-operate with the applicant moving the .... respondent [*insert P's initials*] to the Arcacia Rehabilitation Centre [*insert name of Centre*] with all reasonable requests made by the applicant in connection with the move, and with regard to the applicant's assessment of the .... [*insert P's name*] which shall include the provision of information and any medical or care records within his/her possession, custody or power and with the second respondent further undertaking not to attempt to remove .... [*insert P's initials*] from the Arcacia Rehabilitation Centre nor to encourage .... [*insert P's initials*] to leave or to ask him/her to leave

AND UPON noting that the applicant has undertaken an assessment which concludes that JS [*insert P's initials*] is deprived of his liberty at the .... Home and this is in his best interests

AND UPON the Court indicating that all parties being present this Order shall take immediate effect for the purposes of authorising the move to Arcacia Rehabilitation Centre (such move being anticipated to take place today) notwithstanding that this Order has not been sealed

IT IS DECLARED AND ORDERED IN THE INTERIM AND FURTHER ORDER OF THE COURT THAT:

1.   JS [*insert P's initials*] lacks capacity to litigate/or on the information presently available to the Court there is reason to believe that JS [*insert P's initials*] lacks capacity to make decisions in respect of her residence care and the extent of contact with .... or

2.   By reason of his Learning Disability and Autistic spectrum disorder JS [*insert P's initials*] does not have capacity to make decisions on where he/she should reside and with whom he/she should have contact.

3.   That JS [*insert P's initials*] lacks capacity to make decisions as to his/her:

        (a)   residence;

        (b)   care; and

        (c)   contact.

RESIDENCE

4.   It is lawful and in JS's [*insert P's initials*] best interests to reside at .... [*insert name and address of Home/Rehabilitation Centre etc*] or at her current placement until further order or final determination of the application in accordance with the care plan dated .... (whether or not the same amounts to deprivation of liberty) or

5.   JS [*insert P's initials*] shall be moved immediately from .... to .... so that the applicant may assess his/her capacity and best interests in respect of his/her residence, care and contact with ....

6.   It is in JS's [*insert P's initials*] best interests to continue to reside at accommodation at .... arranged by the .... [*name the local authority*] and to receive care arranged by the LA. In the event that the applicant has to

take steps to remove JS [*insert P's initials*] from the .... Home in order to prevent serious harm to JS [*insert P's initials*], his carers or any other person in such circumstances that it is not possible for the matter to be brought before the Court prior to his removal, then(and only then) it is lawful and in JS's [*insert P's initials*] best interests:

(a)   for him to be removed from the .... Home [*insert the name of the Home/Centre*]; and

(b)   thereafter pending further order of the Court, for him to reside at such other accommodation arranged by the applicant local authority in accordance with the care plan submitted to the Court;

(c)   the applicant shall provide to the other parties full written details of the steps leading up to any removal in the circumstances outlined above and also shall refer the matter to the Court within 48 hours of the removal or as soon thereafter as is practicable.

7.   It is not in JS's [*insert P's initials*] best interests to reside with or be provided with care by ....

AUTHORITY TO USE RESTRAINT/DEPRIVATION OF LIBERTY

8.   The applicant only if necessary may use reasonable and proportionate force to effect the move. Such force may include restraining JS [*insert P's initials*] and to the extent that it deprives him/her of his/her liberty it is justified. The administration of a sedative or other medication is not authorised. Should force be used in the course of the move then the applicant shall file and serve a report specifically addressing that within 7 days.

9.   It is lawful and in JS's [*insert P's initials*] best interests that reasonable and proportionate measures are taken to ensure that JS [*insert P's initials*] continues to reside at .... Home and in the event that he/she absents himself/herself without the approval of the manager of the Home, that reasonable and proportionate measures be taken to return him/her there [or]

10.   It is lawful and proportionate and in the best interests of JS [*insert P's initials*], for the applicant's servants agents to separate JS [*insert P's initials*] and .... [*name person*] by the use of minimal physical contact if necessary, for example taking JS's [*insert P's initials*] arm and leading him/her away at the end of any contact session (whether or not such measures amount to deprivation of liberty) or

11.   It is lawful being in JS's [*insert P's initials*] best interests, that whilst he/she continues to reside in accommodation arranged by the applicant and pending future reviews, reasonable and proportionate measures (including any measures which amount to deprivation of his/her liberty) may be taken to prevent the .... respondents [*insert name*] from removing JS [*insert P's initials*] from such accommodation) or

12.   It is lawful and in the best interests of JS [*insert P's initials*] that while he/she continues to reside at .... Hospital that reasonable and proportionate measures set out in the applicant's Risk Assessment and Management Plan dated .... or the Risk Management Plan referred to below be taken to prevent JS [*insert P's initials*] leaving (including measures which amount to deprivation of liberty). Force in order to prevent JS [*insert P's initials*] leaving the .... Hospital shall not be used upon JS [*insert P's initials*] by any person other than officers of the applicant and/or staff of the NHS Trust/ PCT and only such force as is absolutely necessary should be used and only by person having appropriate training in safe restraint techniques.

13.   [*where necessary*] For the purposes of its assessment at the .... Home the applicant and those it instructs have permission to examine including physically examine him/her.

14.   It is lawful and in JS's [*insert P's initials*] interests whilst resident at the Paradise Care Home to receive health and social care in accordance with the assessment of the applicant and those health clinicians responsible for his/her care subject to the applicant filing and serving its proposals in respect of the future placement of JS and its care plans and restraint policy at the Paradise Care Home by .... [*insert date*].

REVIEW OF DEPRIVATION OF LIBERTY PROVISION (WHERE THERE IS NO
AUTHORISATION IN FORCE)

15.   The applicant/local authority shall review the deprivation of JS's [*insert P's initials*] liberty as regular intervals, the first such review shall be convened within 6 weeks of the date hereof. The Official Solicitor on behalf of JS [*insert P's initials*] shall be invited to attend all such internal reviews pending the final determination of the proceedings.

16.   Prior to each review the applicant shall consider:

   (a)   whether JS [*insert P's initials*] has regained capacity in relation to the issue of residence care and contact and the care package that he/she should receive and what assistance, if any, could be given to assist him/her in making decisions on those issues;

   (b)   whether further expert evidence, if any is required on the issue of capacity and to obtain such evidence if required;

   (c)   whether the deprivation of liberty provisions remain necessary and proportionate and in JS's [*insert P's initials*] interests.

17.   In the event that the applicant has cause to use the deprivation of liberty provisions, the applicant shall:

   (a)   notify the Official Solicitor's representative as soon as reasonably practicable; and

(b)   keep proper records of the events leading up to the use of the deprivation of liberty provisions including the names of those involved, the control used to prevent JS [*insert P's initials*] leaving [*insert the reasons for using the provisions*] any injury suffered by any person involved in any such incident and the treatment, if any received.

18.   The Court shall review the deprivation of liberty provisions at a hearing on .... day of .... 2010 (T/E 1 hour). The hearing shall be by telephone unless any party indicates by midday on the .... [*insert date*] that they require the hearing to be in person. Prior to the hearing the following directions shall apply:

(a)   the HCC [*the local authority*] shall file and serve a position statement by .... ;

(b)   the Official Solicitor for JS [*insert P's initials*] shall file and serve a position statement by ....

CONTACT

19.   It is lawful and in JS's [*insert P's initials*] best interests for him/her to have reasonable contact with .... [*insert name*], the level and frequency of such contact to be arranged between the respective parties and the staff at the .... Home in accordance with JS's [*insert P's initials*] care plans or

20.   It is in JS's [*insert P's initials*] best interests to have contact with .... [*insert name*] in accordance with the Schedule attached to this Order.

21.   It is not in JS's [*insert P's initials*] best interests to have contact with .... [*insert name*] contrary to his expressed wishes save as provided for in the Schedule attached to this order.

22.   It is in JS's [*insert P's initials*] best interests to have only supervised contact with .... [*insert name*] in accordance with the care plan /as provided for in the Schedule attached to this order or

23.   It is in JS's [*insert P's initials*] best interests to have contact with .... [*insert name*] subject to the conditions set out in the Schedule attached to this order which may only be varied by .... after consultation with a representative of the applicant's Social Services Department or on an application to this Court by an order of this Court.

24.   It is in JS's [*insert P's initials*] best interests to have supervised contact with .... [*insert name*] as follows:

[*Set out the venue, frequency, duration/whether it needs to be agreed with the Official Solicitor or nor and whether the applicant can bring contact to an end and if so in what circumstances*]

25.   There shall be a meeting attended by all parties, their legal

representatives, and .... [*insert the names of the person*] at .... [*identify the venue*] on .... [*specify the date*] for the purposes of the parties attempting to try and reach an agreement on a suitable contact schedule – such meeting is to be on a without prejudice basis save as to costs. If such contact is agreed, the parties shall inform the Court immediately. In the event that an agreement is not reached the application be listed for a final hearing before .... on .... day of .... 2010 (T/E ....). [*The Court will also give directions for the filing of evidence – see below*]

Conduct of .... [relevant persons should be named]/Injunctions

26.   AB, CD .... [*name the person who are to be the subject of these orders*] must not by themselves or by instructing encouraging or suggesting to another person.

[*See chapter 14 Enforcement for precedents*]

DISCLOSURE

27.   The applicant shall disclose to the Official Solicitor's representative all social care records, assessments, care plans, reviews relating to JS [*insert P's initials*] which it has in its possession and control by the ....

28.   The Speedwell medical practice shall disclose to the Official Solicitor's representatives JS's [*insert P's initials*] medical records by the .... [*insert date*].

29.   Any third party (including NHS Trusts, Hospitals and other bodies and GP practices) holding information relating to JS [*insert P's initials*] is herby directed to release to the Official Solicitor such information and documents (including clinical records, GP records and social services records) as he may require on behalf of JS [*insert P's initials*] within 7 days of such request.

30.   The .... [*identify any other organization or person*] must forthwith disclose to the applicant copies of all records concerning JS [*insert P's initials*] from the 1 January 2000 to the date hereof and shall thereafter disclose such records to the applicant authority on a continuing basis and the applicant shall upon receipt of such records forthwith serve copies of those records to .... 's legal representatives.

31.   Any third party holding information relating to JS's [*insert P's initials*] finances, state benefits is directed to release to the Official Solicitor such information and documents as he may require on behalf of JS [*insert P's initials*] in the course of his investigations within 7 days of any request.

32.   The Chief Constable of Hellenic CC must within 14 days of receipt of a request from the Official Solicitor, provide full details including any printouts of the relevant incident logs in relation to all incidents involving JS [*insert P's initials*] in his possession and control subject to the following:

(a)   the Chief Constable may redact any such document to remove the sensitive details of third parties;

(b)   the Chief Constable shall have permission to apply to discharge or vary this order within 7 days of receiving the order and on at least two clear days notice on the other parties;

Save that any third party may apply to the Court on 48 hours notice for further directions if they are unable to comply with this order.

33.   The Official Solicitor do provide to the legal representatives of the second respondent [*or as the case may be*] copies of all such disclosed documents.

34.   The Official Solicitor shall have permission to apply to the Court on notice to all the parties, for permission to redact or withhold any such document, if he considers that it would not be in the best interests of JS [*insert P's initials*] for those documents to be disclosed to the other parties.

EXPERTS

35.   A consultant psychiatrist/psychologist agreed between the parties, shall be jointly instructed to prepare a report on JS's [*insert P's initials*] capacity (a) to litigate; (b) to make decisions about his/her residence care and contact arrangements and (d) the impact on him/her of the deprivation of liberty provisions.

36.   An independent social worker agreed between the parties shall be instructed to prepare a report as to JS's [*insert P's initials*] best interests in respect of residence care and contact.

37.   The Joint letter of instructions to the above experts to be drafted by the Official Solicitor/the Official Solicitor's representative shall be agreed by the parties by the .... [*insert date*].

38.   All relevant documents, Court papers, social services files, medical records [*set out any other records or documents*] shall be disclosed to the experts immediately.

39.   There be permission to the social worker to inspect all the relevant papers filed in the proceedings and to interview JS [*insert P's initials*] for the purposes of undertaking the assessment.

40.   There be permission to the psychiatrist/psychologist to inspect all the relevant papers filed in the proceedings and to interview and examine JS [*insert P's initials*] and his/her family for the purposes of providing his/her report.

41.   The reasonable fees of the independent social worker and the experts shall be paid in the first instance by the applicant [or where public

funding has been granted] shall be paid by the parties in equal shares and the Court deems the costs of instructing such experts to be a reasonable and proper disbursement for the purposes of public funding certificates of the publicly funded parties.

42.   The independent social worker and the experts shall file and serve and interim report by .... [*insert date*] and a final report by .... [*insert date*].

LISTING

43.   The matter be adjourned for further directions and consideration of whether any continuing deprivation of liberty remains justified/contact before District Judge .... sitting at .... on .... day of .... 2013 (T/E .... hour).

DIRECTIONS

44.   In preparation for the adjourned hearing:

(a)   the .... respondents shall file and serve their witness statements setting out his/her/their position in respect of JS's [*insert P's initials*] removal/residence/care/contact/assessment and in response to the applicant's statement by 4 pm on .... [*insert date*].

(b)   the applicant and .... shall file and serve their respective position statements and any other evidence they intend to rely on by .... [*insert date*].

45.   The final hearing be listed before a District judge/a nominated circuit judge/a judge of the Family Division of the High Court authorised to sit in the Court of Protection on a date to be fixed (T/E .... days).

46.   In preparation for the final hearing:

(a)   the applicant shall file and serve its final evidence and care plan and any supporting evidence that it intends to rely on by .... [*insert date*].

(b)   the respondents shall file and serve their respective evidence and any supporting evidence he/she/they intend to rely on by .... [*insert date*].

(c)   the Official Solicitor on behalf of JS [*insert P's initials*] shall file and serve a witness statement and any evidence on which he wishes to rely on by .... [*insert date*].

(d)   all parties to agree and the applicant to file at Court not less than 4 clear working days before the hearing a paginated, indexed bundle containing a chronology, case summary, statement of issues, each party's position statement and skeleton arguments and the legal authorities relied on.

LIBERTY TO APPLY

47.   If any person served with this order disagrees with any part of this order and wishes to seek to set aside or vary it, he/she/ they should make an immediate application to this Court to do so and give .... [*insert time limit*] clear days notice to all other parties.

COSTS

48.   No order for costs save detailed assessment of the publicly funded costs of JS [*insert P's initials*] and .... [*insert details of the parties*].

49.   Costs reserved or

50.   Cost in the application and/or

51.   The costs of the Official Solicitor and his solicitors of an incidental to these proceedings shall be paid out of JS's [*insert P's initials*] monies. All invoice and fee notes/vouchers for disbursements on an interim basis shall be paid by JS's [*insert P's initials*] property and affairs deputy within 28 days of receipt unless prior to such date the said Deputy applies to the Court for directions in respect of the payment of the interim invoices/fee notes/vouchers for disbursements.

PRECEDENT FOR AN ORDER APPOINTING A DEPUTY FOR PERSONAL WELFARE

IN THE COURT OF PROTECTION   CASE NO ....

IN THE MATTER OF THE MENTAL CAPACITY ACT 2005

AND IN THE MATTER OF P [*insert forename and surname*]

BETWEEN

	AB	Applicant
	And	
	XY	Respondent

ORDER APPOINTING A DEPUTY FOR PERSONAL WELFARE

Made by ....

At ....

On ....

WHEREAS

(1)   An application has been made for an order under the Mental Capacity Act 2005.

(2)   The Court is satisfied that P [*insert forename and surname*] is unable to make various decisions for herself in relation to a matter or matters concerning her personal welfare because of an impairment of, or a disturbance in the functioning of, her mind or brain.

(3)   The Court is satisfied that the purpose for which the order is needed cannot be as effectively achieved in a way that is less restrictive of her rights and freedom of action.

IT IS ORDERED that:

(a)   **Appointment of deputy**

(a)   .... [*insert full name of deputy*] of [*insert full address and postcode*] is appointed as deputy ("the deputy") to make personal welfare decisions on behalf of P [*insert forename and surname*] that she is unable to make for herself subject to any conditions or restrictions set out in this order.

(b)   The appointment will last until further order.

(c)   The deputy must apply the principles set out in section 1 of the Mental Capacity Act 2005 and have regard to the guidance in the Code of Practice to the Act.

(b)   Authority of deputy

(a)   The Court authorises the deputy to make the following decisions on behalf of P [*insert forename and surname*] that she is unable to make for herself when the decision needs to be made:

   (i)   Where she should live;

   (ii)   With whom she should live;

   (iii)   Decisions on day-to-day care, including diet and dress;

   (iv)   Consenting to medical or dental examination and treatment on her behalf;

   (v)   Making arrangements for the provision of care services;

   (vi)   Whether she should take part in particular leisure or social activities;

   (vii)   Complaints about her care or treatment; [*Delete paragraph if not applicable*]

(b)   For the purpose of giving effect to any decision the deputy may execute or sign any necessary deeds or documents.

(c)   The deputy does not have authority to make a decision on behalf of P [*insert forename and surname*] in relation to a matter if the deputy knows or has reasonable grounds for believing that she had capacity in relation to the matter.

(d)   The deputy does not have the authority to make the following decisions or do the following things in relation to P [*insert forename and surname*]:

   (i)   To prohibit any person from having contact with her;

   (ii)   To direct a person responsible for her health care to allow a different person to take over that responsibility;

   (iii)   To make a decision that is inconsistent with a decision made, within the scope of his authority and in accordance with the Act, by the donee of a lasting power of attorney granted by her (or, if there is more than one donee, by any of them);

(iv)   To consent to specific treatment if she has made a valid and applicable advance decision to refuse that specific treatment;

(v)   To refuse consent to the carrying out or continuation of life sustaining treatment in relation to her;

(vi)   To do an act that is intended to restrain her otherwise then in accordance with the conditions specified in the Act.

(c) Reports

(a)   The deputy is required to keep a record of any decisions made or acts done pursuant to this order and the reasons for making or doing them.

(b)   The deputy must submit an annual report to the Public Guardian.

Requested by: [*solicitors'/applicant's name*]

Your ref: «sols ref»

Our ref: NA/«COP ref no»

PRECEDENT OF ORDER APPOINTING JOINT DEPUTIES FOR PERSONAL AND WELFARE

IN THE COURT OF PROTECTION　　　　　　　　CASE NO ....

IN THE MATTER OF THE MENTAL CAPACITY ACT 2005

AND IN THE MATTER OF P [*insert forename and surname*]

BETWEEN

AB	Applicant

And

XY	Respondent

ORDER APPOINTING JOINT DEPUTIES FOR PERSONAL WELFARE

Made by ....

At ....

On ....

WHEREAS

(1)　An application has been made for an order under the Mental Capacity Act 2005.

(2)　The Court is satisfied that P [*insert forename and surname*] is unable to make various decisions for herself in relation to a matter or matters concerning her personal welfare because of an impairment of, or a disturbance in the functioning of, her mind or brain.

(3)　The Court is satisfied that the purpose for which the order is needed cannot be as effectively achieved in a way that is less restrictive of her rights and freedom of action.

IT IS ORDERED that:

2.　Appointment of deputies

(a)　.... [*insert full name of first deputy*] of .... [*insert address and postcode*] and .... [*insert full name of second deputy*] of [*insert address and postcode*] are appointed as joint deputies ("the joint deputies") to make personal welfare decisions on behalf of P [*insert forename and surname*] that she is unable to make for herself subject to any conditions or restrictions set out in this order.

(b)   The appointment will last until further order.

(c)   The joint deputies must apply the principles set out in section 1 of the Mental Capacity Act 2005 and have regard to the guidance in the Code of Practice to the Act.

3.   Authority of joint deputies

(a)   The Court authorises the joint deputies to make the following decisions on behalf of P [*insert forename and surname*] that she is unable to make for himself when the decision needs to be made:

  (i)   Where she should live

  (ii)   With whom she should live

  (iii)   Decisions on day-to-day care, including diet and dress

  (iv)   Consenting to medical or dental examination and treatment on her behalf

  (v)   Making arrangements for the provision of care services

  (vi)   Whether she should take part in particular leisure or social activities

  (vii)   Complaints about her care or treatment

(b)   For the purpose of giving effect to any decision the joint deputies may execute or sign any necessary deeds or documents.

(c)   The joint deputies do not have authority to make a decision on behalf of P [*insert forename and surname*] in relation to a matter if the joint deputies know or have reasonable grounds for believing that she had capacity in relation to the matter.

(d)   The joint deputies do not have the authority to make the following decisions or do the following things in relation to P [*insert forename and surname*]:

  (i)   To prohibit any person from having contact with her;

  (ii)   To direct a person responsible for her health care to allow a different person to take over that responsibility;

  (iii)   To make a decision that is inconsistent with a decision made, within the scope of her authority and in accordance with the Act, by the donee of a lasting power of attorney granted by her (or, if there is more than one donee, by any of them);

(iv) To consent to specific treatment if she has made a valid and applicable advance decision to refuse that specific treatment;

(v) To refuse consent to the carrying out or continuation of life sustaining treatment in relation to her;

(vi) To do an act that is intended to restrain her otherwise then in accordance with the conditions specified in the Act.

4. Reports

(a) The joint deputies are required to keep a record of any decisions made or acts done pursuant to this order and the reasons for making or doing them.

(b) The joint deputies must submit an annual report to the Public Guardian.

Requested by: [solicitors'/applicant's name]

Your ref: «sols ref»

Our ref: NA/«COP ref no»

PRECEDENT OF ORDER APPOINTING JOINT AND SEVERAL DEPUTIES FOR PERSONAL WELFARE

IN THE COURT OF PROTECTION   CASE NO ....

IN THE MATTER OF THE MENTAL CAPACITY ACT 2005

AND IN THE MATTER OF .... [*insert forename and surname*]

BETWEEN

AB	Applicant
And	
XY	Respondent

ORDER APPOINTING JOINT AND SEVERAL DEPUTIES FOR PERSONAL WELFARE

Made by ....

At ....

On ....

WHEREAS

(1)   An application has been made for an order under the Mental Capacity Act 2005.

(2)   The Court is satisfied that P [*insert forename and surname*] is unable to make various decisions for herself in relation to a matter or matters concerning her personal welfare because of an impairment of, or a disturbance in the functioning of, her mind or brain.

(3)   The Court is satisfied that the purpose for which the order is needed cannot be as effectively achieved in a way that is less restrictive of her rights and freedom of action.

IT IS ORDERED that:

1.   Appointment of deputies

(a)   .... [*insert name of first deputy*] of .... [*insert full address and postcode*] and .... [*insert name of second deputy*] of .... [*insert full address and postcode*] are appointed jointly and severally as deputies to make personal welfare decisions on behalf of P (insert forename and surname) that she is unable to make for herself subject to any conditions or restrictions set out in this order.

(b)   The appointment will last until further order.

(c)   The joint deputies must apply the principles set out in section 1 of the Mental Capacity Act 2005 and have regard to the guidance in the Code of Practice to the Act.

2.   Authority of joint deputies

(a) The Court authorises the deputies jointly and severally to make the following decisions on behalf of P [*insert forename and surname*] that she is unable to make for himself when the decision needs to be made:

(i)   Where she should live

(ii)   With whom she should live

(iii)   Decisions on day-to-day care, including diet and dress

(iv)   Consenting to medical or dental examination and treatment on her behalf

(v)   Making arrangements for the provision of care services

(vi)   Whether she should take part in particular leisure or social activities

(vii)   Complaints about her care or treatment [*Delete paragraph if not applicable*]

(b)   For the purpose of giving effect to any decision the joint and several deputies may execute or sign any necessary deeds or documents.

(c)   The joint and several deputies do not have authority to make a decision on behalf of P [*insert forename and surname*] in relation to a matter if the joint deputies know or have reasonable grounds for believing that she had capacity in relation to the matter.

(d)   The joint and several deputies do not have the authority to make the following decisions or do the following things in relation to P [*insert forename and surname*].

–   To prohibit any person from having contact with her

–   To direct a person responsible for her health care to allow a different person to take over that responsibility

–   To make a decision that is inconsistent with a decision made, within the scope of her authority and in accordance with the Act, by the donee of a lasting power of attorney granted by her (or, if there is more than one donee, by any of them);

–   To consent to specific treatment if she has made a valid and applicable advance decision to refuse that specific treatment;

–   To refuse consent to the carrying out or continuation of life sustaining treatment in relation to her

–   To do an act that is intended to restrain her otherwise then in accordance with the conditions specified in the Act

3. Reports

(a)   The joint and several deputies are required to keep a record of any decisions made or acts done pursuant to this order and the reasons for making or doing them.

(b)   The joint and several deputies must submit an annual report to the Public Guardian.

Requested by: [*solicitors' or applicant's name*]

Your ref: «sols ref»

Our ref: NA/«COP ref no»

CHAPTER 8

URGENT MEDICAL TREATMENT

LAW AND PRACTICE

8.1 INTRODUCTION

At common law intrusive medical treatment upon anyone constitutes an unlawful act, unless carried out with the consent of the person concerned or authorised by statute. Consent given by a competent adult has to be respected no matter how unwise or absurd the decision may appear to others. Common law did not give any other person the right or the power to make decisions for or on behalf of a person who lacked capacity.

For those requiring treatment for illnesses associated with poor mental health the provisions set out in the Mental Health Act 1959 and 1983 are limited to undertaking assessments of and providing treatment to those with a mental illness or suffering from mental disorder as defined by the Acts. The treatment provided must, however, be related to the mental disorder which the person is or believed to be suffering from. These provisions include compulsory powers, provided the strict criteria set out in the Mental Health Act 1983 are met. Generally these powers are exercised irrespective of whether or not the person has capacity to consent to the treatment. The powers do not authorise intrusive treatment generally. The legislation does not deal with the day to day care or provision of treatment to those who lack capacity. Hence before the MCA 2005 came into force these issues were dealt with informally or where there were doubts or concerns relating to serious medical treatment, the High Court's inherent jurisdiction as *parens patriae* was increasingly relied on to obtain a declaration as to capacity or lack of it and to authorise the provision of particular treatment or withholding treatment in the best interests of P.

Following the House of Lords decisions in *Re F (Mental Patient)*[1] and *Airedale NHS Trust v Bland*[2] the High Court under its inherent jurisdiction dealt with many cases in which the common law was developed and which eventually formed the basis of the statutory provisions contained in the Mental Capacity Act 2005 and to which reference is often still made in determining issues under the MCA 2005. These decisions developed the concept of the sanctity of life, respecting a competent person's autonomy to make decisions, the test of

---

[1] [1990] 2 AC 1.
[2] [1993] AC 789.

capacity and the fact that it is issue specific, and the best interests principle, including the 'balance sheet approach' involving medical issues and other factors, not only in relation to medical treatment but other welfare issues.

In addition, the coming into force of the Human Rights Act 1998 made it necessary for appropriate provisions to be made to ensure that a person's rights under the European Convention for the Protection of Human Rights and Fundamental Freedoms (ECHR) and more particularly those set out in Arts 2, 3, 5, 6 and 8 were respected and protected.

The Mental Capacity Act 2005 as amended seeks to provide a comprehensive legal framework which covers all matters relating to an adult person (P) who lacks capacity. It sets out a clear and consistent legal basis and authority for decisions which need to be taken on behalf of, and acts to be done to, P. It reinforces the common law principle that the autonomy of a person who has capacity to make decisions must be respected. It ensures that proper assessments are made to test whether a person lacks capacity to make the specific decision in question; that appropriate steps are taken to enable the person to make a decision for himself/herself and that the person's wishes and feelings are taken into account. The Act and the Code of Practice ensures that a uniform best practice is followed and it provides for a careful planning process to enable advance decisions to be made and for members of the person's family to be consulted.

The key principles set out in s 1 of the Act which underpin the entire statutory provision and the Code of Practice under s 42 must be considered in all applications relating to medical care and treatment as they apply to all other matters. The provisions set out in ss 2 and 3 which relate to issue of capacity and the best interests test as provided in s 4 must also be applied both before any application to the Court is made for a declaration and by the Court when determining any issue which relates to providing medical treatment. Since these sections reinforce the principles developed under common law in decisions of the High Court those decisions continue to be relevant and are referred to in cases under the Act but subject to the specific provisions of the Act.

Section 5 of the Act and the Code of Practice, para 6.5 set out the type of acts, (mainly those which under common law would have been included under the principle of 'necessity') that professionals involved with the health and care of P may provide with the protection from liability for the care and treatment of P as if P had given his consent. The Code of Practice in paras 6.7 and 6.15–6.19 sets out detailed guidance in relation to health care and treatment decisions (see further under 8.13).

The Court's powers to make declarations in respect of P are set out in s 15 of the Act (see 8.15 and chapter 9). Powers relating to the giving or refusal of consent to the carrying out or continuation of treatment by a person giving direction for permission for a different person to take over the responsibility for P's health care are set out in s 17(1)(d) and (e). Section 48 of the Act enables the

Court to make interim orders or give directions where there is reason to believe that P lacks capacity in relation to a matter. This power will be exercised where there is some urgency in providing the care or treatment to P.

8.2 PERSONS WHO LACK CAPACITY – S 2

The starting point in assessing capacity or lack of it is that an adult has full capacity until the contrary is proved. The burden lies on the person who asserts that P lacks capacity. This was the presumption at common law and is now embodied in s 1(2) of the Act and in the Code of Practice, para 2.5. A person lacks capacity in relation to a matter if at the material time he is unable to make a decision himself in relation to the matter *because of an impairment of, or disturbance in the functioning of, the mind or brain* (see under chapter 2). However, a diagnosis or finding of 'an impairment of or a disturbance in the functioning of the mind or brain' or that P is suffering from a mental disorder within the meaning of the Mental Health Act 1983, is not conclusive evidence that P is unable to make the specific decision in question applying the criteria set out in s 3. A person who is suffering from a mental disorder within the Mental Health Act 1983, or 'suffering an impairment of or disturbance in the functioning of the mind or brain' may nonetheless be able to make the specific decision in relation to medical treatment which is not related to his mental illness. Although there is no legal requirement under the Act that lack of capacity has to be established by medical evidence issues relating to medical treatment and the question of whether a person has the capacity to make the decision in question is usually provided by expert evidence which may include evidence from a psychiatrist and or a psychologist. However, it does not follow that the assessment of capacity provided by one or more experts will be considered as determinative by the Court. Once the issue is put before the Court, it is for the Court to assess whether P has capacity to make the specific decision in question and may come to a decision which is different from the evidence of experts. (See *Re C (Adult: Refusal of Treatment)*[3] and cases referred to below.)

The standard of proof required is the civil standard ie on the balance of probabilities. The Act specifically provides that lack of capacity cannot be decided simply by reference to a person's age or appearance or an aspect of behaviour which might lead others to make unjustified assumptions about his capacity.

8.3 INABILITY TO MAKE DECISION – S 3

The criteria to be applied remains similar to that which was applied under common law and set out in the decision in *Re C (Refusal of Medical Treatment)*[4] (see further in chapter 2).

---

[3] [1994] 1 WLR 290.
[4] [1994] 1 FLR 31.

8.4   BEST INTERESTS – S 4

The position under the Act is not dissimilar to that under common law. Cases concerning medical treatment or withdrawal of treatment invariably raise sensitive, emotional and distressing issues and can be highly charged but considerations of the best interests of P necessarily involve facts that are very personal to P and P's family and friends. The Court will invariably need to undertake a careful and in depth analysis of the factual and expert medical evidence and carry out a balancing exercise of the advantages and disadvantages and risks to P of both giving and not giving the proposed treatment or withdrawing treatment; ie conduct 'the balance sheet' approach advocated by Thorpe LJ in *Re A (Male Sterilisation)*[5] and followed by Holman J in *An NHS Trust v (1) K & (2) Another Foundation Trust*[6] and in *Aintree University Hospitals NHS Foundation Trust v James & Others*.[7] The test remains an objective one in that the emphasis is on what is in the best interests of the person concerned with the emphasis being on P's own views as being the central aspect of the objective best interests test (see further under 2.5). The Act sets out a new statutory framework and s 4 sets out the criteria which must be applied when a decision has to be made about what is in P's best interests. It may therefore be argued that in determining issues that arise under it, the Court should approach such cases uninfluenced by previous decisions made under the High Court's inherent jurisdiction. However, since the statutory framework is based on and in some respects replicates case law it is inevitable that some reliance will be placed on such cases, if for no other reason than as a guide and tool to interpret the statutory provision and develop this area of the law. The observations of McFarlane J (as he then was) in *LLBC v TG, JG and KR*[8] and the review of the pre-2005 law by the Supreme Court in *Aintree University Hospitals NHS Foundation Trust v James;* Baker J in *W v M & Others*[9] in relation to withdrawal of treatment are examples of recent cases where reference to pre-2005 case has been made. The case of *Airedale NHS Trust v Bland* is frequently relied on in cases of persistent vegetative state (see also under 9.4 below).

Additionally, there are bound to be cases which are border line or involve a number of issues where it is determined that the person has capacity to make decisions in relation to some matters but not others. In such cases the High Court will need to consider the issues under its dual jurisdiction ie under the Act and its inherent jurisdiction and thus there is likely to be an overlap.[10] The following paragraphs therefore set out how various difficult issues have been dealt with by the High Court under its inherent jurisdiction both to assist decision makers and advisers should similar matters arise for determination under the new statutory regime in future.

---

[5]   [2000] 1 FLR 549, at 560F–560H.
[6]   [2012] EWHC 2922 (COP), [2012] COPLR 694 (COP).
[7]   [2013] UKSC 67; EWCA Civ 65.
[8]   [2007] EWHC 2640 (Fam).
[9]   [2011] EWHC 243 (Fam).
[10] See *Re MM (An Adult)* [2007] EWHC 2689 (Fam).

8.5 REFUSAL OF ASSESSMENT/TREATMENT

Where a person has capacity but refuses to consent he/she cannot be forced to give consent. The position is the same in the case of a person who is incapable and resists intervention.[11] In the past the Mental Health Act 1983 provisions have been resorted to in order to forcibly treat a patient. However, in this event, it would have to be established that the criteria under the relevant provision of that Act are met.

The general principle is that the consent of a mentally competent adult must be obtained before medical or surgical treatment is administered to him.[12] 'Prima facie every adult has the right and capacity to decide whether or not he will accept medical treatment, even if a refusal may risk permanent injury to his health or even lead to premature death' per Lord Donaldson MR in *Re T (An Adult) (Consent to Medical Treatment)*.[13]

Thus, an adult has the right to choose whether he will consent to treatment, refuse it or choose one form of treatment rather than another. This right exists notwithstanding that the reason for making the choice may be rational, irrational, unknown or even non-existent.[14] This principle has been recognised in the MCA 2005 which in s 1(4) provides that a person is not to be treated as unable to make a decision merely because he makes an unwise decision (see *Re SB* (above) and *PC and NC v York County Council*).[15] This widely drawn principle is, however, subject to exceptions and the presumption of the 'capacity to decide' is rebuttable. The following guidelines set out in *Re B (Consent to Treatment: Capacity)*[16] may assist in deciding how best to deal with such situations:

(a)   There is a presumption that a patient has the mental capacity to make decisions whether to consent to or refuse medical or surgical treatment offered to him or her.

(b)   If mental capacity is not in issue and the patient, having been given the relevant information and offered the available options, chooses to refuse the treatment that decision has to be respected by the doctors. Considerations, that the best interest of the patient would indicate that the decision should be to consent to treatment, were irrelevant.

(c)   If there is concern or doubt about the mental capacity of the patient, that doubt should be resolved as soon as possible, by the doctors within the hospital or NHS Trust or by other normal medical procedures.

(d)   Meanwhile, while the question of capacity is being resolved, the patient, of course, has to be cared for in accordance with the judgment of the doctors as to the patient's best interests.

---

[11]   Code of Practice, para 4.59.

[12]   *Re F (Sterilisation: Mental Patient)* [1989] 2 FLR 376.

[13]   [1992] 2 FLR 458, at 473.

[14]   *Re T (An Adult) (Consent to Medical Treatment)* above and see also *Sidaway v Board of Governors of Bethlem Royal Hospital and the Maudsley Hospital* [1985] AC 871.

[15]   [2013] EWCA 478.

[16]   [2002] EWHC 429, [2002] 1 FLR 1090.

(e)   If there are difficulties in deciding whether the patient has sufficient mental capacity, particularly if the refusal might have grave consequences for the patient, it is important that those considering the issue should not confuse the question of mental capacity with the nature of the decision made by the patient, however grave the consequences. The view of the patient might reflect a difference in values rather than an absence of competence, and the assessment of capacity should be approached with that firmly in mind. The doctors should not allow their emotional reaction to, or strong disagreement with, the decision of the patient to cloud their judgment in answering the primary question whether the patient had the mental capacity to make the decision.

(f)   In the rare case where disagreement still exists about capacity, it is of the utmost importance that the patient is fully informed of the steps being taken and be made a party to the process. If the option of enlisting independent outside expertise is being considered, the doctor should discuss that with the patient so that any referral to a doctor outside the hospital would be, if possible, on a joint basis with the aim of helping both sides to resolve the disagreement. It might be crucial to the prospects of a good outcome that the patient is involved before the referral is made and feels equally engaged in the process.

(g)   If the hospital is faced with a dilemma which the doctors do not know how to resolve, it has to be recognised and further steps taken as a matter of priority. Those in charge cannot allow a situation of deadlock or drift to occur.

(h)   If there is no disagreement about competence but the doctors are for any reason unable to carry out the wishes of the patient, their duty is to find other doctors who would do so.

(i)   If all appropriate steps, to seek independent assistance from medical experts outside the hospital fail, the NHS Trust should not hesitate to make an application to the High Court (the Court of Protection) or seek the advice of the Official Solicitor.

(j)   The treating clinicians and the hospital should always have in mind that a seriously physically disabled patient who is mentally competent has the same right to personal autonomy and to make decisions as any other person with mental capacity.

The test of capacity is thus decision specific and based on the understanding of the issues including the advantages and the risks and an acknowledgement of the fact that individuals may not give the same weight to relevant factors in the decision making process but that does not make their decision any the less valid. There is no universal test and it is no longer possible to bring a case within the compulsory regime of the Mental Health Act 1983 regime to justify overruling a decision made by P who has capacity. This was also the position before 2005 (see *Re JT (Adult: Refusal of Medical Treatment)*[17] where it was held that it would be a criminal and tortious act to perform physically invasive treatment without P's consent).

Issues will arise whether a person who is under some disability, for example due to alcohol or drug abuse, should be regarded as having an impairment or disturbance in the functioning of mind or brain. Case law as demonstrated below would suggest that they are likely to be regarded as temporarily incapacitated. Whether such cases will in future be covered under the provisions of MCA 2005 will depend on whether the requirement 'because of impairment or disturbance in the functioning of mind and brain' is construed widely or restrictively. In a number of cases decided under the inherent jurisdiction, the Court has been satisfied that the competent person was unable to make the relevant decision due to factors which destroyed or disabled the person's will and capacity. It is submitted that it is arguable that such cases would come within the definition of 'impairment or disturbance in the functioning of mind and brain'.

Where a person is deprived of capacity or has it reduced by reason of temporary factors such as unconsciousness, confusion, shock, severe fatigue, the effects of drugs, or by panic induced by psychological fear and anxiety, it will be necessary to scrutinise the evidence very carefully because fear may be a rational reason for refusing to undergo an operation. On the other hand it may also have the effect of paralysing the will to the point at which refusal and irrationality tips the usually competent person over into a situation where the capacity to make a decision is destroyed.[18] Sometimes it may be difficult to ascertain whether a person has, in fact, exercised a right to decide and, if so, what that decision is. This is particularly the case in emergency situations. In such cases, although the next of kin have no right to consent or refuse consent on another person's behalf, contact with them may reveal what the patient's anticipated decision would be. If this is clearly established, it would be legally binding on the doctor.

In every case, the doctor must give careful and detailed consideration of the patient's capacity to decide at the time the decision is made. The fact that a person is suffering from mental illness does not preclude him from giving a valid consent. The question is whether the patient is capable of understanding and understands what he is deciding; the more serious the decision, the greater the capacity required. The level of the person's ability to decide will inevitably depend on the nature of treatment to be administered, and the information he is given about the proposed treatment. Doctors and health professionals are under a duty to give the patient full information as to the nature of the treatment proposed and the likely risks (including any special risks attaching to the treatment). Having given the information, the doctor faced with a refusal of consent must give careful consideration to the patient's capacity to make the

---

[17]   [1998] 1 FLR 48.
[18]   *Bolton Hospital NHS Trust v O* [2002] EWHC 2871 (Fam), [2003] 1 FLR 824; *Re MB (Medical Treatment)* [1997] 2 FLR 426.

decision, the true scope and basis of the decision and whether the decision has been or could have been vitiated as a result of the undue influence of others (for the test of competency see chapter 2).

8.6   UNDUE INFLUENCE IN DECISION MAKING

Undue influence of others may be sufficient to cause someone to lose capacity temporarily, as occurred in *Re T (An Adult) (Consent to Treatment)*[19] where a woman, who was in the late stages of her pregnancy, was involved in a road traffic accident. Her refusal to undergo a Caesarean operation was overruled because it was found on the facts that the decision had been made under the influence of her mother who was a Jehovah's Witness. Lord Donaldson MR, at 474 said:

> 'In cases of doubt as to the effect of a purported refusal of treatment, where failure to treat threatens the patient's life or threatens irreparable damage to his health, doctors and health authorities should not hesitate to apply to the Courts for assistance.'

For the test of capacity see s 2 of the Act and 2.4. Practitioners' attention is also drawn to the Code of Practice, para 4.12. In cases where the issue may be very borderline the application should be issued in the Court of Protection with an application for the case to be allocated to the High Court and immediately transferred up.

8.7   PHOBIA

In *Re L (Patient: Non-Consensual Treatment)*[20] a declaration was sought that a patient in labour could be anaesthetised by means of an injection before her child was delivered by emergency operation. The patient had refused to give her consent because she had an extreme phobia against needles. The evidence was that in the absence of intervention the foetus was at risk, deterioration was inevitable and that death would follow. It was held that the patient's fear put her life and that of her unborn child at risk and that her phobia was such, as to deprive her of mental competence to make a decision. The treatment proposed to be administered was in the best interests of the patient as it was necessary in order to save the patient's life and that of her child. It should be noted that the decision turned on whether the patient had 'mental competence' whereas the issue under the Act is one of 'capacity' and the person's lack of capacity to make a decision has to be due to an 'impairment of, or disturbance in the functioning of, the mind or brain'. It is submitted that since the provisions in ss 1–3, which deal with the issue of capacity and how lack of capacity is to be determined, are not dissimilar to the principles developed in case law upon which the decision in *Re L* was made, it is arguable, subject to psychiatric and

---

[19]   [1992] 2 FLR 458.
[20]   [1997] 2 FLR 837.

or psychological evidence in support, that in similar circumstances, the decision on an application under the Act would be the same.

In *Re MB (Medical Treatment)*[21] the patient was a young woman who was pregnant. She had a phobia of needle pricks. This was known to the doctors and those who attended upon her from the 33rd week of the pregnancy because she had refused to allow blood samples to be taken by reason of the phobia. Subsequently, obstetric complications with potential serious consequences for the unborn child developed. The risk to the unborn child was assessed at 50% but there was little physical risk to the mother. A Caesarean section was recommended. The mother consented to the operation but she refused to provide blood samples and refused to allow the anaesthetist to insert the veneflon or allow anaesthesia by way of injection or by mask and eventually withdrew her consent to the operation. The doctor's view was that the patient clearly understood the reasons for the operation and accepted them without reservation. He did not, however, think that the full implications of not being able to accept the advice of the impact of her refusal on her and her baby was as clear to her as he would have wished and his impression was that she lacked the capacity to see very far beyond the immediate situation. She was a naive frightened young woman but was not exhibiting any psychiatric disorder. It was the phobia of needles and the irrational fear of needles that got in the way. By reason of this the doctor confirmed that she was suffering from the abnormal mental condition of needle phobia and that at the moment of panic, her fear dominated all; that at the actual point of and for a period of time after the panic, she was not capable of making a decision at all, ie she was not able to hold the information in the balance and make a choice. The Court of Appeal confirmed the decision at first instance that she was temporarily incompetent and incapable of making a decision. The Court held that in an emergency the doctors would be free to administer the anaesthetic if that was in her best interests. In considering the scope of best interests, the patient has to be treated on similar principles to those which apply to the welfare of a child since the Court and the doctors are concerned with a person unable to make the necessary decision for himself. In coming to such a decision, relevant information about the patient's circumstances and background should be made available to the Court.

A similar dilemma as under *Re L* (above) arises both in relation to the test of capacity and best interests. However, it is clear that in assessing her capacity the four criteria set out in s 3 was applied in the case. Since it was accepted that her incapacity was a temporary one the question arises whether if a similar situation were to arise in an application under the Act it would be appropriate to wait until the patient was in a better frame of mind and/or whether it is essential in the circumstances to take further steps to help the patient to make a decision. Depending on the particular facts of the case an assessment of the need for urgency for a decision and the impact on both the patient and the unborn child of any delay would be relevant particularly in assessing the best

---

[21] [1997] 2 FLR 426.

interests principle. Additionally, there may be evidence of other events during her pregnancy to suggest that even if the case is delayed, the situation would not be any different.

8.8   FEAR, PANIC AND ANXIETY

In *Bolton Hospitals NHS v O*[22] the patient who was 39 weeks pregnant had on four previous occasions given birth, by Caesarean section. She required a Caesarean section to deliver the child she was carrying and, if she did not, there was a greater than 95% chance that she and her baby would die. The patient wished to have the operation but on the four previous occasions, having given her consent, when she had gone down to the theatre to have the operation she experienced panic and withdrew her consent. She was diagnosed as suffering from post-traumatic stress disorder with symptoms of flashbacks, anxiety, and fear arising from previous Caesarean sections. When granting the declaration sought that the patient temporarily did not have capacity to consent to the treatment due to psychological fear and anxiety, the Court held that whilst the patient was entitled to refuse consent without giving any good reason for so doing, there was a point at which refusal and irrationality tipped the usually competent person over, into a situation where the capacity to see through the consequences was inhibited by the panic situation in which the patient found him or herself. However panic, indecisiveness and irrationality in itself does not as such amount to incompetence, but they may be symptoms or evidence of incompetence. Again it is important to review the significance of these pre-2007 cases in the light of the new definition of capacity and how it has been interpreted by case law.

8.9   PAIN

In *Rochdale Healthcare (NHS) Trust v C*[23] the patient was admitted to hospital for the birth of her child. The consultant obstetrician was of the view that a Caesarean section was necessary but the patient would not agree to the operation being carried out as she had previously had a section and had suffered backache and pain around the resulting scar. The consultant obstetrician was also of the opinion that the mental capacity of the patient was not in question and that she seemed to be fully competent. She was able to comprehend and retain information and to believe the information she was given. Although there was no psychiatric evidence available, the Court, however, concluded that she was not capable of weighing-up the information she was given because she was in the throes of labour and that:[24]

> '... a patient who could, in those circumstances, speak in terms which seemed to accept the inevitability of her own death, was not a patient who was able properly

---

22   [2002] EWHC 2871 (Fam), [2003] 1 FLR 824.
23   [1997] 1 FCR 274.
24   Per Johnson J.

to weigh up the considerations that arose so as to make any valid decision, about anything of even the most trivial kind, surely still less one which involved her life.'

The operation in this case was in fact carried out with the patient's consent before the Court had made the decision.

8.10 ABUSE OF DRUGS

In *A Metropolitan Borough Council v DB*[25] the Court found that a 17-year-old crack-cocaine addict, who had refused ante-natal treatment care until shortly before the birth of her child, was not competent to give her consent to medical treatment. The Court permitted reasonable force to be used for the purpose of imposing intrusive medical treatment on her as a life-threatening situation had arisen or a serious deterioration to her health might occur if appropriate treatment was not administered.

8.11 RELIGIOUS BELIEFS

In *Re S (Adult: Surgical Treatment)*[26] the High Court, exercising its inherent jurisdiction, granted a declaration that an emergency Caesarean section, despite the mother's refusal on religious grounds, was lawful where it was necessary in order to protect the patient and her unborn child. The mother in that case had been in labour for 2 days. Her situation and that of her unborn child was described as desperately serious. There was the gravest risk of a rupture of the uterus if the section was not carried out. It was described as a life and death situation. The doctors had done their utmost to persuade the mother that the only means of saving her life and that of the unborn child was to allow the operation to be carried out. Although there was no other English authority directly on the point the Court granted the declaration. The reported judgment is short and does not set out any principles upon which the consent of the mother, who was of sound mind, was overruled. It is thus contrary to the general principle that treatment cannot be imposed upon a competent person because it is believed to be in the patient's interests. It is unlikely that, in an application brought under the Act, the Court would interfere with a person's right to autonomy and right to self determination, in the absence of any evidence to suggest that the person was under pressure or undue influence of another, or other factors which establishes that the person's will was destroyed, even when his/her life depended on receiving treatment and even though the decision appears to be morally repugnant. In any case where there is doubt regarding a person's capacity and the decision relates to surgical intervention or invasive treatment, application should be made to the Court for a declaration as to capacity and for authorisation. See further under chapter 9 and *Re T (An Adult) (Consent to Medical Treatment)*.[27]

---

[25]   [1997] 1 FLR 767.
[26]   [1993] 1 FLR 26.
[27]   [1992] 2 FLR 458.

8.12   THE UNBORN CHILD

At common law an unborn child has no legal status or rights and the unborn child has not been treated as a person. Any rights accorded to the foetus have been held to be contingent upon its subsequent live birth. In *Re MB (Medical Treatment)*,[28] however, although the Court was asked to consider the interests of the unborn child and balance them against the mother's interests, the Court's decision was made on the finding that the mother was not competent. The Court gave consideration to the written submissions made and concluded that, on the present state of English law, the Court did not have the jurisdiction to take the interests of the foetus into account and the judicial exercise of balancing those interests did not arise in such cases. The Court of Appeal outlined the statutory provisions which protected the rights of the unborn child but nevertheless held that:

> '... on the present state of law, it is clear that a competent woman who has the capacity to decide may, for religious reasons, other reasons, or for no reasons at all, choose not to have medical intervention, even though the consequences may be the death or serious handicap of the child she bears or her own death. She may refuse to consent to the anaesthesia injection in the full knowledge that her decision may significantly reduce the chance of the unborn child being born alive. The foetus up to the moment of birth does not have any separate interests capable of being taken into account when a court has to consider an application for a declaration in respect of a Caesarian section operation. The court does not have the jurisdiction to declare that such medical intervention is lawful to protect the interests of the unborn child even at the point of death.'

The observation made by Butler-Sloss LJ was obiter but in *St George's Healthcare NHS Trust v S; R v Collins and others, ex parte S*,[29] the Court of Appeal reviewed the cases on the status of the foetus and confirmed the decision of the Supreme Court in Canada in *Winnipeg Child and Family Services (Northwest Area) v G*,[30] and the observation made in *Re MB* (above) and in *A-G's Reference (No 3 of 1994)*[31] Judge LJ said:

> 'Although human, and protected by the law in a number of different ways set out in the judgment in Re MB, an unborn child is not a separate person from its mother. Its need for medical assistance does not prevail over her rights. She is entitled not to be forced to submit to an invasion of her body against her will, whether her own life or that of her unborn child depends on it. Her right is not reduced or diminished merely because her decision to exercise it may appear morally repugnant. The declaration in this case involved the removal of the baby from within the body of her mother under physical compulsion. Unless lawfully justified, this constituted an infringement of the mother's autonomy. Of themselves, the perceived needs of the foetus did not provide the necessary justification.'

---

28   [1997] 2 FLR 426.
29   [1998] 2 FLR 728, [1998] 3 All ER 673.
30   [1997] 3 BHRC 611.
31   [1998] AC 245, [1997] 3 All ER 936.

The basis of this decision reflects the principles which are now set out in ss 1–3 of the Act.

In *St George's Healthcare NHS Trust v S; R v Collins and Others, ex parte S*[32] a declaration had been obtained without notice to the mother dispensing with her consent to medical treatment. The mother was detained under the Mental Health Act 1983 and delivered of her child by Caesarean section, although she had, with full knowledge and understanding of the risk to her and the baby, and after having taken legal advice, clearly indicated that she wanted her baby to be delivered naturally. The application was nevertheless made without notice to the mother and without her knowledge. No attempt had been made to inform her or her solicitors of the application. No evidence was submitted to the Court and the order did not contain any provision that the mother could apply to vary or discharge the order. The Court of Appeal held that having regard to the right of an individual to autonomy and the right of self-determination, an adult of sound mind was entitled to refuse medical treatment even when his or her own life depended on receiving such treatment (at p 685E). In the case of a pregnant woman, whilst the pregnancy increased her personal responsibilities, it did not diminish her entitlement to decide whether or not to undergo medical treatment, even though her decision to exercise it might appear morally repugnant (at p 692). To avoid any recurrence of the unsatisfactory procedure that was followed, the Court of Appeal repeated and expanded the guidelines set out in *Re MB*. The Court of Appeal also emphasised that the guidelines applied not only to Caesarean section cases, but also to any case involving capacity when surgical or invasive treatment may be needed by a patient, whether female or male. It also extended to medical practitioners and health professionals generally as well as to hospital authorities. However, those who represent the mother/patient in such cases should ensure that the hearing takes place on proper notice; that the fullest information as possible on the mother/patient is given by the applicants; that all the medical documents on the mother/patient are disclosed; that information is received on the practice of the profession and, in particular, on the hospital and medical team concerned, and that the opportunity is made available for a second opinion to be obtained on behalf of the mother.

It is appropriate to point out that at the time when these decisions were made, concerns and misgivings were expressed by some in the medical profession regarding these cases. Practitioners' attention is drawn to the commentaries which have appeared in the British Medical Journal.[33] As to the failure to provide in an order that the respondent in whose absence the order was made has the right to apply for a variation or discharge of the order, see *LLBC v TG, JG, and KR*[34] and *B Borough Council v S (By the Official Solicitor)*.[35]

---

[32]   [1998] 2 FLR 728, [1998] 3 All ER 673.
[33]   BMJ No 7088 [1997] 19 April, pp 1143 and 1183–1187.
[34]   [2007] EWHC 2640 (Fam).
[35]   [2006] EWHC 2584 (Fam), [2007] 1 FLR 1600.

In the first reported case (*Re AA*[36]) under the MCA 2005 the mother had been compulsorily detained under the MHA 1983 suffering from psychotic episodes and delusional beliefs and although it was accepted that this did not necessarily mean that she lacked capacity within s 2 of the Act evidence adduced before the Court demonstrated that in this case the mother lacked capacity within the terms of s 2(1). The medical evidence indicated that the mother, having previously had two children by caesarean section, should have elective Caesarean section in order to avoid not only the risk to the child but to prevent a possible risk to the mother of a ruptured womb. Following the guidelines in *MB (Medical Treatment)*[37] Mostyn J held that it was in the mother's best interests to undergo a caesarean section and that it was in the best interests of her mental health that her child should be born alive and healthy and that it should not be exposed to any risk during its birth. It is however not clear from the short judgment why the application came before the Court as a matter of urgency the day before the procedure was to be carried out and what if any efforts had been made to assist the mother to make an appropriate decision in advance.

In another very recent case of *Great Western Hospital NHS Foundation Trust v AA & Others*[38] AA who suffered from bipolar disorder was detained under s 5(2) of the MHA 1983 when she was 38 weeks pregnant. When her waters broke she became agitated and was uncooperative with the care and treatment proposed by the obstetric team. Her condition deteriorated raising concern of the increased risk of infection to the mother and foetus. Inducement of labour was not an option as she had been unco-operative in the past. The hospital trust sought a declaration that AA lacked capacity to decide whether to undergo a caesarean section and in relation to the care and treatment proposed and more particularly for restraint to be used in order to administer anesthetic and after delivery of the child if she became agitated. In addition because AA was detained under the MHA 1983 it was necessary to consider the appropriate legal framework for exercising restraint or deprivation of liberty. On the facts and the urgency of making a declaration, and given the complex legal interplay between the MHA and MCA the court relied on the inherent jurisdiction in arriving at its decision (see para 21). Hayden J applying Baker J's decision in *A NHS Trust v Dr A*[39] authorised the caesarean section if necessary under general anaesthesia and the use of restraint or force to administer treatment. In explaining to the family the reasons for the need to apply to the court for a declaration in such cases Hayden J stated:[40]

> 'the declaratory relief is sought for two purposes; Firstly, the legal purpose, which is to cloak the Trust with the legal authority to carry out the procedure and to provide them with a defence to any allegation of criminal or tortious liability for trespass to the person (see *Re W (A Minor) (Medical Treatment: Court's Jurisdiction)* [1993] Fam 64); secondly, the clinical purpose, which stems from the

---

[36] [2012] EWHC 4378 (COP).
[37] [1997] 2 FLR 426, CA.
[38] [2014] EWHC 132 (Fam).
[39] [2013] EWHC 2442 (COP).
[40] At para 23.

fact that in many instances the co-operation of a patient, or at least a patient's confidence in the efficacy of the treatment's success. Failure to obtain the consent of a patient not only deprives the patient but the medical staff of this advantage. The court has the jurisdiction over the legal purpose; it does not have jurisdiction over the clinical one, and its approval helps to ameliorate that disadvantage.'

8.13 THE COMMON LAW DOCTRINE OF 'NECESSITY' AND THE POSITION UNDER THE MENTAL CAPACITY ACT 2005

The general rule has been that it is unlawful to carry out any invasive medical treatment on a person without his/her consent unless it is an act specifically authorised by statute law or under the doctrine of necessity.

The common law doctrine of necessity has in the past been relied on to render lawful any treatment carried out by a medical professional, if it could be shown that the treatment was necessary as a matter of urgency and that the act was done in the best interests of the patient notwithstanding the absence of consent. The Act, in ss 5 and 6, confirms that position but the provisions appear to be slightly wider. It remains to be seen how the provisions are interpreted if challenged.

Section 5 of the Act provides that if a person does an act in connection with the care or treatment of another person he will be placed in the same position as if he had done the act on the person who had capacity to consent in relation to the matter and had consented to the particular act or treatment, provided that before doing the act he had taken reasonable steps to establish whether the person lacked consent in relation to the matter and that it was in the person's best interests for the act to be done. In future, (save for cases which come within the category of serious medical treatment) where a decision has to be taken which relates to the care and medical treatment of an incapacitated person the decision can be made and the act done without seeking prior authorisation from the Court. Section 6 of the Act however, excludes the use of restraint unless it is necessary to prevent harm to the patient and the act is a proportionate response to the likelihood of the patient suffering harm and the seriousness of that harm (see s 4B and further under chapter 10). Whatever the circumstances the restraint which amounts to deprivation of liberty within the meaning of Art 5(1) is prohibited unless it is used to provide life-sustaining treatment or the act is done to prevent a serious deterioration in the patient's condition while a decision is sought from the Court. Where such a situation is anticipated an application should be made to the Court of Protection as a matter of urgency for authorisation or declaration. In all other cases, if there is any doubt in relation to the capacity of the patient or the nature of the care or treatment to be provided or whether the treatment proposed (eg where there is a difference of opinion) is in the best interests of the patient, it is desirable to seek the prior approval of the Court. In *D v NHS Trust (Medical Treatment: Consent)*[41] Coleridge J approved this as an appropriate course to take when he said:

> 'In cases of controversy and cases involving momentous and irrevocable decisions, the courts have treated as justiciable any genuine question as to what the best interests of a patient require or justify.'

8.14   PRACTICE AND PROCEDURE

Applications to the Court must follow the procedure set out in COP Rules 2007, Parts 8–10 and the relevant practice directions. The appropriate COP Forms must be used with such variations as the case requires. All information required in the forms must be provided. Every application must be made in Form COP1 and must be filed with Form COP1B. If the applicant is applying in a representative capacity, he/she must state what that capacity is. The application form must identify the issue/s which the applicant wishes the Court to determine and set out the order/s sought. The parties to the application must be identified. The name of the person in respect of whom the application is made (P) must also be identified. The applicant must also file all the supporting documents required under COP Rules 2007, r 64.

8.14.1   Is permission required – s 50 and Part 8

No permission is required if an application is made by:

(a)   a person who lacks or is alleged to lack capacity;

(b)   anyone with parental responsibility for a person who lacks capacity and is under 18 years of age;

(c)   the donor or donee of a lasting power of attorney to which the application relates;

(d)   a deputy appointed by the Court for a person to whom the application relates; or by a person named in an existing order of the Court;

(e)   where the application is made by the Official Solicitor or the Public Guardian.

Permission is required for any other applicant.

8.14.2   How to apply – Parts 8–10 of the COP Rules 2007 and PD 9C and 10A

If permission to apply is required the applicant should file Form COP2 together with the substantive application in Form COP1. The applicant must also file an assessment of capacity in Form COP3. Where a deputy has been appointed the deputy's declaration in Form COP4 should also be filed.

---

[41]   [2004] 1 FLR 1110.

The applicant should indicate on the application form that the application:

- is urgent;
- or should be dealt with by a particular judge or level of judge within the Court;
- requires a hearing; or
- any combination of the above.[42]

8.14.3   What will the Court do if permission is granted to make the application

If permission is granted the Court will issue the application and give the applicant the following Forms:

- the acknowledgment of service Form COP5;
- notice of proceedings to P Form COP14 and the guidance notes COP Form 14A;
- notice that the application has been issued in Form COP15 and the guidance notes COP15A; and
- certificate of service and notification Form COP20.[43]

The Court must also consider the application as soon as practicable after issue to identify whether there are important and or urgent issues which need to be considered immediately. The Court may deal with the application or part of it with or without a hearing. In considering whether to hold a hearing the Court is required to have regard to the following:

(a)   the nature of the proceedings and the orders sought;

(b)   whether the application is opposed by a person who appears to the Court to have an interest in matters relating to P's best interest;

(c)   whether the application involves a substantial issue of facts;

(d)   the complexity of the facts and the law;

(e)   any wider public interest in the proceedings;

(f)   the circumstances of P and any party, particularly as to whether their rights would be adequately protected if a hearing were not held;

(g)   whether the parties agree that the Court should dispose of the application without a hearing;

(h)   any other matter specified in PD 10A.

If the Court considers that a hearing is necessary it will give notice of the hearing date to the parties and to any other relevant person and state on the notice whether the hearing is to dispose of the matter or for directions. Where the Court decides that the matter can be dealt with without a hearing it will make such orders as it thinks fit and serve a copy of the order on all the parties

---

[42]   PD 10A, para 17.
[43]   COP Rules 2007, r 65.

and any relevant person. If the Court makes an order without a hearing the order must contain a provision that the order was made in the absence of the parties and that any party may apply within 21 days of the order being served (or such other period as the Court may direct) for the Court to reconsider the order.[44]

Any party to the proceedings who wishes the Court to reconsider the order made without a hearing must make an application to the Court to do so as required by COP Rules 2007, r 89(3).

The Court may also direct that an application or any part of it will be dealt with by a telephone conference. Where video conferencing is required the person requesting it must apply to the Court for such a direction (see Part 14 of PD 14A).

P will be joined as a party to the proceedings and representation ordered usually by the Official Solicitor as litigation friend.

8.14.4 What the applicant must do if the application is granted

The applicant must:
(a) Serve on the respondent/s the following documents within 21 days:
    (i)   the application Form COP1 and COP1A
    (ii) the accompanying documents Form COP5 and COP15 and COP15A.[45]
(b) Notify the following persons that an application has been issued:
    (i)   P if he is not a party to the proceedings. P must be served with Forms COP 14, 14A and COP5.[46]
    (ii) Any other relevant person who may have an interest in the proceedings of the application. Any other person must be served with Forms COP15 and 15A and Form COP5.[47]
(c) Within 7 days of service and notification file at Court the certificate of service and notification in Form COP20.[48]
(d) If an urgent application is required the applicant must make an application for an urgent hearing in Form COP9.[49]

Any person who is served or notified of the application and who wishes to be heard must file an acknowledgement of service within 21 days of service in Form COP5.[50]

---

[44] COP Rules 2007, r 89(9).
[45] COP Rules 2007, r 66.
[46] COP Rules 2007, r 69.
[47] COP Rules 2007, r 70.
[48] COP Rules 2007, r 70(3).
[49] COP Rules 2007, Part 10 and PD 10A and 10B.
[50] COP Rules 2007, r 72.

8.14.5 What the person served with or notified of the application should do

Where the person is served with the application form he must if he wishes to be a party to the proceedings file an acknowledgement of service, using Form COP5.[51] Where a person is notified of the application he must if he wishes to apply to the Court to be joined as a party file an acknowledgement of notification using Form COP5.[52]

Where a person is neither served nor notified of the application, he must, if he wishes to be a party to the proceedings, apply to the Court to be joined by filing an application in Form COP10.[53]

In the event of an emergency the Court is empowered to make orders:

- on the papers without a hearing;
- at a without notice hearing;
- abridging time.

Where orders are made without notice to respondents a further hearing will be fixed and directions given for the respondents to file a response.

8.14.6 Hearing

The Court will list a hearing to consider the application and give directions and make an interim or final order. At a directions hearing the Court will allocate the case to the appropriate level of the judiciary and consider making the directions set out in COP Rules 2007, r 85. If P is joined as a party, a direction will be given for him/her to be represented by a litigation friend. The Court will also set a timetable for the filing of evidence, disclosure and give directions as to the attendance of witnesses at the final hearing and fix a trial window or, in a case of urgency, it will list the case for a final hearing.

8.15 POWERS OF THE COURT OF PROTECTION IN MEDICAL TREATMENT CASES

Section 15 of the Act empowers the Court to make declaratory orders as the High Court has done and continues to do when exercising its inherent jurisdiction as to:

- Whether a person has or lacks capacity to make a particular decision specified in the declaration.
- Whether a person has or lacks capacity to make decisions on the matters described in the declaration.

---

[51] PD 9C, para 33.
[52] PD 9C, para 4.
[53] COP Rules 2007, r 75 and PD 9C, para 5.

- The lawfulness or otherwise of any act done or yet to be done in relation to that person.

The Court may also appoint a deputy to make decision on behalf of the patient (see further under chapter 3) although a decision of the Court is to be preferred and the appointment of a deputy for welfare issues will not be made routinely as in the case of property and affairs.

An 'act' in this context is defined as including an omission and a course of conduct.

8.16   COSTS

See under chapter 2, at **2.8**.

8.17   APPEALS

Section 53(1) of the Act provides that an appeal lies to the Court of Appeal from any decision of the Court but s 53(2) enables the COP Rules 2007 to provide that an appeal from the district judge or circuit judge lies to a prescribed higher judge of the Court of Protection. COP Rules 2007, Part 20 sets out the detailed provision relating to Appeals as follows:

(a)   appeals from the decision of a district judge will lie to a nominated circuit judge;

(b)   from the decision of the circuit judge to a High Court judge who is nominated to sit in the Court of Protection including the President and the Chancellor of the Chancery Division;

(c)   from the decision of the High Court to the Court of Appeal.

Permission to appeal will be required from the Court making the decision. Permission may be sought at the conclusion of the hearing, or by an appellant's notice to the first instance judge or to the appeal judge (see further under chapter 15).

8.18 PROCEDURAL GUIDE FOR APPLICATIONS FOR URGENT TREATMENT

Permission to apply	Required by everyone except by the person lacking capacity	MCA 2005 s 50 COP Rules 2007, Part 8
	If the person lacking capacity is under 18 anyone with parental responsibility	
	Donee of a LPA to which the application relates	
	Deputy appointed by the Court	
	A person named in an existing order	
	Official Solicitor/Public Guardian	
Applicant must file	Form **COP2** if permission is required	COP Rules 2007, Part 9
	Forms **COP1** and **COP1A**	PD 9A and
	Form **COP3**	COP Rules 2007, rr 62–64
	Form **COP4** where a deputy has been assigned	
Court Office	(1) Issues application and gives to the applicant: • Form **COP5** • Forms **COP14** and **COP14A** • Forms **COP15** and **COP15A** • Form **COP20**	
	(2) Judge considers the application and decides whether to give directions or list for directions/disposal hearing, including joining P as a party and appointing a litigation friend	COP Rules 2007, r 9
	(3) May decide to make order without a hearing in which case order Court will serve order on all the parties	
What the applicant must do	(1) Serve on the respondent/s within 21 days Forms **COP1**, **COP1A**, **COP5**, **COP15** and **COP15A**	
	(2) Notify P on Forms **COP14**, **COP14A** and **COP5** of the application	COP Rules 2007, r 69
	(3) Notify any relevant party on Forms **COP15** and **COP15A**	COP Rules 2007, r 70
	(4) File certificate of service and notification in Form **COP20**	
	(5) If an urgent application is required, file Form **COP9**	COP Rules 2007, Part10 PD 10A ad 10B
What the respondent must do	File an acknowledgement of service in Form **COP5**	PD 9C(3)

What the person notified must do	File an acknowledgement of notification in Form **COP5**	PD 9C(4)
Hearing	The Court will consider the application give directions; allocate the case; set the time table and trial window or, if urgent, list for a disposal hearing; make any other appropriate orders	COP Rules 2007, r 85
Orders that the Court may make at the final hearing	(1) Declare whether a person lacks capacity to make a particular decision specified in the declaration	MCA 2005, s 15
	(2) Declare whether the person lacks capacity on the matters set out in the declaration	
	(3) The lawfulness or otherwise of any act done or yet to be done	
	(4) Any other consequential or protective orders	

PRECEDENTS

PRECEDENT FOR A STATEMENT IN SUPPORT OF AN APPLICATION FOR URGENT TREATMENT

IN THE COURT OF PROTECTION   CASE NO ....

IN THE MATTER OF THE MENTAL CAPACITY ACT 2005

AND IN THE MATTER OF MELAINIS LOVE

BETWEEN

HELLENIC COUNTY   Applicant
COUNCIL

And

MELAINIS LOVE   Respondent

(By her Litigation friend the
Official Solicitor)

I, Hestia Goodlady of the Social Services Department of Hellenic County Council, Hogh Road Hellenic, Social Worker will state as follows:

1.   I make this statement in support of the applicant's application for leave to make the application for a declaration that the respondent Melainis Love lacks capacity to make a decision relating to her medical treatment and that it would be lawful for the medical team at the Blackford Hospital Trust to perform a Caesarean operation on Melainis Love.

2.   I have been the allocated social worker for Melainis Love since she came out of care at the age of 18 years. I graduated in social science in 1998 and then went on to an MSc and Diploma in social work completing my studies in 2002. Since then the focus of my career has been to work with those who have severe learning difficulties and have undertaken special training in this field.

3.   Melainis Love suffers from severe learning difficulties and has been assessed as having the mental age of a 5-year-old. She has from time to time also suffered from delusions.

4.   For the past three years she has been living in a residential unit with other young people of her age and who also suffer from various disabilities. She has been having an emotional relationship with one of the residents. Although every effort has been taken to monitor them she became pregnant.

5.   During the pregnancy every effort has been made by all the professionals involved to make her understand her condition. The pregnancy however has been a difficult one and has involved her being admitted to hospital for various complications.

6.   More recently I and the midwife have tried to explain to her what is involved in giving birth to a child. We were both under the impression, as were the doctors, that she understood what would happen.

7.   Yesterday she went into labour. She has now been in labour for 38 hours and with every hour that has passed Melainis has become more confused and now believes we are all out to take her baby away. Her condition and that of the baby is fast deteriorating and the consultant gynecologist now advises that the life of the baby is at risk unless a Caesarean operation is carried out. We have attempted to explain this to Melainis but she is now under the delusion that we are all trying to cut her open to take the baby away. She has refused to co operate and is utterly confused.

8.   The consultant psychiatrist at the hospital has assessed her and concluded that she is delusional and that she is totally unable to understand what is happening to her, or the advice that she is receiving on her treatment or the risk to her and her unborn child.

9.   I attach with this statement the report of Dr Brilliant, the Consultant gynecologist and Dr Whizkid's assessment of Melainis' mental capacity. The Official Solicitor has been contacted and served with the medical reports and he has agreed to act as Melainis litigation friend. He has also consulted with the medical team. He is in agreement with this application being made.

10.   In the circumstances I apply for permission to make an application to the Court for a declaration on her capacity and for the Caesarean operation to be carried out as a matter of urgency.

PRECEDENT FOR A DRAFT ORDER

IN THE COURT OF PROTECTION   CASE NO ....

IN THE MATTER OF THE MENTAL CAPACITY ACT 2005

AND IN THE MATTER OF MELAINIS LOVE

BETWEEN

HELLENIC COUNTY   Applicant
COUNCIL

And

MELAINIS LOVE   Respondent

(By her Litigation friend the
Official Solicitor)

DRAFT ORDER

Made by ....

At ....

On ....

UPON hearing Counsel for the applicant and Counsel for the PCT and Counsel instructed by the Official Solicitor

AND UPON reading the bundle prepared for this hearing, the letter from the Hellinic County Council (HCC) dated .... and considering the submissions made

IT IS DECLARED THAT:

1. By reason of her severe learning difficulties and delusional condition AA lacks capacity to:

    (a) Make decisions in relation to the serious medical treatment at issue in this application. In particular she lacks capacity to decide whether to undergo a caesarean section and to make decisions generally about her care and treatment in connection with her ongoing pregnancy.

    (b) Litigate these proceedings.

2. Notwithstanding AA's lack of capacity to consent thereto it is lawful

being in her best interests for AA to continue as an in-patient at the applicant trust's hospital and for the medical and midwifery practitioners attending AA to carry out such treatment as may in their opinion be necessary for the management of AA's present pregnancy and delivery, including if in their professional opinion it is necessary in her best interests:

(a)   a formal examination and diagnostic assessment;

(b)   monitoring both the condition of AA and the foetus;

(c)   the taking of blood samples for testing;

(d)   the insertion of needles for the purpose of intravenous infusions;

(e)   the administration of anaesthesia including general anaesthesia;

(f)   delivery by caesarean section;

(g)   pre-, peri-, and post-operative medical care associated with such treatment.

3.   It is lawful being in AA's best interests for staff employed by the applicant NHS Trust and / or those staff from the NHS Trust responsible for AA's clinical care to use reasonable and proportionate measures, including those which constitute a deprivation of AA's liberty:

(a)   to achieve the interventions referred to in paragraph 2(a) to (g) above; and/or

(b)   ensure that she does not leave the ward at the applicant's hospital during the course of such interventions and/or post-operatively until it is clinically appropriate for AA to be discharged from the hospital after those interventions.

PROVIDED THAT:

(i)   anaesthesia and sedation may be used as far as necessary as prescribed by a consultant anaesthetist in consultation with a consultant obstetrician and is to be administered by a registered medical practitioner or registered nurse as appropriate;

(ii)   such physical restraint or force that may be used to administer such treatment/anaesthesia/sedation and/or to prevent AA from leaving the ward at the applicant's hospital shall be the minimum necessary reasonable force; and

(iii)   all reasonable steps are taken to minimise distress to AA and to maintain her greatest dignity.

AND IT IS FURTHER ORDERED AND DIRECTED THAT:

4.   Any restraint used shall be the minimum deemed necessary by those applying that restraint (having consulted with the treating clinical team) in order to facilitate the assessment and treatment of AA and shall be used in a manner to ensure she suffers the least distress and retains the greatest dignity possible in the circumstances.

5.   This hearing is in public.

6.   Any subsequent hearings in this matter shall be in public.

7.   As the matter involves issues of serious medical treatment and deprivation or possible deprivation of liberty, an anonymised version of the judgment in this application shall be published.

8.   There be no order for costs, save that the applicant shall pay half the costs of the Official Solicitor of this application, to be subject to detailed assessment if not agreed.

CHAPTER 9

SERIOUS MEDICAL TREATMENT

LAW AND PRACTICE

9.1 INTRODUCTION

When the Mental Health Acts 1959 and 1983 came into force there were some doubts as to whether the High Court could continue to exercise its inherent jurisdiction in respect of adults who lack capacity. The House of Lord's decision in *Re F (Mental Patient: Sterilisation)*[1] confirmed that the High Court continued to have jurisdiction to make declaratory orders in respect of an adult person who lacked capacity. Thereafter, the question of what medical treatment should or should not be provided to an adult who lacks capacity, and whether or not certain medical procedures should or should not be carried out on such a person, was referred to the Family Division of the High Court for determination. Consequently, the High Court developed the law on issues relating to the health, welfare and medical treatment of those lacking capacity. More significantly the test of capacity, the concept of 'best interests' and best practice guidelines when dealing with cases involving adults who lack capacity and on providing or withholding life-sustaining treatment and other serious medical conditions and procedures were developed in these cases and formed the basis of the provisions which are now contained in the Mental Capacity Act 2005.

The Act provides a statutory framework supplemented by the procedural rules and practice directions for making these decisions. The President's Practice Direction *Applications Relating to Serious Medical Treatment* defines the treatment that is classed as serious and specifically deals with the procedure to be followed when making an application in such cases. Applications relating to medical treatment to an adult who lacks capacity are now dealt with in the Court of Protection.

The inherent jurisdiction may still be relied on in cases which concern a vulnerable adult or where the person's ability to consent is unclear or fluctuates, or where there is uncertainty regarding the vulnerable adult's capacity to decide all the issues relating to his health and welfare.[2] In such cases it is suggested that the application should be issued in the Court of Protection and transferred

---

[1] [1990] 2 AC 1.
[2] See *MM: Local Authority X v MM (by the Official Solicitor) and KM* [2009] 1 FLR 443.

to the High Court to be determined by a nominated judge of the Family Division so that, if necessary, the Court can exercise dual jurisdiction under the Act and under its inherent jurisdiction.

9.2   DEFINITION OF 'SERIOUS MEDICAL TREATMENT' AND 'SERIOUS CONSEQUENCES'

Section 37(6) of the Act defines 'serious medical treatment' as treatment which involves providing, withholding or withdrawing treatment of the kind prescribed by regulations made by the appropriate authority. 'Treatment' includes a diagnostic or other procedure.[3]

The Mental Capacity Act 2005 (Independent Mental Capacity Advocates) (General) Regulations 2006[4] defines 'serious medical treatment' for the purposes of s 37 as treatment which involves providing, withdrawing or withholding treatment in circumstances where:

(a)   in a case where a single treatment is being proposed, there is a fine balance between its benefits to P (person lacking capacity) and the burdens and risks it is likely to entail for him;

(b)   in a case where there is a choice of treatments, a decision as to which one to use is finely balanced; or

(c)   what is proposed would be likely to involve serious consequences for P.

'Serious consequences' are described as 'those which could have a serious impact on P, either from the effects of the treatment, procedure or investigation itself or its wider implications'. This may include treatments, procedures or investigations which:

(a)   cause, or may cause, serious prolonged pain, distress or side effects;

(b)   have potentially major consequences for P; or

(c)   have a serious impact on P's future life choices.

The President's Practice Direction (PD 9E) 'Applications relating to serious medical treatment' also provides a similar definition and in para 5 states that cases involving any of the following decisions should be regarded as serious medical treatment for the purposes of the Rules and the practice direction and should be brought to the Court:

(a)   decisions about the proposed withholding or withdrawal of artificial nutrition and hydration from a person in a permanent vegetative state (PVS) or a minimally conscious state (MCS);

(b)   cases involving organ or bone marrow donation by a person who lacks capacity to consent; and

(c)   cases involving non-therapeutic sterilisation of a person who lacks capacity to consent.

---

[3]   MCA 2005, s 64.
[4]   SI 2006/1832.

The Practice Direction also lists some procedures and treatments which may be considered to be 'serious medical treatment. These are:

(a) certain terminations of pregnancy in relation to a person who lacks capacity to consent to such a procedure;

(b) a medical procedure performed on a person who lacks capacity to consent to it, where the procedure is for the purpose of a donation to another person;

(c) a medical procedure or treatment to be carried out on a person who lacks capacity to consent to it, where that procedure or treatment must be carried out using a degree of force to restrain the person concerned;

(d) an experimental or innovative treatment for the benefit of a person who lacks capacity to consent to such treatment; and

(e) a case involving an ethical dilemma in an untested area.[5]

The categories of medical procedures listed in the Regulations and the PD reflect those which have been considered as serious medical treatment by the High Court exercising its inherent jurisdiction. This list however is not exhaustive . There may be other procedures or treatments not contained in the list above which may, on the specific facts of the case and its consequences for P, be regarded as serious medical treatment. PD 9E, para 5 requires that any case where an adult person lacks capacity and which involves any of the above listed decisions must be referred to the Court. Indeed, proceedings for declaratory relief are the most appropriate means of providing guidance as to the lawfulness of withholding ANH and despite what is set out in the Code of Practice at para 5.33 doctors should as a matter of practice, seek the guidance of the Court by way of an application for declaratory relief before withholding life-prolonging treatment from a PVS patient (*Airedale NHS Trust v Bland* (above) and applied in *W v M & others*[6]).

In determining any issue which arises the overarching principle established under common law and now enshrined in s 1(5) of the Act that any act done or decision made on behalf of a person who lacks capacity must be done, or made in that person's best interest will apply to the Court's decision and the criteria which will determine 'best interests' will include those which are set out in s 4 of the Act. Other wider factors concerning the individual including medical, emotional and welfare, may also be relevant but these factors and the weight to be attached to the various factors will depend on the individual circumstances of the case (see further below). Save in cases of PVS the 'balance sheet approach' will be applied. In determining the issues that have arisen in such cases under the Act, the Court has referred to and applied the principles developed under common law prominent amongst these is the decision in *Airedale NHS Trust v Bland*.[7]

---

5   PD 9E, para 6.
6   [2012] COPLR 222.
7   [1993] 1 FLR 1026.

9.3   BASIS PRINCIPLES

In cases relating to declaration concerning medical treatment the Supreme Court in *Aintree University Hospitals NHS Foundation Trust v James*[8] referred to some basic principles which may assist in identifying how these cases should be approached.

The Act does not give the Court a general power to order how the doctors should treat their patient. It is concerned with enabling the Court to do for the patient what he could do for himself if he had full capacity. The Court thus has no greater powers than the patient would have had if he had capacity. What the Court can do is to withhold consent to treatment of which it disapproves and it can approve treatment proposed by the authority and its doctors (see para 18). This principle reflects the common law as developed in cases decided by the High Court under its inherent jurisdiction (see *Re J (A Minor) (Wardship: Medical Treatment)*[9] and *R v Cambridge District Health Authority, ex p B*[10]).

Whilst both at common law and under the MCA it is accepted that every competent person is entitled to have their autonomy respected, autonomy and the right of self determination does not entitle the patient to insist upon receiving a particular medical treatment so that where a doctor considers a particular treatment to be adverse to the patient's needs, the patient cannot demand that the doctor should administer the treatment (*R (Burke) General Medical Council*[11]) In *Burke's* case the Court also endorsed the following proposition advanced by the General Medical Council which was approved of by the Supreme Court in *Aintree* above:

(i)   the doctor, exercising his professional clinical judgment, decides what treatment options are clinically indicated (ie will provide the overall clinical benefit) for his patient.

(ii)   the doctor offers those treatment options to the patient in the course of which he explains to him/her the risks, benefits, side effects etc involved in each of the treatment options.

(iii)   the patient then decides whether he wishes to accept any of those options and, if so, which one. In the majority of cases, he will of course decide which treatment option he considers to be in his best interests and in doing so, he will or may take into account other, non clinical factors. However, he can, if he wishes, decide to accept (or refuse) the treatment option on the basis of reason which are irrational or for no reason at all.

(iv)   if the patient chooses one of the treatment options offered to him, the doctor will then proceed to provide it.

(v)   if the patient refuses all the treatment options offered to him and instead informs the doctor that he wants a form of treatment which the doctor has not offered him, the doctor will no doubt, discuss that form of treatment

---

[8]   [2013] UKSC 67.
[9]   [1991 Fam 33, para 48.
[10]   [1995] 1 WLR 898, [1995] 1 FLR 1055.
[11]   [2005] EWCA Civ 1003, [2005] 2 FLR 1223, para 55.

with him (assuming that it is a form of treatment known to him) but if the doctor concludes that this treatment is not clinically indicated he is not required (ie he is under no legal obligation) to provide it to the patient although he should offer to arrange a second opinion.

The Court of Protection is not concerned 'with the legality of NHS policy or guidelines for the provision of particular treatments. Its role is to decide whether a particular treatment is in the best interests of a patient who is incapable of making the decision for himself'.[12]

Any treatment which the doctors decide to give must be lawful. Generally, it is the patient's consent which makes invasive medical treatment lawful. It is not lawful to treat a patient who has capacity and refuses that treatment. Nor is it lawful to treat a patient who lacks capacity if he has made a valid and applicable advance decision to refuse it or if he has granted a lasting power of attorney or the Court has appointed a deputy with authority to give or withhold consent to that treatment and that consent is withheld (see s 11(8) and s 20(5) for limitation on such power).

The focus therefore is:[13]

> 'on whether it is in the patient's interests to give the treatment, rather than on whether it is in his best interests to withhold or withdraw it. If the treatment is not in his best interests, the Court will not be able to give its consent on his behalf and it will follow that it will be lawful to withhold or withdraw it. Indeed it will follow that it will not be lawful to give it. It also follows that (provided of course that they have acted reasonably and without negligence) the clinical team will not be in breach of any duty towards the patient if they withhold or withdraw it.'

In deciding what is in the best interests of the patient the guidance set out in s 4 of the Act should be applied (see chapter 2 and above). In determining what is in the best interests of the patient, the patient's past and present wishes and feelings, his beliefs and values and other factors, which would be likely to influence his decision if he had capacity should be taken into account. The patient's preferences are an 'important component in deciding where his best interests lie' (para 24). The Supreme Court in emphasising the need to see 'the patient as an individual with his own values, likes and dislikes and to consider his best interests in a holistic way' (para 26) therefore leaned in favour of the 'substituted judgment' approach and of the patient's wishes being of central importance in best interests' decisions.

9.4 WITHHOLDING /WITHDRAWING ANH FROM A PERSON IN A PERSISTENT VEGETATIVE STATE (PVS)

In all cases where the withholding or withdrawal of ANH is proposed for a P in PVS, the Act confirms, the common law practice set out in *Airedale NHS Trust*

---

[12] [2013] UKSC 67, para 18.
[13] Ibid, para 22.

v Bland,[14] that where it is proposed to withdraw ANH from a P in PVS the matter should be brought before the Court. Prior sanction/opinion of the Court therefore should be sought in all cases on the legality of any proposed discontinuance of life support of a PVS (see PD 9E). The Code of Practice at para 6.18 also confirms that the previous case-law requirement to seek a declaration from the Court in cases where it is proposed to withdraw or withhold life-sustaining treatment from a P in a persistent vegetative state is unaltered by the MCA 2005.

The Practice Direction does not set out any guidelines which apply in such cases. The guidelines and principles applied in the leading case *Airedale NHS Trust v Bland*[15] and subsequently approved in *Frenchay Healthcare NHS Trust v S*[16] and *Re R (Adult: Medical Treatment)*[17] and developed in other cases under common law have been applied in all cases of PVS (VS) under the Act (see eg *W v M & Others*;[18] *NHS Trust v L & Others*[19]). The key principles which apply were succinctly summarised by Baker J in *W v M & Others* as follows:[20]

> '(1) the principle of the sanctity of life is fundamental; (2) that principle is not, however, absolute and may yield in certain circumstances, for example to the principle of self-determination; (3) a decision whether ANH treatment should be initiated or withdrawn must be determined by what is in the best interests of the patient; (4) in the great majority of cases the best interests of the patient were likely to require that the treatment should be given; (5) there was a category of case in which the decision whether to withhold treatment would be made by weighing up relevant and competing considerations but (6) such an approach was inappropriate in the case of Anthony Bland as the treatment had no therapeutic purpose and was 'futile' because he was unconscious and had no prospects of recovery.'

The 'best interests' test which is set out in s 4 of the Act is invariably applied in every case. The Act in s 4(1) states that the person making the determination on what is in the best interests of the patient must consider all the circumstances and the particular matters set out in s 4(1)–(11). Where the determination relates to life-sustaining treatment the person making the decision must not in considering whether the treatment is in the best interests of the person concerned be motivated by a desire to bring about his death. The Code of Practice in paras 5.31–5.33 deals with decisions about life sustaining treatment as follows:

> 'All reasonable steps which are in the person's best interests should be taken to prolong their life. There will be a limited number of cases where treatment is *futile, overly burdensome to the patient or where there is no prospect of recovery*. In circumstances such as these, it may be that an assessment of best interests leads to

---

14   [1993] 1 FLR 1026.
15   [1993] 1 FLR 1026.
16   [1994] 1 FLR 485.
17   [1996] 2 FLR 99.
18   [2011] EWHC 2443 (Fam).
19   [2012] EWHC 2741 (COP).
20   At para 65.

the conclusion that it would in the best interests of the patient to withdraw or withhold life sustaining treatment, even if this may result in the person's death. The decision-maker must make a decision based on the best interests of the person who lacks capacity. They must not be motivated by a desire to bring about the person's death for whatever reason, even if this is from a sense of compassion. Healthcare and social care staff should also refer to relevant professional guidance when making decisions regarding life-sustaining treatment.

5.32 As with all decisions, before deciding to withdraw or withhold life-sustaining treatment, the decision maker must consider the range of treatment options available to work out what would be in the person's best interests. All the factors in the best interests checklist should be considered, and in particular, the decision maker should consider any statements that the person has previously made about their wishes and feelings about life-sustaining treatment.

5.33 Importantly, section 4(5) cannot be interpreted to mean that doctors are under an obligation to provide, or to continue to provide, life-sustaining treatment where that treatment is not in the best interests of the person, even where the person's death his forseen. Doctors must apply the best interests checklist and use their professional skills to decide whether life-sustaining treatment is in the person's best interests. If the doctor's assessment is disputed, and there is no other way of resolving the dispute, ultimately the Court of Protection may be asked to decide what is in the person's best interest.'

The Supreme Court in *Aintree University Hospitals NHS Foundation Trust v James* (above) accepted that this to be an accurate statement of the law (para 29). It also ruled that in determining whether to give or withhold treatment the issue is whether the treatment is in the best interests of the patient.

Applying the principles set out in the authorities the Supreme Court confirmed that the starting point in cases of life-sustaining treatment is a 'a strong presumption that it is in a person's best interests to stay alive' but that this is not an absolute. There are cases where it will not be in a patient's best interests to receive life-sustaining treatment (para 35) but that every patient and every case is different and must be decided on its own facts (*Portsmouth Hospital NHS Trust v Wyatt*[21] applied). With regard to how the 'best interests' test is to be applied the Supreme Court stated that:[22]

'The most that can be said, therefore, is that in considering the best interests of this particular patient at this particular time, decision-makers must look at his welfare in the widest sense, not just the medical but the social and psychological; they must consider the nature of the medical treatment in question, what it involves and its prospects of success; they must consider what the outcome of that treatment for the patient is likely to be; they must try and put themselves in the place of the individual patient and ask what his attitude to the treatment is or would be likely to be; and they must consult others who are looking after him or interested in his welfare, in particular for their view of what his attitude would be.'

---

[21] [2005] 1 FLR 21.
[22] At para 39.

And that:[23]

> 'the purpose of the test is to consider matters from the patient's point of view but accepted that it will not always be possible to ascertain what an incapable patient's wishes are and that even when this is possible to determine what his views were in the past, they might well have changed in the light of the stresses and strains of his current predicament. But where 'it is possible to ascertain the patient's wishes and feelings, his beliefs and values or things which were important to him, it is those which should be taken into account because they are a component in making the choice which is right for him as an individual human being.'

The Court also considered the meaning of terms referred to pre-MCA decisions and in the Code of Practice 'overly burdensome' or 'touchstone of intolerability', 'no prospect of recovery' and 'futility'. As regards 'overly' burdensome/intolerable having reviewed pre MCA 2005 cases the Court found that this factor may arise in those cases where it is necessary to carry out a balancing exercise, eg whether there is any evidence to suggest that having the treatment or operation is going to make the patient's life so awful that life would be intolerable. In such cases account should be taken of the pain and suffering and quality of life which the patient is likely to suffer if life is prolonged and also the pain and suffering involved in administering the treatment. In such cases the issue must be seen through the prism of the individual.

When considering whether the patient has any prospect of recovery, 'recovery' does not mean a return to full health but the resumption of quality of life which the patient would regard as worthwhile not whether others would regard it worthwhile. Where the treatment is likely to be burdensome the burdens have to be weighed against the benefits of a continued existence. Assessments of the medical effects of the treatment was only one factor to be considered. Regard had to be had of the patient's welfare in the widest sense and great weight had to be given to the patient's family life. 'No prospect of recovery' does not mean 'no prospect of recovering such a state of good health as will avert the looming prospect of death if life-sustaining treatment is given'. Where the patient is close to death the object may properly be to make his dying comfortable and as dignified as possible rather than to take invasive steps to prolong his life for a short while. Where the patient is suffering from incurable illness or disability it is not very helpful to talk of recovering to a state of good health. The patient's life may still be well worth living. It is not for others to say that a life which the patient would regard as worthwhile is not worth living.

With regards to 'futility' the Supreme Court disagreed with the statements of the Court of Appeal that 'treatment is futile unless it has a real prospect of curing or at least palliating the life sustaining disease or illness from which the patient is suffering'. It ruled that futility is to be considered as treatment which is ineffective or of no benefit to the patient. Factors such as the particular nature of the treatment, its prospects of success and particularly the risk that, if

---

[23]   At para 45.

revived, the patient would be even more seriously disabled than before may be relevant in determining whether the treatment would be futile.

If when applying the best interests test it is clear that the treatment is futile and 'it can be properly concluded that it is no longer in the best interests of the patient to continue with it' (per Lord Goff in *Airedale NHS Trust v Bland*) it will be lawful to withhold/withdraw life-sustaining treatment. The Code of Practice at paras 5.29–5.36 sets out some guidance on how someone's best interests should be worked out when making decisions about life-sustaining treatment.

Where, P is totally unconscious and there is no prospect of improvement in his condition, it could be argued that there is no balancing exercise to be performed. Medical treatment is not appropriate or requisite simply to prolong P's life when such treatment has no therapeutic purpose, or where it is futile, because P is unconscious and there is no prospect of any improvement in his condition. The invasiveness of the treatment and of the indignity to which a person is likely to be subjected if his life is prolonged by artificial means, and the likelihood of the distress which would be caused to his family are relevant considerations.[24] Where P has remained in a coma wholly dependent on artificial feeding and unaware of anything or anybody and all the evidence establishes that P has no meaningful life whatsoever and that P is suffering a living death the case for withdrawal of ANH will be made out (see *Re D (Medical Treatment)*.[25] Similarly, in *The NHS Trust v AW*[26] where P remained unconscious for 4 years and the unanimous professional diagnosis was supported by detailed SMART and WHIM assessments and P's family and carers, the Court found that her treatment regime was futile and declared that she was in a PVS and that it was lawful and in P's best interests for ANH to be withdrawn but that she should receive such treatment and nursing care as may be appropriate to ensure that she retains the greatest dignity until her life ends.

Other matters established in case law, which may be relevant, include the fact that a diagnosis of irreversible PVS should not be considered confirmed until P has been insentient for at least 12 months. Every effort should be made at rehabilitation.

Of relevance will also be considerations of the rights enshrined under the European Convention for the Protection of Human Rights and Fundamental Freedoms (ECHR).

The burden of proving that treatment should be discontinued is on those who seek to assert that life-sustaining treatment should be discontinued.

---

[24] *Airedale NHS Trust v Bland* [1993] 1 FLR 1026 (per Lord Goff at p 1040). See also *Portsmouth NHS Trust v Wyatt and Wyatt Southampton NHS Intervening* [2004] EWHC 2247 (Fam), [2005] 1 FLR 21 and *Re L (Medical Treatment: Benefit* [2004] EWHC 2713 (Fam), [2005] 1 FLR 491.

[25] [1998] 1 FLR 411.

[26] [2013] EWHC 78 (COP).

9.5   WHAT OF CASES WHERE THERE IS SOME AWARENESS IN P – MINIMALLY CONSCIOUS STATE (MCS)

Although not referred to as MCS in cases decided before 2005, there were a number of cases of MCS in which the High Court under its inherent jurisdiction granted declaratory relief for withholding/withdrawing ANH (see *NHS Trust A v H*,[27] where P had some degree of visual tracking and of response to menace but there had not been any improvement in P's condition for 8 years and *Re H (A Patient)*[28] where P had tracking movements of the eyes and could be roused by clapping or by touch but was wholly unaware of her environment). Thus the principle set out in *Airedale NHS Trust v Bland* (see above) that if treatment is futile it can be properly concluded that it is not in the best interests of P to continue with it was applied to what is now known as MCS.

Section 37 of the Act read together with the Court's powers to grant declaratory relief set out in s 15 of the Act clearly gives the Court of Protection jurisdiction to determine cases of ANH where P is in MVS. The Court of Protection Practice Direction PD 9E specifically provides that decisions relating to ANH where the person is in a 'minimally conscious state' are to be regarded as 'serious medical treatment' and should be brought before the Court. Hence what was regarded as 'good practice' in *R (Burke) v General Medical Council and Others*[29] is now given legal force.

The question of whether P is in MCS or not will very much depend on the facts (see *A Local Health Board v J*[30] where the distinction was made between vocalisation and verbalisation).

Re W v M & Others[31] is the first case of MCS under the Act in which a declaration was sought to discontinue and withhold life – sustaining treatment including artificial nutrition and hydration. The issues which the Court had to determine related to whether it had jurisdiction; the test to be applied; the factors which were relevant and the weight to be attached to the expressed wishes of P which had not been set out in an advance decision within the terms of ss 24–26 of the Act. In determining the issues Baker J comprehensively reviewed case law under the common law where life sustaining treatment had been withdrawn/withheld including where the patient had not been in a PVS. On the facts he concluded that the Court had jurisdiction to determine the withholding/withdrawal of treatment in cases of MCS under the Act; that the test to be applied was the 'best interests' test set out in s 4 of the Act and by reference to pre-2005 case law, principally *Airedale NHS Trust v Bland* (see above). He confirmed that the 'balance sheet approach' applied to decisions regarding the withdrawal of ANH from those in a MCS but whose condition was stable (ie non PVS cases). In applying the s 4 best interests test criteria and

---

27   [2001] 2 FLR 367.
28   [1998] 2 FLR 36.
29   [2005] EWCA Civ 1003.
30   [2012] MHLO 158 (COP).
31   [2011] EWHC 2443 (COP), [2012] COPLR 222.

using the balance sheet approach the factors he took into account were: (i) the preservation of life; (ii) P's wishes and feelings; (iii) pain; (iv) enjoyment of life; (v) prospects of recovery; (vi) dignity; (vii) wishes and feelings of family members.

Baker J also made the following observations approved by the President of the Court of Protection designed to assist in future applications for the withdrawal of ANH:

(a)   A decision to withhold or withdraw ANH from a person in VS or MC must be referred to the Court as stated in COP PD 9E para 5 and all applications must be made to a High Court judge and allocated to one judge.

(b)   Every step should be taken to diagnose the patient's true condition before the application is made to the Court and no application should be made unless a SMART assessment or similarly validated equivalent has been carried out to provide a diagnosis of the patient's disorder of consciousness and in the case of a patient thereby diagnosed as being in an MCS a series of WHIM assessments have been carried out over time with a view to tracking the patient's progress and recovery (if any) through the MCS.

(c)   Given the fundamental issues involved in cases involving the withdrawal of ANH it is alarming that public funding has not been made available to members of the family to assist them in prosecuting their application.

(d)   Provided that the privacy of the individuals involved is fully respected it is imperative in the public interest that the press should be free to report as widely and freely as possible cases of this sort.

Apart from the factors referred to by Baker J as being relevant, case law establishes that other factors may also be relevant. Pre-2005 cases indicate that where the treatment is found to be futile that factor is very much a relevant consideration. The assessment of quality of life must necessarily also involve its intolerabilty and is a relevant factor which should be taken into account. The issue of futility must now be considered in the light of the decision of the Supreme Court in *Aintree University Hospital NHS Trust v James* (see above at **9.4**).

As these cases indicate any decision on what is in the best interests of P is very much dependant on the facts of the individual case.

9.5.1   Strongly held wishes and religious beliefs of patient in minimally conscious state

Where P is in a minimally conscious state but there is clear evidence that he would have wished treatment to be provided no matter what because of, for instance his religious beliefs, the Court may reach a decision on P's behalf which is not consistent with his wishes. Where the medical evidence suggests that it is highly unlikely that any further intensive life-sustaining treatment would result in any meaningful recovery; that the continuation of such treatment would cause harm to the patient; that even CPR would result in further damage to the patient's condition making further interventions contrary to the central medical objectives of intensive care and all ethics the Court's approach will be as set out in *Aintree*. It would not in those circumstances be in P's best interests to require staff to administer treatment that would be entirely futile: *An NHS Foundation Trust v VT and A.*[32] In that case the NHS Foundation Trust applied for a declaration that it would be unlawful to provide intensive care and or resuscitation other than bag and mask resuscitation. For religious reasons the family considered that it was in his best interests for such treatment to be provided, because VT 'would have wanted to avail himself of every possible opportunity for survival in its crudest, most basic sense, no matter what the pain involved, no matter what the prospects for long-term survival might be, no matter what quality of life might lie at the end of the journey or, indeed, during it. Those ultimate decisions they believed to be for Allah alone. They believed that VT's suffering would also cleanse him from sin, would prepare him for death and would be borne by him with stoicism, in recognition of that process'. The family also had strongly held beliefs that to deprive him of the opportunity to suffer is to deprive him of the chance to purify his soul in preparedness for death. They argued that the Court should consider VT not only as 'a raft of medical problems' but broadly as the man he has been throughout his life, his morality, his faith, his ethics and his religious beliefs. Hayden J accepted that VT's wishes were an important factor but that they were not determinative. The overwhelming evidence was that treatment would be ineffective; would not be of benefit to him and was likely to be damaging and compromising to his dignity and would not be in his best interests. It would not only permit him to suffer but require others actively to harm him for no medical reason or benefit. That said Hayden J:

> 'is not only medically contrary to his best interest, it is difficult to reconcile with the underlying theological premise that the family advances. It can hardly be right to expect doctors to cause pain for no justifiable medical reason other than to accommodate the religious or other beliefs of a patient. It would require those who, through medical training and personal beliefs, want to help the patient, to do the exact opposite – that would be neither ethical nor lawful in my judgment.'

Hayden J concluded:

> 'Finally, it is, I think, clear, from my review both of the medical and lay evidence, that to require the team to treat VT in Intensive Care would be wholly futile, in that it would be:
> (i)   Likely to cause distress, discomfort and probably pain.
> (ii)   Unable to achieve any positive medical benefit.
> (iii) Life-threatening, in and of itself.
> (iv) To further compromise VT's vital organs, and therefore medically harmful.'

Although the facts of this case fall outside those where the evidence establishes that the patient is close to death and that the treatment administered to the

---

32   [2013] EWHC B26 (COP).

patient should be to make his dying as comfortable and dignified as possible, the decision suggests that where the patient is not close to death but, where his condition is such that intensive and burdensome treatment will not improve his condition; there is little if any prospect of a meaningful recovery and the treatment is likely to cause him further harm and damage, it is both unethical and not in the patient's best interests to permit the continuation of that treatment notwithstanding the patient's wishes and religious beliefs.

9.6   CARDIO-PULMONARY RESUSCITATION (CPR)

A statement issued by the British Medical Association and the Royal College of Nursing states that:

> 'Cardio-pulmonary resuscitation (CPR) can be attempted on any individual in whom cardiac or respiratory function ceases. Such events are inevitable as part of dying and thus CPR can theoretically be used on every individual prior to death. It is therefore essential to identify patients for whom cardio-pulmonary arrest represents a terminal event in their illness and in whom CPR is inappropriate.'

The publication provides guidelines as a framework within which decisions may be formulated.

Unlike cases of PVS, where the Court is asked to approve a course aimed at terminating life or accelerating death, in cases of CPR the Court will be asked to consider and rule upon the circumstances in which steps should not be taken to prolong life.

At common law the test applied in such cases is the same as in PVS, ie the best interest of P. In *Re J (A Minor) (Wardship: Medical Treatment)*[33] the Court of Appeal, when considering the issue of whether a child, who was not terminally ill but who suffered from convulsions requiring resuscitation, should not, in the event of further convulsions, be revived by means of mechanical ventilation, held that the test in the case of a child was the paramountcy of the child's best interest. Where a child was not terminally ill, the Court in determining where the child's interest lay, would take into account the pain and suffering to the child if life-prolonging treatment were given and assess its effect from the child's position were he able to make a sound judgment. If from this standpoint, his future life might be regarded as intolerable to him the Court might choose a course which did not prevent his death:[34]

> 'the correct approach is for the Court to judge the quality of life the child would have to endure if given treatment, and decide whether in all the circumstances such a life would be so afflicted as to be intolerable to that child.'

---

[33]   [1991] Fam 33, [1991] 1 FLR 366.
[34]   *Re J (A Minor) (Wardship: Medical Treatment)* [1991] 1 FLR 366, at 383, per Taylor LCJ .

In *Re C (Medical Treatment)*[35] the High Court applied the principles set out in *Re J* (above) and exercised its inherent jurisdiction to approve the recommended treatment, which involved the withdrawal of ventilation as advised by the medical team, notwithstanding the objections of the parents on the basis that the best interest of the child (who was 16 months old) required that she be prevented from suffering.

The same principle would be applied in the case of a handicapped incapacitated adult.

In cases where the issue is whether the administration of antibiotics should be withheld in the event of P developing a potentially life-threatening infection, the decision can only be taken at the time by P's responsible medical practitioners in the light of the prevailing circumstances and 'falls fairly and squarely within the clinical responsibility of the consultant treating the patient' (per Sir Stephen Brown P in *Re R (Adult: Medical Treatment)*[36]). Where the Court is satisfied that the medical team having responsibility for P's treatment have P's best interest in mind, the Court will leave the decision to them subject to conditions, for example that the medical practitioner and the consultant, having the responsibility at the time for P's treatment and care, advise the withholding of antibiotics.

9.7   CASES INVOLVING ORGAN OR BONE MARROW DONATION BY A PERSON WHO LACKS CAPACITY

The second category of cases referred to in Practice Direction 9E (para 5) is where an organ or bone marrow donation by a person who lacks capacity is proposed. A declaration must be sought from the Court for an organ or bone marrow donation. In considering such an application, the Court will apply the best interests provision set out in s 4 and adopt an objective approach with an element of subjective factors set out in s 4(6), ie the wishes and feelings, beliefs and values that would be likely to influence the person concerned when making his decision (see above at **9.3**). In *Re W Healthcare NHS Trust v KH*[37] where there was a conflict between the incapacitated person's views and the patient's 'best interests' as demonstrated by the views of the treating doctors, the Court overruled P's views and applying the best interests test permitted the doctor to provide life-sustaining treatment to P. (But see **9.13** under 'Advance decision'.)

At common law, cases involving organ and bone marrow donation require the sanction of the Court. For an example of a case where the Court approved bone marrow donation see *Re Y (Mental Patient: Bone Marrow)*.[38]

---

35   [1998] 1 FLR 384.
36   [1996] 2 FLR 99, at 109.
37   [2004] EWCA Civ 1324.
38   [1997] Fam 110.

9.8   NON-THERAPEUTIC STERILISATION

Non-therapeutic sterilisation cases are classified as 'serious medical treatment' and require a determination by the Court.[39] This reflects the common law position: see *GF (Medical Treatment)*[40] where the Court ruled that no declaration was needed regarding the lawful performance of a hysterectomy, which had the incidental effect of sterilisation on a woman, who lacked capacity and was severely disabled, and who suffered from excessively heavy periods which she was unable to deal with. Two medical practitioners were satisfied that the operation was necessary for therapeutic purposes; was in the best interests of P and there was no other less intrusive means of treating the condition. However, this decision turned on its facts and in a later case of *Re S (Sterilisation)*[41] it was said that the test set in *Re GF* (above) for bringing applications in sterilisation cases was expressed in broad terms and that if a particular case lay anywhere near the boundary line it should be referred to the Court. Sterilisation as a contraceptive procedure in the absence of gynecological pathology would in general not be justified. Consideration should also be given to whether or not other non-invasive or least invasive medical or surgical treatment was available which would resolve the problem. The possibility of pregnancy and its effect on P may also be relevant in assessing the best interests of the incapacitated person. In *Re S* on appeal the declaration that it was lawful to carry out the hysterectomy was overruled on the facts of the case.

The principle set out under common law has been followed in a similar case under the Act. In *A Local Authority v K & Others*[42] K suffered from Down's syndrome and learning difficulties. Her parents were concerned about the risks of her becoming pregnant. They considered that it was in her best interests to undergo sterilisation and threatened to have the procedure carried out outside the jurisdiction. An expert instructed by the local authority and the Official Solicitor concluded that it would not be in K's best interests to take contraception or to undergo sterilisation as a less restrictive option was available. Although at the date of the hearing the parents were no longer supporting sterilisation, the Court nevertheless ruled on the issue as it was possible that the issue could be raised in the future. In evaluating capacity in circumstances concerning sterilisation and contraceptive treatment, Cobb J applied the test formulated by Bodey J in *A Local Authority v Mrs A*.[43] The test for capacity to be applied to ascertain a woman's ability to understand and weigh up the immediate medical issues surrounding contraceptive treatment includes consideration of:

(a) the reason for contraception and what it does (which includes the likelihood of pregnancy if it is not in use during sexual intercourse);

(b) the types available and how each is used;

---

[39] PD 9E, para 5(c).
[40] [1992] 1 FLR 293.
[41] [2000] 2 FLR 389.
[42] [2013] EWHC 242 (COP).
[43] [2010] EWHC 1549 (COP), [2010] COPLR Con Vol 138, at para 64.

(c) the advantages and disadvantages of each type;

(d) the possible side-effects of each and how they can be dealt with;

(e) how easily each type can be changed; and

(f) the generally accepted effectiveness of each.

In reaching his decision Cobb J applied the test in s 1(6) that any decision made or endorsed by the Court should be the least restrictive of K's rights and freedom of action; the s 4 test of best interests and took into consideration the parents' wishes and feelings, medical evidence including the risks and complications of the procedure and the evidence of the social worker. He concluded that:

> 'sterilisation would be a disproportionate (and not the least restrictive) step to achieve contraception for K in the future (absent significant change in her circumstances). Plainly risk management is better than invasive treatment, it is less restrictive. Moreover, I am persuaded by Dr. Rowlands that there are less restrictive methods of achieving the purpose of contraception than sterilisation, and that in the event of a need for contraception, these ought to be attempted.

> It is in K's interests that I should make this declaration now; I do not believe that it is in K's interests that this issue should be left unresolved; plainly it may need to be litigated at some point in the future but only if there has been a significant change in circumstances.'

In relation to male sterilisation in *Re A (Male Sterilisation)*,[44] sterilisation of a man and that in respect of a woman was distinguished. It was suggested that when considering the issue the 'judge at first instance should draw up a balance sheet of factors of actual benefit and counter-balancing dis-benefits. Only if the account was in relatively significant credit should the judge conclude that the application was likely to advance the best interests of the claimant' (Thorpe LJ).

Of relevance is also the application of the best interests test. This will involve consideration of whether vasectomy will result in improving the quality of P's life and or lead to lessened supervision. It will now also involve consideration of P's Art 8 rights and those under the Art 23 of the United Nations Convention on the Rights of Persons with Disabilities (UNCRPD). In *Re A* (above) the application was refused on the facts. In *A NHS Trust v DE*,[45] which is the first case under the Act and the only one in which the Court has authorised sterilisation of a male, the Court pointed out that the decision in each case was very much restricted to its facts. Eleanor King stated:[46]

> 'In my judgment it is overwhelmingly in DE's best interests to have a vasectomy. That being said the court does not make such an order lightly, conscious as it is that for the court to make an order permitting the lifelong removal of a person's fertility for non--medical reasons requires strong justification.'

---

[44] [2000] 1 FLR 549.

[45] [2013] EWHC 2562 (Fam), [2013] COPLR 531.

[46] At para 93.

and:[47]

> 'Every assessment of the best interests of a person under the Mental Capacity Act 2005 is by its very nature fact specific. I have reached the conclusion that a vasectomy is undoubtedly in DE's best interests after having heard all the evidence and having taken into account all the circumstances before conducting the balancing exercise commended by Lord Justice Thorpe. In doing so I have been astute at all times to keep to the forefront of my mind that the consequences of the proposed procedure for DE (ignoring the possibility of reversal), are to sterilise him and render him permanently infertile. The fact that the procedure to achieve this is routine, commonplace and safe should not ever be allowed to mask or minimise that bald fact when a court is considering such an application.'

The factors which the judge took into account when undertaking the balance sheet approach advocated by Thorpe LJ (see above) in this case were (i) the private life of DE and his wishes to continue his relationship with his girlfriend, who had already borne him a child; not to have any more children and his wish to remain with his parents; (ii) his relationship with his parents on whom he was wholly dependent for emotional and physical support and the impact on them and consequently on DE of a second pregnancy; (iii) DE's independence and the need to preserve this. On the downside were consideration of the effect on DE of surgical intervention and procedure which included:

> '(a) The slender risk of DE suffering from long term scrotal pain and or discomfort, a risk further reduced by the fact that it is intended that the procedure would be carried out by a consultant urologist with a consultant anaesthetist. DE has tolerated local anaesthesia in the past and there is no reason to believe that he will not do so again. One or other of his parents will be with him throughout.
>
> (b) The procedure is non therapeutic.
>
> (c) The procedure does not protect against the transmission of STIs or STDs.'

The issue which was raised but not determined is whether a man needs to understand information about female contraceptive options in order to have capacity to make a decision about contraception. This involves whether it is necessary for P to understand only the options for him of condoms and vasectomy; or to understand all the possible options for him and for any female partner which includes understanding of the contraceptive pill, IUDs, the contraceptive injection and sterilisation; and to understand the male options and the female option which are available but which his partner is reluctant or decided not to use. It is thus clear that the case of DE was very much related to its own particular facts and should not be taken as giving a 'green light' for vasectomy to be approved as a matter of course.

---

[47] At para 98.

9.8.1   Guidance on practice and procedure

As there appears to have been some confusion on the part of the doctor and the local authority of the need to refer non-therapeutic sterilisation cases to the Court Cobb J gave guidance on the practice and procedure that should be followed in such cases as follows:

> 'Referral to the Court of Protection in a case such as this could and should always be considered at the earliest moment in accordance with the Rules (see in particular Practice Direction 9E to the Court of Protection Rules 2007, and Para.6.18 and Paras.8.18-8.29 of the Mental Capacity Act 2005 Code of Practice). I take this opportunity to remind medical (and, where relevant, legal) practitioners of the Court of Protection's role in considering a question of non-therapeutic sterilisation. Such a treatment decision is so serious that the Court has to make it. In particular I advise that particular note is made of the process as follows:
>
> (a)   The decision of whether someone who lacks capacity to consent should have a non-therapeutic sterilisation is a question involving "serious medical treatment" (see Practice Direction E (PD9E) – Applications relating to serious medical treatment). Non-therapeutic sterilisation is specifically identified in this category (see Paragraph 5(c));
>
> (b)   A question concerning non-therapeutic sterilisation of a person who lacks capacity to give consent "should be brought to the court" (Para.5 ibid.);
>
> (c)   Where a question arises as to non-therapeutic sterilisation of a person who lacks capacity to consent, the proposed applicant (whether it be carer, local authority or trust), can (indeed I suggest should) usefully discuss the application with the Official Solicitor's department before the application is made (see PD9E para.8): such cases should be addressed to a family and medical litigation lawyer at the Office of the Official Solicitor;
>
> (d)   The organisation which is, or will be, responsible for providing clinical or caring services to P should usually be named as a respondent in the application form (where it is not already the applicant in the proceedings);
>
> (e)   Proceedings of this kind must be conducted by a judge of the Court of Protection who has been nominated as such by virtue of section 46(2)(a) to (c) of the Act (i.e. the President of the Family Division, the Chancellor or a puisne judge of the High Court) (Para.12 PD9E);
>
> (f)   At the first hearing of the application the Court will consider:
>
> > (i)   whether P should be joined as party to the proceedings, and give directions to that effect;
> >
> > (ii)   if P is to be joined as a party to the proceedings, decide whether the Official Solicitor should be invited to act as a litigation friend or whether some other person should be appointed as a litigation friend;
> >
> > (iii)   identify anyone else who has been notified of the proceedings and who has filed an acknowledgment and applied to be joined as a party to proceedings, and consider that application; and
> >
> > (iv)   set a timetable for the proceedings including, where possible, a date for the final hearing;
>
> (g)   Note that the hearing will generally be in public, given the nature of the application, although the Court will ordinarily make an order pursuant to Rule 92 that restrictions be imposed in relation to publication of information about the proceedings.

Where a declaration is needed, the order sought should be in the following or similar terms:

(a) That P lacks capacity to make a decision in relation to the [proposed medical treatment or procedure]. e.g. "That P lacks capacity to make a decision in relation to sterilisation by [named procedure]"; and

(b) That, having regard to the best interests of P, it is lawful for the [proposed medical treatment or procedure] to be carried out by [proposed healthcare provider]; or

(c) That it is not in the best interests of P to undergo [the proposed medical treatment or procedure].'

9.9 OTHER CASES WHERE THE CASE SHOULD BE TREATED AS REQUIRING SERIOUS MEDICAL TREATMENT

Practice Direction 9E lists five specific examples but with the proviso that the list is not an exhaustive one and that there may be other procedures or treatment which can be regarded as serious medical treatment depending on the circumstances and the consequences for P. The general principle established at common law in *D v An NHS Trust (Medical Treatment: Consent)*[48] namely:

'In cases of controversy and cases involving momentous and irrevocable decisions, the courts have treated as justiciable any genuine question as to what the best interests of a patient require or justify ...'

remains the position under the Act. It will be up to the decision maker to decide, having had regard to all the circumstances of the individual case, whether to rely on the protection afforded by s 5 of the Act or to take the safer option of seeking a declaration from the Court particularly where the case is one which may be regarded as borderline.

9.10 TERMINATION OF PREGNANCY

Where termination is carried out in accordance with the requirements of the Abortion Act 1967 and where the issues of capacity and best interests are clear and beyond doubt, an application is generally not necessary. If there is any doubt about capacity or best interests an application should be made. Where, it is a borderline case it should be referred to the Court in good time in particular where:[49]

'(i) there is a dispute as to capacity, or where there is a realistic prospect that P will regain capacity, following a response to treatment, within the period of her pregnancy or shortly thereafter;

(ii) where there is a lack of unanimity amongst the medical professionals as to the best interests of P;

---

[48] [2004] 1 FLR 1110.

[49] *D v NHS Trust (Medical Treatment: Consent: Termination)* [2004] 1 FLR 1110, per Coleridge J.

(iii)   where the procedures under s 1 of the Abortion Act 1967 have not been followed (ie where two medical practitioners have not provided a certificate);

(iv)   where P, members of her immediate family, or the foetus' father have opposed, or expressed views inconsistent with, a termination of the pregnancy; or

(v)   where there are exceptional circumstances (including where the termination may be the last chance to bear a child).'

In *Re SS (Medical Treatment: Late Termination)*[50] a woman who had a history of schizophrenia, psychosis and who was detained under s 3 of the Mental Health Act 1983, applied for a declaration that it was in her best interest to have a termination of her pregnancy at 24 weeks. On assessing the competing risks the Court dismissed her application on the ground that the continuation of the pregnancy carried a lesser detriment to the applicant and thus concluded that termination of the pregnancy was not in the applicant's interests. The Court observed that the delay in seeking a declaration in this case was unacceptable and suggested that each hospital should have a protocol to deal with possible termination of pregnancies of psychiatric Ps in good time, so that termination could be carried out at the earliest opportunity, and that the protocol should ensure P was referred to independent legal advice at an early stage.

Cases of termination may raise issues of whether or not P has the capacity to decide to terminate her pregnancy. In such cases it would assist the Court where possible to hear from P herself in order to make an informed decision as to her capacity. The UNCRPD Art 13 imposes a duty on States to ensure effective access to justice for persons with disabilities on an equal basis with others in order to facilitate their effective role as direct and indirect participants including as witnesses in all legal proceedings including at investigative and other preliminary stages. Recommendation No R (99) of the Committee of Ministers of the Council of Europe on principles concerning the legal protection of incapable adults provides that P should have the right to be heard in person in any proceedings which could affect his or her legal capacity (Principle 13). The COP Rules 2007, r 88 makes provision for P to participate in proceedings. Case law also confirms the need for P to be heard. In *X and Y v Croatia*[51] the ECtHR whilst accepting that domestic courts enjoy a margin of appreciation in cases involving a mentally ill person these measures do not affect the applicant's right to a fair hearing as guaranteed in Art 6 of the ECHR (for an example where P gave oral evidence see Re *SB*.[52] (See also Re *KK*[53].)

---

[50]   [2002] 1 FLR 445.
[51]   [2011] Application No 5193/09, judgment of 11 November 2011, ECtHR.
[52]   [2013] EWHC 1417 (COP).
[53]   [2012] EWHC 2136 (COP).

9.11   USE OF REASONABLE FORCE

In *Tameside and Glossop Acute Services Trust v CH*[54] Wall J left open the question whether the Court had power in common law to authorise the use of force on P. In *Norfolk and Norwich Healthcare Trust v W*,[55] *Rochdale Healthcare (NHS) Trust v C*[56] and *Re C (Detention: Medical Treatment)*,[57] the Court held that it had jurisdiction at common law to grant a declaration that it would be lawful for reasonable force to be used in the course of treatment. In *Re MB* (above), the Court of Appeal, although confirming that, where a P is found to be incompetent to refuse treatment, it may become necessary to use force to give the necessary treatment, and stating that the extent of the force or compulsion which may become necessary will depend on the circumstances of each individual case and can be judged only by the professionals treating P, did not lay down any guidelines. The Court left the question open.

The Act, in ss 5 and 6, sets out the circumstances when restraint and use of force may be permitted where it is necessary to carry out the act in order to prevent harm to P, provided the act is a proportionate response to the likelihood of P's suffering harm and the seriousness of that harm (see further chapter 10). In such cases, it may become necessary for those treating P to carry out a balancing exercise between continuing treatment forcibly and deciding not to continue with it. It is submitted that in all cases where the doctor is doubtful about the use of force or the extent of force to be used, an application should be made to the Court for a declaration.

In any case where treatment may require the use of force, an application should be made to the Court for authorisation to do so before the urgency arises as these cases are bound to raise ethical and legal issues and infringement of P's human rights especially those concerned with Art 5 rights of deprivation of liberty. Cases where this is more likely to arise are those where P is suffering from severe anorexia nervosa and forcible feeding or medical treatment has to be considered where P does not qualify for treatment under the Mental Health Act. If the matter is dealt with under the MCA the issue of whether the action proposed would also amount to deprivation of liberty would need to be considered. Two recent COP cases have resulted in two different outcomes. *Local Authority v E & Others*[58] concerned a 32-year-old intelligent woman who suffered from emotionally unstable borderline personality disorder, alcohol and opiate dependency. She had been compulsorily detained under the Mental Health Act 1983 on numerous occasions and had expressed a wish to end her life. The medical team had concluded that it was in E's interest to die in comfort. Proceedings were commenced and one of the issues before the Court was whether if her advance decision was not valid it was in her best interests to force feed her. The Court had to decide on two options; on the one hand to

---

[54]   [1996] 1 FLR 762.
[55]   [1996] 2 FLR 613.
[56]   [1997] 1 FCR 274.
[57]   [1997] 2 FLR 180.
[58]   [2012] EWHC 1639 (COP).

respect her autonomy and freedom and for palliative care to be given and allow her to die or on the other hand to allow her to be transferred to be stabilised and fed through a nasogastric tube or PEG tube inserted through her stomach wall with any resistance on her part being dealt with by physical restraint or sedation- a process which would continue on a regular basis for a year or more. In concluding that it was in her best interests to be force-fed Jackson J undertook the 'balance sheet' approach and took into account the risks involved; E's wishes and feelings beliefs and values; the wishes of her parents evidence of the consultant gastroenterologist and psychiatrist and considerations of her rights under the ECHR.

However, in *NHS Trust v L and the Psychiatric NHS Trust & Others*[59] where the application was for a declaration that it was not in the best interests of L to be the subject of forcible feeding or medical treatment notwithstanding the fact that this would result in her death. She was critically ill and there had already been a decision made that she should not be resuscitated (DNR-CPR) Her condition further deteriorated. The medical opinion was that in order to force feed her it would be necessary to sedate her and her medical condition was such that the likelihood of death if force feeding were to be attempted on a chemically sedated basis would run at close to 100%. In the unlikely event of her surviving she would suffer severe physical and psychological consequences. Sedation or restraint for the purposes of forced feeding would be disproportionate and would worsen her long term physical and psychological condition. Having determined that L lacked capacity the Court applied the s 4 criteria and her rights under the ECHR, particularly the right to life in assessing her best interests and concluded that it was not in L's best interest to provide her with nutrition and hydration with which she was non-compliant and which could not be delivered without her co-operation and /or without the use of physical force (see under precedent for the full order made in this case). L's case was an extreme case of anorexia nervosa which justified the decision taken to withdraw life-sustaining treatment. Having considered all the evidence King J stated:[60]

> 'In my judgment this one of those few cases where the only possible treatment, namely force feeding under sedation, is not to be countenanced in Ms L's best interests: to do so would be futile, carrying with it a near certainty that it would cause her death in any event. Such a course would be overly burdensome in that every calorie that enters her body is an enemy to Ms L.
>
> Ms L would I am satisfied be appallingly distressed and resistant to any suggestion that she was to be force fed and to what purpose? Her poor body is closing down, organ failure has begun, she can no longer resist infection and she is, at all times in imminent danger of cardiac arrest. When if she could, by some miracle, agree to some miniscule increase in her nutrient intake her organ failure is nevertheless reversible and her anorexia so sever and deep rooted that there could be no real possibility of her maintaining her co-operation. Ms L on some occasion shows

---

some small spark of insight- she said on the 1st August that she was frightened as she cannot help herself from 'messing with the tube.'

Where a patient is non compliant with a medical or surgical procedure the issue sometimes arises whether sedation should be used to make the patient more compliant and whether physical restraint should be used so that the patient can be sedated in order to facilitate the treatment or the operation. These situations obviously raise ethical issues and the legality of administering the sedation. In *DH NHS Foundation Trust v PS*[61] where the patient although agreeable to the surgical procedure suffered from a needle phobia which prevented the operation proceeding, the Court approved a plan which included provision of covert sedation mixed with a soft drink to enable her to be anaesthatised. In *An NHS Trust v K & Others*[62] where the Official Solicitor acting on behalf of K was against the proposal that K should undergo an operation for treatment of cancer because of the considerable risk that she could die during the operation or in the post-operative recovery period and K had been resistant to the operation prior to anaesthesia, the Court on balance ruled that the operation should go ahead but that as it could be very risky to apply physical restraint she should be sedated before being told of the operation in the hope that she might thereby be compliant to it. Holman J declared that it was in K's overall best interests to have the operation and it can be lawful and in her best interests to sedate her to enable it to take place and lawful to do so before she is told. However, he ruled that she should be told after sedation but before anaesthesia, what is planned under the supervision of a qualified anaesthethist. In both cases the Court first determined the issue whether it was in the best interests of P to undergo the medical procedure and then went about deciding how best to achieve it without having to use physical restraint.

9.12 EXPERIMENTAL MEDICAL TREATMENT

Under the MCA 2005 experimental or innovative treatment for the benefit of a person who lacks capacity must be referred to the Court for approval, as has been the case under common law. In *JS v An NHS Trust; JA v An NHS Trust*,[63] two teenagers were at the advanced stages of variant Creutzfeldt-Jakob disease (vCJD). Both had sustained severe brain damage, were confined to their beds with a severely limited enjoyment of life and a limited extent of expressing their feelings. The Court was asked to declare that both Ps had no capacity to consent to treatment and that it would be lawful to subject them to a new experimental treatment, which had not been tested on humans, involving intraventricular administration of a drug. It was known that the treatment would only provide a slight chance of resulting in some benefit to Ps and the very best that could be hoped for was the possibility of slight neurological improvement in their condition, the temporary arresting of the disease's progress, or the prolongation of life but with risks involved to both Ps. The Court held that both Ps lacked capacity to give consent to the treatment; that

[61] [2010] EWHC 1217 (Fam).
[62] [2012] EWHC 2922 (COP).
[63] [2002] EWHC 2734 (Fam), [2003] 1 FLR 879.

where there was a responsible body of relevant professional opinion which supported the innovative treatment, subject to the seriousness of the risks involved and the degree of benefit that might be achieved, the test in *Bolam v Friern Hospital Management Committee*[64] (the 'Bolam test') ought not to be allowed to inhibit medical progress and innovative work. Where there was no alternative treatment available and the disease was progressive and fatal, it was reasonable to consider experimental treatment with unknown risks but risks that did not seem to fall outside the bounds of responsible surgical and medical treatment so as to be unacceptable and without significant risk of increased suffering to P, but where there was a chance of benefit to P by way of some improvement in the present state of the illness. A P who was unable to consent to pioneering treatment ought not to be deprived of a chance in circumstances where he would have been likely to consent if he had been competent.

On the facts, the Court held that it was in the best interest of both Ps for the treatment to be carried out as both had lives worth preserving and any treatment that might be beneficial would be of value to them; that a reduced enjoyment of life even at quite a low level was to be respected and protected and even the prospect of a slightly longer life was a benefit worth having for these Ps. See also *Simms v Simms; A v A (A Child)*.[65]

The Court will also protect P's privacy in such cases by granting an injunction. The terms of the injunction order granted in the above case are reproduced below as a guide to practitioners:

'IT IS ORDERED THAT:
1   No written or photographic material shall be published or broadcast in any form whatsoever to any person whether in writing or electronically which might lead directly or indirectly to any of the following being identified as being connected with these proceedings –
    (a)   ... JA (being a person suffering from variant Creutzfeldt-Jakob disease and for whom treatment with Pentosan Polysulphate (PPS) has been proposed).
    (b)   any member of her family.
    (c)   at any time before PPS treatment for JS or JA commences, any clinician, hospital or NHS trust (including the second defendant trust) as being a clinician, hospital or NHS trust which may be involved in treating either JS or JA.
    (d)   at any time after PPS treatment for JS or JA has commenced, any clinician, hospital or NHS trust as being the clinician, hospital or NHS trust which is actually involved in treating either JS or JA.
    (e)   any clinician, hospital or NHS trust that normally has clinical responsibility for JS or JA.
2   This order shall not prevent the reporting of any information contained in a judgment given in open court or any information already in the public domain (provided that information shall not be considered to be in the public domain on the ground only that it has been published outside the jurisdiction of this court).

---

[64]   [1957] 2 All ER 118, [1957] 1 WLR 582.
[65]   [2003] Fam 83.

3   This order shall remain in effect until the death of both JS and JA has occurred.

4   Copies of this order endorsed with a penal notice may be served by the parties to the proceedings:

(a)   on such newspapers and sound or television broadcasting or cable or satellite programme services as they may think fit in each case by facsimile transmission or pre-paid first class post addressed to the editor in the case of a newspaper or senior news editor in the case of a broadcasting or cable or satellite programme service; and

(b)   on such other persons as they may think fit in each case by personal service,

And the parties and any person affected by the injunction in paragraph 1 above are to be at liberty to apply on 24 hours notice to the parties. Such application to be listed before the President of the Family Division if available.'

9.13   EMERGENCY MEDICAL TREATMENT

Under the common law in a case of an emergency, pursuant to the doctrine of necessity, where the treatment is to preserve life or P's well-being and the doctor acts in accordance with the accepted practice in consultation with other medical opinion, he may administer treatment lawfully to such a P without his/her consent.

Where there is a responsible body of opinion against a proposed treatment it would be prudent to apply to the Court for a declaration. In such cases the opposition to the proposed treatment is a relevant factor which the Court will take into account when applying the best interests of P test and the medical necessity test. It should be noted, however, that where Art 3 of the ECHR is raised, the Court will apply the standard of proof with respect to medical necessity as set out in *Herczegfalvy v Austria*.[66] It must be 'convincingly' shown that treatment is necessary rather than that the particular treatment is a medical necessity on the balance of probability.[67] In cases where it is proposed to administer innovative experimental treatment the Court will take account of whether there is any alternative treatment available and weigh-up the risks involved, the degree of benefit that might be achieved and whether the treatment carries any significant risk of increased suffering to P. Subject to the particular circumstances of each individual case, the views of the patient's family is also a relevant factor and would carry considerable weight.[68]

Where P is incompetent to give consent or there appears to be doubt about his capacity, the assistance of the Court should be obtained; see *Re T (An Adult) (Consent to Medical Treatment)* above, where Lord Donaldson MR, at 474 said:

---

[66]   (1993) EHRR 437.

[67]   *R(N) v Doctor M* [2002] EWCA Civ 1789, [2003] 1 FLR 667.

[68]   *JS v An NHS Trust; JA v An NHS Trust* [2002] EWHC 2734 (Fam), [2003] 1 FLR 879.

'In cases of doubt as to the effect of a purported refusal of treatment, where failure to treat threatens P's life or threatens irreparable damage to his health, doctors and health authorities should not hesitate to apply to the courts for assistance.'

In that case the Court declared treatment to be lawfully administered to an adult.

Similar principles apply under the Act which makes provision for an application to be made under s 15, for a declaration as to capacity and under s 48, which expressly confers powers on the Court to take steps 'pending' the determination of any question relating to capacity, and to make such orders as are expedient in the best interests of P. The court's interim jurisdiction under this section is something less than that required to justify the ultimate declaration. The 'gateway' test for the engagement of the Court's powers under s 48 is lower than that of evidence sufficient, in itself, to rebut the presumption of capacity. When determining such an application the Court in the first instance will consider whether there is evidence giving good cause for concern that the person might lack capacity in some relevant regard. Once that is raised as a serious possibility, the Court will decide what action, if any, it is in the person's best interests to take before a final determination of his or her capacity could be made. Where necessary, the Court will make such orders as may be appropriate to permit safeguarding steps to be undertaken with regard to P's health and as a matter of the emergency, depending on the individual facts of the case and the urgency of the decision in question, balanced against the person's right to autonomy and his best interests; see under 7.5 (interim order) and *Re F (Court of Protection)*.[69]

9.14   ADVANCE DECISION – SS 24–26

Under the common law in cases where P, being an adult and of sound mind, in anticipation of becoming incapable and entering into a condition such as PVS, has given clear instruction, whether orally or in writing, with full understanding of the nature and consequences of his decision that in such an event he was not to be given medical care designed to keep him alive, his wishes are respected and it would be unlawful to administer medical treatment. The principle of a competent adult's autonomy to make decisions for himself is determinative, provided that decision remains valid and unequivocal. This principle was followed in the case of *Re AK (Medical Treatment: Consent)*,[70] where a young man of 19, who had motor neurone disease and was reduced to eye movement only, had indicated clearly and independently that he no longer wished to be kept alive once his last means of communication had gone. The High Court granted the medical team, who were treating the young man, a declaration that they would not be acting unlawfully in withdrawing life support. The Court found that the man was able to see, hear, think and understand. He was capable of making an informed decision and his wishes should be respected. The

---

[69] HHJ Marshall QC, 28 May 2009.
[70] [2001] 1 FLR 129.

advance indication given by P who was of full capacity and sound of mind was effective. However, the Court held that care must be taken to ensure that such advance indications of wishes still represented the current wishes of P. Doctors will need to be satisfied that the patient is of full capacity to give consent and to examine carefully and critically the issue of consent, particularly where communication is difficult.

Where P's wish is clear, the continuation of invasive treatment without the consent of an adult P of sound mind will be unlawful. Where the directive is contained in a 'living will' the same principle applies.

In *Re B (Consent to Treatment: Capacity)*[71] the patient had made a living will in which she had indicated that if she were unable to give instructions she wished for treatment to be withdrawn if she was suffering from a life threatening condition, permanent mental impairment or if she became unconscious. The intensive care team treated her with a ventilator and she underwent surgery. P then asked for the ventilator to be switched off which was declined. Her application for a declaration that she had the mental capacity whether to accept or reject treatment and that the doctors had treated her unlawfully was granted.[72] In the absence of any such expressed intention or views, where the person is totally unconscious, it is the duty of doctors to apply the 'best interest' test, and administer such treatment as in their informed opinion is in P's best interests bearing in mind that although the principle of the sanctity of human life forbids the taking of positive steps to cut short the life of the terminally ill P, it is not an absolute principle and does not forbid the discontinuance of treatment which serves merely to keep alive a P who is terminally ill and to prolong his suffering. In such cases, the wishes of P's immediate family should also be given due weight. The best interest test is broad and flexible and allows room for the exercise of judgment by the doctors as to whether the relevant conditions exist which justify the discontinuance of life support. Before life–sustaining treatment is withheld/withdrawn application must be made to the court for a declaration that the denial in the circumstances is lawful and for direction on palliative care.

This principle is now embodied in ss 24–26 of the Act with additional safeguards. The statutory provisions specifically address the issue of validity and when the decision may not be applicable. It also specifically imposes conditions in relation to advance decisions relating to life-sustaining treatment.

An advance consent will apply only if:

*   the person has reached the age of 18 years;
*   had capacity when he made the decision;

---

[71] [2002] 1 FLR 1090.
[72] See also *HE v A Hospital NHS Trust* [2003] 2 FLR 408.

- the decision is that if, at a later date and in such circumstances as he may specify, a specified treatment is proposed to be carried out or continued by the health care provider and at that time he lacks capacity to consent to that treatment;
- the specified treatment is not to be carried out or continued;
- the advance directive has not been withdrawn by any means at any time when the person had capacity to do so.

The Act does not require that the advance decision should be made in any formal document. It may be expressed in 'layman's terms', but it is desirable to follow the guidance set out in the Code of Practice at paras 9.10–9.37 relating to what should be included in an advance decision and since s 25 of the Act makes a distinction between the requirements of an advance decision for life-sustaining treatments and those that are not (see below **9.14.2**), particular care should be taken to follow the guidance in relation to refusal of life-sustaining treatment set out in para 9.24.[73] The Code of Practice, para 9.19 sets out the information that should be included in a written advance decision. This includes the following:

- full details of the maker of the advance decision including the date of birth, home address and any distinguishing features (in case healthcare professionals need to identify an unconscious person, for example);
- the name and address of the person's GP and whether they have a copy of the document;
- a statement that the document should be used if the person ever lacks capacity to make treatment decisions;
- a clear statement of the decision, the treatment to be refused and the circumstances in which the decision will apply;
- the date the document was written (or reviewed);
- the person's signature (or the signature of someone the person has asked to sign on their behalf and in their presence);
- the signature of the person witnessing the signature, if there is one (or a statement directing somebody to sign on the person's behalf).

Although the signature of the maker of the advance decision is not essential, except where it relates to an advance decision to refuse life-sustaining treatment, if there is a witness it is advised that a description of the relationship between the witness and the person making the advance decision is given. In the case where the witness is a professional, who has assessed the person's capacity, the professional witness should also make a record of the assessment. In the case of a non professional witness the witness's role is not to certify the person's capacity and his/her signature does not prove that there has been an assessment of the maker of the advance decision.

---

[73] MCA 2005, s 24(1).

In the case of a verbal advance decision the Code of Practice, para 9.23 advises healthcare professionals to make a record of the decision to refuse treatment in the person's healthcare record and to ensure that the record includes:

- a note that the decision should apply if the person lacks capacity to make treatment decisions in future;

- a clear note of the decision, the treatment to be refused and the circumstances in which the decision will apply;

- details of someone who was present when the oral advance decision was recorded and the role in which they were present (for example, healthcare professional or family member); and

- whether they heard the decision, took part in it or are just aware that it exists.

9.14.1 Validity of the decision

An advance decision will not be valid if P has:

- withdrawn the decision at any time when he had capacity to do so;

- under a lasting power of attorney created after the advance decision was made, conferred authority on the donee (or if more than one, any of them) to give or refuse consent to the treatment to which the advance decision relates; or

- done anything else clearly inconsistent with the advance decision remaining his fixed decision.[74]

An advance decision will not be applicable to the treatment in question if at the material time the person has capacity to give or refuse consent. It will thus only come into operation if and when the person lacks capacity to make the relevant decision. An advance decision is also not applicable to the treatment in question if:

- that treatment is not the treatment specified in the advance decision;

- any circumstances specified in the advance treatment are absent; or

- there are reasonable grounds for believing that circumstances exist which the person did not anticipate at the time of the advance decision and which would have affected his decision had he anticipated them.

9.14.2 Conditions which must be satisfied for an effective advance decision relating to life-sustaining treatment

To be valid advance decision to refuse life-sustaining treatment must:

- be in writing;

---

[74] MCA 2005, s 25.

- be signed by P (or under his direction and in his presence by another) and the signature must be made or acknowledged by P in the presence of a witness who must sign or acknowledge his signature in the presence of P.[75]

A personal welfare lasting power of attorney which authorises health care decisions cannot override a subsequent advance decision refusing treatment and does not prevent it from being regarded as valid and applicable.[76]

The need to ensure that the advance decision conforms with the above requirements and the difficulties that may result if they are not is best illustrated in *The X Primary Care Trust v XB and YB*[77] where XB who suffered from Motor Neurone Disease, had used a pro forma advance decision downloaded from the internet in which he had stated that he would wish to have life sustaining withdrawn in the event where he was unable to communicate his needs or have control over decisions as to his care and management. The document set out a date for review of 2 May 2012 and the date had also been entered in the box marked 'valid until'. In the light of concerns raised by one of his carers as to the circumstances in which the advance decision was made and the limitation of time set out in the document the PCT brought proceedings for a declaration on the validity of the advance decision and whether it was time limited. On the evidence the court was satisfied that XB lacked capacity to communicate and that his capacity was permanent and the event on which the advance decision was to take effect was met. The Court was also satisfied that the advance decision was validly made and was valid. In relation to the time limits which appeared on the document the judge was satisfied on the evidence that the time limit had not been discussed with or consented to by XB and therefore was inapplicable. In view of the issues raised in the case Theis J made the following three observations:

- In the event that there is an issue raised about an advance decision, it is important it is investigated by the relevant health authorities or relevant bodies as a matter of urgency. This will clarify issues at an early stage. It will enable relevant primary evidence to be gathered (for example, by taking statements) and, if required, an application made to this court. The judges who sit in the Court of Protection are experienced in dealing with urgent applications, as this case has demonstrated.

- There is no set form for advance decisions, because the contents will inevitably vary, depending on the person's wishes and situation. The Mental Capacity Code includes guidance on what should be included in an advanced decision at paras 9.10–9.23

- There are number of pro forma advance decisions available on the internet. One of the difficulties in this case was the inclusion in the pro forma of a 'valid until' date. Those organisations that have such terms in their pro formas may want to look again at the necessity for that being in the pro forma form. It is clearly in the interests of the person who has

---

[75]   MCA 2005, s 25(6).
[76]   MCA 2005, s 25(7).
[77]   [2012] EWHC 1390 (Fam).

made the advance decision, his or her family, and those who have responsibility for providing or withholding treatment that there is clarity in relation to what the terms of the advance decision are.

The difficulties and distress which can be caused when advance decisions fail to comply with the statutory requirements of the Act were highlighted in *An NHS Trust v D*[78] where unaware of the provisions relating to advance decisions to refuse life–sustaining treatment D had made his advance decision in a signed letter 'to whom it may concern' but had not had it witnessed. The result was that when he was in a PVS the medical team was not able to act on it for some 9 months until an application was made to the court for a declaration.

In such an event P's wishes are not totally disregarded as the court under s 4(6) is required to consider as far as is reasonably ascertainable P's past and present wishes and in particular any relevant written statement made by him when he had capacity; his beliefs and values. In such cases the court can only consider this in the balance with other factors. The conclusion the court will reach will depend on the circumstances of the individual case. In *W v M* (above) Baker J considered the wishes expressed by P with other factors in the balance sheet and did not permit the treatment to be withdrawn whereas in *An NHS Trust v D* although the conclusion was inevitable given D's condition the judge stated that 'had there been anything to put in the balance against the other evidence, D's wishes would have carried great weight' as he was 'a very private man before his incapacity, who would have been horrified at the prospect of being kept alive in this condition with the total loss of privacy that his dependency entails' (para 17).

9.14.3   Effect of an advance decision

A valid and applicable advance decision has effect as if the person had capacity to make it at the time when the question arises whether the treatment should be carried out or continued.[79]

The person treating the person concerned will not incur any liability:

(a)   for providing the treatment or continuing the treatment, unless at the material time he is satisfied that an advance decision exists which is valid and applicable; or

(b)   for the consequences of withholding or withdrawing treatment from the P concerned if, at the time, he reasonably believes that an advance decision exists which is valid and applicable to the treatment.

If there is any doubt in relation to the existence of or the validity or applicability of an advance consent, or the capacity of the maker when he/she made the advance decision, an application should be made to the Court for a declaration. The Act, in s 26(5), provides that whilst a decision in respect of any

---

[78]   [2012] EWHC 885 (COP).
[79]   MCA 2005, s 25(1).

relevant issue is sought the treatment provider is not prevented from providing life-sustaining treatment or doing any act he reasonably believes to be necessary to prevent a serious deterioration in that person's condition.[80]

9.15   INDEPENDENT MENTAL CAPACITY ADVOCATES – SS 35–37

9.15.1   The purpose of the IMCA

The provision of an independent mental capacity advocate (IMCA) is a creation of the Act. The need to provide the service was identified by the Joint Parliamentary Committee because it considered that an independent advocacy service plays:

> 'an essential role in assisting people with capacity problems to make and communicate decisions; helping them to enforce their rights and guard against unwarranted intrusion into their lives; providing a focus on the views and wishes of an incapacitated person in the determination of their best interests; providing additional safeguards against abuse and exploitation; and assisting in the resolution of disputes.'

The Act, in s 35, carries this through by imposing a duty on the Secretary of State for Health in England (and the Welsh Assembly in Wales) to make such arrangements as it considers reasonable to enable independent mental capacity advocates to be available to represent and support persons to whom acts or decisions specified in ss 37–39 of the Act apply. It ensures that the objective of this provision is met by identifying in s 35(4) that in making the arrangements for an IMCA the Secretary of State:

> 'must have regard to the principle that a person to whom a proposed act or decision relates should, as far as practicable, be represented and supported by a person who is independent of any person who will be responsible for the act or decision.'

When serious medical treatment is provided or proposed by an NHS body, it imposes a duty on the NHS body to instruct an IMCA to represent P, before it provides or secures the provision of serious medical treatment as defined in s 37(6) of the Act (see **5.1** above) for a P who lacks capacity to consent to treatment if it is satisfied that there is no person other than one engaged in providing care or treatment for P in a professional capacity or for remuneration, whom it would be appropriate to consult in determining what would be in P's best interests.[81] The only exception to this duty is where there is:

(a)   a person nominated by P (in whatever manner) as a person to be consulted on matters to which that duty relates;

---

[80]   MCA 2005, s 26(5).
[81]   MCA 2005, s 37(1).

(b)   a donee of a lasting power of attorney created by P who is authorised to make decisions in relation to those matters; or

(c)   a deputy appointed by the Court for P with power to make decisions in relation to those matters;[82] and

(d)   where the treatment needs to be provided as a matter of urgency. It does not apply to treatment under the Mental Health Act 1983.[83] Where emergency serious medical treatment is required it is more than likely that an application will be made to the Court and the Court will invite the Official Solicitor to act for P who lacks capacity.

Note however that a person appointed under Part 10 of Sch A1 to be P's representative is not by virtue of that appointment, a person nominated by P to be consulted in matters relating to this duty.[84]

Section 37(5) imposes a further duty on the NHS body in providing or securing the provision of treatment for P to take into account any information given, or submissions made by the IMCA.

9.15.2   Definition of clauses referred to above

The Mental Capacity Act 2005 (Independent Mental Capacity Advocates) (General) Regulations 2006[85] (General Regulations) make the necessary provisions which inter alia relate to the provision of serious medical treatment stipulated in the Act and define the terms 'serious medical treatment' and 'NHS body' for this purpose. They also contain provisions as to who can be appointed to act as an IMCA and the IMCA's function when he has been instructed to represent a person who lacks capacity.

The General Regulations 2006 define 'serious medical treatment' for the purposes of s 37 as:

'treatment which involves providing, withdrawing or withholding treatment in circumstances where:
(a)   in a case where a single treatment is being proposed, there is a fine balance between its benefits to the patient and the burdens and risks it is likely to entail for him,
(b)   in a case where there is a choice of treatments, a decision as to which one to use is finely balanced, or
(c)   what is proposed would be likely to involve serious consequences for the patient.'

It defines an NHS body to mean:

(a)   a Strategic Health Authority which is established under s 8 of the National Health Service Act 1977;

---

[82]   MCA 2005, s 40(1).
[83]   MCA 2005, s 37(4).
[84]   MCA 2005, s 40(2).
[85]   SI 2006/1832.

(b) an NHS foundation trust established under s 1 of the National Health Service and Community Care Act 1990;

(c) a Primary Care Trust established under s 16A of the National Health Service Act 1977;

(d) an NHS Trust established under s 5 of the National Health Service and Community Care Act 1990;

(e) a Care Trust designated as a Care Trust under s 45 of the Health and Social Care Act 2001.

9.15.3   Functions of the IMCA

Section 36 of the Act gives powers to make regulations on the functions of the IMCA and specifically identifies the steps the IMCA must take for the purposes of discharging those functions. The IMCA is required to take such steps as he may be required for the purpose of:

(a) providing support to the person whom he has instructed to represent (P) so that P may participate as fully as possible in any relevant decision;

(b) obtaining and evaluating relevant information;

(c) ascertaining what P's wishes and feelings would be likely to be, and the beliefs and values that would be likely to influence P if he had capacity;

(d) ascertaining what alternative courses of action are available in relation to P;

(e) obtaining a further medical opinion where treatment is proposed and the advocate thinks that one should be obtained;

(f) the advocate may challenge or provide assistance for the purpose of challenging any relevant decision.

The General Regulations provide that the IMCA must determine in all the circumstances how best to represent and support P and in particular the IMCA must:

(a) verify that the instructions were issued by an authorised person;

(b) to the extent that it is practicable and appropriate to do so, interview P and examine the records relevant to P to which the IMCA has access under s 35(6) of the Act;

(c) to the extent that it is practicable and appropriate to do so, consult persons engaged in providing care or treatment for P in a professional capacity or for remuneration, and other persons who may be in a position to comment on P's wishes, feelings, beliefs or values;

(d) take all practicable steps to obtain such other information about P or the act or decision that is proposed in relation to P, as the IMCA considers necessary;

(e) evaluate all the information he has obtained for the purpose of ascertaining the extent of the support provided to P to enable him to participate in making any decision about the matter in relation to which the IMCA has been instructed and what the patient's wishes and feeling are likely to be and the beliefs and values that would be likely to influence him/her if he/she had capacity in relation to the proposed act or decision and to consider what alternative courses of action are available and whether P is likely to benefit from a further medical opinion.

In accordance with the provisions of s 37(3) the IMCA is given the right to challenge the decision taken or proposed as if he were a person engaged in caring for P or interested in his welfare. In most cases this can be achieved by using the complaints procedure to resolve disputes but there may be circumstances where the IMCA may be obliged to apply to the Court of Protection for relief.

Regulation 5 of the General Regulations provides certain minimum requirements that a person must meet in order to be appointed as an IMCA. In order to act as an IMCA, a person must be approved by a local authority as meeting the appointment requirements, or he must be a member of a class which has been so approved. The appointment requirements are that:

- he/she must have appropriate experience/training;
- he/she be a person of integrity and good character;
- he/she must be able to act independently of anyone who instructs him to act as an IMCA.

Regulation 5(3) further provides that a criminal record certificate or enhanced criminal record certificate must be obtained.

9.16   PRACTICE AND PROCEDURE

9.16.1   Allocation

The Central Registry for the Court of Protection is now based at First Avenue House High Holborn, London. Regional Courts are located in Birmingham, Bristol, Cardiff, Manchester, Newcastle and Preston. Cases will also be heard at the RCJ. The President of the Family Division is also the President of the Court of Protection. Sir Andrew Morritt, the Chancellor of the Chancery Division has been appointed Vice-President and Denzil Lush, the former Master of the Court of Protection, is the Senior Judge. A number of High Court judges, circuit and district judges have also been nominated to hear Court of Protection cases.

The COP Rules 2007, r 86 allows a practice direction to specify the types of application which may be dealt with only by the President, the Vice-President or one of the other judges nominated by virtue of s 46(2)(a)–(c) of the Act. Practice Directions PD 9E and PD 12A make provision for the allocation of serious medical cases as follows:

(a)   An application involving the lawfulness of withholding or withdrawing artificial nutrition and hydration from a person in a permanent vegetative state, or minimally conscious state or a case involving an ethical dilemma in an untested area must be heard by the President of the Court of Protection or by a judge nominated by the President (including permission, the giving of any directions and any other hearing).[86]

(b) All other application in relation to serious medical treatment or where a declaration of compatibility pursuant to s 4 the Human Rights Act 1998 is sought (including permission, the giving of any directions, and any hearing) must be conducted by the President of the Family Division, the Chancellor or a puisne judge of the High Court.[87]

(c) Non-urgent cases: It will be for the senior judge of the Court of Protection or a judge nominated by him to determine whether the case falls within the Practice Directions or is one which may properly be dealt with by a judge of the Court other than a designated High Court judge.[88]

9.16.2 Steps to be taken pre-proceedings

Those seeking orders or declarations under the MCA 2005 must ensure that all the steps set out in ss 1–4 MCA and the relevant matters set out in the Code of Practice, particularly Chapters 4 and 5 (see above) have been undertaken. The Court of Protection Rules 2007, r 9, PD 9E specifically applies to cases of serious medical treatment (for definition, see above). Parts 8, 10, 12–16 set out the procedure which applies to all applications made to the Court of Protection under MCA 2005. Before an application is issued in relation to serious medical treatment, it is advisable to contact the Official Solicitor (family and medical lawyer) and discuss the issues. The Official Solicitor's offices are at 81, Chancery Lane, London WC2A 1DD; tel: 020 7922 7205; fax: 020 7911 7105; email: enquiries@offsol.gsi.gov.uk. The applicant must seek permission to make the application, unless exempt from doing so (see below).

9.16.3 The application form

(1) The application should be made in Form COP1. Where it relates to serious medical treatment it should be headed 'serious medical treatment' to draw the Court's attention to this fact. It should also be headed with the name of the person to whom the application relates unless an order dispensing with this requirement is obtained pursuant to r 19.

(2) It should state the issues which the Court is asked to determine and the order sought. It is good practice to lodge a draft of the order with the application. Where a declaration is required PD 9E, para 17 requires that the order sought should be in the following or similar terms:

> '(a) That P lacks capacity to make a decision in relation to the ... [*proposed medical treatment or procedure*]; or
>
> (b) That P lacks capacity to make a decision in relation to sterilisation by vasectomy, and

---

[86] PD 9E, para 11 and PD 12A, para 2.

[87] PD 9E, para 12 and PD 12A, para 3.

[88] PD 12A, para 5.

(c)   That having regard to the best interests of P, it is lawful for the ... [*proposed medical treatment or procedure*] to be carried out by ... [*the proposed healthcare provider*].'

Where the order sought is for withdrawal of life-sustaining treatment, the order should be in the following or similar terms:

'(a)   That P lacks capacity to consent to continued life-sustaining treatment measures [*specify what these are*]; and

(b)   That having regard to the best interests of P it is lawful for ... [*name of healthcare provider*] to withdraw the life-sustaining treatment from P.'[89]

It should state:

(i)   the name of the applicant and his/her address;

(ii)   the name and address of P;

(iii)   name and address of each respondent and details of his or her connection with P;

(iv)   the name and addresses of each person whom the applicant intends to notify of the application and details of his or her connection with P.

(3)   The application form must be verified by a statement of truth if it contains evidence on which the applicant seeks to rely.

(4)   The application form must be supported by evidence relied on. If that is contained in a witness statement, the statement must be verified by a statement of truth.

(5)   Part 9, r 64 requires that the following documents must be filed with the application form:

(i)   any evidence on which the applicant relies;

(ii)   copy of the order granting permission;

(iii)   an assessment of capacity form where this is required by the PD;

(iv)   any other document referred to in the application form; and

(v)   any other information and material as may be set out in a PD.

(See further PD 9A, para 12.)

If an assessment of capacity has not been completed and filed, a witness statement must be filed explaining why the assessment has not been obtained; what attempts have been made to obtain it and the basis on which it is believed that P lacks capacity to make the specific decision.

9.16.4   The applicant

The applicant will usually be the organisation which will be responsible for providing the clinical or caring services to P but it could be P (see *Re C (Refusal of Medical Treatment)*,[90] where a schizophrenic P exercised his right to invoke the High Court's inherent jurisdiction in order to obtain a ruling by way of

---

[89]   PD 9E, para 18.
[90]   [1994] 1 FLR 31.

injunction or declaration that he was capable of refusing or consenting to medical treatment) or a family member, eg a parent.

9.16.5   Permission to apply

An applicant will be required to obtain permission to start proceedings unless the applicant is:

(a)   P or if under 18, a person with parental responsibility for the patient;

(b)   a deputy for the person to whom the application relates;

(c)   a donor or donee of LPA to which the application relates;

(d)   a person named in an existing order if the application relates to the order;

(e)   the Official Solicitor or Public Guardian.

If permission is required the applicant must file the application for permission in Form COP2 and must file with it a draft of the application form (COP1) and an assessment of capacity using Form COP3. If the applicant is unable to complete an assessment of capacity form, the applicant should file a witness statement explaining the reasons for the same and why he believes that P lacks capacity.[91] There is no need for the applicant to file any of the annexes to the application form with the permission form.

Factors which the Court will take into account when dealing with an application for permission are set out in s 50(3):

(a)   the applicant's connection with the person who is the subject of the application;

(b)   the reasons for the application;

(c)   whether there is any benefit to the person to whom the application relates if the proposed order or directions were given; and

(d)   whether there are other ways of achieving the same beneficial results for the person concerned.

Within 14 days of the application for permission being filed the Court is obliged to:

(a)   grant the application in whole or part or on condition and the Court may give directions;

(b)   refuse the application or fix a date for the hearing.[92]

It is submitted that where the Court refuses the application without a hearing it should provide that if the applicant disagrees with the Court's decision he/she should apply within a specified period to have the order revoked or varied.

Where the Court fixes a hearing it will notify the applicant and others who it considers should be informed (see PD 9B for those who should be notified) and

---

[91]   PD 8A, para 7.
[92]   COP Rules 2007, Part 8, r 55.

serve a form for acknowledging the notification. Any person who is notified and who wants to take part in the proceedings must, within 21 days of notice of the application, file the acknowledgement notification. If the person served with the acknowledgment notification form does not file it with the information required in r 57(4) within 21 days he will not be permitted to take part in the proceedings.

9.16.6 Court fees

On issuing the application the applicant will be required to pay the Court fee for the application.

The Court of Protection Fees Order 2007[93] applies to applications issued in the Court of Protection. The fee payable for an application is £400 (art 4) and for a hearing £500 (art 6). Article 8 makes provision for exemptions from payment of these fees. A fee is not payable by a person who is in receipt of:

(a) income support;

(b) working tax credit, provided that:
   (i) child tax credit is being paid to the person, or to a couple (as defined in s 3(5)(A) of the Tax Credit Act 2002) which includes the person; or
   (ii) there is a disability element or severe disability element (or both) to the tax credit received by the person;

(c) income-based jobseeker's allowance under the Job Seekers Act 1995;

(d) guarantee credit under the State Pensions Credit Act 2002;

(e) council tax benefit under the Social Security Contributions and Benefits Act 1992;

(f) housing benefit; and

(g) income related employment and support allowance.

Article 9 also provides that where it appears to the Lord Chancellor that the payment of any fee prescribed by the order would, owing to the exceptional circumstances of the particular case, involve undue hardship, he may reduce or remit the fee in that case. A person earning up to £11,500 will be fee exempt. A person earning up to £13,000 will be entitled to a remission of 75% of the fee; between £13,001 and £14,500 to a remission of 50% and £14,5001 to £16,000 a remission of 25% of the fee. Form OPG506A needs to be completed in order to apply for a remission and sent to the Court with supporting documents.

9.16.7 Urgent applications

(a) Where possible, urgent applications should be issued and dealt with within court hours by attendance at the Court. In really serious medical treatment cases which are urgent it may be expedient to go directly to the Clerk of the Rules at the Royal Courts of Justice Family Division to seek an urgent

---

[93] SI 2007/1745 (L 13).

hearing before the first available nominated judge on an undertaking to issue the proceedings at the Court of Protection within a specified period (eg 24 hours or the next working day).

(b)   Cases of extreme urgency may also be dealt with by telephone at the Court during court hours on 084 5330 2900.

(c)   When it is not possible to apply during court hours, contact should be made with the security office at the RCJ on 020 7497 6000[94] without filing the application form at the Court of Protection. However, the Court will require an undertaking that the application form be issued at the Court of Protection on the next working day after the emergency hearing or as the Court directs.[95] Where a case is extremely urgent application may be made directly to the High Court without filing an application form in COP1. If an application form has already been filed and an emergency arises, the applicant should where possible file and serve an application notice in form COP9. In an exceptionally urgent case an application may be made without notice and the notice served later.[96] However, it would be prudent to give any interested party notice by telephone or by other electronic means eg text message, e-mail, fax.[97]

NB where an urgent application has been made outside court hours, if the judge dealing with the application considers that the application could have been made within court hours he/she may require the applicant or the applicant's representative to attend to provide an explanation for the delay.

Where the application is not so urgent the applicant should contact the listing officer at the Court of Protection to ensure that the case is placed before one of the district judges immediately for consideration on whether it should be transferred to the High Court.

9.16.8   Parties to the application

The applicant and the respondent/s who filed the acknowledgment notification in Form COP5 are parties. P is not a party unless the Court otherwise directs[98] but he must be notified (see further Part 7, rr 42–45). The Court however, has a discretion to hear P even if he is not a party.

9.16.9   Respondent to the application

Where, the organisation, which is to provide the treatment etc is not the applicant, it should be made a respondent.[99] Part 9, r 73 provides that unless the Court orders otherwise, P should not be named as a respondent to any

---

[94]   PD 10B, para 3.
[95]   PD 10B, para 9.
[96]   PD 10B, para 8.
[97]   PD 10B, para 8.
[98]   COP Rules 2007, Part 9, r 73(4).
[99]   PD 9E, para 9.

proceedings. However, since the rules require that P should be named, the Official Solicitor should be invited to act for him/her, or steps must be taken to ensure he/she is represented by an advocate or litigation friend.

Any other person, who the applicant reasonably believes to have an interest should be made a respondent. The court may direct a person to be joined as a party to the proceedings if it considers that it is desirable to do so for the purpose of dealing with the application.[100] Any other person who has a connection or interest in P may apply to be joined as a party to the proceedings. (See Part 9, r 75 for the procedure for such application.)

9.16.10   Persons (although not respondents) who should be notified

The applicant must attempt to identify at least three persons who are likely to have an interest in being notified. The members of P's close family will be the most likely to have an interest in him or her. PD 9B, para 7 gives a suggested list of the members of the family who are presumed to have an interest in P. Notice must be sent out to these individuals in Form COP15.[101]

9.16.11   Steps that the respondent/s need to take (PD 9C)

A person who wishes to take part in the proceedings must file an acknowledgment of service within 21 days of service of the application form. The acknowledgement of service must state whether the respondent:

(a)   consents to the order/s sought;

(b)   opposes the application and if so, set out the grounds for so doing;

(c)   seeks alternative orders and give particulars of the order/s sought;

(d)   files a statement and/or report upon which he intends to rely (but see Part 15, r 120 which restricts the filing of experts' reports unless the Court directs);

(e)   if not already a party, states whether he/she wishes to be joined as a party, giving details of the reasons and identifying his interest in the proceedings or connection with P.

9.16.12   First directions

Save in the case where the matter needs to be disposed of urgently, the Court will list the application for a directions hearing. At the hearing the Court will give such directions as it considers appropriate. PD 9E requires the Court to consider whether to give directions on any or all of the following matters at the first hearing:

(a)   decide whether P should be joined as a party to the proceedings and give directions to that effect;

---

[100]   COP Rules 2007, Part 9, r 73(2).
[101]   PD 9B, para 12.

(b)   if P is joined as a party to the proceedings, decide whether the Official Solicitor should be invited to act as a litigation friend or whether some other person should be appointed as a litigation friend;

(c)   identify anyone else who has been notified of the proceedings and who has filed an acknowledgement and applied to be joined as a party to the proceedings, and consider that application; and

(d)   set a timetable for the proceedings including where possible, a date for the final hearing.[102]

The court should also consider what if any of the direction listed in r 85(2) should be given;[103] see under **8.14.6** (Urgent Medical Treatment).

9.16.13   Form of draft order

Precedents of possible orders are set out under **9.16.3**. It is suggested that the precedents of orders in cases of PVS, CPR, use of force, reporting restrictions etc. set out in *Emergency Remedies in the Family Courts* may also be a useful guide. These orders were developed by the High Court in cases of serious medical treatment and can be adapted for use in applications before the Court of Protection.

It is also suggested that when seeking the sanction of the Court in such cases, the procedure set out in *Practice Note of 1 May 2001 (Official Solicitor: Declaratory Proceedings: Medical and Welfare Decisions for Adults who Lack Capacity)*[104] should be used as a guide in conjunction with the procedure set out in PD 9E to the Court of Protection Rules.

---

[102]   PD 9E, para 14.
[103]   PD 9E, para 15.
[104]   [2001] 2 FLR 158.

9.17 PROCEDURAL GUIDE FOR AN APPLICATION IN CASES OF SERIOUS MEDICAL TREATMENT

The applicant	Will usually be the organisation which will be providing the treatment	
Permission to apply	Required by everyone except by the person lacking capacity	MCA 2005, s 50 COP Rules 2007, Part 8
	If the person lacking capacity is under 18 anyone with parental responsibility	
	Donee of a LPA to which the application relates	
	Deputy appointed by the Court	
	A person named in an existing order	
	Official Solicitor/Public Guardian	
Applicant must file	Form **COP2** if permission is required	COP Rules 2007, Part 9
	Forms **COP1** and **COP1B** Form **COP1** should be headed '**Urgent medical treatment**'	PD 9E and COP Rules, rr 62–64
	Form **COP24** (witness statement) setting out reasons connection with P and reasons for the application and benefit to P	
	Statement must be verified by a statement of truth	
	Form **COP3**	
	Form **COP4** where a deputy has been assigned	
	Copy of a LPA if relevant	
	Any other evidence relied on	
Applicant must pay Court Fees	£400	COP Fees Order 2007, art 4
Urgent applications	Apply directly to the Clerk of the Rules High Court Family Division to attend before a nominated Judge	PD 10B
Extreme urgency	May be dealt with by telephone 084 5330 2900 (o ffice hours) 020 7497 6000 (out of hours)	
Respondents	Organisation that will provide treatment (if not the applicant) The O/S as litigation friend Any other person having an interest Any other person directed by the Court	
Court Office	(1) Issues application and gives to the applicant:	
	• Form **COP5**	
	• Forms **COP14** and **COP14A**	

		• Forms **COP15** and **COP15A**	
		• Form **COP20**	
	(2)	Judge considers the application and decide whether to give directions or list for directions/disposal hearing	COP Rules 2007, r 89
	(3)	May decide to make order without a hearing in which case order court will serve order on all the parties	
What the applicant must do	(1)	Serve on the respondent/s within 21 days Forms **COP1, COP1A, COP5, COP15** and **COP15A**	
	(2)	Notify P on Forms **COP14, COP14A** and **COP5** of the application	COP Rules 2007, r 69
	(3)	Notify any relevant party on Forms **COP15** and **COP15A**	COP Rules 2007, r 70
	(4)	File certificate of service and notification in Form **COP20**	
	(5)	If an urgent application is required file Form **COP9**	COP Rules 2007, Part 10 PD 10A and 10B
What the respondent must do		File an acknowledgement of service in Form **COP5** indicating whether R	
	(a)	Consents	
	(b)	opposes the application	
	(c)	seeks alternative remedy	
		File evidence intended to be relied on	
What the person notified must do		File an acknowledgement of notification in Form **COP5** and indicate whether wants to be joined as a party and file Form **COP10**	PD 9C(4)
Hearing		The court will consider the application	
		Give directions	COP Rules 2007, r 85
		Allocate the case	
		Set the time table and trial window or if urgent list for a disposal hearing	
		Make any other appropriate orders	
Orders that the Court may make at the interim hearing	(1)	Declare whether a person lacks capacity to make a particular decision specified in the declaration	MCA 2005, s 15

And at the final hearing (for which fee of £500 is payable)	(2)	Declare whether the person lacks capacity on the matters set out in the declaration
	(3)	Declare the lawfulness or otherwise of any act done or yet to be done
	(4)	Authorise deprivation of liberty in certain circumstances
	(5)	Specify where P should live
	(6)	Define the extent of contact between P and others
	(7)	Grant injunctions
	(8)	Appoint a deputy where appropriate
	(9)	Any other consequential or protective orders

PRECEDENTS

PRECEDENT FOR A DRAFT ORDER SEEKING AUTHORITY TO WITHHOLD CARDIO-PULMONARY RESUSCITATION AND ADMINISTRATION OF ANTIBIOTICS, TO WITHDRAW GASTRO/NASAL FEEDING AND/OR OTHER FORMS OF LIFE SUSTAINING TREATMENT

IN THE COURT OF PROTECTION   CASE NO ....

IN THE MATTER OF THE MENTAL CAPACITY ACT 2005

AND IN THE MATTER OF JOSIE SMITH

BETWEEN

HELLINIC COUNTY   Applicant
COUNCIL

And

BLACKFORD HOSPITAL   1st Respondent
TRUST

And

JOHN SMITH   2nd Respondent
(by his litigation friend the
Official Solicitor)

DRAFT ORDER

Made by ....

At the Royal Courts of Justice Strand

On ....

UPON hearing counsel for all parties

AND UPON reading the bundle of documents filed in the proceedings

AND UPON hearing the oral evidence of ....

IT IS DECLARED THAT:

1.   P lacks capacity to make a decision in relation to his medical condition and treatment

2.   P lacks capacity to make a decision in relation to the proposal to withhold ANH cardio-pulmonary resuscitation and administration of antibiotics and other life sustaining treatment [*or other forms of life sustaining treatment – set these out*].

3.   P is in PVS and has no prospect of recovery.

4.   Having regard to the best interests of P it shall be lawful for the Blackford NHS Trust and responsible medical practitioners having responsibility at the time for the patient's treatment and care:

    (a)   to perform the proposed .... [*set out the details of the surgical operation if appropriate*];

    (b)   to withhold cardio-pulmonary resuscitation of P;

    (c)   to withhold the administration of antibiotics in the event of P developing a potentially life-threatening infection which would otherwise call for the administration of antibiotics, but only if immediately before withholding the same;

        (i)   the applicant is so advised by both the medical practitioner and by the consultant neurologist/psychiatrist [*or as the case may be*] having the responsibility at the time for the treatment and care of P; and

        (ii)   [*set out any other condition that may be appropriate*];

    (d)   to discontinue treatment and/or nourishment thereafter not to furnish medical treatment except for the sole purpose of enabling her to end her life and to die peacefully with the greatest of dignity and least distress; or

    (e)   to furnish such treatment and nursing care as may from time to time be appropriate to ensure that P suffers the least distress and retains the greatest dignity.

5.   An order that in the event of a material change in the existing circumstances occurring before the withholding of treatment any party shall have permission to apply for such further or other declaration or order as may be just.

6.   An injunction forbidding until further order, any person whether by himself or by encouraging or instructing any other person, or in the case of a company whether by its directors or officers, servants, agents or otherwise from:

    (a)   publishing the name and address or otherwise identifying:

        (i)   The applicant;

        (ii)   P;

        (iii)   any hospital at which P is receiving treatment or has been treated;

        (iv)   any medical practitioner or nurse or any other person who has had the care of P;

  (b)   soliciting any information relating to P [*identify any other person to whom the order relates*], any staff at any hospital where P is being treated or has been treated or any other person who may have had the care of P.

7.   Such further or other consequential orders and direction as may be necessary.

8.   That the costs of this application be provided for.

PRECEDENT FOR A DRAFT ORDER FOR DISCONTINUING LIFE-SUSTAINING TREATMENT

IN THE COURT OF PROTECTION   CASE NO ....

IN THE MATTER OF THE MENTAL CAPACITY ACT 2005

AND IN THE MATTER OF JOSIE SMITH

BETWEEN

HELLINIC COUNTY   Applicant
COUNCIL

And

BLACKFORD HOSPITAL   1st Respondent
TRUST

And

JOHN SMITH   2nd Respondent
(by his litigation friend the
Official Solicitor)

DRAFT ORDER

Made by ....

At the Royal Courts of Justice Strand

On ....

UPON hearing counsel for all parties

AND UPON reading the bundle of documents filed in the proceedings

AND UPON hearing the oral evidence of ....

IT IS DECLARED THAT:

1.   P lacks capacity to consent to continued life-sustaining treatment measures [*specify what these are*].

2.   Having regard to the best interests of P it shall be lawful for the responsible medical practitioners [*or the name of the health provider*]:

      (a)   to discontinue/withdraw all life-sustaining treatment and medical support measures designed to keep P alive in her existing [persistent vegetative] state including the termination of ventilation, nutrition and hydration by artificial means; and

(b)   to discontinue and thereafter need not furnish medical treatment/or nourishment to P except for the purpose of enabling her to end her life and to die with the greatest dignity and least distress.

3.   An order that in the event of a material change in the existing circumstances occurring before the withdrawal of artificial feeding and hydration any party shall have permission to apply for such further or other declaration or order as may be just.

IT IS FURTHER ORDERED THAT:

4.   Until further order, it is forbidden for any person whether by himself or by encouraging or instructing any other person, or in the case of a company whether by its directors or officers, servants, agents or otherwise from:

(a)   publishing the name and address or otherwise identifying:

(i)   the applicant;

(ii)   P;

(iii)   any hospital at which P is receiving treatment or has been treated;

(iv)   any medical practitioner or nurse or any other person who has had the care of P;

(b)   soliciting any information relating to P or her parents, any staff at any hospital where P is being treated or has been treated or any other person who may have had the care of P.

5.   Such further or other consequential orders and direction as may be necessary.

6.   That the costs of this application be provided for.

PRECEDENT OF ORDER FOR TREATMENT AND WITHDRAWAL OF TREATMENT AND USE OF FORCE/RESTRAINT IN AN ANOREXIA NERVOSA CASE TAKEN FROM THE ORDER MADE IN THE *NHS TRUST V L & OTHERS*

UPON the NHS Trust agreeing to continue to involve the family of L in discussions about L's future clinical care including any decisions to move to a solely palliative care plan

And Upon the Court having made a reporting restrictions order in respect of the matter

IT IS HEREBY DECLARED THAT:

(1)   L Lacks capacity to:

    (a)   Litigate; and

    (b)   Make decisions in relation to the serous medical treatment at issue in this application. Specifically in relation to whether or not to refuse:

        (i)   Nutrition and hydration, and

        (ii)   Dextrose for hypoglycaemic episodes.

(2)   L has the capacity to make decisions as to antibiotic treatment, analgesia and treatment of her pressure sores.

(3)   The following being in L's best interests, the applicant clinicians shall be permitted:

    (a)   To provide nutrition and hydration and medical treatment, (including treatment for hypoglycaemia) to L in circumstances where she complies with that administration, including where nutrition and/or hydration is delivered by means of naso-gastric tube

    (b)   To administer dextrose solution to L by oral or intravenous route despite her objections where in the opinion of the treating clinicians, such administration is immediately necessary to save the life of L provided that such treatments administered using the minimal degree of force practicable and necessary to achieve the same, and at all times taking such steps as can be taken to ensure that L suffers the least distress and retains the greatest dignity. Save that there be permission not to insert or leave a central line in situ in anticipation of peripheral access being unobtainable.

    (c)   Not to provide L with nutrition and hydration with which she does not comply where such treatment cannot be delivered without her cooperation and/or without the use of physical force.

(i)   For the avoidance of doubt the above declaration shall be of effect notwithstanding that in the opinion of the treating clinician it would be immediately necessary to administer such nutrition to preserve the life of L;

(ii)   Save that the above declaration shall only be of effect if all reasonable steps have been taken to gain L's cooperation (having regard to the distress such steps may cause L) through the use of appropriate verbal explanations and persuasion including where appropriate, involving her parents, or such other person in whom she might have some trust, in attempts to persuade L to accept the said interventions.

(d)   Should L's condition further deteriorate such that in the opinion of the treating clinician she has entered the terminal stage of her illness, to provide L with such palliative care and related treatment (including pain relief and anxiolytics) under medical supervision to ensure that L suffers the least distress and retains the greatest dignity until such time as her life comes to an end.

PRECEDENT FOR AN ORDER FOR THE COVERT USE OF SEDATION TAKEN FROM THE ORDER MADE IN *NHS TRUST V K & OTHERS* [2012] EWHC 2922 (COP)

(1) Subject to paragraph (2) below, it is hereby declared as follows:

(a)   it shall be lawful, notwithstanding K's refusal to consent to such treatment, for Mr J, a consultant surgeon at [........] hospital and his team to perform on K a hysterectomy and bilateral salpingo-ophorectomy under general anaesthetic;

(b)   it shall be lawful, notwithstanding K's refusal to consent thereto, for Dr VB, a consultant anaesthetist at [........] Hospital and her team to administer general anaesthetic and any necessary pre-operative sedation (provided the sedation is administered by, and thereafter continuously monitored by, a qualified anaesthetist) to K for the surgery permitted in paragraph (a) above;

(c)   it shall be lawful for sedation to be administered by, and thereafter continuously monitored by, a qualified anaesthetist before K is informed that it is proposed to carry out the above surgery and anaesthesia;

(d)   it shall be lawful, in the event of K refusing to co-operate with post-operative recovery treatment, for Dr W, a consultant in anaesthesia and intensive care, and her team to sedate K in order to carry out treatment considered necessary to ensure her survival.

(2)

(i)   It shall be a condition of the permission granted by paragraphs (1)(a) to (d) above that a consultant psychiatrist, Professor W, and his team should undertake K's psychiatric care at all stages of her treatment.

(ii)   The declarations in paragraphs (1)(a), (b) and (c) above shall cease until further order to be of any effect if at any stage prior to the actual sedation or anaesthesia or operation any of Mr J, Dr VB, Dr W or Professor W notifies his/her colleagues pursuant to this paragraph of this order that he/she considers that the sedation or anaesthesia or operation should not take place; or if any of the patient's three sons notifies the doctors pursuant to this paragraph of this order that he no longer considers that the operation should take place. In the event of any person making a notification pursuant to this paragraph, the matter may be restored to the court, reserved to myself, Mr. Justice Holman, if available.

(3) An official transcript approved by the judge must be made urgently of the judgment given today, at the expense of the applicant Trust. It and this order must be supplied to, and read by, each of Mr J, Dr VB, Dr W and Professor W before any procedures authorised by this order take place. Copies may also be supplied to all other doctors who gave evidence at the hearing.

Note: The above precedents may be adapted to include some or all of the terms of the draft order set out in chapter 8.

PART IV

DEPRIVATION OF LIBERTY

CHAPTER 10

DEPRIVATION OF LIBERTY

LAW AND PRACTICE

10.1 INTRODUCTION

People who lack capacity are unable to consent to their living arrangements. For those who are resident in institutional care this may mean that they are effectively deprived of their liberty. The Mental Capacity Act 2005 (MCA 2005), as amended, introduced a framework of safeguards not previously available, for those who lack capacity to agree to living arrangements which have the effect of depriving them of their liberty unlawfully. The safeguards are intended to be compliant with the European Convention for the Protection of Human Rights and Fundamental Freedoms (ECHR) and the Strasbourg jurisprudence and have become known as the Deprivation of Liberty Safeguards (DOLS). The effect of the safeguards is to provide a framework for the state to authorise a deprivation of liberty lawfully in respect of those in hospital and residential care homes and to provide a process of challenge for those subject to authorizations. However, the Court of Appeal's decisions in *Cheshire West and Chester Council v P*[1] and *P&Q v Surrey CC (MIG and MEG)*[2] (on which the Supreme Court's judgment is awaited) indicate that there is considerable confusion, misunderstanding and misconception on what constitutes deprivation of liberty of those who lack capacity particularly those who are placed in residential care when and by whom the statutory authorisation procedure set out in Schs 1A and A1 to the MCA 2005 should be utilised. Until the Supreme Court clarifies the law, the principles set out in decisions of the European Court of Human Rights (ECtHR) especially recent ones, provide at least a guide to the approach to be adopted where it is sought to deprive the liberty of an incapacitated adult.

It is thus necessary, as a starting point to consider the reasons which brought about the change, the European jurisprudence, the new regime; the function and the role of the Court of Protection particularly in areas where the DOLS provisions have needed clarification and the principles which should be applied when seeking to apply the statutory provisions.

---

[1] [2012] EWCA Civ 1257, [2012] COPLR 37, [2012] 1 FLR 693.
[2] [2011] EWCA Civ 190, [2011] COPLR Con Vol 931.

10.2   BACKGROUND

An unlawful deprivation of a person's liberty is contrary to Art 5 of the ECHR. For those suffering with a mental disorder, the Mental Health Act 1983 as amended by the Mental Health Act 2007 makes provision for their hospital admission, for assessment and treatment. Section 1(2) of the Mental Health Act 1983 as amended defines 'mental disorder' as 'any disorder or disability of the mind'. The 1983 Act in its original form contained provisions which enabled the compulsory detention in hospital of persons suffering from mental disorder who were either unable or unwilling to consent to such assessment and treatment provided certain conditions set out in the Act were met.[3] The Mental Health Act 2007 extends this power to treatment within the community of patients who are discharged from hospital by introducing compulsory treatment orders. The 1983 Act as amended sets out the conditions and criteria which must be satisfied before a person can be compulsorily detained under these provisions. It also sets out a review and appeal procedure so that the patient can challenge any decision made concerning his detention against his will. These protective rights render the detention lawful. Similar protection was not available for those who lacked capacity to consent to their placement but who were not actually resisting. They were subject to so-called informal admission to hospital or other institutional care by way of an administrative decision made by health or social services departments of local authorities which was not formally authorised. The nature of these placements, effectively deprived them of their liberty even if it was limited to locking of doors for safety reasons. P was in such circumstances unable to consent to the deprivation of liberty through lack of capacity and there were no safeguards in place. The basis of the (then) thinking was that there could be no detention unless the admitted person protested and that the substituted consent or indeed protest of another such as a spouse or relative on behalf of an adult lacking capacity was not recognised in law.

This shortfall in safeguards and lack of protection of P's rights was initially identified by the European Court of Human Rights in *X v United Kigdom*[4] which found that the then UK legislation was in breach of the rights set out in Art 5(4) of the ECHR (see below under **10.3**) because consent was taken as given, in the absence of protest and hence there was no right of appeal. The provisions of the ECHR were incorporated into English law by virtue of Human Rights Act 1998. Although the Act received Royal Assent on 9 November 1998 it did not come into force until 2 October 2000 and the remaining parts until 19 November 2003. This had an enormous impact on English law generally in that it required public authorities to act in a way which was compatible with the ECHR. It also gave a person who was aggrieved to bring proceedings against the authority under the Act or to rely on rights protected by the Convention and intended to be protected under the Act. This together with the numerous cases that followed brought about the need to

---

3   MHA 1983, s 2(2).
4   (Application No 72151/75) [1981] 4 EHHR 188.

review the mental health legislation on detention and treatment of those lacking capacity, and the absence of any procedure available to the person who lacked capacity to challenge such a decision.

The leading case of *HL v UK (Bournewood)*[5] which became known as the 'Bournewood Gap' highlighted the inadequacies and the absence of any procedure in the mental health legislation to safeguard the rights of those lacking capacity who are detained or restrained or restricted to a degree that could be regarded as deprivation of liberty. Mr HL was an autistic man who lacked capacity. He was re-admitted to Bournewood hospital following his placement with carers in the community. He was not 'sectioned' under the Mental Health Act 1983 as he had not resisted the admission to the hospital. His carers were critical of the care and treatment he was being given by the hospital and disapproved of his continued detention. This led to an application for judicial review of the decision on the ground that HL had been unlawfully detained. The carers failed in their application. They appealed to the Court of Appeal which reversed the decision and upheld the carers' claim that he had been unlawfully detained. There was a further appeal to the House of Lords which reinstated the decision of the High Court.

The case was taken to the European Court of Human Rights. The ECtHR identified the following factual factors relating to the case which contributed to a deprivation of liberty:

(a) the nature of the restraint which was used, including sedation, to admit Mr HL to hospital when he was resisting admission;

(b) the staff exercised complete and effective control over his care and movement for a significant period of the day on a daily basis;

(c) the staff exercised control over assessments, treatment, and contact with others;

(d) a decision had been taken that he would be prevented from leaving if he attempted to do so or his carers sought to remove him;

(e) the carers request for his discharge had been refused without any recourse for challenging that decision;

(f) he was not able to make or maintain any outside social contacts due to the restrictions placed on his movements and access by others to him;

(g) he was kept under constant supervision and control and hence lost autonomy.

The Court held that Mr HL had been deprived of his liberty contrary to Art 5(1) of the Convention. His detention had been arbitrary and there was no procedure in place prescribed by law to permit such detention, nor were there any procedures available to him under which he could seek to have the decision reviewed or to challenge the merits of the decision or the conditions for his detention in breach of Art 5(4). The Court referred to the safeguards which were available to a person detained under the Mental Health Act 1983 and the

---

5   (2004) 40 EHRR 761.

lack of such or any procedure for the detention of a person who did not suffer from mental disorder but lacked capacity. The Court in particular highlighted the lack of any formal procedures in place: (a) on who could authorise such detention or admission; (b) for reasons to be given for such admission and detention and whether the admission was for treatment or assessment; (c) for a continuing assessment and review; (d) for the person lacking capacity to be represented; and (e) for the person lacking disability or a representative on his behalf to seek a review of his detention or continued detention or to challenge the decision either on merit or on the ground of his Art 5 rights before a formal independent and appropriate tribunal.

After the decision of the European Court in *HL v UK* (above) and implementation of the Human Rights Act 1998, the issue of deprivation of liberty took on a greater significance in the domestic courts. There was thus a clear and immediate urgency to make the mental health legislation Convention compliant. The domestic courts attempted to bridge the 'gap' in the cases that followed by applying the principles set out by the European Courts. Parliament also had a duty to resolve the issues raised and introduce legislation which contained the appropriate safeguards. The Mental Capacity Act 2005, s 5 addressed some of the issues raised by the Court but the decision of the ECtHR was not handed down in time for all the gaps in the legislation to be dealt with. The Mental Health Act 2007 was subsequently introduced to inter alia add new provisions to the Mental Capacity Act 2005 to fill the gaps identified by the European Court. These provisions are known as the Deprivation of Liberty Safeguards. The Deprivation of Liberty Safeguards – Code of Practice pursuant to ss 42 and 43 of the Act has been issued to provide guidance and information for those implementing Deprivation of Liberty Safeguards on a daily basis to ensure that by following the criteria set out, any decision taken to deprive a person, who lacks capacity, of his or her liberty can be made lawfully. The Code of Practice is intended to apply to paid staff and other professionals who have been appointed to represent the person who lacks capacity and to make decisions on that person's behalf. As with the main Code of Practice this Code has statutory force and must be followed. In addition, a number of regulations have also been issued eg the Mental Capacity (Deprivation of Liberty: Standard Authorisations, Assessments and Ordinary Residence) Regulations 2008[6] and the Mental Capacity (Deprivation of Liberty: Appointment of Relevant Person's Representative) (Amendment) Regulations 2008.[7] Guidance to and for all the relevant professionals and public bodies have also been made available by the Department of Health. These can be accessed on the department's website: www.dh.gov.uk/en/SocialCare/Deliveringadultsocialcare/MentalCapacity/MentalCapacityActDeprivationoflibertySafeguards/index.htm.

The Court of Protection (Amendment) Rules 2009[8] and Practice Directions thereunder (the Deprivation of Liberty Rules) and forms have also been issued to ensure that any application made to the Court is dealt with expeditiously by

---

[6]   SI 2008/1858.
[7]   SI 2008/2368.
[8]   SI 2009/582.

a specially appointed team. The rules and Practice Directions set out the procedure which must be followed when making an application for a declaration for deprivation of liberty in cases of urgency. The provisions relating to 'deprivation of liberty' (DoL) came into force on 1 April 2009.

10.3   WHAT ARE THE ART 5 RIGHTS WHICH MUST BE RESPECTED?

Article 5 of the ECHR protects liberty and security and is relevant to those who lack capacity. The provisions of Art 5 which are generally relevant to cases involving a person lacking capacity or a vulnerable person are Art 5(1)(e), 5(4) and 5(5). Article 5(1)(e) provides that:

> 'Everyone has the right to liberty and security of person. No one shall be deprived of his liberty save in the following cases and in accordance with a procedure prescribed by law ...
> (e)   the lawful detention of persons for the prevention of the spreading of infectious diseases, of persons of unsound mind, alcoholics or drug addicts or vagrants.'

Article 5(4) provides that:

> 'Everyone who is deprived of his liberty by arrest or detention shall be entitled to take proceedings by which the lawfulness of his detention shall be decided speedily by a court and his release ordered if the detention is not lawful.'

Article 5(5) provides that:

> 'Everyone who has been the victim of arrest or detention in contravention of the provisions of this Article shall have an enforceable right to compensation.'

10.4   WHAT AMOUNTS TO A DEPRIVATION OF LIBERTY?

The Deprivation of Liberty Safeguards (DOLS) were introduced by amendments to the MCA 2005 to address the shortcomings of domestic law as it related to the detention and restraint of those lacking capacity. The amendments put in place an administrative process whereby a hospital or care home detaining an incapacitated person has to seek authorisation for the arrangement. The authorisation may be challenged by the incapacitated person either by using the administrative appeal procedure or by way of application to the Court of Protection. In addition the Court of Protection is empowered to order that the incapacitated person be deprived of his liberty where the authorisation regime does not apply. However, what the legislators avoided was to provide a statutory definition of what amounts to deprivation of liberty. The only guidance provided is that which is contained in the DOLS Code of Practice which sets out a summary of decisions of the European Court of Human Rights (ECtHR) and the process which should be followed by those who are responsible for the care of those lacking capacity. Thus the decision makers have to rely on the principles set out in those and subsequent decisions of the ECtHR and domestic case-law for guidance. Health trusts and other public bodies have the advantage of being able to obtain advice from legal professionals experienced in this field but small care homes striving to do their best for their residents have been left marooned with all of the responsibility to apply for authorisations and or court orders with few tools to guide them on what actions will or will not be considered deprivation of liberty under the Convention and the MCA 2005.

How then is it possible to identify what amounts to deprivation of liberty. This takes us on a short tour through the history of how this has been approached by European and domestic jurisdiction.

For the purposes of the Act deprivation of liberty is defined in s 6(5) as having the same meaning as in Art 5(1) of the Human Rights Convention (see under **10.3** above). Lord Hoffman in *Home Secretary v JJ*[9] said that it was not easy to discover the criterion from the majority of the decision: 'the nearest one gets is the situation that "in certain respects the treatment complained of resembles detention in an 'open prison' or committal to a disciplinary unit"', and he referred to the observations made by Judge Matcher in *Guzzardi* (see below) that deprivation of liberty was 'a concept of some complexity, having a core which cannot be the subject of argument but which is surrounded by a "grey zone" where it is extremely difficult to draw the line.'

Baroness Hale in that case said that to be deprived of liberty does not mean deprived of the freedom to live one's life as one wishes:

> 'It must mean forced or obliged to be at a particular place where one does not choose to be. But even that is not enough to amount to deprivation of liberty. There must be a greater degree of control over one's physical liberty than that.'

The European Court and the domestic courts have established certain key principles which should be applied as guidance when assessing a case. In *Guzzardi v Italy*,[10] a case involving a suspected member of the Mafia detained on a small island off the coast of Italy, Judge Matcher said rather said that deprivation of liberty was 'a concept of some complexity, having a core which cannot be the subject of argument but which is surrounded by a "grey zone" where it is extremely difficult to draw the line'. It is those 'grey zones' with which the Court and decision makers have to grapple. *Guzardi*, however was instrumental in confirming that deprivation of liberty was not limited to restriction of movement. It held that:

> 'in proclaiming the "right to liberty" paragraph 1 of Article 5 is contemplating the physical liberty of the person; its aim is to ensure that no one should be dispossessed of this liberty in an arbitrary fashion ... the paragraph is not concerned with the mere restrictions of liberty of movement ... In order to

---

[9]   [2007] UKHL 45.
[10] (1980) 3 EHRR.

determine whether someone has been deprived of his liberty within the meaning of Article 5, the starting point must be his concrete situation and account must be taken of a whole range of criteria such as the type, duration, effects and manner of implementation of the measure in question.'

and:

'The difference between deprivation of and restriction upon liberty is nonetheless merely one of degree or intensity, and not one of nature or substance.'Although the process of classification into one or other of these categories sometimes proves to be no easy task in that some borderline sses are a matter of pure opinion, the court cannot avoid making the selection upon which the applicability or inapplicability of Art.5 depends.'

It is thus not merely one of restriction of movement.

This principle has been repeated and established in a number of decisions of the European Court and applied in cases decided by the High Court.

In *Ashingdane v UK*[11] the Court applied the same principle. In *Neilson v Denmark*[12] a 12 year old boy had been admitted to a psychiatric ward of a hospital for nervous disorder at the request of his mother. He remained in hospital for five and a half months. The restrictions on his movements were no different to that in any hospital. He was free to leave the ward with permission and go out accompanied by a member of the staff. The Court held that his admission to hospital did not constitute deprivation of liberty and that the admission had been a responsible exercise of the mother's parental responsibility and in the best interests of the child.

In *HM v Switzerland*[13] an elderly person was placed in a nursing home on account of neglect to provide her with the necessary medical care and living condition. The nursing home allowed freedom of movement and encouraged her to have social contact between others both within and outside the institution. After moving to the nursing home she had agreed to remain there. As a result of which the placement order had been lifted. In holding that she was not deprived of her liberty, the Court took into account the fact that she had been placed in the home in her own interests to provide her with medical care and living conditions which addressed her personal and welfare needs. The applicant had also been indecisive regarding whether she wanted to stay at the home or not. The Court decided that the placement was a 'responsible measure taken by the competent authorities in the applicant's interests' and the situation was not of a degree or intensity to justify the conclusion that she had been deprived of her liberty.

---

[11]   (1985) 7 EHRR 528.
[12]   (1988) EHRR 175.
[13]   (2002) 38 EHRR 314.

In *HL v UK (Bournewood)*[14] the dispute was between the carers of an autistic person and the hospital and related to his care and treatment. The ECtHR followed the principles set out in *Guzzardi v Italy* and held that the patient was unlawfully deprived of his liberty as his professional carers exercised complete and effective control over his care and his movements and there was no procedure in place prescribed by law or otherwise regarding his admission, and grounds for or authorisation of his detention (see further below). Some factors the Court considered important in finding that HL's detention at Bournewood hospital amounted to deprivation of liberty were:

(a)   detention was arbitrary;

(b)   there was complete and effective control over care and movement;

(c)   there was continuous supervision and control with no freedom to leave;

(d)   there was a regime of enforced medication and restraint; and

(e)   HL was unable to maintain social contact because of the restriction placed on access such that it amount to loss of autonomy.

In *Storck v Germany*[15] an 18 year old was placed in a psychiatric clinic at the request of her father and cared for under constant supervision and was not permitted to leave the clinic. She had on several occasions tried to escape and was chained to a radiator to prevent her leaving. On one occasion having succeeded in escaping from the clinic she had been returned to the clinic by the police. Holding that that she had been deprived of her liberty the Court stated:

> 'the Court is unable to discern any actual basis for the assumption that the applicant – presuming that she had the capacity to consent – agreed to her continued stay in the clinic. In the alternative, assuming that the applicant was no longer capable of consenting following her treatment with strong medication, she cannot, in any event, be considered to have validly agreed to her stay in the clinic.'

The judgment identified three elements:

(a)   An objective view of confinement for not a negligible length of time;

(b)   A subjective assessment for the validity of consent; and

(c)   That the deprivation of liberty must be one for which the state is responsible.

Following the decision in *HL v UK* and before the amendments introduced by the Mental Health Act 2007 came into force, in cases concerning an incapacitaed adult the domestic court considered, applied and developed the principles set out in the decisions of the ECtHR. The majority of these cases were decided under the High Court's inherent jurisdiction, but they are nevertheless relevant for future reference subject to legal developments whether statutory or in case law which have occurred since then. In these cases, the Court acknowledged the difficulty in assessing borderline cases, suggesting that in such cases the decision was one of opinion or judgment and that there is no

---

[14]   (2004) 40 EHRR 761.
[15]   (2005) 43 EHRR 96.

bright line separating the two. Since the DOLS have been put in place as a result of the amendments made to the MCA 2005 the Court of Protection has applied the principles set out by the ECtHR in interpreting the statutory provisions.

In *JE v DE and Surrey County Council*,[16] an application was made by a wife seeking a declaration that the local authority had deprived her husband of his liberty. Her husband was 76 years of age when he was taken into care suffering from dementia after his wife had placed him in a chair on a pavement outside their home clothed only in his pyjama bottoms and a shirt and slippers and refused to have him back home. Whilst in care he was repeatedly expressing a desire to go home. Whilst he was allowed contact with his wife he was restricted from leaving. It was established that he lacked capacity to decide where he should live. Munby J (as he then was) having considered the circumstances and facts in the case and relying on the decision in *HL* said at para 115 of his judgment:

'The crucial question in this case, as it seems to me, is not so much whether (and, if so, to what extent) DE's freedom or liberty was or is curtailed within the institutional setting. The fundamental issue in this case, in my judgment, is whether DE has been and is deprived of his liberty to leave the Y home. And when I refer to leaving the X home and the Y home, I do not mean leaving for the purpose of some trip or outing approved by SCC or by those managing the institution; I mean leaving in the sense of removing himself permanently in order to live where and with whom he chooses, specially removing himself to live at home with JE.'

The local authority had complete control over DE and he had not given a valid consent to these arrangements. The key factor thus was whether the person lacking capacity was or was not free to leave.

In *Home Secretary v JJ*[17] the House of Lords (now known as the Supreme Court) emphasised that the borderline between restriction and deprivation remains indistinct and stated that 'it is essential not to give an over-expansive interpretation to the concept of deprivation of liberty.' The issue is therefore one of whether P was required to live in a confined area. The Court held that in order to determine whether someone has been 'deprived of his liberty' within the meaning of Art 5(1):

'the starting point must be his concrete situation and account must be taken of the whole range of criteria such as the type, duration, effects and manner of implementation of the measure in question.'

Lord Bingham stated that national courts must look to the jurisprudence of the Commission and the European Court in Strasbourg which the UK courts are required by s 2(1) of the Human Rights Act 1998 to take account of. But that jurisprudence must be used as laying down principles and not mandatory

---

[16] [2006] EWHC 3459 (Fam).
[17] [2007] UKHL 45.

solutions because case law shows that the Art 5 rights have been considered in a very wide range of factual situations. Therefore, the national courts must look for guidance inter alia to the principles laid down in *Guzzardi v Italy* reiterated by the courts on many occasions and to seek to give fair effect, on the facts of the case to those principles (para 13) Lord Bingham also warned that it was:

> 'perilous to transpose the outcome of one case to another where the facts are different and all the relevant factors and circumstances related to that specific case must be taken into account.'

The facts of the individual case must be assessed cumulatively and the question answered, whether in combination they amount to deprivation. There may be no deprivation of liberty if a single feature of an individual's situation is taken on its own, but the combination of measures considered together may have that result (see *Guzzardi v Italy*). Locked doors or institutional surroundings are not essential to the concept of deprivation of liberty. These features may be relevant in the assessment of whether a person has been deprived of his liberty (para 16).

Baroness Hale took the view that 'merely being required to live at a particular address ... does not without more amount to deprivation of liberty. There must be greater degree of control over one's physical liberty than that'. On the facts the Court ruled that P had been deprived of his liberty. The Court also added that distinction between 'restraint and deprivation of liberty was one of degree or intensity and not one of nature or substance'.

10.4.1   Restrictions for the benefit of the person

Not all restrictions on a person's liberty will be considered as a deprivation of liberty. There needs to be an assessment of the degree or intensity of such restrictions. Restrictions designed, at least in part for the benefit of the person lacking capacity may be a relevant consideration. In *HM v Switzerland*[18] the European Court treated as relevant, restrictions which were imposed as a responsible measure in the person's best interests. In *Home Secretary v JJ*[19] (a case concerning control orders) Baroness Hale suggested that such restrictions are less likely to be considered as deprivation of liberty than are restrictions designed for the protection of society, but in *JE v DE and Surrey County Council*[20] Munby J (as he then was) observed that it was an error to confuse the question of deprivation of liberty with whether it had been justified in the interests of the person concerned. He held that the fundamental issue was whether DE was free to leave the care home permanently to live where and with whom he chose.

In *LBCC v TG, JG, and KR*[21] a 78 year old man who suffered from dementia and cognitive impairment had been resident in the L care home. That placement

---

[18]   (2002) 38 EHRR 314.
[19]   [2007] UKHL 45.
[20]   [2006] EWHC 3459 (Fam).
[21]   [2007] EWHC 2640 (Fam).

was terminated but before he could be transferred to an alternative home he was admitted to hospital with pneumonia and septicaemia. While he was in hospital one of his daughters and a granddaughter put themselves forward as possible carers for him. The local authority did not consider that he would be well placed with them as he required 24 hour care in a residential home. The local authority found him an alternative care home but before he could be placed there the hospital discharged him into the care of his daughter and granddaughter. The local authority obtained an order without notice requiring the daughter and granddaughter to deliver him to the care home. He was delivered up as ordered. At the final hearing having considered all the evidence the Court directed that he be placed with the daughter and the granddaughter. They had claimed that he had been deprived of his liberty during the period he had been placed in the care home. Their claim was rejected. While the Court accepted that it was a borderline case it found that the evidence demonstrated that the restrictions placed on the claimants' father was no different to the ones in any ordinary care home. He was able to have contact with his family and permitted to go out with them. He was compliant and had expressed that he was happy in the care home.

10.4.2 Relevance of consent

The issue of the relevance of consent will turn on the facts of the particular case. In *HM v Switzerland*[22] the fact that the person detained had not objected to her placement in the nursing home was taken into consideration when deciding the issue of degree or intensity of the restriction and reached the conclusion that in the circumstances she had not been deprived of her liberty. But in *Storck v Germany*[23] where the applicant had attempted to leave the unit on numerous occasions and was chained to a radiator to prevent her from so doing and had been returned to the home by the police when she had escaped the Court concluded that she had not consented to the placement. Similarly in *JE v DE and Surrey County Council*[24] the Court ruled that the local authority was exercising complete and effective control on the person and on every movement of his including social contact and whether he could live with his wife. Account was also taken of the numerous occasions on which he had expressed his wish to independent professionals without any prompting of his wish to live with his wife to conclude that the actions of the local authority constituted deprivation of his liberty.

In *LBCC v TG, JG, and KR*[25] the Court found that the father had spent three years in a care home. He was compliant and expressed himself as happy in the care home.

---

[22] (2002) 38 EHRR 314.
[23] (2005) 43 EHRR 96.
[24] [2006] EWHC 3459 (Fam).
[25] [2007] EWHC 2640 (Fam).

10.4.3   Relevance of the freedom to leave

Locked doors or institutional surroundings are not essential to the concept of deprivation of liberty. These features may be relevant in the assessment of whether a person has been deprived of his liberty. In *JE v DE* (above) Munby J (as he then was) considered that the question of whether the person was free to leave was a relevant factor but in *Home Secretary v JJ*[26] Baroness Hale in her judgment said that:

> 'merely being required to live at a particular address or to keep within a particular geographical area does not, without more amount to a deprivation of liberty. There must be a greater degree of control over one's physical liberty than that.'

10.4.4   Cases post 2009 and the introduction of the DOLS

Decisions made since the amendments to the MCA 2005 came into force have applied the three elements referred to in *Storck v Germany* (see above under 10.4). However, the issue of whether or not detention which is beneficial to the person lacking capacity, amounts to a deprivation of liberty has exercised the courts, with difference of opinion.

P and Q v Surrey County Council[27] was an appeal from the first instance decision, where the case was familiarly known as MIG and MEG. The issue was whether Q, and adult lacking capacity, was deprived of her liberty as a resident of a care home. She was thriving there having being rescued from her abusive family circumstances. Wilson J (as he then was) rejected that the purpose of the placement and the notion of a person's happiness as such were relevant to whether or not a person lacking capacity was being deprived of his/her liberty but held that the purpose of the arrangement and the relevance of the person's happiness were relevant in determining whether any such deprivation was in that person's best interests under s 4(6) of the MCA 2005 and therefore lawful under Art 5(1)(e) of the ECHR (para 24). However, when considering whether there had been an objective deprivation of liberty he did not consider it appropriate to attach significance to the fact that the purpose of the arrangement had been to further the best interests of the person concerned, but considered that the relative normality of the living arrangements was relevant, because 'even when the person lives in an institution, rather than in a family home, there is a wide spectrum between the small children's home or nursing home on the one hand, and a hospital designed for compulsory detention like Bournewood; and it is in my view necessary to place each case along it' (para 28). The enquiry into normality transcends an inquiry into the residential arrangements: of potentially great relevance in the case of children or young adults is whether, they went out to some sort of school or college, and in the case of adults whether they went to college or a day centre or to pursue some form of occupation. Restrictions placed on outside social contact, ie, another major aspect of normal life were also relevant (paras 27–29).

---

[26]   *Home Secretary v JJ* [2007] UKHL 45.
[27]   [2011] EWCA Civ 190, [2011] COPLR Con Vol 931, [2011] 2 FLR 583.

In *Cheshire West and Chester Council v P*[28] Munby LJ (as he then was) comprehensively revisited the case law and applied the principles to the reality of the lives of those who need care and their carers. P was a 30 year old man who was born with cerebral palsy and Down's Syndrome. He had a history of cerebral vascular accidents. He also had significant physical and learning disabilities and lacked capacity. His behaviour was challenging. He lived with his mother from birth until 2009. In December 2008 the mother's health began to deteriorate to the point where the local authority concluded that she was no longer able to care for her son. Following interim proceedings P was placed at Z House, where he remained. The home was cosy and homely but P had no choice about his placement. He was unable to leave and had no control over the treatment and care he received. He needed care of the most intimate nature. He was incontinent and required help with toileting, incontinence and personal hygiene. He could be resistant to intervention. A particularly worrying feature of his behaviour was the fact that he chewed his incontinence pads sometimes including faecal matter. Staff were required to carry out a finger sweep of his mouth to check for and/or remove debris to avoid choking. In addition physical restraint was sometimes necessary to prevent aggressive attacks on the staff. The extent of P's difficulties were enormous and difficult for staff to manage without intrusive interventions.

At first instance Baker J reached the conclusion that P was being deprived of his liberty at Z House. On appeal Munby LJ (as he then was) disagreed. His analysis drew the following conclusion by way of guidance:

(a) The starting point is the 'concrete situation' taking account of a whole range of criteria such as the 'type, duration, effects and manner of implementation' of the measure in question. The difference between deprivation of and restriction upon liberty is merely one of degree or intensity, not nature or substance.

(b) Deprivation of liberty must be distinguished from restraint. Restraint by itself is not deprivation of liberty.

(c) Account must be taken of the individual's whole situation.

(d) The context is crucial.

(e) Mere lack of capacity to consent to living arrangements cannot itself create a deprivation of liberty,

(f) In determining whether or not there is deprivation of liberty, it is legitimate to have regard both to the objective 'reason' why someone is placed and treated as they are and also to the objective 'purpose' (or 'aim') of the placement.

(g) Subjective motive or intentions, on the other hand, have only limited relevance. Any improper motive or intention may have the effect that what would otherwise not be a deprivation of liberty is in fact, and for that very reason, a deprivation. But a good motive or intention cannot render innocuous what would otherwise be a deprivation of liberty. Good intentions are essentially neutral. At most they merely negate the existence

---

[28] [2011] EWCA Civ 1257, [2012] COPLR 37, [2012] 1 FLR 693.

of any improper purpose or of any malign, base or improper motive that might, if present, turn what would otherwise be innocuous into a deprivation of liberty. Thus the test is essentially an objective one.

(h)   In determining whether or not there is a deprivation of liberty, it is always relevant to evaluate and assess the 'relative normality' (or otherwise) of the concrete situation.

(i)   But the assessment must take account of the particular capabilities of the person concerned. What may be a deprivation of liberty for one person may not be for another.

(j)   In most contexts (as, for example, in the control order cases) the relevant comparator is the ordinary adult going about the kind of life which the able-bodied man or woman on the Clapham omnibus would normally expect to lead.

(k)   But not in the kind of cases that come before the Family Division or the Court of Protection. A child is not an adult. Some adults are inherently restricted by their circumstances. The Court of Protection is dealing with adults with disabilities often, as in the present case, adults with significant physical and learning disabilities, whose lives are dictated by their own cognitive and other limitations.

(l)   In such cases the contrast is not with the previous life led by X (nor with some future life that X might lead), nor with the life of the able-bodied man or woman on the Clapham omnibus. The contrast is with the kind of lives people like X would normally expect to lead. The comparator is an adult of similar age with the same capabilities as X, affected by the same condition or suffering the same inherent mental and physical disabilities and limitations as X. Likewise, in the case of a child the comparator is a child of the same age and development as X.

Both the above cases have raised considerable controversy particularly as it leads to the temptation of placing an over reliance upon the 'no realistic alternative' interpretation in difficult cases. So where a person lacking capacity objects to living in a particular care home, find supervision intrusive and security unacceptably restrictive, providers may nonetheless conclude that there has not been any deprivation of his liberty as there is no realistic alternative. This of course means that he will have no recourse to the Deprivation of Liberty Safeguards which includes obliging the authorities to assess and review placement and/or treatment. Nor will there be an obligation to resource alternative arrangements. It has also been suggested that the approach suggested in the case does not sit comfortably with Art 14(1) of the UN Convention on the Rights of Persons with Disabilities. Art 14 provides that:

> 'States shall ensure that persons with disabilities, on an equal basis with others, (a) enjoy the right to liberty and security of person; (b) are not deprived of their liberty unlawfully or arbitrarily... and that the existence of a disability shall in no case justify a deprivation of liberty'.

Both the above cases are subject of conjoined appeals to the Supreme Court. The appeals have been heard and judgment is awaited. The Court of Appeal's decision remains binding on domestic courts. However, since the decision in Cheshire West and Chester there have been a number of cases decided by the ECtHR, which deal with those who are placed in care homes and which shed light on the principles applied by that Court

In *Stanev v Bulgaria* (Application No 3760/06), a decision of the Grand Chamber, S was diagnosed with schizophrenia but had lived in the community. As his family were unable or unwilling to care for him he was placed under guardianship of a guardian who had never met him and who placed him in a social care institution in a remote village in the Bulgarian mountains far from S's home. S alleged that the location of his placement amounted to physical isolation. Absences from the home required permission which was frequently denied and if he overstayed he was liable to be and had been arrested. His activities treatment, personal, social and cultural activities were subject to supervision with no choice given to him. His identity papers were kept by the administration and his finances including his travel costs were managed entirely by the home's management. He had to share his small room with others and lacked privacy. On a formal inspection the care institution the physical conditions at the home were found to amount to inhuman and degrading treatment. Since 2004 he had expressed his wish to leave the home. S alleged that his Convention rights under Arts 3, 5, 6 and 13 had been violated. The European Court held that:[29]

> 'having regard to the particular circumstances of the present case, especially the involvement of the authorities in the decision to place the applicant in the home and its implementation, the rules on leave of absence, the duration of the placement and the applicant's lack of consent, the Court concludes that the situation under examination amounts to a deprivation of liberty within the meaning of Art 5(1) of the Convention. Accordingly, that provision is applicable.'

The European Court also held unanimously that Mr Stanev had been subjected to degrading treatment in violation of Art 3 of the ECHR by being forced to live for more than seven years in unsanitary and unlivable conditions and that domestic law did not provide him any remedy for such violations. This is the first case in which the Court has found a violation of Art 3 in a social care setting. The Court also unanimously found that Mr Stanev's right to a fair trial under Art 6 of the ECHR had been violated. In this regard, the Court referred to the growing emphasis that international law places on the legal autonomy of persons with disabilities, stating that it:

> 'is also obliged to note the growing importance which international instruments for the protection of people with mental disorders are now attaching to granting them as much legal autonomy as possible.'

---

[29] At para 32.

The Court referred in particular to the rights of a person lacking capacity under the United Nations Convention on the Rights of Persons with Disabilities (para 244).

In *DD v Lithuania* (Application No 13469/06), the applicant had a history of mental disorder since 1979 when she experienced shock having discovered that she was an adopted child. A year later she was diagnosed with schizophrenia. Her condition deteriorated over the years and by 1999 she was diagnosed with paranoid schizophrenia. She had been psychiatric hospitals more than 20 times. In 2000 when she was reassessed it was concluded that she was suffering from 'episodic paranoid schizophrenia with a predictable course' and that she was unable to understand her actions or to control them. She was described as unable to care for herself, manage money and hungrily wandering the city streets. She was admitted to a psychiatric hospital for treatment. At the request of her father, who was her guardian, she was admitted to the Kedainiai care home. At the care home the management exercised complete and effective control and supervision over her assessment, treatment care, and movement and who she could see and from whom she could receive telephone contact, for over seven years. She was not free to leave without permission and was brought back by the police when she tried to leave without permission. On one occasion she was placed in a secure ward, drugged and tied down for between 15–20 minutes. She unsuccessfully challenged the state authorities in relations to the guardianship proceedings and, whether the circumstances surrounding the placement and the treatment she received was unlawful. She eventually applied to the ECtHR alleging violations of her rights under numerous Articles of the Convention. In addition to Art 5 of the ECHR the Court also considered the applicant's rights under Arts 12 and 14 of the UN Convention on the Rights of Persons with Disabilities. The European Court found that her rights under Arts 5(4) and 6(1) had been violated. On the issue of the applicant's Art 5 rights the Court held:

> '145. The Court further recalls that the notion of deprivation of liberty within the meaning of Article 5(1) does not only comprise the objective element of a person's confinement in a particular restricted space for a not negligible length of time. A person can only be considered to have been deprived of his liberty if, as an additional subjective element, he has not validly consented to the confinement in question (see, *mutatis mutandis*, *H.M. v. Switzerland*, cited above, para 46).

> 146. In the instant case the Court observes that the applicant's factual situation in the Kėdainiai Home is disputed. Be that as it may, the fact whether she is physically locked in the Kėdainiai facility is not determinative of the issue. In this regard, the Court notes its case-law to the effect that a person could be considered to have been "detained" for the purposes of Article 5(1) even during a period when he or she was in an open ward with regular unescorted access to unsecured hospital grounds and the possibility of unescorted leave outside the hospital (see *H.L. v. the United Kingdom*, no. 45508/99, 92, ECHR 2004-IX). As concerns the circumstances of the present case, the Court considers that the key factor in determining whether Article 5(1) applies to the applicant's situation is that the Kėdainiai Home's management has exercised complete and effective control by medication and supervision over her assessment, treatment, care, residence and

movement from 2 August 2004, when she was admitted to that institution, to this day (ibid., para 91). As transpires from the rules of the Kėdainiai Home, a patient therein is not free to leave the institution without the management's permission. In particular, and as the Government have themselves admitted in their observations on the admissibility and merits, on at least one occasion the applicant left the institution without informing its management, only to be brought back by the police (see paragraph 29 above). Moreover, the director of the Kėdainiai Home has full control over whom the applicant may see and from whom she may receive telephone calls (see paragraph 81 above). Accordingly, the specific situation in the present case is that the applicant is under continuous supervision and control and is not free to leave (see *Storck v. Germany*, no. 61603/00, para 73, ECHR 2005-V). Any suggestion to the contrary would be stretching credulity to breaking point.'

In assessing the subjective element the Court applied the principles adopted in *Stanev* (above) and on the facts found that DD was able to express her wishes and feeling about her situation and had never agreed to her placement at the home.

In *Kedzior v Poland* (Application No 45026/07) K's brother who had been appointed his guardian had him placed in a social care home for adults. Under Polish law the placement was considered to be voluntary. K made several attempts to challenge the lawfulness of his placement and detention at the care home and of his inability to leave the home without success. He then applied to the ECtHR. The Court had to consider whether K was being deprived of his liberty and if so whether the deprivation of liberty was lawful under Art 5(1)(e) and whether his access to justice had been denied in contravention of Art 6 of the Convention. On the issue of deprivation of liberty the Court found:[30]

'that the key factor in determining whether Article 5(1) applies to the applicant's situation is whether the care home's management has exercised complete and effective control over his treatment, care, residence and movement from February 2002, when he was admitted to that institution, to the present day (see paragraph 44 above and *D.D. v. Lithuania*, cited above, para 149). The applicant was not free to leave the institution without the management's permission. Nor could the applicant himself request leave of absence from the home, as such requests had to be made by the applicant's official guardian. Accordingly, and as in the *Stanev* case, although the applicant was able to undertake certain journeys and to spend time with his family the factors mentioned above lead the Court to consider that the applicant was under constant supervision and was not free to leave the home without permission whenever he wished (see *Stanev*, cited above, 128).'

The European Court also found that, although the applicant's admission was requested by his guardian, it was implemented by a state-run institution (the care home), and hence the responsibility of the authorities for the situation complained of was engaged. He was thus deprived of his liberty for purposes of Art 5(1) (para 60). On the issue of whether the deprivation of liberty was nevertheless lawful the Court found that the assessments undertaken on K had

---

[30] At para 57 of the judgment.

been for purposes related to his legal protection and not to determine whether his mental health justified detention. There had been absent any assessment in this regard and therefore his detention had not complied with any procedure prescribed by law under Art 5(1)(e).

In relation to Art 5(4) the European Court applied the decision in *DD v Lithuania* and set out the principles as follows:[31]

> 'Among the principles emerging from the Court's case-law on Article 5(4) concerning "persons of unsound mind" are the following:
> (a)   a person detained for an indefinite or lengthy period is in principle entitled, at any rate where there is no automatic periodic review of a judicial character, to bring proceedings "at reasonable intervals" before a court to put in issue the "lawfulness" – within the meaning of the Convention – of his detention;
> (b)   Article 5(4) requires the procedure followed to have a judicial character and to afford the individual concerned guarantees appropriate to the kind of deprivation of liberty in question; in order to determine whether proceedings provide adequate guarantees, regard must be had to the particular nature of the circumstances in which they take place;
> (c)   the judicial proceedings referred to in Article 5(4) need not always be attended by the same guarantees as those required under Article 6(1) for civil or criminal litigation. Nonetheless, it is essential that the person concerned should have access to a court and the opportunity to be heard either in person or, where necessary, through some form of representation (see *Megyeri v. Germany*, 12 May 1992, 22, Series A no. 237 A; see also *Stanev*, cited above, 171).'

In *Milhailovs v Lativia* (Application No 35939/10) the applicant was suffering from epilepsy and psychotic symptoms. He was confined to a centre for those with mental disorder following an application made by his guardian. He had remained there for over a decade. M claimed that he was being detained there against his will. In determining his case the Court emphasised that the key factor in determining deprivation of liberty is whether the centre exercised 'complete and effective control over his treatment, residence and movements'. The ECtHR found on the facts that the objective element had been proved because M was under constant supervision and was not able to leave without permission. As to the subjective element of the test the ECtHR held that, the fact that M lacked legal capacity to decide matters for himself does not mean that he is de facto unable to understand his situation and act on it. On the facts the ECtHR found that M was able to express his wishes and feelings and the evidence disclosed that he perceived his compulsive admission and detention at the centre to be a deprivation of his liberty. The Court also found that his rights under Art 5(4) had been breached because there was no procedure in place for M to seek a review or to challenge the decision through a judicial process.

In all the above cases the ECtHR has approved and applied the principles set out in its previous decisions and referred to the principle that a person's liberty

---

[31]   At para 75.

is too important in a democratic society for a person to be taken into detention especially when it is not disputed that the person is legally incapable of consenting to or disagreeing with a proposed action because even is he is divested of his capacity he may still be able to understand and act on that understanding. Therefore, if he lacks capacity he cannot consent to his confinement even if he is compliant. The Court also emphasised that access to reviews was necessary in such cases even where the initial detention has been authorised by judicial authority. The purpose behind the measure in question is not necessarily a factor to be taken into account whether there has been a deprivation of liberty but may be relevant in determining whether it was justified under the provisions of Art 5.

Closer to home in *CC v KK and STCC*[32] KK was 82 years of age. She suffered from partial paralysis, Parkinson's Disease and vascular dementia. She was being cared for in a nursing home. She wanted to return home to her bungalow. She was twice made the subject of standard authorisation by CC. She challenged that authorisation and interim orders were made for further independent assessments to be undertaken. Further assessments concluded that KK lacked capacity to make decisions regarding her care needs and residence. The issues before the Court were twofold: (i) whether she lacked capacity to make decisions regarding her care and residence and (ii) whether she was being deprived of her liberty. The evidence before the Court included professional evidence but importantly also that of KK. Baker J concluded that even where there is consensus of professional opinion on a person's lack of capacity to make decisions it was the Court alone that was in a position to weigh up and analyse all the evidence and in particular the evidence of the person who lacks capacity and to make the decision. On the issue of whether there had been deprivation of liberty, Baker J in finding that the circumstances in the case did not amount to a deprivation of liberty, applied the approach adopted by the Court of Appeal in *P and Q v Surrey CC and Cheshire West and Chester CC v P* (above) .

In each of the above decisions the ECtHR has applied to the objective element the approach adopted in *HL v UK* and in none has reliance been placed on issues which has influenced the decisions of the domestic court in *Cheshire West* and *P and S*, namely that of purpose or motive or 'comparator'. The ECtHR has also emphasised that if a person lacks capacity he cannot be said to have consented to the actions taken and even if the person is compliant it does not exclude the fact that the actions are still capable of amounting to deprivation of liberty. In all cases reference is made to the objective element and the subjective element. In relation to the objective element the starting point is to examine the concrete situation of the person concerned. Some of the principles which apply to this test are:

- the deprivation of liberty must be the responsibility of the state;

---

[32] [2012] EWHC 2136 (COP), [2012] COPLR 627.

- freedom to leave and live where P chooses is significant. In this context P's concrete situation is an important factor eg whether P has a home, care and support from family or others;

- the nature of the measure taken to ensure that P remains in the placement such as type, duration, effect and manner o implementation of measures taken (see *HL v UK*);

- locked doors and wards are not necessarily determinative (see *DD v Lithuania* (above);

- physical isolation from P's normal environment, home and family as in *Stanlev* (above);

- restraint policies and enforced regime will be indicative of deprivation of liberty; the distinction between deprivation of liberty and of restraint or restriction of liberty is one of degree or intesnsity and not one of nature (see *Guzzardi v Italy and Storck v Germany* above);

- purpose, motive and comparator tests are not significant;

- control of lifestyle and contact with other is an important factor. Complete and effective control of every aspect of P's life including control of whom P may see and with whom P may have communication is significant (*Stanlev v Bulgaria, DD v Lithuania, Kedzior v Poland*).

In relation to the subjective element the consent of the person lacking capacity, his wishes and feelings are important considerations and in this regard the provisions of the UN Convention of the Rights of Persons with Disabilities will become relevant (see *DD v Lithuania* above) particularly as it emphasises the need to respect the autonomy of the incapacitated person, to ensure his rights of equality and access to justice (see Art 12 and 14 which were referred to).

Finally, it will be necessary to establish that the deprivation of liberty is imputable to the State such as by a public body or authorised by the Court.

The cautionary tale therefore is to apply to the Court for a declaration, assessment or authorisation.

10.5   THE NEW FRAMEWORK OF SAFEGUARDS

The Act, as amended by the Mental Health Act 2007, now sets out the legal framework for depriving a compliant person of his liberty, previously admitted to care informally, without recourse to the Act of 1983. It puts in place safeguards to ensure that any decision, to deprive someone of his/her liberty, is made following a defined process and in consultation with the appropriate authorities. It also provides a process for an application to be made to the Court of Protection for a declaration or as a means of challenging any decision which seeks to deprive a person of his liberty.

The regime in Sch A1 to the MCA 2005 which applies only to those in hospitals and care homes, imposes a duty on provider to protect the Art 5 rights of those they look after and incorporates the following safeguards for the sanctioning of deprivation of liberty:

- duty to identify any deprivation of liberty;
- creation of an authorising body;
- assessments requirements;
- appointment of representatives;
- procedure for authorisation;
- procedure for monitoring and review;
- procedure for challenge either to the supervisory body or the COP;
- administrative requirements, eg for record keeping and or decision making.

Thus there are considerable benefits to P where the Sch A1 regime applies by reason of the checks and balances it imposes in scrutinising Ps placement and treatment. There is also an obligation on decision makers to have regard to the wishes and feelings of the individual and his family and thus P's Art 8 rights too are protected where possible.

The Deprivation of Liberty Safeguards – Code of Practice refers to the relevant cases to identify some of the factors that should in general be considered by the decision maker in considering whether an act done or proposed to be undertaken may amount to a deprivation of liberty. These are:

- All the circumstances of each and every case.
- What measures are being taken in relation to the individual? When are they required? For what period do they endure? What are the effects of any restraints or restrictions on the individual? Why are they necessary? What aim do they seek to meet?
- What are the views of the relevant person, their family or carers? Do any of them object to the measures?
- How are any restraints or restrictions implemented? Do any of the constraints on the individual's personal freedom go beyond 'restraint' or 'restriction' to the extent that they constitute a deprivation of liberty?
- Are there any less restrictive options for delivering care and treatment that avoid deprivation of liberty altogether?
- Does the cumulative effect of all the restrictions imposed on the person amount to a deprivation of liberty, even if individually they would not?

The Code also sets out the steps which should be taken to reduce the risk of deprivation in para 2.7. These may provide some directions regarding the process which should be followed:

- Make sure that all decisions are taken (and reviewed) in a structured way and reasons for the decision recorded.

- Follow established good practice for care planning.

- Make proper assessment of whether the person lacks capacity to decide whether or not to accept the treatment proposed, in line with the principles of the Act.

- Before admitting a person to hospital or residential care in circumstances that amount to deprivation of liberty consider whether the person's needs could be met in a less restrictive way. Any restrictions placed on the person while in hospital or in a care home must be kept to the minimum necessary, and should be in place for the shortest period.

- Take proper steps to help P to retain contact with family, friends and carers. Where local advocacy services are available, their involvement should be encouraged to support the P and his family, friends and carers.

- Review the care plans on an ongoing basis. It may be helpful to include an independent element, possibly via an advocacy service in the review.

The statutory provisions with the Code of Practice form the Deprivation of Liberty Safeguards which provide a regime for the authorities formally to authorise the deprivation of liberty and provide an appeal process to the Court of Protection in the event of challenge.

Decisions of the High Court exercising its inherent jurisdiction have set out some useful guidelines to safeguard the rights of P (see below *Sunderland v PS & Children Act 1989*[33] and *Salford County Council v GJ, MJ & BJ*,[34] *A NHS Trust v Dr A*[35] and under **10.6**)

The Court of Protection (Amendment) Rules 2009[36] and the Practice Directions that supplement the rules and, which came into force on 1 April 2009, set out the procedure and practice in relation to applications for deprivations of liberty and declaration in cases of urgency. The Court of Protection has a dedicated team for the speedy identification and administration of these applications.

10.6 THE COURT OF PROTECTION'S POWERS TO MAKE DECLARATION AUTHORISING DEPRIVATION OF LIBERTY

In its original form the MCA 2005 did not include a specific power to authorise an act of detention. Whether this could be implied has been considered in a number of cases. In *Re PS Incapacitated or Vulnerable Adult*[37] a case under the inherent jurisdiction of the High Court, it was held that the Court has the power to make an order authorising the minimum of force or restraint necessary for detention of an adult who lacks capacity. This issue was further

---

[33] [2007] EWHC 623 (Fam).
[34] [2008] EWHC 1097 (Fam).
[35] [2013] EWHC 2442 (COP).
[36] SI 2009/582.
[37] [2007] 2 FLR 1083.

advanced in *Re GJ (Incapacitated Adults)*[38] where restraint was permitted to provide medical treatment to P, but this case too was decided under the inherent jurisdiction of the High Court. The issue was further argued and considered in *Re P (Adult) Medical Treatment)*.[39] It was held that the provisions of s 15(1)(c) of the Act which confer on the Court the general power to make declarations as to 'the lawfulness or otherwise of any act done, or yet to be done, in relation to' a person who lacks capacity to make a decision, and the provisions of s 48 (interim order and directions, see **2.4.8**) of the Act, were intended to and do empower, the Court of Protection to make orders under the Act similar to those made by the High Court under its inherent jurisdiction before the amendments to the Act by the Mental Health Act 2007 came into effect on 1 April 2009. The Court therefore has power, if the circumstances and the welfare of the person concerned requires, to make a declaration under s 6(1)–(4), to render lawful an act of restraint that would otherwise amount to deprivation of liberty and to a breach under s 6(5) of the Act. The Court also relied on s 17 of the Act, which provides that, in relation to the personal welfare of P, the powers of the Court under s 16 to grant an order making a decision or decisions on behalf of P in respect of issues concerning his welfare extend to 'giving or refusing' consent to the carrying out or continuation of a treatment by a person providing health care' for P. The Code of Practice at para 6.51 also provides that:

> 'in some cases the Court of Protection might grant an order that permits the deprivation of a person's liberty, if it is satisfied that this is in the person's interests.
>
> Thus where the facts justify, and the immediate welfare of an incapacitated adult so dictate, the Court may, by prior declaration in appropriate terms, render lawful an act of restraint under section 6(1)–(4) of the Act, which might otherwise amount to a deprivation of liberty under s 6(5), thus bridging the Bournewood Gap.' (per Sir Mark Potter P).

Since that decision, the amendments made to the Act by the Mental Health Act 2007, s 50 and Schs 7 and 8 came into force on 1 April 2009 by virtue of the Mental Health Act 2007 (Commencement No 10 and Transitional Provisions) Order 2009.[40] Section 4A now empowers the Court of Protection to make an order under the Act (as inserted by the Mental Health Act 2007). Section 4A sets out when a P may be deprived of his liberty. Section 4B of the Act also sets out the condition which must apply before a person may lawfully deprive an incapacitated person of his/ her liberty while a decision is sought from the Court. These are:

(a)   there is a question about whether that person is authorised to deprive the incapacitated person of his liberty under s 4A;

(b)   the deprivation of liberty is wholly or partly for the purpose of giving life sustaining treatment or doing any act which the person doing it reasonably

---

[38]   [2008] 2 FLR 1295.

[39]   [2009] 1 FCR 567.

[40]   SI 2009/239.

believes to be necessary to prevent a serious deterioration in the incapacitated person's condition; and

(c) the deprivation of liberty is necessary in order to give the life sustaining treatment or doing any act which the person undertaking it reasonably believes to be necessary to prevent a serious deterioration in the person's condition.

In any case where the person's lack of capacity is in question or the issues relate to a vulnerable person it is still possible to issue proceedings in the Court of Protection and the High Court if necessary will invoke its inherent jurisdiction to make the relevant orders as it did in cases decided before 1 April 2009. In *PS (Incapacitated or Vulnerable Adult)*[41] it was held that the Court had power to make an order authorising minimum of force or restraint necessary for detention of an adult who lacks capacity and in *Re GJ (Incapacitated Adults)*[42] the Court authorised restraint in order that medical treatment could be provided to the patient.

In *Sunderland v PS & Children Act 1989*[43] a case decided under the inherent jurisdiction of the High Court, the dispute was between the local authority and the daughter of the person concerned, over the care provided for her and her wish to leave the home. The issue was whether the local authority could detain the woman and whether the Court under its inherent jurisdiction could make an order preventing the discharge of the woman from the care of the treatment unit preferred by the local authority and whether it could appoint a receiver to prevent the daughter dissipating her mother's savings and pensions in preference to the local authority applying for orders under the Mental Health Act 1983. Although not a case directly concerned with deprivation of liberty, the Court set out some guidelines which may be relevant if the High Court's powers under it inherent jurisdiction is likely to be relied on. Munby J (as he then was) set the following minimum requirements which must be satisfied:

(a) the detention must be authorised on an application made before the detention commences;

(b) except in an emergency, there must be evidence to establish that the person lacks capacity and that the restrictions or restraint proposed is appropriate;

(c) any order authorising detention must contain provision for an adequate review procedure at reasonable intervals in particular to ascertain whether the lack of capacity persists or detention should continue;

(d) in *Salford County Council v GJ, MJ & BJ*[44] whilst accepting that safeguards would depend on the circumstances of the particular case, Munby J suggested an initial review hearing before the Court within 4 weeks of the court order authorising deprivation of liberty or sooner if the Official Solicitor had not previously been involved in the proceedings;

---

[41] [2007] 2 FLR 1083.
[42] [2008] 2 FLR 1295.
[43] [2007] EWHC 623 (Fam).
[44] [2008] EWHC 1097 (Fam).

(e) regular review by the Court at or about twelve months after the hearing or sooner if so directed by the Court. The Official Solicitor should be involved at each review hearing and should be provided with up to date reports at least 4 weeks in advance of the hearing;

(f) any party to the proceedings should be at liberty to apply for a review at any time, and where necessary at short notice;

(g) there must be regular internal reviews as required usually every 8–10 weeks, such reviews to include the Official Solicitor.

The need for regular reviews is in line with the decisions of the ECtHR which have emphasised that access to reviews was necessary even where the original detention has been authorised by judicial authority.

10.7 AUTHORITY TO RESTRAIN

10.7.1 What is meant by restraint

Section 6(4) of the Act provides that a person restrains an incapacitated person if:

(a) he uses, or threatens to use, force to secure the doing of an act which the person lacking capacity resists, or

(b) restricts that person's liberty of movement, whether or not there is resistance.

In *Guzzardii v Italy*[45] a suspected Mafioso had been made the subject of a compulsory residence order and taken to a small island, Asinara where he was required to live in a confined area. The Court held that in order to determine whether someone has been 'deprived of his liberty' within the meaning of Art 5(1) 'the starting point must be his concrete situation and account must be taken of the whole range of criteria such as the type, duration, effects and manner of implementation of the measure in question'. On the facts, the Court ruled that he had been deprived of his liberty. The Court also added that the distinction between 'restraint and deprivation of liberty was one of 'degree or intensity and not one of nature or substance'.

The Act however, permits the use of some form of restraint in limited circumstances and provided two conditions are satisfied. These are, firstly, that the person using restraint must reasonably believe that it is necessary to do the act in order to prevent harm to P and secondly, that the act done must be a proportionate response to: (i) the likelihood of P suffering harm; and (ii) the seriousness of that harm.[46] The circumstances of P and the situation which necessitates the use of restraint must be assessed and if restraint is used the degree of force used must only be just enough to prevent harm to P.

---

[45] (1980) 3 EHRR 333.
[46] MCA 2005, s 6(2) and (3).

The main Code of Practice, paras 6.40–6.48 also sets out guidance about the appropriate use of restraint. The Code of Practice also makes reference to the relevant cases to assist in identifying the relevant factors that should generally be considered by the decision maker to distinguish 'restraint' from 'deprivation of liberty' (see above at **10.4**).

10.8 RESTRAINT OR DEPRIVATION OF LIBERTY IN A HOSPITAL OR CARE HOME

10.8.1 When do the Deprivation of Liberty Safeguards apply?

The position of those who lack capacity residing in institutional care by reason of administrative decision making, which effectively deprives them of their liberty, was a concern to the government following the decision of the European Court of Human Rights in *HL v UK*.[47] HL, an autistic man, lacking capacity, was readmitted to Bournewood Hospital following his placement with carers in the community. His detention was not regularised by use of the mental health legislation as he was compliant with the decision. It is everyday social policy for people who lack capacity and who are unable to care for themselves to be placed in care or nursing homes on the basis that they are compliant with the placement and do not resist. The route to care is by way of an administrative decision made by health or social services departments of local authorities and is not formally authorised. The nature of these placements may perforce involve a deprivation of liberty even if it is limited to the locking of doors for safety reasons (see above). The point is that P is unable to consent to the deprivation through lack of capacity. The European Court of Human Rights held that these informal arrangements contravened Art 5. The Deprivation of Liberty Safeguards provide a regime for the authorities formally to authorise the deprivation and provides an appeal process to the Court of Protection.

The new regime refers to hospitals and care homes as being the relevant providers for the purposes of the Deprivation of Liberty Safeguards. It is those two residential providers of care which must obtain authorisation to deprive P of his or her liberty. Obvious examples are hospitals which provide care for dementia patients or those with brain injuries. In relation to care homes this would include residential care for older people, nursing homes and EMI (elderly mentally infirm) homes.

Aside from the obvious examples, there exists a range of provision from sheltered housing for older people to semi independent living schemes for those with learning disabilities. It has proved difficult for those involved to decide whether the provision was subject to the regime. It also has to be said that the regime places an enormous administrative burden particularly upon local authorities. This is manifestly difficult in an economic climate where resources and costs are to be constrained rather than expanded. Perhaps understandably, it is likely that imaginative exercises will be carried out in order to classify

---

[47]   *HL v UK (Bournewood)* (2004) 40 EHRR 761.

provisions as being outside the scope of the authorisation and therefore its expense. The case of *G v R, A Local Authority and F*[48] is a good example of failure of such attempts. Additionally, while the statutory provisions at first sight seem to be straightforward it has been acknowledged that the environment in which local authorities operate in this field of adult care is not legally coherent and bristles with intricate regulations so it is essential that care is taken to ensure that the procedures followed with precision and attempts are not made to circumvent them or to look for short cuts.

10.8.2 The s 5 provisions

Section 5 of the Act makes provision to allow carers and, for instance, health and social care professionals to carry out acts in connection with the care or treatment of a person lacking capacity provided before doing the act the carer takes reasonable steps to establish whether the person is lacking capacity in relation to the matter and when doing the act the carer reasonably believes that the person lacks capacity and that it will be in the person's best interests for the act to be done. This allows the carers to do whatever is considered necessary and in the best interests of P in order to safeguard his/her welfare and health. When carrying out such acts the carer must also apply the key principles set out in s 1 and the best interests check list set out in s 4 (see chapter 2). Provided these conditions are met, the carer is afforded protection from liability for their actions and such acts can be carried out as if P had capacity and had given his/her consent. However, the protection from liability does not cover any act which is intended to *restrain* P.[49]

10.8.3 The Sch A1 provisions

Provision contained in Sch A1 of the Act (inserted by the Mental Health Act 2007) sets out the Deprivation of Liberty Safeguards which came into force on 1 April 2009. A managing authority of a hospital or care home is now permitted to deprive a person lacking capacity of his/her liberty by detaining him/her provided three conditions are satisfied. These are:

(a) the incapacitated person is detained in hospital or care home for the purpose of being given care or treatment;

(b) that a standard or urgent authorisation is in force;

(c) the standard or urgent authorisation relates to the incapacitated person and the hospital or care home in which that person is detained.[50]

A person who carries out any act in pursuance of such authorisation and for the purpose of giving care or treatment is excluded from liability and is placed in the same position as if the person lacking capacity had had capacity to consent in relation to the doing of the act and had consented to his/her detention.[51]

---

[48] [2010] EWHC 621 (Fam), [2010] 2 FLR 294.
[49] MCA 2005, s 6(1).
[50] MCA 2005, Sch A1, Part 1, paras 1 and 2.
[51] MCA 2005, Sch A1, Part 1, para 3.

However, the person is not protected from civil or criminal liability resulting from his/her negligence in doing any thing. It is also emphasised that any act done must be done for the purpose of the standard or urgent authorisation and where a standard authorisation is in force it does not authorise a person to do any act which does not comply with the conditions (if any) included in the authorisation.[52]

A standard authorisation is usually requested by the managers of the hospital or care home, where the person is or may be deprived of his/her liberty. The request is made to the supervisory authority. In order to obtain the authorisation the managing authority will have to ensure that the person in respect of whom the authorisation is sought meets the qualifying requirements set out in Sch A1, Part 3, para 12 because, before the authorisation is granted, the supervisory authority will arrange for assessments to be carried out to determine whether these requirements are met in relation to the person detained (see below).

Following the abolition in April 2013 of Primary Care Trusts, the supervisory body for both hospitals and care homes is the local authority for the area where P is ordinarily resident or if the person is not resident in the area of any local authority the supervisory body will be the local authority for the area in which the hospital or care home is situated (DOL Code of Practice para 3.1–3.3). If P's residence remains unclear the local authority which received the application should deal with it (see Mental Capacity (Deprivation of Liberty: Standard Authorisations and Assessments and Ordinary Residence) Regulations 2008).

10.8.4 The qualifying requirements

The following are the qualifying requirements which must be met before a standard authorisation is granted:
(a)   the age requirement;
(b)   the mental health requirement;
(c)   the mental capacity requirement;
(d)   the best interests requirement;
(e)   the eligibility requirement;
(f)   the no refusals requirement.

The age requirement

The person in respect of whom the authorisation is sought must be 18 years of age because for those who are under 18 years of age a different safeguards process applies. In most cases this will not present any difficulty as a birth certificate will be considered sufficient evidence of age.

---

[52]   MCA 2005, Sch A1, Part 1, para 4.

The mental health requirement

The person must be suffering from mental disorder within the meaning of the Mental Health Act 1983 as amended ie, 'any disorder or disability of mind, but including for these purposes a person with learning difficulties whether or not associated with abnormally aggressive behaviour or seriously irresponsible conduct'.[53] The mental health assessment must be carried out by a doctor approved under s 12 of the Mental Health Act 1983 (see also DOL Code of Practice, paras 4.35–4.39).

The mental capacity requirement

The person must lack capacity in relation to the question whether or not he/she should be accommodated in the relevant hospital or care home for the purpose of being given the relevant care or treatment. The key principles set out in s 1 of the Act and the provisions of ss 2 and 3 of the Act must be applied when assessing whether the person lacks capacity (see **2.4**). The assessment of capacity must be undertaken in accordance with the key principles set out in s1 of the MCA 2005 and the provisions of ss 3 and 4 of the Act.

The best interests requirement

Four conditions must be met to satisfy this requirement. These are:
(a)   the person is, or is to be a detained resident;
(b)   the person's detention is in his/her best interests;
(c)   the detention is necessary to prevent harm to the person; and
(d)   the detention is a proportionate response to the likelihood of the person suffering harm and the seriousness of that harm.[54]

The assessors should seek the views of anyone who has been named as someone P would want to be consulted, anyone caring for P, anyone interested in P's welfare (eg, family member or friend) and any attorney or deputy who represents P. The assessor must consult the managing authority and have regard to the conclusions of the mental health assessor on the impact or likely impact on the person's mental health by being detained, any relevant needs assessment and care plan. When providing the assessment the assessor must state the name and address of every interested person consulted. If the report is positive, it must state the maximum authorisation period which should not exceed 12 months, and may provide for different periods to apply in relation to different kinds of standard authorisations. The assessor may also recommend the conditions which should apply to the authorisation. If the conclusion is that deprivation of liberty is not in P's best interests or that there is or has been an unauthorised deprivation of liberty this must be stated in the assessment.

---

[53]   MCA 2005, Sch A1, Part 3, para 14.
[54]   MCA 2005, Sch A1, Part 3, para 16.

The eligibility requirement

A person is ineligible if he/she is already subject to the provision of the Mental Health Act 1983 namely, he/she is detained in a hospital under the Mental Health Act 1983 or meets the criteria for detention but is objecting to being detained in the hospital or to some or all of the treatment in which case he/she should be detained under the powers contained in the 1983 Act. A person would also be ineligible if on leave of absence, or subject to a guardianship, or a community treatment regime, or conditional discharge and subject to a measure which would be inconsistent with an authorisation if granted, or if on leave of absence, or subject to community treatment regime or conditional discharge and the authorisation if granted would be for deprivation of liberty in a hospital for the purpose of treatment for mental disorder.[55] This assessment must be carried out by a mental health assessor who is a doctor approved under s 12 of the MH 1983 or a best interests assessor who is also an approved mental health professional. For those who come within the 1983 Act the process set out in that Act will apply.

In *GJ v Foundation Trust PCT v Secretary of State for Health*[56] Charles J considered the application of the eligibility criteria in relation to a challenge by P to his detention under DOLS. Three important areas were highlighted.

*   Where the person detained comes within the scope of Mental Health Act 1983, this takes primacy regardless of there being alternative solutions under MCA 2005.

*   If detention is for the purpose of physical treatment only, then the person detained is not authorised as a mental health patient.

*   In considering eligibility/ineligibility, there must be reference to the reality of the purpose of detention and the Court must focus upon the position as it is when the case falls to be decided and not what it may have been at the time authorisation was granted.

The no refusals requirement

A person meets this requirement unless he/she has made an effective and valid advance decision refusing some or all of the treatment in question.

There is also a refusal if there is a valid refusal, which is within the scope of his authority, by a donee of a lasting power of attorney or deputy for the person concerned to be accommodated in the hospital or care home for the purposes of receiving some or all of the relevant care or treatment in circumstances which amount to deprivation of the person's liberty or at all.[57]

---

[55]   MCA 2005, Sch A1, Part 3, para 17.
[56]   [2009] EWHC 2972 (Fam), [2010] Fam Law 139.
[57]   MCA 2005, Sch A1, Part 3, para 20.

10.9 STANDARD AUTHORISATION

The managing authority must request a standard authorisation in the following cases:

(a) if it is proposing to accommodate the person who appears to meet all the qualifying requirements, to be detained in the relevant hospital or care home, or is likely to do so within the next 28 days; or

(b) where it appears to the managing authority that the person who is already accommodated in the relevant hospital or care home is likely at some time within the next 28 days to be a detained resident in the relevant hospital or care home or is likely at that time or at some later time within the next 28 days to meet all the qualifying requirements; or

(c) where the person is detained resident in the relevant hospital or care home and meets all the qualifying requirements or is likely to do so at some time within the next 8 days; or

(d) if there is or is likely to be a change in the place of detention provided that a standard authorisation has been given and remains in force.[58]

There is a change in the place of detention if the person concerned ceases to be detained in the stated hospital or care home and becomes detained in a different hospital or care home. In this instance the managing authority will be the managing authority of the new hospital or care home.[59]

Before a standard authorisation is given the supervisory authority must secure an assessment of all the qualifying requirements and be satisfied that these requirements are met. The Mental Capacity (Deprivation of Liberty: Standard Authorisations, Assessments and Ordinary Residence) Regulations 2008[60] provide for who should carry out the assessments, the professional skills and training which the assessors must have and the timeframe within which the assessments must be completed.

10.9.1 The application process for authorisation

The request must be made in writing to the supervisory body. A prescribed form for making the application for standard authorisation is not provided in the Act or the COP Rules 2007 but pursuant to the DOL Code of Practice, para 3.7 the Department of Health has developed standard forms for the assessments and the application. In England the request must include:

• the name and gender of P;

• the age of P or where this is not known whether the managing authority reasonably belives that P is a person aged 18 or over;

• the address at which P is currently located and the telephone number of the managing authority who is dealing with the request;

[58] MCA 2005, Sch 1A, Part 4, para 25.
[59] MCA 2005, Sch A1, Part 4, para 26.
[60] SI 2008/1858.

- the purpose for which the authorisation is requested;
- the date from which the authorisation is sought; and
- whether the managing authority has given an urgent authorisation and if so the date on which it expires.

The request must also include if it is available or could reasonably be obtained:

- any medical information relating to P's health that the managing authority considers to be relevant to the proposed restrictions to P's liberty;
- the diagnosis of the mental disorder (within the meaning of the MHA 1983 but disregarding any exclusion for persons with learning disability) from which P is suffering;
- any care plans and need assessments;
- P's racial ethnic or national origins;
- whether P has any special communication needs;
- details of the proposed restriction on P's liberty;
- whether it is necessary for an independent mental capacity advocate (IMCA) to be instructed;
- where the authorisation is required to give treatment; whether P has made an advance decision that may be valid and applicable to some or all of that treatment;
- whether there is an existing standard authorisation in relation to P and if so the date when it will expire;
- whether P is subject to the requirements of the MHA 1983 and the name address and telephone number of any person named by P as someone to be consulted about his/her welfare; anyone engaged in caring for the P or interested in P's welfare; any done of LPA granted by P or any deputy appointed for P by the Court and any IMCA who has already been instructed (DOL Code of Practice, paras 3.8 and 3.9).

The managing authority must also inform P's family, friends and carers and any IMCA already involved that the application for authorisation of deprivation of liberty has been made unless it is impractical or impossible to do so, or undesirable in terms of the interests of P's health or safety. Any person who is engaged in P's care or interested in his/her welfare or any person who has been named as person to consult must be given an opportunity to input their views on whether DOL is in the best interests of P as part of the best interests assessment. If P has expressed views about who should be informed and consulted those views should be taken into account (DOL Code of Practice, para 3.15)

In order to obtain authorisation the managing authority will have to ensure that P meets the qualifying requirements (see above) because before authorisation is granted the supervisory authority will arrange for assessments to be carried to determine whether these requirements are met. It is best therefore, to be prepared in advance to avoid any delay in providing the appropriate care and treatment plan for P and avoid the need for an urgent authorisation.

10.9.2 Supervisory body

When it receives a request for authorisation of deprivation of liberty, the supervisory body must, as soon as practical and possible consider whether the request is appropriate, valid complete and should be pursued. Any information that it requires from the managing authority to help with the decision should be sought. If the supervisory body has any doubts about proceeding with the request, it should seek to resolve the issue with the managing authority. The supervisory body should also consider whether P has somebody who is not engaged in providing care or treatment in a professional capacity or for remuneration to support P. If there is no such appropriate person who may be consulted, the supervisory body must immediately instruct an IMCA to represent P. This is of even greater importance if an urgent authorisation has been given to ensure that there is someone to make any input on behalf of P. Guidance is set out in Chapter 10 of the Code of Practice in identifying an IMCA who is suitably qualified to represent P (DOL Code of Practice, paras 3.22–3.23).

The supervisory body must also appoint assesors to assess the six qualifying requirements (ee above) and give the assessors any relevant needs assessment or care plan drawn up by them or on their behalf. The supervisory has a legal duty to ensure that the assessors selected are both suitable and eligible to undertake the assessments. The factor which they should consider include the reason for deprivation of liberty, whether the potential assessor has the relevant experience in relation to P's specific disability and his/her cultural background (DOL Code of Practice para 4.4). Provision is made in the Deprivation of Liberty: Standard Authorisations Assessments and Ordinary Residence) Regulations 2008 for the qualification skill and training needed by the person who carries out the assessments and the time frame within which the assessments must be completed. There must be a minimum of two assessors. The mental health and best interests assessments must be undertaken by different assessors. The best interests assessors may be an employee of the supervisory body or the managing authority provided that the person is not involved in the care or treatment of P or in the decisions about P's care. A potential best interests assessor should not be used if/she is in a line management relationship with the professional proposing the deprivation of liberty or the mental health assessors. The assessors should not have any financial interest in the case. An assessor must not be a relative of the person being assessed nor of a person with a financial interest in the person's care (DOL Code of Practice, para 4.13).

The assessment must be completed with 21 days from the date the supervisory body received the request for authorisation. If an urgent authorisation has been granted the assessment must be completed within the period of the urgent authorisation including any extension granted by the supervisory body (DOL Code of Practice, para 4.1).

If any of the assessments is negative, the supervisory body must refuse the authorisation and notify the managing authority, P and any s 39A IMCA and every interested person consulted by the best interests assessor. The supervisory may review a standard authorisation at any time and must do so if requested by P or his/her representative or the managing authority. If a request for review is made the supervisory body must decide whether review of any of the qualifying requirements is needed and if so commission review assessments. Thus in order to ensure that the authorisation process proceeds smoothly the supervisory body should have a procedure in place that identifies the actions they should take, who should take it and within what time scale. As far as practical and possible, they should communicate the procedure to the managing authorities and give them the relevant contact details for making the request for authorisation. The flow chart set out in Annex 3 of the DOL Code of Practice summarises the process that a supervisory body should follow.

If the assessment is a best interests assessment the supervisory body must take into account any information given or submission made by P's representative or any s 39C IMCA or any s 39D IMCA. If P is not currently in the supervisory body's area, it should seek as far as practical and possible, to arrange to use assessors based near where P is currently located (DOL Code of Practice, paras 4.4–4.8). In undertaking the best interests assessment there is duty on the assessor to take account of the impact of any decision taken on P's health and of P's wishes and the views of anyone whose views P wishes to be considered or anyone who has an interest in P's welfare, or anyone who is caring for P. In this regard consideration must be given to the relationship P has with his family to ensure that the rights enshrined under Art 8 of the ECHR are respected. Failure to take these matters into consideration risks the actions taken under any authorisation granted to be deemed unlawful as occurred in *London Borough of Hillingdon v Steven Neary (By the Official Solicitor) and Others*.[61] In that case P who was 20 years of age and who suffered from autism and severe learning difficulties lived with his father. The father received high level of financial and practical support including respite care from the Adult and Social Care Department of the local authority until December 2009 when P was taken into respite care and never returned home despite opposition by the father and P's expressed wishes. The local authority initially retained him under an urgent authorisation and subsequently it made three requests for standard authorisation to the service manager of the supervisory body. When the meeting was convened it was chaired by the team manager who was responsible for the support services team. The father and the Official Solicitor on behalf of P challenged the local authority's decision on the ground that their action had been unlawful and had deprived P of his liberty. Jackson J in rejecting the local authority's opposition concluded that: (i) P had been deprived of his liberty through the relevant period; (ii) the authorisation relied upon by the local

---

[61]   [2011] EWHC 1377 (COP), [2011] COPLR Con Vol 632, [2012] 1 FLR 72.

authority was flawed and even if it had been valid they did not in themselves in the circumstances of the case amount to lawful authority for keeping P at the support unit; and (iii) the mere belief that the local authority was acting in the best interests of P was not relevant. It had acted as if it had the right to make decisions about P and by a combination of turning a deaf ear and force majeure it had tried to wear down the father's resistance. It had thus failed to activate the statutory safeguards. Consequently the local authority had breached P's rights to family life and deprived him of his liberty in contravention of Art 8 and 5 of the ECHR. Additionally the Court found that by failing to refer the matter to the Court of Protection sooner; failing to appoint an IMCA and failing to conduct an effective review it had deprived his Art 6 rights to take proceedings to challenge their actions.

By reference to the actions taken by the local authority Jackson J gave the guidance set out below in relation to the operation of the DOLS regime and the responsibilities of the supervisory body.

10.9.3   The interface between the administrative DOLS regime and the Court of Protection

In cases where there is a disagreement between the local authority and P and/or his famiy the local authority's powers are limited to investigating, providing support and where appropriate applying to the Court to make an order. If a local authority seeks to take any restrictive measures it must have statutory authority or else obtain a decision of the Court (para 22 and see also *Re A and C (Equality and Human Rights Commission Intervening*[62]). Decisions about those lacking capacity are determined by their best interests The burden is always on the state to show that an incapacitated person's welfare cannot be sustained by living with and being looked after by his or her family with or without outside support (see para 24).

The DOL scheme is an important safeguard against arbitrary detention. Where stringent conditions are met, it authorises a managing authority to deprive a person of liberty at a particular place. It is not to be used by a local authority a means of getting its own way on the question of whether is in the person's best interests to be in the place at all. To adopt such an attitude would be to turn the spirit of the MCA 2005 on its head and the code designed to protect the liberty of vulnerable people being sued instead as a instrument of confinement.

Decision making

Where a local authority wears a number of hats, it should be clear about who is responsible for its direction and specific decisions. Welfare planning should be directed by the team to which the allocated social worker belonged, there would of course be the closest liaison with those who ran the support facilities. The 'tail' of service provision, however expert and specialised, should not wag

---

[62]   [2010] EWHC 978 (Fam), [2010] COPLR Con Vol 10, [2010] 2 FLR 1363.

the 'dog' of welfare planning as in this case which was characterised either by the absence of decision making or by a disorganised situation where nobody was truly in charge and it was consequently possible for no one to take responsibility.

Responsibilities of the supervisory body

The best interests assessment is not a routine piece of paper work. Properly viewed it is the corner stone of the DOL safeguarding regime. Its purpose is to ensure that a person is only deprived of his liberty where he is eligible and it in his best interests, necessary and proportionate in relation to the likelihood and seriousness of the harm that he might otherwise suffer. The supervisory body's responsibility is to scrutinise the assessment it receives with independence and with a degree of care that is appropriate to the seriousness of the decision and to the circumstances of the individual case that or should be known to it. The obligation under Sch A1, para 50 requires an authorisation to be granted only if all the assessments are positive and to grant the authorisation only when it is satisfied that the best interests assessment is a thorough piece of work that adequately analyses the four necessary conditions. The supervisory body has control of the terms of the authorisation. It is under no obligation to follow the recommendation fo the best interests assessor and it is open to the supervisory body to require a discussion with the assessor or require further inquiries to be made. To enable the supervisory body to undertake its function responsibly and rationally, it should have sufficient knowledge base about the circumstances of P. Therefore, where a supervisory body grants an authorisation on the basis of perfunctory scrutiny of superficial best interests assessments it cannot expect the authorisation to be valid. A best interests assessment would also be considered flawed if the assessor fails to compare and contrast viable and practically available placements and the supervisory body fails to question this omission before granting the authorisation (see decision of Charles J in *A County Council v MB, JB and A Residential Home*[63]).

10.9.4   Position where equivalent assessments have already been carried out

The supervisory body is not obliged to secure a required assessment if:

(a) it has a written copy of an existing assessment whether or not such an assessment was carried out in connection with a request for a standard authorisation or for some other purpose, and

(b) the assessment complies with all the required requirements under Sch A1;

(c) the existing assessments were carried out within the last 12 months; and

(d) it is satisfied that there is no reason why the existing assessment may no longer be accurate.

---

[63]   [2010] EWHC 2508 (COP), [2010] COPLR Con Vol 65, [2011] 1 FLR 790.

If the assessment is a best interests assessment the supervisory body must take into account any information given or submissions made, by the relevant person's representative (see below), any s 39C IMCA or any s 39D IMCA.

10.9.5   Supervisory body's duty to give authorisation

- The supervisory body must give a standard authorisation if all the assessments are positive and it has written copies of the assessments. All assessments are positive if each assessment concludes that the relevant person meets the qualifying requirements to which the assessment relates.[64]

- The authorisation must set out the period during which the authorisation is to be in force but the period must not exceed the maximum period recommended in the best interests assessment. The commencement date of the period may be a date after the authorisation is given.

- The authorisation may be given subject to conditions.

- The authorisation must be in writing and must name the relevant person, the hospital or care home, the period during which the authorisation is to be in force and the purpose for which it is given, the conditions subject to which the authorisation is given and the reason why the qualifying requirement is met.

- Appoint someone to act as the person's representative during the period of the authorisation (see below).

- Provide a copy of the authorisation to the relevant person's representative, the managing authority; the person being deprived of his/her liberty; any IMCA and every interested person consulted by the best interests assessor.

- Keep records.

The supervisory body may review a standard authorisation at any time and must do so if requested by the person detained under its provision, his/her representative or the managing authority. If a request is made, the supervisory body must decide whether any of the qualifying requirements appear to need a review and if so commission review assessments.

10.9.6   Duty of the managing authority

It must comply with any conditions attached to the authorisation. In the event of any material change in the detained person's circumstances it must request a review. If the conditions on which the authorisation was requested persist when the authorisation expires it may apply for a further authorisation to begin on the date when the original authorisation expires. In this event the full assessment process must be repeated.

---

[64]   MCA 2005, Sch A1, Part 4, para 50.

10.9.7   Rights of third party to require consideration of unauthorised detention by the supervisory body

An eligible third party may request the supervisory body to decide whether or not there is an unauthorised deprivation of liberty, provided the following conditions are met:

(a)   the eligible person must have notified the managing authority that it appears that there is an unauthorised deprivation of liberty;

(b)   the eligible person must have asked the managing authority to request a standard authorisation;

(c)   the managing authority has failed to make a request for standard authorisation within a reasonable period of the request having been made.

Where a request is made by an eligible third party the supervisory body must select and appoint a person to carry out an assessment of whether or not the person to whom the request relates is a detained resident unless it appears to the supervisory body that the request is frivolous or vexatious, or where the issue has already been decided and since that decision there has been no change of circumstances which would merit the question being decided again. The supervisory body's decision must be notified to the eligible person, the person to whom the request relates, the managing authority and any IMCA.[65]

10.10   URGENT APPLICATIONS

The managing authority of the relevant hospital or care home may give an urgent authorisation to provide a lawful basis for deprivation of liberty before a request for a standard authorisation is made, if it is required to make a request for a standard authorisation and they believe that the need for the relevant person to be a detained resident is so urgent that it is appropriate for the detention to begin before they make the request, or where they have made the request for a standard authorisation and they believe that the need for the relevant person to be a detained resident is so urgent that it is appropriate for the detention to begin before the request is disposed of. If the managing authority decide to give an urgent authorisation they must:

• Specify the period during which the authorisation is to be in force not exceeding 7 days.

• Give the urgent authorisation in writing.

• State the name of the relevant person, the name of the relevant hospital or care home, the period of authorisation and the purpose for which the authorisation is given.

• Keep a written record of why they have given the urgent authorisation.

• As soon as practicable after giving the authorisation, give a copy of the authorisation to the relevant person and any s 39A IMCA.

---

[65]   MCA 2005, Sch A1, Part 4, paras 67–69.

- Take such steps as are practicable to ensure that the relevant person understands the effect of the authorisation and the right to make an application to the Court to exercise its jurisdiction under s 21A and give the appropriate information both orally and in writing.[66]

The managing authority may seek an extension of the duration of the urgent authorisation. They must keep a written record of the reasons for the request and give the relevant person notice of the request for an extension. The supervisory body may on request grant an extension of the period of urgent authorisation only if they are satisfied that a request for a standard authorisation has been made; that there are exceptional reasons why it has not yet been possible for the request to be disposed of, and that it is essential for the existing detention to continue until the request is disposed. The extension must not exceed 7 days. If an extension is granted the supervisory body must notify the managing authority stating the period of the extension keep a written record of the outcome of the request and the period of the extension.

10.11 APPOINTMENT OF RELEVANT PERSON'S REPRESENTATIVE

The provision for the appointment of a representative to a person in respect of whom a standard authorisation has been issued are set out in the Act at Sch A1, paras 139–140. It provides that the supervisory body must appoint a person to be the relevant person's representative and that person must if appointed maintain, represent and support the relevant person in matters relating to or connected with his/her deprivation of liberty. The functions of a representative are in addition to and do not affect the authority of any donee, the powers of a deputy or any powers of the Court.[67] The Mental Capacity (Deprivation of Liberty: Appointment of Relevant Person's Representative) Regulations 2008, as amended by SI 2008/2368, provide for the selection and termination of appointment of a representative, and the formalities of the appointment and termination of a representative's appointment.

10.12 CHALLENGING AUTHORISTION

The Deprivation of Liberty Safeguards provide a regime for appropriate assessments to be carried out in relation to P which operate to justify P's detention. However, the regime would be inadequate unless there is available to the person detained, the right to challenge the authorisation together with a system of monitoring. The ECtHR emphasised the need for P to have access to reviews even where the detention has been authorised by judicial authority and Art 5(4) of the ECHR provides that everyone who is deprived of his liberty by arrest or detention shall be entitled to take proceedings b which the lawfulness of his detention shall be decided speedily by a court and his release ordered if the detention is not lawful. The amendments made to the MCA 2005 provide

---

[66] MCA 2005, Sch A1, Part 5, paras 77–83.
[67] MCA 2005, Sch A1, Part 10, para 141(1) and (2).

two routes of challenge to the grant of authorizations. First, by an application to the supervisory body and secondly on an application for review to the Court of Protection.

10.13 REVIEW BY THE SUPERVISORY BODY

Part 8 of Sch A1 provides for a built in monitoring and review procedure where standard authorisations have been given and which remain in force. Monitoring provides an opportunity for quality control in addition to safeguarding the detention. The review process focuses upon the validity of the qualifying requirements and thus the eligibility of P to be subject to the regime. It does not however apply to urgent authorisations.

Paragraph 102(1) of Sch A1 to the MCA 2005 imposes a monitoring responsibility upon the supervisory body to carry out its own review. Whilst this not compulsory, it is unlikely that the supervisory bodies will fail to build into their individual policies on Deprivation of Liberty Safeguards, their own review mechanism particularly having regard to the view expressed by the ECtHR. Failure to do so would inevitably lead to challenge through the courts.

10.13.1 Review

Paragraph 102(2) imposes an obligation to carry out a review if the supervisory body is requested to do so by an eligible person. Those eligible are defined as P, P's representative, or the manager of the relevant hospital or care home. The purpose is to provide an accessible procedure for reconsideration.

The grounds for review are set out in paras 105–107. In summary the grounds for review are that: (i) P does not meet the qualification requirements; or (ii) P is ineligible under Sch A1 (if P is ineligible by reason of being a mental health patient); or (iii) where the reason for the initial authorisation has changed; or (iv) where conditions need to be reconsidered or varied.

The power of the supervisory body in this context is either to terminate the standard authorisation or vary the conditions. Discretion is limited. So for instance where review assessments are carried out and reach a negative conclusion the supervisory body must terminate the authorisation

10.13.2 Procedure

It is suggested that any request for a review should be made in writing although there is no specific stipulation for this and no pro forma for the application. The process of review is detailed ad mandatory. There is no scope for misunderstandings. The supervisory body must:

- Give notice of the review, decide which of the requirements is reviewable, and where there is more than one, ensure they are subject to separate assessments.

- Secure separate review assessments where necessary, e g best interest requirements are non-assessable if a variation of conditions only is sought or there has been no significant change.
- Complete the review by deciding whether or not the requirements are reviewable and if so whether or not to terminate or vary the authorisation.
- Give notice stating the outcome and any variation of terms of authorisation. Made in writing.
- Keep records of their reviews and outcomes.

Paragraph 118 of Sch A1 provides that according to the outcome the individual reviewable assessments the overall review of the standard authorisation is complete at a variety of different stages. For instance the review will be complete if the supervisory body decides that none of the qualifying requirements are reviewable (para 110). In those circumstances the supervisory body need go no further save to report the outcome. Where or more of the review assessments reach a negative conclusion the supervisory body must terminate the authorisation (for full details see the MCA Sch A1 in the Appendices and Annex 4 of the Deprivation of Liberty Code of Practice which sets out a flow chart).

10.14   THE COURT'S POWERS IN RELATION TO STANDARD AND URGENT AUTHORISATION UNDER SCH A1

Section 4A of the MCA 2005 clarifies that the legislation does not authorise deprivation of liberty except by way of court order or authorisation under Sch A1.

The Court of Protection has jurisdiction to ensure that Art 5(4) of the ECHR is complied with by reviewing the lawfulness of the detention of anyone for whom authorisation has been granted to provide care or treatment. The application for a review may be made by the person who has been deprived of his/her liberty or a representative for that person.

Section 21A of the Act provides that where a standard authorisation has been made the Court may determine any questions relating to:

(a)   whether the relevant person meets one or more of the qualifying requirements;

(b)   the period during which the standard authorisation is to be in force;

(c)   the purpose for which the standard authorisation is given;

(d)   the conditions subject to which the standard authorisation is given,

and may make an order varying or terminating the standard authorisation or directing the supervisory body to vary or terminate the standard authorisation.[68]

---

[68]   MCA 2005, s 21A(2) and (3).

Where an urgent authorisation has been given, the Court may determine any question relating to:

(a)   whether the urgent authorisation should have been given;

(b)   the period during which the urgent authorisation is to be in force;

(c)   the purpose for which the urgent authorisation is given;

and may make an order varying or terminating the urgent authorisation or directing the managing authority of the relevant hospital or care home to vary or terminate the urgent authorisation.[69]

A court may, in relation to either of the above applications, consider a person's liability for any act done in connection with the standard or urgent authorisation before its variation or termination, and make an order excluding a person from liability.[70]

As will be observed the legislation is comprehensive and self explanatory. In summary:

(a)   in the case of an application relating to an urgent authorisation the Court can determine whether the authorisation should have been given, the period for which it remain in force and its purpose;

(b)   in the case of a standard authorisation the Court can determine whether the qualifying requirements are met, the period purpose and conditions of the authorisation.

10.15   PROCEDURE

The procedure and practice in relation to deprivation of liberty applications are set out in Part 10A of the Court of Protection Rules 2007 and related Practice Directions. Deprivation of liberty (DoL) applications means applications for orders under s 21A of the Act relating to standard or urgent authorisation under Sch A1 of the Act. It is acknowledged that by their nature such applications are of special urgency. The procedure set out hereunder relates to only such applications. They do not apply to applications concerning other matters, which may also raise issues relating to deprivation of liberty and require urgent attention. This should be explained to the DoL team at the Court so that the applications are handled appropriately.

The Practice Direction relating to applications for a deprivation of liberty identifies the key features of the special DoL procedure as follows:

(a)   special DoL forms ensure that DoL court papers stand out as such and receive special handling by the Court office;

---

[69]   MCA 2005, s 21A(4) and (5).
[70]   MCA 2005, s 21A(6) and (7).

(b) the application is placed before a judge as soon as possible – if necessary before the application is issued – for directions to be given as to the steps to be taken in the application and who is to take each step and by when;

(c) the usual COP Rules 2007 will apply only so far as consistent with the judicial directions given for the particular case;

(d) a dedicated team in the court office (the DoL team) will deal with such application at all stages including liaison with would be applicants/other parties;

(e) the progress of each DoL case will be monitored by a judge assigned to that case, assisted by the DoL team.

10.15.1 When can an application be made to the Court of Protection?

In order to comply with the provisions of Art 5(4) of the ECHR an application made by the person who is deprived of his liberty or on his behalf must be dealt with expeditiously. However, whenever there are concerns about a person being deprived of his liberty, in the first instance attempts must be made to resolve the issue through a conciliatory process rather than through litigation. The main Code of Practice sets out, in Chapter 15, the best ways to settle disagreements and disputes. Where possible these guidelines should be followed. The complaint procedure of the managing authority and the supervisory body should also be used where appropriate and where there is sufficient time to do so. However, since the issue of someone being deprived of his/her liberty relates to a breach of a person's human rights under the ECHR it is important that the vulnerable person or those who are acting on his behalf or concerned about his welfare should not be discouraged from applying to the Court for a declaration and appreciate that an application can be made at any stage of the safeguarding process set out in the Act. The Act, in s 21A, sets out the circumstances in which an application may be made to the Court. In summary the application can be made:

- before standard authorisation is given;

- after a standard authorisation is given;

- where an urgent authorisation is given;

- where an extension of the authorisation is sought.

Where the application is considered before the standard authorisation is given the Court may be asked to declare whether the relevant person has capacity and whether the act done or proposed to be done is lawful and in the best interests of the incapacitated person.

Where an application is made after the supervisory body has given authorisation the relevant person or his/her representative deputy or donee may apply to the Court to determine:

- whether the relevant person meets one or more of the qualifying requirements for deprivation of liberty;

- the period for which the standard authorisation is to remain in force;

- the purposes for which the standard authorisation has been given;
- the conditions attached to the standard authorisation.

Where an urgent authorisation has been given an application to the Court may be made to determine any question relating to:

- whether the authorisation should have been given;
- the period during which the authorisation is to remain in force;
- the purpose for which the urgent authorisation has been given.

10.15.2   Who can apply without permission?

The following person can apply without permission:

- The person who lacks or may lack capacity.
- A donor of a lasting power of attorney to whom an application relates or their donee.
- A deputy who has been appointed by the Court to act for the person concerned.
- A person named in an existing order.
- A person appointed by the supervisory body as the relevant person's representative.
- The Official Solicitor in certain circumstances.
- A Public Guardian.

Permission to apply for the substantive application will need to be applied for by any other person.

10.16   HOW TO APPLY

10.16.1   Steps to be taken before issuing an application

The applicant must contact the deprivation of liberty (DoL) team at the earliest opportunity before making the application to inform the team that the application is to be made and how quickly the Court's decision is required on the merits of the application and when the application is likely to be lodged. Where this is not possible, the applicant should liaise with the DoL team either by telephone or fax at the time when the application is lodged. The information that the DoL team will need in advance is:

(a)   that the DoL application is to be made;

(b)   how urgent the application is (by when should the Court's decision, or interim decision on the merits be given); and

(c)   when the Court will receive the application papers.

In very urgent cases arrangements can be made by the team for directions to be given or an interim order to be obtained by telephone conference before the application is issued. In such cases the Court will require brief details including the following:

(a)   the parties' details and where they live;

(b)   the issue to be decided;

(c)   the date of the urgent or standard authorisation;

(d)   the date of effective detention;

(e)   the parties' legal representatives;

(f)   details of any interested parties, such as a relative; and

(d)   whether there have been any previous proceedings relating to the parties and, if so, details of the same.

In cases of emergency, where it is necessary to make an application out of office hours, the security office at the RCJ should be contacted on 020 7947 6000. The security officer should be informed of the nature of the case. In the Family Division the procedure involves the judge being contacted through the Family Division duty Officer, and the RCJ security officer will need to contact the duty officer and not the judge's clerk. In all other cases the DoL team should be contacted at:

DoLs Application Branch
The Court of Protection
courtofprotectionenquiries@hmcts.gsi.gov.uk
Telephone: 0300 456 4600
Monday to Friday, 9am to 5pm

You can also write to the following address:

PO Box 70185
First Avenue House
42 – 49 High Holborn
London
WC1A 9JA

Emergency applications only – out of office hours
Telephone: 020 7947 6000

In all cases relating to an application for deprivation of liberty, the prescribed forms for such applications must be used. If in such a case it is anticipated that other issues may arise, the DoL forms should identify and describe briefly those issues and any relief which may be sought in respect of them should be set out in the sections 3.5 and 5 of the DLA Form under the heading 'other issues'. This will enable the Court to deal with them immediately or by giving directions for how they should be dealt with. Therefore, unless the Court expressly directs, applicants should not issue a second and separate application (using the standard court forms) relating to any 'other issues'.

Where the application seeks relief concerning a deprivation of liberty other than under s 21A in respect of standard or urgent authorisation eg under s 16(2)(a) the standard court forms and not the DoL forms should be used but it should be made clear on the standard form that relief relating to deprivation of liberty is also being sought and the proposed applicant should contact the DoL team to discuss the handling of the application before the application is issued.

10.16.2   Issuing an application

To make an application where permission to make the DoL application is required:

(a)   the applicant is required to file the following forms:
    (i)   Form DLC where the applicant needs permission to make a DoL.
    (ii)   A draft form DLA.
    (iii)   Form DLB (if the application is urgent) in which the reasons for the application and the urgency must be set out. If the applicant considers that the application needs to be dealt with within a shorter time scale this should be indicated on the form and a proposed timetable should be set out. The directions and order sought must be identified with a draft of the order attached. The DLB should always be placed at the top of the papers and (where this is appropriate) mention that the permission is required and that a completed DLC form is attached.

    Only P and his appointed representative, attorney or deputy have the right to make an application without leave. All other persons including family members are required to seek permission to apply;

(b)   pay the court fee of £400;

(c)   if possible an electronic version of the draft order on disc should be lodged;

(d)   where an application is made out of hours before the application is lodged, an undertaking will be required that the appropriate forms will be lodged and the court fee paid unless an exemption applies.

10.16.3   The Court Office

As soon as the DoL team is notified of the application the team will ensure that the application is placed before a nominated judge. During office hours the application will be placed before a judge at the Court of Protection. During out of office hours the application will be placed before the judge who is most immediately available. Initially, the application will be dealt with by the judge and any orders made without attendance of the applicant or his representatives. Possible directions which the Court may need to give include:

(a) upon whom and by when and how service of the application should be effected;

(b) dispensing with acknowledgement of service of the application or allowing a short period of time for so doing, which in some cases may amount to a few hours only;

(c) whether further lay or expert evidence should be obtained;

(d) whether the detained person should be a party and represented by the Official Solicitor and whether any other person should be a party;

(e) whether any family members should be formally notified of the application and of any hearing and joined as parties;

(f) fixing a date for the first hearing and giving the time estimate;

(g) allocation of the case to the level of judge appropriate to hear the case;

(h) whether the case is such that should be immediately transferred to the High Court for directions;

(i) directions relating to the preparation of a bundle for the judge

As soon as the order is made the DoL team will notify the applicant of the order and carry out any other directions given by the judge and make arrangements for any transfer of the case to another court and for a first hearing

10.16.4 After issue/directions given

After issue and any directions given, the applicant or his legal representatives must:

(a) ensure that any directions given by the judge are complied with;

(b) ensure that the application, any orders made and the acknowledgement of service in Form DLE are served on the respondents to the application;

(c) prepare an indexed and paginated bundle of documents which should include a case summary, skeleton arguments and draft order for the hearing on notice; and

(d) serve an index of the bundle on all parties to the application and, where a party appears in person, serve a copy of the bundle on that person.

10.16.5 The first hearing

The first hearing will be listed for the Court to fix a date and or give directions, make an interim order or final order if appropriate or make such other orders as the appropriate in the case. Section 21A MCA 2005 provides that the Court may determine questions relating to standard authorisation. The Court must determine how it approaches that task; it is not compelled to carry out a full inquiry regardless of the merit. The fact that P's deprivation was to be reviewed is a factor which it will take into consideration. Furthermore in order to deal with an appeal and give it due consdieeration 'may not require any lengthy consideration. A full hearing is not necessarily a lengthy, time consuming or expensive hearing (Moses LJ at para 75 in *TA v AA*.) The hearing is as a general rule held in private.[71] The Court may direct that the hearing takes place in public if the criteria in r 93 apply.

10.16.6   Orders the Court can make

The Court may make any appropriate orders, grant an injunction and given directions. These will include:

(a)   a declaration whether or not the person who is the subject of the proceedings lacks capacity;

(b)   a declaration whether the act done or proposed to be done is lawful or in the best interests of the person who lacks capacity;

(c)   authorising acts which deprive a person of his liberty;

(d)   authorising appropriate restraint to be used;

(e)   orders varying or terminating the standard or urgent authorisation and;

(f)   orders directing the managing authority or supervisory body to comply with any directions the Court gives;

(g)   prohibiting a person from doing certain acts.

The general rule in all cases concerning health and welfare is that there will be no order as to costs of the proceedings.[72] This also applies to DoL applications.

10.17   APPEALS

Part 20 of the COP Rules 2007 applies to appeals from the Court's decision. Permission to appeal will be required[73] (for the consequences of failure to apply to the trial court for permission to appeal see *TA v AA ad Knowsley Metropolitan Borough Council*[74]). Permission will only be granted if the Court considers that the appeal would have a real prospect of success or there is some other compelling reason why the appeal should be heard.[75]

10.17.1   Practice in relation to without notice applications

Concerns have been expressed by the Court that practitioners too regularly do not follow the guidance on the information to be provided and the procedure to be followed in seeking without notice relief and that such failure shows an insufficient appreciation of the exceptional nature of without notice relief and the impact it has or could have on the rights, life and emotions of the person concerned in relation to whom and others against whom the order is made. It is only in exceptional circumstances and in accordance with the guidance set out

---

[71]   COP Rules 2007, r 90 and PD 13A.
[72]   COP Rules 2007, r 157.
[73]   COP Rules 2007, r 172.
[74]   [2013] EWCA Civ 1661.
[75]   COP Rules 2007, r 173.

in the relevant case law and practice guidance should without notice applications be made.[76] It is therefore important to ensure that the evidence in support of an application for deprivation of liberty gives a balanced, fair and particularised account of the events leading up to the application and the facts upon which it is based. Where possible it should include what the applicant thinks the respondent's case is or is likely to be. It should also include an account of the steps the applicant proposes concerning services, the giving of explanation of the order and the implementation of the order. This is of particular importance where emotional issues are involved and family members of a person who lacks capacity are the subject of injunctions and orders. In such cases information of the applicant's intentions is likely to inform issues as to the need, form and the proportionality of the relief sought and granted.[77] Where an order is obtained on a without notice application the term 'liberty to apply' should be replaced with the terms:

> 'If any person served with this order disagrees with any part of this order and wishes to seek to set aside or vary it, they should make an application to this court to set it aside or vary it within 21days of service of it upon them.'

This suggestion endorses the observation made in *B Borough Council v S (By the Official Solicitor)*[78] by Charles J in relation to without notice applications:

> 'There is a natural temptation for applicants to seek, and the Court to grant, relief to protect vulnerable person whether they are children or vulnerable adults. In my view this can lead (and experience as the applications judge confirms that it does lead) to practitioners making without notice applications which are not necessary or appropriate, or which are not properly supported by appropriate evidence. Also there is in my view a general practice of asking the Court to grant without notice orders over fairly extended period with expression permission to apply to vary or discharge on an inappropriately long period of notice (often 48 hours). It seems to me that on occasions this practice pays insufficient regard to the interests of both the person in respect of whom and against whom the orders are made, and that therefore on every occasion without notice relief is sought and granted the choice of the return date and the provisions as to permission to apply should be addressed with care by both applicants and the court. Factors in that consideration will be an estimation of the effect on the person against whom the order is made of service of the order and how that is to be carried out.'

10.18 EXAMPLE OF ORDERS

(a) The first respondent … is eligible to be deprived of his/her liberty at V pursuant to an authority under section 4A of the Mental Capacity Act 2005.

(b) Notwithstanding … P's inability to consent, it shall be lawful and in his/her best interests for his/her clinicians and care workers including the applicant's and the … respondents employees servants or agents to:

---

[76] *B Borough Council v S (By the Official Solicitor)* [2006] EWHC 2584 (Fam), [2007] 1 FLR 1600.

[77] *LLBC v TG, JG and KR* [2007] EWHC 2640 (Fam) (para 38 of the judgment).

[78] [2006] EWHC 2584 (Fam), [2007] 1 FLR 1600.

(i) admit the first respondent ... to units provided by ... At either the A care home or the B care home for the purpose of caring for his/her welfare and providing him/her with psychological, behavioural and psychiatric treatment.

(ii) Provide him/her with psychological, behavioural and psychiatric treatment in accordance with the care plans provided by ...

(iii) Use such reasonable restraint as may be necessary in conveying the First respondent ... to and preventing him/her from leaving the unit, including measures that may amount to the deprivation of liberty for the purpose of caring for his/her welfare and providing him/her with psychological, behavioural and psychiatric treatment.

10.19 PROCEDURAL GUIDE FOR DEPRIVATION OF LIBERTY ORDER

When can an application be made	Before standard authorisation is given	
	After standard authorisation is given	
	After urgent authorisation is given	
Steps to be taken		
Before the application is issued	The applicant must contact the DoL team or at the same time as lodging the application and give the team the following information:	
	(1) that an application is to be made	
	(2) how urgent it is	
	(3) by when the decision should be given	
If an urgent application is to be made	(4) details of the parties and their addresses	
	(5) issue to be decided	
	(6) date of standard/urgent authorisation	
	(7) details of parties' legal representatives	
	(8) details of family members	
	(9) details of previous court proceedings	
Is permission needed	Only the patient and his appointed representative, attorney or deputy have the right to make an application without leave. All other persons including family members must seek permission	MCA 2005, s 50 COP Rules 2007, Parts 8 and 10A
In an emergency	Application can be made out of hours by calling security officer at the RCJ on 020 7947 6000	PD 10A, para 2.5
	In the Family Division judge can be contacted through the FD duty officer. The security officer will contact the duty officer	
How to apply		
The applicant must file	Form DLA Form DLB (plus draft) Form DLC (if permission required) If possible an electronic version of order sought on disc	PD 10A, para 4.1
	In an emergency an undertaking will be required that Forms will be filed and fee paid	
Court fee	£400	PD 10A, para 4.1

Possible directions which may be sought on issue	(1) Upon whom, by whom and how service should be effected	PD 10A, para 5.1
	(2) Dispensing with acknowledgement of service or seeking abridgement of time	
	(3) Whether lay or expert evidence required whether P or OS or other persons should be made parties	
	(4) Whether family member should be notified and joined as a party	
	(5) Fixing trial window or date for hearing allocation	
	(6) Whether it is appropriate to transfer to the High Court	
	(7) Directions for the preparation of bundles	
Court Office	Take steps to place application before a Nominated judge to hear DoL cases will notify the judge to put him/her on stand by and the judge will consider the application and give directions if appropriate	PD 10A, paras 6.1 and 6.2
Steps after judge's order	DoL team will notify parties of order Action every point on judge's note Refer queries to the judge Make arrangements for transfer	
Steps to be taken by applicant	Comply with the order made File DLD if appropriate Serve Form DLE with other documents Prepare indexed and paginated Court bundle to include skeleton arguments and draft order Provide a copy of index to all parties and a copy of bundle to unrepresented party	PD 10A, paras 7.2 and 8.4
First Hearing	Court will attempt to hear case within 5 days. The hearing will be in private unless r 93 applies and Court so directs	PD 10A, para 8.2 COP Rules 2007, r 90
Orders that may be made	See **4.11, 4.13.6, 4.15** above and s 21A of MCA 2005	
Costs	No order	COP Rules 2007, r 157 PD 10A, para 10.1
Appeal	Permission to appeal required	PD 10A, para 11.1 COP Rules 2007, r 172
	Permission will only be granted if Court considers it has a real prospect of success or there are some other compelling reasons	COP Rules 2007, r 173 PD 10A, para 11.1

PART V

CHILDREN

CHAPTER 11

CHILDREN

LAW AND PRACTICE

11.1 INTRODUCTION

Section 2(5) Mental Capacity Act 2005 prevents powers available under the Act from being exercised in relation to anyone under the age of 16. Decisions on behalf of children are generally made by those with parental responsibility in any event, usually parents. In the event of a dispute the appropriate forum for resolution is in the family courts principally through orders made under Children Act 1989. This applies equally to children who lack mental capacity as those who do not lack capacity. Exceptionally s 18(3) enables the court's jurisdiction to be exercised in relation to the property and affairs of children under the age of 16, who lack capacity and who are likely to still lack capacity and be unable to make decisions for themselves at 18. Further there is power under s 21 to transfer to the Court of Protection (usually) the case of personal welfare matters of young people aged between 16–18 years.

11.2 PROPERTY AND AFFAIRS

Children can be entitled to great wealth either by way of inheritance or damages awards in personal injury litigation. For example children in receipt of extensive compensation as a result of a claim for damages in a catastrophic accident will need to have a deputy appointed to manage their property and affairs. Often damages awards for such things as brain injuries at birth attract awards of damages running to in excess of £ millions. The award will need to provide for lifelong care and accommodation. Parents are unlikely to be used to managing these sums. In those circumstances it is often a precondition of the award that an application be made to the Court of Protection for the appointment of a deputy. Where the assets to which a child is entitled are significant, the appointment is most likely to be of a professional to act jointly with parents, certainly to see them through large capital expenditure and the setting of an annual budget. Applications may be urgent either for the deputy to be appointed or for one off orders for the purchase of a home. The procedure follows that set out in Part 11 Chapter 3 as does the procedure for discharge or revocation.

Other orders the Court of Protection may make for children and their property and affairs include:

- appointment of litigation friend;
- gifts;
- sale/purchase of land;
- approval of trusts and trustees.

It is worthy of mention by way of reminder here that despite a child who lacks capacity being wealthy they are not able to make a will by virtue of s 7 of the Wills Act 1837 (as amended) which precludes anyone under age of 18 from validly executing a will. Therefore the provision whereby deputies may apply to the Court for an order authorising the making of a will, known as a 'statutory will' does not extend to those under 18. This is reaffirmed by s 18(2).

11.3   YOUNG PERSON BETWEEN THE AGES OF 16–18 YEARS

Section 2(5) of the Act provides that no one shall exercise powers acquired by virtue of the power which an individual has in relation to a person who lacks capacity, or who is reasonably believed to lack capacity, in relation to a person aged under 16. It is therefore assumed that where a young person aged between 16 and 18 lacks capacity within the meaning of ss 2 and 3 of the Act, the provisions of the Act and the Code of Practice apply when decisions regarding the welfare needs of the young person are in issue. The Code of Practice, para 4.6 provides that the Act generally applies to individuals who are aged 16 or older. Exceptions to the Court or individuals exercising powers in the case of those between 16–18 are in the following circumstances:

- Only those over 18 may execute an LPA.
- Only those over 18 can make an advance decision to refuse medical treatment.
- A will can only be made for those over 18 (see above).

In matters relating to the admission of the young person to a psychiatric hospital, the authorities should be able to rely on the provisions of ss 5 and 6 of the Act (see chapter 10 at **10.8.2**) in conjunction and consultation with the parents of the young person, or a person who has parental responsibility for him/her, to do what is in the best interests of the young person. The Code of Practice, Chapter 12 confirms this position by providing that the protection from liability provided in s 5 of the Act applies as long as the person carrying out the act has taken reasonable steps to establish that the young person lacks capacity and, when doing the act, reasonably believes that the young person lacks capacity and that the act done is in the young person's best interests and follows the general principles. In addition it requires that, when assessing the young person's best interests, the person providing care or treatment must consult those involved in the young person's care and anyone interested in his/her welfare – if it is practical and appropriate to do so. This may include the young person's parents but care should be taken not unlawfully to breach the young person's right to confidentiality. Where a young person has indicated that he/she does not want his/her parent consulted, it may not be appropriate to involve them (for example where there have been allegations of abuse).[1] In cases where the appropriate treatment proposed requires deprivation of liberty, the provisions of the Mental Health Act 1983 should be used to authorise detention.

Where the issues concern the welfare of a young person, the provisions of the Children Act 1989 should be considered alongside those of the Act in carrying out the appropriate assessments and care plans. The Code of Practice acknowledges in para 12.6 that there is an overlap with the Children Act 1989 and that where the young person lacks capacity within the meaning of the Act either MCA 2005 or the Children Act may apply, depending on the circumstances. Where neither of these Acts apply it may be necessary to look to the powers available under the Mental Health Act 1983 or the High Court's inherent jurisdiction. There are no specific rules or criteria to determine when the Act or the Children Act 1989 should apply. The Code of Practice gives some examples including that:

'It may be appropriate for the Court of Protection to make a welfare decision concerning a young person who lacks capacity to decide for themselves (for example, about where the young person should live) if the Court decides that the parents are not acting in the young person's best interests.

It might be appropriate to refer a case to the Court of Protection where there is disagreement between a person interested in the care and welfare of a young person and the young person's medical team about the young person's best interests or capacity.'

Where there is a disagreement about whether the young person lacks capacity and there is no other way of resolving the matter, a declaration or other order should be sought from the Court of Protection and if the Court considers that the issue should be dealt with in the Family Division, the Court will transfer the case to the High Court.[2]

These provisions will be of particular relevance in cases where the young person up to the age of 21 years has been the subject of a care order or is a looked after child. In such cases, conflict may arise between the young person, his/her parents and family members and the local authority and other agencies with regard to issues concerning eg accommodation, contact with, sexual relationships between the young person and a third party and what is deemed to be in the best interests of the young person and how the balance between those issues and the young person's right to autonomy and the rights of those who have parental responsibility for the child should be struck.

---

[1] Code of Practice, para 12.19.
[2] Code of Practice, paras 12.20–12.25.

The Children Act 1989 imposes on the responsible local authority a statutory duty towards looked after and relevant/eligible persons between the age of 16 and 21 years. The statutory provisions which apply to persons within this category are set out in the Children Act 1989, ss 22–24D and Part II, paras 19A–19C of Sch 2 to the Act and the Care and Planning and Case Review (England) Regulations 2010[3] and, in the case of Wales, the Children (Leaving Care) (Wales) Regulations 2001.[4] Under these provisions the local authority has a duty to advise, assist and befriend a looked after child, and befriend him with a view to promoting his welfare when they have ceased to look after him. In relation to an eligible young person the local authority is under a duty to carry out an assessment of his needs with a view to determining what advice, assistance and support it would be appropriate to provide for him and to prepare a pathway plan for him.[5] Paragraph 19C imposes a duty on the local authority to arrange for such a young person to have a personal adviser.

11.3.1   The assessment

The Care and Planning and Case Review (England) Regulations 2010 provide that in carrying out an assessment and in preparing or reviewing the pathway plan the local authority must, to the extent that it is practicable, seek and have regard to the views of the young person to whom it relates and take steps to enable him to attend and participate in any meetings at which his or her case is to be considered. This includes providing the young person with copies of the results of the assessment and the pathway plan and ensuring that the contents of the documents are explained to him or her.

In carrying out the assessment the responsible local authority must take account of the following considerations:
(a)   the child's health (including physical, emotional and mental health) and development;
(b)   the child's continuing need for education, training or employment;
(c)   the support available to the child from parents and other connected persons;
(d)   the child's actual and anticipated financial resources and capacity to manage personal finances;
(e)   the extent to which the child possesses the practical and other skills necessary for independent living; and
(f)   the child's continuing need for care, support and accommodation;
(g)   the wishes and feelings of:
      (i)   the child;
      (ii)   any parent of the child and any person who is not the child's parent but who has parental responsibility for the child;
      (iii) the appropriate person;

---

[3]   SI 2010/959.
[4]   SI 2001/2189.
[5]   Children Act 1989, Sch 2A, Part II, paras 19A and 19B.

(h)   the views of:
   (i)   any person or educational institution that provides the child with education or training, and if the child has a statement of special educational needs, the local authority who maintain the statement (if different);
   (ii)   the independent reviewing officer;
   (iii) any person providing health (whether physical, emotional or mental health) or dental care or treatment to the child;
   (iv)   the personal adviser appointed for the child; and
   (v)   any other person whose views the responsible authority, or the child, consider may be relevant.[6]

11.3.2   The pathway plan

Having carried out the assessment, the responsible local authority is required to prepare a pathway plan which should include the following matters:

(a)   the name of the child's personal adviser;

(b)   the nature and level of contact and personal support to be provided to the child / young person and by whom;

(c)   details of the accommodation the child or young person is to occupy when he/she ceases to be looked after;

(d)   a detailed plan for his or her continuing education or training when he/she ceases to be a looked after;

(e)   where relevant, how the responsible local authority will assist the child or young person in obtaining employment or other purposeful activity or occupation or;

(f)   the support to be provided to enable the child or young person to develop and sustain appropriate family and social relationships;

(g)   a programme to develop the practical and other skills necessary for him or her to live independently;

(h)   the financial support to be provided to the child or young person, to enable him/her to meet his or her accommodation and maintenance costs;

(i)   the child's health care needs, including any physical, emotional or mental health needs and how they are to be met when the child ceases to be looked after;

(j)   the responsible authorty's contingency plans for action to be taken by the responsible local authority, should the pathway plan for any reason cease to be effective.[7]

In respect of each of the above matters the responsible local authority is required to set out the manner in which it proposes to meet the needs of the

---

[6]   SI 2020/959 reg 42.
[7]   SI 2010/959, reg 43 and Sch 8.

child and the date by which any action required to implement any aspect of the plan, will be carried out by the local authority.[8]

11.3.3   The functions of the personal adviser

The functions of the personal adviser in relation to the child are set out in reg 42 and require him/her:

(a)   to provide advice (including practical advice) and support;

(b)   to participate in the reviews of the child's case carried out under Part 6 of the regulations;

(c)   to liaise with the responsible local authority in the implementation of the pathway plan;

(d)   to coordinate the provision of services , and to take reasonable steps to ensure that they child makes use of such services;

(e)   to remain informed about the child's progress and wellbeing; and

(f)   to maintain a written record of any of the adviser's contacts with the child.

The personal adviser should not be a person who is an officer or an employee of the local authority and he/she should not be responsible for undertaking the assessment or the pathway plan.

R (G) v Nottingham City Council and Nottingham University NHS Trust[9] and *R (J) v Caerphilly County Borough Council*,[10] although not determined by the Court of Protection, illustrate the importance of complying with the above provisions when seeking authorisation from the Court for any plan proposed for a young person, in addition to those which apply under the Act.

---

[8]   SI 2010 /959, reg 43.

[9]   [2008] EWHC 400 (Admin).

[10]   [2005] 2 FLR 860.

PART VI

PUBLICITY AND DISCLOSURE

CHAPTER 12

PUBLICITY, RESTRICTIONS ON PUBLICATION AND ATTENDANCE BY REPRESENTATIVES OF THE MEDIA

LAW AND PRACTICE

12.1 INTRODUCTION

The media have been too eager to label the Court of Protection as a 'secret court'. In fact one of Britain's most secretive courts. It has condemned judicial decisions concerning persons who lack capacity (P) and their families as outrageous without knowing the full circumstances of the case which led to the decision being made. It is important therefore to set out here the practice and procedure that exists for restrictions on publicity and on open justice to take place where this is justified in the interests of P and the competing rights of others involved in the case and in the public interest. Often these issues arise on the hoof and practitioners can be taken by surprise.

The Court and especially the President of the Court of Protection are anxious to promote open justice and not to exclude any person who has a legitimate interest in the proceedings from attending court or publishing information about the decision and its subject matter. It is also concerned in protecting private information concerning P and an unjustified intrusion in P's privacy and his or her right to private and family life under Art 8 of the European Convention for the Protection of Human Rights and Fundamental Freedoms (ECHR).

Although the general rule is that hearings are to be held in private, the COP Rules 2007 contain provisions which empower the Court to authorise attendance by any person at a hearing and for the publication of such information relating to the proceedings as it deems fit and necessary. It also provides for the Court to order a public hearing. Where reporting restrictions are imposed by reason of the operation of s 12(1) of the Administration of Justice Act 1960 or are to be imposed under the provision in Part 13 and the Practice Direction that supplements it, provision is made for the media to be notified of the restrictions and for representations to be made. In addition, COP law reports have their own dedicated site on Bailli and dedicated Law Reports published by Jordan Publishing Limited. The President's intention for greater transparency in the family courts and the Court of Protection resulted in draft Guidance on the Publication of Judgments being issued on 12 July 2013 for comment and discussion ([2013] Fam Law 981). This was revised and adjusted to take into account the comments and suggestions received during the consultation process. On 16 Janaury 2014 the President issued *Practice Guidance on Publication of Judgments: Transparency in the Court of Protection* which takes effect from 3 February 2014. The guidance can be found in Part VIII. The proposal to consider the practical steps to enable the media to have access to some at least of the documents used in court is outstanding. Issues that still need to be decided is the nature of documents which should be disclosed; in what form disclosure should take place and the safeguards that need to be put in place. There will no doubt be further public consultation and discussion with the media on these issues but the President's views are re-enforced in his judgment in *Re P (A Child)*[1] when he stated:[2]

> 'The second point is, if anything, even more important. This case must surely stand as final, stark and irrefutable demonstration of the pressing need for radical changes in the way in which both the family courts and the Court of Protection approach what for shorthand I will refer to as transparency. We simply cannot go on as hitherto. Many more judgments must be published. And, as this case so very clearly demonstrates, that applies not merely to the judgments of High Court Judges; it applies also to the judgments of Circuit Judges.'

However unlike, the Family Procedure Rules 2010 (FPR 2010) and the Practice Direction which supplement the rules, the COP Rules 2007 do not set out any specific provisions for the attendance of the media or the procedure that should apply or the factors to be taken into account when an application is made by the media to attend the hearing or report a judgment or decision taken on behalf of P. The authors suggest that in appropriate cases it may be useful in such cases to refer to the FPR 2010 for guidance. Indeed in *P v Independent Print Ltd and others*[3] the Court of Appeal declined to give guidance on how such applications should be managed and expressed the view that it was for the President and the Family Division with their greater experience of the day to day working of the Court and the pressure upon it to establish the proper practice and procedure and the unexpected applications made under Part 13.

12.2 HEARINGS IN PRIVATE

The general rule in the Court of Protection, (as is the case in family proceedings), is that hearings are held in private where the only persons who are entitled to attend are the parties, P, any person acting as the litigation friend in the proceedings, the legal representatives and any court officer (COP Rules 2007, r 90(1) and (2)). The rules do not specifically include attendance by representatives of the media nor do the rules or Practice Direction provide any specific procedure which should be followed if attendance is sought as was

---

[1]   [2013] EWHC 4048 (Fam).
[2]   At para 45.
[3]   [2011] EWCA Civ 756, [2012] COPLR 110.

provided for in the two Practice Directions, *Attendance of Media Representatives at Hearings in Family Proceedings* dated 20th April 2009 made by the President to support the rule changes in the respective courts.

By contrast the FPR 2010, r 27.11(2) includes a duly accredited representative of news gathering and reporting organisations to be present as of right unless excluded and PDs 27B and 27C which supplement the rule give guidance on the handling of applications to exclude media representatives from the whole or part of the proceedings and the exercise of the Court's discretion in such cases whether upon the Court's own motion or an application for exclusion. The absence of any rules or PD in the COP Rules 2007 does not mean that media attendance will be denied in all cases in the Court of Protection. Pursuant to COP Rules 2007, r 90(3) the Court has a discretion to authorise any person or class of persons to attend the hearing or a part of it or to exclude any person or class of person from attending the hearing or a part of it but no guidance is given on how the discretion is to be exercised. Additionally, even if a representative of the media is authorised to attend the hearing, publication of any information about the proceedings will be a contempt of court pursuant to s 12(1) of the Administration of Justice Act 1960, unless the Court has authorised its publication. This then begs the question how should an application be made by the media, on what grounds can such an application be resisted and what are the relevant factors which the Court needs to consider when exercising its discretion whether or not to exclude the media.

12.3   ATTENDANCE OF MEDIA IN PROCEEDINGS

12.3.1   The problems that arise

The problems that the absence of proper procedure for the attendance of the media causes can best be demonstrated by reference to the Court of Appeal's recount of the situation which Hedley J and the legal representatives of the parties had to face in *P v Independent Print Ltd & Others* (above). The Independent newspaper appeared by counsel at the hearing before Hedley J without issuing or serving the application or notifying the parties to the proceedings that they would be attending to make an application 'for permission to attend the hearing and to report the hearing subject to the discretion of the Court to decide which, if any elements may be reported'. Hedley J stated:

> '[2] this application was not effectively served on any of the parties until the day of the hearing. That is clearly unsatisfactory. The reason that that has happened is because the applicants relied on email transmission to the Court of Protection office at Archway and that never yielded what they expected it to yield, namely the sending out of the application form which then be served on the parties.
>
> [3] Two matters flow from that. One is it is the obligation of any applicant to ensure that parties are served in good time and secondly, that reliance on email communications as a way of initiating an application is one that not effective and

the matter will have to be addressed in the conventional way. In the event, it has been accepted on all sides that this matter needs to be dealt with now, as otherwise it would result in an entirely unnecessary adjournment of the review proceedings which would be doubly unfortunate, given that this is a case from [out of London].

[4] The second matter is that it merely illustrates that there are still some difficulties in terms of how the press and media generally play a role in Family and Court of Protection proceedings. It is usually the press that are in the position of complaining about want of notice in injunction proceedings. It merely illustrates that clear working procedures have still not yet been fully worked out in this rather difficult area. That said I intend to entertain and deal with this application.

[5] The second observation is this. This application (succinctly argued though it has been) raises some really quite difficult issues but almost a policy decision has been taken that the court must deal with these applications summarily and therefore I propose to give an ex tempore judgment even though some deliberation might otherwise have been justified. Unless the court accepts the discipline of summary determination and ex tempore judgment, cases are likely to be unnecessarily and significantly delayed each time an application of this sort is made.'

12.3.2   Procedure for making an application for permission to attend and to publish – COP Rules 2007, rr 90 and 91

An application for an order to authorise media representatives to attend the hearing or part of it and to authorise publication of information in the proceedings must be commenced by filing a notice of application in Form COP 9 with supporting evidence upon which reliance is placed in accordance with COP Rules 2007, rr 78(1), (2) and 80(2). The application notice must set out the order or direction the applicant is seeking and briefly the grounds on which the order is sought.[4] The application must be served by the applicant on anyone who is named as a respondent in the application notice (if not already a party); every party in the proceedings and on any other person as the Court may direct as soon as practicable and in any event within 21 days of the date on which the notice was issued.[5] On having effected service, the applicant must file a certificate of service within 7 days beginning with the date on which the documents were served.[6]

12.3.3   Orders that the Court may make to displace privacy

Apart from the order under r 90(3) authorising the attendance of a person not included in the list under r 90(2) (see above) the Court is empowered to authorise publication of information relating to the proceedings and to impose conditions or restrictions on the authorised publication of information. These include the following powers:

---

[4]   COP Rules 2007, r 79.
[5]   COP Rules 2007, r 80(1).
[6]   COP Rules 2007, r 80(3).

(a) Authorisation of the publication of such information relating to the proceedings as it may specify.

(b) The publication of the text or a summary of the whole or part of a judgment or order made by the Court.[7]

(c) The Court may impose such conditions on the authorised publication as it thinks fit and in particular, it may:

   (i) Impose restrictions on the publication of the identity of any party; P; any witness or any other person. These may include for example restrictions on identifying the hospital where P is treated and the identity of the treating medical team; or restrictions on identifying the care home and the staff who are responsible for P's care or the local authority that is responsible for P's care or in whose area the care is provided.

   (ii) Prohibit the publication of any information that may lead to any such person being identified.

   (iii) Prohibit the further publication of any information relating to the proceedings from such date as the Court may specify.

   (iv) Impose such other restrictions on the publication of information relating to the proceedings as the Court may specify.[8]

(d) The Court may order the entire hearing or part of it to be held in public or exclude any person from attending a public hearing or part of it and impose similar conditions and restrictions as those set out under (a) to (d) above.[9]

12.3.4 When may the Court make any of the above orders

The Court may make any of the above orders at any time and either on its own initiative or on an application made by any person in accordance with Part 10 of the COP Rules 2007.

12.3.5 Ground on which the Court may make the orders

Unlike the FPR 2010 which set out in detail the test to be applied by the Court when seeking to exclude any person from the hearing, the only ground set out in COP Rules 2007, r 93(1)(a) is that the Court may make any of the above orders only where it appears to the Court that there is good reason for making the order. No further definition or explanation is given on what would constitute good reason or how it is to be assessed. Guidance however is provided under case law on how the Court should determine the issue.

In the leading case of *Independent News and Media Limited v A*[10] Hedley J set out a two stage process which should be applied where the media seek to attend proceedings and to publish the information within the proceedings. The case

---

7   COP Rules 2007 r 91(2).
8   COP Rules 2007, r 91.
9   COP Rules 2007, r 92.
10 [2009] EWHC 2858 (Fam).

concerned the extraordinary case of a man who suffered from blindness and learning difficulties from birth but who had overcome his disabilities by teaching himself to play the piano to such a standard that he had received international recognition. His story was thus not only in the public domain but was also of 'compelling human interest'.

Hedley J's approach was approved by the Court of Appeal (*Independent News and Media v A*[11]) and has since been approved and applied by it in *P v Independent Print Ltd & Others* (above). The Court of Appeal confirmed that the new statutory structure starts with the assumption that just as the conduct of their lives by adults with the necessary mental capacity is their own affair, so too is the conduct of those who are incapacitated private business. Hearings in the Court of Protection should therefore be held in private unless there is good reason why they should not. This protection mirrors the common law exception to the principle that justice must be done in open court.

The first test therefore, is to consider whether the applicant has established a 'good reason' for allowing the application. If there is, the second stage is to decide whether the requisite balancing exercise applied in *Re S (A Child) (Identification: Restrictions on Publication)*[12] justified the making of the order because 'even when good reason appears, before the necessary authorisation can be granted better reasons may lead the Court to refuse it'. Accordingly, the reality is that provided good reason appears, the Court will then assess all the relevant considerations and make a balanced fact-specific judgment whether the specific authorisation should be granted (para 11).

In addition, the Court when considering whether to exercise its powers must consider whether the Art 8 rights under the ECHR (ie the right to private life) of any party might in some way be infringed if the order was made. If it does, the Court should give great weight to the actual or potential invasive or other effect which an order might have on the private family life of any person whose privacy is intended to be protected by r 90(1). The Court of Appeal however, doubted whether in the great majority of cases considerations under Art 8 would add anything to the reasoning or conclusion of the Court. But 'in rare cases it may intensify the focus on such rights, and in other cases it could conceivably affect the outcome' (para 30).

Article 10 rights of the ECHR of freedom of expression is also relevant more particularly so because s 12(4) of the Human Rights Act 1998 emphasises that when issues relating to freedom of expression may arise the Court must have particular regard to its importance. However, this factor is not engaged until the second stage of the two stage process referred to above ie until the 'good reason' factor is established. The Court went on to explain that:[13]

---

[11]   [2010] EWCA Civ 343, COPLR Con Vol 686.
[12]   [2004] UKHL 47, [2005] 1 FLR 591.
[13]   At para 35.

'The "good reason" relied on by the media will invariably be based on the public interest in the imparting and receiving of information about the particular case, or some of its features, or the functioning of the Court of Protection. As we see it, the statutory structure properly and sufficiently ensures that the Art 10 rights of the media are given their proper weight in the process. The question when Art 10 is engaged will, therefore, at least normally, not matter in any particular case when the court is being asked by the media to make an order under rr 90 to 93. As with Art 8, the factors which the common law would require to be taken into account, and the weight to be given to them, would usually be the same as if the issue was being addressed by reference to Art 10. Nonetheless, again as with Art 8, if Art 10 is engaged it may involve a more intense focus than under the common aw, and it could conceivably sometimes yield a different result.'

The Court after giving due consideration to the numerous decisions of the European Commission of Human Rights concluded that the interests of the public and the media were legitimately engaged in the case because the young man's remarkable situation, including his private life was already in the public domain. Authorising a selected number of media representative to be present during the proceedings would enable those representatives to be fully aware of the issues that might be of legitimate interest to the public and to make representations about the matters for which publication should be authorised. It would be difficult to find a more appropriate hearing before the Court of Protection for media understanding of its processes. It was also valuable for the public to be informed of precisely what happened in a court in which the overwhelming majority of the hearings were conducted in private (see paras 22 and 23).

In *P v Independent Print Ltd & Others* (above) The Court of Appeal approved and applied the approach adopted in its earlier decision in *Independent News and Media v A* (above). The facts in the case were that P who had been adopted suffered from severe uncontrolled epilepsy for which he was treated by specialist. His adoptive parents disagreed with the treatment. P was admitted to hospital in an emergency suffering from life-threatening epileptic seizures. His adoptive parents had withdrawn all his medication prior to his admission to hospital. This had resulted in the hospital issuing proceedings for the Court to determine P's future. Hedley J granted the media's application to attend the hearing and to publish the information disclosed in the proceedings subject to restrictions.

On appeal from this decision the Court of Appeal confirmed that the two stage process prescribed in the earlier case of *Independent News and Media* (above) was the correct approach and that on the facts the judge had been entitled to find that there was good reason for the limited intervention sought by the Independent. In relation to the second stage the judge had properly considered the Art 8 rights of P and the importance of the Convention right to freedom of expression under Art 10. The Court in rejecting the appeal on the grounds that

P's Art 8 rights outweighed the media's Art 10 rights, applied the principle set out in *Lord Browne of Madingley v Associated Newspapers Limited*:[14]

> 'although the exercise upon which the judge was engaged was not the exercise of discretion it was similar in that it involved carrying out a balancing exercise upon which different judges could properly reach different conclusions. In these circumstances it is now well settled that an appellate court should not interfere unless the judge has erred in principle or reached a conclusion which was plainly wrong or, put another way, was outside the ambit of conclusions which a judge could reasonably reach.'[15]

In relation to the weight to be given to P's best interests the Court of Appeal held that:[16]

> 'Permitting the press to attend and permitting the press to report the judgment is not an act done or decision made for or on behalf of the disabled person. Section 1(5) is concerned with acts done or decisions made in relation to the management and administration of that person's property and affairs or to decisions relating to his health or medical treatment. We are concerned with the decision taken by the court about the administration of the court's process and it falls outside s 1(5).'

Applying the test applied in family proceedings and wardship proceedings, the Court concluded that 's 1(5) does not govern or dominate a decision to be taken under rr 90–93. There is no requirement for the decision to be dictated by the best interests of P. Welfare is not the paramount consideration trumping all other considerations. That is very far from saying that his best interests are ignored or are irrelevant. The impact upon him (P) will always be a material factor' but the weight attached to it would be dependent on the particular facts and circumstances of the individual case.

In deciding whether or not there is good reason for the media's attendance or reporting, the judge is bound to have regard to the overriding objective and in particular with the requirement to deal with the case justly. Any ill-effect the attendance of the media or publication of the information may have on P is thus a relevant factor but in weighing that factor against all the others the Court has the power to safeguard any impact on P by imposing conditions and restrictions (see para 49). *Re G v E & Others*[17] is an example of a case of how the Court can and does permit publication whilst at the same time safeguarding the rights of others. When allowing the identity of the local authority to be reported the Court took into account the impact on the children and the social workers who were involved with the case. The proceedings concerned the health and welfare issues before the Court of Protection in which Manchester City Council had been criticised. When determining whether to permit the name of the local authority to be reported the Court balanced the need for

---

[14]   [2007] EWCA Civ 295.
[15]   At para 45.
[16]   [2012] EWCA Civ 110 at para 46.
[17]   [2010] EWHC 2042 (Fam).

openness and accountability and the risk of E and members of his family being identified. On the facts Baker J was satisfied that there was no risk of E or his family being identified but that it was important that the local authority should be named in the public interest and on the ground of accountability. It was also hoped that the publicity would highlight the reforms made by the MCA 2005 and its amendment to include the deprivation of liberty safeguards. Baker J also refused to permit the names of the social workers to be identified because the failures related to those in senior positions. He also refused permission to name the placement where E had lived on the ground that they had not been present at the hearing and had not had the opportunity to make representations and also because the concerns raised during the proceedings in relation to the placement could be brought to the attention of the Care Quality Commission. (By way of an analogy see also *Re X & Y*[18] which concerned the balancing of the Art 8 and 10 rights in relation to a child and the importance of the welfare of a child and its protection.)

12.3.6 Notification of proposed reporting restriction orders

Where the Court intends to make an order on its own initiative or an application is made for an order restricting publication the order should not be made where the person against whom the order is proposed to be made is neither present nor represented unless the Court is satisfied that the applicant has taken all practicable steps to notify the respondent or there are compelling reasons why the respondent should not be notified.[19]

Notice of the possibility that reporting restriction may be imposed should be effected via the Press Association's copy direct service, to which national newspapers and broadcasters subscribe as a means of receiving notice of such applications. Copy direct will be responsible for notifying the individual media organisations. In exceptional circumstances the Court may make an order without notice.[20] It should however be noted that in *Re P (A child)*[21] the President expressed the need for the following information to be widely known:

'There is a page on the Injunctions Alerts Service website – http://www. medialawyer.press.net/courtapplications/mediaorganisations.jsp – which lists the media organisations served, and the relevant telephone numbers, and which states at the top:

"The notification system serves all the national media (newspapers and broadcasters) with the exception of the Financial Times and Sky News. If notice has to be served on these two companies it needs to be served on them directly."

---

[18] [2012] EWCA Civ 1500.
[19] COP Rules 2007, PD 13A, paras 10 and 11.
[20] Ibid, paras 13 and 14.
[21] [2013] EWHC 4048 (Fam).

The service was also established on the basis that subscribing organisations would be taken to have been served with an application if notification was sent via the service.

The system works as follows: Would-be applicants are supposed to call a number, given in the Practice Note, and speak to the Customer Services staff who deal with the service.

They then send the documents, electronically (which is easier) or by fax, to the service. These documents are, if necessary, scanned to be put into electronic form, and are then distributed via e-mail alerts to the national media. Distribution is followed up by calls to each of the subscribing organisations to check that service has been received.

The service does not:

1:   Serve regional and local newspapers, or magazines
2:   Serve orders which have been obtained from the courts (despite the continuing efforts by some law firms to use it for this purpose).

The website's Home page, and the pages for the Practice Direction, Practice Note and for the Notification system all contain a red-bordered box detailing what it does and does not do. The box is the same on all pages. It will be updated in the New Year, due to increasing use of the service by applicants seeking injunctions in the QBD who are also being required to notify the media of their applications. These mostly are cases involving settlements of medical negligence cases involving children.'

12.3.7   Notice of an application seeking restrictions on publication on Convention grounds

A person who applies for restriction on publication on Convention grounds is under a duty to give prior notice of the application to the national media via copy direct service first, by telephone (0870 830 6429) and then a copy of the following documents should be sent either by fax or email to copy direct:

(a)   the application form or application notice seeking the restriction order;

(b)   the witness statement filed in support;

(c)   any legal submissions in support;

(d)   an explanatory note setting out the nature of the proceedings in the form set out in the Annex to PD13A.[22]

The applicant must also serve the documents. If there are reasons for not serving the documents the media should be given details of the reasons so that an informed decision can be made as to whether it wishes to attend a hearing or be legally represented.[23]

---

[22]   Ibid, paras 15 and 16.
[23]   Ibid, para 17.

The Court however has the power to dispense with any of the above requirements.

On receiving notice of the application or of the Court's intention to make the order on its own initiative, if the media wish to make representations it must file an acknowledgement of service using form COP5 and in accordance with r 75 within 21 days beginning with the date on which the notice was given to it by copy direct.

12.3.8   Drafting of orders which include conditions and restrictions

By reason of the fact that publication of information in proceedings held in private in the Court of Protection is a contempt of court. When the Court permits publication subject to conditions and or restrictions it is of the utmost importance that the order is drafted with care and accurately and clearly sets out the extent of the publication permitted and the conditions and restrictions imposed. The need for this was highlighted by Munby LJ (as he then was) in *Re X & Y* (above) – a case involving the children of a parent who had been convicted of a serious offence relating to X – as follows:

> 'Before parting with this case there are two other matters to which I wish to draw attention.
>
> The first relates to the form of the order made by Peter Jackson J. The relevant paragraph for present purposes provided, by way of exception to the injunctions contained in the order, that:
>
>> "Nothing in this Order shall prevent any person from ... publishing the anonymised Executive Summary of the Serious Case Review carried out in relation to [name] and dated July 2012 (this Court having secured assurances from the [local authority] in relation to the form of the Summary and its date of publication)."
>
> This form of order is thoroughly objectionable, for it leaves wholly unclear precisely what document it is that may be published and, consequently, what the intended ambit is of the injunction.
>
> It is an elementary principle of justice and fairness that no order will be enforced by committal unless it is expressed in clear, certain and unambiguous language. So far as this is possible, the person affected should know with complete precision what it is that he is required to do or to abstain from doing. The authorities setting out this sometimes overlooked principle are legion. In *Harris v Harris, Attorney-General v Harris* [2000] EWHC 231 (Fam), [2001] 2 FLR 895, [288], I set out what I said was a no doubt selective anthology. Here I can content myself with what Lord Westbury LC said in *Low v Innes* [1864] EngR 337 (1864) 4 DeGJ&S 286, 295–296: the order must
>
>> "lay down a clear and definite rule ... The Court ... should, in granting an injunction, see that the language of its order is such as to render quite plain what it permits and what it prohibits."

The principle has been endlessly repeated down the years since.

A related principle is that an order should not require the person to whom it is addressed to cross-refer to other material in order to ascertain his precise obligation. In *Ellerman Lines Ltd v Read* [1928] 2 KB 144, 157, Atkin LJ said:

> "That judgment when drawn up, instead of reciting what the order of the Court was and what the defendants were restrained from doing, only refers to continuing an injunction granted by Rowlatt J, varied by Roche J, and continued by Greer J, without stating what it is that the Court was ordering the defendants to abstain from doing. That appears to me to be very bad practice ... It is a matter of very great importance that the orders of the Court ... should make it quite clear what the Court is ordering to be done. There is considerable laxity in this matter ... Practitioners and the officers of the Court should see that orders are not passed unless they are in proper form."

In *Rudkin-Jones v Trustee of the Property of the Bankrupt* (1965) 109 Sol Jo 334 the order as drawn read "It is ordered that an injunction be granted in the terms of Notice of Motion for Injunction". Lord Upjohn said:

> "I do want to protest as strongly as I can at the granting of injunctions in that form. It means then that the person against whom the injunction is granted ... has to look at another document in order to see what it is that he is enjoined from doing ... It cannot be too clearly understood ... that a person is entitled to look and look only at the order to see what it is that he is enjoined from doing. He looks at that order and finds out from the four walls of it and from no other document exactly what it is that he must not do."

In the present case matters were even worse. When we inquired of counsel which was the authentic text of the document referred to in the order they were unable to give us any very confident response. Since the hearing they have investigated the matter very carefully, for which I am grateful. This involved an analysis of a number of emails passing between the parties and between the parties and the court: the first on 23 July 2012 and the last on 31 July 2012. What that analysis reveals, as set out in an agreed note by Ms Meyer and Mr Geekie dated 4 October 2012, is that as at 31 July 2012 "the local authority had declined to accept one of the judge's proposed amendments" (email timed at 15.39), that it was "not altogether clear whether the judge was directing that his amendment should stand" (counsel's comment on email timed at 16.11), that the local authority then "proposed further amendments" (email timed at 16.56) but, as counsel observe, that "their status is not clear from the judge's response" (counsel's comment on email timed at 17.29). The next relevant event was the sealing of the order in the form I have described on 9 August 2012.

I appreciate that all this was happening on the last day of term, but the upshot is that even now, even the lawyers immersed in the litigation are unable to state with confidence what precisely it is that is permitted by the order. It is, in my judgment, a wholly unacceptable state of affairs. It is intolerable that a layman who risks imprisonment – a reporter, perhaps, or a newspaper editor wishing to publish some document which he may think is of public interest and importance – should be left to decipher an order of the court in this way, especially if, when seeking enlightenment, he turns to the local authority who obtained it only to be told that even they are not sure.

There is a perfectly simple remedy. If the order, having referred to the document, then contains words to the following effect

> "being the document entitled [etc] marked 'X' and initialled by the judge a copy of which is annexed to this order"

there will be no doubt as to what it is that the order prohibits and permits. Nor, importantly, will there be any doubt that the document annexed to the order is indeed in the form approved by the judge.'

(For an appropriate form for a reporting restriction order see *Emergency Remedies in the Family Court* Div G).

12.4 PROCEDURAL GUIDE FOR AN APPLICATION BY THE MEDIA FOR PERMISSION TO ATTEND AND REPORTING OF INFORMATION

Applicant	Will usually be a representative of the media or news gathering and reporting organisation. But the Court may make an order on its own initiative	COP Rules 2007, r 93(1)(c)
Applicant must file	Application notice in Form COP 9 which must set out the order sought, the grounds relied on and any other relevant information; and Evidence in support setting out 'good reasons' why the order is sought and dealing with the competing rights of the parties under the ECHR;	COP Rules 2007, Part 10, r 78 COP Rules 2007, r 79 and r 78(2)
There's currently no fee for CoP9		
Court Office	Will issue the application notice and give a date for the hearing	COP Rules 2007, r 78(3)
What the applicant must do next	Serve the application notice and the supporting evidence on: anyone who is named as a respondent (if not already a party to the proceedings); every party in the proceedings and any other person, as the Court may direct, As soon as is practicable and in any event within 21 days of the date on which the notice was issued unless time has been abridged by order of Court	COP Rules 2007, r 80
What the parties served with the application should do	Consent or oppose the application; Seek alternative remedy File evidence intended to rely on	
Hearing and orders that may be made	The Court may make any one or more of the orders set out in COP Rules 2007, rr 90(3)–92 (see **12.2.(c)**	

CHAPTER 13

DISCLOSURE

LAW AND PRACTICE

13.1 INTRODUCTION

Disclosure, non-disclosure and withholding disclosure is troublesome in all fields of litigation. In the Court of Protection it is not made any easier by the lack of uniformity between the disclosure rules under the Civil Procedure Rules 1998 (CPR 1998), Family Procedure Rules 2010 (FPR 2010) and the Court of Protection Rules 2007 (COP Rules 2007) despite the fact that in many respects both the FPR 2010 and the COP Rules 2007 follow the CPR 1998. Unlike the CPR 1998 and the FPR 2010, the COP Rules 2007 does not define 'document' and Part 16 (rr 132–138, which deal with disclosure and inspection generally) does not have a Practice Direction to supplement the rules. Reference should therefore be made to the CPR 1998 and its interpretation where the COP Rules 2007 are found to be unclear or inadequate. Indeed, COP Rules 2007, r 9 specifically provides that 'in any case not expressly provided for by these Rules or the practice directions made under them the Civil Procedure Rules 1998 (including any practice directions made under them) may be applied with any necessary modifications, insofar as is necessary to further the overriding objective'.

Issues which arise in COP cases often have parallels with those in family proceedings especially in relation to decisions relating to welfare issues. In such cases it may be useful to draw on case law in family proceedings and where necessary to the CPR 1998 by analogy or on the basis of common law to seek out an answer.

13.2 MEANING OF DOCUMENT

Document is not defined in the COP Rules 2007, but in both the CPR 1998, r 31.4 and the FPR 2010, r 21.1(3) it is defined: 'anything in which information of any description is recorded'. The definition is thus not limited to paper records but its terms are wide enough to include any material on which information is recorded and extends to audio/video records, computerised records stored on hard drives, disks, memory sticks, software or any other electronic form (see CPR PD 31B and *North Ventures Ltd v Anstead*

Holdings Inc.[1] In line with proceedings in other jurisdictions the term should be given the widest interpretation particularly with the advancement of electronic technology and the drive in court proceedings towards a paperless culture.

13.3   MEANING OF DISCLOSURE

COP Rules 2007, r 132 is based on CPR 1998, r 31.2 and makes it clear that a party discloses a document by stating the document exists or has existed. The rules then go to distinguish between general and specific disclosure and how it operates, but in each case disclosure only takes place if the Court on its own initiative or on the application of a party makes an order either for general or specific disclosure.[2] Under general disclosure a party is required to disclose not only the documents on which he relies but also those which adversely affect his own case or that of another party or support another party's case. In the case of a specific disclosure order the relevant party is required to disclose the specific documents referred to in the order or make a search for the documents to the extent stated in the order or disclose any document located as a result of that search (r 133(3) and see the similarities with CPR 1998, r 31.12(2)). Rule 134 goes on to set out the procedure for making the disclosure ordered by the Court. However unlike CPR 1998, r 31.7 which imposes a duty on a party when giving standard disclosure (referred to as general disclosure in the COP Rules 2007, r 133) to make a reasonable search for documents which adversely affect a party's case or another party's case or support another party's case, the COP Rules 2007, Part 16 is silent on this issue. Although COP Rules 2007, Part 16 does not make any reference to the factors which may be relevant when the Court makes or is requested to make an order under COP Rules 2007, r 133(3) for specific disclosure, including an order to carry out a search, a relevant consideration must necessarily be, as it is under the CPR 1998, r 31.7(1), the reasonableness of such disclosure or search. In deciding the reasonableness of any disclosure and search of information, the factors set out in CPR 1998, r 31.7(2) will be relevant as will consideration of what is in P's best interests and the overriding objectives. The procedure set out in CPR 1998, r 31.10, for providing standard disclosure, and the making of a disclosure statement in relation to the extent of the search that has been made to locate documents, which that party has been required to disclose, should be followed. If it is sought to argue that it would be unreasonable to undertake the search required, the reasons relied upon should be set out in the statement. Of significance will be the issue of proportionality. It will however, be for the Court to determine whether a reasonable search has taken place.

13.4   PRIVILEGED DOCUMENTS

Two types of privilege attaches to legal professional privilege. Communication between a party and his legal advisers whether or not litigation is contemplated carries legal professional privilege and in all cases the privilege is that of the

---

[1]   [2012] EWCA Civ 11.
[2]   COP Rules 2007, r 133(1).

client and not the legal adviser. It is the client alone who can waive the privilege. It is an absolute privilege and cannot be overridden on the ground of public interest or of balancing the competing rights as in the case of public interest immunity (see below under **13.6**).

Secondly, it is also settled law that litigation privilege applies to a document where the document has been produced or came into existence for the purpose of obtaining information or advice in connection with pending or contemplated litigation. This class of documents however, can only be considered as subject to litigation privilege if the document came into existence for the 'dominant purpose' of obtaining information or advice in connection with pending or contemplated litigation (*Tchenguiz & Anr v Director of Serious Fraud Office & Others*[3]).

13.5   ONGOING DUTY OF DISCLOSURE

Once the Court has made an order to give general or specific disclosure, the party to whom the order applies has a continuing duty to provide such disclosure until the proceedings are concluded, so that even if a document is not initially available but comes to a party's notice at any stage during the proceedings he/she is under a duty immediately to notify every other party.[4]

13.6   CONSEQUENCES OF FAILURE TO DISCLOSE

A party who fails to disclose any document or to permit its inspection will not be permitted to rely on it unless the Court gives permission to do so.[5]

13.7   COURT POWERS TO WITHHOLD DISCLOSURE OF DOCUMENTS

The procedure for applications to withhold disclosure and/or for inspection is set out in r 138 but it does not contain any grounds upon which to base the application for withholding disclosure. Rule 138 simply provides that a party seeking to withhold inspection of document or part of a document must state in writing in the list in which the document is disclosed that he has such a right or duty and the grounds on which he claims that right or duty. It will then be for the Court to determine on an application made by a party in accordance with Part 10. By contrast CPR 1998, r 31.19 and FPR 2010, r 21.3 provide that an application without notice may be made for an order to withhold disclosure on the ground that disclosure would damage the public interest and must support the application by evidence. Public interest immunity may include, taking into account consideration of the risk of harm to the subject of the proceedings or the giver of the information. This will necessarily also engage consideration of

---

[3]   [2013] EWHC 2297 (QB).
[4]   COP Rules 2007, r 135.
[5]   COP Rules 2007, r 139.

the competing rights of the parties under the ECHR and balancing those rights. The party seeking to withhold disclosure will claim rights under under Arts 2 and 8 and the right of the other party seeking disclosure will claim rights under Art 6 to a fair trial and also possibly Art 8 rights to family life. In such cases the Court will also need to consider whether disclosure is actually necessary to deal fairly with the case (see *A Chief Constable v YK & Others*[6]).

In relation to other considerations which may apply to those who lack capacity the decision in *RC v CC and X Local Authority*[7] provides some guidance on the Court's approach to such an application. In that case HH Judge Cardinal proceeded on the basis that the presumption in favour of disclosure must be tempered by the Court's paramount duty to address the best interests of P and to weigh up the Art 6 and 8 rights of both of the parties. Applying the test of whether denial is 'strictly necessary' which was adopted in *Durham County Council v Dunn*,[8] he concluded that the starting point must be in favour of disclosure unless good grounds are shown that withholding of disclosure is 'strictly necessary'. In applying the 'strictly necessary' test the Court:

- should take account of the best interests of P principle set out in the Act;
- in determining the best interests of P the Court should weigh up the competing rights of the parties under Arts 6 and 8 of the European Convention for the Protection of Human Rights and Fundamental Freedoms (ECHR);
- in order to determine these issues the Court should read the unredacted documents;
- where an order is granted it should be made the subject of regular review.

The judge, however went further in this case, which was about an adoption, and provided for disclosure of some of the documents to the advocate for the birth mother but strictly on the basis that neither the documents nor the information contained in them would be disclosed by counsel to his client. Although there appears to be no statutory basis for the Court's jurisdiction to impose such a restraint, there is support for such a course to be taken in appropriate cases under common law (see *R (Mohamed) v SSD*[9]).

In *RC v CC* (above) the birth mother was seeking the reintroduction of indirect contact with her adopted daughter CC. CC lacked capacity to make the decision whether to resume contact with her mother whom she had not had contact with for over 18 years. The issue before the Court was whether an un-redacted psychological report and the social worker's statement should be disclosed to the mother. If disclosed the mother would discover the whereabouts of her daughter and the location of the psychological services which were treating the daughter. In determining the issues before him HH Judge Cardinal took into account the birth mother's right under Art 6 of the

---

6   [2010] EWHC 2438 (Fam), [2011] 1 FLR 1493.
7   [2013] EWHC 1424 (COP).
8   [2012] EWCA Civ 1654.
9   [2012] EWHC 3454 (Admin).

ECHR to a fair trial, but he took the view that she was not entitled to examine the private life of the vulnerable daughter. He was also satisfied that it would be disturbing for the daughter for her rights to be invaded, and 'for her to have to be told that private information had been divulged to a party whom in reality she does not know' (para 33), although there was no evidence that the birth mother would act improperly in abusing such information. On the facts however, the judge directed the disclosure of the redacted psychological report to the mother, but that the social worker's statements should only be disclosed to her counsel, with an order restraining the counsel from revealing the contents to the mother. The judge took this step, because he considered that withholding this information was 'strictly necessary' and proceeding in this way would not breach the mother's Convention rights.

The mother was granted permission to appeal by Sir James Munby P under COP Rules 2007, r 173(1)(b) on the basis that permission should be granted because there was need for a ruling on the issue raised. In a reserved judgement handed down on 30 January 2014[10] having considered cases involving children and acknowledging the need for withholding disclosure, the President adopted the test applied in *Re D (Minors) (Adoption Reports: Confidentiality)*,[11] (p 615) and his decision in *Dunn v Durham County Council*[12] namely that:

'Non-disclosure should be the exception and not the rule. The court should be rigorous in its examination of the risk and gravity of the feared harm to the child, and should order nondisclosure only when the case for doing so is compelling.'

In determining whether the power should be exercised the court should consider:

(1) 'Whether disclosure of the material would involve a real possibility of significant harm to the child'.

(2) 'If it would, the court should next consider whether the overall interests of the child would benefit from non-disclosure, weighing on the one hand the interest of the child in having the material properly tested, and on the other both the magnitude of the risk that harm will occur and the gravity of the harm if it does occur'.

(3) If the court is satisfied that the interests of the child point towards non-disclosure, the next and final step is for the court to weigh that consideration, and its strength in the circumstances of the case, against the interest of the parent or other party in having an opportunity to see and respond to the material. In the latter regard the court should take into account the importance of the material to the issues in the case ...'.

(4) '... disclosure is never a simply binary question: yes or no. There may be circumstances ... where a proper evaluation and weighing of the various interests will lead to the conclusion that (i) there should be disclosure but (ii) the disclosure needs to be subject to safeguards. For example,

---

[10]   [2014] EWHC 131 (COP).
[11]   [1996] AC 593.
[12]   [2012] EWCA Civ 1654.

safeguards limiting the use that may be made of the documents and, in particular, safeguards designed to ensure that the release into the public domain of intensely personal information about third parties is strictly limited and permitted only if it has first been anonymised ...'.

(5)   '... that the position initially arrived at is never set in stone and that it may be appropriate to proceed one step at a time'.

(See as examples, to what was said by Hale LJ, as she then was, in *Re X (Adoption: Confidential Procedure)*,[13] and, most recently, by Baroness Hale JSC in *In re A (A Child) (Family Proceedings: Disclosure of Information)*.[14])

Although it is a decision made in family proceedings the Supreme Court's decision in *Re A (Sexual Abuse: Disclosure)*[15] is a useful example of the relevant test to be applied to disclosure of information when consideration of competing rights of the relevant parties is in issue. The decision is particularly relevant, because it concerned disclosure of sexual abuse allegations made against a father of a child, by a young vulnerable woman, who suffered from unexplained but poor mental and physical health, and the possibility of her giving live evidence in family proceedings. The question of disclosure arose in relation to continuation of contact between the father and his daughter in view of the allegations that had been made against the father and the risk he posed to his daughter. Whilst expressing concern about contact taking place, the local authority sought to withhold disclosure of the records of the allegations made by the young woman on the ground of public immunity. It was also resisted by the young woman on the ground that it would violate her Art 3 rights, as disclosure would be potentially detrimental to her mental and psychological health. In addition, it was submitted on her behalf that disclosure would breach her right to private life. The High Court had dismissed the application for disclosure. On appeal the Court of Appeal had allowed disclosure. On further appeal to the Supreme Court the Court upheld the order for disclosure. The Court held that in assessing the competing rights of the parties, the Court must strike a balance between the right to a fair trial and family life of the parties which non-disclosure would entail. The allegations had to be investigated in order to protect the child from risk of harm which her father potentially presented or to enable the child to resume her contact with her father. This could not be done without disclosure of the identity of the young woman and the details and history of the allegations that she had made. The young woman's right to private life was not sufficient justification for the compromise of the fair trial and the family life of the parents and the child. The Court confirmed that in determining the issue the Court had to consider all the circumstances of the case. On the facts of the case it was held that disclosure would not violate the young woman's right under Art 3 as she was currently under specialist care of a consultant physician and psychiatrist, who would no doubt do the utmost to mitigate any further deterioration in her condition.

---

[13]   [2002] EWCA Civ 828, [2002] 2 FLR 476, para 28.
[14]   [2012] UKSC 60, [2012] 3 WLR 1484, para 36.
[15]   [2012] UKSC 60, [2013] 1 FLR 948.

In relation to the issue of the young woman giving evidence, the Court held that if disclosure was not sufficient to resolve the issues before the Court and live evidence was necessary, there were various options now available on how the evidence should be presented. Her medical condition based on up-to-date reports would be relevant to determine how the evidence would be received, to enable the witness to give her evidence in a way which best enabled the Court to assess her reliability.

The principles set out above were applied to cases involving children. However, the President in *RC v CC and X Local Authority* considered whether they apply in cases in the Court of Protection relating to adults. He stated that:[16]

> '... there can, in my judgment, be only one sensible answer: they do. One really needs look no further than *Scott v Scott* to see that the same fundamental principles underlie both jurisdictions. If more is needed, there is, it seems to me, some support to be derived from *In re E (Mental Health Patient)* [1985] 1 WLR 245. More recently, and more to the point, there are the powerful observations of McFarlane J, as he then was, in *Enfield London Borough v SA, FA and KA* [2010] EWHC 196 (Admin), [2009] COPLR Con Vol 362, para 58, with which I respectfully agree.'

In relation to the issue of disclosure being limited to a party's legal representative the President referred to case law (*Official Solicitor to the Supreme Court v K and Anr*;[17] *R v Mohammed v Secretary of State*[18]) to confirm that it was a recognised practice but referred to potential difficulties to such an approach but noted that:[19]

> 'Importantly, such disclosure cannot take place without the consent of the lawyers to whom the disclosure is to be made; and they may find themselves, for reasons they may be unable to communicate to the court, unable to give such consent. Moreover, they cannot consent unless satisfied that they can do so without damage to their client's interests.'

(Cf *AHK, AM, AS, FM V Secretary of State for the Home Dept*[20]).

The President approved Judge Cardinal's decision save in one respect namely, those parts of Judge Cardinal's order which related to the three social worker statements. With the agreement of Counsel this issue was remitted to Judge Cardinal for him to reconsider his decision and judgment in the light of this judgment.

As a matter of practice the President offered guidance that 'in an unusual case such as this it might have been better if, instead of giving RC permission in

---

[16] [2014] EWHC 131 (COP), para 20.
[17] [1965] AC 201.
[18] [2012] EWHC 3454 (Admin).
[19] [2014] EWHC 131 (COP), para 21.
[20] [2013] EWHC 1426 (Admin).

accordance with rule 55(a), the District Judge had fixed a date for the hearing of the application for permission in accordance with rule 55(c)'.

13.8   DISCLOSURE OF SENSITIVE MATERIAL TO COUNSEL OR SPECIAL ADVOCATE

In *RC v CC* (above) HH Judge Cardinal permitted disclosure only to counsel but with a prohibition of disclosure to the client or discussion of the material disclosed with the client. It is however questionable whether the Court has jurisdiction to adopt the approach of injuncting counsel from revealing the document to his client as there appears to be no statutory basis for it within the Act or the Rules. It is also arguable that it breaches the client's right to a fair trial as without knowledge of the material against his/her, the person is unable to answer the claims made against him/her.

The appointment of a special advocate in such cases would also be considered to be inappropriate in most cases (see *A Chief Constable v YK & others*[21] and *Re T (Wardship: Impact of Police Investigation)*[22]). In *Re A (Sexual Abuse: Disclosure)* (above) the issue of special advocate was considered by the Supreme Court. Lady Hale when dealing with the suggestion that disclosure should be made to a special advocate referred to two 'formidable difficulties'. She stated:[23]

> 'The first is that this court has held that there is no power to adopt such a procedure in ordinary civil proceedings: *Al Rawl v Security Service* [2011] UKSC 34, [2012] AC 531, [2011] 3 WLR 388. That case can be distinguished on the ground that it was the fair trial rights of the State that were in issue, and the State does not enjoy European Convention rights. It is arguable that a greater latitude may be allowed in children cases where the child's welfare is the court's paramount concern? But the arguments against making such an inroad into the normal principles of a far trial remain very powerful. The second difficulty lies in the deficiencies of any closed material procedure in a case such as this. We have arrived at a much better understanding of those difficulties in the course of the control order cases, culminating in *Secretary of State for the Home Department v AF* [2009] UKHL 28, [2009] 3 WLR 74. The essential requirement of any fair procedure is that the person who stands to lose his rights has an opportunity effectively to challenge the essence of the case against him. There may be cases in which this can be done by offering him a "gist" of the allegations and appointing a special advocate to scrutinise the whole of the material deployed against him. In a case such as this, however, it is not possible effectively to challenge the allegations without knowing where, when and how the abuse is alleged to have taken place. From this information it is inevitable that X's identity will be revealed. Even if it were theoretically possible to devise some form of closed material procedure, therefore it would not meet the minimum requirements of a fair hearing in this case.

---

21   [2010] EWHC 2438 (Fam), 1 FLR 1493.
22   [2009] EWHC 2440 (Fam), [2010] 1 FLR 1048.
23   At paras 34 and 35.

The only possible conclusion is that the family life and fair trial rights of all three parties to these proceedings are a sufficient justification for the interference with the privacy rights of X. Put the other way round, X's privacy rights are not a sufficient justification for the grave compromise of the fair trial and family rights of the parties which non-disclosure would entail.'

This decision is relevant in COP cases because it concerned the rights of a vulnerable person, and the impact of disclosure and the giving of oral evidence on her, and considerations of how both these issues should be determined.

13.9   EDITING INFORMATION CONTAINED IN DOCUMENTS

Where it is sought to provide disclosure of documents subject to redaction, an application should be made for permission to do so under COP Rules 2007, Part 4, r 19 prior to it being served or disclosed. Although the rules do not set out the criteria which the Court should apply when determining the application, the Court will necessarily consider the reasons for seeking the redaction, P's best interests and the competing rights of others, who may be affected by the redaction, as it would under an application to withhold information (see above **13.6**). The application should be made in accordance with Part 10 of the COP Rules 2007 (see Part 4, r 19(4)).

13.10   PROCEDURE

Applications for disclosure or for withholding disclosure should be made by application notice. In the case of specific disclosure both the application and the order if granted should specify the documents or class of documents which need to be disclosed. Where the order requires a search to be undertaken, the order must specify the extent of the search to be carried out, or disclose any document located as a result of that search.

Where an order is made for a general or specific search, each party must make and serve on every other party a list of documents to be disclosed and a copy of the list must be filed within 7 days of the date of service.[24] The list must identify the documents in a convenient order and manner and as concisely as possible. The list must also indicate the documents in respect of which the party claims a right or duty to withhold inspection and the documents which are no longer in the control of that party setting what has happened to them.[25]

An application to withhold disclosure may be made without notice. It must be supported by a statement in writing setting out the applicant's right or duty to make the application and the reasons.

Where it is intended to withhold disclosure on the ground of public immunity, the statement must set out the circumstances which justify non-disclosure. This

---

[24]   COP Rules 2007, rr 134(2) and (3).
[25]   COP Rules 2007, rr 132(4) and (5).

will include the impact on the mental health of the party in respect of whom the information is sought to be withheld, (in COP that will usually be P), and the need to protect that person's Convention rights. Details of how these rights would be infringed should be set out in detail. Care should also be taken to consider the competing rights of the other parties to the litigation and to deal with these rights and give an explanation and reasons why it is suggested that P's rights outweigh those of any other party. Consideration should also be given to redacting the documents or information under COP Rules 2007, r 19 as a means of addressing the other party's right to a fair trial.

PART VII

ENFORCEMENT AND APPEALS

CHAPTER 14

ENFORCEMENT

LAW AND PRACTICE

14.1 BACKGROUND

It is a common misconception that the Court of Protection has an ongoing supervisory responsibility to investigate misuse and abuse of P's welfare, property and affairs. In fact the Court has no role in this respect beyond the reinforcement or enforcement of its own orders. If physical, emotional or financial abuse of those who lack capacity is suspected, the most effective remedy is to report the matter to the police, and to make a referral to the local social services authority for investigation under the protection of vulnerable adults procedures.

However the Court is empowered to strengthen its orders by imposing restraints by way of freezing orders or injunctions and in the event of non-compliance may enforce in the last resort by committal for contempt. The Court's general powers of enforcement are governed by COP Rules 2007, Part 21 which provides that the following provisions of the Civil Procedure Rules 1998 (CPR 1998) apply 'so far as they are relevant with such modification as may be necessary':

- Part 70 – general rules about enforcement of judgments and orders.
- Part 71 – orders to obtain information from judgment debtors.
- Part 72 – third party debt orders.
- Part 73 – charging orders, stop orders and stop notices.
- RSC Orders 45–47 which include general provisions for the enforcement of judgments and orders; writs of execution and writs of *fieri facias (fi fa)*.

The respective rules should be referred to for the procedure to be followed to obtain any one of the above orders. Where any one of the orders is contemplated it is advisable to issue the application in the Court of Protection where a single fee will be payable and then seek a transfer of the application to the High Court or county court (where a separate fee is payable of each application) for the application to be dealt with as the civil courts are more familiar with dealing with such enforcement proceedings.

The Court of Protection's powers to make restraining orders are very wide and not limited by any statutory provisions such as contained in the Family Law Act 1996 or under the Protection from Harassment Act 1997. The MCA 2005 s 47(1) provides that the Court of Protection has the 'same powers, rights, privileges and authority as the High Court'. The Court of Protection Rules 2007, rr 183–194 also make provisions for the application of the Civil Procedural Rules with appropriate modification to apply to the Court of Protection. PD 21A makes further supplementary provisions in relation to those rules. The Court thus has all the powers available to the High Court and in particular relating to charging orders, freezing orders, stop orders and writ of fieri facias. The Court may also enforce any non-compliance of its orders by way of a committal order provided that the order which has been breached was endorsed with a penal notice and was served personally or in such other manner directed by the Court.

14.2   PENAL NOTICE

Although the Court is empowered to direct that a penal notice be endorsed on an order such a notice is not automatically endorsed on mandatory or prohibitive injunction orders. The COP Rules 2007, r 192 provides that the Court may direct that a penal notice is to be endorsed to any order warning the person to whom the copy of the order is served that disobeying the order would be a contempt of court punishable by imprisonment or fine. Unless such a direction is given by the Court a penal notice may not be attached to any order. It is extremely rare for a penal notice to be attached to a contact order but in extreme situations and where the behaviour of the parties is serious and harmful to P and his/her welfare the Court will direct that the notice be endorsed on a contact order (*E & K v SB & JB*[1] and see also under **3.6**).

In relation to restraint orders against family members concerning personal welfare issues of P, a penal notice would not normally be attached to such an order in the first instance as the Court's approach is to deal with such issues where possible by agreement and in a conciliatory manner, but in extreme cases, where there have been serious and repeated breaches of court orders, the Court has the powers and will make restraining orders to ensure that its orders are complied with and enforced when they are breached (see *E & K v SB & JB* above). However, in relation to issues concerning P's property and financial affairs, such a direction may be necessary to protect and preserve P's assets, particularly if the order is directed to a third party or a deputy/attorney.

14.3   FREEZING ORDERS AND INJUNCTIONS AND CHARGING ORDERS

Where there has been actual or suspected financial irregularity with regard to the management of P's property and affairs resulting in the suspension or

---

[1]   [2012] EWHC 4161 (COP).

discharge of a deputy or attorney it may be necessary for orders to be made protecting P's assets or preventing debts being incurred.

Similarly protective orders may be required where the deputy or attorney is unsuitable to continue to act or where those who have not been properly authorised with financial responsibility are misusing P's assets. Orders may also be appropriate to regulate P's own use of funds pending for instance a declaration regarding capacity.

Orders may be applied for in conjunction with applications to suspend or discharge a deputy or an attorney but may also be applied for as free standing applications.

In common with all other applications there must be evidence of P's incapacity or at the very least s 48 threshold must be met where orders are necessary without delay.

The Courts powers are contained in ss 16 and 18.

Section 16 provides:

'(1) This section applies if a person (P) lacks capacity in relation to a matter or matters concerning
(a) ...
(b) P's property and affairs
(2) The court may
(a) by making an order, make the decision or decisions on P's behalf in relation to the matter or matters.'

Section 18 provides:

'(1) The powers under s 16 as respects P's property and affairs extend in particular to
(a) the control and management of P's property.'

In making its decision the Court is obliged by virtue of s 16(3) to take account of the general principles established by the Act and to make any decision in P's best interests.

The Court's powers are extended to empower it to make interim orders as a matter of urgency and in order to protect P and his property and affairs and where appropriate as a holding measure. The COP Rules 2007, r 82 empowers the Court to grant interim remedies by way of:

- an interim injunction;
- an interim declaration; or
- any other interim order it considers appropriate.

Such orders may be made in pending proceedings or before an application has been issued.[2] An application for restraint orders may also be made without notice, (by telephone if necessary) and a hearing on notice will be directed to enable the person against whom the order is made to be heard and for the Court to consider the issues fully.[3]

Section 16(3):

> '(3) The powers of the Court under this section are subject to the provisions of this Act and, in particular to sections 1 (the principles) and 4 (best interests).'

Of particular importance in this area will be the empowerment of P to take decisions for himself, and the recognition that the making of unwise decisions does not automatically render someone unable to make decisions for themselves.

Having established the need for the Court to make a decision it must be done taking account of the guidance in s 4 which has been set out in detail at chapter 2. Section 4 only comes into play once it has been decided that P lacks capacity or the s 48 criteria are met. The Court has to follow the steps which must be taken to determine what is in P's best interests as set out in the best interests checklist. The purpose is to identify those factors which are most relevant to the individual against the background of the decision the Court has to make. The check list is not exhaustive and points to 'all relevant circumstances' being considered. So for instance in a high value money case where the Court needs to protect P's assets from misuse by a professional deputy, information may be needed from P's accountant or fund manager. By contrast in a case where P is of modest means the appropriate line of enquiry may be to seek views from a relative or care home. Moreover, the Act recognises that it is not always possible to make all relevant enquiries, which is particularly pertinent in an emergency where interim orders are to be made.

Section 4(3) qualifies the extent of investigation by defining relevant circumstances as those:

> '(a) of which the person making the determination is aware, and
> (b) which it would be reasonable to regard as relevant.'

Freezing orders place an embargo on dealings with assets whilst an injunction will restrict a person from so dealing. For example, where there is misuse of funds from a particular bank account the Court may impose a freezing order in respect of any dealings. The order will take the form of a direction to the bank preventing all dealings with the account. On a practical point, caution needs to be exercised here. The Court should avoid making an order which prevents proper payments to be made such as care home fees, especially in cases where there are limited funds paid into only one account. In these circumstances an

---

injunction against named persons making withdrawals may be more effective in terms of managing P's finances. Injunctions are also more appropriate in the case of irregular land or share transactions and the Court can impose an injunction preventing a person signing a contract or transfer document on behalf of P. In a case where it is suspected that P is adversely influenced by a particular person an injunction may be termed so as to restrict their contact with P and in particular the giving of financial advice.

Injunctions are also a useful tool in managing P's welfare needs providing an effective way of regulating contact particularly in a climate of hostile family pressures. Nonetheless where injunctive remedies are sought in the context of domestic abuse, remedies under the Family Law Act 1996 are to be preferred. This is by reason of their more effective enforcement procedure, specifically the change in the law since 1 July 2007, by the Domestic Violence, Crime and Victims Act 2004, which amends the FLA 1996 to make a breach of a non-molestation order a criminal offence. Also in a case where an occupation order under s 33 of the FLA 1996 may be appropriate, the Court when making such an order has a statutory power to attach a power of arrest not available to the Court of Protection.

A charging order is a means of enforcement of an order by the imposition of a charge to secure the payment of money due under an order. The application may be made without notice (CPR 1998, r 73.3(1)). The first step is to apply for an interim charging order over the judgment debtor's interest in the asset to which the application relates. For ease of reference a procedural guide and the law and practice in relation to a charging order can be found in *Emergency Remedies in the Family Courts*.[4]

14.4 PROCEDURE

Applications for freezing orders and injunctions will usually be made in conjunction with a substantive application. In those circumstances the application should simply be included as one of the list of orders required so separate applications and permission applications are unnecessary. Where substantive proceedings have already been issued the application should be made on COP9.

For free standing orders the following applies:

14.4.1 Permission

Permission to make the application will be required unless it is made by:
(a) P;
(b) if P has not reached the age of 18 years, by anyone with parental responsibility for him/her;

---

[4] Looseleaf (Jordan Publishing Ltd).

(c) by the donor or a donee of a lasting power of attorney to which the application relates;

(d) by a deputy appointed by the Court;

(e) by a person named in an existing order of the Court if the application relates to the order;[5]

(f) by the Official Solicitor;[6]

(g) by the Public Guardian;[7]

(h) where the application concerns P's property and affairs, unless the application is of a kind specified in COP Rules 2007, r 52 or a lasting power of attorney, which is or purports to be created under the Act, or an instrument which is or purports to be an enduring power of attorney.

14.4.2   How to apply

If permission is required, the application for permission should be made in Form COP2 and filed with the substantive application in Form COP1. In addition the following accompanying forms should be filed namely, Form COP1A (ie all the supporting information). Form COP3 to confirm that P lacks or continues to lack capacity should also be filed.

The Court fee of £400 will have to be paid when the application is issued.

14.4.3   Issue

Where permission is necessary the Court is required to deal with the application within 14 days. It may grant or refuse the application or list the application for a hearing and give directions including specifying who should be given notice of the hearing.[8] If a hearing is listed a person who is notified of the hearing should file an acknowledgement of service in Form COP5.

If permission is given the application will be issued by the Court. The applicant will receive from the Court Form COP5 (the acknowledgement of service), Form COP14 (the notice of proceedings to P) with the guidance notes in Form COP14A, notice in Form COP15 and guidance notes of the issue of the application and the certificate of service Form COP20.

In an emergency, the Court may also make immediate interim orders:[9]

•   by dealing with the application before issue;

•   by abridging time;

•   by dispensing with service;

•   by telephone;

---

5   MCA 2005, s 50.
6   COP Rules 2007, r 51(1)(a).
7   COP Rules 2007, r 51(1)(b).
8   COP Rules 2007, rr 55, 56 and 89.
9   COP Rules 2007, r 82 and PD 10B.

- by making the order sought on the papers without notice and without a hearing.

In those circumstances the Court will fix a return date and give directions and a timetable for respondents to reply to the application.

14.4.4 Service

It is the duty of the applicant to:

- serve all the necessary documents and Forms on the respondents within 21 days;
- serve P with Forms COP14 and 14A and COP5;
- notify any other relevant person of the application in Forms COP 15 and COP 5;
- file the certificate of service within 7 days of service in Form COP20.

14.4.5 The respondent/s to the application

Every respondent and any person who wishes to take part in the proceedings must file the acknowledgment of service within 21 days. The Court will then either give directions without a hearing or list the matter for a directions hearing. In urgent applications the Court will abridge the applicable time limits.[10]

14.4.6 Orders

The Court has a wide ranging power to make protective/restraining orders to meet the circumstances of each individual case. For menus of orders see the precedent in chapter 3.

14.5 COMMITTALS

Applications for a committal order have been extremely rare in the Court of Protection, but that is not to imply that the remedy is ineffective or not to be considered as an appropriate means of ensuring compliance with orders made by the Court. Indeed in *SCC v LM*[11] following the appalling behaviour of the family and serious and repeated breaches of the court orders the Court made further injunctive orders to cover violence, threats, intimidation and harassment, but when these were breached again a committal order was made.

Where a mandatory or prohibitive order made by the Court has not been complied with or has been disobeyed it can be enforced on an application made to a nominated judge of the Court of Protection. The Court has the same

---

[10] COP Rules 2007, r 26.
[11] [2012] EWHC 1137 (COP).

powers of committal as any other civil court. The COP Rules 2007, rr 185–194 and the PD 21A specifically provide the procedure which must be followed.

Rule 192 empowers the Court to direct that a penal notice be attached to an order warning that the consequences of breach may result in imprisonment or a fine. The direction order is expressed as: '*You must obey this order. If you do not, you may be sent to prison for contempt of court*'. The application for a penal notice to be endorsed to an order must be made on Form COP9 with supporting evidence. If a mode of service other than personal service is required the application should seek a substituted order for service and set out the reasons for the same. It is also important to follow the correct procedure which applies to committals in every court.

Because proceedings for committal for contempt of court are quasi criminal in nature and concern the liberty of the subject the relevant rules must be complied with and the appropriate prescribed forms must be used unless the Court has otherwise directed. Practitioners and the Court must also follow the *Practice Guidance on Committal for Contempt of Court* dated 3 May 2013 and the supplemental guidance issued on 4 June and the Circular issued on 2 August 2013 must be implicitly followed (see *The Family Court Practice* (Jordan Publishing, 2013)).

The CPR PD Committal, para 10 provides that any procedural defect in the commencement or conduct by the applicant of a committal application may be waived by the Court if satisfied that no injustice has been caused to the respondent by the defect. Lord Woolf in *Nicholls v Nicholls*[12] also stated that the requirements are not 'mandatory, in the sense that any non-compliance with the rule means that a committal for contempt is irredeemably invalid'.

Lord Woolf also stated that:

(a)   As committal orders involve the liberty of the subject it is particularly important that the relevant rules are duly complied with. It remains the responsibility of the judge when signing the committal order to ensure that it is properly drawn and that it adequately particularises the breaches which have been proved and for which the sentence has been imposed.

(b)   As long as the contemnor has had a fair trial and the order has been made on valid grounds the existence of a defect whether in the application to commit or in the committal order served will not result in the order being set aside except insofar as the interests of justice require this to be done.

(c)   Interests of justice will not require an order to be set aside where there is no prejudice caused as the result of errors in the application to commit or in the order to commit. When necessary the order can be amended.

(d)   When considering whether to set aside an order, the Court should have regard to the interests of justice of any other party and the need to uphold the reputation of the justice system.

---

[12] [1997] 1 FLR 649.

(e) If there has been a procedural irregularity or some other defect in the conduct of the proceedings which has occasioned injustice, the Court will consider exercising its power to order a new trial unless there are circumstances which indicate that it would not be just to do so.

In a more recent as yet unreported case *S-C v H-C*[13] it was once again stressed by the Court of Appeal that, the formalities of committal proceedings must be strictly observed. Where the order is unusual, where one of the parties is in person, and where one or more of the parties is not English and has little or no understanding of the English language, it is extremely important for the formalities to be observed if it is sought to penalise the contemnor. The order needs to be clear on its face as to precisely what it means, what it forbids and where the order requires a person to do something, the order should clearly state what it is that the person is required to do and the time frame within which what is required of him/her should be done. Where the order requires the person to abstain from doing an act the order must make it clear what the person is abstained from doing.

14.5.1 Service of order to be enforced

Before an application for committal is made it is essential to ensure that a penal notice has been endorsed in an appropriate form on the order to be enforced, and that the order with the penal notice endorsed on it has been served on the person against whom the committal order is sought. The Court may direct some other form of service or in an appropriate case make an order dispensing with service, but such an order must be made before a breach has occurred to make the breach enforceable through committal unless it is a restraining order and the Court is satisfied that the person concerned had knowledge of the terms of the order, or that the terms of the order were brought to his attention, for example by the person being present in court when the order was made.

Where the order requires the person to do an act (mandatory order) the order must give the person sufficient time to comply with the order and the order must be personally served on the person in reasonable time to enable the person to do the act within the time specified by the Court. The Court may in an appropriate case or where the circumstances are exceptional direct for an alternative mode of service. (See *Couzens v Couzens*[14] where the sentence imposed was set aside because the Court form had not been served on the respondent.)

14.5.2 Use and content of prescribed forms and evidence in support

The Court of Protection Rules 2007, r 186 deals with applications for committal orders. The application must be made on Form COP9 and supported

---

[13] [2010] EWCA Civ 21.
[14] [2001] 2 FLR 701, CA.

by an affidavit.[15] The application must set out the grounds on which the committal application is made. Form COP9, in section 2.2, specifically requires the applicant to set out the grounds for the application.[16] The form also, in section 2.3, requires the applicant to set out the grounds on which the committal order is sought. Thus the applicant is required to set out details of the order and the alleged breaches of its terms. The contents to be included in the affidavit are set out at PD 21A, paras 4, 5 and 6. Form COP 9, in section 2.3, states that if the Court requires the evidence to be given by affidavit the applicant needs to use the Form COP25 affidavit form. It is essential that the person against whom the committal order is sought is given sufficient details of the allegations.

The content of the affidavit

The affidavit must contain:

(a)   the name and description of the person making the application;

(b)   the name address and description of the person sought to be committed;

(c)   the grounds on which committal is sought;

(d)   a description of each alleged act of contempt, identifying each act separately and numerically and if known, the date of each act; and

(e)   any additional information required by paras 5 and 6 of the PD;

(f)   if the allegation of contempt relates to prior proceedings the case number and date of those prior proceedings and the name of P;

(g)   the contents of any order, judgment or undertaking which it is alleged has been disobeyed or broken by the person sought to be committed, where the allegation of contempt is made on the grounds that:
- the person required by an order or judgment to do an act has refused or neglected to do it within the time fixed by the judgment or order or any subsequent order;
- a person has disobeyed a judgment or order requiring him to abstain from doing an act; or
- a person has breached the terms of an undertaking which he gave to the Court.

14.5.3   Service of the application for committal

Subject to the Court's power to dispense with service, the application, the affidavit in support and the notice of the date of the hearing of the application must be served personally on the person sought to be committed.[17] The Court will only rely on the grounds set out in the application.

An order dispensing with service of the application for committal is exceptional. Dispensation of service may be granted where it is shown that the

---

[15]   PD 21A, paras 2 and 3.

[16]   See also *Harmsworth v Harmsworth* [1988] 1 FLR 349.

[17]   COP Rules 2007, r 186(2).

person concerned is deliberately evading service. Where a committal order is made without service on the person against whom the order is made the order should provide that the person when arrested should be brought before the Court at the earliest opportunity after his/her arrest.[18]

14.5.4 Oral hearing

Rules 187 and 188 govern the hearing. The person sought to be committed is entitled to give oral evidence and must be given the opportunity to obtain legal representation. If he elects to give oral evidence he may be cross-examined.[19] The person to be committed must also be allowed to cross-examine the applicant and any witness called to give evidence on behalf of the applicant. PD 21A anticipates that the initial hearing may not proceed to determination and provides for directions to be granted for future disposal.

14.5.5 Burden and standard of proof

The burden of proof rests on the applicant to prove the allegations of contempt.

The standard of proof is that a breach must be proved beyond reasonable doubt and the breach must be wilful and deliberate.

14.5.6 Disposal of the committal application

The approach to be taken by the Court will vary in accordance with the background of the case. Where there is simple financial irregularity the approach will be in line with that taken in civil litigation generally. Where breaches are alleged in the context of complex and emotional welfare issues the Court's approach will be similar to that adopted in family cases. The overall aim is to achieve compliance and any punishment is likely to take into account the effect upon P, P's family and significant others.

Imprisonment will be considered in the most serious of cases. The Court may make no order or adjourn the application if there is a likelihood of the order being complied with. It may impose a fine or suspend the committal order or consider other alternative options to achieve compliance with its order such as a writ of sequestration.[20]

Because committal applications are rare in the Court of Protection, notwithstanding the fact that the practice and procedure which apply to such application are set out in the rules and the practice direction it is perhaps understandable that some may not be too familiar with these. As further guidance the following passages from the judgment of Hayden J in *Re*

---

[18] *Lamb v Lamb* [1984] FLR 278.
[19] COP Rules 2007, r 186(10).
[20] See further *Hale v Tanner* [2000] 2 FLR 879.

Whiting[21] is set out below. Hayden J also went on to give further guidance on the importance of and the need for a close working relationship between the social workers and the lawyer to identify the breach and to consider the evidence to support each of the breach to the criminal standard of proof (para 14). By way of guidance Hayden J stated:

> '12. It seems to me to be important to note some crucial features of the committal process:
> (1) the procedure has an essentially criminal law complexion. That is to say, contempt of court must be proved to the criminal standard, i.e. so that the judge is sure. The burden of proof rests throughout on the applicant (see: *Mubarak v Mubarak* [2001] 1 FLR 698);
> (2) contempt of court involves a deliberate contumelious disobedience to the court (see: *Re A (A Child)* [2008] EWCA Civ 1138);
> (3) it is not enough to suspect recalcitrance; it must be proved (see: *London Borough of Southwark v B* [1993] 2 FLR 559);
> (4) committal is not the automatic consequence of a contempt, though the options before the court are limited – for example: (a) do nothing; (b) adjourn where appropriate; (c) levy a fine; (d) sequester assets; (e) where relevant, make orders under the Mental Health Act (see: *Jamie Malcolm Hale v Rachel Tanner* [2000] 2 FLR 879);
> (5) the objectives of the application are usually dual, i.e. to punish for the breach and to ensure future compliance;
> (6) bearing in mind the dual purpose of many committal proceedings, they should be brought expeditiously, whilst primary evidence is available and the incidents are fresh in the mind of the relevant witness. This is particularly important in the Court of Protection where there may be reliance on a vulnerable witness and where capacity might have to be assessed.
>
> 13. It follows, therefore, that where injunctive orders are made, they should be clear, un-ambivalent and drafted with care. In my judgment, simplicity should be the guide. Similarly, where breaches are alleged, they should be particularised with care, both so that the alleged contemnor knows exactly what, where, when and how it is contended that he is in breach, so as to be able to marshal his defence, but also to help the applicant focus on what evidence is likely to be required to establish the breach to the requisite standard of proof.'

In the county court a committal order is enforced by the court baliff and in the High Court by the Tiptaff as enforcement officers. Since pursuant to s 47(1) of the MCA 2005 the Court of Protection is vested with the same powers, rights, privileges, and authority as the High Court, a judge of the Court of Protection has the power to direct the Tipstaff to execute the committal order.

14.5.7 Power of the Court to commit on its own initiative

The Court of Protection Rules 2007, r 194 empowers the Court to make an order for committal on its own initiative against a person who has disobeyed its order. Where a case is considering making an order in such circumstances it

---

[21] [2013] EWHC B27 (COP).

would be desirable to consider the following factors which were referred to by the Court of Appeal in *Re G (Contempt: Committal)*:[22]

- A committal order on the Court's own motion should only be made in exceptional circumstances.
- A committal order is a remedy of last resort to be made only in serious, or intentional or repeated contempts.
- In any event the person to be committed should be given an opportunity of an adjournment to enable him to seek advice and to be represented and to be informed of the acts which constitute the contempt.
- Committal proceedings should be held in public.

14.5.8 Discharge of person committed

A person who has been committed to prison for disobedience of an order of the Court should be given an opportunity to purge his contempt. Where a person has been committed for failing to comply with an order requiring him to deliver anything to some other person or to deposit it in court or elsewhere, a writ of sequestration may be issued to enforce that judgment or order. If a writ is issued, then if the thing is in the custody or power of the person committed, the commissioners appointed by the writ of sequestration may take possession of it as if it were the property of that person. Additionally, and without prejudice to any application made by the contemnor to purge his contempt, the Court may discharge him/her and may give such directions for dealing with the thing taken away by the commissioners as it thinks just.[23]

14.5.9 Form of committal order

There is no provision in the Court of Protection Rules or the Practice Direction for a committal form. Rule 188 provides that when making the committal order the Court must publicly identify the person committed and state in general terms the nature of the contempt in respect of which the order is made and the punishment imposed. The *Practice Guidance on Committal for Contempt of Court* of 13 May and 2 August 2013 should be followed. It is submitted that the order should be drawn in the terms of Form N79 which is used in the county court (Form A85 is used in the High Court). A copy of Form N79 is provided under Precedent for guidance; Forms N78 (notice of an application to commit) and N80 (warrant for committal to prison) are also provided. Practitioners' attention is also drawn to the changes proposed to the form of committal orders. Draft forms of the orders are currently the subject of consultation. The new form of orders will be available on HM Court-service website when they have been approved (see *Emergency Remedies in the Family Courts* where the draft forms are set out).

---

[22] [2003] 2 FLR 58.
[23] COP Rules, r 191.

14.6   PROCEDURAL GUIDE

Before the application is issued	Obtain proof of service of the order endorsed with penal notice before the breach occurred	
Application	Form COP9 (must identify the provisions in the order alleged to have been breached and set out the ways in which it has been breached.)	
Affidavit in support with proof of service of the order	(1) Must identify the parties	PD 21A(4)-(6)
	(2) Must state the grounds, describe each act separately (with dates) and numerically	
	(3) Where appropriate give details of previous proceedings	
	(4) Set out in full details of the order allegedly breached	
Court Office	Fixes date of hearing and issues notice of hearing	PD 21A(7)
Service of application	Applicant must serve COP9, affidavit in Support and notice of hearing on the Contemnor unless otherwise directed	COP Rules 2007, r186(2)
Hearing	In open court	COP Rules 2007, r 188(3)
Orders	Committal order	COP Rules 2007, r 188
	Suspended committal order	COP Rules 2007, r 189
	Fine	COP Rules 2007, r 193
	Writ of sequestration	
	Provide security for good behaviour	
	No order	

PRECEDENT

EXAMPLES OF THE TERMS OF INJUCTIVE RELIEF
THAT MAY BE GRANTED

The respondent/s .... [*insert name*] is/are forbidden whether by himself/herself themselves or by instructing, encouraging or suggesting to another person to do so.

(a)   To remove or attempt to remove JS from the .... Home/Hospital [*as the case may be*] or any other suitable hospital where JS may from time to time reside/or be admitted.

(b)   To remove or attempt to remove JS from the jurisdiction of this Court/England and Wales.

(c)   To obstruct or attempt to obstruct treatment and care while at the .... Hospital or any other suitable hospital where JS may from time to time reside.

(d)   To give or attempt to give any food or drink to JS other than that specified and agreed with the staff at the .... Hospital.

(e)   To administer or attempt to administer any medication to JS.

(f)   To interfere with the arrangements made by the applicant for the care of JS at the Paradise Care Home or any hospital to which JS may be admitted.

(g)   To do or say anything calculated to interfere with the current or any future residence/placement of JS.

(h)   To enter or attempt to enter the Paradise Care Home or any hospital to which JS is admitted without the prior written agreement of the applicant's social services department.

(i)   To see JS at the Paradise Care Home or any hospital to which JS is admitted.

(j)   To telephone the Paradise Care Home or any hospital to which JS may be admitted except at times set out in the schedule of contact attached to this order or times agreed in advance with the applicant's Social Services Department.

(k)   To bring any food or drink for JS when he/she/they visit JS except with the permission of the Manager of the Paradise Care Home.

(l)   To remove any item from JS's room without prior agreement of the Manager or the Paradise Care Home.

(m)   To use or threaten violence or behave in an abusive or aggressive manner towards the staff at the Paradise Care Home/or any employee of the applicant/or a deputy appointed by the Court.

(n)   To interfere in any manner whatsoever when the applicant/social worker/etc has access to JS to assess him/her, speak with him/her or interview him/her.

(o)   To discuss these proceedings with JS.

(p)   To do any act calculated to interfere with JS's co-operation with any member of the HCC's employee or with the independent social worker or experts instructed in the proceedings.

(q)   To do any act which puts at risk the current care arrangements made for JS.

Orders relating to access to JS

The second respondent .... [*or as the case may be*] must allow a social worker of the HCC and the Team manager into the property at .... and to have access to JS alone to see and speak with him/her.

Orders relating to passports

Immediately on receipt of this order or its terms being brought to his/her attention the second respondent [*or as the case may be and insert name of the person*] do hand over to .... the Team Manager JS's passport. Upon receipt of the passport .... the Team Manager shall hand over the same to the legal department of the HCC who will in turn ensure that the passport is delivered to the Official Solicitor for safe keeping until further order of the Court.

FORMS

FORM 78

Notice to Show Good Reason why an Order for Your Committal to Prison should not be made

In the	
	County Court
Case No. *Always quote this*	

Between   **Applicant**

and   **Respondent**

To

of

On the   the Court made an order [*or* you gave an undertaking] as follows:

           has applied for an order that you should be committed to prison. It is alleged that you have disobeyed the order [*or* broken the undertaking] by:

You must attend Court

at

on   at   o'clock to show good reason why you should not be sent to prison.

- If the Court is satisfied that any of the allegations are true, it may order that you be imprisoned for your contempt of this Court.
- **Important instructions about what you should do are set out overleaf.**

The applicant (Solicitor)
Name
Address

Ref

Tel

The court office at

is open between 10 am and 4 pm Monday to Friday. When corresponding with the court, please address forms or letters to the Court Manager and quote the claim number. Tel: Fax:

N78 Notice of an application to commit

Case No.

Important notes

- The Court has the power to send you to prison if it finds that any of the allegations made against you are true. Full details of the allegations are contained in the applicant's sworn statement (the affidavit).

- You must attend court on the date shown on the front of this form. It is in your own interest to do so. At the hearing, the person making this application will tell the Court why they believe you should be sent to prison. You will then have the opportunity to put your case. You should bring any witnesses and documents with you which you think will help you put your side of the case.

- If you need advice you should show this document at once to your solicitor or go to a Citizens' Advice Bureau. If you do not already have a solicitor acting for you the Court can give details of local solicitors. You may be entitled to help towards the cost of legal advice.

- Even if you do not seek advice, you can, if you wish, file a sworn statement at the Court setting out your side of the case. The Court Office can give you a form for this purpose and it can be sworn before a Court Officer. If you have disobeyed the order you can apologise for it on this form. You must still attend court on the date shown, however.

For Court use only

I certify that the notice, of which this is a true copy, was served by me on

(date)...

on   personally.

at the address stated in the notice, or at

Or *in accordance with an order for substituted service.*

Bailiff/Officer of the Court

Notice of Non – Service

I certify that this notice has not been served for the following reasons:

Bailiff/Officer of the Court

The court office at

is open between 10 am and 4 pm Monday to Friday. When corresponding with the court, please address forms or letters to the Court Manager and quote the claim number. Tel: Fax:

N78 Notice of an application to commit

FORM 79

Committal or Other Order upon Proof of Disobedience of a Court Order or Breach of an Undertaking

In the	County Court

Between_____

Applicant
Claimant
Petitioner

Claim No. *Always quote this*

and _____

Respondent
Defendant

seal

Before His (Her) Honour Judge

Sitting at _____ on *(date)*

1 **An application having been made by**[1] for committal of[2] to prison for disobeying the order [breach of the undertaking] dated .The relevant terms of the order (undertaking) and the allegations made by the applicant are recited on the attached notice to show good reason.

or

2 **Whereas**[2] has been suspected of a breach of the attached order dated and has been arrested by a constable and brought before the Judge under section 47(6) of the Family Law Act 1996.

or

3 **Whereas**[2] has been suspected of a breach of the attached order [undertaking] dated and has been arrested under a warrant of arrest and brought before the Judge under [section 47(8) of the Family Law Act 1996] [section 3(3) of the Protection from Harassment Act 1997].

——————————————— **IMMEDIATE CUSTODIAL ORDER** ———————————————

It is ordered that[2] be committed for contempt to Her Majesty's Prison (be detained under section 9(1) of the Criminal Justice Act 1982) at[3] for a (total) period of[4] or until lawfully discharged if sooner, and that a warrant of arrest and committal be issued forthwith.

And the contemnor can apply to the (court) (judge) to purge his contempt and ask for release.

[And, as the court by order dated dispensed with service of the notice of application for a committal order, **It is ordered** that the contemnor be brought before a judge of this court as soon as practicable.]

——————————————— **ALTERNATIVE DISPOSAL** ———————————————

It is ordered that[2] be committed for contempt to prison for a (total) period of[4]

The order is suspended until **20** and will not be put in force if during that time the contemnor[2] complies with the following terms:

And it is further ordered that in the event of non compliance any application for issue of the warrant shall be made to a judge (on notice to the contemnor)

It is ordered that[2] be fined the sum of £ .
Such sum to be paid into the office of the court within 14 days of the date of this order.

It is ordered that consideration of the penalty for the contempts found proved be adjourned until **20** and may be restored for decision if during that time[2] does not comply with the following terms

——————————————— **PROVISION FOR COSTS** ———————————————

And it is ordered that

Date

For record of service, hearing and contempts found proved, see next page

RECORD OF SERVICE, HEARING AND CONTEMPTS FOUND PROVED

At the hearing

(1)   [appeared personally] [was represented by solicitor/counsel] [did not attend]

(2)   [appeared personally] [was represented by solicitor/counsel] [did not attend]

The court read the affidavits of (Names)	Date affidavit(s) sworn

And the court heard oral evidence given by
Name(s)

And the court is satisfied having considered the facts disclosed by the evidence and/or admitted in court by him/her that(2)   has been guilty of contempt of this court by disobeying the order (breaking the undertaking) dated   by (and as set out in the attached schedule)

	And for the particular contempt the court imposed the penalty of:
1.	1.
2.	2.

──────────────────── **RECORD OF SERVICE** ────────────────────

Service of Injunction Order with Penal Notice incorporated or indorsed	Service of Notice to show good reason in form N78	Arrest under warrant of arrest
(Order dated 20	(Order dated 20	Respondent arrested on
(for substituted) (dispensing with) service)	(for substituted) (dispensing with) service)	
Service proved by	Service proved by	by
☐ certificate of service dated 20	☐ certificate of service dated 20	in accordance with a warrant of arrest issued on
☐ certificate of bailiff	☐ certificate of bailiff	
☐ oral evidence of	☐ oral evidence of	

Service of Immediate Custodial Order

I (name of Officer)   certify that I served the contemnor with a copy of this order by:

☐ delivery by hand to the contemnor before he was taken from the court building or other place of arrest to the place of detention

☐ delivery by hand to the contemnor at (time)   on (date)   20   at (place)

Where a suspended committal order is made, the applicant is responsible for service. (Rules of the Supreme Court Order 52 rule 7(2).) Where there is suspended committal order or penalty is adjourned on terms, personal service is advisable.

The court office is open from 10 am to 4 pm Monday to Friday.

When corresponding with the court, please address forms and letters to the Court Manager and quote the case number.

Notes for completion of page 2
(RECORD OF SERVICE, HEARING AND CONTEMPTS FOUND PROVED)

──────── REPRESENTATION (At the hearing) ────────

Name the parties or their legal representative (advocate only).

──────── AFFIDAVIT EVIDENCE (The court read the affidavits) ────────

List only those affidavits which the judge has considered at the hearing. There is unlikely to be any affidavit evidence offered where the respondent has been brought to court under a power of arrest.

──────── ORAL EVIDENCE (And the court heard oral evidence) ────────

Give the names of only those witnesses sworn and examined.

──────── CONTEMPTS FOUND PROVED (And the court is satisfied) ────────

List and give exact details of only those allegations of contempt which the judge has found proved.

If separate penalties are imposed for each contempt found proved these are to be recorded in the right-hand column showing whether or not periods of detention are to run consecutively or concurrently.

If necessary, annex additional page and continue list on it. If an additional page is not used, delete the words *(and as set out in the attached schedule)*.

──────── JUDGE'S APPROVAL ────────

The Judge must be asked to initial the order indicated by the dotted line.

──────── RECORD OF SERVICE ────────

Enter details of certificates of service.

Record of delivery of an undertaking need not be made on this document as it can be found on the form of undertaking.

A sealed copy of the approved order must be served on the contemnor.

Order 29 rule 1(5) CCR states:

If a committal order is made, the order shall be for the issue of a warrant of committal and unless the judge otherwise orders:-

(a) a copy of the order shall be served on the person to be committed either before or at the time of the execution of the warrant; or

(b) where the warrant has been signed by the Judge, the order for issue of the warrant may be served on the person to be committed at any time within 36 hours after execution of the warrant.

Where the respondent is brought before the court under a power of arrest delete record of service of form N78.

Where the respondent is brought before the court under a warrant of arrest delete record of service of form N78 and complete record of service of warrant of arrest.

Terms or names that may be used more than once in the order are numbered in brackets as follows:

(1) Person making application for committal

(2) Person against whom the committal order is made (contemnor)

(3) Name of prison or young offender institution

(4) Period of detention

Notes for Guidance on completion of form N79
(Disobedience of a Court Order or Breach of an Undertaking)

The Court Officer responsible for the forms completion should note the following:

- **Where the respondent is brought before the court after being arrested under a power of arrest** (Section 47(6) of the Family Law Act 1996) a sealed copy of the injunction order giving the power of arrest (not Power of Arrest form FL406) with penal notice indorsed becomes part of form N79 and must be attached to the approved order.

- **Where the respondent is brought before the court after being arrested under a warrant of arrest** (section 47(8) of the Family Law Act 1996) (section 3(3) of the Protection from Harassment Act 1997) a sealed copy of the injunction order becomes part of form N79 and must be attached to the approved order.

- **In all other cases** Form N78 (notice to show good reason why an order for committal should not be made) becomes part of form N79 and a sealed copy of N78 must be attached to the approved order.

- In all cases the warrant is in form N80.

- **When the form has been fully completed it must be passed to the judge for approval.** If the judge is available he/she should be asked to approve and initial or sign the final (typed) version. If this is not possible the judge must be asked to initial or sign the final hand-written draft. In either case the document endorsed by the judge **must be retained on the court file.**

- Before the order is served it must also be checked by an officer of no less than HEO grade.

- Before the order is served these notes should be detached, they are for the guidance of Court Staff only.

When an immediate custodial order is made:

- A copy of N79 (with attached N78 or injunction) must be sent to the Office of the Official Solicitor.

- A sealed copy of the approved order must be served on the contemnor. Order 29 rule 1(5) CCR.

Notes for completion of page 1

Terms or names that may be used more than once in the order are numbered in brackets as follows:

(1) Person making application for committal

(2) Person against whom the committal order is made (contemnor)

(3) Name of prison or young offender institution

(4) Period of detention

CLAUSES 1 TO 3

If the respondent has been brought before the court under a power of arrest (Family Law Act 1996) delete 1 and 3.

If the respondent has been brought before the court under a warrant of arrest (Family Law Act 1996 or Protection from Harassment Act 1997) delete 1 and 2.

In all other cases delete 2 and 3.

Enter the date of order (with penal notice incorporated or indorsed) or undertaking.

Date of form N78 Notice to show good reason (applies to 1 only).

Date of the warrant of arrest (applies to 3 only).

Note: A warrant of arrest cannot be issued on an undertaking under the Protection from Harassment Act 1997.

IMMEDIATE CUSTODIAL ORDER

Complete this section if an immediate custodial order is made otherwise delete and complete section below

Section 9(1) of CJA is for persons aged less than 21 and at least 18.

The total period of detention must be specified by the Judge. The maximum period for contempt of court (including a county court) is 2 years.

If the offence is failure to do a specific act and the judge decides that the application may be made to a district judge upon proof that the act has been done delete (judge) otherwise delete (court).

Complete only if order dispensing with service of notice of application was granted otherwise delete.

ALTERNATIVE DISPOSAL

Delete this section if an immediate custodial order is made otherwise delete alternatives not selected by judge.

Enter the exact terms of any suspended committal order or adjournment of penalty.

There are further possible alternative disposals, eg under sections 35, 37 and 38 of the Mental Health Act and sequestration.

COSTS

Enter any order for costs here or show that no order for costs has been made if applicable.

Give the date of the order.

FORM 80

Warrant of Committal to prison

In the	
	County Court
Claim No.	
Warrant No.	

Between

_____ **Applicant**
Petitioner

and

_____ **Respondent**
Defendant

Seal

To ● the District Judge and Bailiffs of the Court

● every constable within his jurisdiction

 ● the Governor (of Her Majesty's Prison at)(1)

(1) Name of Prison

(2) Name and
(3) address of
person to be
committed.

On the   **day of** |19 ||20 | ,

(enter name of judge) has ordered that (2)

of (3)

(4) Where the
person to
be committed is
aged less than
21 years and
at least 18 delete
all references
to prison
otherwise
delete
reference to
Sec 9(1)CJA

should be committed to Prison (4) (detained under Section 9(1) Criminal Justice Act 1982) for

a period of (5)

You the District Judge and Bailiff are therefore required forthwith to arrest and deliver

(2)

to (Her Majesty's Prison at) (1)

(5) State term of
imprisonment

And you, the Governor, are required to receive and keep (2)

safely (in prison) from the arrest under this warrant for a period of (5)   or until

lawfully discharged, if sooner.

(6) Add if so
ordered
otherwise
delete

[(6) **And**, as the court by order dated   dispensed with service of the notice of

application for a committal order,

It is ordered that you, the Governor, bring (2)

before a judge of this court at such time and place as the court shall specify and afterwards,

return him to the prison unless the court orders his discharge.]

Date

I arrested the person named in this warrant on (date)

and delivered him into the custody of the Governor (of Her Majesty's Prison) at (1)

on *(date)*

Bailiff of the County Court

The Court Office is open from 10am to 4pm Monday to Friday

Address all communications to the Court Manager and quote the above claim number.

N80 Warrant for committal to prison (4.99)   *Printed on behalf of The Court Service*

CHAPTER 15

APPEALS

LAW AND PRACTICE

15.1 INTRODUCTION

The provisions relating to appeals are set out in s 53 of the Act. Subsection (1) states that an appeal lies to the Court of Appeal from any decision of the Court but subsection (2) states that the Court of Protection Rules may provide that where a decision of the Court is made by a person exercising the jurisdiction of the Court by virtue of rules made under s 51(2)(d) (ie an officer of the Court) or a district or a circuit judge, an appeal from that decision lies to a prescribed higher judge of the Court and not to the Court of Appeal.

'Higher judge of the Court' is defined as follows; in relation to an officer, a circuit judge or a district judge; in relation to a district judge, a circuit judge, or a nominated judge.

The COP Rules 2007, Part 20 make provisions relating to whether permission to appeal is required and if required to whom the application should be made and the grounds on which such application can be made and the consideration to be taken into account in relation to granting or refusing permission to appeal.

15.2 AVENUES OF APPEAL

Appeals from a district judge lie to a circuit judge.

Appeals from a decision of a judge which was itself made on appeal (ie second appeal) will be to the Court of Appeal.[1]

Appeals from a circuit judge lies to a High Court Judge nominated to sit in the Court of Protection.

Appeals from the President, Vice Chancellor or a High Court Judge, lie to the Court of Appeal.

---

[1] COP Rules 2007, r 182.

15.3   GROUNDS FOR ALLOWING AN APPEAL

The appeal court will allow an appeal where the decision of the first instance court was:

(a)   wrong; or

(b)   unjust, because of a serious or procedural or other irregularity in the proceedings before the fist instance judge.[2]

15.3.1   The decision below was 'wrong'

It will be for the appellant to establish, particularly if an interim remedy is sought pending the full appeal, that there is merit in the appeal. It may therefore be helpful to refer to decisions in the civil jurisdiction on what is meant by 'wrong'.

The term 'wrong' in this context implies that the Court at first instance erred: (i) in law; or (ii) on its assessment of the facts; or (iii) in the exercise of its discretion but the basis on which an appeal is most likely to be allowed is that the decision of the Court was wrong in law. The appeal is not a rehearing but only a review and the appeal court's review of the facts will be a cautious one because the judge at first instance heard the evidence and had the advantage of assessing the demeanour of the witnesses and their credibility. Baroness Hale in *Re J (Child Returned Abroad: Convention Rights)*[3] at para 12 said that in the exercise of a discretion in which various factors were relevant, the evaluation and balancing of those factors was a matter for the trial judge. Only if his decision was so plainly wrong that he must have given far too much weight to a particular factor was the appellate court entitled to interfere. If trial judges were led to believe that, even if they directed themselves impeccably on the law, make findings of fact which were open to them on the evidence and were careful in their evaluation and weighing of the relevant factors, their decisions were liable to be overturned unless they reached a particular conclusion, they will come to believe that they do not in fact have any choice or discretion in the matter.

Similar observations were made by Lord Hoffman in *Piglowski v Piglowski*[4] that an appellate court had to be very cautious in giving leave and in granting appeals. The appellate court had to bear in mind that the first instance judge had the advantage of seeing the parties and the other witnesses. This is well understood on questions of credibility and findings of primary facts including the evaluation of those facts. Given the exigencies of daily courtroom life the reasons for judgment ought to be read on the assumption that unless the judge

---

[2]   PD 20A, para 179(3).
[3]   [2005] 2 FLR 802.
[4]   [1999] 2 FLR 763.

had demonstrated the contrary he knew how he should perform his functions and which matter he should take into account.[5]

As in cases involving children, the decision made in cases involving persons who lack capacity will be very much dependent on the factual evidence before the Court and the evaluation of that evidence. Where the decision involves the exercise of discretion unless it can be shown that the 'judge has either erred in principle in his approach or has left out of account or has taken into account some feature that he should, or should not, have considered' which throws doubt on the analysis and the basis of the decision it is unlikely that the appeal court will interfere with the decision.[6] Butler Sloss LJ in *Re M and R (Child abuse: Evidence)*[7] succinctly put it:

> 'It is the function of the appellate court to make sure that the judge has correctly directed himself to and applied the correct law, has properly approached his task in deciding disputed facts and has not erred in principle. The appellate court then has to stand back and consider whether his decision is plainly wrong. If it is not, it is not for the appellate court to intervene.'

Guidance on the approach which the appellate court should adopt where errors of fact is alleged was given in *Assicurazioni Generali Spa v Arab Insurance Group*[8] at [6]-[23] by Clarke LJ and at [193]-[197] by Ward LJ but in such cases much will depend on the circumstances of the case and the nature of challenge made against the decision of the judge at first instance. However, the appellate court cannot substitute its own assessment of the evidence for that made by the trial judge.[9]

In relation to the issue of serious procedural or other irregularity the challenge raised must show that the irregularity was a serious one and it must have led to injustice.[10] The issues are likely to relate to the conduct of the proceedings and in particular to issues concerning the Art 6 rights eg refusal to allow a party to call a witness or adduce evidence, or to be heard, and whether the judge at first instance had taken into account matters which were irrelevant or ignored matters which were relevant or arrived at a conclusion which was plainly wrong (see *Breeze v Ahmed*[11] where the Court of Appeal allowed an appeal because the effect of two technical documents had been misrepresented to the Court).

---

[5]   See also *Assicurazioni Generali Spa v Arab Insurance Group* [2002] EWCA Civ 1642, [2003] 1 WLR 577.
[6]   *AEI Rediffusion Music Ltd v Phonographic Performance Ltd* [1999] 1 WLR 1507.
[7]   [1996] 2 FLR 195.
[8]   [2002] EWCA Civ 1642.
[9]   See *Designers Guild Ltd v Russell Williams (Textiles) Ltd* [2000] 1 WLR 2416, HL.
[10]   See *Storer v British Gas Plc* [2000] 1 WLR 1237.
[11]   [2005] EWCA Civ 192.

A review by the appeal court will necessarily involve the Court going through the process before the judge at first instance to determine whether or not there was any error in the steps undertaken before him or in the analysis of the evidence.

In relation to error in the exercise of discretion *G v G (Minors: Custody Appeal)*[12] Lord Fraser summarised the principles which the Court will apply as follows:[13]

> '... the appellate court should only interfere when they consider that the judge of first instance has not merely preferred an imperfect solution which is different from an alternative imperfect solution which the Court of Appeal might or would have adopted, but has exceeded the generous ambit within which a reasonable disagreement is possible.'

Before embarking on an appeal, and in particular seeking any interim relief, the grounds of the appeal will need to identify precisely how it is alleged that the judge at first instance was 'wrong' in matters of law or matters of fact or the exercise of his discretion.

15.4 PERMISSION TO APPEAL

Save in the case of an appeal against an order for committal to prison permission to appeal is required against any decision of the Court. The application for permission may be made to the trial judge or the appeal judge. Where an application for permission is refused by the trial judge a further application may be made as follows:

- Where the decision sought to be appealed is a decision of a district judge permission may be granted or refused by the President, the Vice President, a puisne judge of the High Court or a circuit judge.[14]

- Where the decision sought to be appealed is a decision of a circuit judge permission may be granted or refused by the President, Vice President or a puisne judge of the High Court.

- Where the appeal is from a decision of a judge which was itself made on appeal from a judge of the Court, permission will be required from the Court of Appeal.[15]

---

[12] [1985] FLR 894.

[13] Followed in *Tanfern Ltd v Cameron MacDonald* [2000] 1 WLR and see *AEI Rediffusion Music Ltd v Phonographic Performance Ltd* above and *Price v Price (t/a Popyland Headware)* [2003] EWCA Civ 888.

[14] COP Rules 2007, r 172.

[15] COP Rules 2007, r 182(2).

15.5 MATTERS TO BE TAKEN INTO CONSIDERATION WHEN CONSIDERING AN APPLICATION FOR PERMISSION

Permission to appeal will only be granted where:

(a) the Court considers that the appeal would have a real prospect of success; or

(b) there is some other compelling reason why the appeal should be heard[16] eg serious medical treatment involving life sustaining or withdrawal of treatment.

Where the application for permission is in relation to a second appeal and which must be made to the Court of Appeal, the Court of Appeal will not give permission unless it considers that:

(a) the appeal would raise an important point of principle or practice; or

(b) there is some other compelling reason for the Court of Appeal to hear it.[17]

15.6 APPELLANT'S NOTICE

Where permission to appeal is being sought from the appeal court, it must be requested in the appellant's notice in Form COP35. The notice, with a copy for the Court, must be filed within such period as directed or specified in the order of the trial judge or where no such direction is given within 21 days after the date of the decision being appealed.[18]

The appellant must serve a sealed copy of the appeal notice on each respondent and such other person as the Court directs as soon as practicable and in any event within 21 days of the date on which it is issued. Where permission to appeal has been granted by the trial judge the appellant must also serve a skeleton argument on each respondent.[19] Once service is effected the appellant must file a certificate of service in Form COP20 within 7 days of service.[20]

Where the appellant seeks a remedy incidental to the appeal eg an interim remedy under r 82 the appellant may include this application in the appellant's notice or in an application notice in Form COP9 and must attach this to the appellant's notice.

15.7 EXTENSION OF TIME

Where the time for filing the appellant's notice has expired an application for an extension of time may be made to the appeal judge by filing the appellant's notice in Form COP35 and include an application for an extension of time. The

---

[16] COP Rules 2007, r 173.
[17] COP Rules 2007, r 182(3).
[18] COP Rules 2007, r 175.
[19] PD 20A, para 4.
[20] PD 20A, para 7.

appellant's notice should include the reasons for the delay and any steps that have been taken prior to the application being made. The respondent has a right to be heard on an application for an extension of time.[21]

15.8   DOCUMENTS TO BE FILED WITH THE APPELLANT'S NOTICE

(a)   *Skeleton Arguments*: The appellant's notice must be accompanied by a skeleton argument using or attached to, a skeleton argument in Form COP37. Where the appellant is unable to provide a skeleton argument with the appellant's notice it must be filed and served on each respondent within 21 days of filing of the notice.[22]

The skeleton must contain a concise and numbered list of points which the party wishes to make. These should define and confine the areas of controversy. Each numbered point must also identify the document on which the appellant relies.

If a legal authority is cited the skeleton argument must state the proposition of law that the authority demonstrates and the parts of the authority (identified by page or paragraph references) that support the proposition. If more than one authority is relied upon the skeleton argument must state the reasons, the relevance of the authority or authorities to the argument and that the citation is necessary for the proper presentation of that argument.

(b)   *Suitable record of the judgment*: Where the judgment was recorded an approved transcript should accompany the appellant's notice. If there is no officially recorded judgment, but the Court handed down a written judgment, the Court will accept a written copy of the judgment endorsed with the judge's signature. If the judgment was not recorded or given in writing an agreed note of the judgment should be submitted for approval to the trial judge. If agreement cannot be reached, both parties should submit their respective note to the trial judge. Where permission to appeal is sought the note need not be approved by the respondent or the trial judge for approval.[23] Where the appellant was not represented but the respondent was, it is the duty of the respondent's advocate to make a note of the judgment and provide a copy to the appellant without charge if the judgment was not recorded or handed down in writing.

If permission to appeal is granted a transcript of the evidence should be obtained if the evidence was recorded. If not, a typed version of the judge's note should be obtained. Where the appellant's financial circumstances are such that the cost of the transcript would cause an excessive burden on him, the Court may direct that the transcript be obtained at public expense provided it is satisfied that there are reasonable grounds for appeal.[24]

(c)   A sealed copy of the order being appealed.

---

[21]   PD 20A, para 8.
[22]   PD 20A, paras 16 and 17.
[23]   PD 20A, para 24.
[24]   PD 20A, paras 26–29.

(d) A copy of any order giving or refusing permission to appeal together with a copy of the judge's reasons for allowing or refusing permission to appeal.

(e) Any witness statements or affidavits in support of any application included in the appellant's notice.

(f) The application form and any application notice or response (where relevant to the subject of the appeal).

(g) Any other documents which the appellant reasonably considers necessary to enable the Court to reach its decision on the hearing of the application or appeal.

(h) Such other documents as the Court may direct.[25]

(i) A list of persons who feature in the case, a glossary of technical terms and a chronology of relevant events should also be filed.

If it is not possible to file all the above documents with the appellant's notice, the appellant should identify which documents have not been filed and the reasons for the same and the time estimate within which the missing documents can be filed. The appellant must file the missing documents as soon as reasonably practicable.

15.9 RESPONDENT'S NOTICE

A respondent who wishes to cross appeal must seek permission to do so in accordance with r 172 (see above). If the respondent wishes to appeal or wishes to ask the appeal judge to uphold the order for reasons different from or additional to those given by the trial judge the respondent must file a respondent's notice. If he fails to do so he will not be entitled to rely on any reasons for upholding the decision unless the appeal court gives him permission.

The respondent who seeks permission to appeal or wishes to ask the appeal court to uphold the decision of the trial judge for reasons different from or additional to those given by the trial judge must file his notice in Form COP36 with his skeleton arguments in Form COP37 within the time specified by the trial judge or in any event within 21 days beginning with the date which is the soonest of:

(a) the date on which the respondent is served with the appellant's notice where permission to appeal was given by the trial judge or permission to appeal is not required;

(b) the date on which the respondent is served with notification that the appeal judge has given the appellant permission to appeal; or

(c) the date on which the respondent is served with the notification that the application for permission to appeal and the appeal itself are to be heard together.

---

[25] PD 20A, para 11.

15.10 DOCUMENTS TO BE FILED WITH THE RESPONDENT'S NOTICE

The respondent to the appeal must file the following documents:

(a) a copy of his skeleton argument which must conform to the requirement set out under **15.8**(a);

(b) a sealed copy of the order being appealed;

(c) a copy of any order giving or refusing permission to appeal together with a copy of the judge's reasons for allowing or refusing permission to appeal;

(d) any witness statements or affidavits in support of any application included in the appellant's notice;

(e) any other documents which the respondent reasonably considers necessary to enable the Court to reach its decision on the hearing of the application or appeal;

(f) such other documents as the Court may direct;[26]

(g) a list of persons who feature in the case, a glossary of technical terms and a chronology of relevant events should also be filed.

The respondent's notice and the accompanying documents must be served on the appellant and any other respondent.[27]

15.11 SERVICE

The respondent must serve the respondent's notice on the appellant and any other respondent and on such other parties as the Court may direct, as soon as practicable and in any event within 21 days of the date on which it is issued unless the Court directs otherwise. Within 7 days of service of the respondent's notice the respondent must file a certificate of service in Form COP20.

15.12 POWER OF THE APPEAL JUDGE ON APPEAL

The appeal judge has all the powers of the trial judge whose decision is being appealed and may exercise his powers in relation to the whole or part of an order made by the trial judge. The appeal judge also has the power to:

- affirm, set aside or vary any order made by the trial judge;

- refer any claim or issue to that judge for determination;

- order a new hearing;

- make an order for costs.

---

[26] PD 20A, para 40.

[27] PD 20A, para 43.

15.13 DETERMINATION OF APPEALS

- An appeal is limited to a review of the decision of the trial judge unless the appeal judge considers that in the circumstances of the appeal it would be in the interest of justice to hold a re-hearing.

- The appeal judge will not receive any oral evidence or evidence which was not before the trial judge unless the Court otherwise directs.

- The appeal will only be allowed if the appeal judge considers that the decision at first instance was wrong; or unjust because of a serious procedural or other irregularity in the proceedings before the trial judge.

- The appeal judge will not allow a party to rely on a matter not contained in the appellant's or respondent's notice unless the appeal judge gives permission.

These powers are similar to those that apply in civil proceedings to which the CPR 1998 apply and the grounds on which the appeal court may allow the appeal are identical to those set out in CPR 1998, r 52.11(3). This provides a uniform approach across appeals from all jurisdictions and to all appeal courts.

PART VIII

APPENDICES

APPENDIX 1

MENTAL CAPACITY ACT 2005

PART 1
PERSONS WHO LACK CAPACITY

The principles

1 The principles

(1) The following principles apply for the purposes of this Act.

(2) A person must be assumed to have capacity unless it is established that he lacks capacity.

(3) A person is not to be treated as unable to make a decision unless all practicable steps to help him to do so have been taken without success.

(4) A person is not to be treated as unable to make a decision merely because he makes an unwise decision.

(5) An act done, or decision made, under this Act for or on behalf of a person who lacks capacity must be done, or made, in his best interests.

(6) Before the act is done, or the decision is made, regard must be had to whether the purpose for which it is needed can be as effectively achieved in a way that is less restrictive of the person's rights and freedom of action.

Preliminary

2 People who lack capacity

(1) For the purposes of this Act, a person lacks capacity in relation to a matter if at the material time he is unable to make a decision for himself in relation to the matter because of an impairment of, or a disturbance in the functioning of, the mind or brain.

(2) It does not matter whether the impairment or disturbance is permanent or temporary.

(3) A lack of capacity cannot be established merely by reference to –

    (a) a person's age or appearance, or
    (b) a condition of his, or an aspect of his behaviour, which might lead others to make unjustified assumptions about his capacity.

(4) In proceedings under this Act or any other enactment, any question whether a person lacks capacity within the meaning of this Act must be decided on the balance of probabilities.

(5) No power which a person ('D') may exercise under this Act –

(a)   in relation to a person who lacks capacity, or
(b)   where D reasonably thinks that a person lacks capacity,

is exercisable in relation to a person under 16.

(6) Subsection (5) is subject to section 18(3).

3 Inability to make decisions

(1) For the purposes of section 2, a person is unable to make a decision for himself if he is unable –

(a)   to understand the information relevant to the decision,
(b)   to retain that information,
(c)   to use or weigh that information as part of the process of making the decision, or
(d)   to communicate his decision (whether by talking, using sign language or any other means).

(2) A person is not to be regarded as unable to understand the information relevant to a decision if he is able to understand an explanation of it given to him in a way that is appropriate to his circumstances (using simple language, visual aids or any other means).

(3) The fact that a person is able to retain the information relevant to a decision for a short period only does not prevent him from being regarded as able to make the decision.

(4) The information relevant to a decision includes information about the reasonably foreseeable consequences of –

(a)   deciding one way or another, or
(b)   failing to make the decision.

4 Best interests

(1) In determining for the purposes of this Act what is in a person's best interests, the person making the determination must not make it merely on the basis of –

(a)   the person's age or appearance, or
(b)   a condition of his, or an aspect of his behaviour, which might lead others to make unjustified assumptions about what might be in his best interests.

(2) The person making the determination must consider all the relevant circumstances and, in particular, take the following steps.

(3) He must consider –

(a)   whether it is likely that the person will at some time have capacity in relation to the matter in question, and
(b)   if it appears likely that he will, when that is likely to be.

(4) He must, so far as reasonably practicable, permit and encourage the person to participate, or to improve his ability to participate, as fully as possible in any act done for him and any decision affecting him.

(5) Where the determination relates to life-sustaining treatment he must not, in considering whether the treatment is in the best interests of the person concerned, be motivated by a desire to bring about his death.

(6) He must consider, so far as is reasonably ascertainable –

(a) the person's past and present wishes and feelings (and, in particular, any relevant written statement made by him when he had capacity),
(b) the beliefs and values that would be likely to influence his decision if he had capacity, and
(c) the other factors that he would be likely to consider if he were able to do so.

(7) He must take into account, if it is practicable and appropriate to consult them, the views of –

(a) anyone named by the person as someone to be consulted on the matter in question or on matters of that kind,
(b) anyone engaged in caring for the person or interested in his welfare,
(c) any donee of a lasting power of attorney granted by the person, and
(d) any deputy appointed for the person by the court,

as to what would be in the person's best interests and, in particular, as to the matters mentioned in subsection (6).

(8) The duties imposed by subsections (1) to (7) also apply in relation to the exercise of any powers which –

(a) are exercisable under a lasting power of attorney, or
(b) are exercisable by a person under this Act where he reasonably believes that another person lacks capacity.

(9) In the case of an act done, or a decision made, by a person other than the court, there is sufficient compliance with this section if (having complied with the requirements of subsections (1) to (7)) he reasonably believes that what he does or decides is in the best interests of the person concerned.

(10) 'Life-sustaining treatment' means treatment which in the view of a person providing health care for the person concerned is necessary to sustain life.

(11) 'Relevant circumstances' are those –

(a) of which the person making the determination is aware, and
(b) which it would be reasonable to regard as relevant.

4A Restriction on deprivation of liberty

(1) This Act does not authorise any person ('D') to deprive any other person ('P') of his liberty.

(2) But that is subject to –

  (a)   the following provisions of this section, and
  (b)   section 4B.

(3) D may deprive P of his liberty if, by doing so, D is giving effect to a relevant decision of the court.

(4) A relevant decision of the court is a decision made by an order under section 16(2)(a) in relation to a matter concerning P's personal welfare.

(5) D may deprive P of his liberty if the deprivation is authorised by Schedule A1 (hospital and care home residents: deprivation of liberty).

——————————
Amendment: Mental Health Act 2007.

4B Deprivation of liberty necessary for life-sustaining treatment etc

(1) If the following conditions are met, D is authorised to deprive P of his liberty while a decision as respects any relevant issue is sought from the court.

(2) The first condition is that there is a question about whether D is authorised to deprive P of his liberty under section 4A.

(3) The second condition is that the deprivation of liberty –

  (a)   is wholly or partly for the purpose of –
         (i)   giving P life-sustaining treatment, or
         (ii)   doing any vital act, or

  (b)   consists wholly or partly of –
         (i)   giving P life-sustaining treatment, or
         (ii)   doing any vital act.

(4) The third condition is that the deprivation of liberty is necessary in order to –

  (a)   give the life-sustaining treatment, or
  (b)   do the vital act.

(5) A vital act is any act which the person doing it reasonably believes to be necessary to prevent a serious deterioration in P's condition.

——————————
Amendment: Mental Health Act 2007.

5 Acts in connection with care or treatment

(1) If a person ('D') does an act in connection with the care or treatment of another person ('P'), the act is one to which this section applies if –

  (a)   before doing the act, D takes reasonable steps to establish whether P lacks capacity in relation to the matter in question, and
  (b)   when doing the act, D reasonably believes –
         (i)   that P lacks capacity in relation to the matter, and
         (ii)   that it will be in P's best interests for the act to be done.

(2) D does not incur any liability in relation to the act that he would not have incurred if P –

  (a) had had capacity to consent in relation to the matter, and
  (b) had consented to D's doing the act.

(3) Nothing in this section excludes a person's civil liability for loss or damage, or his criminal liability, resulting from his negligence in doing the act.

(4) Nothing in this section affects the operation of sections 24 to 26 (advance decisions to refuse treatment).

6 Section 5 acts: limitations

(1) If D does an act that is intended to restrain P, it is not an act to which section 5 applies unless two further conditions are satisfied.

(2) The first condition is that D reasonably believes that it is necessary to do the act in order to prevent harm to P.

(3) The second is that the act is a proportionate response to –

  (a) the likelihood of P's suffering harm, and
  (b) the seriousness of that harm.

(4) For the purposes of this section D restrains P if he –

  (a) uses, or threatens to use, force to secure the doing of an act which P resists, or
  (b) restricts P's liberty of movement, whether or not P resists.

(5) (*repealed*)

(6) Section 5 does not authorise a person to do an act which conflicts with a decision made, within the scope of his authority and in accordance with this Part, by –

  (a) a donee of a lasting power of attorney granted by P, or
  (b) a deputy appointed for P by the court.

(7) But nothing in subsection (6) stops a person –

  (a) providing life-sustaining treatment, or
  (b) doing any act which he reasonably believes to be necessary to prevent a serious deterioration in P's condition,

while a decision as respects any relevant issue is sought from the court.

Amendment: Mental Health Act 2007.

7 Payment for necessary goods and services

(1) If necessary goods or services are supplied to a person who lacks capacity to contract for the supply, he must pay a reasonable price for them.

(2) 'Necessary' means suitable to a person's condition in life and to his actual requirements at the time when the goods or services are supplied.

8 Expenditure

(1) If an act to which section 5 applies involves expenditure, it is lawful for D –

- (a) to pledge P's credit for the purpose of the expenditure, and
- (b) to apply money in P's possession for meeting the expenditure.

(2) If the expenditure is borne for P by D, it is lawful for D –

- (a) to reimburse himself out of money in P's possession, or
- (b) to be otherwise indemnified by P.

(3) Subsections (1) and (2) do not affect any power under which (apart from those subsections) a person –

- (a) has lawful control of P's money or other property, and
- (b) has power to spend money for P's benefit.

Lasting powers of attorney

9 Lasting powers of attorney

(1) A lasting power of attorney is a power of attorney under which the donor ('P') confers on the donee (or donees) authority to make decisions about all or any of the following –

- (a) P's personal welfare or specified matters concerning P's personal welfare, and
- (b) P's property and affairs or specified matters concerning P's property and affairs,

and which includes authority to make such decisions in circumstances where P no longer has capacity.

(2) A lasting power of attorney is not created unless –

- (a) section 10 is complied with,
- (b) an instrument conferring authority of the kind mentioned in subsection (1) is made and registered in accordance with Schedule 1, and
- (c) at the time when P executes the instrument, P has reached 18 and has capacity to execute it.

(3) An instrument which –

- (a) purports to create a lasting power of attorney, but
- (b) does not comply with this section, section 10 or Schedule 1,

confers no authority.

(4) The authority conferred by a lasting power of attorney is subject to –

- (a) the provisions of this Act and, in particular, sections 1 (the principles) and 4 (best interests), and
- (b) any conditions or restrictions specified in the instrument.

10 Appointment of donees

(1) A donee of a lasting power of attorney must be –

  (a) an individual who has reached 18, or
  (b) if the power relates only to P's property and affairs, either such an individual or a trust corporation.

(2) An individual who is bankrupt or is a person in relation to whom a debt relief order is made may not be appointed as donee of a lasting power of attorney in relation to P's property and affairs.

(3) Subsections (4) to (7) apply in relation to an instrument under which two or more persons are to act as donees of a lasting power of attorney.

(4) The instrument may appoint them to act –

  (a) jointly,
  (b) jointly and severally, or
  (c) jointly in respect of some matters and jointly and severally in respect of others.

(5) To the extent to which it does not specify whether they are to act jointly or jointly and severally, the instrument is to be assumed to appoint them to act jointly.

(6) If they are to act jointly, a failure, as respects one of them, to comply with the requirements of subsection (1) or (2) or Part 1 or 2 of Schedule 1 prevents a lasting power of attorney from being created.

(7) If they are to act jointly and severally, a failure, as respects one of them, to comply with the requirements of subsection (1) or (2) or Part 1 or 2 of Schedule 1 –

  (a) prevents the appointment taking effect in his case, but
  (b) does not prevent a lasting power of attorney from being created in the case of the other or others.

(8) An instrument used to create a lasting power of attorney –

  (a) cannot give the donee (or, if more than one, any of them) power to appoint a substitute or successor, but
  (b) may itself appoint a person to replace the donee (or, if more than one, any of them) on the occurrence of an event mentioned in section 13(6)(a) to (d) which has the effect of terminating the donee's appointment.

Amendment: SI 2012/2404.

11 Lasting powers of attorney: restrictions

(1) A lasting power of attorney does not authorise the donee (or, if more than one, any of them) to do an act that is intended to restrain P, unless three conditions are satisfied.

(2) The first condition is that P lacks, or the donee reasonably believes that P lacks, capacity in relation to the matter in question.

(3) The second is that the donee reasonably believes that it is necessary to do the act in order to prevent harm to P.

(4) The third is that the act is a proportionate response to –

    (a)   the likelihood of P's suffering harm, and
    (b)   the seriousness of that harm.

(5) For the purposes of this section, the donee restrains P if he –

    (a)   uses, or threatens to use, force to secure the doing of an act which P resists, or
    (b)   restricts P's liberty of movement, whether or not P resists,

or if he authorises another person to do any of those things.

(6) (*repealed*)

(7) Where a lasting power of attorney authorises the donee (or, if more than one, any of them) to make decisions about P's personal welfare, the authority –

    (a)   does not extend to making such decisions in circumstances other than those where P lacks, or the donee reasonably believes that P lacks, capacity,
    (b)   is subject to sections 24 to 26 (advance decisions to refuse treatment), and
    (c)   extends to giving or refusing consent to the carrying out or continuation of a treatment by a person providing health care for P.

(8) But subsection (7)(c) –

    (a)   does not authorise the giving or refusing of consent to the carrying out or continuation of life-sustaining treatment, unless the instrument contains express provision to that effect, and
    (b)   is subject to any conditions or restrictions in the instrument.

Amendment: Mental Health Act 2007.

12 Scope of lasting powers of attorney: gifts

(1) Where a lasting power of attorney confers authority to make decisions about P's property and affairs, it does not authorise a donee (or, if more than one, any of them) to dispose of the donor's property by making gifts except to the extent permitted by subsection (2).

(2) The donee may make gifts –

    (a)   on customary occasions to persons (including himself) who are related to or connected with the donor, or
    (b)   to any charity to whom the donor made or might have been expected to make gifts,

if the value of each such gift is not unreasonable having regard to all the circumstances and, in particular, the size of the donor's estate.

(3) 'Customary occasion' means –

(a) the occasion or anniversary of a birth, a marriage or the formation of a civil partnership, or
(b) any other occasion on which presents are customarily given within families or among friends or associates.

(4) Subsection (2) is subject to any conditions or restrictions in the instrument.

13 Revocation of lasting powers of attorney etc

(1) This section applies if –

(a) P has executed an instrument with a view to creating a lasting power of attorney, or
(b) a lasting power of attorney is registered as having been conferred by P,

and in this section references to revoking the power include revoking the instrument.

(2) P may, at any time when he has capacity to do so, revoke the power.

(3) P's bankruptcy, or the making of a debt relief order (under Part 7A of the Insolvency Act 1986) in respect of P, revokes the power so far as it relates to P's property and affairs.

(4) But where P is bankrupt merely because an interim bankruptcy restrictions order has effect in respect of him or where P is subject to an interim debt relief restrictions order (under Schedule 4ZB of the Insolvency Act 1986), the power is suspended, so far as it relates to P's property and affairs, for so long as the order has effect.

(5) The occurrence in relation to a donee of an event mentioned in subsection (6) –

(a) terminates his appointment, and
(b) except in the cases given in subsection (7), revokes the power.

(6) The events are –

(a) the disclaimer of the appointment by the donee in accordance with such requirements as may be prescribed for the purposes of this section in regulations made by the Lord Chancellor,
(b) subject to subsections (8) and (9), the death or bankruptcy of the donee or the making of a debt relief order (under Part 7A of the Insolvency Act 1986) in respect of the donee or, if the donee is a trust corporation, its winding-up or dissolution,
(c) subject to subsection (11), the dissolution or annulment of a marriage or civil partnership between the donor and the donee,
(d) the lack of capacity of the donee.

(7) The cases are –

(a)   the donee is replaced under the terms of the instrument,
(b)   he is one of two or more persons appointed to act as donees jointly and severally in respect of any matter and, after the event, there is at least one remaining donee.

(8) The bankruptcy of a donee or the making of a debt relief order (under Part 7A of the Insolvency Act 1986) in respect of a donee does not terminate his appointment, or revoke the power, in so far as his authority relates to P's personal welfare.

(9) Where the donee is bankrupt merely because an interim bankruptcy restrictions order has effect in respect of him or where the donee is subject to an interim debt relief restrictions order (under Schedule 4ZB of the Insolvency Act 1986),, his appointment and the power are suspended, so far as they relate to P's property and affairs, for so long as the order has effect.

(10) Where the donee is one of two or more appointed to act jointly and severally under the power in respect of any matter, the reference in subsection (9) to the suspension of the power is to its suspension in so far as it relates to that donee.

(11) The dissolution or annulment of a marriage or civil partnership does not terminate the appointment of a donee, or revoke the power, if the instrument provided that it was not to do so.

Amendment: SI 2012/2404.

14 Protection of donee and others if no power created or power revoked

(1) Subsections (2) and (3) apply if –

(a)   an instrument has been registered under Schedule 1 as a lasting power of attorney, but
(b)   a lasting power of attorney was not created,

whether or not the registration has been cancelled at the time of the act or transaction in question.

(2) A donee who acts in purported exercise of the power does not incur any liability (to P or any other person) because of the non-existence of the power unless at the time of acting he –

(a)   knows that a lasting power of attorney was not created, or
(b)   is aware of circumstances which, if a lasting power of attorney had been created, would have terminated his authority to act as a donee.

(3) Any transaction between the donee and another person is, in favour of that person, as valid as if the power had been in existence, unless at the time of the transaction that person has knowledge of a matter referred to in subsection (2).

(4) If the interest of a purchaser depends on whether a transaction between the donee and the other person was valid by virtue of subsection (3), it is conclusively presumed in favour of the purchaser that the transaction was valid if –

  (a)   the transaction was completed within 12 months of the date on which the instrument was registered, or
  (b)   the other person makes a statutory declaration, before or within 3 months after the completion of the purchase, that he had no reason at the time of the transaction to doubt that the donee had authority to dispose of the property which was the subject of the transaction.

(5) In its application to a lasting power of attorney which relates to matters in addition to P's property and affairs, section 5 of the Powers of Attorney Act 1971 (protection where power is revoked) has effect as if references to revocation included the cessation of the power in relation to P's property and affairs.

(6) Where two or more donees are appointed under a lasting power of attorney, this section applies as if references to the donee were to all or any of them.

General powers of the court and appointment of deputies

15 Power to make declarations

(1) The court may make declarations as to –

  (a)   whether a person has or lacks capacity to make a decision specified in the declaration;
  (b)   whether a person has or lacks capacity to make decisions on such matters as are described in the declaration;
  (c)   the lawfulness or otherwise of any act done, or yet to be done, in relation to that person.

(2) 'Act' includes an omission and a course of conduct.

16 Powers to make decisions and appoint deputies: general

(1) This section applies if a person ('P') lacks capacity in relation to a matter or matters concerning –

  (a)   P's personal welfare, or
  (b)   P's property and affairs.

(2) The court may –

  (a)   by making an order, make the decision or decisions on P's behalf in relation to the matter or matters, or
  (b)   appoint a person (a 'deputy') to make decisions on P's behalf in relation to the matter or matters.

(3) The powers of the court under this section are subject to the provisions of this Act and, in particular, to sections 1 (the principles) and 4 (best interests).

(4) When deciding whether it is in P's best interests to appoint a deputy, the court must have regard (in addition to the matters mentioned in section 4) to the principles that –

- (a) a decision by the court is to be preferred to the appointment of a deputy to make a decision, and
- (b) the powers conferred on a deputy should be as limited in scope and duration as is reasonably practicable in the circumstances.

(5) The court may make such further orders or give such directions, and confer on a deputy such powers or impose on him such duties, as it thinks necessary or expedient for giving effect to, or otherwise in connection with, an order or appointment made by it under subsection (2).

(6) Without prejudice to section 4, the court may make the order, give the directions or make the appointment on such terms as it considers are in P's best interests, even though no application is before the court for an order, directions or an appointment on those terms.

(7) An order of the court may be varied or discharged by a subsequent order.

(8) The court may, in particular, revoke the appointment of a deputy or vary the powers conferred on him if it is satisfied that the deputy –

- (a) has behaved, or is behaving, in a way that contravenes the authority conferred on him by the court or is not in P's best interests, or
- (b) proposes to behave in a way that would contravene that authority or would not be in P's best interests.

16A Section 16 powers: Mental Health Act patients etc

(1) If a person is ineligible to be deprived of liberty by this Act, the court may not include in a welfare order provision which authorises the person to be deprived of his liberty.

(2) If –

- (a) a welfare order includes provision which authorises a person to be deprived of his liberty, and
- (b) that person becomes ineligible to be deprived of liberty by this Act, the provision ceases to have effect for as long as the person remains ineligible.

(3) Nothing in subsection (2) affects the power of the court under section 16(7) to vary or discharge the welfare order.

(4) For the purposes of this section –

- (a) Schedule 1A applies for determining whether or not P is ineligible to be deprived of liberty by this Act;
- (b) 'welfare order' means an order under section 16(2)(a).

Amendment: Mental Health Act 2007.

17 Section 16 powers: personal welfare

(1) The powers under section 16 as respects P's personal welfare extend in particular to –

    (a)   deciding where P is to live;

    (b)   deciding what contact, if any, P is to have with any specified persons;

    (c)   making an order prohibiting a named person from having contact with P;

    (d)   giving or refusing consent to the carrying out or continuation of a treatment by a person providing health care for P;

    (e)   giving a direction that a person responsible for P's health care allow a different person to take over that responsibility.

(2) Subsection (1) is subject to section 20 (restrictions on deputies).

18 Section 16 powers: property and affairs

(1) The powers under section 16 as respects P's property and affairs extend in particular to –

    (a)   the control and management of P's property;

    (b)   the sale, exchange, charging, gift or other disposition of P's property;

    (c)   the acquisition of property in P's name or on P's behalf;

    (d)   the carrying on, on P's behalf, of any profession, trade or business;

    (e)   the taking of a decision which will have the effect of dissolving a partnership of which P is a member;

    (f)   the carrying out of any contract entered into by P;

    (g)   the discharge of P's debts and of any of P's obligations, whether legally enforceable or not;

    (h)   the settlement of any of P's property, whether for P's benefit or for the benefit of others;

    (i)   the execution for P of a will;

    (j)   the exercise of any power (including a power to consent) vested in P whether beneficially or as trustee or otherwise;

    (k)   the conduct of legal proceedings in P's name or on P's behalf.

(2) No will may be made under subsection (1)(i) at a time when P has not reached 18.

(3) The powers under section 16 as respects any other matter relating to P's property and affairs may be exercised even though P has not reached 16, if the court considers it likely that P will still lack capacity to make decisions in respect of that matter when he reaches 18.

(4) Schedule 2 supplements the provisions of this section.

(5) Section 16(7) (variation and discharge of court orders) is subject to paragraph 6 of Schedule 2.

(6) Subsection (1) is subject to section 20 (restrictions on deputies).

19 Appointment of deputies

(1) A deputy appointed by the court must be –

  (a)   an individual who has reached 18, or
  (b)   as respects powers in relation to property and affairs, an individual who has reached 18 or a trust corporation.

(2) The court may appoint an individual by appointing the holder for the time being of a specified office or position.

(3) A person may not be appointed as a deputy without his consent.

(4) The court may appoint two or more deputies to act –

  (a)   jointly,
  (b)   jointly and severally, or
  (c)   jointly in respect of some matters and jointly and severally in respect of others.

(5) When appointing a deputy or deputies, the court may at the same time appoint one or more other persons to succeed the existing deputy or those deputies –

  (a)   in such circumstances, or on the happening of such events, as may be specified by the court;
  (b)   for such period as may be so specified.

(6) A deputy is to be treated as P's agent in relation to anything done or decided by him within the scope of his appointment and in accordance with this Part.

(7) The deputy is entitled –

  (a)   to be reimbursed out of P's property for his reasonable expenses in discharging his functions, and
  (b)   if the court so directs when appointing him, to remuneration out of P's property for discharging them.

(8) The court may confer on a deputy powers to –

  (a)   take possession or control of all or any specified part of P's property;
  (b)   exercise all or any specified powers in respect of it, including such powers of investment as the court may determine.

(9) The court may require a deputy –

  (a)   to give to the Public Guardian such security as the court thinks fit for the due discharge of his functions, and
  (b)   to submit to the Public Guardian such reports at such times or at such intervals as the court may direct.

20 Restrictions on deputies

(1) A deputy does not have power to make a decision on behalf of P in relation to a matter if he knows or has reasonable grounds for believing that P has capacity in relation to the matter.

(2) Nothing in section 16(5) or 17 permits a deputy to be given power –

    (a)   to prohibit a named person from having contact with P;

    (b)   to direct a person responsible for P's health care to allow a different person to take over that responsibility.

(3) A deputy may not be given powers with respect to –

    (a)   the settlement of any of P's property, whether for P's benefit or for the benefit of others,

    (b)   the execution for P of a will, or

    (c)   the exercise of any power (including a power to consent) vested in P whether beneficially or as trustee or otherwise.

(4) A deputy may not be given power to make a decision on behalf of P which is inconsistent with a decision made, within the scope of his authority and in accordance with this Act, by the donee of a lasting power of attorney granted by P (or, if there is more than one donee, by any of them).

(5) A deputy may not refuse consent to the carrying out or continuation of life-sustaining treatment in relation to P.

(6) The authority conferred on a deputy is subject to the provisions of this Act and, in particular, sections 1 (the principles) and 4 (best interests).

(7) A deputy may not do an act that is intended to restrain P unless four conditions are satisfied.

(8) The first condition is that, in doing the act, the deputy is acting within the scope of an authority expressly conferred on him by the court.

(9) The second is that P lacks, or the deputy reasonably believes that P lacks, capacity in relation to the matter in question.

(10) The third is that the deputy reasonably believes that it is necessary to do the act in order to prevent harm to P.

(11) The fourth is that the act is a proportionate response to –

    (a)   the likelihood of P's suffering harm, and

    (b)   the seriousness of that harm.

(12) For the purposes of this section, a deputy restrains P if he –

    (a)   uses, or threatens to use, force to secure the doing of an act which P resists, or

    (b)   restricts P's liberty of movement, whether or not P resists,

or if he authorises another person to do any of those things.

(13) (*repealed*)

Amendment: Mental Health Act 2007.

21 Transfer of proceedings relating to people under 18

(1) The Lord Chief Justice, with the concurrence of the Lord Chancellor, may by order make provision as to the transfer of proceedings relating to a person under 18, in such circumstances as are specified in the order –

    (a)   from the Court of Protection to a court having jurisdiction under the Children Act 1989, or

    (b)   from a court having jurisdiction under that Act to the Court of Protection.

(2) The Lord Chief Justice may nominate any of the following to exercise his functions under this section –

    (a)   the President of the Court of Protection;

    (b)   a judicial office holder (as defined in section 109(4) of the Constitutional Reform Act 2005).

Amendment: SI 2006/1016.

Powers of the court in relation to Schedule A1

Amendment: Mental Health Act 2007.

21A Powers of court in relation to Schedule A1

(1) This section applies if either of the following has been given under Schedule A1 –

    (a)   a standard authorisation;

    (b)   an urgent authorisation.

(2) Where a standard authorisation has been given, the court may determine any question relating to any of the following matters –

    (a)   whether the relevant person meets one or more of the qualifying requirements;

    (b)   the period during which the standard authorisation is to be in force;

    (c)   the purpose for which the standard authorisation is given;

    (d)   the conditions subject to which the standard authorisation is given.

(3) If the court determines any question under subsection (2), the court may make an order –

    (a)   varying or terminating the standard authorisation, or

    (b)   directing the supervisory body to vary or terminate the standard authorisation.

(4) Where an urgent authorisation has been given, the court may determine any question relating to any of the following matters –

    (a)   whether the urgent authorisation should have been given;

    (b)   the period during which the urgent authorisation is to be in force;

(c)   the purpose for which the urgent authorisation is given.

(5) Where the court determines any question under subsection (4), the court may make an order –

(a)   varying or terminating the urgent authorisation, or
(b)   directing the managing authority of the relevant hospital or care home to vary or terminate the urgent authorisation.

(6) Where the court makes an order under subsection (3) or (5), the court may make an order about a person's liability for any act done in connection with the standard or urgent authorisation before its variation or termination.

(7) An order under subsection (6) may, in particular, exclude a person from liability.

Amendment: Mental Health Act 2007.

Powers of the court in relation to lasting powers of attorney

22 Powers of court in relation to validity of lasting powers of attorney

(1) This section and section 23 apply if –

(a)   a person ('P') has executed or purported to execute an instrument with a view to creating a lasting power of attorney, or
(b)   an instrument has been registered as a lasting power of attorney conferred by P.

(2) The court may determine any question relating to –

(a)   whether one or more of the requirements for the creation of a lasting power of attorney have been met;
(b)   whether the power has been revoked or has otherwise come to an end.

(3) Subsection (4) applies if the court is satisfied –

(a)   that fraud or undue pressure was used to induce P –
    (i)   to execute an instrument for the purpose of creating a lasting power of attorney, or
    (ii)   to create a lasting power of attorney, or

(b)   that the donee (or, if more than one, any of them) of a lasting power of attorney –
    (i)   has behaved, or is behaving, in a way that contravenes his authority or is not in P's best interests, or
    (ii)   proposes to behave in a way that would contravene his authority or would not be in P's best interests.

(4) The court may –

(a)   direct that an instrument purporting to create the lasting power of attorney is not to be registered, or
(b)   if P lacks capacity to do so, revoke the instrument or the lasting power of attorney.

(5) If there is more than one donee, the court may under subsection (4)(b) revoke the instrument or the lasting power of attorney so far as it relates to any of them.

(6) 'Donee' includes an intended donee.

23 Powers of court in relation to operation of lasting powers of attorney

(1) The court may determine any question as to the meaning or effect of a lasting power of attorney or an instrument purporting to create one.

(2) The court may –

- (a) give directions with respect to decisions –
  - (i) which the donee of a lasting power of attorney has authority to make, and
  - (ii) which P lacks capacity to make;
- (b) give any consent or authorisation to act which the donee would have to obtain from P if P had capacity to give it.

(3) The court may, if P lacks capacity to do so –

- (a) give directions to the donee with respect to the rendering by him of reports or accounts and the production of records kept by him for that purpose;
- (b) require the donee to supply information or produce documents or things in his possession as donee;
- (c) give directions with respect to the remuneration or expenses of the donee;
- (d) relieve the donee wholly or partly from any liability which he has or may have incurred on account of a breach of his duties as donee.

(4) The court may authorise the making of gifts which are not within section 12(2) (permitted gifts).

(5) Where two or more donees are appointed under a lasting power of attorney, this section applies as if references to the donee were to all or any of them.

Advance decisions to refuse treatment

24 Advance decisions to refuse treatment: general

(1) 'Advance decision' means a decision made by a person ('P'), after he has reached 18 and when he has capacity to do so, that if –

- (a) at a later time and in such circumstances as he may specify, a specified treatment is proposed to be carried out or continued by a person providing health care for him, and
- (b) at that time he lacks capacity to consent to the carrying out or continuation of the treatment,

the specified treatment is not to be carried out or continued.

(2) For the purposes of subsection (1)(a), a decision may be regarded as specifying a treatment or circumstances even though expressed in layman's terms.

(3) P may withdraw or alter an advance decision at any time when he has capacity to do so.

(4) A withdrawal (including a partial withdrawal) need not be in writing.

(5) An alteration of an advance decision need not be in writing (unless section 25(5) applies in relation to the decision resulting from the alteration).

25 Validity and applicability of advance decisions

(1) An advance decision does not affect the liability which a person may incur for carrying out or continuing a treatment in relation to P unless the decision is at the material time –

  (a)   valid, and
  (b)   applicable to the treatment.

(2) An advance decision is not valid if P –

  (a)   has withdrawn the decision at a time when he had capacity to do so,
  (b)   has, under a lasting power of attorney created after the advance decision was made, conferred authority on the donee (or, if more than one, any of them) to give or refuse consent to the treatment to which the advance decision relates, or
  (c)   has done anything else clearly inconsistent with the advance decision remaining his fixed decision.

(3) An advance decision is not applicable to the treatment in question if at the material time P has capacity to give or refuse consent to it.

(4) An advance decision is not applicable to the treatment in question if –

  (a)   that treatment is not the treatment specified in the advance decision,
  (b)   any circumstances specified in the advance decision are absent, or
  (c)   there are reasonable grounds for believing that circumstances exist which P did not anticipate at the time of the advance decision and which would have affected his decision had he anticipated them.

(5) An advance decision is not applicable to life-sustaining treatment unless –

  (a)   the decision is verified by a statement by P to the effect that it is to apply to that treatment even if life is at risk, and
  (b)   the decision and statement comply with subsection (6).

(6) A decision or statement complies with this subsection only if –

  (a)   it is in writing,
  (b)   it is signed by P or by another person in P's presence and by P's direction,
  (c)   the signature is made or acknowledged by P in the presence of a witness, and

(d)   the witness signs it, or acknowledges his signature, in P's presence.

(7) The existence of any lasting power of attorney other than one of a description mentioned in subsection (2)(b) does not prevent the advance decision from being regarded as valid and applicable.

26 Effect of advance decisions

(1) If P has made an advance decision which is –

(a)   valid, and
(b)   applicable to a treatment,

the decision has effect as if he had made it, and had had capacity to make it, at the time when the question arises whether the treatment should be carried out or continued.

(2) A person does not incur liability for carrying out or continuing the treatment unless, at the time, he is satisfied that an advance decision exists which is valid and applicable to the treatment.

(3) A person does not incur liability for the consequences of withholding or withdrawing a treatment from P if, at the time, he reasonably believes that an advance decision exists which is valid and applicable to the treatment.

(4) The court may make a declaration as to whether an advance decision –

(a)   exists;
(b)   is valid;
(c)   is applicable to a treatment.

(5) Nothing in an apparent advance decision stops a person –

(a)   providing life-sustaining treatment, or
(b)   doing any act he reasonably believes to be necessary to prevent a serious deterioration in P's condition,

while a decision as respects any relevant issue is sought from the court.

Excluded decisions

27 Family relationships etc

(1) Nothing in this Act permits a decision on any of the following matters to be made on behalf of a person –

(a)   consenting to marriage or a civil partnership,
(b)   consenting to have sexual relations,
(c)   consenting to a decree of divorce being granted on the basis of two years' separation,
(d)   consenting to a dissolution order being made in relation to a civil partnership on the basis of two years' separation,
(e)   consenting to a child's being placed for adoption by an adoption agency,
(f)   consenting to the making of an adoption order,

(g)   discharging parental responsibilities in matters not relating to a child's property,

(h)   giving a consent under the Human Fertilisation and Embryology Act 1990,

(i)   giving a consent under the Human Fertilisation and Embryology Act 2008.

(2) 'Adoption order' means –

(a)   an adoption order within the meaning of the Adoption and Children Act 2002 (including a future adoption order), and

(b)   an order under section 84 of that Act (parental responsibility prior to adoption abroad).

Amendment: Human Fertilisation and Embryology Act 2008.

28 Mental Health Act matters

(1) Nothing in this Act authorises anyone –

(a)   to give a patient medical treatment for mental disorder, or

(b)   to consent to a patient's being given medical treatment for mental disorder,

if, at the time when it is proposed to treat the patient, his treatment is regulated by Part 4 of the Mental Health Act.

(1A) Subsection (1) does not apply in relation to any form of treatment to which section 58A of that Act (electro-convulsive therapy, etc) applies if the patient comes within subsection (7) of that section (informal patient under 18 who cannot give consent).

(1B) Section 5 does not apply to an act to which section 64B of the Mental Health Act applies (treatment of community patients not recalled to hospital).

(2) 'Medical treatment', 'mental disorder' and 'patient' have the same meaning as in that Act.

Amendments: Mental Health Act 2007; SI 2008/1900.

29 Voting rights

(1) Nothing in this Act permits a decision on voting at an election for any public office, or at a referendum, to be made on behalf of a person.

(2) 'Referendum' has the same meaning as in section 101 of the Political Parties, Elections and Referendums Act 2000.

Research

30 Research

(1) Intrusive research carried out on, or in relation to, a person who lacks capacity to consent to it is unlawful unless it is carried out –

(a)   as part of a research project which is for the time being approved by the appropriate body for the purposes of this Act in accordance with section 31, and

(b)   in accordance with sections 32 and 33.

(2) Research is intrusive if it is of a kind that would be unlawful if it was carried out –

(a)   on or in relation to a person who had capacity to consent to it, but

(b)   without his consent.

(3) A clinical trial which is subject to the provisions of clinical trials regulations is not to be treated as research for the purposes of this section.

(3A) Research is not intrusive to the extent that it consists of the use of a person's human cells to bring about the creation in vitro of an embryo or human admixed embryo, or the subsequent storage or use of an embryo or human admixed embryo so created.

(3B) Expressions used in subsection (3A) and in Schedule 3 to the Human Fertilisation and Embryology Act 1990 (consents to use or storage of gametes, embryos or human admixed embryos etc.) have the same meaning in that subsection as in that Schedule.

(4) 'Appropriate body', in relation to a research project, means the person, committee or other body specified in regulations made by the appropriate authority as the appropriate body in relation to a project of the kind in question.

(5) 'Clinical trials regulations' means –

(a)   the Medicines for Human Use (Clinical Trials) Regulations 2004 and any other regulations replacing those regulations or amending them, and

(b)   any other regulations relating to clinical trials and designated by the Secretary of State as clinical trials regulations for the purposes of this section.

(6) In this section, section 32 and section 34, 'appropriate authority' means –

(a)   in relation to the carrying out of research in England, the Secretary of State, and

(b)   in relation to the carrying out of research in Wales, the National Assembly for Wales.

_____

Amendment: Human Fertilisation and Embryology Act 2008; SI 2009/2232.

31 Requirements for approval

(1) The appropriate body may not approve a research project for the purposes of this Act unless satisfied that the following requirements will be met in relation to research carried out as part of the project on, or in relation to, a person who lacks capacity to consent to taking part in the project ('P').

(2) The research must be connected with –

  (a) an impairing condition affecting P, or
  (b) its treatment.

(3) 'Impairing condition' means a condition which is (or may be) attributable to, or which causes or contributes to (or may cause or contribute to), the impairment of, or disturbance in the functioning of, the mind or brain.

(4) There must be reasonable grounds for believing that research of comparable effectiveness cannot be carried out if the project has to be confined to, or relate only to, persons who have capacity to consent to taking part in it.

(5) The research must –

  (a) have the potential to benefit P without imposing on P a burden that is disproportionate to the potential benefit to P, or
  (b) be intended to provide knowledge of the causes or treatment of, or of the care of persons affected by, the same or a similar condition.

(6) If the research falls within paragraph (b) of subsection (5) but not within paragraph (a), there must be reasonable grounds for believing –

  (a) that the risk to P from taking part in the project is likely to be negligible, and
  (b) that anything done to, or in relation to, P will not –
       (i)   interfere with P's freedom of action or privacy in a significant way, or
       (ii) be unduly invasive or restrictive.

(7) There must be reasonable arrangements in place for ensuring that the requirements of sections 32 and 33 will be met.

32 Consulting carers etc

(1) This section applies if a person ('R') –

  (a) is conducting an approved research project, and
  (b) wishes to carry out research, as part of the project, on or in relation to a person ('P') who lacks capacity to consent to taking part in the project.

(2) R must take reasonable steps to identify a person who –

  (a) otherwise than in a professional capacity or for remuneration, is engaged in caring for P or is interested in P's welfare, and
  (b) is prepared to be consulted by R under this section.

(3) If R is unable to identify such a person he must, in accordance with guidance issued by the appropriate authority, nominate a person who –

  (a) is prepared to be consulted by R under this section, but
  (b) has no connection with the project.

(4) R must provide the person identified under subsection (2), or nominated under subsection (3), with information about the project and ask him –

(a) for advice as to whether P should take part in the project, and

(b) what, in his opinion, P's wishes and feelings about taking part in the project would be likely to be if P had capacity in relation to the matter.

(5) If, at any time, the person consulted advises R that in his opinion P's wishes and feelings would be likely to lead him to decline to take part in the project (or to wish to withdraw from it) if he had capacity in relation to the matter, R must ensure –

(a) if P is not already taking part in the project, that he does not take part in it;

(b) if P is taking part in the project, that he is withdrawn from it.

(6) But subsection (5)(b) does not require treatment that P has been receiving as part of the project to be discontinued if R has reasonable grounds for believing that there would be a significant risk to P's health if it were discontinued.

(7) The fact that a person is the donee of a lasting power of attorney given by P, or is P's deputy, does not prevent him from being the person consulted under this section.

(8) Subsection (9) applies if treatment is being, or is about to be, provided for P as a matter of urgency and R considers that, having regard to the nature of the research and of the particular circumstances of the case –

(a) it is also necessary to take action for the purposes of the research as a matter of urgency, but

(b) it is not reasonably practicable to consult under the previous provisions of this section.

(9) R may take the action if –

(a) he has the agreement of a registered medical practitioner who is not involved in the organisation or conduct of the research project, or

(b) where it is not reasonably practicable in the time available to obtain that agreement, he acts in accordance with a procedure approved by the appropriate body at the time when the research project was approved under section 31.

(10) But R may not continue to act in reliance on subsection (9) if he has reasonable grounds for believing that it is no longer necessary to take the action as a matter of urgency.

33 Additional safeguards

(1) This section applies in relation to a person who is taking part in an approved research project even though he lacks capacity to consent to taking part.

(2) Nothing may be done to, or in relation to, him in the course of the research –

(a)   to which he appears to object (whether by showing signs of resistance or otherwise) except where what is being done is intended to protect him from harm or to reduce or prevent pain or discomfort, or

(b)   which would be contrary to –
   (i)   an advance decision of his which has effect, or
   (ii) any other form of statement made by him and not subsequently withdrawn,

of which R is aware.

(3) The interests of the person must be assumed to outweigh those of science and society.

(4) If he indicates (in any way) that he wishes to be withdrawn from the project he must be withdrawn without delay.

(5) P must be withdrawn from the project, without delay, if at any time the person conducting the research has reasonable grounds for believing that one or more of the requirements set out in section 31(2) to (7) is no longer met in relation to research being carried out on, or in relation to, P.

(6) But neither subsection (4) nor subsection (5) requires treatment that P has been receiving as part of the project to be discontinued if R has reasonable grounds for believing that there would be a significant risk to P's health if it were discontinued.

34 Loss of capacity during research project

(1) This section applies where a person ('P') –

(a)   has consented to take part in a research project begun before the commencement of section 30, but

(b)   before the conclusion of the project, loses capacity to consent to continue to take part in it.

(2) The appropriate authority may by regulations provide that, despite P's loss of capacity, research of a prescribed kind may be carried out on, or in relation to, P if –

(a)   the project satisfies prescribed requirements,

(b)   any information or material relating to P which is used in the research is of a prescribed description and was obtained before P's loss of capacity, and

(c)   the person conducting the project takes in relation to P such steps as may be prescribed for the purpose of protecting him.

(3) The regulations may, in particular, –

(a)   make provision about when, for the purposes of the regulations, a project is to be treated as having begun;

(b)   include provision similar to any made by section 31, 32 or 33.

Independent mental capacity advocate service

35 Appointment of independent mental capacity advocates

(1) The responsible authority must make such arrangements as it considers reasonable to enable persons ('independent mental capacity advocates') to be available to represent and support persons to whom acts or decisions proposed under sections 37, 38 and 39 relate or persons who fall within section 39A, 39C or 39D.

(2) The appropriate authority may make regulations as to the appointment of independent mental capacity advocates.

(3) The regulations may, in particular, provide –

- (a) that a person may act as an independent mental capacity advocate only in such circumstances, or only subject to such conditions, as may be prescribed;
- (b) for the appointment of a person as an independent mental capacity advocate to be subject to approval in accordance with the regulations.

(4) In making arrangements under subsection (1), the responsible authority must have regard to the principle that a person to whom a proposed act or decision relates should, so far as practicable, be represented and supported by a person who is independent of any person who will be responsible for the act or decision.

(5) The arrangements may include provision for payments to be made to, or in relation to, persons carrying out functions in accordance with the arrangements.

(6) For the purpose of enabling him to carry out his functions, an independent mental capacity advocate –

- (a) may interview in private the person whom he has been instructed to represent, and
- (b) may, at all reasonable times, examine and take copies of –
  - (i) any health record,
  - (ii) any record of, or held by, a local authority and compiled in connection with a social services function, and
  - (iii) any record held by a person registered under Part 2 of the Care Standards Act 2000 or Chapter 2 of Part I of the Health and Social Care Act 2008,

which the person holding the record considers may be relevant to the independent mental capacity advocate's investigation.

(6A) In subsections (1) and (4), 'the responsible authority' means –

- (a) in relation to the provision of the services of independent mental capacity advocates in the area of a local authority in England, that local authority, and
- (b) in relation to the provision of the services of independent mental capacity advocates in Wales, the Welsh Ministers.

(6B) In subsection (6A)(a), 'local authority' has the meaning given in section 64(1) except that it does not include the council of a county or county borough in Wales.

(7) In this section, section 36 and section 37, 'the appropriate authority' means –

(a)   in relation to the provision of the services of independent mental capacity advocates in England, the Secretary of State, and
(b)   in relation to the provision of the services of independent mental capacity advocates in Wales, the National Assembly for Wales.

Amendment: Mental Health Act 2007; Health and Social Care Act 2012; SI 2010/813.

36 Functions of independent mental capacity advocates

(1) The appropriate authority may make regulations as to the functions of independent mental capacity advocates.

(2) The regulations may, in particular, make provision requiring an advocate to take such steps as may be prescribed for the purpose of –

(a)   providing support to the person whom he has been instructed to represent ('P') so that P may participate as fully as possible in any relevant decision;
(b)   obtaining and evaluating relevant information;
(c)   ascertaining what P's wishes and feelings would be likely to be, and the beliefs and values that would be likely to influence P, if he had capacity;
(d)   ascertaining what alternative courses of action are available in relation to P;
(e)   obtaining a further medical opinion where treatment is proposed and the advocate thinks that one should be obtained.

(3) The regulations may also make provision as to circumstances in which the advocate may challenge, or provide assistance for the purpose of challenging, any relevant decision.

37 Provision of serious medical treatment by NHS body

(1) This section applies if an NHS body –

(a)   is proposing to provide, or secure the provision of, serious medical treatment for a person ('P') who lacks capacity to consent to the treatment, and
(b)   is satisfied that there is no person, other than one engaged in providing care or treatment for P in a professional capacity or for remuneration, whom it would be appropriate to consult in determining what would be in P's best interests.

(2) But this section does not apply if P's treatment is regulated by Part 4 or 4A of the Mental Health Act.

(3) Before the treatment is provided, the NHS body must instruct an independent mental capacity advocate to represent P.

(4) If the treatment needs to be provided as a matter of urgency, it may be provided even though the NHS body has not been able to comply with subsection (3).

(5) The NHS body must, in providing or securing the provision of treatment for P, take into account any information given, or submissions made, by the independent mental capacity advocate.

(6) 'Serious medical treatment' means treatment which involves providing, withholding or withdrawing treatment of a kind prescribed by regulations made by the appropriate authority.

(7) 'NHS body' has such meaning as may be prescribed by regulations made for the purposes of this section by –

  (a) the Secretary of State, in relation to bodies in England, or
  (b) the National Assembly for Wales, in relation to bodies in Wales.

***

Amendment: Mental Health Act 2007.

38 Provision of accommodation by NHS body

(1) This section applies if an NHS body proposes to make arrangements –

  (a) for the provision of accommodation in a hospital or care home for a person ('P') who lacks capacity to agree to the arrangements, or
  (b) for a change in P's accommodation to another hospital or care home,

and is satisfied that there is no person, other than one engaged in providing care or treatment for P in a professional capacity or for remuneration, whom it would be appropriate for it to consult in determining what would be in P's best interests.

(2) But this section does not apply if P is accommodated as a result of an obligation imposed on him under the Mental Health Act.

(2A) And this section does not apply if –

  (a) an independent mental capacity advocate must be appointed under section 39A or 39C (whether or not by the NHS body) to represent P, and
  (b) the hospital or care home in which P is to be accommodated under the arrangements referred to in this section is the relevant hospital or care home under the authorisation referred to in that section.

(3) Before making the arrangements, the NHS body must instruct an independent mental capacity advocate to represent P unless it is satisfied that –

  (a) the accommodation is likely to be provided for a continuous period which is less than the applicable period, or
  (b) the arrangements need to be made as a matter of urgency.

(4) If the NHS body –

- (a) did not instruct an independent mental capacity advocate to represent P before making the arrangements because it was satisfied that subsection (3)(a) or (b) applied, but
- (b) subsequently has reason to believe that the accommodation is likely to be provided for a continuous period –
  - (i) beginning with the day on which accommodation was first provided in accordance with the arrangements, and
  - (ii) ending on or after the expiry of the applicable period,

it must instruct an independent mental capacity advocate to represent P.

(5) The NHS body must, in deciding what arrangements to make for P, take into account any information given, or submissions made, by the independent mental capacity advocate.

(6) 'Care home' has the meaning given in section 3 of the Care Standards Act 2000.

(7) 'Hospital' means –

- (a) in relation to England, a hospital as defined by section 275 of the National Health Service Act 2006; and
- (b) in relation to Wales, a health service hospital as defined by section 206 of the National Health Service (Wales) Act 2006 or an independent hospital as defined by section 2 of the Care Standards Act 2000.

(8) 'NHS body' has such meaning as may be prescribed by regulations made for the purposes of this section by –

- (a) the Secretary of State, in relation to bodies in England, or
- (b) the National Assembly for Wales, in relation to bodies in Wales.

(9) 'Applicable period' means –

- (a) in relation to accommodation in a hospital, 28 days, and
- (b) in relation to accommodation in a care home, 8 weeks.

(10) For the purposes of subsection (1), a person appointed under Part 10 of Schedule A1 to be P's representative is not, by virtue of that appointment, engaged in providing care or treatment for P in a professional capacity or for remuneration.

Amendments: Mental Health Act 2007; SI 2010/813.

39 Provision of accommodation by local authority

(1) This section applies if a local authority propose to make arrangements –

- (a) for the provision of residential accommodation for a person ('P') who lacks capacity to agree to the arrangements, or
- (b) for a change in P's residential accommodation,

and are satisfied that there is no person, other than one engaged in providing care or treatment for P in a professional capacity or for remuneration, whom it would be appropriate for them to consult in determining what would be in P's best interests.

(2) But this section applies only if the accommodation is to be provided in accordance with –

(a) section 21 or 29 of the National Assistance Act 1948, or
(b) section 117 of the Mental Health Act,

as the result of a decision taken by the local authority under section 47 of the National Health Service and Community Care Act 1990.

(3) This section does not apply if P is accommodated as a result of an obligation imposed on him under the Mental Health Act.

(3A) And this section does not apply if –

(a) an independent mental capacity advocate must be appointed under section 39A or 39C (whether or not by the local authority) to represent P, and
(b) the place in which P is to be accommodated under the arrangements referred to in this section is the relevant hospital or care home under the authorisation referred to in that section.

(4) Before making the arrangements, the local authority must instruct an independent mental capacity advocate to represent P unless they are satisfied that –

(a) the accommodation is likely to be provided for a continuous period of less than 8 weeks, or
(b) the arrangements need to be made as a matter of urgency.

(5) If the local authority –

(a) did not instruct an independent mental capacity advocate to represent P before making the arrangements because they were satisfied that subsection (4)(a) or (b) applied, but
(b) subsequently have reason to believe that the accommodation is likely to be provided for a continuous period that will end 8 weeks or more after the day on which accommodation was first provided in accordance with the arrangements,

they must instruct an independent mental capacity advocate to represent P.

(6) The local authority must, in deciding what arrangements to make for P, take into account any information given, or submissions made, by the independent mental capacity advocate.

(7) For the purposes of subsection (1), a person appointed under Part 10 of Schedule A1 to be P's representative is not, by virtue of that appointment, engaged in providing care or treatment for P in a professional capacity or for remuneration.

Amendments: Mental Health Act 2007.

39A Person becomes subject to Schedule A1

(1) This section applies if –

(a) a person ('P') becomes subject to Schedule A1, and
(b) the managing authority of the relevant hospital or care home are satisfied that there is no person, other than one engaged in providing care or treatment for P in a professional capacity or for remuneration, whom it would be appropriate to consult in determining what would be in P's best interests.

(2) The managing authority must notify the supervisory body that this section applies.

(3) The supervisory body must instruct an independent mental capacity advocate to represent P.

(4) Schedule A1 makes provision about the role of an independent mental capacity advocate appointed under this section.

(5) This section is subject to paragraph 161 of Schedule A1.

(6) For the purposes of subsection (1), a person appointed under Part 10 of Schedule A1 to be P's representative is not, by virtue of that appointment, engaged in providing care or treatment for P in a professional capacity or for remuneration.

Amendment: Mental Health Act 2007.

39B Section 39A: supplementary provision

(1) This section applies for the purposes of section 39A.

(2) P becomes subject to Schedule A1 in any of the following cases.

(3) The first case is where an urgent authorisation is given in relation to P under paragraph 76(2) of Schedule A1 (urgent authorisation given before request made for standard authorisation).

(4) The second case is where the following conditions are met.

(5) The first condition is that a request is made under Schedule A1 for a standard authorisation to be given in relation to P ('the requested authorisation').

(6) The second condition is that no urgent authorisation was given under paragraph 76(2) of Schedule A1 before that request was made.

(7) The third condition is that the requested authorisation will not be in force on or before, or immediately after, the expiry of an existing standard authorisation.

(8) The expiry of a standard authorisation is the date when the authorisation is expected to cease to be in force.

(9) The third case is where, under paragraph 69 of Schedule A1, the supervisory body select a person to carry out an assessment of whether or not the relevant person is a detained resident.

Amendment: Mental Health Act 2007.

39C Person unrepresented whilst subject to Schedule A1

(1) This section applies if –

(a) an authorisation under Schedule A1 is in force in relation to a person ('P'),

(b) the appointment of a person as P's representative ends in accordance with regulations made under Part 10 of Schedule A1, and

(c) the managing authority of the relevant hospital or care home are satisfied that there is no person, other than one engaged in providing care or treatment for P in a professional capacity or for remuneration, whom it would be appropriate to consult in determining what would be in P's best interests.

(2) The managing authority must notify the supervisory body that this section applies.

(3) The supervisory body must instruct an independent mental capacity advocate to represent P.

(4) Paragraph 159 of Schedule A1 makes provision about the role of an independent mental capacity advocate appointed under this section.

(5) The appointment of an independent mental capacity advocate under this section ends when a new appointment of a person as P's representative is made in accordance with Part 10 of Schedule A1.

(6) For the purposes of subsection (1), a person appointed under Part 10 of Schedule A1 to be P's representative is not, by virtue of that appointment, engaged in providing care or treatment for P in a professional capacity or for remuneration.

Amendment: Mental Health Act 2007.

39D Person subject to Schedule A1 without paid representative

(1) This section applies if –

(a) an authorisation under Schedule A1 is in force in relation to a person ('P'),

(b) P has a representative ('R') appointed under Part 10 of Schedule A1, and

(c) R is not being paid under regulations under Part 10 of Schedule A1 for acting as P's representative.

(2) The supervisory body must instruct an independent mental capacity advocate to represent P in any of the following cases.

(3) The first case is where P makes a request to the supervisory body to instruct an advocate.

(4) The second case is where R makes a request to the supervisory body to instruct an advocate.

(5) The third case is where the supervisory body have reason to believe one or more of the following –

- (a) that, without the help of an advocate, P and R would be unable to exercise one or both of the relevant rights;
- (b) that P and R have each failed to exercise a relevant right when it would have been reasonable to exercise it;
- (c) that P and R are each unlikely to exercise a relevant right when it would be reasonable to exercise it.

(6) The duty in subsection (2) is subject to section 39E.

(7) If an advocate is appointed under this section, the advocate is, in particular, to take such steps as are practicable to help P and R to understand the following matters –

- (a) the effect of the authorisation;
- (b) the purpose of the authorisation;
- (c) the duration of the authorisation;
- (d) any conditions to which the authorisation is subject;
- (e) the reasons why each assessor who carried out an assessment in connection with the request for the authorisation, or in connection with a review of the authorisation, decided that P met the qualifying requirement in question;
- (f) the relevant rights;
- (g) how to exercise the relevant rights.

(8) The advocate is, in particular, to take such steps as are practicable to help P or R –

- (a) to exercise the right to apply to court, if it appears to the advocate that P or R wishes to exercise that right, or
- (b) to exercise the right of review, if it appears to the advocate that P or R wishes to exercise that right.

(9) If the advocate helps P or R to exercise the right of review –

- (a) the advocate may make submissions to the supervisory body on the question of whether a qualifying requirement is reviewable;
- (b) the advocate may give information, or make submissions, to any assessor carrying out a review assessment.

(10) In this section –

'relevant rights' means –
- (a) the right to apply to court, and

(b)   the right of review;

'right to apply to court' means the right to make an application to the court to exercise its jurisdiction under section 21A;
'right of review' means the right under Part 8 of Schedule A1 to request a review.

Amendment: Mental Health Act 2007.

39E Limitation on duty to instruct advocate under section 39D

(1) This section applies if an advocate is already representing P in accordance with an instruction under section 39D.

(2) Section 39D(2) does not require another advocate to be instructed, unless the following conditions are met.

(3) The first condition is that the existing advocate was instructed –

(a)   because of a request by R, or
(b)   because the supervisory body had reason to believe one or more of the things in section 39D(5).

(4) The second condition is that the other advocate would be instructed because of a request by P.

Amendment: Mental Health Act 2007.

40 Exceptions

(1) The duty imposed by section 37(3), 38(3) or (4), 39(4) or (5), 39A(3), 39C(3) or 39D(2) does not apply where there is –

(a)   a person nominated by P (in whatever manner) as a person to be consulted on matters to which that duty relates,
(b)   a donee of a lasting power of attorney created by P who is authorised to make decisions in relation to those matters, or
(c)   a deputy appointed by the court for P with power to make decisions in relation to those matters.

(2) A person appointed under Part 10 of Schedule A1 to be P's representative is not, by virtue of that appointment, a person nominated by P as a person to be consulted in matters to which a duty mentioned in subsection (1) relates.

Amendment: Mental Health Act 2007.

41 Power to adjust role of independent mental capacity advocate

(1) The appropriate authority may make regulations –

(a)   expanding the role of independent mental capacity advocates in relation to persons who lack capacity, and
(b)   adjusting the obligation to make arrangements imposed by section 35.

(2) The regulations may, in particular –

    (a)   prescribe circumstances (different to those set out in sections 37, 38 and 39) in which an independent mental capacity advocate must, or circumstances in which one may, be instructed by a person of a prescribed description to represent a person who lacks capacity, and

    (b)   include provision similar to any made by section 37, 38, 39 or 40.

(3) 'Appropriate authority' has the same meaning as in section 35.

Miscellaneous and supplementary

42 Codes of practice

(1) The Lord Chancellor must prepare and issue one or more codes of practice –

    (a)   for the guidance of persons assessing whether a person has capacity in relation to any matter,

    (b)   for the guidance of persons acting in connection with the care or treatment of another person (see section 5),

    (c)   for the guidance of donees of lasting powers of attorney,

    (d)   for the guidance of deputies appointed by the court,

    (e)   for the guidance of persons carrying out research in reliance on any provision made by or under this Act (and otherwise with respect to sections 30 to 34),

    (f)   for the guidance of independent mental capacity advocates,

    (fa)   for the guidance of persons exercising functions under Schedule A1,

    (fb)   for the guidance of representatives appointed under Part 10 of Schedule A1,

    (g)   with respect to the provisions of sections 24 to 26 (advance decisions and apparent advance decisions), and

    (h)   with respect to such other matters concerned with this Act as he thinks fit.

(2) The Lord Chancellor may from time to time revise a code.

(3) The Lord Chancellor may delegate the preparation or revision of the whole or any part of a code so far as he considers expedient.

(4) It is the duty of a person to have regard to any relevant code if he is acting in relation to a person who lacks capacity and is doing so in one or more of the following ways –

    (a)   as the donee of a lasting power of attorney,

    (b)   as a deputy appointed by the court,

    (c)   as a person carrying out research in reliance on any provision made by or under this Act (see sections 30 to 34),

    (d)   as an independent mental capacity advocate,

    (da)   in the exercise of functions under Schedule A1,

    (db)   as a representative appointed under Part 10 of Schedule A1,

    (e)   in a professional capacity,

(f)   for remuneration.

(5) If it appears to a court or tribunal conducting any criminal or civil proceedings that –

(a)   a provision of a code, or
(b)   a failure to comply with a code,

is relevant to a question arising in the proceedings, the provision or failure must be taken into account in deciding the question.

(6) A code under subsection (1)(d) may contain separate guidance for deputies appointed by virtue of paragraph 1(2) of Schedule 5 (functions of deputy conferred on receiver appointed under the Mental Health Act).

(7) In this section and in section 43, 'code' means a code prepared or revised under this section.

Amendments: Mental Health Act 2007.

43 Codes of practice: procedure

(1) Before preparing or revising a code, the Lord Chancellor must consult –

(a)   the National Assembly for Wales, and
(b)   such other persons as he considers appropriate.

(2) The Lord Chancellor may not issue a code unless –

(a)   a draft of the code has been laid by him before both Houses of Parliament, and
(b)   the 40 day period has elapsed without either House resolving not to approve the draft.

(3) The Lord Chancellor must arrange for any code that he has issued to be published in such a way as he considers appropriate for bringing it to the attention of persons likely to be concerned with its provisions.

(4) '40 day period', in relation to the draft of a proposed code, means –

(a)   if the draft is laid before one House on a day later than the day on which it is laid before the other House, the period of 40 days beginning with the later of the two days;
(b)   in any other case, the period of 40 days beginning with the day on which it is laid before each House.

(5) In calculating the period of 40 days, no account is to be taken of any period during which Parliament is dissolved or prorogued or during which both Houses are adjourned for more than 4 days.

44 Ill-treatment or neglect

(1) Subsection (2) applies if a person ('D') –

(a)   has the care of a person ('P') who lacks, or whom D reasonably believes to lack, capacity,

(b) is the donee of a lasting power of attorney, or an enduring power of attorney (within the meaning of Schedule 4), created by P, or

(c) is a deputy appointed by the court for P.

(2) D is guilty of an offence if he ill-treats or wilfully neglects P.

(3) A person guilty of an offence under this section is liable –

(a) on summary conviction, to imprisonment for a term not exceeding 12 months or a fine not exceeding the statutory maximum or both;

(b) on conviction on indictment, to imprisonment for a term not exceeding 5 years or a fine or both.

PART 2
THE COURT OF PROTECTION AND THE PUBLIC GUARDIAN

The Court of Protection

45 The Court of Protection

(1) There is to be a superior court of record known as the Court of Protection.

(2) The court is to have an official seal.

(3) The court may sit at any place in England and Wales, on any day and at any time.

(4) The court is to have a central office and registry at a place appointed by the Lord Chancellor, after consulting the Lord Chief Justice.

(5) The Lord Chancellor may, after consulting the Lord Chief Justice, designate as additional registries of the court any district registry of the High Court and any county court office.

(5A) The Lord Chief Justice may nominate any of the following to exercise his functions under this section –

(a) the President of the Court of Protection;

(b) a judicial office holder (as defined in section 109(4) of the Constitutional Reform Act 2005).

(6) The office of the Supreme Court called the Court of Protection ceases to exist.

Amendments: SI 2006/1016.

46 The judges of the Court of Protection

(1) Subject to Court of Protection Rules under section 51(2)(d), the jurisdiction of the court is exercisable by a judge nominated for that purpose by –

(a) the Lord Chief Justice, or

(b) where nominated by the Lord Chief Justice to act on his behalf under this subsection –

(i) the President of the Court of Protection; or

(ii)   a judicial office holder (as defined in section 109(4) of the Constitutional Reform Act 2005).

(2) To be nominated, a judge must be –

- (a) the President of the Family Division,
- (b) the Chancellor of the High Court,
- (c) a puisne judge of the High Court,
- (d) a circuit judge,
- (e) a district judge.
- (f) a District Judge (Magistrates' Courts),
- (g) a judge of the First-tier Tribunal, or of the Upper Tribunal, by virtue of appointment under paragraph 1(1) of Schedule 2 or 3 to the Tribunals, Courts and Enforcement Act 2007,
- (h) a transferred-in judge of the First-tier Tribunal or of the Upper Tribunal (see section 31(2) of that Act),
- (i) a deputy judge of the Upper Tribunal (whether under paragraph 7 of Schedule 3 to, or section 31(2) of, that Act),
- (j) the Chamber President, or Deputy Chamber President, of a chamber of the First-tier Tribunal or of a chamber of the Upper Tribunal,
- (k) the Judge Advocate General,
- (l) a Recorder,
- (m) the holder of an office listed in the first column of the table in section 89(3C) of the Senior Courts Act 1981 (senior High Court Masters etc),
- (n) a holder of an office listed in column 1 of Part 2 of Schedule 2 to that Act (High Court Masters etc),
- (o) a deputy district judge appointed under section 102 of that Act or under section 8 of the County Courts Act 1984,
- (p) a member of a panel of Employment Judges established for England and Wales or for Scotland,
- (q) a person appointed under section 30(1)(a) or (b) of the Courts-Martial (Appeals) Act 1951 (assistants to the Judge Advocate General),
- (r) a deputy judge of the High Court,
- (s) the Senior President of Tribunals,
- (t) an ordinary judge of the Court of Appeal (including the vice-president, if any, of either division of that court),
- (u) the President of the Queen's Bench Division,
- (v) the Master of the Rolls, or
- (w) the Lord Chief Justice.

(3) The Lord Chief Justice, after consulting the Lord Chancellor, must –

- (a) appoint one of the judges nominated by virtue of subsection (2)(a) to (c) to be President of the Court of Protection, and
- (b) appoint another of those judges to be Vice-President of the Court of Protection.

(4) The Lord Chief Justice, after consulting the Lord Chancellor, must appoint one of the judges nominated by virtue of subsection (2)(d) to (q) to be Senior

Judge of the Court of Protection, having such administrative functions in relation to the court as the Lord Chancellor, after consulting the Lord Chief Justice, may direct.

Amendments: Crime and Courts Act 2013; SI 2006/1016; SI 2013/2200.

Supplementary powers

47 General powers and effect of orders etc

(1) The court has in connection with its jurisdiction the same powers, rights, privileges and authority as the High Court.

(2) Section 204 of the Law of Property Act 1925 (orders of High Court conclusive in favour of purchasers) applies in relation to orders and directions of the court as it applies to orders of the High Court.

(3) Office copies of orders made, directions given or other instruments issued by the court and sealed with its official seal are admissible in all legal proceedings as evidence of the originals without any further proof.

48 Interim orders and directions

The court may, pending the determination of an application to it in relation to a person ('P'), make an order or give directions in respect of any matter if –

(a)   there is reason to believe that P lacks capacity in relation to the matter,
(b)   the matter is one to which its powers under this Act extend, and
(c)   it is in P's best interests to make the order, or give the directions, without delay.

49 Power to call for reports

(1) This section applies where, in proceedings brought in respect of a person ('P') under Part 1, the court is considering a question relating to P.

(2) The court may require a report to be made to it by the Public Guardian or by a Court of Protection Visitor.

(3) The court may require a local authority, or an NHS body, to arrange for a report to be made –

(a)   by one of its officers or employees, or
(b)   by such other person (other than the Public Guardian or a Court of Protection Visitor) as the authority, or the NHS body, considers appropriate.

(4) The report must deal with such matters relating to P as the court may direct.

(5) Court of Protection Rules may specify matters which, unless the court directs otherwise, must also be dealt with in the report.

(6) The report may be made in writing or orally, as the court may direct.

(7) In complying with a requirement, the Public Guardian or a Court of Protection Visitor may, at all reasonable times, examine and take copies of –

  (a) any health record,
  (b) any record of, or held by, a local authority and compiled in connection with a social services function, and
  (c) any record held by a person registered under Part 2 of the Care Standards Act 2000 or Chapter 2 of Part 1 of the Health and Social Care Act 2008,

so far as the record relates to P.

(8) If the Public Guardian or a Court of Protection Visitor is making a visit in the course of complying with a requirement, he may interview P in private.

(9) If a Court of Protection Visitor who is a Special Visitor is making a visit in the course of complying with a requirement, he may if the court so directs carry out in private a medical, psychiatric or psychological examination of P's capacity and condition.

(10) 'NHS body' has the meaning given in section 148 of the Health and Social Care (Community Health and Standards) Act 2003.

(11) 'Requirement' means a requirement imposed under subsection (2) or (3).

Amendment: SI 2010/813.

Practice and procedure

50 Applications to the Court of Protection

(1) No permission is required for an application to the court for the exercise of any of its powers under this Act –

  (a) by a person who lacks, or is alleged to lack, capacity,
  (b) if such a person has not reached 18, by anyone with parental responsibility for him,
  (c) by the donor or a donee of a lasting power of attorney to which the application relates,
  (d) by a deputy appointed by the court for a person to whom the application relates, or
  (e) by a person named in an existing order of the court, if the application relates to the order.

(1A) Nor is permission required for an application to the court under section 21A by the relevant per-son's representative.

(2) But, subject to Court of Protection Rules and to paragraph 20(2) of Schedule 3 (declarations relating to private international law), permission is required for any other application to the court.

(3) In deciding whether to grant permission the court must, in particular, have regard to –

(a) the applicant's connection with the person to whom the application relates,

(b) the reasons for the application,

(c) the benefit to the person to whom the application relates of a proposed order or directions, and

(d) whether the benefit can be achieved in any other way.

(4) 'Parental responsibility' has the same meaning as in the Children Act 1989.

Amendment: Mental Health Act 2007.

51 Court of Protection Rules

(1) Rules of court with respect to the practice and procedure of the court (to be called 'Court of Protection Rules') may be made in accordance with Part 1 of Schedule 1 to the Constitutional Reform Act 2005.

(2) Court of Protection Rules may, in particular, make provision –

(a) as to the manner and form in which proceedings are to be commenced;

(b) as to the persons entitled to be notified of, and be made parties to, the proceedings;

(c) for the allocation, in such circumstances as may be specified, of any specified description of proceedings to a specified judge or to specified descriptions of judges;

(d) for the exercise of the jurisdiction of the court, in such circumstances as may be specified, by its officers or other staff;

(e) for enabling the court to appoint a suitable person (who may, with his consent, be the Official Solicitor) to act in the name of, or on behalf of, or to represent the person to whom the proceedings relate;

(f) for enabling an application to the court to be disposed of without a hearing;

(g) for enabling the court to proceed with, or with any part of, a hearing in the absence of the person to whom the proceedings relate;

(h) for enabling or requiring the proceedings or any part of them to be conducted in private and for enabling the court to determine who is to be admitted when the court sits in private and to exclude specified persons when it sits in public;

(i) as to what may be received as evidence (whether or not admissible apart from the rules) and the manner in which it is to be presented;

(j) for the enforcement of orders made and directions given in the proceedings.

(3) Court of Protection Rules may, instead of providing for any matter, refer to provision made or to be made about that matter by directions.

(4) Court of Protection Rules may make different provision for different areas.

Amendments: SI 2006/1016.

52 Practice directions

(1) Directions as to the practice and procedure of the court may be given in accordance with Part 1 of Schedule 2 to the Constitutional Reform Act 2005.

(2) Practice directions given otherwise than under subsection (1) may not be given without the approval of –

    (a)   the Lord Chancellor, and
    (b)   the Lord Chief Justice.

(3) The Lord Chief Justice may nominate any of the following to exercise his functions under this section –

    (a)   the President of the Court of Protection;
    (b)   a judicial office holder (as defined in section 109(4) of the Constitutional Reform Act 2005).

Amendments: SI 2006/1016.

53 Rights of appeal

(1) Subject to the provisions of this section, an appeal lies to the Court of Appeal from any decision of the court.

(2) Court of Protection Rules may provide that where a decision of the court is made by –

    (a)   a person exercising the jurisdiction of the court by virtue of rules made under section 51(2)(d),
    (b)   a district judge, or
    (c)   a circuit judge,

an appeal from that decision lies to a prescribed higher judge of the court and not to the Court of Appeal.

(3) For the purposes of this section the higher judges of the court are –

    (a)   in relation to a person mentioned in subsection (2)(a), a circuit judge or a district judge;
    (b)   in relation to a person mentioned in subsection (2)(b), a circuit judge;
    (c)   in relation to any person mentioned in subsection (2), one of the judges nominated by virtue of section 46(2)(a) to (c).

(4) Court of Protection Rules may make provision –

    (a)   that, in such cases as may be specified, an appeal from a decision of the court may not be made without permission;
    (b)   as to the person or persons entitled to grant permission to appeal;
    (c)   as to any requirements to be satisfied before permission is granted;
    (d)   that where a higher judge of the court makes a decision on an appeal, no appeal may be made to the Court of Appeal from that decision unless the Court of Appeal considers that –
        (i)   the appeal would raise an important point of principle or practice, or

    (ii)   there is some other compelling reason for the Court of Appeal to hear it;

(e)   as to any considerations to be taken into account in relation to granting or refusing permission to appeal.

Fees and costs

54 Fees

(1) The Lord Chancellor may with the consent of the Treasury by order prescribe fees payable in respect of anything dealt with by the court.

(2) An order under this section may in particular contain provision as to –

(a)   scales or rates of fees;
(b)   exemptions from and reductions in fees;
(c)   remission of fees in whole or in part.

(3) Before making an order under this section, the Lord Chancellor must consult –

(a)   the President of the Court of Protection,
(b)   the Vice-President of the Court of Protection, and
(c)   the Senior Judge of the Court of Protection.

(4) The Lord Chancellor must take such steps as are reasonably practicable to bring information about fees to the attention of persons likely to have to pay them.

(5) Fees payable under this section are recoverable summarily as a civil debt.

55 Costs

(1) Subject to Court of Protection Rules, the costs of and incidental to all proceedings in the court are in its discretion.

(2) The rules may in particular make provision for regulating matters relating to the costs of those proceedings, including prescribing scales of costs to be paid to legal or other representatives.

(3) The court has full power to determine by whom and to what extent the costs are to be paid.

(4) The court may, in any proceedings –

(a)   disallow, or
(b)   order the legal or other representatives concerned to meet,

the whole of any wasted costs or such part of them as may be determined in accordance with the rules.

(5) 'Legal or other representative', in relation to a party to proceedings, means any person exercising a right of audience or right to conduct litigation on his behalf.

(6) 'Wasted costs' means any costs incurred by a party –

  (a) as a result of any improper, unreasonable or negligent act or omission on the part of any legal or other representative or any employee of such a representative, or
  (b) which, in the light of any such act or omission occurring after they were incurred, the court considers it is unreasonable to expect that party to pay.

56 Fees and costs: supplementary

(1) Court of Protection Rules may make provision –

  (a) as to the way in which, and funds from which, fees and costs are to be paid;
  (b) for charging fees and costs upon the estate of the person to whom the proceedings relate;
  (c) for the payment of fees and costs within a specified time of the death of the person to whom the proceedings relate or the conclusion of the proceedings.

(2) A charge on the estate of a person created by virtue of subsection (1)(b) does not cause any interest of the person in any property to fail or determine or to be prevented from recommencing.

The Public Guardian

57 The Public Guardian

(1) For the purposes of this Act, there is to be an officer, to be known as the Public Guardian.

(2) The Public Guardian is to be appointed by the Lord Chancellor.

(3) There is to be paid to the Public Guardian out of money provided by Parliament such salary as the Lord Chancellor may determine.

(4) The Lord Chancellor may, after consulting the Public Guardian –

  (a) provide him with such officers and staff, or
  (b) enter into such contracts with other persons for the provision (by them or their sub-contractors) of officers, staff or services,

as the Lord Chancellor thinks necessary for the proper discharge of the Public Guardian's functions.

(5) Any functions of the Public Guardian may, to the extent authorised by him, be performed by any of his officers.

58 Functions of the Public Guardian

(1) The Public Guardian has the following functions –

  (a) establishing and maintaining a register of lasting powers of attorney,
  (b) establishing and maintaining a register of orders appointing deputies,

(c) supervising deputies appointed by the court,

(d) directing a Court of Protection Visitor to visit –
   (i) a donee of a lasting power of attorney,
   (ii) a deputy appointed by the court, or
   (iii) the person granting the power of attorney or for whom the deputy is appointed ('P'),
   and to make a report to the Public Guardian on such matters as he may direct,

(e) receiving security which the court requires a person to give for the discharge of his functions,

(f) receiving reports from donees of lasting powers of attorney and deputies appointed by the court,

(g) reporting to the court on such matters relating to proceedings under this Act as the court requires,

(h) dealing with representations (including complaints) about the way in which a donee of a lasting power of attorney or a deputy appointed by the court is exercising his powers,

(i) publishing, in any manner the Public Guardian thinks appropriate, any information he thinks appropriate about the discharge of his functions.

(2) The functions conferred by subsection (1)(c) and (h) may be discharged in co-operation with any other person who has functions in relation to the care or treatment of P.

(3) The Lord Chancellor may by regulations make provision –

(a) conferring on the Public Guardian other functions in connection with this Act;

(b) in connection with the discharge by the Public Guardian of his functions.

(4) Regulations made under subsection (3)(b) may in particular make provision as to –

(a) the giving of security by deputies appointed by the court and the enforcement and discharge of security so given;

(b) the fees which may be charged by the Public Guardian;

(c) the way in which, and funds from which, such fees are to be paid;

(d) exemptions from and reductions in such fees;

(e) remission of such fees in whole or in part;

(f) the making of reports to the Public Guardian by deputies appointed by the court and others who are directed by the court to carry out any transaction for a person who lacks capacity.

(5) For the purpose of enabling him to carry out his functions, the Public Guardian may, at all reasonable times, examine and take copies of –

(a) any health record,

(b) any record of, or held by, a local authority and compiled in connection with a social services function, and

(c)   any record held by a person registered under Part 2 of the Care Standards Act 2000 or Chapter 2 of Part 1 of the Health and Social Care Act 2008,

so far as the record relates to P.

(6) The Public Guardian may also for that purpose interview P in private.

Amendment: SI 2010/813.

59 (*Repealed*)

Amendment: SI 2012/2401.

60 Annual report

(1) The Public Guardian must make an annual report to the Lord Chancellor about the discharge of his functions.

(2) The Lord Chancellor must, within one month of receiving the report, lay a copy of it before Parliament.

Court of Protection Visitors

61 Court of Protection Visitors

(1) A Court of Protection Visitor is a person who is appointed by the Lord Chancellor to –

(a)   a panel of Special Visitors, or
(b)   a panel of General Visitors.

(2) A person is not qualified to be a Special Visitor unless he –

(a)   is a registered medical practitioner or appears to the Lord Chancellor to have other suitable qualifications or training, and
(b)   appears to the Lord Chancellor to have special knowledge of and experience in cases of impairment of or disturbance in the functioning of the mind or brain.

(3) A General Visitor need not have a medical qualification.

(4) A Court of Protection Visitor –

(a)   may be appointed for such term and subject to such conditions, and
(b)   may be paid such remuneration and allowances,

as the Lord Chancellor may determine.

(5) For the purpose of carrying out his functions under this Act in relation to a person who lacks capacity ('P'), a Court of Protection Visitor may, at all reasonable times, examine and take copies of –

(a)   any health record,
(b)   any record of, or held by, a local authority and compiled in connection with a social services function, and

(c)   any record held by a person registered under Part 2 of the Care Standards Act 2000 or Chapter 2 of Part 1 of the Health and Social Care Act 2008,

so far as the record relates to P.

(6) A Court of Protection Visitor may also for that purpose interview P in private.

Amendment: SI 2010/813.

PART 3
MISCELLANEOUS AND GENERAL

Declaratory provision

62 Scope of the Act

For the avoidance of doubt, it is hereby declared that nothing in this Act is to be taken to affect the law relating to murder or manslaughter or the operation of section 2 of the Suicide Act 1961 (assisting suicide).

Private international law

63 International protection of adults

Schedule 3 –

(a)   gives effect in England and Wales to the Convention on the International Protection of Adults signed at the Hague on 13th January 2000 (Cm. 5881) (in so far as this Act does not otherwise do so), and

(b)   makes related provision as to the private international law of England and Wales.

General

64 Interpretation

(1) In this Act –

'the 1985 Act' means the Enduring Powers of Attorney Act 1985,
'advance decision' has the meaning given in section 24(1),
'authorisation under Schedule A1' means either –

(a)   a standard authorisation under that Schedule, or
(b)   an urgent authorisation under that Schedule;

'the court' means the Court of Protection established by section 45,
'Court of Protection Rules' has the meaning given in section 51(1),
'Court of Protection Visitor' has the meaning given in section 61,
'deputy' has the meaning given in section 16(2)(b),
'enactment' includes a provision of subordinate legislation (within the meaning of the Interpretation Act 1978),

'health record' has the meaning given in section 68 of the Data Protection Act 1998 (as read with section 69 of that Act),

'the Human Rights Convention' has the same meaning as 'the Convention' in the Human Rights Act 1998,

'independent mental capacity advocate' has the meaning given in section 35(1),

'lasting power of attorney' has the meaning given in section 9,

'life-sustaining treatment' has the meaning given in section 4(10),

'local authority', except in section 35(6A)(a) and Schedule A1, means –

    (a)   the council of a county in England in which there are no district councils,

    (b)   the council of a district in England,

    (c)   the council of a county or county borough in Wales,

    (d)   the council of a London borough,

    (e)   the Common Council of the City of London, or

    (f)   the Council of the Isles of Scilly,

'Mental Health Act' means the Mental Health Act 1983,

'prescribed', in relation to regulations made under this Act, means prescribed by those regulations,

'property' includes any thing in action and any interest in real or personal property,

'public authority' has the same meaning as in the Human Rights Act 1998,

'Public Guardian' has the meaning given in section 57,

'purchaser' and 'purchase' have the meaning given in section 205(1) of the Law of Property Act 1925,

'social services function' has the meaning given in section 1A of the Local Authority Social Services Act 1970,

'treatment' includes a diagnostic or other procedure,

'trust corporation' has the meaning given in section 68(1) of the Trustee Act 1925, and

'will' includes codicil.

(2) In this Act, references to making decisions, in relation to a donee of a lasting power of attorney or a deputy appointed by the court, include, where appropriate, acting on decisions made.

(3) In this Act, references to the bankruptcy of an individual include a case where a bankruptcy restrictions order under the Insolvency Act 1986 has effect in respect of him.

(3A) In this Act references to a debt relief order (under Part 7A of the Insolvency Act 1986) being made in relation to an individual include a case where a debt relief restrictions order under the Insolvency Act 1986 has effect in respect of him.

(4) 'Bankruptcy restrictions order' includes an interim bankruptcy restrictions order.

(4A) 'Debt relief restrictions order' includes an interim debt relief restrictions order.

(5) In this Act, references to deprivation of a person's liberty have the same meaning as in Article 5(1) of the Human Rights Convention.

(6) For the purposes of such references, it does not matter whether a person is deprived of his liberty by a public authority or not.

Amendment: Mental Health Act 2007; Health and Social Care Act 2012; SI 2012/2404.

65 Rules, regulations and orders

(1) Any power to make rules, regulations or orders under this Act, other than the power in section 21 –

(a)   is exercisable by statutory instrument;
(b)   includes power to make supplementary, incidental, consequential, transitional or saving provision;
(c)   includes power to make different provision for different cases.

(2) Any statutory instrument containing rules, regulations or orders made by the Lord Chancellor or the Secretary of State under this Act, other than –

(a)   regulations under section 34 (loss of capacity during research project),
(b)   regulations under section 41 (adjusting role of independent mental capacity advocacy service),
(c)   regulations under paragraph 32(1)(b) of Schedule 3 (private international law relating to the protection of adults),
(d)   an order of the kind mentioned in section 67(6) (consequential amendments of primary legislation), or
(e)   an order under section 68 (commencement),

is subject to annulment in pursuance of a resolution of either House of Parliament.

(3) A statutory instrument containing an Order in Council under paragraph 31 of Schedule 3 (provision to give further effect to Hague Convention) is subject to annulment in pursuance of a resolution of either House of Parliament.

(4) A statutory instrument containing regulations made by the Secretary of State under section 34 or 41 or by the Lord Chancellor under paragraph 32(1)(b) of Schedule 3 may not be made unless a draft has been laid before and approved by resolution of each House of Parliament.

(4A) Subsection (2) does not apply to a statutory instrument containing regulations made by the Secretary of State under Schedule A1.

(4B) If such a statutory instrument contains regulations under paragraph 42(2)(b), 129, 162 or 164 of Schedule A1 (whether or not it also contains other regulations), the instrument may not be made unless a draft has been laid before and approved by resolution of each House of Parliament.

(4C) Subject to that, such a statutory instrument is subject to annulment in pursuance of a resolution of either House of Parliament.

(5) An order under section 21 –

(a)   may include supplementary, incidental, consequential, transitional or saving provision;

(b)   may make different provision for different cases;

(c)   is to be made in the form of a statutory instrument to which the Statutory Instruments Act 1946 applies as if the order were made by a Minister of the Crown; and

(d)   is subject to annulment in pursuance of a resolution of either House of Parliament.

Amendments: SI 2006/1016, Mental Health Act 2007.

66 Existing receivers and enduring powers of attorney etc

(1) The following provisions cease to have effect –

(a)   Part 7 of the Mental Health Act,

(b)   the Enduring Powers of Attorney Act 1985.

(2) No enduring power of attorney within the meaning of the 1985 Act is to be created after the commencement of subsection (1)(b).

(3) Schedule 4 has effect in place of the 1985 Act in relation to any enduring power of attorney created before the commencement of subsection (1)(b).

(4) Schedule 5 contains transitional provisions and savings in relation to Part 7 of the Mental Health Act and the 1985 Act.

67 Minor and consequential amendments and repeals

(1) Schedule 6 contains minor and consequential amendments.

(2) Schedule 7 contains repeals.

(3) The Lord Chancellor may by order make supplementary, incidental, consequential, transitional or saving provision for the purposes of, in consequence of, or for giving full effect to a provision of this Act.

(4) An order under subsection (3) may, in particular –

(a)   provide for a provision of this Act which comes into force before another provision of this Act has come into force to have effect, until the other provision has come into force, with specified modifications;

(b)   amend, repeal or revoke an enactment, other than one contained in an Act or Measure passed in a Session after the one in which this Act is passed.

(5) The amendments that may be made under subsection (4)(b) are in addition to those made by or under any other provision of this Act.

(6) An order under subsection (3) which amends or repeals a provision of an Act or Measure may not be made unless a draft has been laid before and approved by resolution of each House of Parliament.

68 Commencement and extent

(1) This Act, other than sections 30 to 41, comes into force in accordance with provision made by order by the Lord Chancellor.

(2) Sections 30 to 41 come into force in accordance with provision made by order by –

    (a)   the Secretary of State, in relation to England, and
    (b)   the National Assembly for Wales, in relation to Wales.

(3) An order under this section may appoint different days for different provisions and different purposes.

(4) Subject to subsections (5) and (6), this Act extends to England and Wales only.

(5) The following provisions extend to the United Kingdom –

    (a)   paragraph 16(1) of Schedule 1 (evidence of instruments and of registration of lasting powers of attorney),
    (b)   paragraph 15(3) of Schedule 4 (evidence of instruments and of registration of enduring powers of attorney).

(6) Subject to any provision made in Schedule 6, the amendments and repeals made by Schedules 6 and 7 have the same extent as the enactments to which they relate.

69 Short title

This Act may be cited as the Mental Capacity Act 2005.

SCHEDULES

Schedule A1
Hospital and Care Home Residents: Deprivation of Liberty

Amendment: Mental Health Act 2007.

PART 1
AUTHORISATION TO DEPRIVE RESIDENTS OF LIBERTY ETC

1 Application of Part

(1) This Part applies if the following conditions are met.

(2) The first condition is that a person ('P') is detained in a hospital or care home –for the purpose of being given care or treatment –in circumstances which amount to deprivation of the person's liberty.

(3) The second condition is that a standard or urgent authorisation is in force.

(4) The third condition is that the standard or urgent authorisation relates –

    (a)   to P, and
    (b)   to the hospital or care home in which P is detained.

The managing authority of the hospital or care home may deprive P of his liberty by detaining him as mentioned in paragraph 1(2).

3 No liability for acts done for purpose of depriving P of liberty

(1) This paragraph applies to any act which a person ('D') does for the purpose of detaining P as mentioned in paragraph 1(2).

(2) D does not incur any liability in relation to the act that he would not have incurred if P –

  (a)   had had capacity to consent in relation to D's doing the act, and
  (b)   had consented to D's doing the act.

4 No protection for negligent acts etc

(1) Paragraphs 2 and 3 do not exclude a person's civil liability for loss or damage, or his criminal liability, resulting from his negligence in doing any thing.

(2) Paragraphs 2 and 3 do not authorise a person to do anything otherwise than for the purpose of the standard or urgent authorisation that is in force.

(3) In a case where a standard authorisation is in force, paragraphs 2 and 3 do not authorise a person to do anything which does not comply with the conditions (if any) included in the authorisation.

Amendment: Mental Health Act 2007.

PART 2
INTERPRETATION: MAIN TERMS

5 Introduction

This Part applies for the purposes of this Schedule.

6 Detained resident

'Detained resident' means a person detained in a hospital or care home –for the purpose of being given care or treatment –in circumstances which amount to deprivation of the person's liberty.

7 Relevant person etc

In relation to a person who is, or is to be, a detained resident –

'relevant person' means the person in question;
'relevant hospital or care home' means the hospital or care home in question;
'relevant care or treatment' means the care or treatment in question.

8 Authorisations

'Standard authorisation' means an authorisation given under Part 4.

9 'Urgent authorisation' means an authorisation given under Part 5.

10 'Authorisation under this Schedule' means either of the following –

    (a)   a standard authorisation;

    (b)   an urgent authorisation.

11 (1) The purpose of a standard authorisation is the purpose which is stated in the authorisation in accordance with paragraph 55(1)(d).

(2) The purpose of an urgent authorisation is the purpose which is stated in the authorisation in accordance with paragraph 80(d).

Amendment: Mental Health Act 2007.

PART 3
THE QUALIFYING REQUIREMENTS

12 The qualifying requirements

(1) These are the qualifying requirements referred to in this Schedule –

    (a)   the age requirement;

    (b)   the mental health requirement;

    (c)   the mental capacity requirement;

    (d)   the best interests requirement;

    (e)   the eligibility requirement;

    (f)   the no refusals requirement.

(2) Any question of whether a person who is, or is to be, a detained resident meets the qualifying requirements is to be determined in accordance with this Part.

(3) In a case where –

    (a)   the question of whether a person meets a particular qualifying requirement arises in relation to the giving of a standard authorisation, and

    (b)   any circumstances relevant to determining that question are expected to change between the time when the determination is made and the time when the authorisation is expected to come into force,

those circumstances are to be taken into account as they are expected to be at the later time.

13 The age requirement

The relevant person meets the age requirement if he has reached 18.

14 The mental health requirement

(1) The relevant person meets the mental health requirement if he is suffering from mental disorder (within the meaning of the Mental Health Act, but disregarding any exclusion for persons with learning disability).

(2) An exclusion for persons with learning disability is any provision of the Mental Health Act which provides for a person with learning disability not to be regarded as suffering from mental disorder for one or more purposes of that Act.

15 The mental capacity requirement

The relevant person meets the mental capacity requirement if he lacks capacity in relation to the question whether or not he should be accommodated in the relevant hospital or care home for the purpose of being given the relevant care or treatment.

16 The best interests requirement

(1) The relevant person meets the best interests requirement if all of the following conditions are met.

(2) The first condition is that the relevant person is, or is to be, a detained resident.

(3) The second condition is that it is in the best interests of the relevant person for him to be a detained resident.

(4) The third condition is that, in order to prevent harm to the relevant person, it is necessary for him to be a detained resident.

(5) The fourth condition is that it is a proportionate response to –

    (a)   the likelihood of the relevant person suffering harm, and
    (b)   the seriousness of that harm,

for him to be a detained resident.

17 The eligibility requirement

(1) The relevant person meets the eligibility requirement unless he is ineligible to be deprived of liberty by this Act.

(2) Schedule 1A applies for the purpose of determining whether or not P is ineligible to be deprived of liberty by this Act.

18 The no refusals requirement

The relevant person meets the no refusals requirement unless there is a refusal within the meaning of paragraph 19 or 20.

19 (1) There is a refusal if these conditions are met –

    (a)   the relevant person has made an advance decision;
    (b)   the advance decision is valid;
    (c)   the advance decision is applicable to some or all of the relevant treatment.

(2) Expressions used in this paragraph and any of sections 24, 25 or 26 have the same meaning in this paragraph as in that section.

20 (1) There is a refusal if it would be in conflict with a valid decision of a donee or deputy for the relevant person to be accommodated in the relevant hospital or care home for the purpose of receiving some or all of the relevant care or treatment –

(a) in circumstances which amount to deprivation of the person's liberty, or

(b) at all.

(2) A donee is a donee of a lasting power of attorney granted by the relevant person.

(3) A decision of a donee or deputy is valid if it is made –

(a) within the scope of his authority as donee or deputy, and

(b) in accordance with Part 1 of this Act.

Amendment: Mental Health Act 2007.

PART 4
STANDARD AUTHORISATIONS

21 Supervisory body to give authorisation

Only the supervisory body may give a standard authorisation.

22 The supervisory body may not give a standard authorisation unless –

(a) the managing authority of the relevant hospital or care home have requested it, or

(b) paragraph 71 applies (right of third party to require consideration of whether authorisation needed).

23 The managing authority may not make a request for a standard authorisation unless –

(a) they are required to do so by paragraph 24 (as read with paragraphs 27 to 29),

(b) they are required to do so by paragraph 25 (as read with paragraph 28), or

(c) they are permitted to do so by paragraph 30.

24 Duty to request authorisation: basic cases

(1) The managing authority must request a standard authorisation in any of the following cases.

(2) The first case is where it appears to the managing authority that the relevant person –

(a) is not yet accommodated in the relevant hospital or care home,

(b) is likely –at some time within the next 28 days –to be a detained resident in the relevant hospital or care home, and

(c) is likely –

    (i)   at that time, or
    (ii)   at some later time within the next 28 days,

to meet all of the qualifying requirements.

(3) The second case is where it appears to the managing authority that the relevant person –

    (a)   is already accommodated in the relevant hospital or care home,
    (b)   is likely – at some time within the next 28 days – to be a detained resident in the relevant hospital or care home, and
    (c)   is likely –
            (i)   at that time, or
            (ii)   at some later time within the next 28 days,

to meet all of the qualifying requirements.

(4) The third case is where it appears to the managing authority that the relevant person –

    (a)   is a detained resident in the relevant hospital or care home, and
    (b)   meets all of the qualifying requirements, or is likely to do so at some time within the next 28 days.

(5) This paragraph is subject to paragraphs 27 to 29.

25 Duty to request authorisation: change in place of detention

(1) The relevant managing authority must request a standard authorisation if it appears to them that these conditions are met.

(2) The first condition is that a standard authorisation –

    (a)   has been given, and
    (b)   has not ceased to be in force.

(3) The second condition is that there is, or is to be, a change in the place of detention.

(4) This paragraph is subject to paragraph 28.

26 (1) This paragraph applies for the purposes of paragraph 25.

(2) There is a change in the place of detention if the relevant person –

    (a)   ceases to be a detained resident in the stated hospital or care home, and
    (b)   becomes a detained resident in a different hospital or care home ('the new hospital or care home').

(3) The stated hospital or care home is the hospital or care home to which the standard authorisation relates.

(4) The relevant managing authority are the managing authority of the new hospital or care home.

27 Other authority for detention: request for authorisation

(1) This paragraph applies if, by virtue of section 4A(3), a decision of the court authorises the relevant person to be a detained resident.

(2) Paragraph 24 does not require a request for a standard authorisation to be made in relation to that detention unless these conditions are met.

(3) The first condition is that the standard authorisation would be in force at a time immediately after the expiry of the other authority.

(4) The second condition is that the standard authorisation would not be in force at any time on or before the expiry of the other authority.

(5) The third condition is that it would, in the managing authority's view, be unreasonable to delay making the request until a time nearer the expiry of the other authority.

(6) In this paragraph –

  (a) the other authority is –
    (i) the decision mentioned in sub-paragraph (1), or
    (ii) any further decision of the court which, by virtue of section 4A(3), authorises, or is expected to authorise, the relevant person to be a detained resident;

  (b) the expiry of the other authority is the time when the other authority is expected to cease to authorise the relevant person to be a detained resident.

28 Request refused: no further request unless change of circumstances

(1) This paragraph applies if –

  (a) a managing authority request a standard authorisation under paragraph 24 or 25, and
  (b) the supervisory body are prohibited by paragraph 50(2) from giving the authorisation.

(2) Paragraph 24 or 25 does not require that managing authority to make a new request for a standard authorisation unless it appears to the managing authority that –

  (a) there has been a change in the relevant person's case, and
  (b) because of that change, the supervisory body are likely to give a standard authorisation if requested.

29 Authorisation given: request for further authorisation

(1) This paragraph applies if a standard authorisation –

  (a) has been given in relation to the detention of the relevant person, and
  (b) that authorisation ('the existing authorisation') has not ceased to be in force.

(2) Paragraph 24 does not require a new request for a standard authorisation ('the new authorisation') to be made unless these conditions are met.

(3) The first condition is that the new authorisation would be in force at a time immediately after the expiry of the existing authorisation.

(4) The second condition is that the new authorisation would not be in force at any time on or before the expiry of the existing authorisation.

(5) The third condition is that it would, in the managing authority's view, be unreasonable to delay making the request until a time nearer the expiry of the existing authorisation.

(6) The expiry of the existing authorisation is the time when it is expected to cease to be in force.

30 Power to request authorisation

(1) This paragraph applies if –

    (a)   a standard authorisation has been given in relation to the detention of the relevant person,

    (b)   that authorisation ('the existing authorisation') has not ceased to be in force,

    (c)   the requirement under paragraph 24 to make a request for a new standard authorisation does not apply, because of paragraph 29, and

    (d)   a review of the existing authorisation has been requested, or is being carried out, in accordance with Part 8.

(2) The managing authority may request a new standard authorisation which would be in force on or before the expiry of the existing authorisation; but only if it would also be in force immediately after that expiry.

(3) The expiry of the existing authorisation is the time when it is expected to cease to be in force.

(4) Further provision relating to cases where a request is made under this paragraph can be found in –

    (a)   paragraph 62 (effect of decision about request), and
    (b)   paragraph 124 (effect of request on Part 8 review).

31 Information included in request

A request for a standard authorisation must include the information (if any) required by regulations.

32 Records of requests

(1) The managing authority of a hospital or care home must keep a written record of –

    (a)   each request that they make for a standard authorisation, and
    (b)   the reasons for making each request.

(2) A supervisory body must keep a written record of each request for a standard authorisation that is made to them.

33 Relevant person must be assessed

(1) This paragraph applies if the supervisory body are requested to give a standard authorisation.

(2) The supervisory body must secure that all of these assessments are carried out in relation to the relevant person –

  (a)   an age assessment;
  (b)   a mental health assessment;
  (c)   a mental capacity assessment;
  (d)   a best interests assessment;
  (e)   an eligibility assessment;
  (f)   a no refusals assessment.

(3) The person who carries out any such assessment is referred to as the assessor.

(4) Regulations may be made about the period (or periods) within which assessors must carry out assessments.

(5) This paragraph is subject to paragraphs 49 and 133.

34 Age assessment

An age assessment is an assessment of whether the relevant person meets the age requirement.

35 Mental health assessment

A mental health assessment is an assessment of whether the relevant person meets the mental health requirement.

36 When carrying out a mental health assessment, the assessor must also –

  (a)   consider how (if at all) the relevant person's mental health is likely to be affected by his being a detained resident, and
  (b)   notify the best interests assessor of his conclusions.

37 Mental capacity assessment

A mental capacity assessment is an assessment of whether the relevant person meets the mental capacity requirement.

38 Best interests assessment

A best interests assessment is an assessment of whether the relevant person meets the best interests requirement.

39 (1) In carrying out a best interests assessment, the assessor must comply with the duties in sub-paragraphs (2) and (3).

(2) The assessor must consult the managing authority of the relevant hospital or care home.

(3) The assessor must have regard to all of the following –

  (a) the conclusions which the mental health assessor has notified to the best interests assessor in accordance with paragraph 36(b);
  (b) any relevant needs assessment;
  (c) any relevant care plan.

(4) A relevant needs assessment is an assessment of the relevant person's needs which –

  (a) was carried out in connection with the relevant person being accommodated in the relevant hospital or care home, and
  (b) was carried out by or on behalf of –
      (i) the managing authority of the relevant hospital or care home, or
      (ii) the supervisory body.

(5) A relevant care plan is a care plan which –

  (a) sets out how the relevant person's needs are to be met whilst he is accommodated in the relevant hospital or care home, and
  (b) was drawn up by or on behalf of –
      (i) the managing authority of the relevant hospital or care home, or
      (ii) the supervisory body.

(6) The managing authority must give the assessor a copy of –

  (a) any relevant needs assessment carried out by them or on their behalf, or
  (b) any relevant care plan drawn up by them or on their behalf.

(7) The supervisory body must give the assessor a copy of –

  (a) any relevant needs assessment carried out by them or on their behalf, or
  (b) any relevant care plan drawn up by them or on their behalf.

(8) The duties in sub-paragraphs (2) and (3) do not affect any other duty to consult or to take the views of others into account.

40 (1) This paragraph applies whatever conclusion the best interests assessment comes to.

(2) The assessor must state in the best interests assessment the name and address of every interested person whom he has consulted in carrying out the assessment.

41 Paragraphs 42 and 43 apply if the best interests assessment comes to the conclusion that the relevant person meets the best interests requirement.

42 (1) The assessor must state in the assessment the maximum authorisation period.

(2) The maximum authorisation period is the shorter of these periods –

    (a)   the period which, in the assessor's opinion, would be the appropriate maximum period for the relevant person to be a detained resident under the standard authorisation that has been requested;

    (b)   1 year, or such shorter period as may be prescribed in regulations.

(3) Regulations under sub-paragraph (2)(b) –

    (a)   need not provide for a shorter period to apply in relation to all standard authorisations;

    (b)   may provide for different periods to apply in relation to different kinds of standard authorisations.

(4) Before making regulations under sub-paragraph (2)(b) the Secretary of State must consult all of the following –

    (a)   each body required by regulations under paragraph 162 to monitor and report on the operation of this Schedule in relation to England;

    (b)   such other persons as the Secretary of State considers it appropriate to consult.

(5) Before making regulations under sub-paragraph (2)(b) the National Assembly for Wales must consult all of the following –

    (a)   each person or body directed under paragraph 163(2) to carry out any function of the Assembly of monitoring and reporting on the operation of this Schedule in relation to Wales;

    (b)   such other persons as the Assembly considers it appropriate to consult.

43 The assessor may include in the assessment recommendations about conditions to which the standard authorisation is, or is not, to be subject in accordance with paragraph 53.

44 (1) This paragraph applies if the best interests assessment comes to the conclusion that the relevant person does not meet the best interests requirement.

(2) If, on the basis of the information taken into account in carrying out the assessment, it appears to the assessor that there is an unauthorised deprivation of liberty, he must include a statement to that effect in the assessment.

(3) There is an unauthorised deprivation of liberty if the managing authority of the relevant hospital or care home are already depriving the relevant person of his liberty without authority of the kind mentioned in section 4A.

45 The duties with which the best interests assessor must comply are subject to the provision included in appointment regulations under Part 10 (in particular, provision made under paragraph 146).

46 Eligibility assessment

An eligibility assessment is an assessment of whether the relevant person meets the eligibility requirement.

47 (1) Regulations may –

- (a) require an eligibility assessor to request a best interests assessor to provide relevant eligibility information, and
- (b) require the best interests assessor, if such a request is made, to provide such relevant eligibility information as he may have.

(2) In this paragraph –

'best interests assessor' means any person who is carrying out, or has carried out, a best interests assessment in relation to the relevant person;

'eligibility assessor' means a person carrying out an eligibility assessment in relation to the relevant person;

'relevant eligibility information' is information relevant to assessing whether or not the relevant person is ineligible by virtue of paragraph 5 of Schedule 1A.

48 No refusals assessment

A no refusals assessment is an assessment of whether the relevant person meets the no refusals requirement.

49 Equivalent assessment already carried out

(1) The supervisory body are not required by paragraph 33 to secure that a particular kind of assessment ('the required assessment') is carried out in relation to the relevant person if the following conditions are met.

(2) The first condition is that the supervisory body have a written copy of an assessment of the relevant person ('the existing assessment') that has already been carried out.

(3) The second condition is that the existing assessment complies with all requirements under this Schedule with which the required assessment would have to comply (if it were carried out).

(4) The third condition is that the existing assessment was carried out within the previous 12 months; but this condition need not be met if the required assessment is an age assessment.

(5) The fourth condition is that the supervisory body are satisfied that there is no reason why the existing assessment may no longer be accurate.

(6) If the required assessment is a best interests assessment, in satisfying themselves as mentioned in sub-paragraph (5), the supervisory body must take into account any information given, or submissions made, by –

- (a) the relevant person's representative,
- (b) any section 39C IMCA, or

(c) any section 39D IMCA.

(7) It does not matter whether the existing assessment was carried out in connection with a request for a standard authorisation or for some other purpose.

(8) If, because of this paragraph, the supervisory body are not required by paragraph 33 to secure that the required assessment is carried out, the existing assessment is to be treated for the purposes of this Schedule –

(a) as an assessment of the same kind as the required assessment, and
(b) as having been carried out under paragraph 33 in connection with the request for the standard authorisation.

50 Duty to give authorisation

(1) The supervisory body must give a standard authorisation if –

(a) all assessments are positive, and
(b) the supervisory body have written copies of all those assessments.

(2) The supervisory body must not give a standard authorisation except in accordance with sub-paragraph (1).

(3) All assessments are positive if each assessment carried out under paragraph 33 has come to the conclusion that the relevant person meets the qualifying requirement to which the assessment relates.

51 Terms of authorisation

(1) If the supervisory body are required to give a standard authorisation, they must decide the period during which the authorisation is to be in force.

(2) That period must not exceed the maximum authorisation period stated in the best interests assessment.

52 A standard authorisation may provide for the authorisation to come into force at a time after it is given.

53 (1) A standard authorisation may be given subject to conditions.

(2) Before deciding whether to give the authorisation subject to conditions, the supervisory body must have regard to any recommendations in the best interests assessment about such conditions.

(3) The managing authority of the relevant hospital or care home must ensure that any conditions are complied with.

54 Form of authorisation

A standard authorisation must be in writing.

55 (1) A standard authorisation must state the following things –

(a) the name of the relevant person;

  (b)   the name of the relevant hospital or care home;

  (c)   the period during which the authorisation is to be in force;

  (d)   the purpose for which the authorisation is given;

  (e)   any conditions subject to which the authorisation is given;

  (f)   the reason why each qualifying requirement is met.

(2) The statement of the reason why the eligibility requirement is met must be framed by reference to the cases in the table in paragraph 2 of Schedule 1A.

56 (1) If the name of the relevant hospital or care home changes, the standard authorisation is to be read as if it stated the current name of the hospital or care home.

(2) But sub-paragraph (1) is subject to any provision relating to the change of name which is made in any enactment or in any instrument made under an enactment.

57 Duty to give information about decision

(1) This paragraph applies if –

  (a)   a request is made for a standard authorisation, and

  (b)   the supervisory body are required by paragraph 50(1) to give the standard authorisation.

(2) The supervisory body must give a copy of the authorisation to each of the following –

  (a)   the relevant person's representative;

  (b)   the managing authority of the relevant hospital or care home;

  (c)   the relevant person;

  (d)   any section 39A IMCA;

  (e)   every interested person consulted by the best interests assessor.

(3) The supervisory body must comply with this paragraph as soon as practicable after they give the standard authorisation.

58 (1) This paragraph applies if –

  (a)   a request is made for a standard authorisation, and

  (b)   the supervisory body are prohibited by paragraph 50(2) from giving the standard authorisation.

(2) The supervisory body must give notice, stating that they are prohibited from giving the authorisation, to each of the following –

  (a)   the managing authority of the relevant hospital or care home;

  (b)   the relevant person;

  (c)   any section 39A IMCA;

  (d)   every interested person consulted by the best interests assessor.

(3) The supervisory body must comply with this paragraph as soon as practicable after it becomes apparent to them that they are prohibited from giving the authorisation.

59 Duty to give information about effect of authorisation

(1) This paragraph applies if a standard authorisation is given.

(2) The managing authority of the relevant hospital or care home must take such steps as are practicable to ensure that the relevant person understands all of the following –

(a) the effect of the authorisation;
(b) the right to make an application to the court to exercise its jurisdiction under section 21A;
(c) the right under Part 8 to request a review;
(d) the right to have a section 39D IMCA appointed;
(e) how to have a section 39D IMCA appointed.

(3) Those steps must be taken as soon as is practicable after the authorisation is given.

(4) Those steps must include the giving of appropriate information both orally and in writing.

(5) Any written information given to the relevant person must also be given by the managing authority to the relevant person's representative.

(6) They must give the information to the representative as soon as is practicable after it is given to the relevant person.

(7) Sub-paragraph (8) applies if the managing authority is notified that a section 39D IMCA has been appointed.

(8) As soon as is practicable after being notified, the managing authority must give the section 39D IMCA a copy of the written information given in accordance with sub-paragraph (4).

60 Records of authorisations

A supervisory body must keep a written record of all of the following information –

(a) the standard authorisations that they have given;
(b) the requests for standard authorisations in response to which they have not given an authorisation;
(c) in relation to each standard authorisation given: the matters stated in the authorisation in accordance with paragraph 55.

61 Variation of an authorisation

(1) A standard authorisation may not be varied except in accordance with Part 7 or 8.

(2) This paragraph does not affect the powers of the Court of Protection or of any other court.

62 Effect of decision about request made under paragraph 25 or 30

(1) This paragraph applies where the managing authority request a new standard authorisation under either of the following –

(a)   paragraph 25 (change in place of detention);
(b)   paragraph 30 (existing authorisation subject to review).

(2) If the supervisory body are required by paragraph 50(1) to give the new authorisation, the existing authorisation terminates at the time when the new authorisation comes into force.

(3) If the supervisory body are prohibited by paragraph 50(2) from giving the new authorisation, there is no effect on the existing authorisation's continuation in force.

63 When an authorisation is in force

(1) A standard authorisation comes into force when it is given.

(2) But if the authorisation provides for it to come into force at a later time, it comes into force at that time.

64 (1) A standard authorisation ceases to be in force at the end of the period stated in the authorisation in accordance with paragraph 55(1)(c).

(2) But if the authorisation terminates before then in accordance with paragraph 62(2) or any other provision of this Schedule, it ceases to be in force when the termination takes effect.

(3) This paragraph does not affect the powers of the Court of Protection or of any other court.

65 (1) This paragraph applies if a standard authorisation ceases to be in force.

(2) The supervisory body must give notice that the authorisation has ceased to be in force.

(3) The supervisory body must give that notice to all of the following –

(a)   the managing authority of the relevant hospital or care home;
(b)   the relevant person;
(c)   the relevant person's representative;
(d)   every interested person consulted by the best interests assessor.

(4) The supervisory body must give that notice as soon as practicable after the authorisation ceases to be in force.

66 When a request for a standard authorisation is 'disposed of'

A request for a standard authorisation is to be regarded for the purposes of this Schedule as disposed of if the supervisory body have given –

(a)   a copy of the authorisation in accordance with paragraph 57, or
(b)   notice in accordance with paragraph 58.

67 Right of third party to require consideration of whether authorisation needed

For the purposes of paragraphs 68 to 73 there is an unauthorised deprivation of liberty if –

  (a)   a person is already a detained resident in a hospital or care home, and
  (b)   the detention of the person is not authorised as mentioned in section 4A.

68 (1) If the following conditions are met, an eligible person may request the supervisory body to decide whether or not there is an unauthorised deprivation of liberty.

(2) The first condition is that the eligible person has notified the managing authority of the relevant hospital or care home that it appears to the eligible person that there is an unauthorised deprivation of liberty.

(3) The second condition is that the eligible person has asked the managing authority to request a standard authorisation in relation to the detention of the relevant person.

(4) The third condition is that the managing authority has not requested a standard authorisation within a reasonable period after the eligible person asks it to do so.

(5) In this paragraph 'eligible person' means any person other than the managing authority of the relevant hospital or care home.

69 (1) This paragraph applies if an eligible person requests the supervisory body to decide whether or not there is an unauthorised deprivation of liberty.

(2) The supervisory body must select and appoint a person to carry out an assessment of whether or not the relevant person is a detained resident.

(3) But the supervisory body need not select and appoint a person to carry out such an assessment in either of these cases.

(4) The first case is where it appears to the supervisory body that the request by the eligible person is frivolous or vexatious.

(5) The second case is where it appears to the supervisory body that –

  (a)   the question of whether or not there is an unauthorised deprivation of liberty has already been decided, and
  (b)   since that decision, there has been no change of circumstances which would merit the question being decided again.

(6) The supervisory body must not select and appoint a person to carry out an assessment under this paragraph unless it appears to the supervisory body that the person would be –

  (a)   suitable to carry out a best interests assessment (if one were obtained in connection with a request for a standard authorisation relating to the relevant person), and

    (b)   eligible to carry out such a best interests assessment.

(7) The supervisory body must notify the persons specified in sub-paragraph (8) –

    (a)   that the supervisory body have been requested to decide whether or not there is an unauthorised deprivation of liberty;

    (b)   of their decision whether or not to select and appoint a person to carry out an assessment under this paragraph;

    (c)   if their decision is to select and appoint a person, of the person appointed.

(8) The persons referred to in sub-paragraph (7) are –

    (a)   the eligible person who made the request under paragraph 68;

    (b)   the person to whom the request relates;

    (c)   the managing authority of the relevant hospital or care home;

    (d)   any section 39A IMCA.

70 (1) Regulations may be made about the period within which an assessment under paragraph 69 must be carried out.

(2) Regulations made under paragraph 129(3) apply in relation to the selection and appointment of a person under paragraph 69 as they apply to the selection of a person under paragraph 129 to carry out a best interests assessment.

(3) The following provisions apply to an assessment under paragraph 69 as they apply to an assessment carried out in connection with a request for a standard authorisation –

    (a)   paragraph 131 (examination and copying of records);

    (b)   paragraph 132 (representations);

    (c)   paragraphs 134 and 135(1) and (2) (duty to keep records and give copies).

(4) The copies of the assessment which the supervisory body are required to give under paragraph 135(2) must be given as soon as practicable after the supervisory body are themselves given a copy of the assessment.

71 (1) This paragraph applies if –

    (a)   the supervisory body obtain an assessment under paragraph 69,

    (b)   the assessment comes to the conclusion that the relevant person is a detained resident, and

    (c)   it appears to the supervisory body that the detention of the person is not authorised as mentioned in section 4A.

(2) This Schedule (including Part 5) applies as if the managing authority of the relevant hospital or care home had, in accordance with Part 4, requested the supervisory body to give a standard authorisation in relation to the relevant person.

(3) The managing authority of the relevant hospital or care home must supply the supervisory body with the information (if any) which the managing authority would, by virtue of paragraph 31, have had to include in a request for a standard authorisation.

(4) The supervisory body must notify the persons specified in paragraph 69(8) –

(a)   of the outcome of the assessment obtained under paragraph 69, and
(b)   that this Schedule applies as mentioned in sub-paragraph (2).

72 (1) This paragraph applies if –

(a)   the supervisory body obtain an assessment under paragraph 69, and
(b)   the assessment comes to the conclusion that the relevant person is not a detained resident.

(2) The supervisory body must notify the persons specified in paragraph 69(8) of the outcome of the assessment.

73 (1) This paragraph applies if –

(a)   the supervisory body obtain an assessment under paragraph 69,
(b)   the assessment comes to the conclusion that the relevant person is a detained resident, and
(c)   it appears to the supervisory body that the detention of the person is authorised as mentioned in section 4A.

(2) The supervisory body must notify the persons specified in paragraph 69(8) –

(a)   of the outcome of the assessment, and
(b)   that it appears to the supervisory body that the detention is authorised.

Amendment: Mental Health Act 2007.

PART 5
URGENT AUTHORISATIONS

74 Managing authority to give authorisation

Only the managing authority of the relevant hospital or care home may give an urgent authorisation.

75 The managing authority may give an urgent authorisation only if they are required to do so by paragraph 76 (as read with paragraph 77).

76 Duty to give authorisation

(1) The managing authority must give an urgent authorisation in either of the following cases.

(2) The first case is where –

- (a)   the managing authority are required to make a request under paragraph 24 or 25 for a standard authorisation, and
- (b)   they believe that the need for the relevant person to be a detained resident is so urgent that it is appropriate for the detention to begin before they make the request.

(3) The second case is where –

- (a)   the managing authority have made a request under paragraph 24 or 25 for a standard authorisation, and
- (b)   they believe that the need for the relevant person to be a detained resident is so urgent that it is appropriate for the detention to begin before the request is disposed of.

(4) References in this paragraph to the detention of the relevant person are references to the detention to which paragraph 24 or 25 relates.

(5) This paragraph is subject to paragraph 77.

77 (1) This paragraph applies where the managing authority have given an urgent authorisation ('the original authorisation') in connection with a case where a person is, or is to be, a detained resident ('the existing detention').

(2) No new urgent authorisation is to be given under paragraph 76 in connection with the existing detention.

(3) But the managing authority may request the supervisory body to extend the duration of the original authorisation.

(4) Only one request under sub-paragraph (3) may be made in relation to the original authorisation.

(5) Paragraphs 84 to 86 apply to any request made under sub-paragraph (3).

78 Terms of authorisation

(1) If the managing authority decide to give an urgent authorisation, they must decide the period during which the authorisation is to be in force.

(2) That period must not exceed 7 days.

79 Form of authorisation

An urgent authorisation must be in writing.

80 An urgent authorisation must state the following things –

- (a)   the name of the relevant person;
- (b)   the name of the relevant hospital or care home;
- (c)   the period during which the authorisation is to be in force;
- (d)   the purpose for which the authorisation is given.

81 (1) If the name of the relevant hospital or care home changes, the urgent authorisation is to be read as if it stated the current name of the hospital or care home.

(2) But sub-paragraph (1) is subject to any provision relating to the change of name which is made in any enactment or in any instrument made under an enactment.

82 Duty to keep records and give copies

(1) This paragraph applies if an urgent authorisation is given.

(2) The managing authority must keep a written record of why they have given the urgent authorisation.

(3) As soon as practicable after giving the authorisation, the managing authority must give a copy of the authorisation to all of the following –

- (a)   the relevant person;
- (b)   any section 39A IMCA.

83 Duty to give information about authorisation

(1) This paragraph applies if an urgent authorisation is given.

(2) The managing authority of the relevant hospital or care home must take such steps as are practicable to ensure that the relevant person understands all of the following –

- (a)   the effect of the authorisation;
- (b)   the right to make an application to the court to exercise its jurisdiction under section 21A.

(3) Those steps must be taken as soon as is practicable after the authorisation is given.

(4) Those steps must include the giving of appropriate information both orally and in writing.

84 Request for extension of duration

(1) This paragraph applies if the managing authority make a request under paragraph 77 for the supervisory body to extend the duration of the original authorisation.

(2) The managing authority must keep a written record of why they have made the request.

(3) The managing authority must give the relevant person notice that they have made the request.

(4) The supervisory body may extend the duration of the original authorisation if it appears to them that –

- (a)   the managing authority have made the required request for a standard authorisation,

(b)   there are exceptional reasons why it has not yet been possible for that request to be disposed of, and

(c)   it is essential for the existing detention to continue until the request is disposed of.

(5) The supervisory body must keep a written record that the request has been made to them.

(6) In this paragraph and paragraphs 85 and 86 –

(a)   'original authorisation' and 'existing detention' have the same meaning as in paragraph 77;

(b)   the required request for a standard authorisation is the request that is referred to in paragraph 76(2) or (3).

85 (1) This paragraph applies if, under paragraph 84, the supervisory body decide to extend the duration of the original authorisation.

(2) The supervisory body must decide the period of the extension.

(3) That period must not exceed 7 days.

(4) The supervisory body must give the managing authority notice stating the period of the extension.

(5) The managing authority must then vary the original authorisation so that it states the extended duration.

(6) Paragraphs 82(3) and 83 apply (with the necessary modifications) to the variation of the original authorisation as they apply to the giving of an urgent authorisation.

(7) The supervisory body must keep a written record of –

(a)   the outcome of the request, and

(b)   the period of the extension.

86 (1) This paragraph applies if, under paragraph 84, the supervisory body decide not to extend the duration of the original authorisation.

(2) The supervisory body must give the managing authority notice stating –

(a)   the decision, and

(b)   their reasons for making it.

(3) The managing authority must give a copy of that notice to all of the following –

(a)   the relevant person;

(b)   any section 39A IMCA.

(4) The supervisory body must keep a written record of the outcome of the request.

87 No variation

(1) An urgent authorisation may not be varied except in accordance with paragraph 85.

(2) This paragraph does not affect the powers of the Court of Protection or of any other court.

88 When an authorisation is in force

An urgent authorisation comes into force when it is given.

89

(1) An urgent authorisation ceases to be in force at the end of the period stated in the authorisation in accordance with paragraph 80(c) (subject to any variation in accordance with paragraph 85).

(2) But if the required request is disposed of before the end of that period, the urgent authorisation ceases to be in force as follows.

(3) If the supervisory body are required by paragraph 50(1) to give the requested authorisation, the urgent authorisation ceases to be in force when the requested authorisation comes into force.

(4) If the supervisory body are prohibited by paragraph 50(2) from giving the requested authorisation, the urgent authorisation ceases to be in force when the managing authority receive notice under paragraph 58.

(5) In this paragraph –

'required request' means the request referred to in paragraph 76(2) or (3);
'requested authorisation' means the standard authorisation to which the required request relates.

(6) This paragraph does not affect the powers of the Court of Protection or of any other court.

90 (1) This paragraph applies if an urgent authorisation ceases to be in force.

(2) The supervisory body must give notice that the authorisation has ceased to be in force.

(3) The supervisory body must give that notice to all of the following –

(a) the relevant person;
(b) any section 39A IMCA.

(4) The supervisory body must give that notice as soon as practicable after the authorisation ceases to be in force.

Amendment: Mental Health Act 2007.

PART 6
ELIGIBILITY REQUIREMENT NOT MET: SUSPENSION OF STANDARD AUTHORISATION

91 (1) This Part applies if the following conditions are met.

(2) The first condition is that a standard authorisation –

    (a)   has been given, and
    (b)   has not ceased to be in force.

(3) The second condition is that the managing authority of the relevant hospital or care home are satisfied that the relevant person has ceased to meet the eligibility requirement.

(4) But this Part does not apply if the relevant person is ineligible by virtue of paragraph 5 of Schedule 1A (in which case see Part 8).

92 The managing authority of the relevant hospital or care home must give the supervisory body notice that the relevant person has ceased to meet the eligibility requirement.

93 (1) This paragraph applies if the managing authority give the supervisory body notice under paragraph 92.

(2) The standard authorisation is suspended from the time when the notice is given.

(3) The supervisory body must give notice that the standard authorisation has been suspended to the following persons –

    (a)   the relevant person;
    (b)   the relevant person's representative;
    (c)   the managing authority of the relevant hospital or care home.

94 (1) This paragraph applies if, whilst the standard authorisation is suspended, the managing authority are satisfied that the relevant person meets the eligibility requirement again.

(2) The managing authority must give the supervisory body notice that the relevant person meets the eligibility requirement again.

95 (1) This paragraph applies if the managing authority give the supervisory body notice under paragraph 94.

(2) The standard authorisation ceases to be suspended from the time when the notice is given.

(3) The supervisory body must give notice that the standard authorisation has ceased to be suspended to the following persons –

    (a)   the relevant person;
    (b)   the relevant person's representative;
    (c)   any section 39D IMCA;

(d)   the managing authority of the relevant hospital or care home.

(4) The supervisory body must give notice under this paragraph as soon as practicable after they are given notice under paragraph 94.

96 (1) This paragraph applies if no notice is given under paragraph 94 before the end of the relevant 28 day period.

(2) The standard authorisation ceases to have effect at the end of the relevant 28 day period.

(3) The relevant 28 day period is the period of 28 days beginning with the day on which the standard authorisation is suspended under paragraph 93.

97 The effect of suspending the standard authorisation is that Part 1 ceases to apply for as long as the authorisation is suspended.

Amendment: Mental Health Act 2007.

PART 7
STANDARD AUTHORISATIONS: CHANGE IN SUPERVISORY RESPONSIBILITY

98 Application of this Part

(1) This Part applies if these conditions are met.

(2) The first condition is that a standard authorisation –

(a)   has been given, and
(b)   has not ceased to be in force.

(3) The second condition is that there is a change in supervisory responsibility.

(4) The third condition is that there is not a change in the place of detention (within the meaning of paragraph 25).

99 For the purposes of this Part there is a change in supervisory responsibility if –

(a)   one body ('the old supervisory body') have ceased to be supervisory body in relation to the standard authorisation, and
(b)   a different body ('the new supervisory body') have become supervisory body in relation to the standard authorisation.

100 Effect of change in supervisory responsibility

(1) The new supervisory body becomes the supervisory body in relation to the authorisation.

(2) Anything done by or in relation to the old supervisory body in connection with the authorisation has effect, so far as is necessary for continuing its effect after the change, as if done by or in relation to the new supervisory body.

(3) Anything which relates to the authorisation and which is in the process of being done by or in relation to the old supervisory body at the time of the change may be continued by or in relation to the new supervisory body.

(4) But –

    (a)   the old supervisory body do not, by virtue of this paragraph, cease to be liable for anything done by them in connection with the authorisation before the change; and

    (b)   the new supervisory body do not, by virtue of this paragraph, become liable for any such thing.

Amendment: Mental Health Act 2007.

PART 8
STANDARD AUTHORISATIONS: REVIEW

101 Application of this Part

(1) This Part applies if a standard authorisation –

    (a)   has been given, and
    (b)   has not ceased to be in force.

(2) Paragraphs 102 to 122 are subject to paragraphs 123 to 125.

102 Review by supervisory body

(1) The supervisory body may at any time carry out a review of the standard authorisation in accordance with this Part.

(2) The supervisory body must carry out such a review if they are requested to do so by an eligible person.

(3) Each of the following is an eligible person –

    (a)   the relevant person;
    (b)   the relevant person's representative;
    (c)   the managing authority of the relevant hospital or care home.

103 Request for review

(1) An eligible person may, at any time, request the supervisory body to carry out a review of the standard authorisation in accordance with this Part.

(2) The managing authority of the relevant hospital or care home must make such a request if one or more of the qualifying requirements appear to them to be reviewable.

104 Grounds for review

(1) Paragraphs 105 to 107 set out the grounds on which the qualifying requirements are reviewable.

(2) A qualifying requirement is not reviewable on any other ground.

105 Non-qualification ground

(1) Any of the following qualifying requirements is reviewable on the ground that the relevant person does not meet the requirement –

- (a)   the age requirement;
- (b)   the mental health requirement;
- (c)   the mental capacity requirement;
- (d)   the best interests requirement;
- (e)   the no refusals requirement.

(2) The eligibility requirement is reviewable on the ground that the relevant person is ineligible by virtue of paragraph 5 of Schedule 1A.

(3) The ground in sub-paragraph (1) and the ground in sub-paragraph (2) are referred to as the non-qualification ground.

106 Change of reason ground

(1) Any of the following qualifying requirements is reviewable on the ground set out in sub-paragraph (2) –

- (a)   the mental health requirement;
- (b)   the mental capacity requirement;
- (c)   the best interests requirement;
- (d)   the eligibility requirement;
- (e)   the no refusals requirement.

(2) The ground is that the reason why the relevant person meets the requirement is not the reason stated in the standard authorisation.

(3) This ground is referred to as the change of reason ground.

107 Variation of conditions ground

(1) The best interests requirement is reviewable on the ground that –

- (a)   there has been a change in the relevant person's case, and
- (b)   because of that change, it would be appropriate to vary the conditions to which the standard authorisation is subject.

(2) This ground is referred to as the variation of conditions ground.

(3) A reference to varying the conditions to which the standard authorisation is subject is a reference to –

- (a)   amendment of an existing condition,
- (b)   omission of an existing condition, or
- (c)   inclusion of a new condition (whether or not there are already any existing conditions).

108 Notice that review to be carried out

(1) If the supervisory body are to carry out a review of the standard authorisation, they must give notice of the review to the following persons –

(a)   the relevant person;

(b)   the relevant person's representative;

(c)   the managing authority of the relevant hospital or care home.

(2) The supervisory body must give the notice –

(a)   before they begin the review, or

(b)   if that is not practicable, as soon as practicable after they have begun it.

(3) This paragraph does not require the supervisory body to give notice to any person who has requested the review.

109 Starting a review

To start a review of the standard authorisation, the supervisory body must decide which, if any, of the qualifying requirements appear to be reviewable.

110 No reviewable qualifying requirements

(1) This paragraph applies if no qualifying requirements appear to be reviewable.

(2) This Part does not require the supervisory body to take any action in respect of the standard authorisation.

111 One or more reviewable qualifying requirements

(1) This paragraph applies if one or more qualifying requirements appear to be reviewable.

(2) The supervisory body must secure that a separate review assessment is carried out in relation to each qualifying requirement which appears to be reviewable.

(3) But sub-paragraph (2) does not require the supervisory body to secure that a best interests review assessment is carried out in a case where the best interests requirement appears to the supervisory body to be non-assessable.

(4) The best interests requirement is non-assessable if –

(a)   the requirement is reviewable only on the variation of conditions ground, and

(b)   the change in the relevant person's case is not significant.

(5) In making any decision whether the change in the relevant person's case is significant, regard must be had to –

(a)   the nature of the change, and

(b)   the period that the change is likely to last for.

112 Review assessments

(1) A review assessment is an assessment of whether the relevant person meets a qualifying requirement.

(2) In relation to a review assessment –

    (a)   a negative conclusion is a conclusion that the relevant person does not meet the qualifying requirement to which the assessment relates;

    (b)   a positive conclusion is a conclusion that the relevant person meets the qualifying requirement to which the assessment relates.

(3) An age review assessment is a review assessment carried out in relation to the age requirement.

(4) A mental health review assessment is a review assessment carried out in relation to the mental health requirement.

(5) A mental capacity review assessment is a review assessment carried out in relation to the mental capacity requirement.

(6) A best interests review assessment is a review assessment carried out in relation to the best interests requirement.

(7) An eligibility review assessment is a review assessment carried out in relation to the eligibility requirement.

(8) A no refusals review assessment is a review assessment carried out in relation to the no refusals requirement.

113 (1) In carrying out a review assessment, the assessor must comply with any duties which would be imposed upon him under Part 4 if the assessment were being carried out in connection with a request for a standard authorisation.

(2) But in the case of a best interests review assessment, paragraphs 43 and 44 do not apply.

(3) Instead of what is required by paragraph 43, the best interests review assessment must include recommendations about whether –and, if so, how –it would be appropriate to vary the conditions to which the standard authorisation is subject.

114 Best interests requirement reviewable but non-assessable

(1) This paragraph applies in a case where –

    (a)   the best interests requirement appears to be reviewable, but

    (b)   in accordance with paragraph 111(3), the supervisory body are not required to secure that a best interests review assessment is carried out.

(2) The supervisory body may vary the conditions to which the standard authorisation is subject in such ways (if any) as the supervisory body think are appropriate in the circumstances.

115 Best interests review assessment positive

(1) This paragraph applies in a case where –

    (a)   a best interests review assessment is carried out, and

    (b)   the assessment comes to a positive conclusion.

(2) The supervisory body must decide the following questions –

    (a)   whether or not the best interests requirement is reviewable on the change of reason ground;

    (b)   whether or not the best interests requirement is reviewable on the variation of conditions ground;

    (c)   if so, whether or not the change in the person's case is significant.

(3) If the supervisory body decide that the best interests requirement is reviewable on the change of reason ground, they must vary the standard authorisation so that it states the reason why the relevant person now meets that requirement.

(4) If the supervisory body decide that –

    (a)   the best interests requirement is reviewable on the variation of conditions ground, and

    (b)   the change in the relevant person's case is not significant,

they may vary the conditions to which the standard authorisation is subject in such ways (if any) as they think are appropriate in the circumstances.

(5) If the supervisory body decide that –

    (a)   the best interests requirement is reviewable on the variation of conditions ground, and

    (b)   the change in the relevant person's case is significant,

they must vary the conditions to which the standard authorisation is subject in such ways as they think are appropriate in the circumstances.

(6) If the supervisory body decide that the best interests requirement is not reviewable on –

    (a)   the change of reason ground, or

    (b)   the variation of conditions ground,

this Part does not require the supervisory body to take any action in respect of the standard authorisation so far as the best interests requirement relates to it.

116 Mental health, mental capacity, eligibility or no refusals review assessment positive

(1) This paragraph applies if the following conditions are met.

(2) The first condition is that one or more of the following are carried out –

    (a)   a mental health review assessment;

    (b)   a mental capacity review assessment;

    (c)   an eligibility review assessment;

    (d)   a no refusals review assessment.

(3) The second condition is that each assessment carried out comes to a positive conclusion.

(4) The supervisory body must decide whether or not each of the assessed qualifying requirements is reviewable on the change of reason ground.

(5) If the supervisory body decide that any of the assessed qualifying requirements is reviewable on the change of reason ground, they must vary the standard authorisation so that it states the reason why the relevant person now meets the requirement or requirements in question.

(6) If the supervisory body decide that none of the assessed qualifying requirements are reviewable on the change of reason ground, this Part does not require the supervisory body to take any action in respect of the standard authorisation so far as those requirements relate to it.

(7) An assessed qualifying requirement is a qualifying requirement in relation to which a review assessment is carried out.

117 One or more review assessments negative

(1) This paragraph applies if one or more of the review assessments carried out comes to a negative conclusion.

(2) The supervisory body must terminate the standard authorisation with immediate effect.

118 Completion of a review

(1) The review of the standard authorisation is complete in any of the following cases.

(2) The first case is where paragraph 110 applies.

(3) The second case is where –

- (a) paragraph 111 applies, and
- (b) paragraph 117 requires the supervisory body to terminate the standard authorisation.

(4) In such a case, the supervisory body need not comply with any of the other provisions of paragraphs 114 to 116 which would be applicable to the review (were it not for this sub-paragraph).

(5) The third case is where –

- (a) paragraph 111 applies,
- (b) paragraph 117 does not require the supervisory body to terminate the standard authorisation, and
- (c) the supervisory body comply with all of the provisions of paragraphs 114 to 116 (so far as they are applicable to the review).

119 Variations under this Part

Any variation of the standard authorisation made under this Part must be in writing.

120 Notice of outcome of review

(1) When the review of the standard authorisation is complete, the supervisory body must give notice to all of the following –

- (a)   the managing authority of the relevant hospital or care home;
- (b)   the relevant person;
- (c)   the relevant person's representative;
- (d)   any section 39D IMCA.

(2) That notice must state –

- (a)   the outcome of the review, and
- (b)   what variation (if any) has been made to the authorisation under this Part.

121 Records

A supervisory body must keep a written record of the following information –

- (a)   each request for a review that is made to them;
- (b)   the outcome of each request;
- (c)   each review which they carry out;
- (d)   the outcome of each review which they carry out;
- (e)   any variation of an authorisation made in consequence of a review.

122 Relationship between review and suspension under Part 6

(1) This paragraph applies if a standard authorisation is suspended in accordance with Part 6.

(2) No review may be requested under this Part whilst the standard authorisation is suspended.

(3) If a review has already been requested, or is being carried out, when the standard authorisation is suspended, no steps are to be taken in connection with that review whilst the authorisation is suspended.

123 Relationship between review and request for new authorisation

(1) This paragraph applies if, in accordance with paragraph 24 (as read with paragraph 29), the managing authority of the relevant hospital or care home make a request for a new standard authorisation which would be in force after the expiry of the existing authorisation.

(2) No review may be requested under this Part until the request for the new standard authorisation has been disposed of.

(3) If a review has already been requested, or is being carried out, when the new standard authorisation is requested, no steps are to be taken in connection with that review until the request for the new standard authorisation has been disposed of.

124 (1) This paragraph applies if –

(a)   a review under this Part has been requested, or is being carried out, and

(b)   the managing authority of the relevant hospital or care home make a request under paragraph 30 for a new standard authorisation which would be in force on or before, and after, the expiry of the existing authorisation.

(2) No steps are to be taken in connection with the review under this Part until the request for the new standard authorisation has been disposed of.

125 In paragraphs 123 and 124 –

(a)   the existing authorisation is the authorisation referred to in paragraph 101;

(b)   the expiry of the existing authorisation is the time when it is expected to cease to be in force.

Amendment: Mental Health Act 2007.

PART 9
ASSESSMENTS UNDER THIS SCHEDULE

126 Introduction

This Part contains provision about assessments under this Schedule.

127 An assessment under this Schedule is either of the following –

(a)   an assessment carried out in connection with a request for a standard authorisation under Part 4;

(b)   a review assessment carried out in connection with a review of a standard authorisation under Part 8.

128 In this Part, in relation to an assessment under this Schedule –

'assessor' means the person carrying out the assessment;
'relevant procedure' means –
    (a)   the request for the standard authorisation, or
    (b)   the review of the standard authorisation;

'supervisory body' means the supervisory body responsible for securing that the assessment is carried out.

129 Supervisory body to select assessor

(1) It is for the supervisory body to select a person to carry out an assessment under this Schedule.

(2) The supervisory body must not select a person to carry out an assessment unless the person –

(a) appears to the supervisory body to be suitable to carry out the assessment (having regard, in particular, to the type of assessment and the person to be assessed), and

(b) is eligible to carry out the assessment.

(3) Regulations may make provision about the selection, and eligibility, of persons to carry out assessments under this Schedule.

(4) Sub-paragraphs (5) and (6) apply if two or more assessments are to be obtained for the purposes of the relevant procedure.

(5) In a case where the assessments to be obtained include a mental health assessment and a best interests assessment, the supervisory body must not select the same person to carry out both assessments.

(6) Except as prohibited by sub-paragraph (5), the supervisory body may select the same person to carry out any number of the assessments which the person appears to be suitable, and is eligible, to carry out.

130 (1) This paragraph applies to regulations under paragraph 129(3).

(2) The regulations may make provision relating to a person's –

(a) qualifications,
(b) skills,
(c) training,
(d) experience,
(e) relationship to, or connection with, the relevant person or any other person,
(f) involvement in the care or treatment of the relevant person,
(g) connection with the supervisory body, or
(h) connection with the relevant hospital or care home, or with any other establishment or undertaking.

(3) The provision that the regulations may make in relation to a person's training may provide for particular training to be specified by the appropriate authority otherwise than in the regulations.

(4) In sub-paragraph (3) the 'appropriate authority' means –

(a) in relation to England: the Secretary of State;
(b) in relation to Wales: the National Assembly for Wales.

(5) The regulations may make provision requiring a person to be insured in respect of liabilities that may arise in connection with the carrying out of an assessment.

(6) In relation to cases where two or more assessments are to be obtained for the purposes of the relevant procedure, the regulations may limit the number, kind or combination of assessments which a particular person is eligible to carry out.

(7) Sub-paragraphs (2) to (6) do not limit the generality of the provision that may be made in the regulations.

131 Examination and copying of records

An assessor may, at all reasonable times, examine and take copies of –

(a)   any health record,
(b)   any record of, or held by, a local authority and compiled in accordance with a social services function, and
(c)   any record held by a person registered under Part 2 of the Care Standards Act 2000 or Chapter 2 of Part 1 of the Health and Social Care Act 2008,

which the assessor considers may be relevant to the assessment which is being carried out.

132 Representations

In carrying out an assessment under this Schedule, the assessor must take into account any information given, or submissions made, by any of the following –

(a)   the relevant person's representative;
(b)   any section 39A IMCA;
(c)   any section 39C IMCA;
(d)   any section 39D IMCA.

133 Assessments to stop if any comes to negative conclusion

(1) This paragraph applies if an assessment under this Schedule comes to the conclusion that the relevant person does not meet one of the qualifying requirements.

(2) This Schedule does not require the supervisory body to secure that any other assessments under this Schedule are carried out in relation to the relevant procedure.

(3) The supervisory body must give notice to any assessor who is carrying out another assessment in connection with the relevant procedure that they are to cease carrying out that assessment.

(4) If an assessor receives such notice, this Schedule does not require the assessor to continue carrying out that assessment.

134 Duty to keep records and give copies

(1) This paragraph applies if an assessor has carried out an assessment under this Schedule (whatever conclusions the assessment has come to).

(2) The assessor must keep a written record of the assessment.

(3) As soon as practicable after carrying out the assessment, the assessor must give copies of the assessment to the supervisory body.

135 (1) This paragraph applies to the supervisory body if they are given a copy of an assessment under this Schedule.

(2) The supervisory body must give copies of the assessment to all of the following –

    (a)   the managing authority of the relevant hospital or care home;
    (b)   the relevant person;
    (c)   any section 39A IMCA;
    (d)   the relevant person's representative.

(3) If –

    (a)   the assessment is obtained in relation to a request for a standard authorisation, and
    (b)   the supervisory body are required by paragraph 50(1) to give the standard authorisation,

the supervisory body must give the copies of the assessment when they give copies of the authorisation in accordance with paragraph 57.

(4) If –

    (a)   the assessment is obtained in relation to a request for a standard authorisation, and
    (b)   the supervisory body are prohibited by paragraph 50(2) from giving the standard authorisation,

the supervisory body must give the copies of the assessment when they give notice in accordance with paragraph 58.

(5) If the assessment is obtained in connection with the review of a standard authorisation, the supervisory body must give the copies of the assessment when they give notice in accordance with paragraph 120.

136 (1) This paragraph applies to the supervisory body if –

    (a)   they are given a copy of a best interests assessment, and
    (b)   the assessment includes, in accordance with paragraph 44(2), a statement that it appears to the assessor that there is an unauthorised deprivation of liberty.

(2) The supervisory body must notify all of the persons listed in sub-paragraph (3) that the assessment includes such a statement.

(3) Those persons are –

    (a)   the managing authority of the relevant hospital or care home;
    (b)   the relevant person;
    (c)   any section 39A IMCA;
    (d)   any interested person consulted by the best interests assessor.

(4) The supervisory body must comply with this paragraph when (or at some time before) they comply with paragraph 135.

Amendment: Mental Health Act 2007; SI 2010/813.

PART 10
RELEVANT PERSON'S REPRESENTATIVE

137 The representative

In this Schedule the relevant person's representative is the person appointed as such in accordance with this Part.

138 (1) Regulations may make provision about the selection and appointment of representatives.

(2) In this Part such regulations are referred to as 'appointment regulations'.

139 Supervisory body to appoint representative

(1) The supervisory body must appoint a person to be the relevant person's representative as soon as practicable after a standard authorisation is given.

(2) The supervisory body must appoint a person to be the relevant person's representative if a vacancy arises whilst a standard authorisation is in force.

(3) Where a vacancy arises, the appointment under sub-paragraph (2) is to be made as soon as practicable after the supervisory body becomes aware of the vacancy.

140 (1) The selection of a person for appointment under paragraph 139 must not be made unless it appears to the person making the selection that the prospective representative would, if appointed –

(a)   maintain contact with the relevant person,
(b)   represent the relevant person in matters relating to or connected with this Schedule, and
(c)   support the relevant person in matters relating to or connected with this Schedule.

141 (1) Any appointment of a representative for a relevant person is in addition to, and does not affect, any appointment of a donee or deputy.

(2) The functions of any representative are in addition to, and do not affect –

(a)   the authority of any donee,
(b)   the powers of any deputy, or
(c)   any powers of the court.

142 Appointment regulations

Appointment regulations may provide that the procedure for appointing a representative may begin at any time after a request for a standard authorisation is made (including a time before the request has been disposed of).

143 (1) Appointment regulations may make provision about who is to select a person for appointment as a representative.

(2) But regulations under this paragraph may only provide for the following to make a selection –

- (a)   the relevant person, if he has capacity in relation to the question of which person should be his representative;
- (b)   a donee of a lasting power of attorney granted by the relevant person, if it is within the scope of his authority to select a person;
- (c)   a deputy, if it is within the scope of his authority to select a person;
- (d)   a best interests assessor;
- (e)   the supervisory body.

(3) Regulations under this paragraph may provide that a selection by the relevant person, a donee or a deputy is subject to approval by a best interests assessor or the supervisory body.

(4) Regulations under this paragraph may provide that, if more than one selection is necessary in connection with the appointment of a particular representative –

- (a)   the same person may make more than one selection;
- (b)   different persons may make different selections.

(5) For the purposes of this paragraph a best interests assessor is a person carrying out a best interests assessment in connection with the standard authorisation in question (including the giving of that authorisation).

144 (1) Appointment regulations may make provision about who may, or may not, be –

- (a)   selected for appointment as a representative, or
- (b)   appointed as a representative.

(2) Regulations under this paragraph may relate to any of the following matters –

- (a)   a person's age;
- (b)   a person's suitability;
- (c)   a person's independence;
- (d)   a person's willingness;
- (e)   a person's qualifications.

145 Appointment regulations may make provision about the formalities of appointing a person as a representative.

146 In a case where a best interests assessor is to select a person to be appointed as a representative, appointment regulations may provide for the variation of the assessor's duties in relation to the assessment which he is carrying out.

147 Monitoring of representatives

Regulations may make provision requiring the managing authority of the relevant hospital or care home to –

(a) monitor, and

(b) report to the supervisory body on,

the extent to which a representative is maintaining contact with the relevant person.

148 Termination

Regulations may make provision about the circumstances in which the appointment of a person as the relevant person's representative ends or may be ended.

149 Regulations may make provision about the formalities of ending the appointment of a person as a representative.

150 Suspension of representative's functions

(1) Regulations may make provision about the circumstances in which functions exercisable by, or in relation to, the relevant person's representative (whether under this Schedule or not) may be –

(a) suspended, and

(b) if suspended, revived.

(2) The regulations may make provision about the formalities for giving effect to the suspension or revival of a function.

(3) The regulations may make provision about the effect of the suspension or revival of a function.

151 Payment of representative

Regulations may make provision for payments to be made to, or in relation to, persons exercising functions as the relevant person's representative.

152 Regulations under this Part

The provisions of this Part which specify provision that may be made in regulations under this Part do not affect the generality of the power to make such regulations.

153 Effect of appointment of section 39C IMCA

Paragraphs 159 and 160 make provision about the exercise of functions by, or towards, the relevant person's representative during periods when –

(a) no person is appointed as the relevant person's representative, but

(b) a person is appointed as a section 39C IMCA.

Amendment: Mental Health Act 2007.

PART 11
IMCAS

154 Application of Part

This Part applies for the purposes of this Schedule.

155 The IMCAs

A section 39A IMCA is an independent mental capacity advocate appointed under section 39A.

156 A section 39C IMCA is an independent mental capacity advocate appointed under section 39C

157 A section 39D IMCA is an independent mental capacity advocate appointed under section 39D.

158 An IMCA is a section 39A IMCA or a section 39C IMCA or a section 39D IMCA.

159 Section 39C IMCA: functions

(1) This paragraph applies if, and for as long as, there is a section 39C IMCA.

(2) In the application of the relevant provisions, references to the relevant person's representative are to be read as references to the section 39C IMCA.

(3) But sub-paragraph (2) does not apply to any function under the relevant provisions for as long as the function is suspended in accordance with provision made under Part 10.

(4) In this paragraph and paragraph 160 the relevant provisions are –

    (a)   paragraph 102(3)(b) (request for review under Part 8);
    (b)   paragraph 108(1)(b) (notice of review under Part 8);
    (c)   paragraph 120(1)(c) (notice of outcome of review under Part 8).

160 (1) This paragraph applies if –

    (a)   a person is appointed as the relevant person's representative, and
    (b)   a person accordingly ceases to hold an appointment as a section 39C IMCA.

(2) Where a function under a relevant provision has been exercised by, or towards, the section 39C IMCA, there is no requirement for that function to be exercised again by, or towards, the relevant person's representative.

161 Section 39A IMCA: restriction of functions

(1) This paragraph applies if –

    (a)   there is a section 39A IMCA, and

(b) a person is appointed under Part 10 to be the relevant person's representative (whether or not that person, or any person subsequently appointed, is currently the relevant person's representative).

(2) The duties imposed on, and the powers exercisable by, the section 39A IMCA do not apply.

(3) The duties imposed on, and the powers exercisable by, any other person do not apply, so far as they fall to be performed or exercised towards the section 39A IMCA.

(4) But sub-paragraph (2) does not apply to any power of challenge exercisable by the section 39A IMCA.

(5) And sub-paragraph (3) does not apply to any duty or power of any other person so far as it relates to any power of challenge exercisable by the section 39A IMCA.

(6) Before exercising any power of challenge, the section 39A IMCA must take the views of the relevant person's representative into account.

(7) A power of challenge is a power to make an application to the court to exercise its jurisdiction under section 21A in connection with the giving of the standard authorisation.

Amendment: Mental Health Act 2007.

PART 12
MISCELLANEOUS

162 Monitoring of operation of Schedule

(1) Regulations may make provision for, and in connection with, requiring one or more prescribed bodies to monitor, and report on, the operation of this Schedule in relation to England.

(2) The regulations may, in particular, give a prescribed body authority to do one or more of the following things –

(a) to visit hospitals and care homes;
(b) to visit and interview persons accommodated in hospitals and care homes;
(c) to require the production of, and to inspect, records relating to the care or treatment of persons.

(3) 'Prescribed' means prescribed in regulations under this paragraph.

163 (1) Regulations may make provision for, and in connection with, enabling the National Assembly for Wales to monitor, and report on, the operation of this Schedule in relation to Wales.

(2) The National Assembly may direct one or more persons or bodies to carry out the Assembly's functions under regulations under this paragraph.

164 Disclosure of information

(1) Regulations may require either or both of the following to disclose prescribed information to prescribed bodies –

   (a)   supervisory bodies;
   (b)   managing authorities of hospitals or care homes.

(2) 'Prescribed' means prescribed in regulations under this paragraph.

(3) Regulations under this paragraph may only prescribe information relating to matters with which this Schedule is concerned.

165 Directions by National Assembly in relation to supervisory functions

(1) The National Assembly for Wales may direct a Local Health Board to exercise in relation to its area any supervisory functions which are specified in the direction.

(2) Directions under this paragraph must not preclude the National Assembly from exercising the functions specified in the directions.

(3) In this paragraph 'supervisory functions' means functions which the National Assembly have as supervisory body, so far as they are exercisable in relation to hospitals (whether NHS or independent hospitals, and whether in Wales or England).

166 (1) This paragraph applies where, under paragraph 165, a Local Health Board ('the specified LHB') is directed to exercise supervisory functions ('delegated functions').

(2) The National Assembly for Wales may give directions to the specified LHB about the Board's exercise of delegated functions.

(3) The National Assembly may give directions for any delegated functions to be exercised, on behalf of the specified LHB, by a committee, sub-committee or officer of that Board.

(4) The National Assembly may give directions providing for any delegated functions to be exercised by the specified LHB jointly with one or more other Local Health Boards.

(5) Where, under sub-paragraph (4), delegated functions are exercisable jointly, the National Assembly may give directions providing for the functions to be exercised, on behalf of the Local Health Boards in question, by a joint committee or joint sub-committee.

167 (1) Directions under paragraph 165 must be given in regulations.

(2) Directions under paragraph 166 may be given –

   (a)   in regulations, or
   (b)   by instrument in writing.

168 The power under paragraph 165 or paragraph 166 to give directions includes power to vary or revoke directions given under that paragraph.

169 Notices

Any notice under this Schedule must be in writing.

171 Regulations

(1) This paragraph applies to all regulations under this Schedule, except regulations under paragraph 162, 163, 167 or 183.

(2) It is for the Secretary of State to make such regulations in relation to authorisations under this Schedule which relate to hospitals and care homes situated in England.

(3) It is for the National Assembly for Wales to make such regulations in relation to authorisations under this Schedule which relate to hospitals and care homes situated in Wales.

171 It is for the Secretary of State to make regulations under paragraph 162.

172 It is for the National Assembly for Wales to make regulations under paragraph 163 or 167.

173 (1) This paragraph applies to regulations under paragraph 183.

(2) It is for the Secretary of State to make such regulations in relation to cases where a question as to the ordinary residence of a person is to be determined by the Secretary of State.

(3) It is for the National Assembly for Wales to make such regulations in relation to cases where a question as to the ordinary residence of a person is to be determined by the National Assembly.

Amendment: Mental Health Act 2007.

PART 13
INTERPRETATION

174 Introduction

This Part applies for the purposes of this Schedule.

175 Hospitals and their managing authorities

(1) 'Hospital' means –

   (a)   an NHS hospital, or
   (b)   an independent hospital.

(2) 'NHS hospital' means –

   (a)   a health service hospital as defined by section 275 of the National Health Service Act 2006 or section 206 of the National Health Service (Wales) Act 2006, or

   (b)   a hospital as defined by section 206 of the National Health Service (Wales) Act 2006 vested in a Local Health Board.

(3) 'Independent hospital' –

   (a)   in relation to England, means a hospital as defined by section 275 of the National Health Service Act 2006 that is not an NHS hospital; and

   (b)   in relation to Wales, means a hospital as defined by section 2 of the Care Standards Act 2000 that is not an NHS hospital.

176 (1) 'Managing authority', in relation to an NHS hospital, means –

   (a)   if the hospital –

      (i)   is vested in the appropriate national authority for the purposes of its functions under the National Health Service Act 2006 or of the National Health Service (Wales) Act 2006, or

      (ii)   consists of any accommodation provided by a local authority and used as a hospital by or on behalf of the appropriate national authority under either of those Acts,

the Local Health Board or Special Health Authority responsible for the administration of the hospital;

   (aa)   in relation to England, if the hospital falls within paragraph (a)(i) or (ii) and no Special Health Authority has responsibility for its administration, the Secretary of State;

   (b)   if the hospital is vested in a National Health Service trust or NHS foundation trust, that trust;

   (c)   if the hospital is vested in a Local Health Board, that Board.

(2) For this purpose the appropriate national authority is –

   (a)   in relation to England: the Secretary of State;

   (b)   in relation to Wales. the National Assembly for Wales;

   (c)   in relation to England and Wales: the Secretary of State and the National Assembly acting jointly.

177

'Managing authority', in relation to an independent hospital, means –

      (a)   in relation to England, the person registered, or required to be registered, under Chapter 2 of Part 1 of the Health and Social Care Act 2008 in respect of regulated activities (within the meaning of that Part) carried on in the hospital, and

      (b)   in relation to Wales, the person registered, or required to be registered, under Part 2 of the Care Standards Act 2000 in respect of the hospital.

178 Care homes and their managing authorities

'Care home' has the meaning given by section 3 of the Care Standards Act 2000.

179

'Managing authority', in relation to a care home, means –
- (a) in relation to England, the person registered, or required to be registered, under Chapter 2 of Part 1 of the Health and Social Care Act 2008 in respect of the provision of residential accommodation, together with nursing or personal care, in the care home, and
- (b) in relation to Wales, the person registered, or required to be registered, under Part 2 of the Care Standards Act 2000 in respect of the care home.

180 Supervisory bodies: hospitals

(1) The identity of the supervisory body is determined under this paragraph in cases where the relevant hospital is situated in England.

(2) If the relevant person is ordinarily resident in the area of a local authority in England, the supervisory body are that local authority.

(3) If the relevant person is not ordinarily resident in England and the National Assembly for Wales or a Local Health Board commission the relevant care or treatment, the National Assembly are the supervisory body.

(4) In any other case, the supervisory body are the local authority for the area in which the relevant hospital is situated.

(4A) 'Local authority' means –
- (a) the council of a county;
- (b) the council of a district for which there is no county council;
- (c) the council of a London borough;
- (d) the Common Council of the City of London;
- (e) the Council of the Isles of Scilly.

(5) If a hospital is situated in the areas of two (or more) local authorities, it is to be regarded for the purposes of sub-paragraph (4) as situated in whichever of the areas the greater (or greatest) part of the hospital is situated.

181 (1) The identity of the supervisory body is determined under this paragraph in cases where the relevant hospital is situated in Wales.

(2) The National Assembly for Wales are the supervisory body.

(3) But if the relevant person is ordinarily resident in the area of a local authority in England, the supervisory body are that local authority.

(4) 'Local authority' means –
- (a) the council of a county;

(b)   the council of a district for which there is no county council;
(c)   the council of a London borough;
(d)   the Common Council of the City of London;
(e)   the Council of the Isles of Scilly.

182 Supervisory bodies: care homes

(1) The identity of the supervisory body is determined under this paragraph in cases where the relevant care home is situated in England or in Wales.

(2) The supervisory body are the local authority for the area in which the relevant person is ordinarily resident.

(3) But if the relevant person is not ordinarily resident in the area of a local authority, the supervisory body are the local authority for the area in which the care home is situated.

(4) In relation to England 'local authority' means –

(a)   the council of a county;
(b)   the council of a district for which there is no county council;
(c)   the council of a London borough;
(d)   the Common Council of the City of London;
(e)   the Council of the Isles of Scilly.

(5) In relation to Wales 'local authority' means the council of a county or county borough.

(6) If a care home is situated in the areas of two (or more) local authorities, it is to be regarded for the purposes of sub-paragraph (3) as situated in whichever of the areas the greater (or greatest) part of the care home is situated.

183 Supervisory bodies: determination of place of ordinary residence

(1) Subsections (5) and (6) of section 24 of the National Assistance Act 1948 (deemed place of ordinary residence) apply to any determination of where a person is ordinarily resident for the purposes of paragraphs 180, 181 and 182 as those subsections apply to such a determination for the purposes specified in those subsections.

(2) In the application of section 24(6) of the 1948 Act by virtue of subsection (1) to any determination of where a person is ordinarily resident for the purposes of paragraph 182, section 24(6) is to be read as if it referred to a hospital vested in a Local Health Board as well as to hospitals vested in the Secretary of State and the other bodies mentioned in section 24(6).

(3) Any question arising as to the ordinary residence of a person is to be determined by the Secretary of State or by the National Assembly for Wales.

(4) The Secretary of State and the National Assembly must make and publish arrangements for determining which cases are to be dealt with by the Secretary of State and which are to be dealt with by the National Assembly.

(5) Those arrangements may include provision for the Secretary of State and the National Assembly to agree, in relation to any question that has arisen, which of them is to deal with the case.

(6) Regulations may make provision about arrangements that are to have effect before, upon, or after the determination of any question as to the ordinary residence of a person.

(7) The regulations may, in particular, authorise or require a local authority to do any or all of the following things –

  (a) to act as supervisory body even though it may wish to dispute that it is the supervisory body;
  (b) to become the supervisory body in place of another local authority;
  (c) to recover from another local authority expenditure incurred in exercising functions as the supervisory body.

184 Same body managing authority and supervisory body

(1) This paragraph applies if, in connection with a particular person's detention as a resident in a hospital or care home, the same body are both –

  (a) the managing authority of the relevant hospital or care home, and
  (b) the supervisory body.

(2) The fact that a single body are acting in both capacities does not prevent the body from carrying out functions under this Schedule in each capacity.

(3) But, in such a case, this Schedule has effect subject to any modifications contained in regulations that may be made for this purpose.

185 Interested persons

Each of the following is an interested person –

  (a) the relevant person's spouse or civil partner;
  (b) where the relevant person and another person of the opposite sex are not married to each other but are living together as husband and wife: the other person;
  (c) where the relevant person and another person of the same sex are not civil partners of each other but are living together as if they were civil partners: the other person;
  (d) the relevant person's children and step-children;
  (e) the relevant person's parents and step-parents;
  (f) the relevant person's brothers and sisters, half-brothers and half-sisters, and stepbrothers and stepsisters;
  (g) the relevant person's grandparents;
  (h) a deputy appointed for the relevant person by the court;
  (i) a donee of a lasting power of attorney granted by the relevant person.

186 (1) An interested person consulted by the best interests assessor is any person whose name is stated in the relevant best interests assessment in accordance with paragraph 40 (interested persons whom the assessor consulted in carrying out the assessment).

(2) The relevant best interests assessment is the most recent best interests assessment carried out in connection with the standard authorisation in question (whether the assessment was carried out under Part 4 or Part 8).

187 Where this Schedule imposes on a person a duty towards an interested person, the duty does not apply if the person on whom the duty is imposed –

  (a)   is not aware of the interested person's identity or of a way of contacting him, and
  (b)   cannot reasonably ascertain it.

188 The following table contains an index of provisions defining or otherwise explaining expressions used in this Schedule –

age assessment	paragraph 34
age requirement	paragraph 13
age review assessment	paragraph 112(3)
appointment regulations	paragraph 138
assessment under this Schedule	paragraph 127
assessor (except in Part 8)	paragraph 33
assessor (in Part 8)	paragraphs 33 and 128
authorisation under this Schedule	paragraph 10
best interests (determination of)	section 4
best interests assessment	paragraph 38
best interests requirement	paragraph 16
best interests review assessment	paragraph 112(6)
care home	paragraph 178
change of reason ground	paragraph 106
complete (in relation to a review of a standard authorisation)	paragraph 118
deprivation of a person's liberty	section 64(5) and (6)
deputy	section 16(2)(b)
detained resident	paragraph 6
disposed of (in relation to a request for a standard authorisation)	paragraph 66
eligibility assessment	paragraph 46

non-qualification ground	paragraph 105
old supervisory body	paragraph 99(a)
positive conclusion	paragraph 112(2)(b)
purpose of a standard authorisation	paragraph 11(1)
purpose of an urgent authorisation	paragraph 11(2)
qualifying requirements	paragraph 12
refusal (for the purposes of the no refusals requirement)	paragraphs 19 and 20
relevant care or treatment	paragraph 7
relevant hospital or care home	paragraph 7
relevant managing authority	paragraph 26(4)
relevant person	paragraph 7
relevant person's representative	paragraph 137
relevant procedure	paragraph 128
review assessment	paragraph 112(1)
reviewable	paragraph 104
section 39A IMCA	paragraph 155
section 39C IMCA	paragraph 156
section 39D IMCA	paragraph 157
standard authorisation	paragraph 8
supervisory body (except in Part 8)	paragraph 180, 181 or 182
supervisory body (in Part 8)	paragraph 128 and paragraph 180, 181 or 182
unauthorised deprivation of liberty (in relation to paragraphs 68 to 73)	paragraph 67
urgent authorisation	paragraph 9
variation of conditions ground	paragraph 107

Amendment: Mental Health Act 2007, s 50(5), Sch 7, Health and Social Care Act 2012, s 55(2), Sch 5, paras 133, 136(1)–(6), SI 2010/813.

Schedule 1
Lasting Powers of Attorney: Formalities

Section 9

PART 1
MAKING INSTRUMENTS

1 General requirements as to making instruments

(1) An instrument is not made in accordance with this Schedule unless –

(a) it is in the prescribed form,
(b) it complies with paragraph 2, and
(c) any prescribed requirements in connection with its execution are satisfied.

(2) Regulations may make different provision according to whether –

(a) the instrument relates to personal welfare or to property and affairs (or to both);
(b) only one or more than one donee is to be appointed (and if more than one, whether jointly or jointly and severally).

(3) In this Schedule –

(a) 'prescribed' means prescribed by regulations, and
(b) 'regulations' means regulations made for the purposes of this Schedule by the Lord Chancellor.

2 Requirements as to content of instruments

(1) The instrument must include –

(a) the prescribed information about the purpose of the instrument and the effect of a lasting power of attorney,
(b) a statement by the donor to the effect that he –
    (i) has read the prescribed information or a prescribed part of it (or has had it read to him), and
    (ii) intends the authority conferred under the instrument to include authority to make decisions on his behalf in circumstances where he no longer has capacity,
(c) a statement by the donor –
    (i) naming a person or persons whom the donor wishes to be notified of any application for the registration of the instrument, or
    (ii) stating that there are no persons whom he wishes to be notified of any such application,
(d) a statement by the donee (or, if more than one, each of them) to the effect that he –
    (i) has read the prescribed information or a prescribed part of it (or has had it read to him), and

> (ii) understands the duties imposed on a donee of a lasting power of attorney under sections 1 (the principles) and 4 (best interests), and

(e) a certificate by a person of a prescribed description that, in his opinion, at the time when the donor executes the instrument –

> (i) the donor understands the purpose of the instrument and the scope of the authority conferred under it,
> (ii) no fraud or undue pressure is being used to induce the donor to create a lasting power of attorney, and
> (iii) there is nothing else which would prevent a lasting power of attorney from being created by the instrument.

(2) Regulations may –

(a) prescribe a maximum number of named persons;
(b) provide that, where the instrument includes a statement under sub-paragraph (1)(c)(ii), two persons of a prescribed description must each give a certificate under sub-paragraph (1)(e).

(3) The persons who may be named persons do not include a person who is appointed as donee under the instrument.

(4) In this Schedule, 'named person' means a person named under sub-paragraph (1)(c).

(5) A certificate under sub-paragraph (1)(e) –

(a) must be made in the prescribed form, and
(b) must include any prescribed information.

(6) The certificate may not be given by a person appointed as donee under the instrument.

3 Failure to comply with prescribed form

(1) If an instrument differs in an immaterial respect in form or mode of expression from the prescribed form, it is to be treated by the Public Guardian as sufficient in point of form and expression.

(2) The court may declare that an instrument which is not in the prescribed form is to be treated as if it were, if it is satisfied that the persons executing the instrument intended it to create a lasting power of attorney.

PART 2
REGISTRATION

4 Applications and procedure for registration

(1) An application to the Public Guardian for the registration of an instrument intended to create a lasting power of attorney –

(a) must be made in the prescribed form, and
(b) must include any prescribed information.

(2) The application may be made –

  (a)   by the donor,
  (b)   by the donee or donees, or
  (c)   if the instrument appoints two or more donees to act jointly and severally in respect of any matter, by any of the donees.

(3) The application must be accompanied by –

  (a)   the instrument, and
  (b)   any fee provided for under section 58(4)(b).

(4) A person who, in an application for registration, makes a statement which he knows to be false in a material particular is guilty of an offence and is liable –

  (a)   on summary conviction, to imprisonment for a term not exceeding 12 months or a fine not exceeding the statutory maximum or both;
  (b)   on conviction on indictment, to imprisonment for a term not exceeding 2 years or a fine or both.

5 Subject to paragraphs 11 to 14, the Public Guardian must register the instrument as a lasting power of attorney at the end of the prescribed period.

6 Notification requirements

(1) A donor about to make an application under paragraph 4(2)(a) must notify any named persons that he is about to do so.

(2) The donee (or donees) about to make an application under paragraph 4(2)(b) or (c) must notify any named persons that he is (or they are) about to do so.

7 As soon as is practicable after receiving an application by the donor under paragraph 4(2)(a), the Public Guardian must notify the donee (or donees) that the application has been received.

8 (1) As soon as is practicable after receiving an application by a donee (or donees) under paragraph 4(2)(b), the Public Guardian must notify the donor that the application has been received.

(2) As soon as is practicable after receiving an application by a donee under paragraph 4(2)(c), the Public Guardian must notify –

  (a)   the donor, and
  (b)   the donee or donees who did not join in making the application,

that the application has been received.

9 (1) A notice under paragraph 6 must be made in the prescribed form.

(2) A notice under paragraph 6, 7 or 8 must include such information, if any, as may be prescribed.

10 Power to dispense with notification requirements

The court may –

  (a) on the application of the donor, dispense with the requirement to notify under paragraph 6(1), or
  (b) on the application of the donee or donees concerned, dispense with the requirement to notify under paragraph 6(2),

if satisfied that no useful purpose would be served by giving the notice.

11 Instrument not made properly or containing ineffective provision

(1) If it appears to the Public Guardian that an instrument accompanying an application under paragraph 4 is not made in accordance with this Schedule, he must not register the instrument unless the court directs him to do so.

(2) Sub-paragraph (3) applies if it appears to the Public Guardian that the instrument contains a provision which –

  (a) would be ineffective as part of a lasting power of attorney, or
  (b) would prevent the instrument from operating as a valid lasting power of attorney.

(3) The Public Guardian –

  (a) must apply to the court for it to determine the matter under section 23(1), and
  (b) pending the determination by the court, must not register the instrument.

(4) Sub-paragraph (5) applies if the court determines under section 23(1) (whether or not on an application by the Public Guardian) that the instrument contains a provision which –

  (a) would be ineffective as part of a lasting power of attorney, or
  (b) would prevent the instrument from operating as a valid lasting power of attorney.

(5) The court must –

  (a) notify the Public Guardian that it has severed the provision, or
  (b) direct him not to register the instrument.

(6) Where the court notifies the Public Guardian that it has severed a provision, he must register the instrument with a note to that effect attached to it.

12 Deputy already appointed

(1) Sub-paragraph (2) applies if it appears to the Public Guardian that –

  (a) there is a deputy appointed by the court for the donor, and
  (b) the powers conferred on the deputy would, if the instrument were registered, to any extent conflict with the powers conferred on the attorney.

(2) The Public Guardian must not register the instrument unless the court directs him to do so.

13 Objection by donee or named person

(1) Sub-paragraph (2) applies if a donee or a named person –

    (a)   receives a notice under paragraph 6, 7 or 8 of an application for the registration of an instrument, and

    (b)   before the end of the prescribed period, gives notice to the Public Guardian of an objection to the registration on the ground that an event mentioned in section 13(3) or (6)(a) to (d) has occurred which has revoked the instrument.

(2) If the Public Guardian is satisfied that the ground for making the objection is established, he must not register the instrument unless the court, on the application of the person applying for the registration –

    (a)   is satisfied that the ground is not established, and

    (b)   directs the Public Guardian to register the instrument.

(3) Sub-paragraph (4) applies if a donee or a named person –

    (a)   receives a notice under paragraph 6, 7 or 8 of an application for the registration of an instrument, and

    (b)   before the end of the prescribed period –

        (i)   makes an application to the court objecting to the registration on a prescribed ground, and

        (ii)   notifies the Public Guardian of the application.

(4) The Public Guardian must not register the instrument unless the court directs him to do so.

14 Objection by donor

(1) This paragraph applies if the donor –

    (a)   receives a notice under paragraph 8 of an application for the registration of an instrument, and

    (b)   before the end of the prescribed period, gives notice to the Public Guardian of an objection to the registration.

(2) The Public Guardian must not register the instrument unless the court, on the application of the donee or, if more than one, any of them –

    (a)   is satisfied that the donor lacks capacity to object to the registration, and

    (b)   directs the Public Guardian to register the instrument.

15 Notification of registration

Where an instrument is registered under this Schedule, the Public Guardian must give notice of the fact in the prescribed form to –

    (a)   the donor, and

(b)   the donee or, if more than one, each of them.

16 Evidence of registration

(1) A document purporting to be an office copy of an instrument registered under this Schedule is, in any part of the United Kingdom, evidence of –

(a)   the contents of the instrument, and
(b)   the fact that it has been registered.

(2) Sub-paragraph (1) is without prejudice to –

(a)   section 3 of the Powers of Attorney Act 1971 (proof by certified copy), and
(b)   any other method of proof authorised by law.

PART 3
CANCELLATION OF REGISTRATION AND NOTIFICATION OF SEVERANCE

17 (1) The Public Guardian must cancel the registration of an instrument as a lasting power of attorney on being satisfied that the power has been revoked –

(a)   as a result of the donor's bankruptcy or a debt relief order (under Part 7A of the Insolvency Act 1986) having been made in respect of the donor, or
(b)   on the occurrence of an event mentioned in section 13(6)(a) to (d).

(2) If the Public Guardian cancels the registration of an instrument he must notify –

(a)   the donor, and
(b)   the donee or, if more than one, each of them.

18 The court must direct the Public Guardian to cancel the registration of an instrument as a lasting power of attorney if it –

(a)   determines under section 22(2)(a) that a requirement for creating the power was not met,
(b)   determines under section 22(2)(b) that the power has been revoked or has otherwise come to an end, or
(c)   revokes the power under section 22(4)(b) (fraud etc).

19 (1) Sub-paragraph (2) applies if the court determines under section 23(1) that a lasting power of attorney contains a provision which –

(a)   is ineffective as part of a lasting power of attorney, or
(b)   prevents the instrument from operating as a valid lasting power of attorney.

(2) The court must –

(a)   notify the Public Guardian that it has severed the provision, or

    (b)   direct him to cancel the registration of the instrument as a lasting power of attorney.

20 On the cancellation of the registration of an instrument, the instrument and any office copies of it must be delivered up to the Public Guardian to be cancelled.

PART 4
RECORDS OF ALTERATIONS IN REGISTERED POWERS

21 Partial revocation or suspension of power as a result of bankruptcy

If in the case of a registered instrument it appears to the Public Guardian that under section 13 a lasting power of attorney is revoked, or suspended, in relation to the donor's property and affairs (but not in relation to other matters), the Public Guardian must attach to the instrument a note to that effect.

22 Termination of appointment of donee which does not revoke power

If in the case of a registered instrument it appears to the Public Guardian that an event has occurred –

    (a)   which has terminated the appointment of the donee, but
    (b)   which has not revoked the instrument,

the Public Guardian must attach to the instrument a note to that effect.

23 Replacement of donee

If in the case of a registered instrument it appears to the Public Guardian that the donee has been replaced under the terms of the instrument the Public Guardian must attach to the instrument a note to that effect.

24 Severance of ineffective provisions

If in the case of a registered instrument the court notifies the Public Guardian under paragraph 19(2)(a) that it has severed a provision of the instrument, the Public Guardian must attach to it a note to that effect.

25 Notification of alterations

If the Public Guardian attaches a note to an instrument under paragraph 21, 22, 23 or 24 he must give notice of the note to the donee or donees of the power (or, as the case may be, to the other donee or donees of the power).

Amendments: SI 2012/2404.

Schedule 1A
Persons Ineligible to be Deprived of Liberty by this Act

PART 1
INELIGIBLE PERSONS

1 Application

This Schedule applies for the purposes of –

    (a)   section 16A, and
    (b)   paragraph 17 of Schedule A1.

2 Determining ineligibility

A person ('P') is ineligible to be deprived of liberty by this Act ('ineligible') if –

    (a)   P falls within one of the cases set out in the second column of the following table, and
    (b)   the corresponding entry in the third column of the table – or the provision, or one of the provisions, referred to in that entry – provides that he is ineligible.

	Status of P	*Determination of ineligibility*
Case A	P is – (a) subject to the hospital treatment regime, and (b) detained in a hospital under that regime.	P is ineligible.
Case B	P is – (a) subject to the hospital treatment regime, but (b) not detained in a hospital under that regime.	See paragraphs 3 and 4.
Case C	P is subject to the community treatment regime.	See paragraphs 3 and 4.
Case D	P is subject to the guardianship regime.	See paragraphs 3 and 5.
Case E	P is – (a) within the scope of the Mental Health Act, but (b) not subject to any of the mental health regimes.	See paragraph 5.

3 Authorised course of action not in accordance with regime

(1) This paragraph applies in cases B, C and D in the table in paragraph 2.

(2) P is ineligible if the authorised course of action is not in accordance with a requirement which the relevant regime imposes.

(3) That includes any requirement as to where P is, or is not, to reside.

(4) The relevant regime is the mental health regime to which P is subject.

4 Treatment for mental disorder in a hospital

(1) This paragraph applies in cases B and C in the table in paragraph 2.

(2) P is ineligible if the relevant care or treatment consists in whole or in part of medical treatment for mental disorder in a hospital.

5 P objects to being a mental health patient etc

(1) This paragraph applies in cases D and E in the table in paragraph 2.

(2) P is ineligible if the following conditions are met.

(3) The first condition is that the relevant instrument authorises P to be a mental health patient.

(4) The second condition is that P objects –

(a)   to being a mental health patient, or
(b)   to being given some or all of the mental health treatment.

(5) The third condition is that a donee or deputy has not made a valid decision to consent to each matter to which P objects.

(6) In determining whether or not P objects to something, regard must be had to all the circumstances (so far as they are reasonably ascertainable), including the following –

(a)   P's behaviour;
(b)   P's wishes and feelings;
(c)   P's views, beliefs and values.

(7) But regard is to be had to circumstances from the past only so far as it is still appropriate to have regard to them.

PART 2
INTERPRETATION

6 Application

This Part applies for the purposes of this Schedule.

7 Mental health regimes

The mental health regimes are –

(a) the hospital treatment regime,
(b) the community treatment regime, and
(c) the guardianship regime.

8 Hospital treatment regime

(1) P is subject to the hospital treatment regime if he is subject to –

(a) a hospital treatment obligation under the relevant enactment, or
(b) an obligation under another England and Wales enactment which has the same effect as a hospital treatment obligation.

(2) But where P is subject to any such obligation, he is to be regarded as not subject to the hospital treatment regime during any period when he is subject to the community treatment regime.

(3) A hospital treatment obligation is an application, order or direction of a kind listed in the first column of the following table.

(4) In relation to a hospital treatment obligation, the relevant enactment is the enactment in the Mental Health Act which is referred to in the corresponding entry in the second column of the following table.

Hospital treatment obligation	*Relevant enactment*
Application for admission for assessment	Section 2
Application for admission for assessment	Section 4
Application for admission for treatment	Section 3
Order for remand to hospital	Section 35
Order for remand to hospital	Section 36
Hospital order	Section 37
Interim hospital order	Section 38
Order for detention in hospital	Section 44
Hospital direction	Section 45A
Transfer direction	Section 47
Transfer direction	Section 48
Hospital order	Section 51

9 Community treatment regime

P is subject to the community treatment regime if he is subject to –

(a) a community treatment order under section 17A of the Mental Health Act, or

    (b)   an obligation under another England and Wales enactment which has the same effect as a community treatment order.

10 Guardianship regime

P is subject to the guardianship regime if he is subject to –

    (a)   a guardianship application under section 7 of the Mental Health Act,
    (b)   a guardianship order under section 37 of the Mental Health Act, or
    (c)   an obligation under another England and Wales enactment which has the same effect as a guardianship application or guardianship order.

11 England and Wales enactments

(1) An England and Wales enactment is an enactment which extends to England and Wales (whether or not it also extends elsewhere).

(2) It does not matter if the enactment is in the Mental Health Act or not.

12 P within scope of Mental Health Act

(1) P is within the scope of the Mental Health Act if –

    (a)   an application in respect of P could be made under section 2 or 3 of the Mental Health Act, and
    (b)   P could be detained in a hospital in pursuance of such an application, were one made.

(2) The following provisions of this paragraph apply when determining whether an application in respect of P could be made under section 2 or 3 of the Mental Health Act.

(3) If the grounds in section 2(2) of the Mental Health Act are met in P's case, it is to be assumed that the recommendations referred to in section 2(3) of that Act have been given.

(4) If the grounds in section 3(2) of the Mental Health Act are met in P's case, it is to be assumed that the recommendations referred to in section 3(3) of that Act have been given.

(5) In determining whether the ground in section 3(2)(c) of the Mental Health Act is met in P's case, it is to be assumed that the treatment referred to in section 3(2)(c) cannot be provided under this Act.

13 Authorised course of action, relevant care or treatment & relevant instrument

In a case where this Schedule applies for the purposes of section 16A –

    'authorised course of action' means any course of action amounting to deprivation of liberty which the order under section 16(2)(a) authorises;
    'relevant care or treatment' means any care or treatment which –
        (a)   comprises, or forms part of, the authorised course of action, or
        (b)   is to be given in connection with the authorised course of action;

'relevant instrument' means the order under section 16(2)(a).

14 In a case where this Schedule applies for the purposes of paragraph 17 of Schedule A1 –

'authorised course of action' means the accommodation of the relevant person in the relevant hospital or care home for the purpose of being given the relevant care or treatment;
'relevant care or treatment' has the same meaning as in Schedule A1;
'relevant instrument' means the standard authorisation under Schedule A1.

15 (1) This paragraph applies where the question whether a person is ineligible to be deprived of liberty by this Act is relevant to either of these decisions –

(a)   whether or not to include particular provision ('the proposed provision') in an order under section 16(2)(a);
(b)   whether or not to give a standard authorisation under Schedule A1.

(2) A reference in this Schedule to the authorised course of action or the relevant care or treatment is to be read as a reference to that thing as it would be if –

(a)   the proposed provision were included in the order, or
(b)   the standard authorisation were given.

(3) A reference in this Schedule to the relevant instrument is to be read as follows –

(a)   where the relevant instrument is an order under section 16(2)(a): as a reference to the order as it would be if the proposed provision were included in it;
(b)   where the relevant instrument is a standard authorisation: as a reference to the standard authorisation as it would be if it were given.

16 Expressions used in paragraph 5

(1) These expressions have the meanings given –

'donee' means a donee of a lasting power of attorney granted by P;
'mental health patient' means a person accommodated in a hospital for the purpose of being given medical treatment for mental disorder;
'mental health treatment' means the medical treatment for mental disorder referred to in the definition of 'mental health patient'.

(2) A decision of a donee or deputy is valid if it is made –

(a)   within the scope of his authority as donee or deputy, and
(b)   in accordance with Part 1 of this Act.

17 Expressions with same meaning as in Mental Health Act

(1) 'Hospital' has the same meaning as in Part 2 of the Mental Health Act.

(2) 'Medical treatment' has the same meaning as in the Mental Health Act.

(3) 'Mental disorder' has the same meaning as in Schedule A1 (see paragraph 14).

Amendment: Mental Health Act 2007.

Schedule 2
Property and Affairs: Supplementary Provisions

Section 18(4)

1 Wills: general

Paragraphs 2 to 4 apply in relation to the execution of a will, by virtue of section 18, on behalf of P.

2 Provision that may be made in will

The will may make any provision (whether by disposing of property or exercising a power or otherwise) which could be made by a will executed by P if he had capacity to make it.

3 Wills: requirements relating to execution

(1) Sub-paragraph (2) applies if under section 16 the court makes an order or gives directions requiring or authorising a person ('the authorised person') to execute a will on behalf of P.

(2) Any will executed in pursuance of the order or direction –

  (a)   must state that it is signed by P acting by the authorised person,
  (b)   must be signed by the authorised person with the name of P and his own name, in the presence of two or more witnesses present at the same time,
  (c)   must be attested and subscribed by those witnesses in the presence of the authorised person, and
  (d)   must be sealed with the official seal of the court.

4 Wills: effect of execution

(1) This paragraph applies where a will is executed in accordance with paragraph 3.

(2) The Wills Act 1837 has effect in relation to the will as if it were signed by P by his own hand, except that –

  (a)   section 9 of the 1837 Act (requirements as to signing and attestation) does not apply, and

(b)   in the subsequent provisions of the 1837 Act any reference to execution in the manner required by the previous provisions is to be read as a reference to execution in accordance with paragraph 3.

(3) The will has the same effect for all purposes as if –

(a)   P had had the capacity to make a valid will, and
(b)   the will had been executed by him in the manner required by the 1837 Act.

(4) But sub-paragraph (3) does not have effect in relation to the will –

(a)   in so far as it disposes of immovable property outside England and Wales, or
(b)   in so far as it relates to any other property or matter if, when the will is executed –
      (i)   P is domiciled outside England and Wales, and
      (ii)   the condition in sub-paragraph (5) is met.

(5) The condition is that, under the law of P's domicile, any question of his testamentary capacity would fall to be determined in accordance with the law of a place outside England and Wales.

5 Vesting orders ancillary to settlement etc

(1) If provision is made by virtue of section 18 for –

(a)   the settlement of any property of P, or
(b)   the exercise of a power vested in him of appointing trustees or retiring from a trust,

the court may also make as respects the property settled or the trust property such consequential vesting or other orders as the case may require.

(2) The power under sub-paragraph (1) includes, in the case of the exercise of such a power, any order which could have been made in such a case under Part 4 of the Trustee Act 1925.

6 Variation of settlements

(1) If a settlement has been made by virtue of section 18, the court may by order vary or revoke the settlement if –

(a)   the settlement makes provision for its variation or revocation,
(b)   the court is satisfied that a material fact was not disclosed when the settlement was made, or
(c)   the court is satisfied that there has been a substantial change of circumstances.

(2) Any such order may give such consequential directions as the court thinks fit.

7 Vesting of stock in curator appointed outside England and Wales

(1) Sub-paragraph (2) applies if the court is satisfied –

  (a) that under the law prevailing in a place outside England and Wales a person ('M') has been appointed to exercise powers in respect of the property or affairs of P on the ground (however formulated) that P lacks capacity to make decisions with respect to the management and administration of his property and affairs, and

  (b) that, having regard to the nature of the appointment and to the circumstances of the case, it is expedient that the court should exercise its powers under this paragraph.

(2) The court may direct –

  (a) any stocks standing in the name of P, or
  (b) the right to receive dividends from the stocks,

to be transferred into M's name or otherwise dealt with as required by M, and may give such directions as the court thinks fit for dealing with accrued dividends from the stocks.

(3) 'Stocks' includes –

  (a) shares, and
  (b) any funds, annuity or security transferable in the books kept by any body corporate or unincorporated company or society or by an instrument of transfer either alone or accompanied by other formalities,

and 'dividends' is to be construed accordingly.

8 Preservation of interests in property disposed of on behalf of person lacking capacity

(1) Sub-paragraphs (2) and (3) apply if –

  (a) P's property has been disposed of by virtue of section 18,
  (b) under P's will or intestacy, or by a gift perfected or nomination taking effect on his death, any other person would have taken an interest in the property but for the disposal, and
  (c) on P's death, any property belonging to P's estate represents the property disposed of.

(2) The person takes the same interest, if and so far as circumstances allow, in the property representing the property disposed of.

(3) If the property disposed of was real property, any property representing it is to be treated, so long as it remains part of P's estate, as if it were real property.

(4) The court may direct that, on a disposal of P's property –

  (a) which is made by virtue of section 18, and
  (b) which would apart from this paragraph result in the conversion of personal property into real property,

property representing the property disposed of is to be treated, so long as it remains P's property or forms part of P's estate, as if it were personal property.

(5) References in sub-paragraphs (1) to (4) to the disposal of property are to –

(a) the sale, exchange, charging of or other dealing (otherwise than by will) with property other than money;
(b) the removal of property from one place to another;
(c) the application of money in acquiring property;
(d) the transfer of money from one account to another;

and references to property representing property disposed of are to be construed accordingly and as including the result of successive disposals.

(6) The court may give such directions as appear to it necessary or expedient for the purpose of facilitating the operation of sub-paragraphs (1) to (3), including the carrying of money to a separate account and the transfer of property other than money.

9 (1) Sub-paragraph (2) applies if the court has ordered or directed the expenditure of money –

(a) for carrying out permanent improvements on any of P's property, or
(b) otherwise for the permanent benefit of any of P's property.

(2) The court may order that –

(a) the whole of the money expended or to be expended, or
(b) any part of it,

is to be a charge on the property either without interest or with interest at a specified rate.

(3) An order under sub-paragraph (2) may provide for excluding or restricting the operation of paragraph 8(1) to (3).

(4) A charge under sub-paragraph (2) may be made in favour of such person as may be just and, in particular, where the money charged is paid out of P's general estate, may be made in favour of a person as trustee for P.

(5) No charge under sub-paragraph (2) may confer any right of sale or foreclosure during P's lifetime.

10 Powers as patron of benefice

(1) Any functions which P has as patron of a benefice may be discharged only by a person ('R') appointed by the court.

(2) R must be an individual capable of appointment under section 8(1)(b) of the 1986 Measure (which provides for an individual able to make a declaration of communicant status, a clerk in Holy Orders, etc to be appointed to discharge a registered patron's functions).

(3) The 1986 Measure applies to R as it applies to an individual appointed by the registered patron of the benefice under section 8(1)(b) or (3) of that Measure to discharge his functions as patron.

(4) 'The 1986 Measure' means the Patronage (Benefices) Measure 1986 (No 3).

Schedule 3
International Protection of Adults

Section 63

PART 1
PRELIMINARY

1 Introduction

This Part applies for the purposes of this Schedule.

2 The Convention

(1) 'Convention' means the Convention referred to in section 63.

(2) 'Convention country' means a country in which the Convention is in force.

(3) A reference to an Article or Chapter is to an Article or Chapter of the Convention.

(4) An expression which appears in this Schedule and in the Convention is to be construed in accordance with the Convention.

3 Countries, territories and nationals

(1) 'Country' includes a territory which has its own system of law.

(2) Where a country has more than one territory with its own system of law, a reference to the country, in relation to one of its nationals, is to the territory with which the national has the closer, or the closest, connection.

4 Adults with incapacity

(1)'Adult' means (subject to sub-paragraph (2) a person who –

    (a)   as a result of an impairment or insufficiency of his personal faculties, cannot protect his interests, and

    (b)   has reached 16.

(2) But 'adult' does not include a child to whom either of the following applies –

    (a)   the Convention on Jurisdiction, Applicable Law, Recognition, Enforcement and Co-Operation in respect of Parental Responsibility and Measures for the Protection of Children that was signed at The Hague on 19 October 1996;

(b)   Council Regulation (EC) No 2201/2003 concerning jurisdiction and the recognition and enforcement of judgments in matrimonial matters and the matters of parental responsibility.

5 Protective measures

(1) 'Protective measure' means a measure directed to the protection of the person or property of an adult; and it may deal in particular with any of the following –

(a)   the determination of incapacity and the institution of a protective regime,
(b)   placing the adult under the protection of an appropriate authority,
(c)   guardianship, curatorship or any corresponding system,
(d)   the designation and functions of a person having charge of the adult's person or property, or representing or otherwise helping him,
(e)   placing the adult in a place where protection can be provided,
(f)   administering, conserving or disposing of the adult's property,
(g)   authorising a specific intervention for the protection of the person or property of the adult.

(2) Where a measure of like effect to a protective measure has been taken in relation to a person before he reaches 16, this Schedule applies to the measure in so far as it has effect in relation to him once he has reached 16.

6 Central Authority

(1) Any function under the Convention of a Central Authority is exercisable in England and Wales by the Lord Chancellor.

(2) A communication may be sent to the Central Authority in relation to England and Wales by sending it to the Lord Chancellor.

Amendment: SI 2010/1898.

PART 2
JURISDICTION OF COMPETENT AUTHORITY

7 Scope of jurisdiction

(1) The court may exercise its functions under this Act (in so far as it cannot otherwise do so) in relation to –

(a)   an adult habitually resident in England and Wales,
(b)   an adult's property in England and Wales,
(c)   an adult present in England and Wales or who has property there, if the matter is urgent, or
(d)   an adult present in England and Wales, if a protective measure which is temporary and limited in its effect to England and Wales is proposed in relation to him.

(2) An adult present in England and Wales is to be treated for the purposes of this paragraph as habitually resident there if –

(a)   his habitual residence cannot be ascertained,

(b)   he is a refugee, or

(c)   he has been displaced as a result of disturbance in the country of his habitual residence.

8 (1) The court may also exercise its functions under this Act (in so far as it cannot otherwise do so) in relation to an adult if sub-paragraph (2) or (3) applies in relation to him.

(2) This sub-paragraph applies in relation to an adult if –

(a)   he is a British citizen,

(b)   he has a closer connection with England and Wales than with Scotland or Northern Ireland, and

(c)   Article 7 has, in relation to the matter concerned, been complied with.

(3) This sub-paragraph applies in relation to an adult if the Lord Chancellor, having consulted such persons as he considers appropriate, agrees to a request under Article 8 in relation to the adult.

9 Exercise of jurisdiction

(1) This paragraph applies where jurisdiction is exercisable under this Schedule in connection with a matter which involves a Convention country other than England and Wales.

(2) Any Article on which the jurisdiction is based applies in relation to the matter in so far as it involves the other country (and the court must, accordingly, comply with any duty conferred on it as a result).

(3) Article 12 also applies, so far as its provisions allow, in relation to the matter in so far as it involves the other country.

10 A reference in this Schedule to the exercise of jurisdiction under this Schedule is to the exercise of functions under this Act as a result of this Part of this Schedule.

PART 3
APPLICABLE LAW

11 Applicable law

In exercising jurisdiction under this Schedule, the court may, if it thinks that the matter has a substantial connection with a country other than England and Wales, apply the law of that other country.

12 Where a protective measure is taken in one country but implemented in another, the conditions of implementation are governed by the law of the other country.

13 Lasting powers of attorney, etc

(1) If the donor of a lasting power is habitually resident in England and Wales at the time of granting the power, the law applicable to the existence, extent, modification or extinction of the power is –

(a)   the law of England and Wales, or
(b)   if he specifies in writing the law of a connected country for the purpose, that law.

(2) If he is habitually resident in another country at that time, but England and Wales is a connected country, the law applicable in that respect is –

(a)   the law of the other country, or
(b)   if he specifies in writing the law of England and Wales for the purpose, that law.

(3) A country is connected, in relation to the donor, if it is a country –

(a)   of which he is a national,
(b)   in which he was habitually resident, or
(c)   in which he has property.

(4) Where this paragraph applies as a result of sub-paragraph (3)(c), it applies only in relation to the property which the donor has in the connected country.

(5) The law applicable to the manner of the exercise of a lasting power is the law of the country where it is exercised.

(6) In this Part of this Schedule, 'lasting power' means –

(a)   a lasting power of attorney (see section 9),
(b)   an enduring power of attorney within the meaning of Schedule 4, or
(c)   any other power of like effect.

14 (1) Where a lasting power is not exercised in a manner sufficient to guarantee the protection of the person or property of the donor, the court, in exercising jurisdiction under this Schedule, may disapply or modify the power.

(2) Where, in accordance with this Part of this Schedule, the law applicable to the power is, in one or more respects, that of a country other than England and Wales, the court must, so far as possible, have regard to the law of the other country in that respect (or those respects).

15 Regulations may provide for Schedule 1 (lasting powers of attorney: formalities) to apply with modifications in relation to a lasting power which comes within paragraph 13(6)(c) above.

16 Protection of third parties

(1) This paragraph applies where a person (a 'representative') in purported exercise of an authority to act on behalf of an adult enters into a transaction with a third party.

(2) The validity of the transaction may not be questioned in proceedings, nor may the third party be held liable, merely because –

(a) where the representative and third party are in England and Wales when entering into the transaction, sub-paragraph (3) applies;

(b) where they are in another country at that time, sub-paragraph (4) applies.

(3) This sub-paragraph applies if –

(a) the law applicable to the authority in one or more respects is, as a result of this Schedule, the law of a country other than England and Wales, and

(b) the representative is not entitled to exercise the authority in that respect (or those respects) under the law of that other country.

(4) This sub-paragraph applies if –

(a) the law applicable to the authority in one or more respects is, as a result of this Part of this Schedule, the law of England and Wales, and

(b) the representative is not entitled to exercise the authority in that respect (or those respects) under that law.

(5) This paragraph does not apply if the third party knew or ought to have known that the applicable law was –

(a) in a case within sub-paragraph (3), the law of the other country;

(b) in a case within sub-paragraph (4), the law of England and Wales.

17 Mandatory rules

Where the court is entitled to exercise jurisdiction under this Schedule, the mandatory provisions of the law of England and Wales apply, regardless of any system of law which would otherwise apply in relation to the matter.

18 Public policy

Nothing in this Part of this Schedule requires or enables the application in England and Wales of a provision of the law of another country if its application would be manifestly contrary to public policy.

PART 4
RECOGNITION AND ENFORCEMENT

19 Recognition

(1) A protective measure taken in relation to an adult under the law of a country other than England and Wales is to be recognised in England and Wales if it was taken on the ground that the adult is habitually resident in the other country.

(2) A protective measure taken in relation to an adult under the law of a Convention country other than England and Wales is to be recognised in England and Wales if it was taken on a ground mentioned in Chapter 2 (jurisdiction).

(3) But the court may disapply this paragraph in relation to a measure if it thinks that –

    (a)   the case in which the measure was taken was not urgent,
    (b)   the adult was not given an opportunity to be heard, and
    (c)   that omission amounted to a breach of natural justice.

(4) It may also disapply this paragraph in relation to a measure if it thinks that –

    (a)   recognition of the measure would be manifestly contrary to public policy,
    (b)   the measure would be inconsistent with a mandatory provision of the law of England and Wales, or
    (c)   the measure is inconsistent with one subsequently taken, or recognised, in England and Wales in relation to the adult.

(5) And the court may disapply this paragraph in relation to a measure taken under the law of a Convention country in a matter to which Article 33 applies, if the court thinks that that Article has not been complied with in connection with that matter.

20 (1) An interested person may apply to the court for a declaration as to whether a protective measure taken under the law of a country other than England and Wales is to be recognised in England and Wales.

(2) No permission is required for an application to the court under this paragraph.

21 For the purposes of paragraphs 19 and 20, any finding of fact relied on when the measure was taken is conclusive.

22 Enforcement

(1) An interested person may apply to the court for a declaration as to whether a protective measure taken under the law of, and enforceable in, a country other than England and Wales is enforceable, or to be registered, in England and Wales in accordance with Court of Protection Rules.

(2) The court must make the declaration if –

    (a)   the measure comes within sub-paragraph (1) or (2) of paragraph 19, and
    (b)   the paragraph is not disapplied in relation to it as a result of sub-paragraph (3), (4) or (5).

(3) A measure to which a declaration under this paragraph relates is enforceable in England and Wales as if it were a measure of like effect taken by the court.

23 Measures taken in relation to those aged under 16

(1) This paragraph applies where –

    (a) provision giving effect to, or otherwise deriving from, the Convention in a country other than England and Wales applies in relation to a person who has not reached 16, and

    (b) a measure is taken in relation to that person in reliance on that provision.

(2) This Part of this Schedule applies in relation to that measure as it applies in relation to a protective measure taken in relation to an adult under the law of a Convention country other than England and Wales.

24 Supplementary

The court may not review the merits of a measure taken outside England and Wales except to establish whether the measure complies with this Schedule in so far as it is, as a result of this Schedule, required to do so.

25 Court of Protection Rules may make provision about an application under paragraph 20 or 22.

PART 5
CO-OPERATION

26 Proposal for cross-border placement

(1) This paragraph applies where a public authority proposes to place an adult in an establishment in a Convention country other than England and Wales.

(2) The public authority must consult an appropriate authority in that other country about the proposed placement and, for that purpose, must send it –

    (a) a report on the adult, and

    (b) a statement of its reasons for the proposed placement.

(3) If the appropriate authority in the other country opposes the proposed placement within a reasonable time, the public authority may not proceed with it.

27 A proposal received by a public authority under Article 33 in relation to an adult is to proceed unless the authority opposes it within a reasonable time.

28 Adult in danger etc

(1) This paragraph applies if a public authority is told that an adult –

    (a) who is in serious danger, and

(b) in relation to whom the public authority has taken, or is considering taking, protective measures,

is, or has become resident, in a Convention country other than England and Wales.

(2) The public authority must tell an appropriate authority in that other country about –

(a) the danger, and
(b) the measures taken or under consideration.

29 A public authority may not request from, or send to, an appropriate authority in a Convention country information in accordance with Chapter 5 (co-operation) in relation to an adult if it thinks that doing so –

(a) would be likely to endanger the adult or his property, or
(b) would amount to a serious threat to the liberty or life of a member of the adult's family.

PART 6
GENERAL

30 Certificates

A certificate given under Article 38 by an authority in a Convention country other than England and Wales is, unless the contrary is shown, proof of the matters contained in it.

31 Powers to make further provision as to private international law

Her Majesty may by Order in Council confer on the Lord Chancellor, the court or another public authority functions for enabling the Convention to be given effect in England and Wales.

32 (1) Regulations may make provision –

(a) giving further effect to the Convention, or
(b) otherwise about the private international law of England and Wales in relation to the protection of adults.

(2) The regulations may –

(a) confer functions on the court or another public authority;
(b) amend this Schedule;
(c) provide for this Schedule to apply with specified modifications;
(d) make provision about countries other than Convention countries.

33 Exceptions

Nothing in this Schedule applies, and no provision made under paragraph 32 is to apply, to any matter to which the Convention, as a result of Article 4, does not apply.

34 Regulations and orders

A reference in this Schedule to regulations or an order (other than an Order in Council) is to regulations or an order made for the purposes of this Schedule by the Lord Chancellor.

35 Commencement

The following provisions of this Schedule have effect only if the Convention is in force in accordance with Article 57 –

(a) paragraph 8,
(b) paragraph 9,
(c) paragraph 19(2) and (5),
(d) Part 5,
(e) paragraph 30.

Schedule 4
Provisions Applying to Existing Enduring Powers of Attorney

Section 66(3)

PART 1
ENDURING POWERS OF ATTORNEY

1 Enduring power of attorney to survive mental incapacity of donor

(1) Where an individual has created a power of attorney which is an enduring power within the meaning of this Schedule –

(a) the power is not revoked by any subsequent mental incapacity of his,
(b) upon such incapacity supervening, the donee of the power may not do anything under the authority of the power except as provided by sub-paragraph (2) unless or until the instrument creating the power is registered under paragraph 13, and
(c) if and so long as paragraph (b) operates to suspend the donee's authority to act under the power, section 5 of the Powers of Attorney Act 1971 (protection of donee and third persons), so far as applicable, applies as if the power had been revoked by the donor's mental incapacity,

and, accordingly, section 1 of this Act does not apply.

(2) Despite sub-paragraph (1)(b), where the attorney has made an application for registration of the instrument then, until it is registered, the attorney may take action under the power –

(a) to maintain the donor or prevent loss to his estate, or
(b) to maintain himself or other persons in so far as paragraph 3(2) permits him to do so.

(3) Where the attorney purports to act as provided by sub-paragraph (2) then, in favour of a person who deals with him without knowledge that the attorney

is acting otherwise than in accordance with sub-paragraph (2)(a) or (b), the transaction between them is as valid as if the attorney were acting in accordance with sub-paragraph (2)(a) or (b).

2 Characteristics of an enduring power of attorney

(1) Subject to sub-paragraphs (5) and (6) and paragraph 20, a power of attorney is an enduring power within the meaning of this Schedule if the instrument which creates the power –

- (a)   is in the prescribed form,
- (b)   was executed in the prescribed manner by the donor and the attorney, and
- (c)   incorporated at the time of execution by the donor the prescribed explanatory information.

(2) In this paragraph, 'prescribed' means prescribed by such of the following regulations as applied when the instrument was executed –

- (a)   the Enduring Powers of Attorney (Prescribed Form) Regulations 1986,
- (b)   the Enduring Powers of Attorney (Prescribed Form) Regulations 1987,
- (c)   the Enduring Powers of Attorney (Prescribed Form) Regulations 1990,
- (d)   the Enduring Powers of Attorney (Welsh Language Prescribed Form) Regulations 2000.

(3) An instrument in the prescribed form purporting to have been executed in the prescribed manner is to be taken, in the absence of evidence to the contrary, to be a document which incorporated at the time of execution by the donor the prescribed explanatory information.

(4) If an instrument differs in an immaterial respect in form or mode of expression from the prescribed form it is to be treated as sufficient in point of form and expression.

(5) A power of attorney cannot be an enduring power unless, when he executes the instrument creating it, the attorney is –

- (a)   an individual who has reached 18 and is not bankrupt or is not subject to a debt relief order (under Part 7A of the Insolvency Act 1986), or
- (b)   a trust corporation.

(6) A power of attorney which gives the attorney a right to appoint a substitute or successor cannot be an enduring power.

(7) An enduring power is revoked by the bankruptcy of the donor or attorney or the making of a debt relief order (under Part 7A of the Insolvency Act 1986) in respect of the donor or attorney.

(8) But where the donor or attorney is bankrupt merely because an interim bankruptcy restrictions order has effect in respect of him or where the donor or attorney is subject to an interim debt relief restrictions order, the power is suspended for so long as the order has effect.

(9) An enduring power is revoked if the court –

    (a)   exercises a power under sections 16 to 20 in relation to the donor, and
    (b)   directs that the enduring power is to be revoked.

(10) No disclaimer of an enduring power, whether by deed or otherwise, is valid unless and until the attorney gives notice of it to the donor or, where paragraph 4(6) or 15(1) applies, to the Public Guardian.

3 Scope of authority etc of attorney under enduring power

(1) If the instrument which creates an enduring power of attorney is expressed to confer general authority on the attorney, the instrument operates to confer, subject to –

    (a)   the restriction imposed by sub-paragraph (3), and
    (b)   any conditions or restrictions contained in the instrument,

authority to do on behalf of the donor anything which the donor could lawfully do by an attorney at the time when the donor executed the instrument.

(2) Subject to any conditions or restrictions contained in the instrument, an attorney under an enduring power, whether general or limited, may (without obtaining any consent) act under the power so as to benefit himself or other persons than the donor to the following extent but no further –

    (a)   he may so act in relation to himself or in relation to any other person if the donor might be expected to provide for his or that person's needs respectively, and
    (b)   he may do whatever the donor might be expected to do to meet those needs.

(3) Without prejudice to sub-paragraph (2) but subject to any conditions or restrictions contained in the instrument, an attorney under an enduring power, whether general or limited, may (without obtaining any consent) dispose of the property of the donor by way of gift to the following extent but no further –

    (a)   he may make gifts of a seasonal nature or at a time, or on an anniversary, of a birth, a marriage or the formation of a civil partnership, to persons (including himself) who are related to or connected with the donor, and
    (b)   he may make gifts to any charity to whom the donor made or might be expected to make gifts,

provided that the value of each such gift is not unreasonable having regard to all the circumstances and in particular the size of the donor's estate.

Amendment: SI 2012/2404.

PART 2
ACTION ON ACTUAL OR IMPENDING INCAPACITY OF DONOR

4 Duties of attorney in event of actual or impending incapacity of donor

(1) Sub-paragraphs (2) to (6) apply if the attorney under an enduring power has reason to believe that the donor is or is becoming mentally incapable.

(2) The attorney must, as soon as practicable, make an application to the Public Guardian for the registration of the instrument creating the power.

(3) Before making an application for registration the attorney must comply with the provisions as to notice set out in Part 3 of this Schedule.

(4) An application for registration –

    (a)   must be made in the prescribed form, and
    (b)   must contain such statements as may be prescribed.

(5) The attorney –

    (a)   may, before making an application for the registration of the instrument, refer to the court for its determination any question as to the validity of the power, and
    (b)   must comply with any direction given to him by the court on that determination.

(6) No disclaimer of the power is valid unless and until the attorney gives notice of it to the Public Guardian; and the Public Guardian must notify the donor if he receives a notice under this sub-paragraph.

(7) A person who, in an application for registration, makes a statement which he knows to be false in a material particular is guilty of an offence and is liable –

    (a)   on summary conviction, to imprisonment for a term not exceeding 12 months or a fine not exceeding the statutory maximum or both;
    (b)   on conviction on indictment, to imprisonment for a term not exceeding 2 years or a fine or both.

(8) In this paragraph, 'prescribed' means prescribed by regulations made for the purposes of this Schedule by the Lord Chancellor.

PART 3
NOTIFICATION PRIOR TO REGISTRATION

5 Duty to give notice to relatives

Subject to paragraph 7, before making an application for registration the attorney must give notice of his intention to do so to all those persons (if any) who are entitled to receive notice by virtue of paragraph 6.

6 (1) Subject to sub-paragraphs (2) to (4), persons of the following classes ('relatives') are entitled to receive notice under paragraph 5 –

(a)   the donor's spouse or civil partner,
(b)   the donor's children,
(c)   the donor's parents,
(d)   the donor's brothers and sisters, whether of the whole or half blood,
(e)   the widow, widower or surviving civil partner of a child of the donor,
(f)   the donor's grandchildren,
(g)   the children of the donor's brothers and sisters of the whole blood,
(h)   the children of the donor's brothers and sisters of the half blood,
(i)   the donor's uncles and aunts of the whole blood,
(j)   the children of the donor's uncles and aunts of the whole blood.

(2) A person is not entitled to receive notice under paragraph 5 if –

(a)   his name or address is not known to the attorney and cannot be reasonably ascertained by him, or
(b)   the attorney has reason to believe that he has not reached 18 or is mentally incapable.

(3) Except where sub-paragraph (4) applies –

(a)   no more than 3 persons are entitled to receive notice under paragraph 5, and
(b)   in determining the persons who are so entitled, persons falling within the class in sub-paragraph (1)(a) are to be preferred to persons falling within the class in sub-paragraph (1)(b), those falling within the class in sub-paragraph (1)(b) are to be preferred to those falling within the class in sub-paragraph (1)(c), and so on.

(4) Despite the limit of 3 specified in sub-paragraph (3), where –

(a)   there is more than one person falling within any of classes (a) to (j) of sub-paragraph (1), and
(b)   at least one of those persons would be entitled to receive notice under paragraph 5,

then, subject to sub-paragraph (2), all the persons falling within that class are entitled to receive notice under paragraph 5.

7 (1) An attorney is not required to give notice under paragraph 5 –

(a)   to himself, or
(b)   to any other attorney under the power who is joining in making the application,

even though he or, as the case may be, the other attorney is entitled to receive notice by virtue of paragraph 6.

(2) In the case of any person who is entitled to receive notice by virtue of paragraph 6, the attorney, before applying for registration, may make an application to the court to be dispensed from the requirement to give him notice; and the court must grant the application if it is satisfied –

(a)   that it would be undesirable or impracticable for the attorney to give him notice, or

    (b)   that no useful purpose is likely to be served by giving him notice.

8 Duty to give notice to donor

(1) Subject to sub-paragraph (2), before making an application for registration the attorney must give notice of his intention to do so to the donor.

(2) Paragraph 7(2) applies in relation to the donor as it applies in relation to a person who is entitled to receive notice under paragraph 5.

9 Contents of notices

A notice to relatives under this Part of this Schedule must –

    (a)   be in the prescribed form,
    (b)   state that the attorney proposes to make an application to the Public Guardian for the registration of the instrument creating the enduring power in question,
    (c)   inform the person to whom it is given of his right to object to the registration under paragraph 13(4), and
    (d)   specify, as the grounds on which an objection to registration may be made, the grounds set out in paragraph 13(9).

10 A notice to the donor under this Part of this Schedule –

    (a)   must be in the prescribed form,
    (b)   must contain the statement mentioned in paragraph 9(b), and
    (c)   must inform the donor that, while the instrument remains registered, any revocation of the power by him will be ineffective unless and until the revocation is confirmed by the court.

11 Duty to give notice to other attorneys

(1) Subject to sub-paragraph (2), before making an application for registration an attorney under a joint and several power must give notice of his intention to do so to any other attorney under the power who is not joining in making the application; and paragraphs 7(2) and 9 apply in relation to attorneys entitled to receive notice by virtue of this paragraph as they apply in relation to persons entitled to receive notice by virtue of paragraph 6.

(2) An attorney is not entitled to receive notice by virtue of this paragraph if –

    (a)   his address is not known to the applying attorney and cannot reasonably be ascertained by him, or
    (b)   the applying attorney has reason to believe that he has not reached 18 or is mentally incapable.

12 Supplementary

Despite section 7 of the Interpretation Act 1978 (construction of references to service by post), for the purposes of this Part of this Schedule a notice given by post is to be regarded as given on the date on which it was posted.

PART 4
REGISTRATION

13 Registration of instrument creating power

(1) If an application is made in accordance with paragraph 4(3) and (4) the Public Guardian must, subject to the provisions of this paragraph, register the instrument to which the application relates.

(2) If it appears to the Public Guardian that –

(a) there is a deputy appointed for the donor of the power created by the instrument, and

(b) the powers conferred on the deputy would, if the instrument were registered, to any extent conflict with the powers conferred on the attorney,

the Public Guardian must not register the instrument except in accordance with the court's directions.

(3) The court may, on the application of the attorney, direct the Public Guardian to register an instrument even though notice has not been given as required by paragraph 4(3) and Part 3 of this Schedule to a person entitled to receive it, if the court is satisfied –

(a) that it was undesirable or impracticable for the attorney to give notice to that person, or

(b) that no useful purpose is likely to be served by giving him notice.

(4) Sub-paragraph (5) applies if, before the end of the period of 5 weeks beginning with the date (or the latest date) on which the attorney gave notice under paragraph 5 of an application for registration, the Public Guardian receives a valid notice of objection to the registration from a person entitled to notice of the application.

(5) The Public Guardian must not register the instrument except in accordance with the court's directions.

(6) Sub-paragraph (7) applies if, in the case of an application for registration –

(a) it appears from the application that there is no one to whom notice has been given under paragraph 5, or

(b) the Public Guardian has reason to believe that appropriate inquiries might bring to light evidence on which he could be satisfied that one of the grounds of objection set out in sub-paragraph (9) was established.

(7) The Public Guardian –

(a) must not register the instrument, and

(b) must undertake such inquiries as he thinks appropriate in all the circumstances.

(8) If, having complied with sub-paragraph (7)(b), the Public Guardian is satisfied that one of the grounds of objection set out in sub-paragraph (9) is established –

(a) the attorney may apply to the court for directions, and

(b) the Public Guardian must not register the instrument except in accordance with the court's directions.

(9) A notice of objection under this paragraph is valid if made on one or more of the following grounds –

(a) that the power purported to have been created by the instrument was not valid as an enduring power of attorney,

(b) that the power created by the instrument no longer subsists,

(c) that the application is premature because the donor is not yet becoming mentally incapable,

(d) that fraud or undue pressure was used to induce the donor to create the power,

(e) that, having regard to all the circumstances and in particular the attorney's relationship to or connection with the donor, the attorney is unsuitable to be the donor's attorney.

(10) If any of those grounds is established to the satisfaction of the court it must direct the Public Guardian not to register the instrument, but if not so satisfied it must direct its registration.

(11) If the court directs the Public Guardian not to register an instrument because it is satisfied that the ground in sub-paragraph (9)(d) or (e) is established, it must by order revoke the power created by the instrument.

(12) If the court directs the Public Guardian not to register an instrument because it is satisfied that any ground in sub-paragraph (9) except that in paragraph (c) is established, the instrument must be delivered up to be cancelled unless the court otherwise directs.

14 Register of enduring powers

The Public Guardian has the function of establishing and maintaining a register of enduring powers for the purposes of this Schedule.

PART 5
LEGAL POSITION AFTER REGISTRATION

15 Effect and proof of registration

(1) The effect of the registration of an instrument under paragraph 13 is that –

(a) no revocation of the power by the donor is valid unless and until the court confirms the revocation under paragraph 16(3);

(b) no disclaimer of the power is valid unless and until the attorney gives notice of it to the Public Guardian;

(c) the donor may not extend or restrict the scope of the authority conferred by the instrument and no instruction or consent given by him after registration, in the case of a consent, confers any right and, in the case of an instruction, imposes or confers any obligation or right on or creates any liability of the attorney or other persons having notice of the instruction or consent.

(2) Sub-paragraph (1) applies for so long as the instrument is registered under paragraph 13 whether or not the donor is for the time being mentally incapable.

(3) A document purporting to be an office copy of an instrument registered under this Schedule is, in any part of the United Kingdom, evidence of –

    (a)   the contents of the instrument, and
    (b)   the fact that it has been so registered.

(4) Sub-paragraph (3) is without prejudice to section 3 of the Powers of Attorney Act 1971 (proof by certified copies) and to any other method of proof authorised by law.

16 Functions of court with regard to registered power

(1) Where an instrument has been registered under paragraph 13, the court has the following functions with respect to the power and the donor of and the attorney appointed to act under the power.

(2) The court may –

    (a)   determine any question as to the meaning or effect of the instrument;
    (b)   give directions with respect to –
        (i)   the management or disposal by the attorney of the property and affairs of the donor;
        (ii)   the rendering of accounts by the attorney and the production of the records kept by him for the purpose;
        (iii)   the remuneration or expenses of the attorney whether or not in default of or in accordance with any provision made by the instrument, including directions for the repayment of excessive or the payment of additional remuneration;

    (c)   require the attorney to supply information or produce documents or things in his possession as attorney;
    (d)   give any consent or authorisation to act which the attorney would have to obtain from a mentally capable donor;
    (e)   authorise the attorney to act so as to benefit himself or other persons than the donor otherwise than in accordance with paragraph 3(2) and (3) (but subject to any conditions or restrictions contained in the instrument);
    (f)   relieve the attorney wholly or partly from any liability which he has or may have incurred on account of a breach of his duties as attorney.

(3) On application made for the purpose by or on behalf of the donor, the court must confirm the revocation of the power if satisfied that the donor –

    (a)   has done whatever is necessary in law to effect an express revocation of the power, and

(b)   was mentally capable of revoking a power of attorney when he did so (whether or not he is so when the court considers the application).

(4) The court must direct the Public Guardian to cancel the registration of an instrument registered under paragraph 13 in any of the following circumstances –

(a)   on confirming the revocation of the power under sub-paragraph (3),
(b)   on directing under paragraph 2(9)(b) that the power is to be revoked,
(c)   on being satisfied that the donor is and is likely to remain mentally capable,
(d)   on being satisfied that the power has expired or has been revoked by the mental incapacity of the attorney,
(e)   on being satisfied that the power was not a valid and subsisting enduring power when registration was effected,
(f)   on being satisfied that fraud or undue pressure was used to induce the donor to create the power,
(g)   on being satisfied that, having regard to all the circumstances and in particular the attorney's relationship to or connection with the donor, the attorney is unsuitable to be the donor's attorney.

(5) If the court directs the Public Guardian to cancel the registration of an instrument on being satisfied of the matters specified in sub-paragraph (4)(f) or (g) it must by order revoke the power created by the instrument.

(6) If the court directs the cancellation of the registration of an instrument under sub-paragraph (4) except paragraph (c) the instrument must be delivered up to the Public Guardian to be cancelled, unless the court otherwise directs.

17 Cancellation of registration by Public Guardian

The Public Guardian must cancel the registration of an instrument creating an enduring power of attorney –

(a)   on receipt of a disclaimer signed by the attorney;
(b)   if satisfied that the power has been revoked by the death or bankruptcy of the donor or attorney or the making of a debt relief order (under Part 7A of the Insolvency Act 1986) in respect of the donor or attorney or, if the attorney is a body corporate, by its winding up or dissolution;
(c)   on receipt of notification from the court that the court has revoked the power;
(d)   on confirmation from the court that the donor has revoked the power.

Amendments –SI 2012/2404.

PART 6
PROTECTION OF ATTORNEY AND THIRD PARTIES

18 Protection of attorney and third persons where power is invalid or revoked

(1) Sub-paragraphs (2) and (3) apply where an instrument which did not create a valid power of attorney has been registered under paragraph 13 (whether or not the registration has been cancelled at the time of the act or transaction in question).

(2) An attorney who acts in pursuance of the power does not incur any liability (either to the donor or to any other person) because of the non-existence of the power unless at the time of acting he knows –

    (a)   that the instrument did not create a valid enduring power,
    (b)   that an event has occurred which, if the instrument had created a valid enduring power, would have had the effect of revoking the power, or
    (c)   that, if the instrument had created a valid enduring power, the power would have expired before that time.

(3) Any transaction between the attorney and another person is, in favour of that person, as valid as if the power had then been in existence, unless at the time of the transaction that person has knowledge of any of the matters mentioned in sub-paragraph (2).

(4) If the interest of a purchaser depends on whether a transaction between the attorney and another person was valid by virtue of sub-paragraph (3), it is conclusively presumed in favour of the purchaser that the transaction was valid if –

    (a)   the transaction between that person and the attorney was completed within 12 months of the date on which the instrument was registered, or
    (b)   that person makes a statutory declaration, before or within 3 months after the completion of the purchase, that he had no reason at the time of the transaction to doubt that the attorney had authority to dispose of the property which was the subject of the transaction.

(5) For the purposes of section 5 of the Powers of Attorney Act 1971 (protection where power is revoked) in its application to an enduring power the revocation of which by the donor is by virtue of paragraph 15 invalid unless and until confirmed by the court under paragraph 16 –

    (a)   knowledge of the confirmation of the revocation is knowledge of the revocation of the power, but
    (b)   knowledge of the unconfirmed revocation is not.

19 Further protection of attorney and third persons

(1) If –

(a) an instrument framed in a form prescribed as mentioned in paragraph 2(2) creates a power which is not a valid enduring power, and

(b) the power is revoked by the mental incapacity of the donor,

sub-paragraphs (2) and (3) apply, whether or not the instrument has been registered.

(2) An attorney who acts in pursuance of the power does not, by reason of the revocation, incur any liability (either to the donor or to any other person) unless at the time of acting he knows –

(a) that the instrument did not create a valid enduring power, and

(b) that the donor has become mentally incapable.

(3) Any transaction between the attorney and another person is, in favour of that person, as valid as if the power had then been in existence, unless at the time of the transaction that person knows –

(a) that the instrument did not create a valid enduring power, and

(b) that the donor has become mentally incapable.

(4) Paragraph 18(4) applies for the purpose of determining whether a transaction was valid by virtue of sub-paragraph (3) as it applies for the purpose or determining whether a transaction was valid by virtue of paragraph 18(3).

PART 7

JOINT AND JOINT AND SEVERAL ATTORNEYS

20 Application to joint and joint and several attorneys

(1) An instrument which appoints more than one person to be an attorney cannot create an enduring power unless the attorneys are appointed to act –

(a) jointly, or

(b) jointly and severally.

(2) This Schedule, in its application to joint attorneys, applies to them collectively as it applies to a single attorney but subject to the modifications specified in paragraph 21.

(3) This Schedule, in its application to joint and several attorneys, applies with the modifications specified in sub-paragraphs (4) to (7) and in paragraph 22.

(4) A failure, as respects any one attorney, to comply with the requirements for the creation of enduring powers –

(a) prevents the instrument from creating such a power in his case, but

(b)   does not affect its efficacy for that purpose as respects the other or others or its efficacy in his case for the purpose of creating a power of attorney which is not an enduring power.

(5) If one or more but not both or all the attorneys makes or joins in making an application for registration of the instrument –

(a)   an attorney who is not an applicant as well as one who is may act pending the registration of the instrument as provided in paragraph 1(2),

(b)   notice of the application must also be given under Part 3 of this Schedule to the other attorney or attorneys, and

(c)   objection may validly be taken to the registration on a ground relating to an attorney or to the power of an attorney who is not an applicant as well as to one or the power of one who is an applicant.

(6) The Public Guardian is not precluded by paragraph 13(5) or (8) from registering an instrument and the court must not direct him not to do so under paragraph 13(10) if an enduring power subsists as respects some attorney who is not affected by the ground or grounds of the objection in question; and where the Public Guardian registers an instrument in that case, he must make against the registration an entry in the prescribed form.

(7) Sub-paragraph (6) does not preclude the court from revoking a power in so far as it confers a power on any other attorney in respect of whom the ground in paragraph 13(9)(d) or (e) is established; and where any ground in paragraph 13(9) affecting any other attorney is established the court must direct the Public Guardian to make against the registration an entry in the prescribed form.

(8) In sub-paragraph (4), 'the requirements for the creation of enduring powers' means the provisions of –

(a)   paragraph 2 other than sub-paragraphs (8) and (9), and
(b)   the regulations mentioned in paragraph 2.

21 Joint attorneys

(1) In paragraph 2(5), the reference to the time when the attorney executes the instrument is to be read as a reference to the time when the second or last attorney executes the instrument.

(2) In paragraph 2(6) to (8), the reference to the attorney is to be read as a reference to any attorney under the power.

(3) Paragraph 13 has effect as if the ground of objection to the registration of the instrument specified in sub-paragraph (9)(e) applied to any attorney under the power.

(4) In paragraph 16(2), references to the attorney are to be read as including references to any attorney under the power.

(5) In paragraph 16(4), references to the attorney are to be read as including references to any attorney under the power.

(6) In paragraph 17, references to the attorney are to be read as including references to any attorney under the power.

22 Joint and several attorneys

(1) In paragraph 2(7), the reference to the bankruptcy of the attorney is to be read as a reference to the bankruptcy of the last remaining attorney under the power; and the bankruptcy of any other attorney under the power causes that person to cease to be an attorney under the power.

(1A) In paragraph 2(7), the reference to the making of a debt relief order (under Part 7A of the Insolvency Act 1986) in respect of the attorney is to be read as a reference to the making of a debt relief order in respect of the last remaining attorney under the power; and the making of a debt relief order in respect of any other attorney under the power causes that person to cease to be an attorney under the power.

(2) In paragraph 2(8), the reference to the suspension of the power is to be read as a reference to its suspension in so far as it relates to the attorney in respect of whom the interim bankruptcy restrictions order has effect.

(2A) In paragraph 2(8), the reference to the suspension of the power is to be read as a reference to its suspension in so far as it relates to the attorney in respect of whom the interim debt relief restrictions order has effect.

(3) The restriction upon disclaimer imposed by paragraph 4(6) applies only to those attorneys who have reason to believe that the donor is or is becoming mentally incapable.

Amendments –SI 2012/2404.

PART 8
INTERPRETATION

23 (1) In this Schedule –

'enduring power' is to be construed in accordance with paragraph 2,
'mentally incapable' or 'mental incapacity', except where it refers to revocation at commonlaw, means in relation to any person, that he is incapable by reason of mental disorder of managing and administering his property and affairs and 'mentally capable' and 'mental capacity' are to be construed accordingly,
'notice' means notice in writing, and
'prescribed', except for the purposes of paragraph 2, means prescribed by regulations made for the purposes of this Schedule by the Lord Chancellor.

(1A) In sub-paragraph (1), 'mental disorder' has the same meaning as in the Mental Health Act but disregarding the amendments made to that Act by the Mental Health Act 2007.

(2) Any question arising under or for the purposes of this Schedule as to what the donor of the power might at any time be expected to do is to be determined

by assuming that he had full mental capacity at the time but otherwise by reference to the circumstances existing at that time.

Amendments –Mental Health Act 2007, ss 1(4), 55, Sch 1, Pt 2, para 23(1)-(3), Sch 11, Pt 1.

Schedule 5
Transitional Provisions and Savings

Section 66(4)

PART 1
REPEAL OF PART 7 OF THE MENTAL HEALTH ACT 1983

1 Existing receivers

(1) This paragraph applies where, immediately before the commencement day, there is a receiver ('R') for a person ('P') appointed under section 99 of the Mental Health Act.

(2) On and after that day –

    (a)   this Act applies as if R were a deputy appointed for P by the court, but with the functions that R had as receiver immediately before that day, and

    (b)   a reference in any other enactment to a deputy appointed by the court includes a person appointed as a deputy as a result of paragraph (a).

(3) On any application to it by R, the court may end R's appointment as P's deputy.

(4) Where, as a result of section 20(1), R may not make a decision on behalf of P in relation to a relevant matter, R must apply to the court.

(5) If, on the application, the court is satisfied that P is capable of managing his property and affairs in relation to the relevant matter –

    (a)   it must make an order ending R's appointment as P's deputy in relation to that matter, but

    (b)   it may, in relation to any other matter, exercise in relation to P any of the powers which it has under sections 15 to 19.

(6) If it is not satisfied, the court may exercise in relation to P any of the powers which it has under sections 15 to 19.

(7) R's appointment as P's deputy ceases to have effect if P dies.

(8) 'Relevant matter' means a matter in relation to which, immediately before the commencement day, R was authorised to act as P's receiver.

(9) In sub-paragraph (1), the reference to a receiver appointed under section 99 of the Mental Health Act includes a reference to a person who by virtue of Schedule 5 to that Act was deemed to be a receiver appointed under that section.

2 Orders, appointments etc

(1) Any order or appointment made, direction or authority given or other thing done which has, or by virtue of Schedule 5 to the Mental Health Act was deemed to have, effect under Part 7 of the Act immediately before the commencement day is to continue to have effect despite the repeal of Part 7.

(2) In so far as any such order, appointment, direction, authority or thing could have been made, given or done under sections 15 to 20 if those sections had then been in force –

    (a)   it is to be treated as made, given or done under those sections, and

    (b)   the powers of variation and discharge conferred by section 16(7) apply accordingly.

(3) Sub-paragraph (1) –

    (a)   does not apply to nominations under section 93(1) or (4) of the Mental Health Act, and

    (b)   as respects receivers, has effect subject to paragraph 1.

(4) This Act does not affect the operation of section 109 of the Mental Health Act (effect and proof of orders etc) in relation to orders made and directions given under Part 7 of that Act.

(5) This paragraph is without prejudice to section 16 of the Interpretation Act 1978 (general savings on repeal).

3 Pending proceedings

(1) Any application for the exercise of a power under Part 7 of the Mental Health Act which is pending immediately before the commencement day is to be treated, in so far as a corresponding power is exercisable under sections 16 to 20, as an application for the exercise of that power.

(2) For the purposes of sub-paragraph (1) an application for the appointment of a receiver is to be treated as an application for the appointment of a deputy.

4 Appeals

(1) Part 7 of the Mental Health Act and the rules made under it are to continue to apply to any appeal brought by virtue of section 105 of that Act which has not been determined before the commencement day.

(2) If in the case of an appeal brought by virtue of section 105(1) (appeal to nominated judge) the judge nominated under section 93 of the Mental Health Act has begun to hear the appeal, he is to continue to do so but otherwise it is to be heard by a puisne judge of the High Court nominated under section 46.

5 Fees

All fees and other payments which, having become due, have not been paid to the former Court of Protection before the commencement day, are to be paid to the new Court of Protection.

6 Court records

(1) The records of the former Court of Protection are to be treated, on and after the commencement day, as records of the new Court of Protection and are to be dealt with accordingly under the Public Records Act 1958.

(2) On and after the commencement day, the Public Guardian is, for the purpose of exercising any of his functions, to be given such access as he may require to such of the records mentioned in sub-paragraph (1) as relate to the appointment of receivers under section 99 of the Mental Health Act.

7 Existing charges

This Act does not affect the operation in relation to a charge created before the commencement day of –

(a)   so much of section 101(6) of the Mental Health Act as precludes a charge created under section 101(5) from conferring a right of sale or foreclosure during the lifetime of the patient, or

(b)   section 106(6) of the Mental Health Act (charge created by virtue of section 106(5) not to cause interest to fail etc).

8 Preservation of interests on disposal of property

Paragraph 8(1) of Schedule 2 applies in relation to any disposal of property (within the meaning of that provision) by a person living on 1st November 1960, being a disposal effected under the Lunacy Act 1890 as it applies in relation to the disposal of property effected under sections 16 to 20.

9 Accounts

Court of Protection Rules may provide that, in a case where paragraph 1 applies, R is to have a duty to render accounts –

(a)   while he is receiver;
(b)   after he is discharged.

10 Interpretation

In this Part of this Schedule –

(a)   'the commencement day' means the day on which section 66(1)(a) (repeal of Part 7 of the Mental Health Act) comes into force,

(b)   'the former Court of Protection' means the office abolished by section 45, and

(c)   'the new Court of Protection' means the court established by that section.

PART 2
REPEAL OF THE ENDURING POWERS OF ATTORNEY ACT 1985

11 Orders, determinations, etc

(1) Any order or determination made, or other thing done, under the 1985 Act which has effect immediately before the commencement day continues to have effect despite the repeal of that Act.

(2) In so far as any such order, determination or thing could have been made or done under Schedule 4 if it had then been in force –

    (a)   it is to be treated as made or done under that Schedule, and

    (b)   the powers of variation and discharge exercisable by the court apply accordingly.

(3) Any instrument registered under the 1985 Act is to be treated as having been registered by the Public Guardian under Schedule 4.

(4) This paragraph is without prejudice to section 16 of the Interpretation Act 1978 (general savings on repeal).

12 Pending proceedings

(1) An application for the exercise of a power under the 1985 Act which is pending immediately before the commencement day is to be treated, in so far as a corresponding power is exercisable under Schedule 4, as an application for the exercise of that power.

(2) For the purposes of sub-paragraph (1) –

    (a)   a pending application under section 4(2) of the 1985 Act for the registration of an instrument is to be treated as an application to the Public Guardian under paragraph 4 of Schedule 4 and any notice given in connection with that application under Schedule 1 to the 1985 Act is to be treated as given under Part 3 of Schedule 4,

    (b)   a notice of objection to the registration of an instrument is to be treated as a notice of objection under paragraph 13 of Schedule 4, and

    (c)   pending proceedings under section 5 of the 1985 Act are to be treated as proceedings on an application for the exercise by the court of a power which would become exercisable in relation to an instrument under paragraph 16(2) of Schedule 4 on its registration.

13 Appeals

(1) The 1985 Act and, so far as relevant, the provisions of Part 7 of the Mental Health Act and the rules made under it as applied by section 10 of the 1985 Act are to continue to have effect in relation to any appeal brought by virtue of section 10(1)(c) of the 1985 Act which has not been determined before the commencement day.

(2) If, in the case of an appeal brought by virtue of section 105(1) of the Mental Health Act as applied by section 10(1)(c) of the 1985 Act (appeal to

nominated judge), the judge nominated under section 93 of the Mental Health Act has begun to hear the appeal, he is to continue to do so but otherwise the appeal is to be heard by a puisne judge of the High Court nominated under section 46.

14 Exercise of powers of donor as trustee

(1) Section 2(8) of the 1985 Act (which prevents a power of attorney under section 25 of the Trustee Act 1925 as enacted from being an enduring power) is to continue to apply to any enduring power –

(a)   created before 1st March 2000, and
(b)   having effect immediately before the commencement day.

(2) Section 3(3) of the 1985 Act (which entitles the donee of an enduring power to exercise the donor's powers as trustee) is to continue to apply to any enduring power to which, as a result of the provision mentioned in sub-paragraph (3), it applies immediately before the commencement day.

(3) The provision is section 4(3)(a) of the Trustee Delegation Act 1999 (which provides for section 3(3) of the 1985 Act to cease to apply to an enduring power when its registration is cancelled, if it was registered in response to an application made before 1st March 2001).

(4) Even though section 4 of the 1999 Act is repealed by this Act, that section is to continue to apply in relation to an enduring power –

(a)   to which section 3(3) of the 1985 Act applies as a result of sub-paragraph (2), or
(b)   to which, immediately before the repeal of section 4 of the 1999 Act, section 1 of that Act applies as a result of section 4 of it.

(5) The reference in section 1(9) of the 1999 Act to section 4(6) of that Act is to be read with sub-paragraphs (2) to (4).

15 Interpretation

In this Part of this Schedule, 'the commencement day' means the day on which section 66(1)(b) (repeal of the 1985 Act) comes into force.

Schedule 6
Minor and Consequential Amendments

Section 67(1)

1 Fines and Recoveries Act 1833

(1) The Fines and Recoveries Act 1833 is amended as follows.

(2) In section 33 (case where protector of settlement lacks capacity to act), for the words from 'shall be incapable' to 'is incapable as aforesaid' substitute 'lacks capacity (within the meaning of the Mental Capacity Act 2005) to manage his property and affairs, the Court of Protection is to take his place as protector of the settlement while he lacks capacity'.

(3) In sections 48 and 49 (mental health jurisdiction), for each reference to the judge having jurisdiction under Part 7 of the Mental Health Act substitute a reference to the Court of Protection.

2 Improvement of Land Act 1864

In section 68 of the Improvement of Land Act 1864 (apportionment of rentcharges) –

- (a)   for ', curator, or receiver of' substitute 'or curator of, or a deputy with powers in relation to property and affairs appointed by the Court of Protection for,', and
- (b)   for 'or patient within the meaning of Part VII of the Mental Health Act 1983' substitute 'person who lacks capacity (within the meaning of the Mental Capacity Act 2005) to receive the notice'.

3 Trustee Act 1925

(1) The Trustee Act 1925 is amended as follows.

(2) In section 36 (appointment of new trustee) –

- (a)   in subsection (6C), for the words from 'a power of attorney' to the end, substitute 'an enduring power of attorney or lasting power of attorney registered under the Mental Capacity Act 2005', and
- (b)   in subsection (9) –
    - (i)   for the words from 'is incapable' to 'exercising' substitute 'lacks capacity to exercise', and
    - (ii) for the words from 'the authority' to the end substitute 'the Court of Protection'.

(3) In section 41(1) (power of court to appoint new trustee) for the words from 'is incapable' to 'exercising' substitute 'lacks capacity to exercise'.

(4) In section 54 (mental health jurisdiction) –

- (a)   for subsection (1) substitute –

    '(1) Subject to subsection (2), the Court of Protection may not make an order, or give a direction or authority, in relation to a person who lacks capacity to exercise his functions as trustee, if the High Court may make an order to that effect under this Act.',

- (b)   in subsection (2) –
    - (i)   for the words from the beginning to 'of a receiver' substitute 'Where a person lacks capacity to exercise his functions as a trustee and a deputy is appointed for him by the Court of Protection or an application for the appointment of a deputy',
    - (ii) for 'the said authority', in each place, substitute 'the Court of Protection', and
    - (iii) for 'the patient', in each place, substitute 'the person concerned', and

- (c)   omit subsection (3).

(5) In section 55 (order made on particular allegation to be conclusive evidence of it) –

    (a)   for the words from 'Part VII' to 'Northern Ireland' substitute 'sections 15 to 20 of the Mental Capacity Act 2005 or any corresponding provisions having effect in Northern Ireland', and

    (b)   for paragraph (a) substitute –

        '(a)   that a trustee or mortgagee lacks capacity in relation to the matter in question;'.

(6) In section 68 (definitions), at the end add –

'(3) Any reference in this Act to a person who lacks capacity in relation to a matter is to a person –

    (a)   who lacks capacity within the meaning of the Mental Capacity Act 2005 in relation to that matter, or

    (b)   in respect of whom the powers conferred by section 48 of that Act are exercisable and have been exercised in relation to that matter.'.

4 Law of Property Act 1925

(1) The Law of Property Act 1925 is amended as follows.

(2) In section 22 (conveyances on behalf of persons who lack capacity) –

    (a)   in subsection (1) –

        (i)   for the words from 'in a person suffering' to 'is acting' substitute ', either solely or jointly with any other person or persons, in a person lacking capacity (within the meaning of the Mental Capacity Act 2005) to convey or create a legal estate, a deputy appointed for him by the Court of Protection or (if no deputy is appointed', and

        (ii)   for 'the authority having jurisdiction under Part VII of the Mental Health Act 1983' substitute 'the Court of Protection',

    (b)   in subsection (2), for 'is incapable, by reason of mental disorder, of exercising' substitute 'lacks capacity (within the meaning of that Act) to exercise', and

    (c)   in subsection (3), for the words from 'an enduring power' to the end substitute 'an enduring power of attorney or lasting power of attorney (within the meaning of the 2005 Act) is entitled to act for the trustee who lacks capacity in relation to the dealing.'.

(3) In section 205(1) (interpretation), omit paragraph (xiii).

5 Administration of Estates Act 1925

(1) The Administration of Estates Act 1925 is amended as follows.

(2) In section 41(1) (powers of personal representatives to appropriate), in the proviso –

    (a)   in paragraph (ii) –

(i)   for the words from 'is incapable' to 'the consent' substitute 'lacks capacity (within the meaning of the Mental Capacity Act 2005) to give the consent, it', and

(ii)   for 'or receiver' substitute 'or a person appointed as deputy for him by the Court of Protection', and

(b)   in paragraph (iv), for 'no receiver is acting for a person suffering from mental disorder' substitute 'no deputy is appointed for a person who lacks capacity to consent'.

(3) Omit section 55(1)(viii) (definitions of 'person of unsound mind' and 'defective').

6 National Assistance Act 1948

In section 49 of the National Assistance Act 1948 (expenses of council officers acting for persons who lack capacity) –

(a)   for the words from 'applies' to 'affairs of a patient' substitute 'applies for appointment by the Court of Protection as a deputy', and

(b)   for 'such functions' substitute 'his functions as deputy'.

7 USA Veterans' Pensions (Administration) Act 1949

In section 1 of the USA Veterans' Pensions (Administration) Act 1949 (administration of pensions) –

(a)   in subsection (4), omit the words from 'or for whom' to '1983', and

(b)   after subsection (4), insert –

'(4A) An agreement under subsection (1) is not to be made in relation to a person who lacks capacity (within the meaning of the Mental Capacity Act 2005) for the purposes of this Act if –

(a)   there is a donee of an enduring power of attorney or lasting power of attorney (within the meaning of the 2005 Act), or a deputy appointed for the person by the Court of Protection, and

(b)   the donee or deputy has power in relation to the person for the purposes of this Act.

(4B) The proviso at the end of subsection (4) also applies in relation to subsection (4A).'.

8 Intestates' Estates Act 1952

In Schedule 2 to the Intestates' Estates Act 1952 (rights of surviving spouse or civil partner in relation to home), for paragraph 6(1) substitute –

'(1) Where the surviving spouse or civil partner lacks capacity (within the meaning of the Mental Capacity Act 2005) to make a requirement or give a consent under this Schedule, the requirement or consent may be made or given by a deputy appointed by the Court of Protection with power in that respect or, if no deputy has that power, by that court.'.

9 Variation of Trusts Act 1958

In section 1 of the Variation of Trusts Act 1958 (jurisdiction of courts to vary trusts) –

(a) in subsection (3), for the words from 'shall be determined' to the end substitute 'who lacks capacity (within the meaning of the Mental Capacity Act 2005) to give his assent is to be determined by the Court of Protection', and

(b) in subsection (6), for the words from 'the powers' to the end substitute 'the powers of the Court of Protection'.

10 Administration of Justice Act 1960

In section 12(1)(b) of the Administration of Justice Act 1960 (contempt of court to publish information about proceedings in private relating to persons with incapacity) for the words from 'under Part VIII' to 'that Act' substitute 'under the Mental Capacity Act 2005, or under any provision of the Mental Health Act 1983'.

11 *Industrial and Provident Societies Act 1965*] [Co-operative and Community Benefit Societies and Credit Unions Act 1965]

In section 26 of the *Industrial and Provident Societies Act 1965* [Co-operative and Community Benefit Societies and Credit Unions Act 1965] (payments for mentally incapable people), for subsection (2) substitute –

'(2) Subsection (1) does not apply where the member or person concerned lacks capacity (within the meaning of the Mental Capacity Act 2005) for the purposes of this Act and –

(a) there is a donee of an enduring power of attorney or lasting power of attorney (within the meaning of the 2005 Act), or a deputy appointed for the member or person by the Court of Protection, and

(b) the donee or deputy has power in relation to the member or person for the purposes of this Act.'.

12 Compulsory Purchase Act 1965

In Schedule 1 to the Compulsory Purchase Act 1965 (persons without power to sell their interests), for paragraph 1(2)(b) substitute –

'(b) do not have effect in relation to a person who lacks capacity (within the meaning of the Mental Capacity Act 2005) for the purposes of this Act if –

(i) there is a donee of an enduring power of attorney or lasting power of attorney (within the meaning of the 2005 Act), or a deputy appointed for the person by the Court of Protection, and

(ii) the donee or deputy has power in relation to the person for the purposes of this Act.'.

13 Leasehold Reform Act 1967

(1) For section 26(2) of the Leasehold Reform Act 1967 (landlord lacking capacity) substitute –

> '(2) Where a landlord lacks capacity (within the meaning of the Mental Capacity Act 2005) to exercise his functions as a landlord, those functions are to be exercised –
>
> > (a) by a donee of an enduring power of attorney or lasting power of attorney (within the meaning of the 2005 Act), or a deputy appointed for him by the Court of Protection, with power to exercise those functions, or
> > (b) if no donee or deputy has that power, by a person authorised in that respect by that court.'.

(2) That amendment does not affect any proceedings pending at the commencement of this paragraph in which a receiver or a person authorised under Part 7 of the Mental Health Act is acting on behalf of the landlord.

14 Medicines Act 1968

In section 72 of the Medicines Act 1968 (pharmacist lacking capacity) –

(a) in subsection (1)(c), for the words from 'a receiver' to '1959' substitute 'he becomes a person who lacks capacity (within the meaning of the Mental Capacity Act 2005) to carry on the business',

(b) after subsection (1) insert –

> '(1A) In subsection (1)(c), the reference to a person who lacks capacity to carry on the business is to a person –
>
> > (a) in respect of whom there is a donee of an enduring power of attorney or lasting power of attorney (within the meaning of the Mental Capacity Act 2005), or
> > (b) for whom a deputy is appointed by the Court of Protection, and in relation to whom the donee or deputy has power for the purposes of this Act.',

(c) in subsection (3)(d) –

> (i) for 'receiver' substitute 'deputy', and
> (ii) after 'guardian' insert 'or from the date of registration of the instrument appointing the donee', and

(d) in subsection (4)(c), for 'receiver' substitute 'donee, deputy'.

15 Family Law Reform Act 1969

For section 21(4) of the Family Law Reform Act 1969 (consent required for taking of bodily sample from person lacking capacity), substitute –

> '(4) A bodily sample may be taken from a person who lacks capacity (within the meaning of the Mental Capacity Act 2005) to give his consent, if consent is given by the court giving the direction under section 20 or by –
>
> > (a) a donee of an enduring power of attorney or lasting power of attorney (within the meaning of that Act), or

(b)   a deputy appointed, or any other person authorised, by the Court of
      Protection,
with power in that respect.'.

16 Local Authority Social Services Act 1970

(1) Schedule 1 to the Local Authority Social Services Act 1970 (enactments
conferring functions assigned to social services committee) is amended as
follows.

(2) In the entry for section 49 of the National Assistance Act 1948 (expenses of
local authority officer appointed for person who lacks capacity) for 'receiver'
substitute 'deputy'.

(3) At the end, insert –

'Mental Capacity
Act 2005

Section 39	Instructing independent mental capacity advocate before providing accommodation for person lacking capacity.
Section 49	Reports in proceedings.'.

17 Courts Act 1971

In Part 1A of Schedule 2 to the Courts Act 1971 (office-holders eligible for
appointment as circuit judges), omit the reference to a Master of the Court of
Protection.

18 Local Government Act 1972

(1) Omit section 118 of the Local Government Act 1972 (payment of pension
etc where recipient lacks capacity).

(2) Sub-paragraph (3) applies where, before the commencement of this
paragraph, a local authority has, in respect of a person referred to in that
section as 'the patient', made payments under that section –

(a)   to an institution or person having the care of the patient, or
(b)   in accordance with subsection (1)(a) or (b) of that section.

(3) The local authority may, in respect of the patient, continue to make
payments under that section to that institution or person, or in accordance with
subsection (1)(a) or (b) of that section, despite the repeal made by
sub-paragraph (1).

19 Matrimonial Causes Act 1973

In section 40 of the Matrimonial Causes Act 1973 (payments to person who
lacks capacity) (which becomes subsection (1)) –

(a) for the words from 'is incapable' to 'affairs' substitute '('P') lacks capacity (within the meaning of the Mental Capacity Act 2005) in relation to the provisions of the order',

(b) for 'that person under Part VIII of that Act' substitute 'P under that Act',

(c) for the words from 'such persons' to the end substitute 'such person ('D') as it may direct', and

(d) at the end insert –

'(2) In carrying out any functions of his in relation to an order made under subsection (1), D must act in P's best interests (within the meaning of that Act).'.

20 Juries Act 1974

In Schedule 1 to the Juries Act 1974 (disqualification for jury service), for paragraph 3 substitute –

'3 A person who lacks capacity, within the meaning of the Mental Capacity Act 2005, to serve as a juror.'.

21 Consumer Credit Act 1974

For section 37(1)(c) of the Consumer Credit Act 1974 (termination of consumer credit licence if holder lacks capacity) substitute –

'(c) becomes a person who lacks capacity (within the meaning of the Mental Capacity Act 2005) to carry on the activities covered by the licence.'.

22 Solicitors Act 1974

(1) The Solicitors Act 1974 is amended as follows.

(2) *(repealed)*

(3) In section 62(4) (contentious business agreements made by clients) for paragraphs (c) and (d) substitute –

'(c) as a deputy for him appointed by the Court of Protection with powers in relation to his property and affairs, or

(d) as another person authorised under that Act to act on his behalf.'.

(4) In paragraph 1(1) of Schedule 1 (circumstances in which Law Society may intervene in solicitor's practice), for paragraph (f) substitute –

'(f) a solicitor lacks capacity (within the meaning of the Mental Capacity Act 2005) to act as a solicitor and powers under sections 15 to 20 or section 48 of that Act are exercisable in relation to him;'.

23 Local Government (Miscellaneous Provisions) Act 1976

In section 31 of the Local Government (Miscellaneous Provisions) Act 1976 (the title to which becomes 'Indemnities for local authority officers appointed as deputies or administrators'), for the words from 'as a receiver' to '1959' substitute 'as a deputy for a person by the Court of Protection'.

24 Sale of Goods Act 1979

In section 3(2) of the Sale of Goods Act 1979 (capacity to buy and sell) the words 'mental incapacity or' cease to have effect in England and Wales.

25 Limitation Act 1980

In section 38 of the Limitation Act 1980 (interpretation) substitute –

   (a)   in subsection (2) for 'of unsound mind' substitute 'lacks capacity (within the meaning of the Mental Capacity Act 2005) to conduct legal proceedings', and

   (b)   omit subsections (3) and (4).

26 Public Passenger Vehicles Act 1981

In section 57(2)(c) of the Public Passenger Vehicles Act 1981 (termination of public service vehicle licence if holder lacks capacity) for the words from 'becomes a patient' to 'or' substitute 'becomes a person who lacks capacity (within the meaning of the Mental Capacity Act 2005) to use a vehicle under the licence, or'.

27 Judicial Pensions Act 1981

In Schedule 1 to the Judicial Pensions Act 1981 (pensions of Supreme Court officers, etc), in paragraph 1, omit the reference to a Master of the Court of Protection except in the case of a person holding that office immediately before the commencement of this paragraph or who had previously retired from that office or died.

28 Senior Courts Act 1981

In Schedule 2 to the Senior Courts Act 1981 (qualifications for appointment to office in Supreme Court), omit paragraph 11 (Master of the Court of Protection).

29 Mental Health Act 1983

(1) The Mental Health Act is amended as follows.

(2) In section 134(3) (cases where correspondence of detained patients may not be withheld) for paragraph (b) substitute –

   '(b)   any judge or officer of the Court of Protection, any of the Court of Protection Visitors or any person asked by that Court for a report under section 49 of the Mental Capacity Act 2005 concerning the patient;'.

(3) In section 139 (protection for acts done in pursuance of 1983 Act), in subsection (1), omit from 'or in, or in pursuance' to 'Part VII of this Act,'.

(4) Section 142 (payment of pension etc where recipient lacks capacity) ceases to have effect in England and Wales.

(5) Sub-paragraph (6) applies where, before the commencement of sub-paragraph (4), an authority has, in respect of a person referred to in that section as 'the patient', made payments under that section –

(a)   to an institution or person having the care of the patient, or
(b)   in accordance with subsection (2)(a) or (b) of that section.

(6) The authority may, in respect of the patient, continue to make payments under that section to that institution or person, or in accordance with subsection (2)(a) or (b) of that section, despite the amendment made by sub-paragraph (4).

(7) In section 145(1) (interpretation), in the definition of 'patient', omit '(except in Part VII of this Act)'.

(8) In section 146 (provisions having effect in Scotland), omit from '104(4)' to 'section),'.

(9) In section 147 (provisions having effect in Northern Ireland), omit from '104(4)' to 'section),'.

30 Administration of Justice Act 1985

In section 18(3) of the Administration of Justice Act 1985 (licensed conveyancer who lacks capacity), for the words from 'that person' to the end substitute 'he becomes a person who lacks capacity (within the meaning of the Mental Capacity Act 2005) to practise as a licensed conveyancer.'.

31 Insolvency Act 1986

(1) The Insolvency Act 1986 is amended as follows.

(2) In section 389A (people not authorised to act as nominee or supervisor in voluntary arrangement), in subsection (3) –

(a)   omit the 'or' immediately after paragraph (b),
(b)   in paragraph (c), omit 'Part VII of the Mental Health Act 1983 or', and
(c)   after that paragraph, insert –
      ', or
      (d)   he lacks capacity (within the meaning of the Mental Capacity Act 2005) to act as nominee or supervisor'.

(3) In section 390 (people not qualified to be insolvency practitioners), in subsection (4) –

(a)   omit the 'or' immediately after paragraph (b),
(b)   in paragraph (c), omit 'Part VII of the Mental Health Act 1983 or', and
(c)   after that paragraph, insert –
      ', or
      (d)   he lacks capacity (within the meaning of the Mental Capacity Act 2005) to act as an insolvency practitioner.'.

32 Building Societies Act 1986

In section 102D(9) of the Building Societies Act 1986 (references to a person holding an account on trust for another) –

(a) in paragraph (a), for 'Part VII of the Mental Health Act 1983' substitute 'the Mental Capacity Act 2005', and

(b) for paragraph (b) substitute –

'(b) to an attorney holding an account for another person under –

(i) an enduring power of attorney or lasting power of attorney registered under the Mental Capacity Act 2005, or

(ii) an enduring power registered under the Enduring Powers of Attorney (Northern Ireland) Order 1987;'.

33 Public Trustee and Administration of Funds Act 1986

In section 3 of the Public Trustee and Administration of Funds Act 1986 (functions of the Public Trustee) –

(a) for subsections (1) to (5) substitute –

'(1) The Public Trustee may exercise the functions of a deputy appointed by the Court of Protection.',

(b) in subsection (6), for 'the 1906 Act' substitute 'the Public Trustee Act 1906', and

(c) omit subsection (7).

34 Patronage (Benefices) Measure 1986 (No 3)

(1) The Patronage (Benefices) Measure 1986 (No 3) is amended as follows.

(2) In section 5 (rights of patronage exercisable otherwise than by registered patron), after subsection (3) insert –

'(3A) The reference in subsection (3) to a power of attorney does not include an enduring power of attorney or lasting power of attorney (within the meaning of the Mental Capacity Act 2005).'

(3) In section 9 (information to be sent to designated officer when benefice becomes vacant), after subsection (5) insert –

'(5A) Subsections (5B) and (5C) apply where the functions of a registered patron are, as a result of paragraph 10 of Schedule 2 to the Mental Capacity Act 2005 (patron's loss of capacity to discharge functions), to be discharged by an individual appointed by the Court of Protection.

(5B) If the individual is a clerk in Holy Orders, subsection (5) applies to him as it applies to the registered patron.

(5C) If the individual is not a clerk in Holy Orders, subsection (1) (other than paragraph (b)) applies to him as it applies to the registered patron.'

35 Courts and Legal Services Act 1990

(1) The Courts and Legal Services Act 1990 is amended as follows.

(2) In Schedule 11 (judges etc barred from legal practice), for the reference to a Master of the Court of Protection substitute a reference to each of the following –

    (a)   Senior Judge of the Court of Protection,
    (b)   President of the Court of Protection,
    (c)   Vice-President of the Court of Protection.

(3) In paragraph 5(3) of Schedule 14 (exercise of powers of intervention in registered foreign lawyer's practice), for paragraph (f) substitute –

> '(f)   he lacks capacity (within the meaning of the Mental Capacity Act 2005) to act as a registered foreign lawyer and powers under sections 15 to 20 or section 48 are exercisable in relation to him;'.

36 Child Support Act 1991

In section 50 of the Child Support Act 1991 (unauthorised disclosure of information) –

    (a)   in subsection (8) –
        (i)   immediately after paragraph (a), insert 'or',
        (ii)   omit paragraphs (b) and (d) and the 'or' immediately after paragraph (c), and
        (iii)   for ', receiver, custodian or appointee' substitute 'or custodian', and

    (b)   after that subsection, insert –

> '(9) Where the person to whom the information relates lacks capacity (within the meaning of the Mental Capacity Act 2005) to consent to its disclosure, the appropriate person is –
>
>   (a)   a donee of an enduring power of attorney or lasting power of attorney (within the meaning of that Act), or
>   (b)   a deputy appointed for him, or any other person authorised, by the Court of Protection,
> with power in that respect.'.

37 Social Security Administration Act 1992

In section 123 of the Social Security Administration Act 1992 (unauthorised disclosure of information) –

    (a)   in subsection (10), omit –
        (i)   in paragraph (b), 'a receiver appointed under section 99 of the Mental Health Act 1983 or',
        (ii)   in paragraph (d)(i), 'sub-paragraph (a) of rule 41(1) of the Court of Protection Rules 1984 or',
        (iii)   in paragraph (d)(ii), 'a receiver ad interim appointed under sub-paragraph (b) of the said rule 41(1) or', and
        (iv)   'receiver,', and

    (b)   after that subsection, insert –

'(11) Where the person to whom the information relates lacks capacity (within the meaning of the Mental Capacity Act 2005) to consent to its disclosure, the appropriate person is –

  (a)   a donee of an enduring power of attorney or lasting power of attorney (within the meaning of that Act), or

  (b)   a deputy appointed for him, or any other person authorised, by the Court of Protection,

with power in that respect.'.

38 Judicial Pensions and Retirement Act 1993

(1) The Judicial Pensions and Retirement Act 1993 is amended as follows.

(2) In Schedule 1 (qualifying judicial offices), in Part 2, under the cross-heading 'Court officers', omit the reference to a Master of the Court of Protection except in the case of a person holding that office immediately before the commencement of this sub-paragraph or who had previously retired from that office or died.

(3) In Schedule 5 (retirement: the relevant offices), omit the entries relating to the Master and Deputy or temporary Master of the Court of Protection, except in the case of a person holding any of those offices immediately before the commencement of this sub-paragraph.

(4) In Schedule 7 (retirement: transitional provisions), omit paragraph 5(5)(i)(g) except in the case of a person holding office as a deputy or temporary Master of the Court of Protection immediately before the commencement of this sub-paragraph.

39 Leasehold Reform, Housing and Urban Development Act 1993

(1) For paragraph 4 of Schedule 2 to the Leasehold Reform, Housing and Urban Development Act 1993 (landlord under a disability), substitute –

'**4** (1) This paragraph applies where a Chapter I or Chapter II landlord lacks capacity (within the meaning of the Mental Capacity Act 2005) to exercise his functions as a landlord.

(2) For the purposes of the Chapter concerned, the landlord's place is to be taken –

  (a)   by a donee of an enduring power of attorney or lasting power of attorney (within the meaning of the 2005 Act), or a deputy appointed for him by the Court of Protection, with power to exercise those functions, or

  (b)   if no deputy or donee has that power, by a person authorised in that respect by that court.'.

(2) That amendment does not affect any proceedings pending at the commencement of this paragraph in which a receiver or a person authorised under Part 7 of the Mental Health Act 1983 is acting on behalf of the landlord.

40 Goods Vehicles (Licensing of Operators) Act 1995

(1) The Goods Vehicles (Licensing of Operators) Act 1995 is amended as follows.

(2) In section 16(5) (termination of licence), for 'he becomes a patient within the meaning of Part VII of the Mental Health Act 1983' substitute 'he becomes a person who lacks capacity (within the meaning of the Mental Capacity Act 2005) to use a vehicle under the licence'.

(3) In section 48 (licence not to be transferable, etc) –

   (a)   in subsection (2) –
      (i)   for 'or become a patient within the meaning of Part VII of the Mental Health Act 1983' substitute ', or become a person who lacks capacity (within the meaning of the Mental Capacity Act 2005) to use a vehicle under the licence,', and
      (ii)   in paragraph (a), for 'became a patient' substitute 'became a person who lacked capacity in that respect', and

   (b)   in subsection (5), for 'a patient within the meaning of Part VII of the Mental Health Act 1983' substitute 'a person lacking capacity'.

41 Disability Discrimination Act 1995

In section 20(7) of the Disability Discrimination Act 1995 (regulations to disapply provisions about incapacity), in paragraph (b), for 'Part VII of the Mental Health Act 1983' substitute 'the Mental Capacity Act 2005'.

42 Trusts of Land and Appointment of Trustees Act 1996

(1) The Trusts of Land and Appointment of Trustees Act 1996 is amended as follows.

(2) In section 9 (delegation by trustees), in subsection (6), for the words from 'an enduring power' to the end substitute 'an enduring power of attorney or lasting power of attorney within the meaning of the Mental Capacity Act 2005'.

(3) In section 20 (the title to which becomes 'Appointment of substitute for trustee who lacks capacity') –

   (a)   in subsection (1)(a), for 'is incapable by reason of mental disorder of exercising' substitute 'lacks capacity (within the meaning of the Mental Capacity Act 2005) to exercise', and
   (b)   in subsection (2) –
      (i)   for paragraph (a) substitute –

      '(a)   a deputy appointed for the trustee by the Court of Protection,',
      (ii)   in paragraph (b), for the words from 'a power of attorney' to the end substitute 'an enduring power of attorney or lasting power of attorney registered under the Mental Capacity Act 2005', and
      (iii)   in paragraph (c), for the words from 'the authority' to the end substitute 'the Court of Protection'.

43 Human Rights Act 1998

In section 4(5) of the Human Rights Act 1998 (courts which may make declarations of incompatibility), after paragraph (e) insert –

> '(f)   the Court of Protection, in any matter being dealt with by the President of the Family Division, the Vice-Chancellor or a puisne judge of the High Court.'

44 *(repealed)*

45 Adoption and Children Act 2002

In section 52(1)(a) of the Adoption and Children Act 2002 (parental consent to adoption), for 'is incapable of giving consent' substitute 'lacks capacity (within the meaning of the Mental Capacity Act 2005) to give consent'.

46 Licensing Act 2003

(1) The Licensing Act 2003 is amended as follows.

(2) In section 27(1) (lapse of premises licence), for paragraph (b) substitute –

> '(b)   becomes a person who lacks capacity (within the meaning of the Mental Capacity Act 2005) to hold the licence,'.

(3) In section 47 (interim authority notice in relation to premises licence) –

(a)   in subsection (5), for paragraph (b) substitute –
> '(b)   the former holder lacks capacity (within the meaning of the Mental Capacity Act 2005) to hold the licence and that person acts for him under an enduring power of attorney or lasting power of attorney registered under that Act,',

and

(b)   in subsection (10), omit the definition of 'mentally incapable'.

47 Courts Act 2003

(1) The Courts Act 2003 is amended as follows.

(2) In section 1(1) (the courts in relation to which the Lord Chancellor must discharge his general duty), after paragraph (a) insert –

> '(aa) the Court of Protection,'.

(3) In section 64(2) (judicial titles which the Lord Chancellor may by order alter) –

(a)   omit the reference to a Master of the Court of Protection, and
(b)   at the appropriate place insert a reference to each of the following –
   (i)   Senior Judge of the Court of Protection,
   (ii)   President of the Court of Protection,
   (iii) Vice-president of the Court of Protection.

Amendments: Constitutional Reform Act 2005; Legal Services Act 2007; Legal Aid, Sentencing and Punishment of Offenders Act 2012.

Prospective Amendments: Para 11 heading: words "Industrial and Provident Societies Act 1965" prospectively repealed and subsequent words in square brackets prospectively substituted by virtue of the Co-operative and Community Benefit Societies and Credit Unions Act 2010, s 2, with effect from a date to be appointed. Para 11: words "Industrial and Provident Societies Act 1965" in italics prospectively repealed and subsequent words in square brackets prospectively substituted by virtue of the Co-operative and Community Benefit Societies and Credit Unions Act 2010, s 2.

Schedule 7
Repeals

Section 67(2)

Short title and chapter	Extent of repeal
Trustee Act 1925	Section 54(3).
Law of Property Act 1925	Section 205(1)(xiii).
Administration of Estates Act 1925	Section 55(1)(viii)
U.S.A. Veterans' Pensions (Administration) Act 1949	In section 1(4), the words from 'or for whom' to '1983'.
Mental Health Act 1959	In Schedule 7, in Part 1, the entries relating to –
	section 33 of the Fines and Recoveries Act 1833,
	section 68 of the Improvement of Land Act 1864,
	section 55 of the Trustee Act 1925,
	section 205(1) of the Law of Property Act 1925,
	section 49 of the National Assistance Act 1948, and
	section 1 of the Variation of Trusts Act 1958.
Courts Act 1971	In Schedule 2, in Part 1A, the words 'Master of the Court of Protection'.
Local Government Act 1972	Section 118.
Limitation Act 1980	Section 38(3) and (4).
Senior Courts Act 1981	In Schedule 2, in Part 2, paragraph 11.
Mental Health Act 1983	Part 7.
	In section 139(1) the words from 'or in, or in pursuance' to 'Part VII of this Act,'.

	In section 145(1), in the definition of 'patient' the words '(except in Part VII of this Act)'.
	In sections 146 and 147 the words from '104(4)' to 'section),'.
	Schedule 3.
	In Schedule 4, paragraphs 1, 2, 4, 5, 7, 9, 14, 20, 22, 25, 32, 38, 55 and 56.
	In Schedule 5, paragraphs 26, 43, 44 and 45.
Enduring Powers of Attorney Act 1985	The whole Act.
Insolvency Act 1986	In section 389A(3) –
	the 'or' immediately after paragraph (b), and in paragraph (c), the words 'Part VII of the Mental Health Act 1983 or'.
	In section 390(4) –
	the 'or' immediately after paragraph (b), and in paragraph (c), the words 'Part VII of the Mental Health Act 1983 or'.
Public Trustee and Administration of Funds Act 1986	Section 2.
	Section 3(7).
Child Support Act 1991	In section 50(8) –
	paragraphs (b) and (d), and the 'or' immediately after paragraph (c).
Social Security Administration Act 1992	In section 123(10) –
	in paragraph (b), 'a receiver appointed under section 99 of the Mental Health Act 1983 or',
	in paragraph (d)(i), 'sub-paragraph (a) of rule 41(1) of the Court of Protection Rules Act 1984 or',
	in paragraph (d)(ii), 'a receiver ad interim appointed under sub-paragraph (b) of the said rule 41(1) or', and

	'receiver,'.
Trustee Delegation Act 1999	Section 4.
	Section 6.
	In section 7(3), the words 'in accordance with section 4 above'.
Care Standards Act 2000	In Schedule 4, paragraph 8.
Licensing Act 2003	In section 47(10), the definition of 'mentally incapable'.
Courts Act 2003	In section 64(2), the words 'Master of the Court of Protection'.

Amendment: Constitutional Reform Act 2005.

APPENDIX 2

TRANSPARENCY IN THE COURT OF PROTECTION PUBLICATION OF JUDGMENTS

PRACTICE GUIDANCE

issued on 16 January 2014 by

SIR JAMES MUNBY, PRESIDENT OF THE COURT OF PROTECTION

The purpose of this Guidance

1 This Guidance (together with similar Guidance issued at the same time for the family courts) is intended to bring about an immediate and significant change in practice in relation to the publication of judgments in family courts and the Court of Protection.

2 In both courts there is a need for greater transparency in order to improve public understanding of the court process and confidence in the court system. At present too few judgments are made available to the public, which has a legitimate interest in being able to read what is being done by the judges in its name. The Guidance will have the effect of increasing the number of judgments available for publication (even if they will often need to be published in appropriately anonymised form).

3 In July 2011 Sir Nicholas Wall P issued, jointly with Bob Satchwell, Executive Director of the Society of Editors, a paper, *The Family Courts: Media Access & Reporting* (Media Access & Reporting), setting out a statement of the current state of the law. In their preface they recognised that the debate on increased transparency and public confidence in the family courts would move forward and that future consideration of this difficult and sensitive area would need to include the questions of access to and reporting of proceedings by the media, whilst maintaining the privacy of the families involved. The paper is to be found at:

http://www.judiciary.gov.uk/Resources/JCO/Documents/Guidance/family-courts-media-july2011.pdf

4 In April 2013 I issued a statement, *View from the President's Chambers: the Process of Reform*, [2013] Fam Law 548, in which I identified transparency as one of the three strands in the reforms which the family justice system is currently undergoing. I said:

> "I am determined to take steps to improve access to and reporting of family proceedings. I am determined that the new Family Court should not be saddled, as the family courts are at present, with the charge that we are a system of secret and unaccountable justice. Work, commenced by my predecessor, is well underway. I hope to be in a position to make important announcements in the near future."

5 That applies just as much to the issue of transparency in the Court of Protection.

6 Very similar issues arise in both the Family Court (as it will be from April 2014) and the Court of Protection in relation to the need to protect the personal privacy of children and vulnerable adults. The applicable rules differ, however, and this is something that needs attention. My starting point is that so far as possible the same rules and principles should apply in both the family courts (in due course the Family Court) and the Court of Protection.

7 I propose to adopt an incremental approach. Initially I am issuing this Guidance. This will be followed by further Guidance and in due course more formal Practice Directions and changes to the Rules (the Court of Protection Rules 2007 and the Family Procedure Rules 2010). Changes to primary legislation are unlikely in the near future.

8 As provided in paragraph 14 below, this Guidance applies only to judgments delivered by certain judges. In due course consideration will be given to extending it to judgments delivered by other judges.

The legal framework

9 The effect of section 12 of the Administration of Justice Act 1960 is that it is a contempt of court to publish a judgment in a Court of Protection case unless either the judgment has been delivered in public or, where delivered in private, the judge has authorised publication. In the latter case, the judge normally gives permission for the judgment to be published on condition that the published version protects the anonymity of the person who is subject of the proceedings and members of their family.

10 In every case the terms on which publication is permitted are a matter for the judge and will be set out by the judge in a rubric at the start of the judgment.

11 The normal terms as described in paragraph 9 may be appropriate in a case where no-one wishes to discuss the proceedings otherwise than anonymously. But they may be inappropriate, for example, where family members wish to discuss their experiences in public, identifying themselves and making use of the judgment. Equally, they may be inappropriate in cases where findings have been made against a person and someone else contends and/or the court concludes that it is in the public interest for that person to be identified in any published version of the judgment.

12 If any party wishes to identify himself or herself, or any other party or person, as being a person referred to in any published version of the judgment, their remedy is to seek an order of the court and a suitable modification of the

rubric: Media Access & Reporting, para 82; *Re RB (Adult) (No 4)* [2011] EWHC 3017 (Fam), [2012] 1 FLR 466, paras [17], [19].

13 Nothing in this Guidance affects the exercise by the judge in any particular case of whatever powers would otherwise be available to regulate the publication of material relating to the proceedings. For example, where a judgment is likely to be used in a way that would defeat the purpose of any anonymisation, it is open to the judge to refuse to publish the judgment or to make an order restricting its use.

Guidance

14 This Guidance takes effect from 3 February 2014. It applies to all judgments in the Court of Protection delivered by the Senior Judge, nominated Circuit Judges and High Court Judges.

15 The following paragraphs of this Guidance distinguish between two classes of judgment:

(i) those that the judge *must* ordinarily allow to be published (paragraphs 16 and 17); and

(ii) those that *may* be published (paragraph 18).

16 Permission to publish a judgment should always be given whenever the judge concludes that publication would be in the public interest and whether or not a request has been made by a party or the media.

17 Where a judgment relates to matters set out in the Schedule below and a written judgment already exists in a publishable form or the judge has already ordered that the judgment be transcribed, the starting point is that permission should be given for the judgment to be published unless there are compelling reasons why the judgment should not be published.

SCHEDULE

Judgments arising from:

(i) any application for an order involving the giving or withholding of serious medical treatment and any other hearing held in public;

(ii) any application for a declaration or order involving a deprivation or possible deprivation of liberty;

(iii) any case where there is a dispute as to who should act as an attorney or a deputy;

(iv) any case where the issues include whether a person should be restrained from acting as an attorney or a deputy or that an appointment should be revoked or his or her powers should be reduced;

(v) any application for an order that an incapacitated adult (P) be moved into or out of a residential establishment or other institution;

(vi) any case where the sale of P's home is in issue

(vii) any case where a property and affairs application relates to assets (including P's home) of £1 million or more or to damages awarded by a court sitting in public;

(viii) any application for a declaration as to capacity to marry or to consent to sexual relations;

(ix) any application for an order involving a restraint on publication of information relating to the proceedings.

18 In all other cases, the starting point is that permission may be given for the judgment to be published whenever a party or an accredited member of the media applies for an order permitting publication, and the judge concludes that permission for the judgment to be published should be given.

19 In deciding whether and if so when to publish a judgment, the judge shall have regard to all the circumstances, the rights arising under any relevant provision of the European Convention on Human Rights, including Articles 6 (right to a fair hearing), 8 (respect for private and family life) and 10 (freedom of expression), and the effect of publication upon any current or potential criminal proceedings.

20 In all cases where a judge gives permission for a judgment to be published:

(i) public authorities and expert witnesses should be named in the judgment approved for publication, unless there are compelling reasons why they should not be so named;

(ii) the person who is the subject of proceedings in the Court of Protection and other members of their family should not normally be named in the judgment approved for publication unless the judge otherwise orders;

(iii) anonymity in the judgment as published should not normally extend beyond protecting the privacy of the adults who are the subject of the proceedings and other members of their families, unless there are compelling reasons to do so.

21 Unless the judgment is already in anonymised form, any necessary anonymisation of the judgment shall be carried out as the judge orders. The version approved for publication will contain such rubric as the judge specifies. Unless the rubric specified by the judge provides expressly to the contrary every published judgment shall be deemed to contain the following rubric:

> "This judgment was delivered in private. The judge has given leave for this version of the judgment to be published on condition that (irrespective of what is contained in the judgment) in any published version of the judgment the anonymity of the incapacitated person and members of their family must be strictly preserved. All persons, including representatives of the media, must ensure that this condition is strictly complied with. Failure to do so will be a contempt of court."

22 The judge will need to consider who should be ordered to bear the cost of transcribing the judgment. Unless the judge otherwise orders:

(i) in cases falling under paragraph 18, the cost of transcribing the judgment shall be borne by the party or person applying for publication of the judgment;

(ii) in other cases, the cost of transcribing the judgment shall be at public expense.

23 In all cases where permission is given for a judgment to be published, the version of the judgment approved for publication shall be made available, upon payment of any appropriate charge that may be required, to any person who requests a copy. Where a judgment to which paragraph 16 or 17 applies is approved for publication, it shall as soon as reasonably practicable be placed by the court on the BAILII website. Where a judgment to which paragraph 18 applies is approved for publication, the judge shall consider whether it should be placed on the BAILII website and, if so, it shall as soon as reasonably practicable be placed by the court on the BAILII website.

* * *

COURT OF PROTECTION FORMS

For recent Court of Protection forms, please see:

http://www.justice.gov.uk/forms/hmcts/cop-packs

INDEX

References are to paragraph numbers.